International Economics

in the Age of Globalization

International Economics

in the Age of Globalization

Wilson B. Brown
Jan S. Hogendorn

broadview press

CANADIAN CATALOGUING IN PUBLICATION DATA

Main entry under title:

Brown, Wilson B., 1938–
    International economics in the age of globalization

Includes bibliographical references and index.

ISBN 1-55111-261-2

1. International economic relations.   I. Hogendorn, Jan S.   II. Title

HF1359.B768 2000   337   C00-930302-2

BROADVIEW PRESS, LTD.
is an independent, international publishing house, incorporated in 1985.

North America
Post Office Box 1243, Peterborough, Ontario, Canada K9J 7H5
3576 California Road, Orchard Park, New York, USA 14127
tel (705) 743-8990 · fax (705) 743-8353 · e-mail customerservice@broadviewpress.com

United Kingdom and Europe
Turpin Distribution Services, Ltd., Blackhorse Rd.,
Letchworth, Hertfordshire, SG6 1HN
tel (1462) 672555 · fax (1462) 480947 · e-mail turpin@rsc.org

Australia
St. Clair Press, Post Office Box 287, Rozelle, NSW 2039
tel (02) 818-1942 · fax (02) 418-1923

www.broadviewpress.com

Broadview Press gratefully acknowledges the financial support of the Ministry of Canadian Heritage through the Book Publishing Industry Development Program.

Art director: Zack Taylor, Black Eye Design, Inc.
Cover design: Zack Taylor. Typesetting: Zack Taylor. Figures: Liz Broes.

Boxed text on page 631 "Join the Army, Make a Killing" reprinted with permission. © 1998 The Economist Newspaper Group, Inc. Further reproduction prohibited. www.economist.com

Printed in Canada

Contents

5

PART TWO **INTERNATIONAL MACROECONOMICS: SAVING, GROWTH, AND FINANCE**

Preface

This book seeks to fill a serious gap in the texts available to students of international economics—the lack of institutional context for the theory they study. While institutional emphasis is normal for courses and texts in money and banking, economic development, and industrial organization, it is rare in international economic texts. Instead, the texts model themselves on intermediate theory books, stressing theoretical development and discussing policy only occasionally when it might apply to some theory. The opportunity cost of stressing the theory over the institutions is high, restricting accessibility (and enrollment) to economics majors and leaving them with little sense of how the theory relates to the world in which they work and live. To remedy this, we striven to present the basic theory needed to understand most of the issues of the emerging twenty-first century within a rich institutional and historical context. Our emphasis is not so much on the learning of new theory, but on consolidating what the students already know and so that they can use it to handle the more complex and open-ended processes of analysis, synthesis, and evaluation.

The choice of material and the level of our explanations make the text fit well into both second- and third-year economics courses. Serious non-majors with good backgrounds in political science or history, and advanced management students will join and do well. We assume the student is taking other relevant courses (particularly monetary economics for the second half of this text), but may not have had an intermediate theory course. The book can also serve in graduate courses in business and international affairs, and as a supplement in economics. Because the book reads like an extended essay, with metaphors, parables, allusions, and wordplay, liberal arts students will enjoy reading the book more than they would the typical economics text. In this regard, then, the book is more closely related to a liberal arts curriculum than most economics texts.

This is our third book on international economics. Those familiar with *International Economics: Theory and Context* will be pleased to see that we have kept its stronger parts, while revising and updating. We have recast the second half, in particular, to fit in better with financial systems and monetary economics courses. This book has served a wide range of markets—many international and domestic universities, on both graduate and undergraduate levels, as well as various government agencies. The present edition has a much fortified and updated content, and reaches a market that may at last have decided that international economics goes beyond offer curves.

Despite the absence of some advanced economic modelling, this is a challenging text, as students who have used it in manuscript form or its predecessors will testify. This is because it deals directly with the major issues of the day, in themselves challenging and ill-understood. More than many texts, it problematizes concepts and theories, avoiding some of the outdated positivism that haunts so many textbooks. We want students to learn how to apply what they know and are learning, to synthesize ideas, and to evaluate theory and policies in the absence of "correct" answers. They can see how, in issue after issue, we present the theory and the evidence, and then draw conclusions and offer some evaluation.

To the extent that a textbook can have a theme, it is that globalization is not new, nor, on balance, to be feared—which is not to deny it presents some very serious problems. After the devastation of two world wars and a world economic depression, foresighted leaders set in motion means to increase global economic integration in order to encourage prosperity and reduce militant nationalism. With the demise of communism and the end of serious military threats to Europe and North America, however, the pressures to promote and maintain integration are less, leading to a resurgent protectionism, increased concerns about capital flows, and more intense criticism of such institutions as the World Trade Organization and the International Monetary Fund. Obviously, globalization has its challenges and problems, sometimes requiring more imaginative (and economically sound) ways of achieving important goals, but trying to stop its progress is costly in economic and political terms. It is passing strange that free trade (and the World Trade Organization) should still be so suspect. Part of the blame may fall on international economics courses and texts that offer students only theory, rather than a hard look at what is actually involved in protectionism and international capital movements.

Authors' debts are always enormous, but we would like to extend special thanks to our students who have helped us hone our presentations and have used the manuscript, to Michael Harrison and Barbara Conolly at Broadview Press, and to our assiduous copy editor, Richard Tallman. We express special thanks to Iva Ilieva for three years of work on the material, and to Nicole

Fallat, Jennifer Blume, and Leah Dering, who helped at Colby College. Thanks also to Greg Rushford for his advice and encouragement.

Wilson B. Brown
WINNIPEG, MANITOBA

Jan S. Hogendorn
OXFORD, U.K., AND
EAST VASSALBORO, MAINE

Chapter One

The Nature of
International Economics

OBJECTIVES

OVERALL OBJECTIVE To demonstrate the extent of interconnectedness of modern national economies, giving historical perspective, and to suggest some of the ways in which the growth of the modern state interacts positively and negatively with the globalized economy.

MORE SPECIFICALLY
- To show how the world economy has become more and more integrated, often in subtle ways that people do not notice.
- To demonstrate that higher degrees of integration have been associated with improvements in communication and transportation and with increasing prosperity.
- To explain that the process today called "globalization" began more than a century ago.
- To convey how, as governments have grown larger and more pervasive within their own economies, they have created many economic differences that would not otherwise exist.
- To illustrate that many special interest groups make use of the state apparatus to gain economic advantages, thereby disadvantaging others, and that these processes are particularly important in international trade and in poor macroeconomic behavior, which in turn causes international financial problems.
- To show that means of achieving many of the important social and political goals of the modern state have to be changed or adjusted in a more global economy.

GLOBALIZATION

Globalization is the increasing economic integration of the world. It began a century and a half ago with the introduction of the railway, steamship, and telegraph, and continues today with the Internet. Increasing integration is virtually unstoppable—or at least stopping it is enormously costly. For the most part increased integration is beneficial (which is why stopping it is costly), but any economic process has harmful effects, sometimes hurting a small group of people, sometimes the society as a whole. If the world is to continue to ride the wave of globalization, it must understand both how to make the best use of globalization's benefits and how to mitigate the more negative things it brings.

Globalization reduces the power of governments to control their economies, including banking regulation, money supply, the ability to bene-fit from creating inflation, environmental regulation, and the ability to favor certain industries or groups of people over others. Many examples in this book suggest that some of the effects of weakening powers are good—that protectionism or inflation protects the politically strong, not the weak. In other cases, however, globalization undermines the effectiveness of estab-lished means of achieving widely accepted and legitimate goals of the govern-ment. Banking, health and environmental regulations, and measures to reduce poverty or narrow income gaps are cases in point. Globalization also con-strains common but less widely accepted measures, such as the policies designed to determine the direction of economic or cultural development within a country.

It is essential to distinguish the goals from the methods. The country may still reach its goals, but may have to devise new methods. Often, as the chap-ters here will show, admirable goals are more a smokescreen for political favors than an end in themselves, or the measures more or less achieve the goals but distribute a lot of unnecessary favors along the way. If at times the arguments in this book come down hard on particular policies, it does not mean that we disagree about the goals of the policies; rather, we do not think the means are particularly effective in achieving the ends. Surely, there are other ways.

On a political level, the stability of a country depends to some degree on the ability of those in power to grant rewards to those who cooperate with them. Countries isolated from the rest of the world can use the power of the modern state much more freely than those more highly integrated. Tariffs and quantitative restrictions on imports allow the government to reward certain groups of supporters. Financial isolation allows governments to run budgetary deficits, financed through inflation. The higher expenditure rewards followers, either directly in the form of putting them or their families on the payroll or indirectly by granting them contracts and various development projects.

Countries more integrated into the world economy must use different means. The choice of an ally rather than a foe from two equally qualified candidates for a position is a perquisite of power that is neither gross nor uneconomic. The choice between two roughly equal development projects, one by supporters, the other benefiting opponents, is also unconstrained by any increased international integration. Governments and politicians should be capable of finding fruitful, not wasteful, ways of keeping themselves in power; greater international integration pressures them to do so.

All the chapters of the book discuss questions of integration and many look at the political forces that shape national reactions to that integration. It is easy to argue in economic terms for a greater freedom of trade and capital movements and for the importance of having an economy in which capital and labor are mobile and in which prices and wages have some flexibility. The political support for such policies is widespread but weak. Typically, benefits that are small per person fail to win out over policies that give a large benefit to a narrower group of beneficiaries. Moreover, the small and better-financed groups often put forth plausible, if disingenuous, arguments that make the policies acceptable. In other cases, some groups may value highly some goals (such as the reduction of pollution), but have not been able to devise ways to pursue their goals without reducing the extent of international integration.

Columnist Tom Friedman[1] a few years back observed that American politics had two dimensions: the extent of international integration and the extent of the use of the state apparatus, particularly to provide social safety nets. Labor in most countries, for instance, favors extensive use of the government, but it tends to be non-integrationist. Most left-of-center parties have within them severe critics of further integration, as well as more traditional internationalists. But those right-of-center parties also harbor virtual isolationists within their ranks. The coalition to support NAFTA, for instance, included former Republican presidents and the very conservative Speaker of the House, Newt Gingrich, while its opposition included the Minority Leader, Richard Gephart, and many Republicans.

This book argues the integrationist side and the necessity to adjust other goals to accommodate the effects of international integration. While it is true that the authors are less confident in the abilities of the state than they were as youths, neither has given up entirely, and their personal preferences would probably put them somewhere in the middle (in North American terms) for use of the state apparatus. They are of that generation that grew up in the wartime and postwar America, haunted by the war and the Depression. As a young child in Hawaii, Professor Hogendorn saw the smoke rising from the bombing of Pearl Harbor, and Professor Brown grew up in a family impoverished by the Great Depression, dimly aware that something had gone terribly wrong. Both depression and war were profoundly international affairs, and both had roots in isolationist and protectionist economic policies. Foresighted leaders after the war tried to construct a world economic and political system that would be closely integrated economically and politically. While their success may be debated, the world has not seen another world war or global depression.

INTERNATIONAL ECONOMICS IN DAILY LIFE

The Sony clock radio (Japanese-made, with a number of parts from Korea and Thailand) awoke Mr. and Mrs. Peoria one morning in their home in America's Midwest, the announcer babbling about the latest crisis in the Middle East. Mr. P. wondered vaguely whether the events would increase the cost of gasoline and whether he should buy that (German-made) Mercedes he always wanted on the excuse it had a diesel engine, or stick to his stylish and peppier but far less classy (Japanese-made) Honda. Mrs. P. was already up, deciding which blouse to wear (both carried the names of European designers, although one was made under license in the United States, the other in Bangkok) when Mr. P. meandered to the bathroom and debated for a few seconds whether he should shave with his Philips (Holland) electric razor or his Gillette (an American modification of the 2-track device designed in Britain).

The stock market had done well this morning (principally due to foreigners' heavy buying in the market). Mr. P. had ordered his broker to sell some shares that day, so he was feeling in a good mood. The dollar was strong, which always gave Mr. P. some satisfaction, even if there was the usual trade deficit, which didn't bother Mr. P. so long as other things were going well. Even interest rates were low, something the man on the "News Hour" had said was related to foreign recession (in fact, a major crisis triggered by panic in some Asian financial markets). Admittedly, with the price of corn down (due to Europe's debatable health regulations and sky-high tariffs on grain and meat), business in town was not as good as before, but it seemed that something was taking up the slack locally (indeed, a number of smaller manufacturers had seen their exports increase). Mrs. P. suggested that instead of a new car they should add a room to the house, but they were concerned because the price of lumber had just risen. (They had not noticed or understood how the U.S. government had just forced Canada to raise the price of its lumber exports to the United States.) Maybe, they thought, that long-awaited trip to see Iguazu Falls in South America would be a better thing, but they worried about the cost of the Argentine peso and Brazilian *real*, since their friends who had traveled there a few years ago had been rather shocked by the prices. Maybe the recent decline of the *real* would help. They understood the Brazilian side of the Falls was nicer, anyway.

The Peorias downed their (Brazilian) orange juice as the doorbell (assembled in Chicago by immigrants from Mexico) rang. It was Maria, come to clean the house (and send some of her earnings to her family in Guatemala). The French coffee-maker (at that moment powered by energy released as a Canadian river gushed through a dam on its way to the Arctic Ocean) sent the aroma of freshly ground (in a grinder made by a German company owned by Gillette) coffee, a blend of Indonesian, Brazilian, and Colombian beans, into the air (which was also carrying pollutants to Canada). Mr. P. paused as he heard the whistle of an Illinois Central (owned by Canadian National Railways) train wafted in on the warm south wind. "Oh well," Mr. Peoria said, finishing his muesli (Swiss-made) and toast with strawberry jam (Bulgarian) and butter (for which they paid an unnecessary premium due to import restrictions), "perhaps we should just keep our money here; it's certainly good to have a 100% American day."

Like Mr. and Mrs. Peoria, everyone is affected by international economics, but rarely and then only dimly do we realize how and in what ways it affects us. In 1997 Americans spent about 13% of their income (GDP) on foreign goods and services, three-quarters of that on goods and the rest on services, including foreign travel. They paid another 3% of GDP abroad for interest on debts and for the profits of foreign firms located in the United States. They earned slightly less, about 11.6% of their income coming from exports of goods and services, and another 3% coming from income received on their foreign investments. Since they spent somewhat more than they earned, they borrowed about 1.5% of GDP from abroad. Even Mr. Peoria helped the borrowing because he sold his bonds to a Japanese company, thus transferring abroad another claim on American assets.

Mr. and Mrs. Brandon, average Canadians, had a similar day, awaking on the western plains and watching CTV news (U.S.-produced) on cable (made by Corning Glass from New York, but using Canadian Nortel equipment) TV (made by a Japanese company manufacturing in the Philippines), but their connection to the world's economy was even stronger. In 1997 Canadians earned (an astounding) 43.5% of their incomes (GNP) from abroad, over 82% of that from exports of goods, 12% from services (including tourism), and the remaining 8% from earnings on foreign investments. They spent about the same amount abroad, 72% of that on goods, 13% on services, and 15% to service foreign debts. The Brandons, being typical Canadians for 1997, borrowed about 2% (net of what they lent) from abroad; part of their mortgage was from funds their Canadian bank borrowed in the United States, but when Mrs. Brandon received an unexpectedly large royalty check (earned from sales in several countries), the Brandons placed the money in American debt securities, so made no net borrowing.

Both the Peorias and the Brandons had income from abroad. Some of the Peorias' income from their holdings of stocks and bonds had its origins in the profits and interest payments from foreign sources. The United States in 1997 received about $253 billion in interest, dividends, and profits of American corporate subsidiaries—nearly $1,000 per person, about 3.1% of GNP, and double what it was as recently as 1991. Countries that have invested substantially abroad over the years such that they have a great stock of wealth in foreign countries find that their returns exceed their payments; those that have been net borrowers over the years have net outflows. Americans earn slightly less investment income abroad than they spend; Canadians pay out around US$1,400 per person, about $700 more than they receive. As the examples of the Brandons and Peorias show, countries differ greatly in the extent and nature of their involvement and integration with the international economy. Figure 1.1 shows the foreign earnings of 10 countries to illustrate the kinds of variation that occur.

Numbers like those in Figure 1.1 often surprise people who are unfamiliar with them. Generally speaking, smaller nations have higher percentages of international trade than do larger ones. The three largest countries in the charts, the United States (270 million people), Brazil (160 million), and Japan (125 million) have the lowest percentages of trade. That is a physical fact having to do with the number of possible interactions. If California were a separate nation, all its trade with the other U.S. states would be international trade; if Belgium were merely part of a United Europe, all its trade with other European countries would be subtracted. The United States is the world's largest trader—12% of all the world's traded goods originated in the U.S. in 1997, and 15% of trade ended up in the U.S.—despite the fact that American trade as a percentage of GDP is one of the lowest among those countries listed. Like the United States, Japan also has a vigorous and large internal economy; it is the third most important trader, yet trade in goods makes up only around 9% of its GDP. The country with the highest percentage of GDP accounted for by exports among industrial countries is Belgium, with around 70% of its GDP exported. Among the G-7, Canada is the highest. It is quite extraordinary, given all the expenditures not much traded internationally—housing, haircuts, medical services, elementary schooling, government services—that still over 40 cents out of every dollar Canadians spend or earn are foreign.

Some of the low figures, however, stem from economic policies that have made it difficult to trade. Chile's population is two-thirds that of Malaysia, but its economic integration is not nearly so high. Chile's low tariffs and more open economy are only about two decades old, while Malaysia has always had

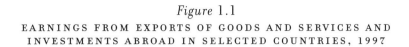

Figure 1.1

EARNINGS FROM EXPORTS OF GOODS AND SERVICES AND
INVESTMENTS ABROAD IN SELECTED COUNTRIES, 1997

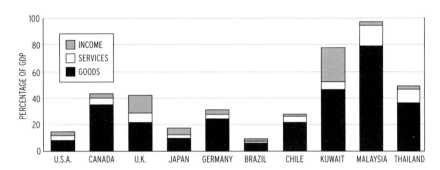

Note: The percentages earned from foreign sources vary greatly between countries. The extremes in this diagram are Brazil, with little over 8% of its income from outside the country, and Malaysia, which earns an astounding 97% of its GDP from abroad. Among the G-7 leading industrial countries, Canada has the greatest amount of its national income coming from abroad, with the United Kingdom (counting the investment income) a close second.

Source: International Financial Statistics, CD-ROM (Washington: IMF, March 1999), charts for national accounts and balance of payments for each country. (Hereafter *IFS,* 1999.)

a very open economy. As subsequent chapters show, high import tariffs discourage both imports and exports, lowering trade as a percentage of GDP, which partially explains why Brazil's figure is so low. Japanese agricultural protectionism also partly explains Japan's relatively low proportion.

Figure 1.1 also shows the large trade in services. The services counted here include expenditures on such things as shipping, tourism and travel, royalties, insurance, consulting, and data processing. Service payments and receipts vary considerably from nation to nation. Britain, with its well-developed financial, insurance, and shipping base, has always had a large percentage of its income in the form of services. Among developing world countries, high receipts of services are usually associated with tourism. In Thailand, for instance, tourism has replaced rice, that country's leading export for over a century, as the number-one foreign exchange earner.

Modern trade is not simply a matter of a German toaster, a Japanese car, or a Chinese-made shirt. Rather, many of the products themselves contain parts or ingredients made in other countries. Some years ago, someone figured Ford's Escort made in Europe has parts from 15 different nations and is assembled in both Britain and Germany. Even at the level of parts, however, we miss other elements—the rubber to make the tires, the nickel for the stainless steel, the payment for the technology used, the rewards for marketing skills and strategies developed, and ultimately the return to the management and capital necessary for it all to work.

Capital flows are another part of global integration. In 1996, for instance, $1.6 trillion dollars of fresh capital flowed between countries. Figure 1.2 shows the various forms that the capital took.

Figure 1.2

NET CAPITAL FLOWS IN 1996

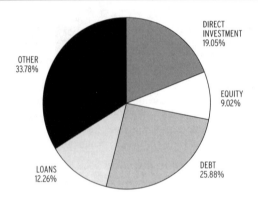

Note: Figures are the sum of the reports of all the individual countries.
Source: Balance of Payments Statistics Yearbook, vol. 2, Tables B23–B30.

At the end of 1996, an additional $1.6 trillion of assets were held outside the countries of origin, in the form of direct investment (foreign corporate subsidiaries), equity (holdings of shares of corporations), debt assets (bonds and notes), bank loans, and "other," which includes central bank and government holdings. Borrowings, of course, matched the lending.

Not only capital, but labor is also mobile. Two statistics give some idea of the impact of mobile labor. *Workers' remittances* estimates the amount of money that immigrant employees send back to their home countries. This item grew from $10 billion (1990 dollars) a year in 1970 to $54 billion (1990 dollars) in 1996. *Compensation to employees* measures the pay of non-residents (people in a country temporarily, as, for instance, a British orchestra conductor working for a short period in Canada or an American playing for a Canadian hockey team (see Chapter 11). This figure was $33 billion in 1996, up from $11 billion (nominal) in 1984.[2]

The extent of the integration of the world economy has profound significance not only for individuals, but for policy-makers and economic

GNP AND GDP

Economists use two closely related figures for measurement of what a country produces—gross national product and gross domestic product. They differ by a number called *net factor payments*, which is principally the difference between the income earned by residents from lending their capital abroad and what they paid for their use of foreign capital, items explained in detail in Chapters 10 and 11. GDP includes all the interest and profits earned by foreign individuals and companies in the country, but does not include any income earned from lending capital abroad; it thus emphasizes what happens in the country. GNP includes the factor payments and receipts, and thus emphasizes what happens to the countries' residents. As an example, Ford's profits from its Brazilian operations would not be counted in American GDP, but are counted in American GNP.

Until the 1970s, it was customary for economists to talk principally about the GNP, and, indeed, some older figures are normally given in terms of GNP. The shift to GDP was to emphasize more what happened within the country, where presumably national monetary and fiscal policies would have most of their effect. Ford's Brazilian profits, for instance, have little to do with American fiscal policy and much to do with Brazilian policy.

We use both GNP and GDP figures in the text. Where the factor payments are important, the logical comparison is with GNP, as it is with the profits of firms that operate abroad or even with the measures of exports and imports. Where they are likely to be unimportant, we use GDP. In some cases, one or the other figure is simply unavailable. Older work may not use GDP, and very recent figures sometimes lack a GNP because it takes longer to gather factor payments numbers. For broad-scale comparisons, the use of one or the other is inconsequential because the difference between them is generally small—normally under 3% of GDP.

institutions in their nations. Today's interpenetration is part of a long historical process and is unlikely to be reversed. Simultaneously, national governments, which control currencies, manage the microeconomic environment, and determine macroeconomic policies, have grown strong and have played an increasing role in shaping their national economies. Yet, almost paradoxically, extensive economic integration has meant that the national governments are less and less able to control economic activity within their own borders. In the following section we look at how this all happened. In the rest of the book, we examine the way the world economy affects the individual nation, and how the nation reacts.

THE GROWTH OF ECONOMIC INTERDEPENDENCE

Trade and Currencies before the Modern Era

The study of international economics can make a claim to be the oldest branch of the discipline. The first acceptable figures for gross national product date from the 1930s—anything before is guesswork, however sophisticated—but foreign trade data can be traced back to medieval times. English trade statistics, for instance, date back to 1355, in the reign of Edward III. Agents of the Crown or city-state could tax and measure foreign trade funneled through relatively few ports or highways. Domestic trade, however, was far too various and complicated to control or count. For the same reasons, economists today find that in many less developed countries trade statistics are reasonable while many other economic figures are not.

Trade among kingdoms and empires is of great antiquity. A recent underwater archaeological find highlights the early origins. It is of a Bronze Age merchant ship, likely headed for some port of Asia Minor laden, not surprisingly, with bronze, that sank off the coast of Turkey some 3,000 years before the Christian era. Some two millennia later, but still a thousand years before the Christian era, we have evidence of agreements between kingdoms. A case in point is the story of Solomon's temple. In the King James Bible's version:

> And Hiram sent to Solomon saying, I have considered the things which thou sentest to me for: and I will do all thy desire concerning timber of cedar, and concerning timber of fir.
>
> My servants shall bring them down from Lebanon unto the sea: and I will convey them by sea in floats unto the place that thou shalt appoint me....
>
> So Hiram gave Solomon cedar trees and fir trees, according to all his desire.
>
> And Solomon gave Hiram twenty thousand measures of wheat for food to his household, and twenty measures of pure oil: thus gave Solomon to Hiram year by year.

This was not the last time that oil and wheat have figured in trade agreements.

Ancient times saw not only extensive trade but also problems of currency exchange. Currency changers were common throughout the ancient world; indeed, it was foreign exchange traders whom Jesus drove out of the temple (for profaning the temple, not for changing coin). Kingdoms used a variety of metals for coinage—gold and silver, electrum (a gold-silver alloy), copper, bronze, and even iron, though gold and silver came to predominate. The prices of these metals varied against one another as the demand and supply of the metals changed, making the job of trading the coins even more difficult. In addition, rulers frequently debased their coins, manufacturing them from less precious metal than their markings indicated. Cleopatra and her father unleashed a serious inflation in Egypt, as did Nero (who rebuilt Rome with the profits from debasement) and many of the late Roman emperors. In Egypt, the value of a pound of gold increased from 1,125 denarii in AD 179 to 3,000 denarii by AD 191, and to over 3 billion denarii at the end of the third century. The currency problems of recent years are hardly new—nor are the means of handling them. Even such seemingly modern and sophisticated devices as forward exchange rates (discussed in Chapter 13) and the use of units of account to denominate debt date back at least to medieval times.[3]

The ancient trade of the West diminished in the early Middle Ages. A decline in public safety, with a rise of marauders and pirates, the collapse of the Roman roads, the decline in literacy, and the disappearance of good coinage all discouraged growth and trade. Signs of revival occurred in the twelfth century, and the invention of sailing vessels that could sail against the wind helped lower the cost of trade. Still, it was not until the fifteenth century that pre-modern institutions—banks, well-integrated markets, credits for trade, double-entry accounting, insurance—developed.[4]

While international trade grew in these centuries, it never penetrated people's lives the way it does today. Only a small part of national production could be exported or imported. A sailing ship had a small capacity to carry goods, and internal roads were usually too miserable to sustain extensive or heavy shipments. Normally, each city or rural estate was supplied almost entirely from the countryside around it, and only the items with a high value per cubic foot could be transported great distances. There was a silk trade, a carpet trade, a fur trade, a spice trade, but no wheat trade, coal trade, or meat trade—indeed, there was very little wine trade until means of preservation were improved. Travel was very difficult—the word itself is a twin to "travail" and derives from a medieval torture instrument in which people were confined so they could not move. It was not undertaken lightly or for fun until well into modern times. Tourism did not begin until the eighteenth century.

The nineteenth and early twentieth centuries brought enormous changes of dimension not seen earlier. In 1800, it took a hard full day to get from New York to Philadelphia and a week to get to the Alleghenies. In 1830, the persistent traveler could get somewhat further west into Pennsylvania in a day, but not much further in a week. Yet by 1857, the traveler could be well into Ohio at the end of the first day and across the Mississippi at the end of the week. The steamboat, railway, telegraph, and telephone all allowed trade on a vastly greater scale. The amount of goods that could be carried in railway cars and steamboats was vastly greater than wagons, barges, and sailing ships could carry. (Steamships at first were not faster than sailing ships, just more reliable and far more capacious.) Wheat from Argentina, Saskatchewan, and North Dakota, beef cattle grazed in the plains and slaughtered in the prairie cities of North and South America, or bananas grown in the Caribbean could be shipped thousands of miles to hungry buyers. Transportation costs, which frequently accounted for 100% or more of the original cost of the goods, fell to small fractions (10-20%) of the costs, often with the remarkable result that prices rose for the exporter while falling for the importer. Thus the price received in the Argentine pampas by the producers of grain or meat rose, at the same time that the price the Londoner paid to consume these commodities fell.

Communications improved the flow of trade. What was needed in the importing country and what was available in the exporting country could be matched, and the ship owner no longer had to wait until his ship came into port to find out what was on board. Payment could be made by telegraph (the line across the Atlantic was established in 1868). By the early years of the twentieth century trade and international finance were no longer affecting only small groups within nations or just a few key products—in many countries 20% and 30% of all wealth was being generated by goods and services that were traded, and that figure was destined to rise even more in the last half of the century.

Historical figures are difficult to evaluate, but Table 1.3 helps us to visualize how the changes in the nineteenth century stimulated trade. The period 1720-1820 saw slow growth of both national economies and commerce; the period after 1820 until World War I, which was the period described above, showed a growth of trade far in excess of the growth of income. The increased protectionism of the 1920s and 1930s and the Great Depression depressed both trade and income. The vigorous postwar growth slowed with the increase in oil prices in the 1970s (Chapter 18), and trade and income growth declined, rising slightly in the last decade.

Trade in the Twentieth Century

The basic technological changes allowing the expansion of trade had been set in place before World War I. While the cost of transportation has continued to decline to an important degree, it cannot have had the same impact as nineteenth-century changes. If the cost of moving $100 worth of goods fell from $100 to $20, another fall of even 50% in costs would represent only 10% of the price of the good. Only air traffic, with its ability to move vast numbers of tourists, has made a difference as dramatic as the nineteenth-century changes did. Indeed, the only comparable change has been the development of the Internet, with its related communications and personal computers.

Figure 1.3

GROWTH OF EXPORTS AND GDP 1720—1997

Note: Britain and France for 1720-1820; these plus Germany and the U.S. for 1820-1870; these four plus Italy and Japan for the later dates.

Sources: For 1720-1979: *World Development Report, 1987* (Oxford: Oxford University Press, 1987), 40; for 1979-1997: *IFS,* 1999, national accounts, deflated by the GDP deflator.

Trade in the present century, as Figure 1.3 shows, is divided into two distinct periods. In the interwar period, both income growth and trade growth were low, and it is the only period when trade grew at a slower rate than income. The two wars disrupted trade itself, but national policies of high tariffs, and later quantitative barriers, also made trade difficult. Finally, the Great Depression of the 1930s reduced incomes and, combined with the protectionism of the period, depressed imports.

The third quarter of the twentieth century saw dramatic declines in tariff barriers, reductions of capital controls, and attempts at international standardization of safety, health, and labeling requirements (see Chapter 5). This period experienced enormous capital movements on a scale never before witnessed—whether or not desired by governments. Transportation costs declined sharply and speed of delivery rose with the introduction of large, highly automated ships capable of unloading their cargoes in a single day. (Indeed, the problem today is to store and move the cargo that has been unloaded. Thus the New York City piers are rotting, while the New Jersey ports of Newark and Elizabeth, with their enormous meadows of marsh that

27

can be used for storage, have virtually all the business.) With rising fuel costs, too, ocean transport became relatively cheaper than land transport. Once a ship is loaded, the marginal cost of sailing another 100 miles is very low. Astonishingly, it is cheaper today to move cars from Japan to California than it is to get them there from Detroit. Sea-rail links have made coastal cities in Japan little more than a week away from Chicago. Winnipeg, not far from the geographical center of North America, regularly has fresh fruits from Argentina, Chile, and, in season, rambutans and lychee from Southeast Asia. A map of the world drawn according to freight rates, not geographical distances, would show the oceans shrunken to the size of the Mediterranean Sea.

National tastes, too, have been converging. As large parts of the developing world come to enjoy high per capita incomes, high levels of education, and high levels of urbanization, they evolve many tastes similar to those of the developed world. The spread of motion pictures, magazines, television programs, books, and the extensive interpersonal contact of people through Internet communications all press toward a certain uniformity in taste. The once uniquely Western business suit, for instance, is well nigh ubiquitous among business leaders and government people. Blue jeans and Coca-Cola seem as popular in Japan and France as in the United States. The cuisines of India, Thailand, and Mexico have supplemented the blander traditional fare in Canada and the United States, where salsa now outsells ketchup. Mechanization has brought with it its own physical demands, lending a certain sameness to cities and factories everywhere. Except for some surface styling, an elevator is an elevator even when it is called a lift, a petrochemical factory is just that; even automobiles vary little from country to country.

The third quarter of the century also saw the rise of a great deal of non-governmental cross-border activity—what has come to be called transnational activity, as opposed to international activities involving relations between governments. The ready communications of satellite, fiber optics, the Internet, and fast jets put people into contact with an ease never before imagined. Net connections, both within a corporation (an "intranet') and between individuals allow close and regular communications so that geographic distance seems unimportant. It is not unusual, though, for an executive to fly across the Atlantic to meet with other executives in some airport hotel for a few hours and then fly back. As a result of this easy communication, growth has mushroomed with all kinds of transnational contacts—charities like Foster Parents, service organizations like the Rotary, a myriad of professional societies of engineers, architects, and economists, interest groups like the Audubon Society, and, not least, those profit-making enterprises known as multinational corporations. Solomon's temple today might have been built by international contractors from Rome, designed by an international

Figure 1.4
GROWTH OF WORLD TRADE

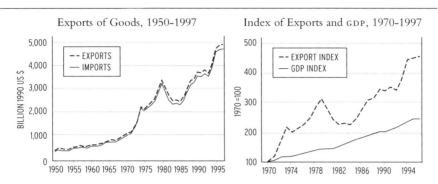

Sources: Left panel: *IFS* 1999; right panel: adapted from *IFS Yearbook*, 1998, Table 23.

architectural firm in New York, and constructed of wood supplied by an international conglomerate.

Statistics support these observations, even though the public is little aware of the extent to which the growth of trade has surpassed the growth of output and income over the past 40 years or so. This enormous increase in trade made new kinds of goods broadly available, contributed to real output growth because of scale economies and specialization that could not be realized in small national markets, increased competition in national markets, and was a major contributor to the high growth rates of GNP that characterized the global economy after World War II. The decline in trade from 1981 to 1985 reflects the decline in petroleum prices (the largest single item of trade), the slow growth in developed countries, and the debt crisis that followed (see Chapter 18).

The left panel in Figure 1.4 reveals the large expansion of trade. World trade in goods grew nearly 13 times in real terms between 1950 and 1997. The right panel, taking the more recent stretch of 1970 to 1997, shows how the sum of all countries' GDPs expanded by 2.5 times, compared with exports, which rose 4.5 times. Some of the figures are affected by the oil crises (see Chapter 18). Oil prices rose sharply in 1972 and 1978, increasing the value of trade, while decreasing its volume. They then fell precipitously in 1982, a period also accompanied by recession and a sharp drop in commodity trade.

Figure 1.4 is for goods only. Exports of services and receipts on investment and some kinds of labor performed abroad, known as income (or factor payments), also make up important parts of trade, and they, too, have expanded. Figure 1.5 shows the exports of goods plus those in the other categories.

Figure 1.5

RECEIPTS FROM EXPORTS OF GOODS AND SERVICES
AND FOR CAPITAL AND LABOR SERVICES

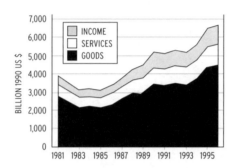

Source: *Balance of Payments Statistics Yearbook*, 1988, 1990, 1997.

As an inevitable result of trade growing faster than domestic economies, nearly all nations have seen trade rise as a percentage of national income. In the early 1950s, only 4-5% percent of American GDP came from exports and services; by 1991 it had climbed to 11%, and by 1997 to 12%. Canada's exports rose from 19% of GNP in 1965 to 40% in 1997, and the pattern is similar in many other countries, as the sampling in Figure 1.6 reveals.

Figure 1.6

GOODS AND SERVICES EXPORTS AS PERCENTAGE
OF GDP, 1975 AND 1997; SELECTED COUNTRIES

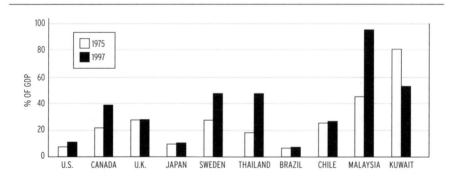

Source: *IFS,* 1999, country tables.

Most countries have seen trade increase sharply as a proportion of GDP, in some cases quite dramatically, as illustrated by Canada, Sweden, Thailand, and Malaysia. In a few countries, such as Kuwait, trade declined as a proportion of GDP as the price and production of oil fell, and trade failed to rise significantly in Japan, Brazil, and Great Britain. While American trade is a small percentage of its GDP, a rise of trade by 1% of American GDP is over $80 billion—an amount equivalent to, for instance, 14% of Canada's GDP.

The historical thrust has been for greater interdependence of the world economy. The forces behind that thrust have been powerful; later chapters will show that those nations that have chosen—or been compelled—to buck the forces of integration have generally not done well. With the exception of big oil exporters, virtually all the nations with trade declining as a percentage of national income, or those with low percentages of trade, have very low growth in income per capita. When the world as a whole has tried to resist the forces of interdependence, as between 1914 and 1950, incomes have fallen or risen only sluggishly.

STATISTICS WITH SOME GRAINS OF SALT

The numbers cited above give the broad sweep of the changes over the last half century. Words of caution, however, are in order. Aggregation of numbers collected in 187 different countries, some of them very difficult to gather and assess, can be only a broad approximation of what probably happened. Year after year, the sum of all countries' imports always exceeds the sum of their exports, and the figures are way off in the early days—17% for 1952, although well below 10% in recent years. Taken literally, this means that countries as a whole are importing more than they are exporting. From whom? Extraterrestrials? The International Monetary Fund (IMF) statisticians have found a number of places to make adjustments (one country's good might be another's service, etc.), but discrepancies in all the measures persist. The IMF adjusts the total figures but not for each individual country, so no country is made to feel better balanced.

Most observers believe that countries pay more attention to imports, which pay tariffs and domestic sales or value-added taxes, than they do to exports, which are generally free of taxes. An understatement on exports is likely to go unnoticed but an understatement (or even an accurate statement) on imports is likely to be challenged. At first blush, it may appear that the errors arise from illegal activity, but $100 million of illegal cocaine is unlikely to be reported *either* as a Colombian export or an American import, so would not affect the figures either way.

A second problem with trade figures—as with most macroeconomic figures—is that they are very inaccurate when the information would be most useful to policy-makers. Perhaps the financial papers headline "October's trade deficit reaches unprecedented levels," and a year later statisticians figure out that it really had not. After more revisions over the next two years as supplementary data come in, the figures are revised again and once again. Do the newspapers report, "October 1998's balance of trade deficit not as bad as once thought"? Can the central bank cancel the interest rate increase it put through three years before?

National account figures such as GDP, investment, and the proper figure for deflation are also dicey. We use them in this book, but we also hope to pass on the idea that they have to be interpreted with caution. As an example, look at the Malaysian figures in Figure 1.6. and consider a few grains of salt. (1) Not all exports were entirely made within the country. *Re-exports*, such as raw rubber from Thailand that Malaysia processes before exporting, cloth from abroad that is turned into clothing, and imported parts that are assembled account for part of the high trade figure. (2) National accounts weigh market transactions more heavily than transactions in the informal sector of the economy, such as housing. The informal sectors of an economy that has large rural areas and is developing rapidly are much larger than in developed countries, so traded goods tend to be overstated. (3) Last, though not a grain of salt, is that Malaysia has many opportunities for small cross-border trading. It is a small country in two distinct parts (the peninsular states and those in North Borneo), with long borders through populated regions. Such a configuration increases trade. Just opposite the economically huge city–state of Singapore is Johore, and a Malaysian could indeed go to Singapore for an evening of entertainment and dining, and a Singaporian might stop for a haircut in Johore while checking out a subsidiary plant there. Chile, in contrast, has only tiny towns along its borders, which essentially exist only because that is where the border posts are. The highly populated central valley has the Andes to the east and the vast Pacific to the west.

Trade and the Nation-State

While the forces of interpenetration are great, nation-states themselves tend to resist, seeking to increase their own distinctiveness, or at least to slow the process of integration.

INTERNATIONAL AND INTERREGIONAL TRADE

Ask the layperson why international trade exists and the answer is likely to have something to do with national characteristics. Malaysia is in the tropics and exports rubber. Industrious Germans produce high-quality cars. Creative French designers produce the latest clothing styles. That type of explanation, clothed in its proper theoretical vestments, is only partially correct. Natural differences of soil, climate, even national temperament often do coincide with nations. Oceans, seas, jungles, deserts, and mountain ranges not only form militarily defensible lines and concentrate populations, but more or less incidentally serve to hold a nation within climatological boundaries. Often, too, national borders delineate cultural differences, as cultural groups have struggled to preserve themselves or eliminated competing cultural groups within the borders. Religions change with the border, as from Israel to Jordan, Pakistan to India, and Thailand to Malaysia. Languages change, as from Mexico to the United States and Uruguay to Brazil, and with that comes much other cultural baggage. Surely an exposition of cultural and climatic differences should explain trade between such nations.

But such explanations also serve to explain why Florida sends oranges to Massachusetts and Massachusetts sends computers to Florida—that is, they are basically explanations of interregional, not international, trade. To the extent that nations have different regional characteristics, the explanations are useful but in themselves insufficient.

To make the point more conclusively, look at something that is international but not interregional. Consider the satellite photograph in Figure 1.7 of part of the border between the United States and Canada. The border stands out as clearly as the edge of a carpet: the American side has farming and the Canadian side ranching. Yet the land is the same. The winter wind blows just as coldly, the summer's grasshoppers munch just as greedily; in short, geography does not explain why the land-use patterns should vary

Figure 1.7

PART OF U.S.-CANADA BORDER
BETWEEN ALBERTA AND MONTANA

Source: Landsat image courtesy of Canada Centre for Remote Sensing, Department of Energy, Mines, and Resources, Ottawa.

33

so sharply. Nor does culture suffice: both Canadians and Americans eat wheat and beef, and each country has both farmers and ranchers. Both groups of farmers are English-speaking of European ancestry. Indeed, the 49th parallel is just a line drawn by far-away negotiators. Yet that "artifact" has determined, somehow, a pattern of land use.

Follow Mr. and Mrs. Peoria, who decide to visit the Brandons in Canada. They drive north across that border some miles east of where the satellite picture was taken. Consider what differences they would see that are not due to regional variations.

1. They have to pick their route more carefully to find a place to cross the border. The transportation system, built largely by government money or subsidies, is not as dense near the border, and access is controlled. It certainly is not a serious problem for their car, but it is for a truck because the roads leading to many crossings are not all that suitable for heavy transport. What is more, there are only two railway crossings between the Winnipeg area (where there are several) and the Rockies.

2. Immigration is controlled. The Peorias spot this immediately when a uniformed customs officer walks over to their car to inquire about their citizenship. Since they are not Canadians, the officer inquires further as to the purpose of their visit and when they intend to leave. As usual, he is satisfied, but young people, especially those traveling in a van might raise suspicions, and be subjected to a long session of questions, for fear they might wish to stay on and find work in Canada. People from a rather long list of countries have to have passports to enter, and some even are required to obtain visas before arriving in the country. Without these, they will be turned back at the border or will not be allowed to land, and the process can at times be rather arbitrary.*

3. Imports are controlled. The officer will inquire what the Peorias are bringing in that they will not be taking back and whether they have any firearms or liquor (one bottle per person is allowed). If they had any gifts for Canadians, they might find themselves paying a tariff, plus the far more costly sales taxes levied by the government and provinces, which could amount to nearly 15% of the value of their purchases.

4. They go for a bite to eat and find they need a different currency. (Yes, the restaurants will take their U.S. dollars in the border areas, but not always at the best rates because they cannot use the U.S. dollars to pay their bills and

---

* Author WBB, crossing into Canada at Sarnia, Ontario, and stopping briefly at immigration, met a bearded young man dressed in a white robe and wearing sandals. Immigration seemed troubled about him and his partner. "What difference does it make," he asked in an airy and distant voice, "what I was doing five years ago, or last year? Can't he feel the good vibes coming from me?" No one had told him that immigration officials are rarely sensitive to good vibes.

have to take them to the bank, which has to send them back across the border.)

5. The Peorias' youngest daughter, Gloria, is 20 years old, and they all want a beer. In North Dakota, she could not be served; indeed, she was not even supposed to be in a place serving beer. In Manitoba, she is of legal drinking age.

6. The Brandons' daughter, Regina, is expecting a child in a few months. Mr. P. asks about her medical coverage, and she tells them that her employer does not provide any insurance, but that she gets a great deal of coverage through the province. To most people in industrial economies, that would be familiar, but to the Peorias, whose health insurance is privately provided and who are aware that part-timers often are not covered by their employers' policy, the Canadian system seems surprising.

7. The Peorias worry, however, at what might be the resultant higher taxes, but find that in the brief discussion they cannot really discover whether Canadian taxes are higher or lower than those paid by Americans because deductions, exemptions, tax rates, and the like are all so different.*

8. Half the label on the ketchup bottle is in French. They learn that a company cannot sell ketchup in Canada without a label in French and English, even if its target market is 1,000 miles away from any concentration of French speakers and even further from any monolingual Francophones.

THE SOURCES OF NATIONAL DIFFERENCES

None of the differences noted above is regional; all deal with the existence of separate governments. Each nation has different codes or rules that make its economy different from those of its neighbors. Taxes may be principally on income in one nation and on value added in another. One nation may subsidize farming, another industry. Pollution, safety, labeling, and branding requirements differ enormously—and often for no better reason than that they have evolved separately. Basically customary habits become sanctioned by law—as in which side of the road to drive on, and therefore which side of the car the steering wheel is on.

National laws also tend to isolate each nation from its neighbors, making a considerable difference in the way trade is conducted within a country and between countries. Within the United States, for example, labor, management, and capital move freely. Great movements these can be, as with the pioneers to the frontier, Blacks to northern cities, or businesses to the so-called Sunbelt. In Europe one finds the Welsh moving to London, provincial

---

* In the mid-1990s, Canadian federal, provincial, and local taxes took about 43% of GDP, compared to the American take of 36%. About 3% of GDP went to medical services in Canada, somewhat more than in the U.S. Net of medical expenses, Canadians pay more taxes.

French to Paris, and Germans to Bavaria. Capital moves, too. New textile plants are built in the American South, leaving old ones idle in New England; electronics firms have moved to the circumferential highway around Boston, robotics plants to the road between Detroit and Ann Arbor; and capital raised through the sale of stocks and bonds sold in any area of the United States can serve to finance operations in any other area.

Between countries the situation is different. In the United States, Ellis Island, the point of entry for millions of immigrants for over a century, is a museum, and legal immigration slowed to a trickle (but has recently risen substantially). Canada and Australia, which until recently had virtually open doors for immigrants (at least those of European origin), now have them open just a crack, and the bulk of new immigrants are refugees. While the number of people working across borders is still substantial, the flow is not what it used to be.

Modern governments also try to restrict the movement of capital, although they are often unsuccessful. Many nations require a business or individual to have government permission before sending money abroad—what is called exchange control. Several nations have tried to restrict the inflow of capital; the Swiss, for instance, actually charge foreigners a fee instead of paying interest on Swiss accounts. Many nations limit any capital movement associated with a controlling ownership, particularly of natural resources. A firm may be able to move 1,500 miles from New York to Alabama, but in the 1960s and 1970s, if it went just across the border into Quebec, it would have to fill out a long document explaining why it was investing and why it should be allowed to make its investment, and could easily have been rejected. For years, in Japan, Mexico, and most of the Andean countries, foreign firms could not invest unless they shared ownership with domestic citizens. Communist countries, of course, prohibited extensive private ownership on principle, but that era appears to have ended.

The nation-state shapes its own economy in many subtle, often unintended, and frequently ill-understood ways. Every tax, subsidy, and regulation causes economic reactions, which economists only partially understand. Economics demonstrates something about the incidence of taxes (who ultimately pays a tax) or the incidence of a subsidy (who ultimately benefits). But answers to such questions are difficult, both theoretically and statistically. The costs and benefits from regulation are even more difficult. Find two side-by-side nations and the differences, as with the 49th parallel, may be clear, but the causes of those differences may not be at all so apparent. Is the difference between U.S. and Canadian land-use patterns caused by a U.S. subsidy to grain farmers? (The picture was taken when subsidies were not high.) Canadian subsidies to meat? Transportation policy? Tax structures? The value of the Canadian dollar? The cause of an obvious difference is in itself quite obscure.

THE NATURE OF THE MODERN STATE

Many of the differences just described derive from the nature of the modern nation-state, both in its jurisdiction and in the extent of its activities. A law made in Paris applies in equal force anywhere in France, and stops at the border. It was not always so—a medieval king could hardly hope to have his laws applied equally in all parts of the country because many of the nobles who were presumably loyal to him were not willing to enforce them, and there was nothing the king could do about it. It is even true today in many countries that the power of the central government diminishes in distant areas. Burmese control over its northeastern area or Colombian control over the illegal drug-producing regions resembles more the struggles of some medieval king dealing with half-rebellious barons than the patterns of a modern state. In this sense, we must have modern, consolidated nation-states to speak of international economics.

The second element in modern nation-states is the extent of their intervention in the economy, which in turn determines the degree to which the governments shape those economies. Certainly, the kings of Europe had intervened in the economy, created monopolies, even tried to set prices, but their power and scope were limited. Large, centrally controlled standing armies and even police forces are basically nineteenth-century developments. The percentage of national income the government could extract in taxes was necessarily small because there was little surplus income above subsistence. Heavy taxation is essentially a phenomenon of the last 100 years. Gathering the historical data is necessarily difficult, but the following sampling should help make the point. The left-hand panel in Figure 1.8 combines some early estimates with more recent figures to give an idea of the American federal government's share of the country's income. The right-hand panel is a snapshot of expenditures in developed countries for 1994. The reason American expenditure takes up about 15% more of GDP in this panel is that it includes American state and local expenditures, which have tended to rise as federal taxes have leveled off. The right panel also separates the amounts governments spend on their own consumption activities from their transfers. Transfers, such as pensions, social security, Medicare, and welfare, were not large percentages of the budgets until the 1940s. Presently they make up half or more of government expenditures (Government investments, which these figures do not break out, run about 3-4% of GDP).

The rise in taxation and expenditure has increased the government's effect on the national economy. Tax rates of 5-10% are unlikely to alter substantially firms' or households' actions, particularly if those taxes are collected from many different tax bases (some excise, some imports, some real estate). When taxes and expenditures are at current levels, however, they have major

37

Figure 1.8
SOME VIEWS OF GOVERNMENT EXPENDITURES

American Federal Government
Expenditures as Percentage of
Estimated National Income

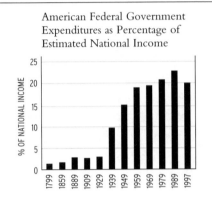

Government Expenditure on
Goods, Services, and Transfers

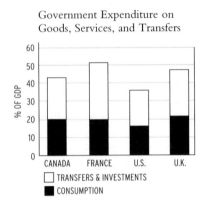

Sources: Left panel: Dennis C. Mueller, "The Growth of Government," *IMF Staff Papers* 34, 1 (March 1987): 116; *Government Financial Statistics Yearbook, 1997.* (The 1799 and 1859 figures are estimated national income; 1889 through 1929 are estimated GDP; more recent years are GDP.) Right panel: *Government Financial Statistics Yearbook, 1997*; *IFS,* 1999, national accounts.

effects in changing (or distorting, to use a more loaded word) the allocation of resources. Since the taxation and subsidies are different in each nation, the shape of their economies differs as well.

POLITICAL-ECONOMIC CONSIDERATIONS

Political considerations loom large in the way the state confers benefits and extracts penalties. The national state is the focus for compromise and trade-offs, carrying a legitimacy that far exceeds its ultimate physical powers to enforce its laws. Citizens pay taxes, albeit grudgingly, to support many things they individually do not wish, and they each get the benefit of subsidies and expenditures paid for by others. All recognize that, among other things, the state is an arena in which various interest groups contend for their piece of the pie, but most also feel that much of what the state does is good for virtually everyone. The vast bulk of the population accepts the compromises and trade-offs made at a national level. Many citizens may begrudge the import controls that cause them to pay extra money for their shoes or chickens, all in support of people in some far-off town, but they expect to get some compensating benefits in the tit-for-tat of national politics.

Internationally, there is less sense of legitimacy and trade-off, and trade-off is much harder to accomplish between nations. People accept the domestic shaping of the economy, even if it involves major "distortions" from a hypothetical free-market result and those distortions hurt many individually. They do not accept similar distortions when the distortions arise abroad. With the focus of political activity on the national level, the international arena is secondary, even when it is not secondary in importance.

Subsequent chapters will demonstrate what occurs when small groups are able to harness the considerable powers of the modern state to their own ends, frequently fighting integrative pressures that will increase economic efficiency at their expense. To prevent the state from bridling as the harness is placed on, they use smooth and soothing phrases, explaining the benefits of some greater good and disguising or ignoring its actual costs, to provide their actions with the moral legitimacy required for acceptance.[*] As economists our concern is with a demonstration of costs and benefits. As students of policy, however, we take our roots to Adam Smith and J.S. Mill seriously; we are still moral philosophers.

LOOKING FORWARD

The chapters that follow explore how international and national economies are related and the patterns of policy that emerge domestically. Part I of the book explores the microeconomic side of the economy: the benefits of trade, the problems of trying to restrict trade, and the development of free trade between groups of countries. Part II delves into financial and macroeconomic questions—trade and national income accounts, the balance of payments, unemployment and growth, inflation, money, foreign exchange, and international capital markets, concluding with a historical overview of the international financial economy.

VOCABULARY AND CONCEPTS

Capital flows
Factor Payments
Globalization
GNP and GDP
International and interregional trade

Legitimacy
Trade in goods
Trade in services
Transnational activity
Workers' remittances

----

[*] Dennis C. Mueller states, "Groups whose interests have public good or externality attributes are more likely to be successful than those seeking pure redistribution." See Mueller, "The Growth of Government," *Quarterly Journal of Economics* (August 1983): 132-33.

QUESTIONS

1. Consider the slice of life in the Peoria vignette. List the (a) imported products they used, (b) things they used that would have contributed to the payment of licensing fees to foreigners, (c) non-imports they used that would have contributed to profits of foreign corporations, (d) income they may have had from foreign sources, (e) ways in which foreign government laws were affecting his welfare, (f) ways in which his own government's trade laws were affecting his welfare, (g) possible foreign services they might consume, (h) contributions their spending might make to the transfer of income abroad.

2. What evidence is there that globalization is not something new, but rather the continuation of a process that has been going on for many years?

3. In your own experience (and in the countries you know) does internationalism appear on both the left and right?

4. What strike you as the most interesting or dramatic of the statistics on the extent of international integration? Why?

5. What changes in the nineteenth century stimulated increased economic integration?

6. What are the forces in the late twentieth century that have led to increased globalization? What figures support the idea of increased globalization?

7. How does the example of the border between the United States and Canada demonstrate that national laws or customs, not climate, create international differences? What are the possible causes for such a difference in land use?

8. "The nation-state shapes its own economy in many subtle, often unintended, and frequently ill-understood ways. Every tax, every subsidy, every regulation causes economic reactions that economists only partially understand." Comment, relating this to the way that national economies become different.

9. Demonstrate that the modern state has considerably more impact on its economy than those of 100 years ago.

10. What is the importance of a sense of legitimacy to the trade-offs that occur within a political body? How can the lack of a similar strong international sense lead to restrictions on trade and capital movements?

NOTES

1. "The New American Politics," reprinted in the *Globe and Mail,* November 17, 1997, from an earlier column in the *New York Daily News.*

2. *Balance of Payments Statistics Yearbook,* Tables B12, B19.

3. Paul Einzig, *The History of Foreign Exchange* (London: St. Martin, 1964), chs. 1-6.

4. We draw from Fernand Braudel's trilogy *Civilization and Capitalism: 15th-18th Century,* vol. 3, *The Perspective of the World* (London: William Collins & Sons, 1984), which describes the city-states. Vol. 1, *The Structures of Everyday Life* (1979), notes that in the thirteenth century, English grain increased in price by 15% for every 50 miles of overland travel.

Part One

International Trade

Chapter Two

The Theory of
Comparative Advantage

OBJECTIVES

OVERALL OBJECTIVE To explain the well-accepted and still powerful proof of the benefits of international trade known as the theory of comparative advantage.

MORE SPECIFICALLY
- To contrast the ideas of absolute advantage and comparative advantage.
- To demonstrate the theory of comparative advantage in numerical and diagrammatic ways.
- To show why becoming more productive may not affect comparative advantage.
- To use supply and demand diagrams to discuss the gains from trade, identifying some gainers and losers.
- To modify some of the key assumptions about the number of products and transport costs.

As noted in the first chapter, the creation of a national border running across a region should not change the economic rationale for trade. If Vienna traded with Budapest before Austria-Hungary was broken up, or Moscow with Kiev in the old Soviet Union, or St. Paul with Winnipeg before there was significant control or taxes along the 49th parallel, the economic gains should still be there afterwards. Yet somehow the advantages of trade we assume to exist domestically must be argued again in an international setting.

The proposition that international trade brings gains to the participants is one that generally unites economists, who on many other questions are more fractious. When the Nobel Prize-winning economist Paul Samuelson wrote that "our subject puts its best foot forward when it speaks out on international trade," he was thinking of the gains to the world from trade.[1] Yet the unity was not always so. In the history of economics the investigation of the costs and benefits of international trade was one of the first great issues faced by the discipline, and the question is still alive, especially in politics and in the business community. The questions posed sound simple. Will countries be better off if they trade with one another? What goods will they trade? Will their welfare be greater if they buy only at home from their own producers?

Plato (427?-347 BC) believed that unnecessary imports should be banned and necessities should not be exported, and Aristotle (384-322 BC) seconded his high opinion of *autarky*. (Autarky means economic self-sufficiency, with no trade between nations. The word "autarky" should not be confused with its homonym, autarchy, which refers to autocratic or dictatorial rule.) A thousand years later a school of thought called mercantilism had evolved.[2] The mercantilist economists viewed exports as productive but imports as wasteful. The country that exported more than it imported would receive from foreigners an inflow of money (gold and silver primarily). This treasure would pay for defense and make for easy credit and the investment that would bring economic development. The mercantilists viewed imports as unfavorable. But even among their ranks there were skeptics. One of them, Roger Coke, observed very aptly in 1670, "The Dutch we see import all, yet thrive upon trade, and the Irish export eight times more than they import, yet grow poorer."

Adam Smith changed the landscape, as he did in so many other areas of economics, with his *Wealth of Nations* (1776). Smith spoke of the obvious gain that occurs when a shoemaker sells shoes to a tailor from whom he buys his clothes.

> What is prudence in the conduct of every private family can scarce be folly in that of a great kingdom. If a foreign country can supply us with a commodity cheaper than we ourselves can make it, better buy it of them with some part of the produce of our own industry employed in a way in which we have some advantage.[3]

Smith's famous concept of opportunity cost was a central discovery for the theory of international trade. The cost of producing some item for ourselves would be some quantity of another item that we could have produced. Producing something we do inefficiently could have great costs in the forgone production of something we produce efficiently.

The great English economist David Ricardo (1772-1823) developed this idea. In his *Principles of Political Economy and Taxation* (1817), he presented a more elaborate theory of the gains from trade, known as the *theory of*

RICARDO AND HIS MODEL

David Ricardo was one of history's greatest economists. He was also one of the richest, making a large fortune on the London stock exchange within 30 years of his birth. Public spirited, he used part of his wealth to buy a seat in Parliament, in which he served with distinction. His new theory of comparative advantage eventually moved British economic policy radically away from the old mercantilist idea that one country's gains from trade were another country's losses. In a relatively short period of time, the mercantilist belief that limiting imports and maximizing foreign exchange receipts were good goals in foreign trade was replaced by a broad new concept that liberal trading rules would best promote the public welfare. For nearly a century thereafter, Britain had the most open trade policy of any industrial nation.

For his model, Ricardo used cloth and wine produced in England and Portugal to make his famous examples. These were contentious topics in his day. The Methuen Treaty of 1703 had reduced British tariffs on wine and Portuguese tariffs on cloth, the two products in which the countries were relatively inefficient, and this had provoked a long and bitter controversy.[4] The modern reader might think one of the product choices not apt. It is impossible to produce wine in England, one might say. But it *is* possible! English wines were indeed bottled from grapes grown along the warm southern coast in Ricardo's time, and a little is produced even today, with output boosted by the price support of the European Union's Common Agricultural Policy. The main reason we do not simply duplicate Ricardo's presentation is not the rarity of good English wine, but the fact that Ricardo used the labor theory of value to measure costs of production (the costs being only the man hours of labor employed to make the products). Later economists considered also the value of land and capital. Even so, the approach followed is Ricardo's.

comparative advantage. This chapter presents that theory, albeit in modern dress. It shows the gains from international trade in both the Ricardian general equilibrium, where the functioning of an entire economy is analyzed with production possibilities and indifference curves, and the Marshallian partial equilibrium, which works through demand and supply curves to analyze a single good. In the process of doing so, the chapter develops the modern theory of comparative advantage. Subsequent chapters examine more deeply why certain trading patterns develop and the vast political, tax, and legal machinery that has arisen to block trade.

THE GAINS FROM TRADE IN GENERAL EQUILIBRIUM

To begin, follow Ricardo in postulating a world of two countries (plausible enough) and (implausible, but absolutely essential for a two-dimensional diagram with any clarity) two products. The products in this 2 × 2 analysis are wheat and cloth, the nations Agricola (the wheat producer, naturally) and Fabrica (the cloth producer). We will also assume that competition is perfect, with all relevant costs known and any idled resources quickly re-employed at their next-highest opportunity costs. This model encompasses only real flows of goods, and it does not incorporate factor flows such as international lending, or the holding of deposits abroad, or the movement of labor from one country to another. Because there are no capital flows, trade must therefore balance, with exports always equaling imports. At this stage there are no transport costs or barriers to trade, such as tariffs or quotas. Nor is it necessary to specify the type of economic system—whether this is market-driven, socialist planned, or simply a computer game with the reader as Grand Coordinator. Furthermore, the present model has no dynamic effects such as changing tastes or production abilities. In other words, Ricardo's model is "static," that is, comparative advantage does not change. Each of these assumptions will be relaxed, in turn, during the course of the next few chapters. After completing that process, some of the conclusions stemming from Ricardo's model are altered in detail, but the fundamental strength remains.

Table 2.1 illustrates the possible production combinations for two goods available to each nation in the absence of international trade between them (autarky). The table shows, among other things, that Fabrica can at any volume of production get 15 more bolts of cloth in return for giving up 30 bushels of wheat; that is, if it wishes to increase its wheat production from 30 to 60, there is an opportunity cost: it must decrease cloth production from 60 to 45. Agricola can at any point get 30 more bushels of wheat by giving up 10 bolts of cloth.

Note that these production trade-offs mean that prices will be different in the two countries. In Fabrica the price of 30 bushels of wheat is 15 bolts of cloth, or half a bolt of cloth per bushel of wheat. Similarly, the price of 15 bolts of cloth is 30 bushels of wheat, or two bushels of wheat for a bolt of cloth. In Agricola, however, prices are different. The price of 30 bushels of wheat is 10 bolts of cloth, or one-third of a bolt for a bushel. The price of 10 bolts of cloth is 30 bushels, or three bushels for a bolt.

Now begin trade between the two nations. Fabrica can buy its wheat in Agricola for one-third of a bolt—one-sixth of a bolt cheaper than if it produced the wheat itself. Agricola can buy one bolt of cloth in Fabrica for two bushels of wheat, one less bushel than it would have cost to buy the cloth at home. If Agricola specialized completely in wheat, it could produce 240 bushels; if Fabrica specialized completely in cloth, it could produce 75 bolts.

Table 2.1

PRODUCTION POSSIBILITIES FOR FABRICA AND AGRICOLA

Fabrica		Agricola	
Wheat (bushels)	Cloth (bolts)	Wheat (bushels)	Cloth (bolts)
150	0	240	0
120	15	180	20
90	30	120	40
60	45	60	60
30	60	30	70
0	75	0	80

No other combination will give so high a total "world" output of wheat and cloth—try it and see. Surely the Grand Coordinator, in allocating resources, would want Agricola producing wheat and Fabrica producing cloth.

Suppose, further, that Agricola and Fabrica have the same population, wealth, and capital stocks. Agricola, however, can produce more of *either* wheat or cloth than Fabrica. Because the same amount of resources can produce more in Agricola, we can say that Agricola has a higher *productivity* than Fabrica. Agricola can make either a bushel of wheat or a bolt of cloth with fewer resources (land, labor, capital) than Fabrica. In Ricardo's language, Agricola has an *absolute advantage* in both products. *An absolute advantage is said to exist when a country uses fewer resources to produce a product than does another country.*

Comparative Advantage Introduced

The absolute advantage does not prevent trade, however. Agricola still has to contend with the fact that its opportunity cost for making an extra bolt of cloth is three bushels of wheat, while Fabrica's is only two bushels of wheat. The trade that springs up between Agricola and Fabrica is determined by *comparative advantage*—that is, the ratio of the trade-offs within one country compared to the ratio in the other country. We compare costs, not productivity. The cost in Agricola is not the number of man-hours, quantity of land used, and value of capital engaged, but the cloth those resources could have produced. Agricola may very well have higher productivity, but that means that the wheat sacrificed to produce cloth is greater. Costs, which are always opportunity costs, are higher. Any nation may be capable of making quite efficiently any number of the things it imports, but only at a sacrifice if it is able to make other products even more efficiently. *A comparative advantage is said to exist when one country can produce a product at lower cost in terms of opportunities forgone than can another country.*

THE COMMON SENSE OF COMPARATIVE ADVANTAGE

The idea of comparative advantage is all around us, affecting our daily lives all the time. Here are four common-sense examples among many thousands of possibilities (remembering that common sense is not always correct in economics, though it is in these cases).

1. You are your town's best surgeon, but you are also a very careful, fast, and efficient mower of lawns. You hire the teen next door to mow your lawn even though the teen works more slowly at the job than you do because your high earnings from an extra hour of surgery far outweigh the cost of paying the (less productive) teen.

2. Consider a law firm where both of us are junior members arguing criminal and corporate cases. Though I am better at arguing both kinds of cases than you are, I argue the corporate cases with relatively greater success. It seems to make sense that if I take all of the corporate cases and you take all the criminal cases, the results will generate more victories for us and will make us partners in the firm at an early age.

3. You are chief of a large surburban fire department in southern California. Vast brush fires have engulfed your area. You have a fleet of fire trucks consisting of modern, powerful La France engines and many older and less capable Buffalos and Pierces. The La France engines are tremendous at snuffing potentially very costly house fires, very much better at that than the older models. They are also far superior to the older engines at extinguishing brush fires along the uninhabited hillsides, which, however, cause less costly damage to property owners. As fire chief directing the firefighting, how would you optimize the outcome as you fight the many fires with your different models? Well, you would say, the La France engines have the absolute advantage in both activities, but their comparative advantage is in extinguishing house fires. That is, the opportunity cost of time spent in fighting brush fires is high for the La France. Using one to save a house makes much more sense than saving an acre of uninhabited brush. Use the older models for the brush fires and minimize your town's bill for the damage.

4. The last example of the common sense of comparative advantage is perhaps our all-time favorite economics anecdote. It was unearthed by Charles P. Kindleberger of MIT. A famous and wealthy impresario of stage and screen in the 1940s named Billy Rose had an unusual hobby, typing and stenography. His speed was legendary, he entered competitions, and he actually won a world championship in the tournaments of that era. Obviously, he would have encountered enormous difficulty in hiring a secretary who could work nearly as well as he himself could. So should he hire secretaries? Yes, because even though he was the world's best at the job, he could still earn much more in an hour spent manipulating his stage and screen empire than he could in typing.

Table 2.2

PRODUCTION POSSIBILITIES AFTER A PRODUCTIVITY CHANGE

Fabrica		Agricola	
Wheat (bushels)	Cloth (bolts)	Wheat (bushels)	Cloth (bolts)
300	0	120	0
240	30	90	10
180	60	60	20
120	90	30	30
60	120	15	35
0	150	0	40

Economic pundits frequently intone that a nation must "increase its productivity" to improve its trading position. False. A nation of beavers and a nation of goof-offs have ample reason to trade, and neither the industry of the beavers nor the lethargy of the goof-offs will change the trading pattern. Suppose that Fabrica is taken over by an efficiency-minded government, while Agricolan industry and farming suffer major efficiency losses as a new spirit of fun-loving and leisure-mindedness infects the population. Productivity doubles in Fabrica and falls to half of its old levels in Agricola. Do trade patterns change? Interestingly, no. Table 2.2 shows that Fabrica can now produce double the amount it could previously make, 180 bushels of wheat and 60 bolts of cloth, for example. Remarkably, however, the ratio of the trade-off of wheat to cloth in more productive Fabrica is still the same: an extra two bushels of wheat must be sacrificed to get an extra bolt of cloth. Agricola, in spite of its now-lower productivity, still has a 3:1 trade-off ratio. While Fabrica is clearly far better off than it was before, it will not overwhelm Agricola with trade. Agricola undoubtedly has fewer goods and services to enjoy, but trade will still leave it better off than it would be under autarky.

Comparative Advantage with Production Possibilities Curves

The data from Table 2.1 produce the solid lines in Figures 2.1a, 2.1b, and 2.1c. The lines are what most students know as production possibilities curves (PPCs), though they are often called production frontiers and occasionally transformation curves. The PPCs here are straight lines, indicating that no matter how specialized or generalized each nation is, the trade-off of wheat for cloth will be the same. This temporary expedient, consistent with Ricardo's illustration, will soon be relaxed. Figure 2.1a shows the production possibilities curve of Fabrica, 2.1b the PPC of Agricola, while 2.1c shows the two curves on the same diagram. It is immediately apparent that the two curves have different slopes, which is to say they represent different prices for wheat and cloth. Consider what the slopes show. The slopes indicate the price of cloth in terms of wheat, 1:2 in Fabrica and 1:3 in Agricola.

Where the curves are located, that is, where they intercept the axes, depends on productivity. If we wished to represent Fabrica after it became a nation of beavers, we would just move the production possibilities curve outward, as suggested by the broken line (curve) on Figure 2.1a. To show Agricola becoming a nation of goof-offs, we would move its PPC inward, as represented by the broken line on Agricola's diagram.

The simple diagram can answer only some questions about trade. It suggests that Agricola would specialize entirely in wheat, and Fabrica in cloth, but it does not provide enough information to tell just how much each nation would keep for its own use or how much welfare would improve. To begin that analysis, we turn to our more normal production possibilities curve, which is bowed, as in Figure 2.2. Such production possibilities curves represent increasing costs—that is, the more wheat a nation wants, the more cloth it will have to sacrifice to get it; the more cloth it wants, the more

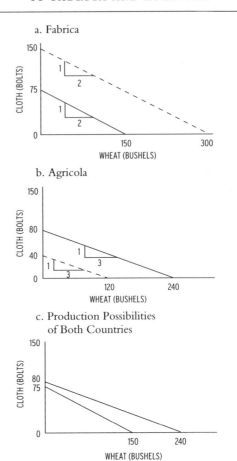

Figure 2.1

PRODUCTION POSSIBILITIES
OF FABRICA AND AGRICOLA

a. Fabrica

b. Agricola

c. Production Possibilities
of Both Countries

Note: Figure 2.1a incorporates the data on Tables 2.1 and 2.2 for Fabrica. If productivity doubles for both wheat and cloth, the slope of the schedule does not change, and therefore the price of one product in terms of the other does not change. Figure 2.1b does the same for Agricola, showing the same thing. Figure 2.1c presents the two original schedules, showing that Agricola can produce either more cloth or more wheat than Fabrica, but that it is still to its advantage not to produce cloth.

Figure 2.2

PRODUCTION POSSIBILITIES CURVES WITH INCREASING COSTS

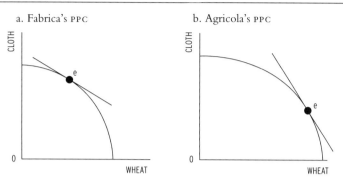

Note: The introduction of increasing costs produces production possibility curves that are concave to the point of origin. The slope at a combination of wheat and cloth the community wants is represented by the line at the point *e*.

wheat it will sacrifice. The assumptions are more realistic and consistent with demand and supply. Supply curves slope upward, meaning that greater and greater opportunity costs are being incurred as production increases. An unbent production possibilities curve suggests a perfectly elastic supply curve for either of the two goods in question.

The problem with using a bowed PPC is that there are a great number of slopes to choose from, ranging from the nearly horizontal to the nearly vertical. To determine what is traded and what gains there might be, we have to know where on the PPC the nation would produce under autarky—what mix of the two products is the one it wants. We could initially just mark the mix desired, as with the points labeled *e* on each of the PPCs in Figures 2.2a and 2.2b. At those points the price ratio in the economy can be represented by a straight line drawn tangent to the PPC at *e*. The slope of that line shows the cost ratio between wheat and cloth, that is, the amount of cloth that must be traded off to get more wheat and vice versa. Under competitive conditions, the cost ratio must also be the price ratio.

As long as the two points *e* are on the PPCs at places where the slopes are different, there is an incentive to trade, just as with the unbent PPCs of Figure 2.1. The lines tangent to the PPCs of Figure 2.2a and 2.2b at point *e* show the slope of the PPCs at *e*. Clearly, Fabrica has a great desire for cloth, Agricola for wheat, so the attempt to specialize that much has caused the price of cloth to be expensive in Fabrica and the price of wheat to be high in Agricola. Note that it is not just the difference in the set of production possibilities here, but the location of points like *e* on the production possibilities curve that causes the differences in cost structures.

Adding Indifference Curves

Production possibilities curves define the range of combinations of goods available to the economy. The reason price and production settle at any given point, however, depends on community preferences. We can show this with *community indifference curves*. Some readers will have encountered indifference curves before, others not, since they are often an optional topic in introductory courses. An *individual* indifference curve marks out all the combinations of goods that are equally satisfactory to an individual. In Figure 2.3, for instance, the indifference curves I, I_1, and I_2 mark out various combinations of wheat and cloth the individual would prefer. Each curve identifies combinations at which the person would be equally well off. Let us take wheat a little more broadly to mean food, and cloth to mean clothing. Then imagine a person thinking: "Well, given various sets of possible combinations of the two things, both of which I want, what is my own personal trade-off between the two? Clearly I need both to eat and to be clothed, and I need some kind of balance between the two. I'll take more clothing in exchange for less food to a point, but I will demand more and more clothing to compensate because I'll have to eat poorer quality and less tasty food, and eventually, I'll start to get

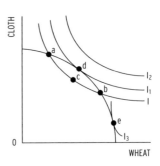

Figure 2.3

ADDING INDIFFERENCE
CURVES TO THE PPC

Note: Community indifference curves allow a statement of the amount the community would prefer of the two goods. A point where the production possibility curve just touches the highest possible indifference curve gives the optimal point of production.

hungry. An extra shirt isn't going to be worth as much to me as a good meal. Similarly, I'll take more food for clothing, but as my wardrobe wears out I'll be willing to sacrifice more of my good meals in order to get some decent clothes."

This means that the individual's indifference curve has a bowed shape convex to the point of origin (that is, the "cave" opens away from the origin), because the person requires more and more of one good to compensate for additional losses of the other good. Any point on the same indifference curve is considered a point at which the individual is indifferent between the various combinations of goods shown along the curve. Moreover, an individual's welfare is increased if he can move to a higher indifference curve (*I* to *I₁*), since that means more of *both* goods.

A *community* indifference curve reflects the community's preference and can, with some welfare reservations noted below, be viewed as the summation of individuals' indifference curves. The indifference curve *I* in Figure 2.3 indicates one possible set of combinations of wheat and cloth that would leave the community indifferent. Note, however, that points *a*, *b*, and *c* would be inferior to production at point *d*, which lies on the highest attainable indifference curve *I₁*.

An indifference curve marks out combinations that would leave the community indifferent at some given level of satisfaction. If we consider another level of satisfaction, we can suppose the community should have a new set of combinations that would leave the community indifferent. This allows us to draw an indifference curve for *any* level of satisfaction. In Figure 2.3, *I₁* represents a higher level of satisfaction than shown by curve *I*, and is an indifference curve that the nation can reach. The country would be even better off, being able to have more of both goods, if it could produce enough to reach *I₂*, but it cannot do so.

With any given output, the community is best off producing where the production possibilities curve and the indifference curve are tangent, just touching each other. As we have seen, *I₁* is the highest curve the nation can reach, and it can only reach that curve if it produces at point *d*. Any other production combination would put the nation on a curve lying under *I₁*.* If the community has a different set of preferences, as for example the greater desire for wheat shown by indifference curve *I₃*, then it would produce a different combination of goods shown by point *e*.

Now with two sets of production possibilities curves and two sets of indifference curves, we can analyze several ways in which trade between nations would improve welfare.

The Model Showing Similar Tastes but Different Production Possibilities

Consider two nations with the same tastes but different production patterns. Figure 2.5 shows both Agricola and Fabrica possessing the same set of

---

* Those with a background in intermediate micro theory will recognize that this is the point where the marginal costs of the production of either product equal their marginal utilities or $MC_a / MC_b = P_a / P_b = MU_a / MU_b$. The terms "marginal rate of substitution in production" and "marginal rate of substitution in consumption" are often used instead of marginal cost and marginal utility. The equation fulfills the condition known as Pareto Optimality, named after the Italian economist Vilfredo Pareto (1848-1923). Given an initial distribution of income, this is the best welfare situation that can emerge.

WELFARE LIMITATIONS OF
COMMUNITY INDIFFERENCE CURVES

Economists do a little dance around community indifference curves. It is no problem to say that an indifference curve represents a community's set of preferences or that given certain production possibilities, the point of production is that which the community prefers. Where we get into trouble is in handling the trade-offs between individuals. Economic welfare theory itself says only that we can be sure that welfare is improved when an individual moves to a higher indifference curve. Summing the curves for more than one individual presents difficulties.

Consider Figure 2.4 on which we have summed two indifference curves, one for Abel and the other for Baker. This is supposed to show the combinations of cloth and wheat that would leave the community equally well off. But a problem occurs when the community is able to obtain a greater quantity of both goods. Suppose the community can now reach a point such as C' on I'_{a+b} instead of C on I_{a+b}. We cannot be certain whether there has been a welfare gain or not because we do not know whether some redistribution of goods has occurred between Abel and Baker. Abel may have been an exporter who gained from free trade, while Baker, who was making something that was in competition with imports, lost from free trade. While the community may gain, this may be because the Abels have gained more than the Bakers lost.

Economists cannot prove an unambiguous gain in this case because economics has no way to make welfare comparisons between persons. A large gain to Abel cannot be proven to offset even a small loss for Baker. Baker may weep and thrash about with the loss of a few shirts while Abel would be only mildly pleased by a whole packet of new goods. If we could put a utility meter on their heads to measure relative satisfaction and dissatisfaction, Baker's unhappiness would overwhelm Abel's increased pleasure.

Welfare economists attempt to cope with the problem of interpersonal welfare by employing the *compensation principle*.[5] This principle states that if the gainers can gain enough to compensate the losers, actually do make these payments, and still have something left over, then there is an unambiguous gain to society as a whole. (It is normally assumed that the compensation would be undertaken through the political process, involving taxes and subsidies. It might, however, under some circumstances be arranged privately.) Suppose the Abels realized that the Bakers would resist any opening of trade and bought them all out at voluntary free market prices and then closed them down or shifted their production to their next best alternative. We would then know the gain would be unambiguous.

Be wary. An argument that says economists are not sure every increase in trade improves welfare does not mean that trade should be restricted unless there

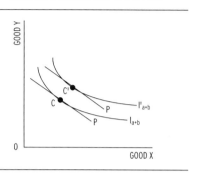

Figure 2.4

THE PROBLEM
POSED BY COMMUNITY
INDIFFERENCE CURVES

is compensation. A dash of skepticism should not provoke violent protectionist reaction. In the wider scope of economic growth, the compensation question is only a minor issue. Like most other decisions, trade decisions are taken with uncertain information and uncertain consequences, and are to a considerable extent judgment calls. Economists are rarely going to judge that the lack of compensation overwhelms the beneficial effects of additional trade.

After all, nations do not operate solely on the basis of unambiguous trade-offs. In the continual economic readjustment to technological and market changes, many people are displaced without compensation, and in practice we make many ambiguous decisions about what increases welfare. Certainly in numerous small-group situations, individuals take losses so that others may gain (or get their gains in psychological satisfaction). In a well-functioning body politic, some groups of people also take losses with a sense that the nation is the better for it. Every new product, every managerial reorganization, every change in production technology can mean layoffs and bankruptcies. Government-built highways bypass small towns, government-funded construction changes shopping and living patterns, all creating losses for some businesses and gains for others with no compensation paid. Indeed, if we were to assure ourselves that all economic gainers fully compensated all losers, we probably would make very few gains.

indifference curves but different production possibilities curves. Because the production possibilities differ, however, Agricola and Fabrica have different prices. Wheat is relatively expensive to produce in Fabrica, and cloth is relatively cheap; consumers respond by consuming more cloth than wheat, at point *w*. The price in Fabrica is indicated by the slope of the tangent line $P_f P_f$. In Agricola, cloth is expensive to produce, and wheat is cheap; consumers choose to consume at point *x*. The price in Agricola is indicated by the tangent line $P_a P_a$.

Trade now opens. There being no transport costs or trade barriers, a single equilibrium price ratio (called the "equilibrium terms of trade") will result, so that the price line must have an identical slope in the two countries.

Figure 2.5

FABRICA AND AGRICOLA BEFORE TRADE: SAME INDIFFERENCE
CURVES, DIFFERENT PRODUCTION POSSIBILITIES CURVES

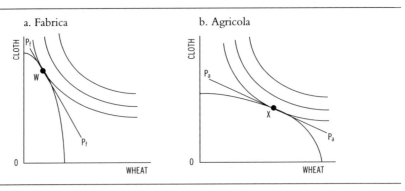

Furthermore, the exports of a product from one country must equal the imports of that product into the other country.

With a little experimentation, we can determine whether an equilibrium price has been reached. Say we have chosen the price represented by the lines $Q_f A$ on Figure 2.6a and BQ_a on 2.6b. Both these lines have the same slope, meaning that both nations pay the same price for goods. But they satisfy other conditions as well. At that price, Fabrica will produce at Q_f, but consume at point A, on an indifference curve that is *beyond* its production possibilities curve. It can do this because it *imports* M_f of wheat from Agricola and *exports* X_f to Agricola. These exports and imports form a triangle, the base of which is the trade in wheat (the product on the horizontal axis), the height of which is the trade in cloth (the product on the vertical axis), and the hypotenuse of which is the price line indicating the price ratio that occurs after trade has taken place. Because Fabrica is an *importer* of wheat, the line showing imports extends beyond the production possibilities curve; Fabrica on its own could not make wheat beyond its production possibilities curve.

Agricola also shows a move to a higher indifference curve at point B. In its case, cloth is imported, so the vertical of the triangle extends beyond the PPC. Wheat is exported. We have arranged the diagram so that Agricola's exports match exactly Fabrica's imports and Fabrica's exports match Agricola's imports. That is, $M_f = X_a$ and $X_f = M_a$ at the equilibrium terms of trade. If this were not the case, then we would not have an equilibrium situation and whatever good was in surplus would continue to fall in price against the scarcer commodity. The gain to trade is represented by the move to the higher indifference curves. As is typical of situations with differing production possibilities curves, each nation becomes more specialized in what it produces but less specialized in what it consumes.

Figure 2.6

FABRICA AND AGRICOLA AFTER TRADE,
SHOWING GAINS; SAME INDIFFERENCE CURVES,
DIFFERENT PRODUCTION POSSIBILITIES CURVES

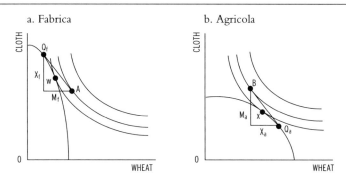

Note: After trade, Fabrica produces cloth at Q_f, exports X_f of cloth, while importing M_f of wheat. It thus moves out to an indifference curve beyond its autarkal reach. A similar process occurs in Agricola with X_a wheat exported and M_a cloth imported. Note that the side of the triangle that represents the exported good must lie entirely within the production possibility curve, and the lines for the traded good extend outside it.

The Model Showing Similar Production Possibilities but Different Tastes

Now change the model around and assume that the production possibilities curves are the same, but that tastes are dissimilar so that the indifference curves vary. Figure 2.7 shows this situation, with Fabrica and Agricola having the same PPC, but with Agricola wanting much more cloth (at point *w*) and Fabrica wanting much more wheat (at point *x*). Before trade the price ratios, as shown by the price lines, are different, so trade can take place. The price, as usual, will be between the two that exist. We have chosen a price, *AQF*, that will yield two identical triangles and be tangent to the production possibilities curve and an indifference curve from both countries. We find that both nations' output becomes less specialized, with production at *Q*. Neither nation has to suffer the increasing costs it was experiencing to produce the mix of cloth and wheat it wanted. Consumption, however, has become more specialized, with the foppish Agricolans buying plenty of clothing and the hungry Fabricans eating more food.

The obvious problem in handling the production possibilities and indifference curve diagrams such as those in Figures 2.6 and 2.7 is finding triangles that have just the right size and slope to fit the curves in both countries. The basic principle is simple. Find the market-clearing price, where the imports of a given good by one country are equal to the exports of the same good by the other country. Yet it takes imagination and a keen eye to draw the

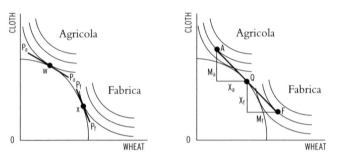

Note: With similar production possibility curves, but different tastes, a gain from trade is still possible. Before trade, Fabrica is producing at *x* to satisfy its great desire for wheat, while Agricola is at *w* so it can have more cloth. Trade allows more specialized consumption and less specialized production, as both nations move to point *Q* to produce.

triangles correctly. Another tool, called the *offer curve*, is visually easier and gives us another way to examine the equilibrium in a two-country, two-commodity setting. Offer curves are explored in an appendix to this chapter.

The Gains from Trade Come from Two Different Sources

The gains from trade, shown by a movement to a higher indifference curve, can be divided into two parts: the gain from trading at the world price rather than the old home price under autarky, and the gain from specialization as production is altered. Figure 2.8 shows a nation that in autarky would produce at *A*, with relative prices shown as P_aP_a. If this nation began to participate in world trade but did not shift its own production pattern, it could move out to wherever the world price is tangent to the highest indifference curve that can be reached. In this case, the world price is represented by the slope of P_wP_w, and it touches indifference curve I_2. The move to I_2, accordingly, is the gain from the lower world prices for its imports and higher world prices for its exports.

A further gain, however, is likely as the nation specializes in the good in which it has a comparative advantage. When production shifts to point *B*, which is the equilibrium where prices and costs are equal with the world price P_wP_w tangent to its production possibilities curve, it can reach a higher indifference curve I_3. Therefore the distance between I_2 and I_3 is the gain from altering production.

Figure 2.8

GAINS FROM TRADE

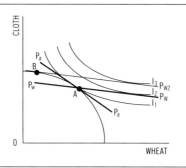

Note: *Pa* (autarkal price) shows the price and production before trade. *Pw* (world price) shows what happens if the country can buy and sell at world prices, but does not specialize in production. *Pw2*, also the world price ratio, touches point *B*, showing that gains are increased when the country is able to shift its production into more cloth-making.

Some Conclusions from the 2 × 2 Analysis

1. Increased foreign trade, with countries following their comparative advantage by exporting what they produce at lesser opportunity cost and importing what they would have to produce at greater opportunity cost, is in a country's economic self-interest. While there are often political reasons for increased trade, that is icing on the cake. There is great unanimity among economists on this point—in a paper published in 1992, fully 93.5% of the U.S. economists surveyed in a large random sample agreed with the proposition that "tariffs and import quotas usually reduce general economic welfare." That was the highest level of agreement in the 40-question survey, tied with the 93.5% concurring that "a ceiling on rents reduces the quantity and quality of housing available."[*] Contrast this unanimity among economists with the statement by the chairman of the USX Corporation (largest U.S. steelmaker) that the theory of comparative advantage is a "combination of rhetoric, smoke, and mirrors."[6] Many business people and politicians have yet to be convinced.

2. Trade increases output and hence consumption. Once two nations enter into trade, the same total quantity of labor, capital, and land is able to

---

[*] Richard M. Alston, J.R. Kearl, and Michael B. Vaughan, "Is There a Consensus Among Economists in the 1990's?" *American Economic Review* 82, 2 (May 1992): 204. It is fair to add, however, that some slippage has occurred over the years. A survey of the members of the American Economics Association published in 1979 showed that 97% of the membership agreed that interference with trade by tariffs and import quotas reduced the general welfare. See J.R. Kearl et al., "A Confusion of Economists?" *American Economic Review* 69, 2 (1979): 30. There are also a few countries where, according to similar surveys, a majority of economists approve of trade barriers—53% in Switzerland, 56% in Austria, and 73% in France, for example. See Stephen P. Magee, "The Political Economy of Trade Policy," in David Greenaway and L. Alan Winters, eds., *Surveys in International Trade* (Oxford: Basil Blackwell, 1994), 141.

produce a greater output of goods because the two countries can move toward specialization in what they do best. It is just as if some highly productive technical change has taken place, as if some necromancer had found a way to convert cheap products into more expensive ones.[7]

3. There is no basic difference, in economic terms, between the gains to specialization and trade that occur between firms or individuals domestically and those that occur internationally.

4. Gains are mutual. Both countries that enter into trade improve their welfare, such that one nation's gains are not at another nation's expense. Thus the theory of comparative advantage states that both sides gain from trade even if one country has an absolute advantage in the production of both goods. Note, however, that the theory does *not* say whether A gains more than B, or B more than A.

5. It is comparative, not absolute, advantage that determines the gains from and the direction of trade. When one nation has higher productivity than another—that is, any given combination of land, labor, and capital will produce more of any good than the same combination will in another nation—there is just as much reason to trade as when productivity is the same. The only situation where trade would bring no gains is when the price ratios in the two countries are exactly the same, for then there is no economic motive either to export or to import.

6. A small country trading with a large country stands to gain more than the larger one does.[8] Though people who live in small countries often bewail their fate, actually there are special economic advantages to living in Luxembourg or Iceland or Belgium. Such countries are likely to be trading at the price levels that hold in their large-country trading partner. Because of their small size, their exports of goods in which they have a comparative advantage will have little effect on the higher price level in the large country. Meanwhile, imports from the large country will be sufficiently small in total so that the prices of these goods do not rise in the large country. All the benefits of specialization and trade will thus go to the small country, and living standards there will receive a mighty boost. These great gains from trade are bought at some cost, however. The small country will be more specialized and more dependent on trade than the large one, involving risks if trade barriers arise, demand patterns alter, or technical changes occur. But the risks of not trading are higher yet, for the small country that chooses not to trade will be poor and poverty is risky.

THE GAINS FROM TRADE IN PARTIAL EQUILIBRIUM

The general equilibrium conclusions can be usefully compared to the results in partial equilibrium using only the tools of supply and demand, with which welfare changes can be viewed by means of the alteration in consumer and producer surplus. Such a model is much simpler, because we look at only one good at a time—the simultaneous changes that occur in general equilibrium cannot be shown directly when looking at the supply and demand for just one good. Yet the partial equilibrium analysis has many uses, and conclusions drawn from it reinforce rather than contradict the judgments arrived at in general equilibrium.

The Gains from Importing

Figure 2.9a shows the demand and supply in Hibernia for strawberries. The supply curve slopes upward, implying increasing costs, and the demand curve downward, implying decreasing marginal utility, consistent with our general equilibrium assumptions. Assume, to begin, that Hibernia is in autarky. With no trade, the market clears at a price of P_e and a volume of Q_2. With trade, however, Hibernia can purchase strawberries from other countries for price P_m. At P_m the quantity consumed is Q_3 and the quantity produced is only Q_1. Is Hibernia better off importing strawberries?

Figure 2.9

THE GAINS FROM TRADE IN PARTIAL EQUILIBRIUM

a. Quantity of Strawberries   b. Quantity of Tomatoes

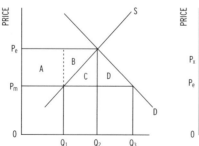
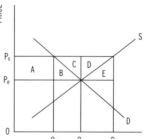

Note: P_e is the price in autarkal equilibrium, P_m the world price for the import, and P_x the world price for the export. Each of the lettered areas is important to understand the benefits (and some of the difficulties) of trade.

Consumers certainly are. The buyers of Q_2 were willing to pay the price P_e for their berries but can now buy them for P_m; their benefit is the rectangle formed by the rectangle A and the triangles B and C, essentially $P_m P_e$ times $0 Q_2$. Their *consumer surplus*—the difference between what they pay and what the good is worth to them, which is the area above the price and below the demand curve—has increased. The increase is the difference between what they were previously willing to pay and what they *actually* pay for it. (A good example of a consumer surplus would be the benefit received when customers have already decided to buy an item and then find it is on sale. They were clearly willing to pay the regular price but obtain it for the sale price. The difference is the change in their consumer surplus.)

The buyers of the strawberries from Q_2 to Q_3 are not equally better off, however. The woman buying the extra quart of berries just to the right of Q_2 would not have bought that quart at price P_e before—she would have needed a few cents off for encouragement. Since she has more than just a few cents off, her benefit is almost as high as the buyers to the left of Q_2. The man just to the left of Q_3 would not, however, have bought the strawberries if they had been the least bit more costly; indeed, his decision to buy was very painful as he struggled in his classical economic mind to compare the benefit of strawberries with all the other possible things he could do with the money spent on the berries. His added benefit from the lower price was therefore very small. We thus consider the increase in consumer surplus for consumers between Q_2 and Q_3 to be the triangle D, which reflects this declining value. The total consumer surplus gained is therefore the area $A + B + C + D$.

Producers of strawberries have, of course, lost, but they are not put out of work. The supply curve sketches the opportunity costs of the strawberry producers in alternative occupations (or the land and capital in alternative uses). A supply curve, after all, represents costs, and costs are always opportunity costs. Producers from 0 to Q_1 simply stay in the strawberry business.* Their loss, or change in producers' surplus, is the area A. The producers from Q_1 to Q_2, however, suffer less of a loss because they are able to do other things. The farmer just to the left of Q_2 was thinking about producing another crop anyway: so close were his calculations that a penny less per quart on strawberries would have driven him to rhubarb production. His loss would be very little. The farmer down just to the right of Q_1, however, only found alternative crops or other occupations sensible when the price of strawberries fell

---

* We cannot tell if these were the most efficient producers or if costs have fallen in the strawberry business as some producers have exited. If we assume that all strawberry producers are identical—a normal assumption under pure competition—then we would have to assume that each producer had a mixture of excellent and mediocre land, and the decline in production was because each producer cut back on its less-good land or turned land over from strawberries to a crop such as rhubarb that it would be best at producing, given the lower strawberry prices.

to near P_m. His loss is nearly the entire distance between P_e and P_m. The change in producers' surplus, then, is the area $A + B$. The gain for the economy from importing the strawberries is the gain in consumers' surplus $A + B + C + D$ less the loss in producers' surplus $A + B$. The consumers' gain outweighs the producers' loss, leaving the triangles $C + D$ as the net gain.

The Gains from Exporting

The analysis is not yet complete, because we still must consider the new export, in this case tomatoes; their foreign price will be above the autarkal (no-trade) equilibrium point, as in Figure 2.9b. As prices rise from P_e to P_x the quantity produced rises from Q_2 to Q_3, while the quantity demanded falls to Q_1. This allows exports of Q_1Q_3. Using the same analysis employed for the decline in price, we see that consumers are worse off, many paying higher prices (rectangle A) and a number shifting to other less satisfactory purchases (triangle B). Producers, however, gain back all of rectangle A, and triangles B and C, which comprise the added revenue for the same amount of production they had before (rectangle A and triangle B are from Hibernia's consumers, triangle C from the rest of the world). The rectangle formed by triangles D and E represents the value of the expanded production Q_2Q_3. Only triangle D, however, is a true gain, because triangle E is the value of the goods that the resources producing Q_2Q_3 could have made in domestic sales. Like the diagram in Figure 2.9a, we have a producers' surplus ($A + B + C + D$) and a consumers' surplus ($A + B$). This time, however, the consumers' surplus is smaller than the producers' surplus, but it is the consumers' surplus that declines and the producers' that rises. The net gain from exporting is thus $C + D$.

Conclusions

The conclusion from the partial equilibrium analysis reinforces what we found in general equilibrium: for society, trade involves overall gains. For imports of strawberries, the gain to consumers outweighs the loss to producers. For exports of tomatoes, the gain to producers outweighs the loss to consumers. There is a net gain both from importing and from exporting. This powerful conclusion has an obvious corollary: reducing trade by means of barriers will reduce a country's welfare.

Now consider the question of compensation. If both sets of producers and consumers are the same (that is, the same farms switch from strawberries to tomatoes, and the same consumers switch from tomatoes to strawberries), then an improvement in welfare takes place. If, however, there are different farmers and different consumers, then there is at least a case that welfare has not improved unless the tomato farmers transfer income to the strawberry farmers and the strawberry eaters compensate the tomato eaters.

As in general equilibrium analysis, the compensation principle discussed in the box titled "Welfare Limitations of Community Indifference Curves" is necessary to prove that trade results in an overall net gain in welfare.

RELAXING THE ASSUMPTIONS

The basic analysis of comparative advantage in a two-country, two-commodity model has now been completed. The next task is to relax, one by one, the restrictive assumptions that have been operative to this point.

Dynamic Effects

The model of comparative advantage as viewed thus far in the chapter has been a static one, with no dynamic effects such as changing production possibilities or changing tastes. At this point we relax the assumption of static conditions and consider a number of dynamic effects that can alter comparative advantage, sometimes very greatly.

CHANGING TASTES

Tastes change frequently, leading to changes in trading patterns. We could show a simple change of tastes by altering the location of the indifference curve, relative to the production possibilities curve; and in partial equilibrium, by changing the location of the demand curve. An example might be the increasing taste for fish in the United States, spurred by health concerns about red meat and the general move toward lighter foods. The taste change has caused American fish imports from Canada to rise sharply. Japan was once the world's major exporter of silk, but as high fashion moved away from silk the Japanese moved toward products in greater demand. (The share of silk in Japan's textile and clothing exports was 99% in 1880-82, still 88% in 1900-02, down to 62% in 1924-26, and only 4% in 1953-55.[9]) One country's very name reflects an old and now outmoded taste. Côte d'Ivoire (Ivory Coast) in West Africa was once a major supplier of the ivory used for piano keys, billiard balls, and Victorian parlor knick-knacks. But the demand for ivory disappeared (before the elephants did), and Côte d'Ivoire switched to coffee and cocoa exporting.

Sometimes the taste change is a result of trade itself. Ragnar Nurkse (1907-59) hypothesized a *demonstration effect*, wherein consumers in less-developed countries acquired new tastes as they were exposed to a wide range of goods through international trade. The result was that changing taste caused a change in comparative advantage as the indifference curves moved. Some South American countries shifted from domestic foods such as corn to imported wheat and rice, from domestic meats to imported beef. Virtually the entire Third World has changed from native dress to more European clothes, often even when the clothing is quite uncomfortable in the local climate. Even the sins of the developed world, such as tobacco smoking and overuse of infant formula, have spread extensively to the developing world.

SCALE AND SPECIALIZATION

For certain goods, and in certain conditions elaborated more fully in the following chapter, increasing production may lower costs. If there are major economies of scale for production, or if a high degree of specialization brings with it substantial cost savings, the economy may not face increasing costs. Specialization in rice, for instance, may bring some economies of scale, but more importantly, it will bring with it specialized traders, chemical companies, seed companies, agricultural extension agents, and even irrigation and water-control activities that will lower the cost of producing rice.

CHANGING FACTOR ENDOWMENTS

Factor endowments change, causing a change in the position of the production possibilities curve. Sometimes the situation is obvious, as when a raw material source gives out or diseases hit important crops. Indeed, some countries have had periods in which major exports rose and then nearly disappeared, reflecting enormous changes in comparative advantage. Peru, for instance, exported gold and silver in colonial times; guano, a fertilizer consisting of bird droppings, in the early nineteenth century; and later nitrates, until they were seized by the Chileans in 1878. Each product dominated and squeezed out other exports, then collapsed unexpectedly.

When factor endowments grow production possibilities curves move outward, often reflecting the growth of one factor relative to the others.[*] In newly industrializing countries, the stock of capital grows in relation to the labor force. As these nations manage to reinvest 25% or 30% of their GDPs into their economies, boosting net investment rates sometimes to over 20%, wages rise relative to the returns on capital. As a result, labor-intensive exports no longer have comparative advantages over capital-intensive exports. Japan began this century exporting labor-intensive goods, but by the 1960s was

---

[*] If the production possibilities curve moves outward, obviously that reason alone will allow a country to touch a higher indifference curve than it otherwise could, increasing the gains from trade.

exporting mostly capital- or technology-intensive products. Similarly, both the United States and Germany were primarily agricultural exporters in the mid-nineteenth century, but by the end of that century they were increasingly exporters of more capital-intensive manufactures.

Improving skills and education can alter PPCs, as historically in Germany, in Japan, and more lately in South Korea, Taiwan, and elsewhere in East Asia. Closely linked to skills and education are research and development (R&D) advances, which can have the same effect of altering PPCs.

Trade itself may be the vehicle for the changes in the factor endowments.[10] For example, contact with foreigners may result in favorable effects on entrepreneurial behavior and methods. Imports might allow new markets to be identified and developed so that risks of entering these markets are reduced for domestic producers. The potential for copying the imports themselves, or importing the technology through which they were produced, might be large, with investment increasing and becoming more productive as a result. If local production develops, the continuing competition from imports might increase efficiency and police monopoly power. Later, local production may develop into exporting, and if so, the new markets abroad can bring economies of scale. In turn, the potential profits from successful exporting can be a strong stimulus for further research and development and investment.

CONCLUSION

In each of the cases discussed in this section, the dynamic changes in supply (PPCs) and demand (indifference curves) are likely to result in a new equilibrium terms of trade. That is to say, dynamic changes can yield new price ratios and can thus alter comparative advantage.

Many Products, Many Countries

The fundamental conclusions of a two-country, two-commodity model survive when the model expands to include many countries and many goods.[11] In the higher mathematics of a multi-country, multi-commodity model explored in graduate-level texts, a *chain of comparative advantage* emerges, each country having a list, as it were, of all potential exportables and importables. At or near the upper end of the list are goods whose factor endowments, demand, and/or technological differences combine to give a comparative advantage so great in terms of relative costs that the country is sure to be an exporter of those commodities. At the other end of the list are goods whose comparative disadvantage is so great that the country is certain to be an importer of these goods. In the center of the list is a gray area where costs are so similar between countries, or transport costs so prohibitive for trade, that trade cannot take place. The dividing line between what is imported and what is exported will be a function wholly of relative costs and prices.

Transport Costs and the Models

Throughout this chapter, the analysis has proceeded as if there were no transportation costs or other special costs of trade and thus international exchange equalized the prices of traded commodities between the trading countries. That is sufficiently unrealistic to require some adjustment. We develop in this final section a model that is useful for handling not only transport costs, but tariffs, export taxes, and other special costs of trade.

It is easiest to show the effect of transport costs in partial equilibrium, looking at the supply and demand for just one product. Return to our consideration of strawberry imports. In Figure 2.10, we use back-to-back diagrams, as if we have flipped over the one on the left. Demand and supply appear to run the wrong way, but since the horizontal axis starts at zero in the center and increases as it goes to the left, D and S are actually correct. The importer is on the left and the exporter on the right, showing that the economies establish different prices for strawberries in autarky. We can show trade without any transportation costs simply by finding a level of exports that happens to equal the imports of the partner country—that is, where Q_1Q_4 on the left diagram, the imports, equals Q_5Q_8 on the right diagram. We then bring the price line across from the left to the right half of the diagram. Equilibrium comes about when $Q_1Q_4 = Q_5Q_8$, which is at P.

To allow for transportation costs we put a crook into the price line, to indicate that there is a difference between the costs when the good leaves one nation and what its costs are when it arrives at the other. That crook in the line, equal to the transportation cost, causes adjustments in both diagrams. In essence, we have to fit a vertical distance like that on the bottom of Figure 2.10 into the D and S diagrams such that the quantities exported and imported are equal. If the same level of exports were produced, the importer would not buy them all at the higher price with transportation costs included. If the importers tried to import the same amount, the exporters could not afford to produce that amount and pay the transportation cost. The result is that the price settles at some intermediate point, where imports and exports equal each other and the transportation cost is covered, as indicated by Q_2Q_3 and Q_6Q_7 of Figure 2.10. Note, in particular, that if transport cost exceeds the original price difference between the importer and exporter, then no trade will occur.

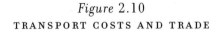

Figure 2.10

TRANSPORT COSTS AND TRADE

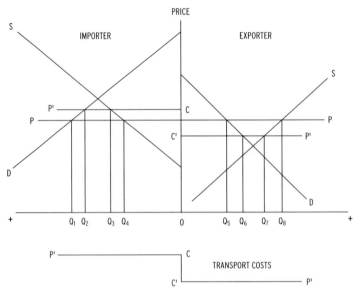

Note: Prices in an importing and an exporting country differ by the transportation costs between them, being higher in the importer and lower in the exporter.

NATURAL PROTECTION AND LOCATION THEORY

An industry that has higher costs than a foreign industry but whose product faces high transportation costs is said to be naturally protected. A vast number of service jobs, from haircutting to medicine to legal advice, are protected by the considerable cost, relative to the value of the service, of transportation. Many of us who have lived in developing countries would love to have a hidden door opening to our old homes or offices, not just to enjoy the sights and flavors, but so we could sneak out for haircuts, watch repairs, or dining at a fraction of our industrial world prices. Some products, such as cement, gravel, bottled water, and beer, are heavy relative to their value, so transport is relatively expensive. Some products are difficult to ship—natural gas when no pipeline is feasible, as from Algeria to the United States—and that also means a much higher price. Some are perishable and are thus sold only as premium products. Apples and peaches do get to Southeast Asia and rambutans and mangosteens (to say nothing of the fabled durian, which smells like coal tar and is said to taste like heaven) are sold in North America. But as with imported beers, what is commonplace at home is at its destination a luxury provided at a luxury price.

With transport costs present, the location of industry as predicted by the model of comparative advantage may be modified by natural protection, which helps to explain both the existence and the siting of the affected industry, and why some goods and services are simply not traded at all. Such modifications of comparative advantage are the subject of location theory.

Transport costs can be important in deciding where to locate an industry. There are three possible cases: (1) supply-oriented industry, (2) market-oriented industry, and (3) footloose industry. In the first two of these cases transport costs influence the degree of comparative advantage. In the third case they do not.

SUPPLY-ORIENTED INDUSTRY

Supply-oriented industries must, because of transport costs, be located near raw materials or fuel. Typical examples are those raw material inputs that lose weight in processing. The ores of zinc or copper, for example, contain much waste material, and gold and platinum even more. They lose considerable weight in refining. It is thus more economical to refine near the site of the mine than to ship heavy, useless waste material. Large-scale fuel consumption can mean economies in producing at or near a source of fuel. This is most true of fuels that are hard to ship, applying in particular to coal, at least historically. Coal was a tremendous attraction for the steel industry, more so than the iron ore itself, because it involved greater totally lost weight, as seen in the German Ruhr, Polish Silesia, the English Midlands, and the region around Pittsburgh in the United States.* Aluminum refining, which is done by passing a strong electric current through the dissolved concentrate, is inevitably close to good sources of electric, often hydroelectric, power. Agricultural commodities requiring immediate preservation or grading are also supply-oriented. Tobacco must be hung for curing within a few hours of being picked; tea should be processed within eight hours; and many frozen and canned fruits and vegetables have only a few hours or days before their quality begins to decline. Grains, on the other hand, do not need to be processed particularly quickly. Rural Thailand, for instance, has very little in the way of rice processing, but considerable tobacco, pineapple, vegetable, and fruit processing.

In other cases there are economies of assortment, where sorting and grading is best done before goods are shipped many miles. Sorting prevents

---

* Recent technical changes have reduced the attraction of coal or iron ore to steel. The new steel minimills use scrap metal and electric arc furnaces so they do not have to be built near either input. They can locate near the market and save on the transport costs. Minimill production had taken about a quarter of the U.S. market by the early 1990s.

certain grades or qualities from being shipped to inappropriate locations. Some mines, as those of highland Peru, produce ores heavy in several minerals—lead, zinc, silver, and perhaps antimony may all be jumbled together, and the ultimate destination of each of those elements is quite different, so it is cheapest to separate them out near the mines. Tobacco and coffee come in many grades in any one nation, but each of their ultimate markets wants only some of those grades. There is no sense in shipping a tar-laden, heavy-nicotine leaf to the United States when other peoples are dying for it. National (indeed, regional) tastes in coffees differ considerably, and the beans from any one estate must be sorted out before being shipped.

MARKET-ORIENTED INDUSTRY

The cost of transport requires some commodities to be produced near the market. Perishable goods such as bread, milk, fresh corn on the cob, and asparagus may survive some long trips, but they lose considerable value in so doing. Services, of course, are heavily market-oriented. It is impossible to import a haircut. Any product that gains weight or bulk in processing will tend to be market-oriented, such as beer and soft drinks, which, being mostly water, are invariably locally produced, with tiny portions of the market provided by imports. In addition, products that have to be changed for each local or national market tend to be produced closer to those markets. Tobacco may be cured near the farm and sorted near the port, but it is assembled and made into cigarettes near its final market. Coffee receives its initial processing as well as its grading at its source, but the differences in national tastes are such that the final blending and roasting take place close to the market.

FOOTLOOSE INDUSTRY

Transport costs are not so important with footloose industries, which can locate at the source of supply, at the market, or in between. Generally such industries produce products that neither lose nor gain weight in processing. Textiles provide a good example: they can be made near the source of the cotton and then be shipped to the market, or the cotton can be shipped to textile mills near the market. Either way, the transport cost is about the same. Many electronic goods can be shipped about for assembly, often with different parts of the operation being done in different countries. Relative to their value, computers and high-tech electronic equipment are very light. The whole of the world's semiconductor production, for instance, would fit into just 10 Boeing 747s.[12] As we shall see, the declining transportation costs of the postwar period have meant that locational factors are less and less important in the siting of an industry.

Figure 2.11, taken from the work of E.M. Hoover, shows how to sum the procurement costs of obtaining raw materials and the distribution costs associated with shipping the final product.[13] Procurement costs, shown by a dashed line, are highest at the market, lowest near the source of supply. Distribution costs for the final product, shown by a dotted line, are highest at the source of the raw materials, lowest at the market. When added vertically, the two together indicate the total cost of transport, seen in Figure 2.11 to be lowest when production of the good is undertaken at the source of raw materials supply. This particular good is therefore supply-oriented.

Figure 2.11

LOCATION OF PRODUCTION AND TRANSPORT COST

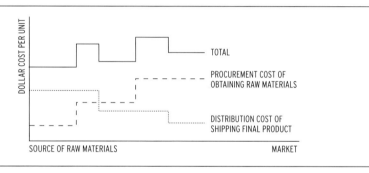

THE FALL IN THE IMPORTANCE OF TRANSPORT COSTS

The role of transport costs in shaping international trade is falling. For one thing, trade has shifted from raw commodities such as agricultural products and minerals, which are heavy and costly to transport, to finished manufactured products whose value is not related to their weight or size. At the same time the manufactured goods are themselves becoming lighter and smaller, especially because of plastics and microprocessors. The total weight of U.S. production today is thought to be only a little larger than it was 100 years ago.

In addition, the transport costs themselves are declining.[14] Ocean freight and port charges in the 1990s were just a quarter of what they were in the 1920s. A major contributor has been containerization, with stackable metal containers shipped by truck and train and loaded directly on board container ships.* The decline in cost has been even greater in communications. Satellite

---

* Specialized container ships first appeared in about 1967. The total capacity of the container fleet grew by about six times between the early 1980s and the mid-1990s. Better "intramodal" organization has furthered the cost reduction, with overhead cranes able to move a container from train to truck or truck to ship in 30 seconds or less. See *The Economist*, November 15, 1997.

charges are now less than a tenth of what they were around 1970. The cost of a three-minute phone call from New York to London is only a hundredth of what it was in 1940.

But there are still many cases where high transport costs limit trade very sharply. In some landlocked African countries such as Burkina Faso, Chad, Niger, Mali, Malawi, Zambia, and the Central African Republic, bad roads mean transport costs absorb an average of 42% of the value of exports, almost 25 percentage points more than the figure for the more accessible countries in Africa.[15] And even where transport costs are less burdensome, borders still raise them because formalities at frontiers mean delays and because crossing points may be infrequent.

CONCLUSION

This chapter has presented the standard trade theory of comparative advantage, with its long heritage and powerful conclusions. An economist of 40 years ago might reasonably have considered the subject to be a settled one. In the next chapter, however, we shall see that controversy has arisen and continues on the question of what gives a country a comparative advantage and what causes it to change. These aspects of trade theory are among the more contentious in economics.

APPENDIX: OFFER CURVES

Offer curves, invented before the turn of the century by two British econo-mists, Alfred Marshall and Francis Edgeworth, give an alternative way to find the size and shape of the triangles of trade developed in this chapter in Figures 2.6 and 2.7.

In the body of the chapter, all price ratios were presented as in Figure 2.12a, where a line runs from axis to axis showing a ratio such as 10 cloth to 20 wheat. Exactly the same ratio can be shown, however, as in Figure 2.12b, running out from the point of origin. This, too, shows the quantity of cloth (10) that will be exchanged for a quantity of wheat (20). This, too, is thus a price ratio.

Figure 2.12

TWO WAYS OF EXPRESSING A PRICE RATIO

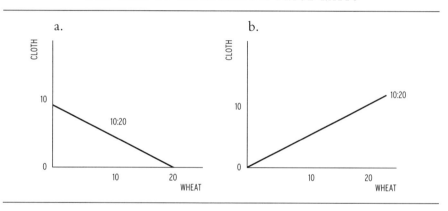

Fabrica's Offer Curve

Let us use price ratios drawn in this second way to construct an offer curve showing the amount of cloth Fabrica is willing to give up (export) in exchange for imports of wheat from Agricola. This curve will show simul-taneously the supply and demand for the two commodities entering into trade. Assume that trade opens between Fabrica and Agricola. If prices do not change from their initial level, say 10:10, or 1:1, then it will make no differ-ence to Fabrican consumers whether they buy their unit of wheat for one of cloth at home or abroad. So only a little trade is likely to spring up, as at *A* in Figure 2.13.

Figure 2.13
CONSTRUCTING FABRICA'S OFFER CURVE

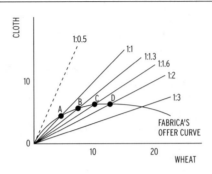

If prices change, however, more trade will develop. We do not need to consider a price movement in Fabrica in the direction of, say, 1:0.5, because that would mean cloth had become cheaper and wheat more expensive after trade. Who in Fabrica would give up *more* Fabrican cloth in exchange for Agricolan wheat than the quantity of cloth that must be given up for wheat in Fabrica *without* international trade? A reduced price of wheat, and an increased price of cloth, say to a ratio of 1:1.3, will, however, cause Fabrica to desire more trade, as at point *B*. There, a larger quantity of cloth will be offered in exchange for a larger quantity of wheat.

Because at point *B* more wheat is available than before, the Fabricans will offer less cloth per unit of wheat. In other words, a doubling of wheat imports will less than double exports of cloth. At the even more favorable price ratio of 1:1.6, Fabrica at point *C* gives up more cloth to get more wheat, but not quite so much per unit as it was willing to give up before. The twin reasons for this are (1) Fabrica wants wheat less, and (2) each unit of cloth is now more valuable because some of it is exported.

If the price ratio were to change further, say to 1:1.7 or 1:1.8, with cloth more expensive and wheat cheaper, the same process would occur. More cloth would be given up for more wheat, though again not so much per unit. Finally, say at a price ratio of 1:2, Fabrica will not give up *any more cloth at all* for wheat, no matter how much more wheat could be obtained in further trade. (See point *D*.) The offer curve may even bend back far to the right in the diagram, as huge stocks of wheat lead to unwanted supplies and problems of storage, while consumers refuse to reduce their cloth consumption any further. Fabrica would then take more wheat only if it had to give up less cloth.

Agricola's Offer Curve

Now we turn to Agricola's offer curve. Agricola's price ratio before trade was 1:3, with one unit of cloth exchanging for three units of wheat, as in Figure 2.14. Agricola would be willing to undertake a little trade with Fabrica even if the price ratio stays unchanged, as at *A* in the figure. Fabrica would certainly have preferred to obtain four, five, or six wheat for one cloth, but Agricola would not trade with Fabrica at those prices because home-produced cloth is cheaper than that.

Thus with trade, the price line swings counterclockwise. At a higher price for wheat and a lower price for cloth, Agricola will be eager for more trade. See how at point *B*, at a price ratio of 1:2, Agricola is willing to exchange more wheat for imported cloth. The analysis is the same as that for Fabrica in the last figure, except that the Agricolan offer curve swings around in the opposite direction.

Figure 2.14

CONSTRUCTING AGRICOLA'S OFFER CURVE

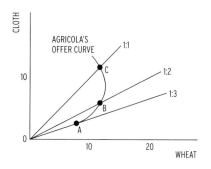

The final step is to put both offer curves, one for Fabrica and another for Agricola, in the same figure (see Figure 2.15). Notice that the two offer curves cross at point *P*. This crossing is important. Only there, at a price ratio shown by the line running from the origin through *P*, will Agricola want to export just the amount of wheat that Fabrica wants to import, as read along the *x*- (horizontal) axis. Also at a price *0P*, and *only* there, will Agricola want to import just the amount of cloth that Fabrica wants to export. The price *0P* is thus called the *equilibrium terms of trade*, and at that price the value of Fabrican imports equals the value of Agricolan exports, both in turn equal to the value of Agricolan imports and Fabrican exports. A country's exports exchange for an equal value of imports at the equilibrium terms of trade.

Figure 2.15

THE EQUILIBRIUM TERMS OF TRADE

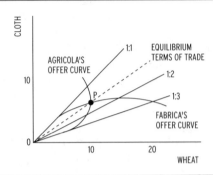

The connection between the offer curves developed here and the diagrams using production possibilities and indifference curves presented in the body of the chapter is reasonably straightforward. The offer curves define the size and shape of the triangles that determine the gains from trade. The reading on the *y*-axis identifies the amount of cloth traded by both countries, and is thus the height of the triangles. The reading on the *x*-axis reveals the length of the triangles. The price ratio is the slope (though it must be reversed) of the hypotenuse of the triangles. If we draw carefully, all will work out well.

VOCABULARY AND CONCEPTS

Absolute advantage
Autarky
Chain of comparative advantage
Comparative advantage
Compensation principle
Consumer surplus
Factor endowments
Footloose industry
Gains from trade

General equilibrium analysis
Indifference curve
Market-oriented industry
Natural protection
Partial equilibrium analysis
Producer surplus
Production possibility curve
Productivity
Supply-oriented industry

QUESTIONS

1. Demonstrate, using numbers only, Ricardo's theory of comparative advantage.
2. Construct a table that shows one country with an absolute advantage in both products, yet trade still takes place.

3. Explain the theory of comparative advantage using Figures 2.5 and 2.6. Identify the gains from trade. Try the same exercise, drawing a diagram for each country freehand, using different production possibility curves and the same pattern of indifference curves. Be careful about what part of the triangle remains entirely inside the production possibility curve and what part extends outside it (the most common error on tests). Technically, the triangles should be the same size (or else one country would be exporting more than the other imports); see how close you can come. (This takes a keen eye, patience, and some experimentation.)

4. Explain, drawing on Figure 2.7, what the gain from trade is and what occurs on that figure. Now try drawing a similar diagram freehand. (You will find it easier than the previous one.)

5. Why does a small country usually benefit more than a large country in a trading relationship? Show with a diagram.

6. Trade theory uses community indifference curves, yet uses them with caution. Why does it (a) use them and (b) take care in so doing?

7. A guru spoke: "There is no international competition; there is only domestic competition." (He is partially right, and right where most people do not think about it.) What did he mean?

8. Given the theory of trade, is it reasonable to ask which side won a trade negotiation?

9. Thus spake the guru: "A nation of beavers will gain no trading advantage over a nation of goof-offs." What did he mean?

10. Both your authors believe that increasing productivity is good for the economy. Both believe that an industry that increases its productivity more than others will move up on the chain of comparative advantage. Neither believes that increasing productivity will improve a country's trade balance. Explain.

11. Sometimes demand and supply diagrams explain better the gains from trade. Show what would happen if two nations entered into trade, using demand and supply diagrams for both the importer and the exporter.

12. Explain, using diagrams like those in Figure 2.9, the gain from trade. Point to the consumer surplus, the producer surplus, and the triangles that show the gain from trade.

13. Explain the distribution of gains and losses from trade, using Figure 2.9.

14. What are the dynamic effects of trade, and why might they be more important than the comparative statics we use in this chapter's models?

15. What is meant by natural protection? Show how transportation costs affect the amount of trade and the extent of reallocation of resources.

16. Distinguish supply-oriented, market-oriented, and footloose industries, giving an example of each.

NOTES

1. See "Paul Samuelson," *The New Palgrave Dictionary of Economics*, vol. 4 (London: Macmillan, 1987), 238.

2. The classic work is Thomas Mun, *England's Treasure by Foreign Trade* (1664). Mun wrote that "The ordinary means ... to increase our wealth and treasure is by foreign trade, wherein we must ever observe this rule: to sell more to strangers yearly than we consume of theirs in value." This paragraph draws on Douglas A. Irwin, *Against the Tide: An Intellectual History of Free Trade* (Princeton, N.J.: Princeton University Press, 1996), 14-15, 34-35, 44, 48.

3. Adam Smith, *The Wealth of Nations* (New York: Random House, Cannan Edition, 1937) [London, 1776], 424.

4. See Peter B. Kenen, *The International Economy* (Englewood Cliffs, N.J.: Prentice-Hall, 1985), 5-6.

5. The principle is surveyed by Irwin, *Against the Tide*, ch. 12, "The Welfare Economics of Free Trade."

6. *Wall Street Journal*, June 14, 1989.

7. Russell D. Roberts's fine allegory of trade, *The Choice* (Englewood Cliffs, N.J.: Prentice-Hall, 1994), calls this "roundabout production." In addition, see Melvyn Krauss, *How Nations Grow Rich: the Case for Free Trade* (New York: Oxford University Press, 1997).

8. On the greater specialization of small countries and the risks involved, see Paul Streeten, "The Special Problems of Small Countries," *World Development* 21, 2 (February 1993): 197-202.

9. Young-Il Park and Kym Anderson, "The Rise and Demise of Textiles and Clothing in Economic Development: The Case of Japan," *Economic Development and Cultural Change* 39, 3 (April 1991): 531-48.

10. See Paul M. Romer and Luis A. Rivera-Batiz, "International Trade with Endogenous Technological Change," *European Economic Review* 35 (May 1991): 971-1004.

11. For more advanced treatment of the 2 × 2 model that confirms its strength, see W.J. Ethier, "Higher Dimensional Issues in Trade Theory," in Ronald W. Jones and Peter B. Kenen, eds., *Handbook of International Economics*, vol. 1 (Amsterdam: Elsevier, 1984), 181.

12. *The Economist*, February 16, 1985.

13. See Edgar M. Hoover, *The Location of Economic Activity* (New York: McGraw-Hill, 1963): 39. The diagram is simplified in our text. Many comments relevant to transport can be found in Paul Krugman, *Geography and Trade* (Cambridge, Mass.: MIT Press, 1991).

14. See World Bank, *World Development Report 1995* (Washington, 1995), 51.

15. Alexander J. Yeats, Azita Amjadi, Ulrick Reincke, and Francis Ng, "What Caused Sub-Saharan Africa's Marginalization in World Trade," *Finance and Development* (December 1996): 38-41.

Chapter Three

The Sources of Comparative Advantage

OBJECTIVES

OVERALL OBJECTIVE   To understand what determines which goods are exported and which are imported.

MORE SPECIFICALLY
- To develop an ability to explain and manipulate the factor-proportions (Heckscher-Ohlin) model verbally and by means of diagrams.
- To examine factor-price equalization.
- To explain how the Leontief Paradox and intraindustrial trade have challenged factor-proportions theory.
- To build more dynamic models based on decreasing costs.
- To develop an understanding of the role of demand in shaping what goods develop comparative advantages.
- To incorporate the role of managerial and governmental choice in contingent and dynamic trade models.

....

Comparative advantage explains why trade brings gains. It does not, however, in itself explain why countries' production possibilities curves have different shapes, and therefore why comparative advantage should be in one good rather than another. It is a satisfactory explanation for the gains from trade, but it does not predict precisely what patterns of exchange will emerge from trade.

Ricardo thought natural differences were a major explanation for the patterns of comparative advantage, as when Portugal's sun and soil favored wine production while the sheep runs of England favored woolen cloth. It is not hard to find natural differences of the Ricardian sort when dealing with goods heavily dependent on climate and other natural resources. Yet

Ricardian natural advantage explains only a smallish part of trade today, and it has a much more difficult time explaining why Sweden exports Volvos and imports Volkswagens or why the United States exports glass-fiber cable and imports radios. If we are to develop some sense of what is likely to be traded and a more specific understanding of the gains from trade, we have to move beyond simple comparative advantage to explore why such advantages exist.

To do so, this chapter first examines the by now classic factor-proportions approach, which is quite satisfactory for working with many standard products or broad industrial groupings. The problem is that a factor-proportions approach does not handle very well a large share of modern trade, which tends to be among relatively similar industrial countries exporting and importing goods within the same industry. The balance of the chapter explores the newer theoretical and more dynamic models that can better explain this trade.

FACTOR PROPORTIONS: THE HECKSCHER-OHLIN MODEL

In the 1920s and 1930s the Swedish economists Eli Heckscher and Bertil Ohlin expanded the Ricardian view of natural advantage to one based on differing quantities and qualities of the factors of production. The *Heckscher-Ohlin (H-O) model* and the many factor-proportions models that are its offspring typically focus on only land, labor, and capital, and most often on just labor and capital. Sometimes, however, they also incorporate additional factors, such as human capital, technology, or entrepreneurship, to provide an explanation of trading patterns that otherwise do not seem readily explicable.

Basically, the Heckscher-Ohlin idea is that nations export goods that use their most abundant factor intensively, and they import goods that use their scarce factor intensively. The country with much labor and little capital will find that labor is comparatively cheap and capital is comparatively expensive. It will export goods that contain much labor relative to capital and import goods that contain much capital relative to labor. In the Heckscher-Ohlin model, a country's factor proportions determine and predict both what it will export and what it will import. (In large part because of this discovery, Ohlin shared the 1977 Nobel Prize in economics. Active in politics, he led the Swedish Liberal Party for over 20 years.)

Exploring the Heckscher-Ohlin Model with the Tools of Microeconomics

The observation is at base relatively simple. It can be explored more thoroughly by using a tool of microeconomic theory, production isoquants.

The production isoquants (labeled *PI*) in Figure 3.1 are the starting point. The quantity of capital is shown on the vertical axis, and the quantity of labor is on the horizontal. The isoquant PI_{100} shows that 100 units of some good can be produced with various factor combinations. The 100 units might be produced with lots of labor (L_2) and only a little capital (K_1), as at point *a*, or with much less labor (L_1) and much more capital (K_2), as at point *b*. Another isoquant could be drawn to show a higher level of output, say 125 units as with PI_{125}. A lower isoquant such as PI_{75} could be drawn to show 75 units of output. Any different level of output would be indicated by other isoquants drawn in the intermediate space.

The convex-to-the-origin shape of the production isoquants reflects the standard microeconomic argument of diminishing returns to a factor. If much capital is already being used to produce the 100 units, as at *b*, then it is difficult to substitute yet more capital for labor. See that to produce 100 units at point *c*, a great deal more capital had to be used because the labor force was already small.

Figure 3.1

GOODS CAN USUALLY BE PRODUCED
WITH VARIOUS FACTOR COMBINATIONS

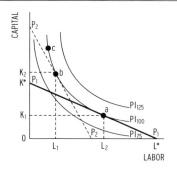

Note: PI_{100} shows the different combinations of capital and labor that will produce 100 units of some good, and PI_{125} the combinations that will produce 125 units. The lines P_1 and P_2 represent two different prices of labor in terms of capital. With much labor exchanging for little capital (P_1), the country will produce at point *a*; with the more expensive labor and cheaper capital, the country will produce at point *b*.

Whether producers will choose to employ considerable labor and little capital, or vice versa, will depend on the relative prices of capital and labor. The line P_1P_1 in Figure 3.1 is a price line; it shows the relative price of labor and capital. It is derived as follows: Let's assume a given amount is available for hiring factors. If the entire amount were devoted to hiring labor, a quantity of labor L^* could be obtained. If the entire amount were devoted to acquiring capital, a quantity of capital K^* could be obtained. Here labor is cheap and capital is expensive, because the same amount of money would bring lots of labor L^* but much less capital K^*. Any combination of labor and capital along P_1P_1 is also obtainable for the fixed sum of money.

In Figure 3.1, a price line P_1P_1 will cause the product to be produced with L_2 labor and K_1 capital, as shown by the point at a. With the affordable combinations of labor and capital along P_1P_1, producers could not reach a higher output quantity such as 125. Not enough labor and capital are available to permit that. An output of 75 would not be satisfactory, however, as it is possible with the available factors to reach 100 units of output at isoquant PI_{100}.

What if labor, however, were much more expensive and capital much cheaper, as shown along price line P_2P_2? In that case production would be undertaken at point b, with more capital used (K_2) than labor (L_1). Again no higher isoquant than PI_{100} can be reached and no lower one would be tolerated.

In the case shown in Figure 3.1, the good can be made either in a labor-intensive manner, with a high ratio of labor to capital as at a, or in a capital-intensive way, with a high ratio of capital to labor as at b. Indeed, most goods can be produced in either a labor-intensive or capital-intensive manner. The Asian farmer walks for hours behind a bullock and plow to break the ground, spends yet more hours on back-bending labor to plant and weed by hand, at harvest swings a sickle, and follows that with hand-threshing to get the crop ready for storage. An American farmer prepares the soil with a \$125,000 tractor pulling gang plows and then discs; attaches specialized implements for the planting, fertilizing, and weeding; watches the harvesting being done by giant combine-harvesters hired for the purpose; and then transfers the harvested crop to large trucks for the move to the local grain elevator.* Very few people are involved per unit of output, compared to many in Asia.

Just looking at Figure 3.1 does not, however, make it apparent which country will have the comparative advantage in producing the product. If labor is cheap enough, then labor-intensive production might win out in world markets. If capital is cheap enough, world markets might be captured by capital-intensive producers. The good shown is not one that *intrinsically* requires more labor than capital or vice versa.

The Heckscher–Ohlin model comes into its own when we consider goods that intrinsically require capital-intensive or labor-intensive production. Figure 3.2 shows two different products from the textile and clothing industry. The set of isoquants labeled *PIK* (*K* for capital-intensive) shows various levels of output for standard, machine-made synthetic fabric such as polyester.

---

* Even more dramatically different is U.S. rice farming. By contrast to the highly labor-intensive age-old techniques of Asia, rice production in California is astoundingly capital-intensive. The clay soils of the California fields are precision-leveled by laser-controlled earthmovers so water can be delivered evenly. The rice is seeded from airplanes. At harvest the drivers of the giant combines sit 14 feet above the ground, and the machines are able to strip off the grain without cutting down the whole plant. While on the move, the combines transfer their rice by tube to so-called bankout wagons. One combine can harvest 160 tons of rice per day.

The production of this item is intrinsically capital-intensive; that is, shifts between labor and capital can be made, but only within limits. Substantial machinery and chemical apparatus are needed to obtain polyester shirts, no matter how cheap labor might be. That is why the *PIK* isoquants for different quantities of polyester all cluster nearer to the vertical (capital) axis. The capital requirements always exceed the labor requirements even though some shifting between the two factors is possible.

Now consider the set of isoquants labeled *PIL* (*L* for labor-intensive) in Figure 3.2. Perhaps these represent fancy hand-sewn rodeo shirts. The production of these shirts is intrinsically labor-intensive. Again, shifts between labor and capital can be made, but the shifting has to be within limits. So much hand sewing is needed to obtain rodeo shirts that no matter how cheap capital might be, a large amount of labor time has to be devoted to producing the good. Thus the *PIL* isoquants for different quantities of rodeo shirts all cluster nearer to the horizontal (labor) axis. The labor requirements always exceed the capital requirements, and that intrinsic property does not change even though some shifting between capital and labor is possible.

Figure 3.2

ISOQUANTS SHOWING CAPITAL-INTENSIVE
AND LABOR-INTENSIVE PRODUCTION

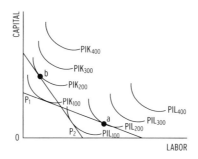

Assume that the country shown in the figure would always prefer to reach an isoquant with a greater number (200 rather than 100), whether the product is polyester shirts or rodeo shirts.* If a country had large amounts of labor relative to capital, then its labor would be relatively cheap, as indicated by the

---

* We say it this way to take into account that each polyester shirt has a lower value than each rodeo shirt. The 100 polyester shirts may thus actually be "100 dozen" whereas the 100 rodeo shirts are "100 units," with the 100 dozen cheap shirts equal in value to the 100 expensive ones. A country would always prefer to be on a "200" isoquant rather than on a "100" isoquant.

price line P_1P_1. The figure shows—and it accords completely with intuition—that with cheap labor it would be advantageous to produce the item that requires relatively more labor than capital—the rodeo shirts, at point *a*.

If, on the other hand, that same country had been relatively well-endowed with capital but labor was scarce, then its capital would be comparatively cheap and its labor expensive, as shown by price line P_2P_2. In this case it would be advantageous to produce the good—polyester shirts, as at point *b*—that requires relatively more capital than labor.

It may be useful to summarize and reiterate this case. Rodeo shirts, as noted, require a great deal of hand labor, while polyester shirts require a great deal of capital, so the isoquants that show expanding production lie in quite different paths. Though it is possible to make rodeo shirts in more or less capital-intensive manners, both P_1 and P_2 being tangent to some rodeo shirt isoquant, they are more labor-intensive than polyester shirts. A country with lots of capital and a P_2 price ratio will therefore specialize in polyester shirts, producing at *b*, and the labor-rich country with a P_1 price ratio will specialize in rodeo shirts, producing at *a*.

FACTOR-INTENSITY REVERSALS

The relation between factor proportions and production opens the possibility that a shift in relative factor prices might cause a major change in technique in the production of a given good. See in Figure 3.3 how as long as the cost of labor relative to capital is shown by the price line P_1P_1, then production will continue in a labor-intensive manner, as at point *a*. Yet a modest rise in the price of labor and fall in the price of capital, shown by price line P_2P_2, will cause producers to adopt the capital-intensive method as indicated by point *b*. Such a shift is an example of a *factor-intensity reversal*, a change in technique that in this case comes after only a small shift in relative factor prices. As an example, the rather rapid movement away from more labor-intensive rice farming in California to extremely capital-intensive methods was highly dramatic, but it was triggered by a decrease in the price of capital relative to labor that was not of very great magnitude.

Figure 3.3

A FACTOR-INTENSITY REVERSAL

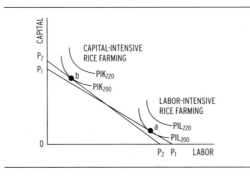

Factor Proportions Determine Comparative Advantage in the Heckscher-Ohlin Analysis

The Heckscher-Ohlin model suggests that comparative advantage will tend to be determined by factor proportions. The consequences for international trade are substantial. The capital-rich country will tend to export products that require proportionally large amounts of capital (that is, capital-intensive products). It will import products that require proportionally large amounts of labor (that is, labor-intensive products).[*]

In the H-O approach, the price system sends signals concerning factor proportions that then mold international trade. In high-wage countries, it would be foolish to try to produce products that require large inputs of costly labor when such products can be imported from cheap-labor countries. Doing so frees costly labor for more productive uses in exporting industries and in services where import competition cannot occur. In cheap-labor countries, however, it would be equally foolish to use scarce, expensive capital to produce products that can be more efficiently produced in countries where capital is cheap. For one thing, not enough capital is available to allow everyone to find jobs producing capital-intensive items. For another, the resulting output would be high in cost and unsellable abroad. Better to produce labor-intensive items with the cheap labor, export some of them, and import the goods that require much capital.

The Rybczynski Theorem: Changes in Factor Proportions Alter Comparative Advantage

It follows that an increase in the quantity of one factor of production (e.g., capital) relative to the other factors (e.g., labor) changes comparative advantage in favor of products that use the increasing factor intensively. The cheaper capital will cause a country's comparative advantage to shift to goods the production of which is basically capital-intensive. The new advantage will cause the output of these capital-intensive export products to rise, at the same time causing the domestic output of the labor-intensive goods to fall as imports of these goods increase. This is called the *Rybczynski Theorem*, after T.M. Rybczynski of City University, London, who first formulated this corollary to the Heckscher-Ohlin model.

The Rybczynski Theorem is illustrated in Figure 3.4. See how a country where labor is the abundant factor, and with a price line P_1P_1 has an advantage in producing a labor-intensive good, as at *a*, rather than a capital-

---

[*] Theoretically, it is possible (though surely rare) that a labor-intensive country might have such strong domestic demand for goods produced with labor-intensive methods that wages are pushed up to the point where labor-intensive goods do not have the comparative advantage.

intensive good. If over time the capital stock grows relative to the labor force, then capital will become relatively cheaper and labor more expensive, shown along price line P_2P_2. (This line is further out than P_1P_1 because the economy is now richer; both more capital and more labor can be purchased, but capital has become relatively cheaper.) Comparative advantage swings to the capital-intensive good, as at point b. Over time, growth in the capital stock has caused a factor-intensity reversal.

Figure 3.4
COMPARATIVE ADVANTAGE MAY SHIFT AS FACTOR INTENSITIES CHANGE

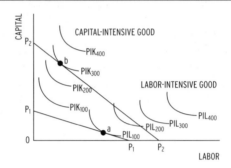

Thus, as a country accumulates more capital and wages rise relative to capital costs, one expects exports and imports to reflect the change. For example, Japan's textile and clothing industry contributed 51% of all Japanese exports, 1900-09, 38% in 1950-59, but just 4% during the period 1980-87. The British data reflect the same trend: textile and clothing exports were 38% of all British exports in 1900-19, when that industry was still Britain's largest. The proportion was down to 11% in 1950-59, and 4% in 1980-88. In both countries, the part of the industry comprising labor-intensive finished textiles and standard clothing was the first to decline, while the capital-intensive synthetic fiber and fabric producers may not decline at all, or only later.

Factor-Price Equalization

The import of labor-intensive items into economies where labor is expensive and items that are capital-intensive into economies where capital is expensive can possibly have a dramatic outcome. If such a pattern of trade continues, then the ratio of labor costs to capital costs will tend to come together internationally. Wages will rise relative to capital in the labor-abundant countries and fall in the scarce-labor countries in a process called *factor-price equalization*.

Start with a country where labor is scarce and capital is abundant, such as the United States. As imported labor-intensive products flow in, labor is released for other uses. This labor is absorbed in the more capital-intensive industries and in areas not subject to competition in foreign trade, but, nonetheless, there is downward pressure on wages. Meanwhile, exports of capital-intensive products raise the demand for capital, the returns to which increase.

Conversely, in the cheap-labor country (e.g. Mexico) the exports of labor-intensive items raise the demand for labor and thus put an upward pressure on wages. Imports of capital-intensive items have the opposite effect, reducing the returns to scarce and expensive capital. As the price of labor falls relative to capital in the United States, and rises in Mexico, the economic structure of the two areas begins to bear a closer resemblance.

The tendency of international trade to move factor prices toward equality is strictly limited, however. The actual likelihood of a full equalization occurring is remote, and the conditions under which it could occur are very restrictive.[1] For one thing, transport costs make many products and most services non-tradeable, so in most countries the pressure toward equalization is felt only by a minority of industries. For another, many trade barriers still exist even where goods are tradeable, lessening competition in the industries involved and further reducing the movement toward equalization. Finally, as international trade increases efficiency and raises incomes (the prediction of Chapter 2), people will want to consume more services. This tendency will provide considerably more employment in services, and at rising wages in the long run because it is difficult to raise productivity in most services that are labor-intensive.[*] These are major reasons why, despite years of increasing trade, the share of U.S. income going for employee compensation has changed very little. In the European Union, labor income has converged, rising faster in the poorer members than in the richer, but it has not fallen even in the richest.[2] Thus, the assumption that real wages will actually be lowered in an absolute sense is unrealistic.

It must, however, be realized that because international trade does tend to reduce the returns to the scarce factor and increase the returns to the abundant factor, then lower wages could occur in given labor-intensive industries because of the imports. The subject is treated in depth in Chapter 8, but for now it is enough to say that because trade raises the returns to the cheap factor, it substitutes to some extent for the free migration of labor and unhindered movement of capital. This has some interesting implications:

---

[*] The mathematical proof of full factor-price equalization requires restrictive assumptions well beyond no transport costs and trade barriers. Others are identical technology and tastes, no factor-intensity reversals, no scale effects, and incomplete specialization so all countries produce both capital-intensive and labor-intensive goods.

1. Groups that oppose immigration because of its effect on wages will also tend to oppose free trade. American labor unions, prosperous in a land of scarce labor, have never welcomed extensive immigration. The attempt to dam up the inflow of Mexican labor across the Rio Grande, even if it succeeds, will not help less-skilled American labor much if the Mexican labor goes to work on the Mexican side of the border producing labor-intensive goods for the U.S. market.

2. Groups that are owners of capital in capital-scarce lands—the wealthy classes of many less-developed nations—oppose free importation of capital because that will depress their returns. They must also oppose the free importation of capital-intensive goods, for that will have the same effect. Again, the conclusion that the returns to capital will fall for economies as a whole is more difficult to document than is the conclusion that it will fall in certain industries subject to the competition of capital-intensive imports.

Empirical Evidence

A number of cross-country studies of international trade have been reasonably consistent with the Heckscher-Ohlin model.[3] That by Bowen, Leamer, and Sveikauskas shows H-O receiving some empirical support in the exports and imports of Britain, France, Germany, and Japan.[4] Furthermore, the Heckscher-Ohlin model tends to hold strongly for less developed countries. Low-income nations appear to export similar labor-intensive manufactured products, the likes of which are not relatively so important in the exports of high-income countries.[5] The objection is sometimes made that Heckscher-Ohlin theory would seem to require that trade between rich and poor countries be huge in volume, whereas it is not. The LDCs have the cheapest labor and the developed countries have the cheapest capital, but trade between them is actually only 19% of world trade. In rebuttal, we must note that trade barriers are very high in the LDCs, while considerable protection also exists in the developed countries against products from the LDCs.[6]

A very large body of evidence exists, however, on the other side. Generally, a substantial amount of international trade, including especially much U.S. trade, does not appear to conform to Heckscher-Ohlin predictions, and the proportion is growing. That is the major concern of much of the remainder of the chapter.

TWO CHALLENGES TO THE HECKSCHER-OHLIN MODEL

The problem with the Heckscher-Ohlin model is that in spite of its logical appeal and its ability to account for some of the world's trade, its explanatory power has proved to be limited. Much of international trade, and an increasing proportion at that, has stubbornly refused to pattern itself along the lines predicted by the theory. Countries rich in capital often export labor-intensive goods, and most trade is between countries with similar factor proportions. Furthermore, much intraindustrial trade takes place in goods produced by the same industry, as when cars exported from Germany to Sweden pass cars exported from Sweden to Germany. For example, intraindustrial trade in automobiles and parts between the United States and Canada, which have similar factor proportions, is very large. The trade in these items alone exceeds all trade between the United States and Mexico in all classes of goods, even though U.S. and Mexican factor proportions are very different.

We begin by examining two major challenges to the Heckscher-Ohlin factor proportions model: Leontief's Paradox and intraindustrial trade. Then we consider several alternative models now attracting considerable attention.

The Leontief Paradox

It was almost dogma among economists that in the United States labor was the relatively scarce and expensive factor, while capital was the relatively abundant and cheap factor. The Heckscher-Ohlin model would therefore predict that U.S. exports would be capital-intensive, while its imports would be labor-intensive. The first sophisticated statistical test of that model (in 1954) did not, however, support that prediction. Indeed, it suggested the theory might be wrong.

Wassily Leontief was a Harvard professor, a pioneer in econometrics, and the winner of the 1973 Nobel Prize in Economics. Using the year 1947 as his base, Leontief compared the labor intensity of U.S. export industries with the labor intensity of U.S. imports. (Lacking good foreign data, he used the labor intensities of goods in the United States that competed with imports as the proxies for foreign labor intensities.) His results were surprising: for every man-year of labor, U.S. exports contained $14,010 of capital (a 1:14 ratio), but to produce the imports domestically, each man-year of labor would require $18,180 worth of capital (a 1:18 ratio). Exports were less capital-intensive than imports! This was hardly what Leontief expected or what the Heckscher-Ohlin model predicted.

The findings created quite a stir among trade theorists and came to be known as the *Leontief Paradox*. Economists could be forgiven for some initial skepticism, despite the eminence of its author. But the literature on the subject within a few years would have filled a good-sized bookcase, with the paradox persisting stubbornly in the data. It appeared again in U.S. data for 1951 and 1962, as analyzed by Leontief himself, and in Robert Baldwin's study of 1971; and it has been confirmed by the work of other scholars as well.[7]

The Heckscher-Ohlin model still thrives because it works well for many countries, particularly the less-developed ones. For all that, the long survival of the Leontief Paradox in the U.S. trade data poses a major challenge for the H-O model.

Intrafactoral and Intraindustrial Trade

The debates over the Leontief Paradox had already shaken the confidence with which economists viewed the Heckscher-Ohlin model of trade when additional remarkable evidence arose, presenting a further challenge to that model. In the 1950s observers began to note an unexpected pattern of trade not common before. Much exporting and importing was taking place among nations that seemed rather similar in their factor proportions and demand conditions. The pattern is quite clear today. Labor-scarce countries trade far more with other labor-scarce countries than the Heckscher-Ohlin theory would anticipate. Industrial countries buy only about 25% of their (non-oil) imports from less-developed countries. The 12 most industrialized countries do about two-thirds of their trade with one another. Trade in the old European Free Trade Association, which included very diverse countries such as Ireland, Iceland, Portugal, and Denmark, never expanded like that of the original European Economic Community, whose economies were far more similar to one another. Trade between the United States and Canada, both of which have high labor costs, is about twice as much as the value of U.S.-Mexican trade, despite Mexico's cheap labor. In short, a considerable amount of international trade involves countries whose factor proportions cause them to specialize in capital-intensive goods trading with other countries whose factor proportions also lead to capital-intensive production.[8]

Detailed studies of the issue added to the perplexity. Vast amounts of trade taking place among industrial nations turned out to be intraindustrial, meaning within the same industry.[9] As one example, the value of French exports of photographic supplies was within 2% of its imports of the same supplies. This is closer than usual, but such figures are not that rare. A substantial portion of the *growth* of trade in recent years has also been intraindustrial. Not only does most trade take place between nations similar in factor proportions, but most of that trade is actually within the same industry! The trade is not only intraindustrial, but intrafactoral, involving like nations trading with like. How could this kind of trade be explained by the Heckscher-Ohlin model?

THE INDEX OF INTRAINDUSTRIAL TRADE

Let us start with the data. It is now common to employ an index of intraindustrial trade in a form originally suggested by Bela Balassa:

$$(Eq.\ 3.1) \quad IIT = 1.0 - \frac{|X - M|}{X + M}$$

Here IIT is the index of intraindustrial trade. The highest possible number, 1, would occur when exports (X) equaled imports (M) within that industry.

Say $X = 10$ and $M = 10$. In that case

$$(Eq.\ 3.2) \quad \frac{X - M}{X + M} = \frac{0}{20} \text{ and therefore } IIT = 1.0 - 0 = 1.$$

The index of intraindustrial trade is thus 1 when exports and imports are equal in that industry.

The lowest number, 0, will occur when there is no intraindustrial trade. Say $X = 0$ and $M = 10$. In that case:

$$(Eq.\ 3.3) \quad \frac{X - M}{X + M} = \frac{10}{10} = 1 \text{ and therefore } IIT = 1.0 - 1 = 0.$$

$X - M$ is expressed as an absolute value, without regard to sign; hence the lines are drawn around it in the original expression so the figure will not turn out to be negative.

The index of intraindustrial trade for 10 industrial countries, only 0.36 in 1959 and 0.48 in 1967, had reached 0.60 by 1985 and it remains in that area.[10] Table 3.1 shows recent figures.

The low ranking for Japan, only about half the rich-country average, will be addressed in Chapter 8. That country imports above-average quantities of natural resources, is resource poor, and has a distribution system that has been rather difficult for foreign firms to penetrate; and there are other reasons, as we shall see.

The less-developed countries, which often export a high proportion of agricultural commodities and minerals and maintain high barriers to imported manufactured goods, engage in little intraindustrial trade. The index numbers for them are usually very low, often under 0.10, and sometimes as low as 0.04 (Sri Lanka) or even 0.02 (Nigeria,

Table 3.1

SHARE OF INTRA-INDUSTRY TRADE IN MANUFACTURING, 1990 (%)

France	81
Germany	69
Great Britain	81
Japan	33
Netherlands	84
United States	60

Source: Peter A.G. van Bergeijk and Dick L. Kabel, "Strategic Trade Theories and Trade Policy," *Journal of World Trade* 27, 6 (December 1993): 177.

Philippines), though the figures are much higher for newly industrializing countries such as Korea and Malaysia.

Explaining the Leontief Paradox

Thus the two major challenges to Heckscher-Ohlin theory are the Leontief Paradox and the existence of intraindustrial trade. Several orthodox explanations (that is, consistent with the Heckscher-Ohlin thesis and the neoclassical tradition) have been offered in explanation of both challenges.

We begin with the Leontief Paradox, that the United States appears to export labor-intensive goods and import capital-intensive goods. Here each of the orthodox explanations appears to contribute something, though not much, to a resolution of this knotty problem. One such explanation involves U.S. trade barriers. What if the U.S. tariffs and other barriers are relatively high on labor-intensive products, so that the United States imports relatively less of these? Imports of these products would be artificially reduced, which would make it appear that factor proportions were less important in determining trade flows. The evidence on this issue is mixed, but some studies do point to this explanation.

Perhaps the importance of U.S. imports of natural resources, which are capital-intensive, contributes to resolving the paradox. Jaroslav Vanek did indeed find that U.S. exports embody only about half as much natural resource content as is the case for U.S. imports, representing a shift from an earlier period when exports were resource-intensive.[11]

PRODUCTIVITY EXPLANATIONS: HUMAN CAPITAL AND TECHNOLOGY

Leontief himself believed the explanation lay in the productivity, that is, the effectiveness, of labor, which is enhanced by the presence of human capital working with advanced technology. Education is a form of capital in that it involves a saving from current consumption to improve productivity later on. Wealthy nations have the ability, in essence, to "save" the labor of millions of secondary school and university students who would otherwise be engaged in contributing to the GDP. Human capital formation can come not only from formal education, but also from on-the-job training, health care, and nutrition, all serving to raise the quality of labor and management. In addition, the education of U.S. managers is considerably greater than that of foreign managers. We can also consider technology a factor of production. Like human capital, it alters the relation of land and labor. Unlike human capital, which makes labor more productive, technology could make land, labor, or capital, or some combination of all three, more productive. Like human capital, technology is to some extent the result of past investment in research, and may be a form of capital. Hence high-quality labor is more akin to capital than it is to labor *per se*. Leontief argued that once international differences in labor productivity are incorporated, the predictions of the Heckscher-Ohlin model are significantly improved.

The productivity argument holds that one U.S. worker, whose output is increased by education, acquired skills, and other human capital, as well as by working with high-level technology, might be the equivalent of several low-paid foreign workers, with the American producing sufficiently more per hour so that the cost of that labor is actually lower per unit of output. If this were the case, then the United States could actually be labor abundant as measured in productivity-equivalent workers. Considerable evidence bears this out. Workers in Bangladesh are on average paid about 5% of U.S. wages, but their labor productivity is only 2% of U.S. labor productivity. Sri Lankan workers are paid 7% of U.S. wages, but their productivity is only 4%; Colombian workers are paid 29% of the U.S. level but their productivity is only 22% of the U.S. figure, and so on.[12]

Admittedly, human capital and technology arguments have inherent weaknesses. Both are difficult to measure. Some education is more consumption than production, much being rather a waste—though that is also true of some physical capital. Technology is an awkward concept, hard to work with statistically and conceptually. The R&D spending that leads to new technology can, of course, be measured, but it is not clear whether the expenditure on R&D can be directly correlated to technical advances. Technology, unlike land, labor, and capital, is dynamic and not innate, as technological gaps appear and disappear. Moreover, technology need not necessarily make labor relatively more productive than capital. The opposite is also possible—technology could make capital more productive than labor. Factor-proportions models that embody human capital and technical change are thus likely to be more complicated and less sure in their prediction.

Even so, human capital and technology can aid greatly in explaining a particular pattern of industrial trade by pointing out that the United States, for example, is exporting sophisticated telecommunications equipment, while it imports unsophisticated radios and television sets. Studies do indeed show that U.S. exports are correlated by industry to the proportion of the labor force employed in highly skilled categories and also by the amount of investment directed toward research and development spending.

Scholarship on the idea that human capital and technical change enhance productivity and alter comparative advantage has become a growth industry. One of the more famous examples is Michael Porter's influential book, *The Competitive Advantage of Nations*.[16] Porter's work offers illuminating analysis concerning what gives advantage in modern trade. Porter goes well beyond standard neoclassical analysis to posit a qualitative difference between "basic

TECHNOLOGY CAN ALTER COMPARATIVE ADVANTAGE

The semiconductor (microchip) provides an intriguing example of capital substituting for labor as a result of technical change. This tiny artifact allowed many types of electrical circuits to be miniaturized and inserted by mechanical means. It replaced the large circuit boards of wires and transistors that required labor-intensive assembly. Suddenly, low-labor-cost countries lost their advantage in production and assembly of a wide range of electronic goods. By the early 1980s, for instance, Hong Kong's cost advantage in electronics assembly had fallen from 66% to only 8% below U.S. costs.[13] There are many similar instances; recent changes sketched below have allowed many firms to see their manufacturing labor costs fall to figures between 5% and 15% of total production costs. This is a key statistic: if wages are below 15% of all production costs then wage differentials would have to be very high—say as much as 50%—to overcome the various costs of importing the product, such as transport, communications, travel for executives, insurance, and finance.[14] As a result, some Japanese TV producers have pulled their operations out of South Korea and back to Japan, GE has closed some of its Southeast Asian offshore factories and switched its foreign buying to Japanese producers; and other pull-backs have affected the garment and auto industries. Later in the chapter we turn to a further discussion of managerial and technological developments that have increased the ability of capital, and the human capital of skilled labor and good management, to substitute for labor.

Another example of the power of technology to affect comparative advantage appears in the data for exports from the newly industrializing countries, including Korea, Taiwan, Malaysia, Thailand, and several others. The original advantage of these countries was in goods manufactured by cheap labor—over 80% of their manufactured exports to the industrial countries in the mid-1960s were categorized as low technology and only 2% were high technology. As their incomes grew, the skills of their labor forces improved, and wages rose, these countries became technically more sophisticated. By 1985 the proportion of their exports described as low technology had fallen to 53% and the high technology component had risen to 25%.[15]

factors" and "advanced factors," which are created and not innate. Highly trained personnel with specific human capital, "knowledge resources," and a supporting scientific base, such as flows from government and private research institutes, leading universities, and industry associations, all combine to alter comparative advantage. Recently, the effectiveness of human capital development and technical change in promoting new paths for international trade have been impressively demonstrated in much of East Asia, including first in

Japan, and later in Taiwan, Malaysia, Thailand, and a few others. Porter's work suggests strongly that a country might engage in deliberate development of advanced factors to promote trade and hence growth, a subject we return to in Chapter 8.

Explaining Intraindustrial Trade

Orthodox explanations have also been advanced in the case of the other major challenge to the Heckscher-Ohlin theory, the existence of intraindustrial trade. The basic problem is whether factor proportions can explain intraindustrial trade.

STATISTICAL PROBLEMS

Traditional approaches based on factor proportions can certainly be the reason for some intraindustrial trade. The statistics may hide deep factor differences. We think of an industry as being a group of firms making similar products, technologically related to one another. Sometimes, however, the firms making up an industry may have quite different input requirements. Examples might include furniture made of wood or steel, or fabric made of wool or artificial fiber. American intraindustrial trade in floor coverings, for instance, is often very close to 1—but it is vinyl flooring that is exported and oriental carpets that are imported. Such trade may be intraindustrial, but it may also be based on factor differences and consistent with Heckscher-Ohlin principles. Though this serves as a partial explanation, it cannot explain *increasing* intraindustrial trade. We must look further.

TRANSPORTATION COSTS

Where products are homogeneous, such as copper, aluminum, red no. 1 wheat, or cement, it is easy to see that transport costs could be one reason for such exchange. The transport costs give rise to border trade. If Canada needs fertilizer in Alberta and has a surplus in Quebec it is certainly not going to haul it 2,500 miles to get it there. Far better to import it to Alberta from Montana, and export it from Quebec to the eastern United States.* The U.S. trade in oil, imported to the east coast and exported from the Southwest, is a similar case; Canada does the same by exporting oil from the prairie provinces and importing it to the Atlantic provinces.

---

* Canada's national news network recently reported with some degree of horror that Canadians were exporting live cattle to the United States and simultaneously importing beef. The fact that the cattle were exported from Alberta and slaughtered to feed American westerners, while the beef was imported 2,000 miles away in Quebec, only appeared later in the story.

Similarly, storage can be a reason for intraindustrial trade in standardized homogeneous goods. If it is cheaper to trade a product than to store it, as with perishables that have different growing seasons in two different countries, then exports will occur in one season and imports in another. Often this is a north-south trade between the hemispheres. Such trade can occur in an east-west direction as well, as when electricity is generated and transmitted over high-tension lines to areas where the load is at its peak, the flow reversed a few hours later as use peaks in the first area.

DIFFERING FACTOR PROPORTIONS BY STAGE OF MANUFACTURE

Another form of intraindustrial trade occurs in the sending of semi-finished goods to low-wage countries for assembly or preparation and their re-importation as finished products.[17] Currently, the most important examples of this trade are apparel and electronic goods. Trade of this kind, with the developed country as exporter of component and importer of final product, depends on transport costs being low enough as a proportion of the value of a given item to stand both the outward and the inward shipment. It includes some unlikely cases. For example, Haiti takes the cores of baseballs exported from the United States, sews their covers on, and flies them back—95% of U.S. baseballs follow this route. Elsewhere, Southeast Asia, Mexico, and the West Indies take semi-finished clothes, gloves, and leather luggage and sew them together for re-export. Growth in Mexico's trade of this type with the United States has been phenomenal. Nowadays about 30% of all U.S. exports to Mexico involve production sharing between U.S. and Mexican plants, and that is true of over 40% of all U.S. imports from Mexico. There are many other examples of trade in components based on differing factor proportions, as discussed in the box on the following page.

Such trade involving stage of manufacture is clearly consistent with the Heckscher-Ohlin model, and is based on factor costs, the capital/labor ratio in particular. Multinational firms foster a fair proportion of this trade, especially in electronics, but they are by no means the only conduit through which this type of processing takes place. If the economic pressure is strong enough, the market is quite capable of arranging deals by subcontracting, as is typical in apparel. Whether by market or by administrative decision of multinational firms, the basic cost pressures created by differing factor proportions determine what is produced where. Thus we have another example of trade that is intraindustrial, but quite different in factor proportions. The remarkable development of such trade has been assisted by the willingness of rich countries to apply their tariffs only to the value added abroad, rather than to the value of the complete product when the finished goods are re-exported back to where

---

EXPORT OF SEMI-FINISHED GOODS FOR PROCESSING OR ASSEMBLY

Over 20 American companies have located their data processing in the Caribbean, about half in Barbados, with other important centers in the Dominican Republic and Jamaica. India, China, and some countries in Southeast Asia also participate. They take data tapes flown from the United States for keypunching; sometimes they obtain the data via satellite. This new industry is supported mostly by airlines, hotels, credit card companies, and car rental agencies. The pioneer firm was American Airlines. The workers are mostly women, who sit behind keyboards with video-display terminals. Taiwan, Korea, Mexico, Thailand, and India work on auto components from and for developed countries. The semiconductors, valves, and tuners for a wide variety of electronic equipment are manufactured in Hong Kong, Singapore, Taiwan, Mexico, and elsewhere.

Clothing manufacture demonstrates clearly how far this kind of trade has developed. Most firms that market brand-name labels now do not take part directly in any manufacturing activities at all, but do only design, marketing, and retailing. These "makers without factories" farm out their manufacturing activities to networks of independent subcontractors around the world. The brand-name firms buy fabric from foreign fabric mills, arrange for the fabric and the garment patterns to go to cutting contractors, after which the cut fabric, buttons, zippers, or other components are delivered to sewing contractors who finish the job and ship the garment to the brand-name company's warehouses. Often the trail is a long one running from the United States or Europe to subcontractors in Hong Kong, Singapore, Taiwan, or South Korea where these firms then further subcontract the least-skilled work to factories in even lower-wage locations such as China, Sri Lanka, Malaysia, Myanmar, Thailand, Indonesia, Honduras, Guatemala, and the Dominican Republic. In many cases U.S. or European managers never even visit these far frontiers of unskilled labor.[18]

---

they started their journey. In the United States, numerous bills have been introduced in Congress to repeal these provisions, so far without success.

Continuing the Search

Statistical problems, transportation problems, and differences by stage of manufacture surely explain some intraindustrial trade, just as the invocation of human capital and technology may explain some of the Leontief Paradox. A great many economists, however, believe that *they do not explain enough of it.*

WHY TRADE ARISES AMONG SIMILAR COUNTRIES

The search for further explanations of trade among countries with similar factor proportions has been dominated by two groups of arguments suggesting that *specialization brings decreasing costs*. Models analyzing why costs decrease include: (1) learning by doing, in which previous experience leads to lower costs, and (2) extensions of the well-accepted logic of scale economies based on specialization. As the remainder of the chapter demonstrates, decreasing cost based on specialization is a principal source of comparative advantage in modern trade.

In some aspects, the Heckscher-Ohlin factor-proportions model is quite compatible with decreasing-cost models in both general and partial equilibrium. Yet most of the decreasing cost models are quite different from the H-O formulation in that they are *indeterminate and contingent*. That is, several outcomes are possible depending on the industries in which countries originally specialize, and comparative advantage can be established partly by that original selection. Our task in the remainder of the chapter is to discuss several such decreasing-cost models. Interestingly, we shall find some reason to believe that much of the trade arising because of specialization and decreasing costs is not as disruptive as trade that arises because of Heckscher-Ohlin conditions.

Economies of Scale and Decreasing Costs

Explanations that provide alternatives to the Heckscher-Ohlin factor-proportions approach invoke some form of scale economies that lead to decreasing costs. Such models usually involve a considerable degree of choice and indeterminacy, with comparative advantage established because costs decrease as a nation becomes more specialized.

Alfred Marshall, the great synthesizer of classical economics, held that decreasing costs were the normal situation in industry:

> The general argument of the present book shows that an increase in the aggregate volume of production of anything will generally increase the size, and therefore the internal economies possessed by this representative firm; that it will always increase the external economies to which such a firm has access; and thus will enable it to manufacture at a less proportionate cost of labour and sacrifice than before.
>
> In other words, we say broadly that while the part which nature plays in production shows a tendency to diminishing returns, the part which man plays shows a tendency to increasing returns. The *law of increasing returns* may be worded thus:—An increase of capital and labour leads generally to an improved organization; and therefore in those industries

which are not engaged in raising raw produce, it generally gives a return increased more than in proportion; and further this improved organization tends to diminish or even override any increased resistance which nature may offer to raising increased amounts of raw produce.[19]

DECREASING COSTS IN GENERAL EQUILIBRIUM

We begin with an overall view of the gains from specialization. Picture two identical countries in autarky, but with decreasing costs. Figure 3.5 shows these countries' production possibilities with decreasing costs. Their identical PPCs showing the trade-off between Good 1 and Good 2 are convex to the point of origin. While the PPCs of Chapter 2 showed goods that were very different in manufacture and use, these production possibilities curves take two goods that are similar. The two goods could actually just be variations of one another, like minivans and sedans, or they could be quite different but both incorporate advanced technology, such as glass-fiber cable and cellular telephones, or memory chips and integrated circuits. The production possibilities curves indicate that the more of either good the nation makes, the fewer of the other good it gives up. In the absence of trade, however, neither country can specialize because the structure of demand is such that people want about the same amount of each good, shown by their identical map of indifference curves I_1 and I_2. Both countries are originally consuming at point Z, which involves quantity W of Good 1 and quantity X of Good 2.

As Figure 3.5 shows, in a decreasing-cost situation specialization brings lower costs. The three triangles in the figure all have the same height ($AB = CD = EF$). Their bases narrow, however, as the country becomes more specialized. (See how $FG > DE > BC$.) That means that producing the same amount of Good 1 requires the sacrifice of less and less of Good 2 the more specialized the country becomes. In autarky,

Figure 3.5

A DECREASING-COST MODEL

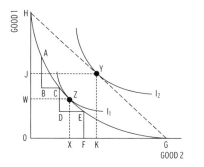

Note: In a decreasing-cost model, the production possibility curve is convex to the point of origin. An economy moving from A to C to E to G gives up the same amount of Good 1, but gets ever-larger amounts of Good 2. Trade would lead to complete specialization with one country at G and the other at H.

the countries produce and consume at point Z, and while Good 1 would be cheaper to make at a more specialized point, consumers would not buy it because the falling production of Good 2 would drive up its price, and vice versa. If both countries could specialize, one producing all of Good 1 and the other all of Good 2 (a "corner" solution), then they could enter into trade with each other. In the figure, the country producing at H could export HJ of Good 1 in return for imports of JY of Good 2; the country producing at G could export GK of Good 2 in return for imports of KY of Good 1. Each country could consume at point Y. Both would be much better off, now touching indifference curve I_2.

It is noteworthy that when trade opens, prices do not signal to firms which way they should move. Once movement starts, however, the first country to specialize in a good will find it has a growing comparative advantage in that good. It will move to the corner indicating complete specialization in that good. The other nation will move to the opposite corner. The gains from trade will be ZY in both countries.

A decreasing-cost model in this form suggests a major issue in modern trade theory: What might cause the movement toward specialization to occur in the first place? That question recurs for the balance of the chapter.

Learning By Doing and Decreasing Costs

One way to analyze decreasing costs as output increases is to consider learning by doing. Learning curve analysis (LCA) is a means for doing so. LCA is a recent development, originally applied in management economics within a single country, but it can also show how the experience from greater output lowers costs, thereby possibly establishing a comparative advantage. LCA relates the increasing skills of labor and improved efficiency in production not to investment in education and research, which are assumed to be constant, but to the total quantity of products of any given type produced over time.[20]

In the 1920s, analysts noted an interesting pattern in the rate of labor's ability to learn.[*] The man-hours spent on manufacturing a given product tended to fall by some regular percentage every time production doubled. Suppose a shipyard found that it took 10,000 man-hours to produce the first tugboat it made, and then discovered with the second tugboat that it took only 8,000 man-hours. From these two points management could project that the fourth tugboat would take only 6,400 man-hours, the eighth 5,120 man-hours, and

---

[*] Economic historians have spotted signs of the effect of learning at a much earlier time than this. Historically, the first indication that labor productivity could be systematically increased by cumulative work experience appeared at the Horndal steelworks in Sweden. This plant was built in 1835-36 and then maintained in an unchanged physical condition for the next 15 years, with the labor force also unchanged in size. Yet output rose by about 2% per year. The

Figure 3.6
A LEARNING CURVE

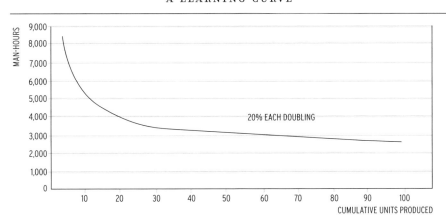

so on, with man-hours falling by 20% for each doubling of production. The points sketched out on a diagram produce a learning curve, as in Figure 3.6. As firms and workers accumulate experience in making a product, the costs of doing so fall in a predictable manner. Every time the firm manages to double its production, costs tend to decline by about the same percentage, as shown in Figure 3.6.

World War II provided major examples of learning curves in practice, with convincing evidence for their existence in airframe production, Liberty ship construction, and destroyer output, among others. For example, excellent data are available for the labor time expended in the construction of large numbers of Sumner and Gearing class destroyers at Maine's Bath Iron Works between 1943 and 1945. These ships were virtually identical; no important alterations in the capital stock were made in this period; and the shipyard's employment did not grow. Yet between the first ships and the last, man-hours expended per ship fell by 52.3%, a result that could only be due to the effect of learning by doing.[21] The figure is, of course, a wartime one, when the motive to learn was boosted by the life-or-death nature of the struggle. Even so, it is very impressive.

There is reason to believe that not only labor costs, but capital and management costs also decline according to cumulative experience. The amount of technical innovation, scale changes, improvements implemented at the shop floor and so forth apparently correlate more closely with total production experience than to either elapsed time or even research expenditure.

phenomenon came to be known as the "Horndal effect." See Paul A. David, *Technical Choice, Innovation, and Economic Growth* (Cambridge: Books on Demand, 1975), 174, citing the original work of E. Lundberg, *Produktivitet och Rantabilitet* (Stockholm, 1961), 129-33.

TRADE BARRIERS CAN INHIBIT LEARNING

An automobile industry was established in India in the late 1940s. One of the firms was founded at the same time that Toyota was founded in Japan. In the late 1970s, India was still producing more cars than Korea. Unfortunately, the stagnant industry showed little sign that cumulative learning was much of an advantage to it. The drive to learn is obviously lessened in the presence of high protection against foreign competition, a monopoly position at home, and lack of incentives to do anything but sit back and rake in profits.[22] The learning advantages are thus probably less for poor countries with high trade barriers and numerous monopolies.

Such changes are, of course, affected by higher spending on R&D, or good management, but production experience, with normal expenditures on those other factors, is arguably the most important variable.

The Boston Consulting Group has pioneered modern learning-curve analysis, constructing many curves from data gathered on various U.S. industries. Experience tended to show, however, that consistent curves are hard to draw, and some economists have concluded that in practice learning curves are insufficiently reliable for making major business decisions.[23] But there is no doubting that learning effects do exist and that they have significant implications for international economics.

With learning taken into account, comparative advantage can change. The nation that has produced the greatest quantity of a good has the lowest cost not because of unusual expenditures on capital, education, or research, but because it has learned to use its labor, and to a lesser extent its capital, more efficiently. A comparative advantage is not given but created. Low costs do not cause a nation to specialize; rather, the specialization causes the low costs. Unlike many other economic models, models based on learning are not reversible. While a plant that must reduce its size to adjust to a smaller market will suffer diseconomies of scale, reduced output will not cancel the experience workers have already gained.

COMBINING MODELS: PIONEERS AND LATE ENTRANTS

Comparing one world with identical countries entering into trade with another world where countries have very different costs is a neat pedagogical device, but a combination of both is actually closer to the reality. Countries with small "innate" cost disparities would often tend to trade heavily in goods where cost differences are largely created by the advantages of learning. Where the innate gap between the cost of labor and capital is high, however,

Figure 3.7

LEARNING CURVES FOR A PIONEER AND A LATE ENTRANT

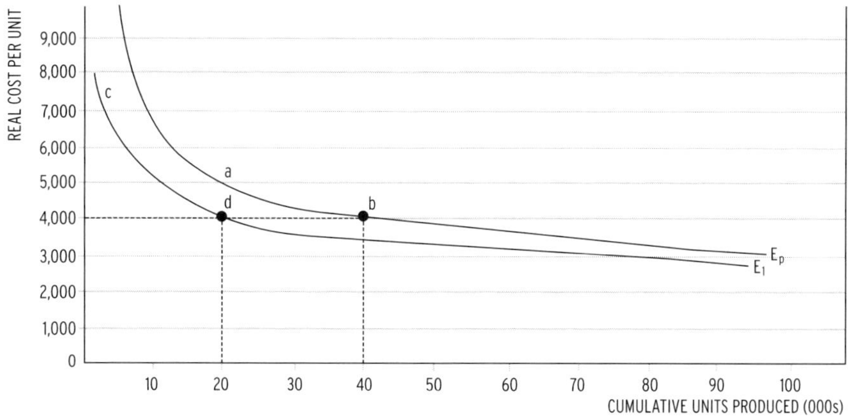

Note: A nation pioneering a product whose costs are E_p can keep ahead of late entrants with lower cost structures only so long as it can keep expanding its production. If the pioneer moves from *a* to *b* at the same time the late entrant moves from *c* to *d*, both countries expanding production by 20,000 units, it will cease to have any advantage.

even large learning effects might not overcome the cost differences, and the predictions of the Heckscher-Ohlin model would prevail.

To illustrate this, assume there are two nations, a "pioneer" that first started the production of a labor-intensive product, and a late-entry nation that starts production at a subsequent period. Further assume that the late entrant's costs are lower (its economic development is occurring after that of the pioneer). Since the product is labor-intensive, the late entrant's lower labor costs should give it a comparative advantage. Because the late entrant is inexperienced, however, it cannot initially compete. Figure 3.7 shows this with two learning curves. E_p represents the learning curve of the pioneering nation, while E_l represents that of the late entrant. Curve E_l lies below E_p, indicating that at any point at which two nations have the same experience, the late entrant's costs would be lower. The late entrant's innate cost differences allow it to achieve a lower cost with less experience than the pioneering nation.

The intriguing aspect of this model is that the pioneering nation can keep the gap between it and the late entrant only so long as it can continue to double its production as fast as the latter. But it becomes increasingly difficult for the pioneering nation to continue doubling its production because the base grows so large. Consider how long it would take General Motors, Toyota, or Volkswagen to produce the quantity of cars equal to the entirety of its production since its founding. Accordingly, the rate of cost decline in the pioneer slows, while the late entrant's costs fall rapidly. Return to Figure 3.7 and suppose the pioneering nation is at point a on curve E_p when the late entrant (using some borrowed technology) starts at point c on its curve. Both nations now raise their sales by equal amounts of the product, say 20,000. The pioneering nation's new sales move it down its learning curve from a to b. For the same sales, however, the late entrant has moved from c to d. Unfortunately for the pioneer, point b and point d reflect the same cost of production. Comparative advantage and factor proportions thus appear to reassert themselves once the technological head start is overcome.

How, you might ask, could the late entrant ever move down its learning curve if the pioneer keeps ahead? It would not have any sales if the leading country always had the lower price. A competitive market would, however, support the late entrant if financiers had the knowledge that it would eventually displace the pioneer. They would then agree to finance the late entrant through loans or very low dividends, until it caught up to the pioneer, using as their rationale the future earnings of the late entrant. To be sure, knowledge is not perfect, nor is the financial market, so this may not happen. But it could and does some of the time. In a situation of imperfect competition, the pioneering nation may also be producing at low costs, but not selling at low costs because its firms had some degree of monopoly control. If these firms fail to observe or respond to the new entrant, as American automobile firms failed to respond to the invasion of Europeans and Japanese in the small and luxury car markets, the new entrant can get a good start. From these considerations it appears likely that late entrants with more suitable factor endowments in the production of some particular good will eventually catch up to the pioneering nation.

It is possible that either pioneer or latecomer will find expected cost reductions cut short, so that the advantages of learning by doing are lost. An early freezing of work rules by trade unions, such as occurred in Great Britain, is a case in point and can stop the process by making impossible the reorganizations and shifts in tasks that learning allows. A resistance to skill acquisition on the job or a non-cooperative workforce can substantially erode the advantages of experience.

The existence of learning curves does not disprove the Heckscher-Ohlin model, but adds to it. Learning is a form of information, and simple equilibrium models with a classical base assume that producers have all relevant information. Used judiciously and in the correct, presumably long-run, context, models incorporating this assumption are highly useful. We know, of course, that nations and companies do not have the same knowledge and that some production and marketing skills are exceedingly difficult to transfer. If we want to ask questions with the realistic assumption that production knowledge is imperfect, then learning curves make fascinating tools for so

A PENALTY FOR TAKING THE LEAD?

There may be a penalty for taking the lead that the pioneer has to bear. High-cost capital equipment that takes a long time to depreciate may eventually become obsolete and hence a drawback to the pioneering nation. Britain's Industrial Revolution in the first half of the nineteenth century saddled it with an inadequate railway system compared to the later networks of the United States and Germany. In order to negotiate the sharp curves of the system, British boxcars were (and are) small, with limited carrying capacity. Given the economic development along the rail lines, buying property to rectify the situation would now be extremely expensive. Similarly, the British iron and steel industry was trapped for many years by its heavy investment in Bessemer converters, at a time when Germany had gone on to the more efficient open-hearth method for steelmaking. (Then, after World War II, the United States and Britain were still stuck with their open-hearth systems while their bombing had done a splendid job of depreciating the German and Japanese mills, which were replaced with more modern facilities.) It is true, as economists point out, that sunk costs should ordinarily have no bearing on future investment decisions.[*] To some extent, however, in practice they do.[24] For one example, large costs may be associated with dismantling the old plant. For another, a heavy burden of outstanding loans on the now-outmoded capital may still have to be repaid, which may weaken the financial performance of firms and mean that they may have to face higher interest rates on subsequent loans. Finally, investment is risky and there may thus be a bias toward the status quo. All may represent penalties borne by the pioneer. The result may then be a momentum, or hysteresis as physicists would say, to exporting. Once the costs of plant and equipment, information, brand loyalty, and established marketing channels have been incurred, firms may continue for a long time to produce and even export as long as variable costs can be covered.[25]

doing. If we wish to assert that factor proportions still hold in the abstract or in the long run, we can also do that.

The Microeconomics of Specialization and Decreasing Cost

The general idea is that trade among nations with similar factor proportions can occur because of scale economies that result in decreasing costs. The greater learning by doing as scale expands is one possible explanation.

[*] A fine historical example: all the huge investment in the Russian-American telegraph project, a line that was to cross the Bering Strait and ran through Siberia, was abandoned unfinished when the Atlantic Cable was successfully completed.

Another explanation involves a more traditional view of decreasing costs, as recently modified by advances in the study of specialization. The conventional microeconomic notion of what actually generates scale economies has focused on *plant-size economies of scale*, wherein costs fall as plants expand in size. Larger plants might allow greater division of labor, more specialized equipment and processes, assembly-line techniques, fuel savings, and the like. *Firm economies of scale*, in which a single company may have many plants but through its coordinative mechanism manages to keep its costs lower than smaller single-plant firms, have also received attention.

In a more significant departure from the neoclassical tradition, *industry economies of scale* or *economies of agglomeration* may exist as great numbers of plants in a single industry cluster in certain areas. In the United States, for instance, there are regional concentrations of microchip plants in California's Silicon Valley and of robotic equipment along Michigan's Route 94 west of Detroit. The clustering occurs because of the need for a pool of specialized labor, specialized inputs and services such as machine shops, technical advisers, and so forth—the infrastructure of an industry. In smaller nations, an excessive diversity could prevent the growth of such specialized infrastructure and the lower costs that go with it.

Organizational economists often distinguish among three types of clusters. A Marshallian cluster (named for the ones Alfred Marshall described) consists of firms with no formal connections; they just share the same talent pool and supporting industries. A North Italian (or "Third Italy") cluster has small firms that have formal arrangements with one another for sharing common facilities, such as accounting, purchasing, and marketing. A Chandlerian firm and associated cluster (after Alfred Chandler, who described the growth of large firms in the United States) has much more formal ownership, joint holdings, or formal alliances.[26]

PLANT-SIZE ECONOMIES

We normally represent plant-size economies of scale with a long-run average cost curve. Typically (or probably) such curves are more or less U-shaped, with a long flat bottom, meaning that beyond a certain minimum amount, the minimum efficient scale (MES) costs per unit stay about the same over quite a range of plant sizes. They begin to rise again with very large plants, at the maximum efficient scale (MXES). Automobile assembly plants, for instance, may reach minimum efficient scale somewhere between 150,000 and 200,000 units a year and have fairly constant costs through 300,000 or 400,000 units. In a small market, a firm might have to build a plant at suboptimal size. If it tried to build a plant at MES but supplied only the small

Figure 3.8

PLANT ECONOMIES OF SCALE

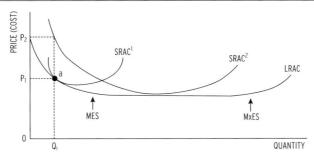

Note: A firm operating on a short-run average cost curve that is less than minimum efficient scale (SRAC[1]) will have higher costs than one operating on an efficient scale SRAC, such as SRAC[2], providing the latter has a market large enough to absorb its production. LRACs typically have rather long flat bottoms, with a minimum efficient scale (MES) and a maximum efficient scale (MXES).

market, it would be operating so far under capacity that it would be a very high-cost operation indeed.

Figure 3.8 shows a long-run average cost curve and two short-run average cost curves, which would apply to the firm once it built a plant. The firm building the sub-MES plant (SRAC[1]), can operate at point *a*, with quantity Q_1 and price P_1, while the firm building at MES (SRAC[2]) would be unable to sell more than Q_1 and, unable to spread its fixed costs over much volume, would thereby face very high costs, at P_2.

Typically, processing plants using large amounts of heat have high MESs. Industrial gases (oxygen, chlorine, ethylene), petroleum refining, petrochemicals, milk processing, beer brewing, fruit and vegetable canning, sugar refining, papermaking, fabrication of metal tubes and pipes, manufacture of cosmetics and perfume, glassmaking, and soapmaking are all among the industries with very high MESs. Gas and oil pipelines, together with satellite and glass-fiber communication systems, have perhaps the highest MESs of all.[*] Next come what can be called the metal-bashing industries, particularly those with continuous production lines such as motor vehicles and appliances.

---

[*] One reason is that pipes and storage tanks do not have to be twice as big to carry twice the capacity. Compare a pipe that is 10 feet wide with one that is five feet wide. The formula for the area of a circle, which is key to the carrying capacity, is πr^2; the 10-foot wide pipe has an area of $\pi 5^2$ or about 79 sq. feet; the five-foot pipe has an area of just under 20 sq. feet. Also, larger plants use little more labor and are better at conserving energy. It is said that a petrochemical plant producing 400,000 tons of ethylene a year costs only about 50% more, and uses only about 15% more labor, than one producing 200,000 tons.

Below that are industries that are batch processors, although these are general rules of thumb, not economic precepts.[*]

Empirical evidence on the matter is not entirely conclusive. Joe S. Bain's pioneering work on U.S. and European data suggested that scale economies were overrated.[27] Bain believed that most major countries had domestic markets large enough to support several plants of optimal size in most industries. Studies of Western Europe's plant sizes before the integration of the European Community also suggested they were about the same size as U.S. plants, which were presumably built to scale. It followed that integration would not increase scale economies by that much.

Bain's figures led to the conclusion that most major countries can support several plants of optimal size in most industries, both light and heavy; the very existence of multiplant firms demonstrated that. Further research by F.M. Scherer and others working with him confirmed the broad thrust of Bain's pioneering efforts.[28] Studies of specific industries do indicate that scale economies are not as important as might be expected in such industries as computers, diesel engines, generators, machine tools, rubber goods, shoes, and fish canning. To the extent that Bain, Scherer, and others are correct, the explanatory power of plant-size economies of scale is reduced.

In general, however, it appears that scale economies have been becoming *more* important in both exporting and import-competing industries.[29] It is especially clear that for countries with inadequate domestic markets, the diseconomies of small plant size can deliver a crucial cost penalty. The Australian petrochemical industry, for instance, has been operating at twice the cost of world-scale chemical plants, being both terribly under scale and, because of overly optimistic market forecasts, under capacity.[30] Many Canadian petrochemical operations, and a number of other industries, are seriously under scale and costly to operate—not because Canada's market is not big enough, but because transportation costs are much too great between market centers, which are mostly strung out along the U.S. border.

In such circumstances the achievement of plant-size scale economies through international trade can be critically important and can outweigh other considerations. Belgium's industry specializes in auto parts and some machinery inputs, Denmark's in furniture, the Netherlands' in electrical equipment, Luxembourg's in steel, Sweden's in telecommunications, and Switzerland's in drugs and watches. In each case, without the scale economies made possible by trade, exporting these items would be difficult if not impossible. The same

---

[*] Changes over time in plant economies have been noted as technology is standardized or altered. Thus with color TVs, MES in the early 1960s was observed to be about 50,000 sets a year, whereas by the late 1970s MES had risen to about 2 million. In steel, the old integrated steel mills had to produce about 2 million tons to reach MES; new mills reach MES with about half-a-million tons.

SCALE PROBLEMS IN UNEXPECTED PLACES

Inability to realize economies of scale can discourage trade in unusual ways. It is not worthwhile to produce a textbook in international economics specifically for the Canadian or Australian markets. Typically, only the large introductory courses have books adjusted to national circumstances; a Canadian or New Zealand student studying international economics, industrial organization, or even plain old intermediate theory finds more discussion of the United States or Britain than is remotely necessary. Even newspaper comic strips need wide markets to be successful—and there are relatively few the United States uses from abroad. *Andy Capp* and *Fred Basset* (British) and *For Better or For Worse* (Canadian) are among this tiny group.

---

consideration affects the newly industrializing countries (NICs). Virtually *every* major manufactured good produced in Singapore or Hong Kong would be impossibly costly if it were not for the scale provided by the world market. For these countries it is unarguable that high trade barriers to their exports will damage their welfare by inflicting scale diseconomies.

INDUSTRY ECONOMIES

Industry economies of scale may be more significant than plant scale economies. Each firm may face a normal long-run average cost curve, $LRAC^1$ in Figure 3.9 for example, but as more firms enter the industry, this curve begins to shift downward, say to $LRAC^2$ and $LRAC^3$, as the essential industrial infrastructure comes into existence. As industry output increases, the firm finds that it faces lower costs. So a firm's LRAC (1, 2, and 3) represents that firm's long-run cost structure at some given industry output. But $LRAC_I$ represents the declining long-run average cost of the industry. $LRAC_I$ slopes downward because as individual firms expand, they create benefits for other firms (externalities). They do so by enlarging the pool of skilled labor and management, supporting local universities and community colleges, and creating markets for a plethora of specialized suppliers and services.

In this reading, clusters of small and medium-size firms can achieve industrial economies of scale. The absence of clustered firms may mean extra transport costs to specialized suppliers, lack of an adequate labor market pool, and no knowledge spillovers of the sort that occur when specialists meet. The successful specialized industries of Belgium, Luxembourg, the Netherlands, Denmark, Sweden, and Switzerland are good examples. They are dependent not just on plant-size scale economies, as already discussed, but on industrial scale economies as well. An industrial strategy that encourages new plants

Figure 3.9

INDUSTRY ECONOMIES OF SCALE

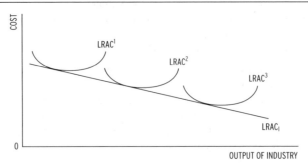

Note: Long-run average costs may fall when a number of firms operate in the same area due to economies of agglomeration. Thus the industry's LRAC (LRAC$_I$) slopes downward.

simply because they meet existing MESs, yet are unrelated to other plants in the region, may never build the industrial infrastructure required to lower costs.

SEGMENTED MARKETS AS AN EXPLANATION FOR TRADE

The demand and supply diagram all students learn in the first year has a horizontal axis labeled "cars" or "bushels of wheat" or, more abstractly, "widgets." The goods have to be identical, or the differences between them clearly quantifiable, for the model to work, and that simplification is enormously useful. Most goods in the economy are not identical, however, and we do not want them to be identical either. Students' clothing may not fit the more rotund bodies of many of their instructors, and many students and teachers would feel foolish or stuffy in the other group's outfits.

The degree of difference is in essence a compromise between the economies of mass production and the rather specific needs of the consumers. In the developing world, inexpensive labor often allows individual tailoring, but the capital-intensive techniques of the developed world have, at least until recently, favored a great degree of standardization—whether in clothing, cars, or breakfast cereal. We buy standardized clothes because of price. Unless we are very wealthy, we do not have our own tailors to match our sizes and shapes precisely. The market makes its own compromises—sport shirts come in four adult sizes, long-sleeved dress shirts in over 30. Consumers buy a good that is somewhat less than perfect because its price compensates—Oreo cookies may not be as good as Mom's, but Mom's are far more expensive, in that she would have to take time off from work, while Oreos can be bought in a bag at the supermarket. The shirt may be a little long in the sleeve or a little tight at the waist, but the buyer saves a few dollars that can be used to buy something else.

Increasingly, however, consumers everywhere (in developed countries at any rate) have shown that their demand shifts away from standardized products as their incomes rise. When the affluence of these consumers increases, they become less interested in the saving on price alone and more anxious to acquire a product that accurately meets their own tastes and needs. Rather than saving $75 on a washing machine to spend elsewhere, they buy a machine with extra washing cycles. Firms accommodate them to get their business. Since each consumer is somewhat different, the firm produces a line of goods with various features to serve various groups of customers—which, evidence indicates, is easier to accomplish when production is capital-intensive rather than labor-intensive.[31] Complete personal customization is impossible, but the firm can divide its market into market segments and manufacture products meeting the desires of each segment. This procedure, usually described as market segmentation, is discussed more fully in the accompanying box.

A FURTHER LOOK AT MARKET SEGMENTATION

Marketers sometimes distinguish between a segmentation based on market characteristics such as age, gender, income, lifestyle—young/old, black/white, yuppie/retired, ad infinitum—and those based on product characteristics—15-, 25-, 50-, 75-, 110-horsepower outboards, or the amount of chocolate in cakes and cookies. The product preferences for each motor or cake fall rather randomly across any market segment; and the purchase is determined by the function the goods are to perform.

Inevitably, market segmentation adds to costs, but it produces benefits consumers want. Hence, even under highly competitive conditions, one could expect a considerable degree of market segmentation as firms try to answer the economic question of what to produce. Under oligopolistic situations there may be rather more market segmentation because firms fear to engage in price wars. If Coke fights with Pepsi through a price cut, Pepsi can match it tomorrow, but if Coke comes out with a new flavor (say diet cherry), Pepsi would take months or longer to produce a competitive drink. Often the market is just not responsive enough to price cuts to make them worthwhile. If *Better Homes and Gardens* lowers its price, it is unlikely to gain customers from *House Beautiful*. Under such conditions firms speak of "deepening their market" and move toward a greater effort to identify market segments and produce goods specifically designed for each. In extreme cases there may be little redesign and merely an assertion that the product is for a particular group, as in a man's deodorant, a woman's laxative, a blue-collar beer. As a result, there is no inexpensive brand X but only more expensive customized products.[32]

Market segments do not necessarily follow national borders. Not all Americans like big cars and all Europeans small ones. Not all Frenchmen love French cars. Blue jeans and jean jackets are popular worldwide, particularly among young people, and their design does not change at the borders. What this means is that companies are able to plan and design for a world market involving a niche for some particular product variety. No single national market can support the BMW or the Volvo—there are not enough buyers in any one market. But the world as a whole makes the market large enough. Even textbooks, particularly those for the upper levels, benefit enormously from world market sales and are increasingly designed (like this one) with those sales in mind.

"IN-FIRM" DISECONOMIES OF MULTIPLE MODELS

Even when a firm can produce locally in multiple models, it is likely to find that its costs rise as the models proliferate. First are the additional costs that occur within a firm that decides to multiply its models. A major example involves the additional pre-production costs for market research, design, prototypes, and testing. Before a company decides to come up with a new model of car, a new textbook, or a new deodorant, it must identify a need or desire, often through market research. It must design a product and build prototypes. Finally, formally or informally it must test-market the product, often at considerable expense. A new automobile model, for instance, could easily cost $100 million before the first car is sold. If the company expects to sell only 200,000 units of that model (the output of one assembly plant for one year), those costs are $500 per car. A new textbook requires the labor of one or two authors, several editors, and another set of critical readers before it is edited or goes to the printer—and that can easily be $10 or more per book. Late-generation DRAM (dynamic random-access memory) computer chips probably cost about $2 billion before even one is sold.[33]

Additional costs will be incurred for advertising and the provision of information, as it will be necessary to bring each different model to the attention of the public. Furthermore, inventory costs will rise greatly as models proliferate. With numerous models, it will be necessary for a firm to increase its holding of parts and components, which will not be fully interchangeable. More finished items must be held in inventory as well, because consumers must be able to see examples of the product at stores or showrooms. Much of the inventory of finished items will not be sold for months, and some of it might not be sold at all.

Finally, if the product is a durable, then providing service for it will be more difficult if there are multiple models. Repair people will need more varied training and diagnostic equipment will have to be more complex. A more complicated stock of spare replacement parts will also be necessary.

Each of the cases discussed above involves the firm with an increased burden of decision-making associated with the proliferation of models. Whether to introduce an additional model will involve weighing the costs against the benefits of marketing that new model. This burden on management is another extra cost of production.

"IN-PLANT" DISECONOMIES OF MULTIPLE MODELS

In addition to the costs affecting an entire firm, there is another set of costs involving the actual production within a plant.[34] The introduction of new models into a production line, with no deletion of any of the existing models, increases the costs of all products in that line. More specifically, these in-plant costs involve the following:

1. *Changeover time.* Down time is the period when a machine or factory is being changed over for new production runs, idling machinery and manpower. One Australian factory, for instance, reported that the set-up time on a machine was eight hours. The machine was used for two hours to turn out a supply of parts that would last many months, and was then reset for something else. The American parent firm, with its larger market, used the same machine for weeks after the set-up.[35] The cost of the changeover must fall on the products involved.

2. *Equipment usage rates.* Specialized dies and machinery are needed for each of the different models. Many of these must be left idle while other products are run, giving low usage rates. When the accountants go over the figures, they find that they must assign higher per-product costs as they divide the cost of the machine by the products it produces.

3. *Automation and the use of specialized equipment.* Many kinds of specialized equipment are justified only with high volumes of particular items. To quote an Australian manager:

> Where we use a two- or three-cavity die, the U.K. company uses a twenty-four cavity die…. And where we have a machine on which we

113

do five different processes consecutively, stripping down the machine between each process, the U.K. company does the five processes simultaneously on one machine—but their machine costs about £400,000.

And another Australian:

Where we use an ordinary turret lathe, the U.K. company uses a multistation loading lathe, and the U.S. company uses a twelve spindle machine which performs twelve operations simultaneously.[36]

Automation is only economical for longer production runs. Workers can be taught to switch tasks, but the machine that replaces them has a more limited range. If there are many different models to turn out, the process cannot be extensively automated, so labor costs must be higher.

4. *Labor's learning curve.* The repetition of tasks leads to a decline in labor costs, as we indicated previously, but if there are many models, the repetition is lessened and much of the learning is forgone.

Computer-aided design and managerial changes are making it easier to produce multiple models within a single plant, but multiple models are still more costly to produce than a few standard ones. According to the rule of thumb adopted by the Boston Consulting Group, reducing product-line variety by half cuts costs on average by 17%; reducing variety again by half yields another cost saving averaging 13%.[37] Studies in Canada have suggested that automobile companies saved 10-15% of their costs by orienting their production toward the U.S. market as well as the Canadian one.

Trade in market-segmented goods carries with it the same kind of convex production possibilities curve we showed in Figure 3.8 for plant-size scale effects. Whatever the country decides to specialize in is cheaper than the product it decides not to specialize in. The effects of factor proportions are just too small to have much of an influence compared with the returns to specialization.

Factories Focused and Flexible

Firms that solve the problem of bringing a wide variety of models to their customers while controlling costs have an obvious edge. At the same time, firms' solutions to the problems have significant international implications. Firms are following one of two paths: (1) toward more specialized plants—*focused factories*, and (2) toward plants that can change very quickly and inexpensively from producing one model to producing another—*flexible factories*.

FOCUSED FACTORIES

If firms can limit the variety of their product lines, producing in focused factories for one or a few of the ever-increasing number of market segments or niches, they can reap substantial in-plant economies. The economies are based on the scale effects of assembly lines and repetitive tasks, "Fordism" as it is called, after Henry Ford, the auto pioneer. In each separate national market, the market segments or niches are often not large enough to allow scale economies, but the world market *is* large enough and exporting allows access to it. The result is likely to be more intra-industrial trade because different but related products will often be made in different countries. Typically, a multinational firm may decide to produce all of a given product line in one plant, which happens to be located in one country, and all of another line of products in a second plant, which happens to be in a second country. Even a domestic company might decide to "source" part of its product line from an independent firm in another country. Shoe and fastener companies have been doing this for years. For example, a fastener firm in Rockford, Illinois, has for some time imported the standard nuts and bolts of its product line from various foreign companies, while using its own production facilities for high-tech aerospace work. (Note how this contributes to the Leontief Paradox because the work the firm maintains at home is far more labor-and-technology-intensive than the items it imports.)

Focused factories possess an inherent disadvantage, however. As market segmentation increases and as changes in consumer tastes occur more rapidly, a focused factory may find itself running up against growth constraints because its product variety is too limited and its response to taste changes too slow. Some authorities now argue that the dedicated equipment of a focused factory represents increasingly risky investment because a market segment may shrink rather suddenly.[38] Hence the development of the flexible factory, with the ability to produce multiple models without the many costs associated with doing so and less risk of being locked into a single model. The aim is to offer customized products priced as close as possible to mass-produced goods.

FLEXIBLE FACTORIES

The term "flexible factories" is not yet definitely set in the literature. Other terms used include "lean production" or "lean manufacturing," "the Toyota system" (from the company made famous by first introducing the idea), and "Japanese Management Techniques" (JMT). Whatever it is called, several components are involved in the concept. All combine with each other to achieve flexibility and save time in production. The components include reform of inventory management, better quality control, the use of computers and robotics, and reorganization of labor use. In effect, the flexible factory has the ability to deliver both volume and variety, allowing rapid shifts among models and fast response to changing consumer demand. Management does not make goods or their components until it senses a real need for them, and then it makes and delivers them quickly.[39]

Inventory reform. Modern inventory control methods were developed by the Japanese, in what is known as just-in-time (JIT) delivery.* JIT reduces inventories dramatically, as much as 90%, because the firms do not make products until they are needed, nor do the suppliers make the components until just before use. Hence the name "just-in-time," implying that there is little inventory, often eight hours or less of major parts, semi-finished, or finished goods.[40]

Improved quality control. The just-in-time inventory system interacts with quality control because quality improvement means less frequent parts rejection, in turn allowing for reduced parts inventories. Indeed, inventory in a JIT situation *must* be reliably delivered and have very few defects since there is no buffer stock that would allow for errors. Firms that supply inputs now provide much more quality control information than previously. In the auto industry, for example, as the 1990s began 92% of suppliers were providing statistical process control charts on defects, compared to only 16% in 1984.[41] These supplying firms must in turn participate in raising the quality of inputs delivered just-in-time from *their* suppliers. In effect, the suppliers have taken over much of the quality control from the final assembler.

An implication of the just-in-time system and its associated quality control is that suppliers are tied more closely to producers, therefore limiting the geographic or cultural scope of the suppliers. The ability to work closely with a producer or supplier, or the technical knowledge needed to fulfill the demands (on time) of a producer, has a considerable value. Frequently, this value is far greater than the price savings offered when purchasing inputs from an unrelated firm. A closely related supplier can often respond within one to three days, rather than taking two weeks or more to do so. That supplier can often be persuaded to originate new ideas and suggest improved manufacturing methods, as well as to police better quality controls—especially since such relations often lead to long-term contracts that reward the commitment. The related supplier may allow the buyer to inspect operations and demand changes almost as if it were a subsidiary. At the least, fewer suppliers tend to give more consistency in quality. In pursuit of what business schools call total quality control (TQC), every employee is expected to assist in checking on quality.

---

* The Japanese call it *kanban* from the little card that was originally placed in a stack of inventory to remind managers to add to inventory immediately.

Computerization (CAD/CAM). The flexible factory combines JIT inventory and advanced quality control with pervasive computerization that saves time. Computers allow for fast response to changing consumer demand. Rapid shifts among models and varieties are central. The flexible factories are often linked digitally to sales outlets, such as automakers to auto showrooms and clothing manufacturers to retail outlets. For example, to track variations and trends in consumer demand and respond immediately, Benetton has linked its factories by computer to the advanced cash registers in its retail outlets.[*]

Computerization also allows much more rapid introduction of new models and new innovations. Computer-assisted design (CAD) means that design changes, initially made by means of math models rather than by means of mock-ups, can be made late in the design process without boosting costs. CAD can be combined with techniques to build models bit by bit or drop by drop with wax, nylon, or other material.[42] Introduction of new innovations to a wide range of product varieties that used to take years now can be made in a matter of months or weeks. Lockheed-Martin, for example, has reduced the time spent on manufacture and design of sheet metal parts from an average of 52 days to just two days.[43]

Production is also different in a flexible factory, with computer-assisted manufacture (CAM) allowing for quick changes in models. The ease with which the programmable machines can be shifted among product varieties sharply cuts the downtime associated with low-volume batch production. A dozen different models can come out of the same production line without any increase in labor or idled machinery. In a computerized factory, round-the-clock operation needs to be interrupted for only a few minutes to reprogram the computerized numerically controlled (CNC) tools to cut or shape for a different model according to programmable instructions. The CNC tools may be directed from central computer work stations, The method often involves programmable robotics. Typically, preassembled and pretested modules held in closely monitored inventory are fitted into products by programmed insertion devices. Automatic guided vehicles, unmanned and electronic, may deliver parts and material under central computer control. Again, the pioneer was Japan: in 1990, about 60% of the world's over 400,000 robots were in that country.[44]

Flexible factories often run for 24 hours a day. They *must* do so to spread their overhead of costly machinery, engineers, and programmers. The result

---

[*] The company maintains inventories of undyed sweaters, shirts, and scarves, scans its sales data on a continuous basis, and decides immediately on changes in the colors of these garments. It used to take months to make these decisions. See Ludovico Alcorta, "The Impact of New Technologies on Scale in Manufacturing Industries: Issues and Evidence," *World Development* 22, 5 (May 1994): 764.

THE NEED TO COORDINATE THESE INNOVATIONS

Observers note the importance of introducing all of these features at the same time rather than one by one. Because their effect is cumulative, it may not even be profitable to introduce just one or two of the innovations separately.[45]

General Motors' introduction of robotics is a case in point.[46] GM had problems with a bloated bureaucracy and antiquated work rules that it thought to bypass by investing in computerized robotics. The showcase for these ideas was to be GM's Hamtramck plant, a newly built Cadillac plant outside Detroit equipped with 260 robots for assembly, welding, and painting. But workers received minimal new training, management structures were left unchanged, and backup systems were weak. When the robots failed, it often took hours to fix them, during which the assembly line was idle. The quality of the cars themselves declined. It was a lesson in how not to do it.

Volvo, the Swedish automaker, was a pioneer in cell manufacturing, with groups of workers at fixed work stations replacing assembly on a traditional production line. But Volvo introduced insufficient automation via CAM, found that costs went up, and eventually returned to production lines.[47]

of CAD/CAM is that consumer demand for quality improvements can be met much more quickly than before.

Reorganized use of labor. Finally, the flexible factory concept involves new methods of organizing the labor force. Labor rules are more pliable, as is the individual worker, who must possess greater abilities to deal with many tasks.[48] With several sorts of skills needed to keep a computerized production process up and running, rewards for broader knowledge and abilities increase. In some flexible factories this has gone to the point of abolishing job titles and specific job descriptions. A premium is put on education, and pay is based on the number of skills mastered. One of the best known of the new applications is the creation of self-managing work groups in which cooperation and informality are emphasized. Such "cell manufacturing," with small groups making the entire product, is currently being tried at more than half of U.S. manufacturing plants.[49] In some plants the goal is to have every worker capable of operating the system; in others, each worker engaged in patrolling the assembly line has a switch that can stop the line. The greater teamwork, group interaction, and commitment in the labor force have led to a surge in useful employee suggestions for improvements in operations. (To be sure, some workers have resisted this development because they do not like or accept the greater responsibility.)

The Impact of Flexible Factories on Comparative Advantage

As we have seen, flexible factories involve a combination of inventory management, quality control, rapid response through CAD/CAM, and reorganization of a multi-skilled labor force. The goods these factories produce have a comparative advantage partly because of the embodied technology, and partly because of skilled and versatile labor and management employed in them. Note that these requirements are fully consistent with a Heckscher–Ohlin factor approach. Partly, however, the output of flexible factories has a comparative advantage because of scale considerations. These plants develop the ability to overcome in-plant diseconomies involved in producing many models and at the same time realize the traditional scale economies from large operations.* They generate new trade because they lower the costs of the products they produce. With such trade, any technological lead already taken by pioneers is likely to be enhanced. Intraindustry or intrafirm trade may slow, but intrafactoral trade will not, with trade continuing to rise among the developed nations.

A Ladder of Comparative Advantage

The forces that determine comparative advantage, as discussed in this chapter, can be viewed as something like a ladder, broad at the bottom and narrow at the top, where few countries are able to meet the technology and human capital requirements.[50] In the great majority of cases, the most developed countries are likely to cluster at the top of the ladder while the less-developed countries will be toward the middle (for the newly industrializing ones) or bottom for many years to come.[51]

---

* Originally, some authorities argued that flexible factories would promote descaling. That is, flexible factories would be profitable at lower levels of output than is the case with focused factories. But the evidence indicates the contrary, that they require a larger scale of total output (spread among models) or at least about the same level of output as focused factories. Descaling appears to be uncommon. Employment typically declines considerably, perhaps by as much as about half (United States), two-thirds (Europe), and even three-quarters (Japan), though labor costs fall by less than this because of higher pay per worker and greater need for training. Other cost reductions occur because rejects are reduced and waste is minimized. But the capital costs are of course very much higher; CNC machines cost 50-100% more than conventional equipment. Because overall total costs so frequently rise, it is necessary to produce a greater amount to realize a fall in average costs. Moreover, there will be increasing costs of research (for a continuous flow of new products has to come from the R&D effort) and marketing (including advertising) for many models and innovations. These also require greater production to spread the overhead. Finally, software that is often specific to the firm that uses it has to be written, and that, too, raises costs that must be spread over all output. See Alcorta, "The Impact of New Technologies on Scale in Manufacturing Industries," 761-64.

Figure 3.10

LADDER OF COMPARATIVE ADVANTAGE

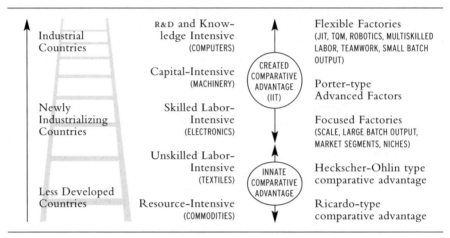

WHAT COULD TRIGGER THE DIRECTION OF SPECIALIZATION?

Our analysis thus far has pointed to a variety of factors that in combination with one another could give a comparative advantage in some particular type of production. These have included traditional economies of scale, decreasing costs due to economies of agglomeration, learning effects, in-plant economies when goods are produced specifically for segmented goods in focused factories, and flexible factories insofar as they involve scale economies. All of these fit into the pattern of decreasing costs with specialization, that is, production possibilities curves convex to the origin like the decreasing cost-curve introduced in Figure 3.5.

The Problem

There is an analytical problem whenever specialization brings an advantage because it has to be explained why the specialization originally took place. An implication of convex PPCs is that the market did not command the direction of specialization. Two identical countries could both start out somewhere midway along their production possibilities curves, as at *a* in the left-hand nation of Figure 3.11 and at *A* for the right one. They could start with the same prices, as shown, and according to theory they would not trade. Yet a slight movement in one direction or the other would initiate a rapid

120

movement toward complete specialization. Strikingly, with imperfect knowledge this movement could occur even if potential gains were greater in a different pattern of specialization.

Figure 3.11
INDETERMINACY AND OPTIMIZATION

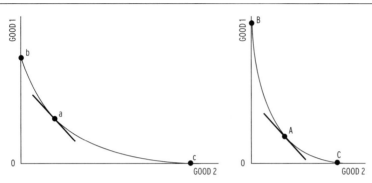

Note: Given convex production possibility curves and insufficient knowledge of the potential cost structure, countries could specialize toward either corner. This would be suboptimal if the right-hand country specialized at *C* and the left-hand one at *b*.

If the left nation begins to move its production toward *b*, its prices will move in favor of Good 1, forcing the right nation to move toward more production of Good 2, toward *C*. Every little movement toward *b* on the left makes Good 1 cheaper, while every slight increase toward *C* on the right makes Good 2 cheaper there. The specialization will become complete at *b* and *C* even though, had the countries only known it, the preferable points were *c* and *B*.

No one, of course, can see the curves because they are a figment, albeit useful, of economists' imaginations, so they would not know which way to go. Once the countries start to move toward specialization, they will continue to do so, whether or not the corner they are moving toward gives the largest gain. With a normal concave production possibilities curve, countries moving in the wrong direction would soon find their prices rising and would be forced to move toward the correct corner in a specialization that would be less than complete. With convex PPCs, however, a movement in either direction represents a gain to countries engaged in trade, but the size of the gain will be smaller should the initial price signals begin movement in the less optimal direction.

The last few pages have suggested that a push toward specializing will bring lower costs and create a comparative advantage. When the road is once taken,

121

the alternative road will never be tried. What, then, pushes a nation to one side or another? We suggest several models, all of which feature a degree of indeterminacy and contingency.

Demand as a Determinant of Costs: Linder's Model of Invention and Development

Suppose a nation sits on an inwardly curved (convex) production possibilities curve such as in Figure 3.11. What is likely to give it a push in one direction or another? One possibility is domestic demand. The country that has a considerable domestic demand for a product will begin to make more of it, thus sliding down its learning curve. The increased production represents a move along its production possibilities curve as well. The price differentials that would accordingly spring up will drive each nation toward the corner in which its initial domestic demand was highest.

The Swedish economist Staffan Burenstam Linder has a more elaborate and subtle explanation of the role of demand in creating comparative advantage. His model examines how goods are invented and how their use expands, rather than looking at initial cost differentials among products whose use is already widespread.[52] New product inventions and introductions, Linder held, are closely tied to differing national tastes and income levels, which thus become major determinants of trade.

To come up with an invention or innovation, one must perceive a need, have an inspiration, and then work and rework that initial idea to fit the market. Often this means not only making the product, but informing people about it and rendering it acceptable to them. Hence, the key factor in determining where production begins is not the cost of the good, but the market for it. Only by working closely with the market can one invent and develop a good. Inventions and innovations thus occur in a quality range that appeals to and is profitable in a given national market. Research on the boundary between economics and psychology in attempts to explain the establishment of different tastes in different national markets is now attracting more attention, but such work is still limited.[53]

Sometimes the reasons why production springs up in one place and not another seem clear enough. The cold Swedish climate provided the right environmental breeding ground for Swedish stoves; long distances, cheap gasoline, and lots of parking space led to large American cars (and the cheap energy also promoted large houses and large appliances in American kitchens); a dispersed population fostered Canadian strength in telecommunications. Pronounced inequalities in British incomes just before and after World War I were surely a major reason for the initial development and success of autos such as the Jaguar, Bentley, and Rolls-Royce, even though

British roads were narrow and winding. Other cases are harder to explain—British liking for darker, heavier beers; bourbon's popularity in the United States but not in Europe; the Central European preference for Turkish tobaccos versus the British preference for Virginia blends; the Canadian love for snowmobiles and the Norwegian ban on such vehicles (except for the rescue services).* We may not know why the nation's particular tastes begin, but the consequence is that specializing on it lowers the cost of producing whatever it is the nation prefers. The demand causes the cost to fall, which in turn generates the comparative advantage.

Whatever the explanations, as inventions are developed for national markets, consumers in other nations with similar needs discover the new products. Trade arises between nations with similar tastes and similar factor proportions, not the reverse. The sewing machine was invented and developed in the United States, but early exports were all to Britain, particularly the textile centers at Glasgow. Indeed, Singer built a plant in the area in 1868. Textile-making machinery moved in the other direction, from Britain to the United States, as did thread production. The Model T Ford, the cigarette, the vacuum cleaner (still known as a Hoover in England), and the elevator (or lift) all moved from the United States to Britain. Aspirin moved from Germany to Britain and the United States.

As Linder notes, the reason products like the vacuum cleaner or the washing machine spread was because the countries had similar economic structures. Both Britain and the United States had high incomes, increasing labor costs, declining availability of servants, and rising mass markets (larger, albeit, in the States than in Britain). They therefore wanted each other's goods. Trade with less-developed countries, interestingly, also follows much the same pattern, with the bulk of the industrial nations' consumer goods going to the rather narrow but wealthy urban sectors. The spread from the home market to an overseas market is likely to be most rapid when foreign buyers are insensitive to price due to the product's unique characteristics. In that event the inelastic demand allows the exporter to build up experience while maintaining a good return on investment. Cases in point are the premium prices U.S. consumers are willing to pay for BMW and Mercedes automobiles.

---

* Guesses are possible, but they are just that. Here are the authors'. Light lager beer is rather unpleasant when not chilled, and the British had little access to ice for cooling and later they were slow to adopt refrigeration. Dark beer does not require chilling. The U.S. taste for bourbon probably dates to farmers' difficulty in transporting corn from areas that produced a lot of it. The corn could be turned into bourbon, which could stand the transport costs (higher value per unit of weight), and drinkers got used to it. The tobacco preference is probably historical as well. Much of Central Europe was occupied for centuries by the Turks, who twice besieged Vienna. Meanwhile, Virginia was a British colony. The snowmobile case may be rather pure psychology; introverted personalities may detest noise and commotion while outgoing personalities may think both are great.

Other examples are the prices that IBM used to be able to charge for its computers and Kodak for its film.

Linder goes on to point out another curious phenomenon: the importing country is the most logical next entrant into the export market. This is particularly true if that country has a large market for the good. Typically, domestic production follows importation. As experience is gained and domestic adjustments are made, exports often ensue as cost levels similar to the original exporter's are reached and new variants of the product are created.

Although Linder's ideas are useful ones and logically sound, it has been difficult to test them empirically. The avidity with which large manufacturing firms have recently been setting up research centers in their overseas markets provides circumstantial evidence that national tastes develop differently and are important for commercial success. Some direct support has emerged from data based on Swedish trade, for which the models were originally formulated. The testing has had less success elsewhere. One complicating factor has been that countries very similar in incomes and class structures (and thus with similar market segments) are often located quite close together, and the lower transportation costs make it difficult to identify Linder-type developments.[54] Like most of the modern trade models, Linder's depends on knowledge imperfections (on the part of both the producer and the consumer). Unlike most, it gives primacy to the role of demand, which determines not only what is consumed, but ultimately the cost of what is produced. While it may not be able to predict exactly what product might be produced, it narrows the constraints by better identifying the contingent factors.

Managerial Choice: A Visible Hand

Consider the situation of a firm producing many differentiated goods in several countries. It knows that it can cut costs by perhaps 20% if it moves to focused factories, but it is unclear that any country is going to have a sustained advantage over another in producing the goods. So it takes existing factories and personnel and cuts down the variety of goods they produce. While the companies may make some studies of different costs, the decision is in most cases quite arbitrary as to which plant is to produce what. The point is not to find what the nation is good at, but simply to specialize, for that in turn will yield a cost advantage. When Chrysler decided to make its Caravans in Windsor, Ontario, it made Canada the low-cost producer. Nowhere else could an extra Caravan be made with the sacrifice of fewer other automobiles. Again, the decision is contingent on Canada having automobile plants, a workforce capable of making cars, and a supportive infrastructure, but the choice of models is not *determined* by those factors.

As we shall see in Chapter 8, governments may also take a role in deciding the direction of specialization. We are not overly optimistic about such approaches. Governments' decisions, it would seem, will be too slow or too laden with political objectives, and so will fail to take into account the constraints already imposed by history and by what is happening elsewhere. Both firms and governments must also be aware that although there are many possible paths to success, success is not random but is contingent on what has gone before.

Product Life Cycles as Influencing Specialization

Both the Linder and the learning curve approaches to why specialization occurs lay a foundation for (or certainly are consistent with) a more elaborate analysis based on life cycles of products and industries. Product life-cycle (PLC) analysis is a common tool among managerial strategists and provides a dynamic to trade analysis that some economists find appealing.[55]

Basically, a PLC model sketches the relationship of a product's sales per year to its age. Figure 3.12 shows the PLC of a typical successful product.

Figure 3.12

A PRODUCT LIFE CYCLE

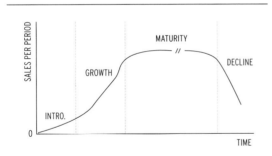

In the figure, time (unspecified) is on the horizontal axis while sales per period are on the vertical. The pattern of sales growth divides into four basic periods—introductory, growth, maturity, and decline—although different writers have subdivided these further. The typical product has an introductory period of uncertain length, sometimes many years, sometimes only a few months, in which sales are low. Following that is a period in which growth is quite rapid, then a long period of stable sales, and eventually a decline. These periods are closely related to changes in demand and supply conditions.

1. On the demand side, consumers have to learn how to use the product and what its benefits are. (We are again operating without all relevant knowledge.) At the same time, other goods and services that are part of the same usage system undergo development. The automobile had a small market when there were few paved roads, gasoline stations were scarce, and mechanics were hard to find. The consumers were a group called "pioneers"

or "early adopters," who could fix their own tires, crank their own engines, and put up with impassable roads. When personal computers first came out, operators had to do their own programming, programs themselves were scarce, and repair people were hard to find. The benefits of owning one were uncertain, particularly in the highly important word-processing areas. Only people who had already had experience with computers in offices, or teenagers with a mathematical and mechanical bent and plenty of spare time to learn computer programming, were interested in purchasing them.

As the product becomes more standardized, more reliable, and more beneficial, sales expand rapidly. Again, in the case of the personal computer, the machines became user-friendly, the number of available programs expanded almost bewilderingly, and the benefits became much clearer to a large number of people. It is a common process. Sixty years earlier the automobile had become more user-friendly with the addition of the electric starter, closed cabs, and pneumatic tires; roads were paved, and gasoline and repairs became easily available, leading to a rapid increase in automobile sales.

Once a product becomes widely accepted, its sales growth rate falls. All the people who have the skills to use the product or who appreciate its benefit (and can afford it) have it. While there may be some marginal buyers who would find some use for the good and some benighted individuals who still have not really been exposed to the good's possible benefits, the majority have. Sales thus become limited to upgrading and replacement markets. This is the mature phase. Finally, the good is no longer even needed; or it may not die completely, maintaining some tiny residual market, as do black-and-white TVs and chewing tobacco.

2. On the technological side, costs tend to fall throughout the life of a product. When there is both rapid consumer acceptance and a steep experience curve, the two factors reinforce each other. The additional production lowers costs, and the lower costs open up new markets, further increasing production. Products that have had slow acceptance and long introductory periods, such as the electric typewriter, which was first produced in the 1920s but did not become standard until the 1960s, fail to benefit from the rapidly declining costs that production experience provides.

3. Competitive patterns also change as a product matures. Early on, there are many competitors, often with competing technologies (the electric, gasoline, and steam car; the 33-RPM and 45-RPM record, the Apple and IBM formats, VHS and Beta videotape formats). As the growth period moves on, the technology for making the product becomes more standardized, and the buyers move toward the standardized forms, both because of price and because the support systems are there. For example, the number of VHS-format movies soon grew to be overwhelmingly larger than those for Beta, and the production of new Beta machines was suspended in 1988. There

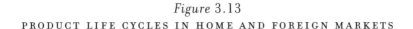

Figure 3.13
PRODUCT LIFE CYCLES IN HOME AND FOREIGN MARKETS

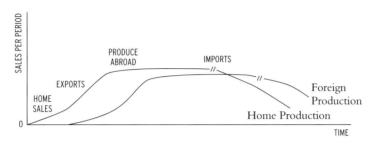

Note: It may be that the product life cycle is connected with the location of production, the pioneer country tending to sell at home during the introductory stage, then to export during growth, then to produce abroad, and finally to import in the declining stage. The PLC in other countries begins later, but has the same shape; it begins with importing and ends in exporting.

tends to be a shake-out in the industry, with only a few successful firms remaining or those remaining shifting to the standardized operations. Well into the mature phase technology becomes diffused, allowing the growth of some new firms, often foreign, as we described in the learning curve discussion. The onslaught of automobile imports into North America occurred because the technology to make the product was widely diffused, while the particular gains from additional production experience were small.

The first attempt to relate PLC models to international trade came from Louis Wells and Raymond Vernon of the Harvard Business School.[56] The Wells-Vernon model provides a thought-provoking historical analysis of U.S. trade. For many years the United States had the highest per capita income in the world, and with that high income came the introduction of many new consumer goods plus a great quantity of new capital goods. U.S. consumers saw the first widespread use of the refrigerator, the radio, the clothes washer, and then later televisions and dishwashers. Initially, export sales of these products were small because few foreign consumers could afford them. Thereafter, as incomes rose abroad, export markets grew. We show this as a product life cycle first involving production for the home market only, and then involving exports that begin at a later time period. (See the uppermost curve in Figure 3.13.)

As foreign markets grew, however, foreign producers were tempted to compete, first with production for local consumers, and then for export. The process was feasible because the technology was more widely available and the technological lead of U.S. firms was shrinking, as our learning curve

Figure 3.14

PRODUCTION AND EXPORTING
FOLLOWING IMPORTS: "WILD GEESE FLYING"

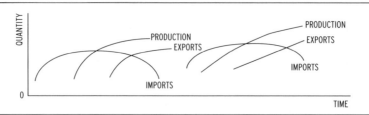

models showed. Though the foreign production may have been initially more expensive, trade barriers, transportation costs, and local preferences served to protect the foreign producers. American manufacturers at this stage also moved their production facilities abroad to be close to the expanding market—if they had not done so already. Note in Figure 3.13 how home production in the top part of the diagram levels off as production picks up in the imitator countries.

Finally, production *falls* in the home country as exports begin from the foreigner. Why? Because the technological gap has been closed or is at least small, but foreign wages and incomes are still below the home country's, such that in the mature stage the foreign country will export and the home country will import. As we noted in our discussion of the learning curve, this is a distinct possibility and it may well explain why the United States now imports vastly more radios, televisions, and automobiles than it exports.

The process can be repeated over the years, with third-country exporting of a product (e.g., by South Korea and Taiwan) succeeding the exporting of the country (e.g., Japan) that dethroned the export pioneer (e.g., Great Britain), and so on. In rather poetic terms for economists, Japanese writers have called this cycle a "wild geese flying" pattern of trade development. The reason for the name is seen in Figure 3.14.

Actually, in the historical record there is very little evidence to support the notion that the pioneer nation loses its early advantages so completely that the industry it first developed shuts down or even that it stops exporting. Rather, the mature stage of the product life cycle is much more likely to be a stage of considerable interpenetration. New variations on old products, such as razor blades, detergents, or car models, increase the amount of market segmentation. Trade at this point becomes a matter not so much of technology, but of specialized production and consumption of goods. Managerial choice, constrained, of course, by past experience and various innate costs, may be the key factor in determining the direction of specialization.

For all that there are arguments about the mature stage, life-cycle models do correctly emphasize the role of human capital and knowledge in giving a *temporary* comparative advantage. The original location of an industry may be explained by the existence of pioneering firms in initial home markets, whose patent protection and learning by doing that moves them down their learning curves give them an advantage. Maturation of the industry eventually occurs as technology settles down, as imitation grows more important, and as learning by doing becomes less significant. The normal Heckscher-Ohlin predictions based on factor proportions then take over, and comparative advantage swings toward countries with the most appropriate factor proportions.

DISLOCATION AND INTRAINDUSTRIAL TRADE

The process of intraindustrial specialization involves much less dislocation than we would expect from the older trade theory. In that theory, if Portuguese wine replaces English cloth, that is too bad for the English producers, who must find other work. If foreign cane sugar replaces domestic sugar beets in Europe and North America, the farmers will have to find something else to plant or go out of business. Under classical theory, trade is supposed to shift resources out of the weak industry into the strong, but it does this by driving the weaker industry to the wall. That does not happen, however, with intraindustrial trade: Canada and the United States still have an automobile business, and while imports have certainly penetrated both markets, that penetration has surely been slowed by the lower costs of production arising from free trade in automobiles. After 40 years of trade in Europe, no country has lost its automobile industry (though, admittedly, Britain's is now almost entirely foreign-owned). These industrial survivals are not because the companies are being nice or politically astute. It is instead because there are no particularly strong factor-proportions pressures that will force the automobile industry into one nation.

The consequences for labor are considerable. Suppose there are 10,000 workers in textiles and freer trade forces clothing prices lower and electronics prices higher, such that somehow 10,000 workers must be shifted out of clothing and another 10,000 into electronics. That is a major dislocation, involving a devaluation of job skills in textiles, movement to other regions, and lowered pay for some—even if all people are re-employed. With intraindustrial specialization, however, the only change is in the workers lost due to the increased efficiency. If the automobile industry manages to increase productivity by 10%, it will need 10% less labor. One thousand people, not 10,000, are displaced and have to find new work. The remaining 9,000 would stay just where they were working before. In fact, the 10% reduction might be small enough to be covered by natural turnover and some early retirements.

Because intraindustrial trade causes less dislocation, it is politically more acceptable. The old models of international trade are thus not only inappropriate for a great deal of modern trade but are politically dangerous. Displacement, even if it is for the greater good, is not politically popular. The most liberal-minded and economically sophisticated senators or members of Parliament are going to defend their constituencies' interest if they are threatened. Arguing that specialization will take place within the industry may be not only more realistic, but politically more astute.

CONCLUSION

Thirty years ago a text could view comparative advantage as based on factor-proportions theory. That still remains a fundamental idea. But the thrust of trade in the late twentieth century has been and continues to be in directions awkwardly handled by a simple factor-proportions approach. Indeterminate and contingent models with decreasing costs may serve as a better basis for understanding modern patterns of international trade. Such models are still consistent with the existence of comparative advantage. They simply offer a different explanation of what determines it. In doing so, they emphasize its changeability, with the shifts likely to be more rapid than once realized. This is important because countries' abilities to react to such changes are elemental in determining how rich they will be.

VOCABULARY AND CONCEPTS

Capital-intensive production
Contingent models
Decreasing-cost models
Economies of agglomeration
Economies of scale
Experience curves
Factor-intensity reversals
Factor proportions
Factor-price equalization
Focused and flexible factories
Heckscher–Ohlin theory
Human capital explanation
In-firm diseconomies
Indeterminacy and optimization
Indeterminate models

Intrafactoral trade
Intraindustrial trade
Isoquant
Labor-intensive production
Learning by doing
Learning curves
Leontief Paradox
Linder model
Natural differences
Pioneers and late entrants
Product life cycles (PLCs)
Rybczynski Theorem
Segmented markets
Technology explanation
Wells-Vernon model
"Wild geese flying"

QUESTIONS

1. Explain in words the Heckscher–Ohlin theory of factor proportions, indicating what its essential assumptions are.
2. Since virtually all goods can be made in capital-intensive or labor-intensive ways, how can we decide if a good is capital- or labor-intensive?
3. Apply the Rybczynski Theorem to Korean trade. What do you think will happen as Korea's workers get shorter hours and more pay?
4. Use factor-proportions theory to suggest what the effect might be on U.S. trading patterns of large numbers of Latin American immigrants.
5. What explanations have been offered for the Leontief Paradox? Which ones appeal to you the most? Why?
6. What is intra-industrial trade? How is it measured? Why is there so much trade of that sort when our factor-proportions theory suggests otherwise?
7. What are the implications of a production possibility curve that is convex to the point of origin (that is, bends inward)? In what sense would it be an appropriate model to apply to many kinds of international trade?
8. Most economic models assume that costs rise with specialization, yet costs could fall. What might cause them to do so?
9. Explain the importance of scale economies in trade between industrial nations. Is it normally plant scale that is of the highest importance?
10. Explain what learning curves (or experience) are. What evidence is there for their existence? What do they imply for specialization?
11. "The advantages of experience may be temporary if other nations, with lower cost structures for producing the particular good in question, can gain equal experience." Demonstrate and discuss.
12. If factor proportions are highly important, we would expect that most trade would be between dissimilar nations. Is it? Explain.
13. What is the role of market demand in determining what goods are traded in decreasing-cost situations?
14. Why would a nation demanding many different models of products be likely to benefit from international trade?
15. "When production possibility curves are convex, we cannot view managers as responding automatically to prices. They create their own comparative advantages. What we trade is to a considerable extent determined by conscious choice, not the invisible hand." Explain.
16. Does the idea that specialization creates its own comparative advantage increase the value of national industrial policies in modern Western economies?
17. What do you believe are the policy implications of using models that are indeterminate and contingent?
18. Adjustments to an increase in intraindustrial trade involve considerably less dislocation of labor than do cross-industrial adjustments. Why?

19. Linder's model, despite the difficulty in demonstrating some of it, has considerable appeal as an explanation of trade among industrial nations. Why?

20. The product life-cycle model combines elements of both cost and demand, but at least in its Wells-Vernon form it has not been a particularly good predictor of trade patterns. Why?

NOTES

1. See Paul A. Samuelson, "International Trade and the Equalization of Factor Prices," *Economic Journal* (June 1948), and "International Factor-Price Equalization Once Again," *Economic Journal* (June 1949). There is a good survey in the various editions of Bo Södersten, *International Economics* (New York: HarperCollins).

2. Dan Ben-David, "Equalizing Exchange: A Study of the Effects of Trade Liberalization," NBER Working Paper No. 3706, 1991.

3. The ability of factor proportions to explain a considerable amount of trade is treated at length in Edward E. Leamer, *Sources of International Comparative Advantage: Theory and Evidence* (Cambridge, Mass.: MIT Press, 1984). For a recent examination of trade theory, see Jim Levinsohn, Alan V. Deardorff, and Robert M. Stern., eds., *New Directions in Trade Theory* (Ann Arbor: University of Michigan Press, 1995).

4. Harry P. Bowen, Edward E. Leamer, and Leo Sveikauskas, "Multicountry, Multifactor Tests of the Factor Abundance Theory," *American Economic Review* 77, 5 (December 1987): 791-809. The testing was accomplished by estimating the proportion of each country's factor supplies to the total world supply of that factor, and then calculating factor embodiments in exports.

5. The study by Bowen et al. showed Brazil, Hong Kong, Mexico, and the Philippines conforming much more to H-O predictions than did the developed countries. Other evidence for the less developed countries is reviewed in Jan S. Hogendorn, *Economic Development*, 3rd ed. (New York: HarperCollins, 1996), ch. 14.

6. James R. Markusen and Randall M. Wiglee, "Explaining the Volume of North-South Trade," *Economic Journal* 100, 403 (December 1990): 1206-15. Markusen and Wiglee present evidence that high protection explains the low levels of trade between the LDCs and the developed countries, which is consistent with a Heckscher-Ohlin view.

7. See A.V. Deardorff, "Testing Trade Theories," in Ronald W. Jones and Peter B. Kenen, eds., *Handbook of International Economics* 1 (Amsterdam: Elsevier, 1984), 480-85; Bowen, Leamer, and Sveikauskas, "Multicountry, Multifactor Tests"; Daniel Trefler, "International Factor Price Differences: Leontief Was Right!" *Journal of Political Economy* 101 (December 1993): 961-87.

8. The data on trade flows are from the quarterly issues of the International Monetary Fund's *Direction of Trade Statistics*, Washington, D.C.

9. See Herbert G. Grubel and P.J. Lloyd, *Intra-Industry Trade* (New York: Wiley, 1975).

10. The early figures are from Grubel and Lloyd, *Intra-Industry Trade.* For the 1985 figure (covering 11 countries), see Margaret Kelly, Naheed Kirmani, Miranda Xafa, Clemens Boonekamp, and Peter Winglee, *Issues and Developments in International Trade Policy,* Occasional Paper No. 63 (Washington: IMF, 1988), 9. The U.S., British, and French figures, and some of the LDC figures are from O. Havrylyshyn and E. Civan, "Intra Industry Trade Among Developing Countries," *Journal of Development Economics* 18 (1985): 260. The great rise since 1958 in the IIT for the members of the European Union is noted by André Sapir, "Regional Integration in Europe," *Economic Journal* 102, 415 (November 1992): 1496. Also see David Greenaway and Chris Milner, "On the Measurement of Intra-Industrial Trade," *Economic Journal* 93 (December 1983): 900-08.

11. Jaroslav Vanek, *The Natural Resource Content of Foreign Trade 1870-1955* (Cambridge, Mass.: MIT Press, 1963).

12. Trefler, "International Factor Price Differences."

13. See *The Economist,* April 11, 1987.

14. The labor cost figures are from the special article, "High Technology," in *The Economist,* August 23, 1986, S15.

15. *The Newly-Industrializing Countries: Challenges and Opportunities for OECD Industries* (Paris: OECD, 1988), 24.

16. Michael E. Porter, *The Competitive Advantage of Nations* (New York: Free Press, 1990).

17. For overseas assembly activities, see Joseph Grunwald and Kenneth Flamm, *The Global Factory: Foreign Assembly in International Trade* (Washington: Brookings Institution, 1985).

18. See Brad Christerson and Richard P. Appelbaum, "Global and Local Subcontracting: Space, Ethnicity, and the Organization of Apparel Production," *World Development* 23, 8 (August 1995): esp. 1363-71.

19. Alfred Marshall, *Principles of Economics,* 397-98.

20. Learning curves and decreasing costs received early formal treatment in the work of Armen Alchian and Jack Hershleifer, although both treated decreasing costs as a special case rather than the normal case. See Armen Alchian, "Costs and Outputs," in Moses Abramowitz et al., eds., *The Allocation of Economic Resources* (Stanford, Calif.: Stanford University Press, 1959), 23-40; and Jack Hershleifer, "The Firm's Cost Function: A Successful Reconstruction?" *Journal of Business* 35, 3 (July 1962): 235-54.

21. Henry A. Gemery and Jan S. Hogendorn, "The Microeconomic Bases of Short-Run Learning Curves: Destroyer Production in World War II," in Gregory T. Mills and Hugh Rockoff, *The Sinews of War: The Economics of World War II* (Ames: Iowa State University Press, 1993).

22. Paul Krugman, *Peddling Prosperity* (New York: Basic Books, 1994), 252.

23. T.N. Srinivasan, "Comment on 'The Noncompetitive Theory of International Trade and Trade Policy,' by Helpman," *Proceedings of the World Bank Annual Conference on Development Economics 1989* (Washington: World Bank, 1989), 217-21.

24. For the case that sunk costs do matter in ways that standard theory suggests should not matter, see William J. Baumol, "Toward a Newer Economics: The Future Lies Ahead," *Economic Journal* 10, 104 (January 1991): 6.

25. Mark J. Roberts and James R. Tybout, "An Empirical Model of Sunk Costs and the Decision to Export," World Bank Policy Research Working Paper No. 1436, 1995.

26. Richard N. Langlois and Paul L. Robertson, *Firms, Markets, and Economic Change* (New York: Routledge, 1995), 120-42.

27. See Joe S. Bain, *Barriers to New Competition* (Cambridge, Mass: Kelley, 1956).

28. The research of F.M. Scherer et al. is in *The Economics of Multi-Plant Operation: An International Comparisons Study* (Cambridge, Mass.: Harvard University Press, 1975). It is surveyed together with the work of Leonard Weiss and C.F. Pratten in Scherer's *Industrial Market Structure and Economic Performance,* 2nd edition (Chicago: Houghton Mifflin, 1980), 91-98.

29. Farhang Niroomand and W. Charles Sawyer, "The Extent of Scale Economies in U.S. Foreign Trade," *Journal of World Trade* 23, 6 (December 1989): 137-46.

30. T.G. Parry, "Plant Size, Capacity Utilization, and Economic Efficiency: Investment in the Australian Chemical Industry," *The Economic Record* 50 (June 1974): 218-44.

31. See Jeffrey E. Bergstrand, "The Heckscher-Ohlin-Samuelson Model, the Linder Hypothesis and the Determinants of Bilateral Intra-Industry Trade," *Economic Journal* 100, 403 (December 1990): 1216-29.

32. Surprisingly little work has been done on the optimal number of products per firm. See Kelvin Lancaster, "Socially Optimal Product Differentiation," *American Economic Review* (September 1975): 567-85. Lancaster demonstrates that under monopolistically competitive conditions there will be more than an optimal number of models produced. Also see F.M. Scherer, "The Welfare Economics of Product Variety: An Application to the Ready-to-Eat Cereals Industry," *Journal of Industrial Economics* 28, 4 (December 1979): 113-34. Scherer discusses the costs of the large number of product introductions in the industry.

33. See *The Economist*, February 3, 1990.

34. See Wilson Brown, "Market Segmentation and International Competitiveness," *Nebraska Journal of Economics* (Summer 1972): 333-48, for development of the list. Some of the ideas were drawn from Bela Balassa, *Trade Liberalization among Industrial Countries* (Baltimore: Johns Hopkins University Press, 1967), ch. 5.

35. Reported in Donald T. Brash, *American Investment in Australian Industry* (Cambridge, Mass.: Harvard University Press, 1966), 157-76.

36. Both quotations ibid., 158.

37. According to the BCG's George Stalk, Jr., "Time—The Next Source of Comparative Advantage," *Harvard Business Review* 66, 4 (July/August 1988): 41-51.

38. Ludovico Alcorta, "The Impact of New Technologies on Scale in Manufacturing Industries: Issues and Evidence," *World Development* 22, 5 (May 1994): 760.

39. See Richard J. Schonberger, *World Class Manufacturing* (New York, Free Press, 1986).

40. For JIT, see Jane Sneddon Little, "Changes in Inventory Management: Implications for the U.S. Recovery," *New England Economic Review* (November-December 1992): 37-65; Uday Karmarkar, "Getting Control of Just-In-Time," *Harvard Business Review* (September-October 1989): 122-31; *The Economist*, March 4, 1995.

41. See Susan Helper, "How Much Has Really Changed Between Automakers and Their Suppliers?" *Sloan Management Review* (Summer 1991): 15-28.

42. *The Economist*, March 5, 1994.

43. See Paul Milgrom and John Roberts, "The Economics of Modern Manufacturing: Technology, Strategy, and Organization," *American Economic Review* 80, 3 (June 1990), citing work of Otis Port and Warren Hausman.

44. See Ludovico Alcorta, "The Impact of New Technologies on Scale in Manufacturing Industries: Issues and Evidence," *World Development* 22, 5 (May 1994): 758-59.

45. See Roy B. Helfgott, "America's Third Industrial Revolution," *Challenge* 29, 5 (November-December 1986): 41-46.

46. See *The Economist*, January 14, 1995.

47. Milgrom and Roberts, "The Economics of Modern Manufacturing," citing work of Walter Kiechel and Ronald Henkoff.

48. Richard J. Murnane and Frank Levy, *Teaching the New Basic Skills* (New York: Free Press, 1996), 202.

49. See *The Economist*, January 14, 1995.

50. The idea of a ladder is taken from Gerald M. Meier, *Leading Issues in Economic Development* (Oxford: Oxford University Press, 1995), 458, with alterations by the authors.

51. Raphael Kaplinsky, "Technique and System: The Spread of Japanese Management Techniques to Developing Countries," *World Development* 23, 1 (January 1995): 64.

52. Staffan Burenstam Linder, *An Essay on Trade and Transformation* (New York, Garland, 1961).

53. See the survey by Mathew Rabin, "Psychology and Economics," *Journal of Economic Literature* 36, 1 (March 1998): 11–46, and the many sources cited there. Groundbreaking works were Tibor Scitovsky, *The Joyless Economy* (London: Oxford University Press, 1976); Shlomo Maitel, *Minds, Markets, and Money* (New York: Basic Books, 1982).

54. The argument can be transposed: with transport costs low, exporting a good to a particular market segment located in a foreign country would be the more feasible. Alan Deardorff, "Testing Trade Theories," in Jones and Kenen, eds., *Handbook of International Economics* 1, 505-06, gives a skeptical view of Linder's ideas. An informative volume on this and other issues involving intra-industry trade is Elhanan Helpman and Paul Krugman, *Market Structure and Foreign Trade: Increasing Returns, Imperfect Competition, and the International Economy* (Cambridge, Mass.: MIT Press, 1985).

55. PLC analysis is explained in most marketing texts. A good advanced treatment of the subject is Chester A. Wasson, *Dynamic Competitive Strategy and Product Life Cycles* (Austin, Texas: Austin Press, 1978).

56. Louis Wells, Jr., "A Product Life Cycle for International Trade," *Journal of Marketing* (July 1968): 1-6; Raymond Vernon, *Sovereignty at Bay* (New York: Basic Books, 1971).

Chapter Four

Tariffs, Quotas, and VERs

OBJECTIVES

OVERALL OBJECTIVE   To convey the sense and reasoning that barriers to trade not only cause economic inefficiency, but redistribute income, frequently in ways that are unfair and reward political rather than economic skills.

MORE SPECIFICALLY
- To convey the numerous effects of tariffs on efficiency and income distribution.
- To show the importance of some institutional factors such as the type of tariff and its measurement.
- To introduce the idea of rent and demonstrate how tariffs and quotas produce rents.
- To compare import quotas to tariffs to show the greater difficulties that quotas create.
- To examine tariff-rate quotas (TRQs) and voluntary export restraints (VERs) and their effects.

....

The analysis in the last two chapters has shown that the benefits arising from trade are considerable. Yet governments persist in indulging in numerous distortions to the free flow of trade despite ample demonstration, both theoretical and statistical, that by so doing they reduce the welfare of the whole. The very persistence of the distortions suggests deeply rooted political-economic factors, which a later section addresses. One of these political factors is ignorance—the public does not know how high the costs of protectionism are. At the minimum, we can help dispel some of that ignorance.

Broadly speaking, the distortions to trade fall into two groups: (1) those created by taxes, principally taxes on imports, called *tariffs*, but also taxes on exports, common in many less-developed countries; and (2) those not related to taxes, including *non-tariff barriers* (NTBs) and many sorts of subsidies. NTBs include primarily the quantitative restrictions on imports known as *quotas*, the combination of tariffs and quotas called *tariff-rate quotas* (TRQs), the special type of quota known as a *voluntary export restraint* (VER), and a host of government regulations and laws that interfere (sometimes purposefully, sometimes incidentally) with the free flow of trade. This chapter explores the best-known distortions to trade: tariffs, quotas, TRQs, and VERs. It investigates the nature of these barriers and presents the basic economic analysis. The next chapter considers a variety of other distortions, many of which have arisen only recently, and then goes on to cast a spotlight on several industries that have been major beneficiaries of these instruments. The following two chapters then examine the public policy implications of the analysis.

TARIFFS

Artificial barriers to trade seem as old as trade itself. An ancient caravan entering an Arab area had to offer a *ta'rif*, in Arabic merely a "notification," to be allowed entry; but since the notification of arrival also involved a tax, *ta'rif* came to mean a tax on trade.* Still today in most Western languages, tariff and its cognates generally mean a tax on imports, or more rarely, on exports. (Occasionally the word "tariff" is also used simply to mean any tax.) Travelers to Hadrian's Wall, the Roman defense work running across the hills of northern England, find at almost every gate in the rampart the remains of a little room that once housed the tax collector, who imposed the tariff (generally 12.5%) on goods moving into the Roman Empire. Today walls may be absent, but there are still gates and little houses for tax collectors at borders. Nothing appears more certain than borders and tariffs.

---

* Many of these tariffs were internal, collected like modern turnpike tolls on the movement of goods within a country. In the thirteenth to fifteenth centuries there were as many as 60 tariff collection points along the Rhine River, and internal tolls along 200 miles of France's Seine River raised the fifteenth century price of grain by 50%. Such taxation lasted for a long time. It was not until 1790 that revolutionary France eliminated internal barriers to trade. Sixty years before there had been over 4,000 internal tolls. Austria eliminated internal barriers to trade in 1775. The U.S. Constitution of 1789 abolished tariffs between the states; under the Articles of Confederation, which prevailed from the Revolutionary War until that year, New York charged tariffs for some time on a number of imports from Connecticut. In some countries with internal turmoil, such as Sierra Leone and Congo (Zaire), internal tariffs have sprung up once again, usually collected by the army or paramilitary units. A good source is John A.C. Conybeare, *Trade Wars* (New York: Columbia University Press, 1987).

138

Specific and Ad Valorem Tariffs

Tariffs can be specific, defined as a flat rate such as $10 per pound, 5¢ a yard, $2 a pair. Or the tariff can be *ad valorem* (Latin for "on the value"), a percentage such as 10% or 20% of a good's value. A specific duty of $10 or an *ad valorem* duty of 20% would be equal on a good valued at $50; at other prices they would not be the same. Occasionally, some aspects of specific and *ad valorem* duties are combined into a compound tariff.* Specific duties were once found most frequently, but today *ad valorem* tariffs are more common by far.

Each type of tariff has its own characteristics. Specific duties are easier to administer because imports do not have to be valued as they enter the country. All the customs official has to do is to decide which category an item is in and how much of it there is. Specific duties also provide more protection against price-cutting. If textiles from Hong Kong cost 20¢ a yard and the duty is 5¢ a yard, or 25% *ad valorem*, then a big cut in the Hong Kong price, of say 10¢, means that the specific duty remains at 5¢, now 50% *ad valorem*. Meanwhile, an *ad valorem* tariff of 25% would fall to 2.5¢. The extra protection against price cuts is thought to be the major reason why the U.S. Republican Party favored specific tariffs for most of the century after the Civil War, when about two-thirds of U.S. tariffs were specific. Perhaps they were also favored because they concealed the actual amount of protection.[1]

Specific duties also may be regressive, in that a low-priced version of a good will pay more tax as a percentage of the original price than a high-priced version of the same good. If poor consumers buy the low-priced variant, then they are taxed more heavily than the wealthy. Furthermore (though to economists this is a benefit, not a problem), specific duties lose their protective effect in inflations. If prices double, any given specific levy will be only half in *ad valorem* terms what it was before; indeed, about half of the decline in protection from the onset of the Great Depression to the early 1960s was due to the rise in prices while specific tariffs stayed unchanged.[2]

Ad valorem tariffs behave quite differently. They are not regressive (though they are not progressive either), and there is no need to alter them as prices change. They are easier to apply to unique goods such as paintings, which may be of very high or very low value. The principal disadvantage of *ad valorem* tariffs is that customs officials have to place a value on each item

---

* For example, the famous English Corn Laws against grain imports were specific duties on a sliding scale. Under the legislation of 1791, when grain brought 54 shillings in England, the tariff was only a nominal 6 pence; between 50 and 54 shillings the duty was higher at 2 shillings 6 pence; while under 50 shillings the duty amounted to a nearly prohibitive 24 shillings 3 pence. The tariff thus rose with any decrease in price. The modern variable levy of the European Union resembles the old Corn Laws: the duty on many agricultural imports is adjusted upward when price falls and downward when price rises so as to keep prices stable within the EU. This is called an *equalizing duty*.

entering the country. Rather than simply checking to see that the bill of lading describes what is being brought in, the officials must also assess whether the value given is correct. The information on the invoice or bill of lading may not be accurate, and the checking of such documentation is a nuisance to traders and customs officials alike. Facing *ad valorem* tariffs, importers try to keep their invoice values down, being anywhere from merely careful to out-right dishonest.

It is possible that a customs official will assess a higher value than a good is worth, thus turning what looked like a low *ad valorem* tariff into one that is considerably higher. Indeed, sometimes governments have instructed customs officers to assess high. (The over- or under-valuation would, incidentally, find its way into the trade statistics, thus introducing an inaccuracy.)[*] With *ad valorem* tariffs, the problem arises as to whether transport costs will be included in the price subject to tariff. Most countries use c.i.f. values of imports (cost, insurance, freight, that is, including the transportation costs), thus also taxing these costs. The United States and Canada are exceptions, using the f.o.b. values (free on board, that is, before transportation costs). Their *ad valorem* tariffs are actually somewhat lower than those of countries that assess on a c.i.f. basis.

Worldwide, the United Nations estimates that lack of trained customs personnel able to make accurate assessments, arbitrary valuations, long delays, and outright dishonesty raise the costs of trade by about 10%. That has caused a number of less-developed countries to establish what is called preshipment inspection. They contract with developed-country private firms that carry out inspecting and valuation when the good is *exported*.[3] Other countries have found that computerizing their customs has reduced some of the transactions costs substantially.

Categorization of Goods

A customs official has to decide which category an import falls into, and this is particularly important if the tariffs for various categories differ greatly. They certainly *can* differ greatly—recently in the United States there were almost 9,000 tariff lines, or categories of dutiable items, ranging from 1% *ad valorem* to 458%. Furthermore, the product might be a new one for which there is no existing category. The question of whether radar sets were measuring devices (highly protected) or radios (with little protection) tied up U.S. courts

---

[*] For many years, the governments of both the United States and Australia found a legal way for customs to value high. They levied some tariffs on the *domestic selling price*, which, because it included the tariff, was higher than the imported price. These venomous ASPs (American or Australian selling prices) were finally done away with as the result of protests by foreign exporters, consumers, and economists.

in a long legal battle. Traders are ever anxious to find opportunities ("loopholes" to their detractors) to have a product come in under a low-tariff category when it seemingly is blocked by a higher tariff. The accompanying box contains some of the anecdotes that have surfaced concerning the categorization of goods. The stories are apparently endless, though their meaning, when we find one, is perhaps pathetic—that rules and tariffs, even when they are not major economic blockages, can cause such petty distortions.

THE DESIRABILITY OF UNIFORM TARIFFS

Economists have argued for many years that the stories would not arise if uniform *ad valorem* tariffs—the same on all categories of goods—were adopted. A uniform tariff would not distort incentives and cause resource misallocation. It would simplify administration. Above all, it would eliminate the all-too-enticing opportunities for corrupt dealing between customs officials and importers.[4] Non-uniformity presently exists in a pronounced way even among goods that are clearly very similar. For example, the U.S. chinaware tariff ranges from 8% to 35% depending on what type of chinaware it is; the earthenware tariff is beween 4.5% and 35%; the tariff on tuna packed in oil, 35%, is six times higher than the 6% tariff on tuna packed in water; casual footwear (athletic footwear, sneakers, sports oxfords, etc.) pay 20% to 67% though the duty on women's leather footwear is only 10%, and so on.[5]

CAR OR TRUCK? MOUSE OR RAT? SOLDIER OR DOLL?

In the 1960s during a long-forgotten trade dispute the United States put a 25% duty on small trucks, 10 times the 2.5% duty on cars. (The small vw pickup, new at that time, was the main target.) That high duty remains in place to this day. A whole class of light utility vehicles and minivans sporting car-like features, including the Nissan Pathfinder, Subaru Brat, Suzuki Samurai, Toyota 4Runner, Mazda MPV, and GEO Tracker thereupon sprang up to avoid the truck tariff.[6] In January 1989, the U.S. Customs Service slammed the loophole shut by classifying all these vehicles as trucks. Lobbying by importers resulted in a 1990 Treasury Department compromise: if it had four doors like the Mitsubishi Montero, or if it was a van with windows or doors on the sides and back and seats additional to the front one, it was a car; but if it had two doors, like the Nissan Pathfinder or Suzuki Samurai, it was a truck. That virtually stopped imports of two-door light utility vehicles. Then in 1993 a judge of the U.S. Court of International Trade ruled that some two-door light utility vehicles are intended to carry over 50% passengers rather than cargo, and so the duty should be 2.5%.[7] (This decision was upheld on appeal in 1994). Cinderella-like, some trucks were turned back into cars.

A shipment of sewing kits, little bags containing needles and thread, was recently stopped by customs officials in Seattle, who insisted that the bags should be classified as luggage at nearly three times the duty. The importer involved had to plead his case in New York before this decision was reversed, but not before many orders were lost and much expense incurred. U.S. opera companies accustomed to importing their sets as duty-free works of art were recently told that they were instead utility items subject to duty ($24,000 in one case). U.S. customs raised the tariff on a shipment of 33,000 girls' ski jackets from 10.6% to 27.5% because the jackets had corduroy trim on the sleeves. That 2% of the material in the jacket changed it, according to customs, from "garments designed for rainwear, hunting, fishing, or similar uses" to "other girls' wearing apparel, not ornamented."[8]

In other cases, the rulings promote accommodation and subterfuge. The U.S. slammed tariffs on jogging shoes, defined as "footwear made of rubber and plastic." But if 50% or more of the shoe uppers were made of leather, the shoe would be categorized as a different type of footwear with a much lower tariff. Hence the introduction of spiffy leather stripes and trim on jogging shoes. A high tariff on jeans stitched with a decorative design hardly fazed one U.S. importer. He had the back pockets cut in two and stitched together again in what, however decorative the design, was clearly a functional stitch subject to a lower tariff. Digital watches, importers' lawyers argued, were not watch movements under the tariff, since they had no moving parts; they were instead "electrical articles not provided for elsewhere." That argument saved a tariff of 50¢ on a $3.00 item.

Of all the silly cases that have occurred, perhaps the winners are the long-tailed mice and "G.I. Joe." U.S. duties on toys are high, but they are low on magic items and products used for jokes. A rodent with a short tail is surely a mouse and therefore a toy; if it has a long tail, it is surely a rat and therefore a joke. In a Darwinian survival of the fittest, the mice found in toy stores have long tails and pay low duties. G.I. Joe (or his lawyers) proved less able at escaping the tariff. That long-popular little fighting man recently lost a battle when he was found in customs court to be a doll (12% duty) and not a model soldier (duty-free).

Nominal and Effective Tariffs (Tariff Escalation)

When considering a tariff, one normally thinks of the duty compared to the cost of the import; thus a $25 tax on a $100 item would be a 25% tariff. Economists refer to this as the *nominal tariff*, although perhaps a better term is *apparent tariff*. The words "nominal" and "apparent" hint that something is misleading in our everyday observations, and well they should. The actual amount of protection is measured by something called an *effective tariff*, a concept developed in the early 1960s, but not at all current among economists until much later.[9] The effective rate compares the tariff to the value added in the country, not to the total value of the product.

One of the first expositions of the theory incorporated a most illustrative tale out of the annals of U.S. tariff history. The duty on strung pearls entering the United States was $50, back in the days when the string itself could be purchased in Greece for $100. This nominal duty of 50% was designed to protect the U.S. jewelry industry. Since pearl fishing was not protected, there was no tariff at all on raw pearls, or even on temporarily strung pearls, which, sized, holes bored, and threaded on a simple string, could be imported without paying any tariff. The cost of removing the pearls from their temporary string and rethreading them on a permanent string and clasp was about $1. No sane Greek exporter would therefore ever export strung pearls and pay a $50 tariff when he could arrange for the process to be done in the United States for $1. Effectively, the tariff on the strung pearls was $50 protecting $1 worth of labor, or 5000%![10]

The formula to figure the effective rate of protection is as follows:

(Eq. 4.1)
$$\frac{(y - b) - (x - a)}{x - a}$$

where x = the international price of the finished commodity, y = the domestic price of the finished commodity, including the tariff, a = the international price of the imported component, and b = the domestic price, including the tariff, of the imported component. (But note that several restrictive assumptions are embodied in the formula, and these are not easy to relax. It assumes producers do not substitute cheaper inputs for more expensive ones as tariffs are imposed, and it does not take into account any effect of quotas.[11])

For ease of calculation, say the nominal tariff on strung pearls is only $1; the cost of stringing of $100 worth of raw pearls is also $1; and there is no duty on unstrung raw pearls. The price of strung pearls in the absence of a tariff would be $101. With a tariff of $1 (nominally about 1%), the price of strung pearls would be $101 + $1 = $102. Given these numbers, the *effective* tariff is:

(Eq. 4.2)
$$\frac{(102 - 100) - (101 - 100)}{101 - 100} = \frac{1}{1} = 100\%$$

It may look like a 1% tariff, but it is 100% protection for the value added.

In the vast majority of cases, the effective tariff is positive; that is, the more finished product pays the higher tariffs. Bela Balassa compared average nominal tariffs to average effective tariffs, based on rates as they were several years ago. (Effective rates are difficult to calculate because of the need to gather extensive information on value added domestically, so studies often rely on older work.) Balassa's calculations showed effective rates 72% higher than nominal rates in the United States, 81% higher in Great Britain, 84% higher in Japan, and 54% higher in the (old) European Economic Community.

When effective tariffs are much higher on finished goods than they are on raw materials, economists speak of the phenomenon as *tariff escalation*. The greater the extent of processing, the greater the effective tariff. The examples in Table 4.1 show some of the many examples where average tariff rates are higher for processed items than for raw materials, meaning high effective protection for the processing. Other wide disparities between nominal duties on raw and processed items, and therefore high effective rates on processing, include fish, tobacco, textiles, and metals. Some cases are egregious.[12] Recently, the EU duty on fresh mangoes was 7%, while on canned mangoes it was 30% and on mango juice 40%. Peanuts enter the EU free of duty but peanut butter pays a 17% tariff. Japan allows cocoa beans entry without tariff but charges 27.4% on chocolate. The United States has no duty on hides and skins but puts a 14.4% charge on leather goods.

Ongoing tariff reductions will bring little improvement in the situation. Currently, developed country tariffs on industrial imports from less-developed countries, other than petroleum, are falling from 2.1% to 0.8% on raw materials, from 5.4% to 2.8% on semi-manufactured or partly processed goods, and from 9.1% to 6.2% on finished products.[13] Thus, even with average nominal tariffs significantly lower than in the past, substantial tariff escalation still exists.* Table 4.1 shows some of the differences in tariff rates for specific raw materials and finished products.

The tariff system, in effect, is rigged against the developing countries that wish to export more manufactures or to export their primary products in a more finished form.[14] A United Nations study suggests that if the escalation could be removed, then the potential increase in the annual exports of 10 important commodities would be about one-and-a-half times the value of the unprocessed commodities themselves.[15] The World Bank has stated that removal of tariffs on processed items by the developed countries would increase exports of the processed products by about 80% in the case of coffee, by 76% for wool, and by 52% for cocoa.[16] It certainly appears that the less-developed countries have a legitimate complaint in the cases where they

---

* The degree of escalation in the United States, the EU, and Japan is very similar. With the development of large econometric models in the rich countries, it has become possible to trace more carefully the effects of any change in nominal tariffs. Thus the subject has gone somewhat out of fashion in those countries, though it remains a very important issue for the less-developed countries, as is discussed in the text. See Peter Kenen, *The International Economy* (Englewood Cliffs, N.J.: Prentice-Hall, 1985), 184.

Table 4.1

TARIFF ESCALATION: AVERAGE
DEVELOPED-COUNTRY TARIFFS, 1980 (%)

Coffee	6.8	Processed coffee	9.4
Cocoa	2.6	Chocolate	11.8
Rubber	2.3	Rubber articles	6.7
Hides and skins	0.0	Leather goods	8.2
Semi-manufactured wood	1.8	Furniture	6.6

Source: World Bank, *World Development Report 1987* (Washington, 1987), 138.

would otherwise have a comparative advantage in processing and manufacturing. (Incidentally, there is no special malevolence against poor countries
involved in this situation. It is obvious that developed-country manufacturers
would lobby for low tariffs on their inputs and high tariffs on imports that
compete with their output.)

Occasionally the effective tariff is less than the nominal tariff, which occurs
when raw material inputs to production pay a higher nominal tariff than the
finished good. When inputs are subject to a tariff, then a product that uses
these taxed inputs is at a relative disadvantage. That creates an incentive to do
the processing abroad.

ANALYSIS OF TARIFFS: THEIR EFFECTS

The analysis of tariffs may be undertaken with the supply-and-demand curves
for one good in one country. Such partial-equilibrium supply-and-demand
analysis allows for a considerable degree of insight into the benefits and costs
of tariffs, as well as into a number of other related questions concerning these
trade barriers. To begin, take the explanations of the benefits of freer trade
and modify them to show the harm caused by a tariff. In the simplest
proposition, consider a tariff high enough to stop all trade, then reverse the
explanation of the benefits of trade given in Figure 2.9a. Rather than a tariff
that leaves no imports, however, it is more realistic to show some imports
remaining. Figure 4.1 is the key to the analysis. It shows a tariff high enough
to restrict but not stop trade. In the absence of a tariff, the equilibrium price
is P_w, with consumption of Q_4 made up partly from imports Q_1Q_4 and partly
from domestic production Q_1. The tariff in Figure 4.1 raises the price from a
world level of P_w to a domestic price P_d, which includes the value of the
tariff.* We will assume that the change in tariff has no impact on the world

---

* It is certainly conceivable that rather than leading to an increase in price, the tariff might lead
  instead to a decline in quality of the domestically produced good.

Figure 4.1

EFFECT OF A TARIFF IN PARTIAL EQUILIBRIUM

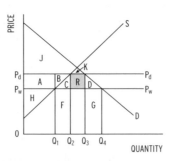

Note: P_w is the world price and P_d is the domestic price when a tariff is applied. With a tariff, consumption drops from Q_4 to Q_3, production increases from Q_1 to Q_2, and imports fall from Q_1Q_4 to Q_2Q_3. The letters *A-K* indicate areas that represent numerous welfare, revenue, and redistributive effects of the tariff.

price. In effect, the suppliers making up the world market will supply any quantity at a price P_w plus the tariff. The assumption is realistic when the importing country consumes only a small share of the world output of this product.

The resulting Figure 4.1 has an appearance similar to Figure 2.9, but it has acquired another rectangle—*R*, the revenue gained by the government. *R* is the amount of imports remaining after the tariff (Q_2Q_3) times the tariff (P_wP_d). We can now describe a number of the principal effects of the tariff in terms of the diagram.

Welfare and Revenue Effects: Demand and Supply Approach

To build the explanation, take first the simple quantity effects of the tariff as seen along the horizontal axis, then the more complex ones.

1. *Production effect*. Domestic producers increase production from Q_1 to Q_2. (If there was no domestic output at all before the tariff, then any production caused by the high price would be from new producers entering the market.)

2. *Consumption effect*. With higher prices, consumers reduce purchases of the protected good from Q_4 to Q_3, buying less satisfactory substitutes or doing without the good altogether.

3. *Import effect*. Imports are reduced from Q_1Q_4 to Q_2Q_3. The consumer buys a greater quantity Q_1Q_2 domestically, replacing imports, and further reduces imports by Q_3Q_4.

Now examine the more complex effects indicated by the triangles and rectangles.

4. *Revenue effect*. The rectangle R is the tariff revenue, found by multiplying the imports that remain after the tariff by the value of the tariff, or $(Q_2Q_3)(P_wP_d)$. For centuries tariffs were the major source of most countries' government revenue. In the United States, the first tariff of 1789 was a revenue tariff, and such revenue funded 90-95% of the U.S. budget until the 1850s. The figure was still 50% in 1900. (It is a little over 1% at present, about $18 billion in 1998.) Even today tariff revenue is an important area of public finance in many countries, furnishing 25% of government revenue in Russia, for example.[17] In the less-developed countries, especially in the poorer ones, it collects an even greater percentage of revenue, over 50% in some cases.*

5. *Producers' subsidy effect*. The new revenue accruing to producers is $A + B + C + F$. Of this new revenue, the portion $C + F$ goes to paying the higher factor costs incurred because of the increased production. $A + B$, however, is not required to increase output; it is extra. $A + B$ can thus be looked at as equivalent to a subsidy to producers, transfered to them by consumers. This subsidy effect explains why an industry's low-cost firms, perhaps those that are better managed, or more efficient, or produce a more desirable differentiated product, may be as eager to obtain a tariff as are the high-cost firms being harmed by imports. The tariff acts as a windfall gain to them. (The waste of this subsidy effect might possibly be avoided by made-to-measure tariffs, carefully worded so as not to apply to the firms that would otherwise receive the windfall. But this would be possible only if the products were highly differentiated, and in any case the legal, political, and bureaucratic problems would probably be insurmountable.)

6. *Consumer tax equivalent*. With a tariff additional costs must be paid by consumers, and these are the equivalent of a tax on consumption. These costs are found by multiplying the total amount purchased after the tariff (Q_3) by the higher price paid (P_wP_d). They total $A + B + C + R$. Consumers pay the entire bill: $A + B$ as a subsidy to producers over and above the costs of production, C as the higher costs of the additional output, and R as revenue collected by the government.

The welfare changes caused by the tariff can also be traced. In partial equilibrium welfare changes can be explored by means of producer and consumer surplus, as follows.

7. *Producer surplus*. Producer surplus is the area above the supply curve but below the price. In Figure 4.1 the original producer surplus is H, showing the amount paid to producers in excess of the actual marginal cost of producing the quantity Q_1. A tariff that raises the price from P_w to P_d raises producer

---

* Earlier we spoke of the advantages of a uniform tariff, but uniformity would not be chosen by a country whose goal is to raise tariff revenue. The most revenue would be received if higher tariffs were put on items for which the price elasticity of demand is low. This would be an example of a "Ramsey Tax," named for the British economist who propounded the principle.

surplus from an original area H to a new enlarged area $H + A + B$. Rectangle A plus triangle B show the increase in producer surplus. (Say the good on the horizontal axis is corn. Rectangle A would be the added revenue accruing to the acres already in corn. B would be the revenue over and above resource costs accruing to the corn grown on land that was planted in soybeans before the tariff, but that is now more valuable when planted in corn.)

8. *Consumer surplus.* The consumer surplus before the tariff was the entire area under the demand curve and above the price P_w, a triangle made up of $J + K + A + B + C + R + D$. When the tariff is imposed those consumers between Q_3 and Q_4 cease to buy while those between 0 and Q_3 continue to purchase the protected good but have to pay a higher price. The loss in consumer surplus is $A + B + C + R + D$.[*]

9. *The deadweight loss.* When a tariff is imposed, the gain in producer surplus and the gain to the government are not as large as the lost consumer surplus. See how producers gain $A+B$ (number 7 above), the government gains the revenue effect R, which we can assume is returned in the form of lower taxes (number 4 above), but consumers lose $A + B + C + R + D$ (number 8 above). The As, Bs, and Rs cancel one another, being both gains and losses, but there are two leftover areas of loss, triangle C and triangle D. This combined net loss is the deadweight loss effect of a tariff, occurring because the tariff harms consumers more than producers and government are helped.

The deadweight losses involved in these two triangles have different root causes. Area C is the producers' deadweight loss, an extra cost of producing the protected good. Consider a tariff on corn with land as the major input. The rectangle F represents the cost of the soybean land transferred into corn production, but that land cannot produce corn as efficiently as it could soybeans. C is the extra cost incurred when some land in soybeans has to be used for corn and is thus a deadweight loss. Area D is consumers' deadweight loss, reflecting their lost satisfaction as they shift away from the purchase of the newly protected good. Consumers between Q_3 and Q_4 shift to other, less desired goods, say from corn-based to wheat-based foods. Those near Q_4 suffer little loss, while those near Q_3 are almost ready to pay the higher import price, but in the end decide to buy the less satisfactory substitute.

The Problem of the Redistribution Effect

Even if the size of the deadweight loss is relatively small, we still have an important *redistribution effect* because income is redistributed from consumers

---

[*] In the presentation here, a tariff is placed atop an unchanged world price. Other variants are possible, however. The tariff may be in response to a fall in the world price, perhaps because one's own currency has appreciated or because costs have declined abroad. In that case, the tariff offsets the losses that domestic producers would otherwise endure and the gains that would accrue to domestic consumers.

THE SIZE OF THE DEADWEIGHT LOSSES

Note that the deadweight losses are not large in these diagrams, and probably not large in most economies. A rough estimate is not hard to make if you know the value of all sales of the protected good, and the tariff on an *ad valorem* basis, and are willing to hazard a guess about the elasticities of demand and supply. Suppose a country is protecting shoes with a 10% tariff, sells a million dollars' worth of shoes, and shoes have a demand elasticity of 1. Assuming the shoes sell for $10 including a tariff of $1, then the height of triangle *D* will be 10% of the price. The width of triangle *D* will also be 10% because we have stated that the elasticity of demand is 1. Use the formula for elasticity, $\%\Delta Q / \%\Delta P = \varepsilon$; if $\varepsilon = 1$ and $\%\Delta P = .10$, $\%\Delta Q$ has to be .10 also. So if sales were 100,000 pairs, they would fall to 90,000. Triangle *D* is actually quite small: is .005, or just 0.5 of 1% of the value of all sales. Triangle *C* is drawn to look about the same, so we can guess that the deadweight losses amount to about 1% of sales—not the kind of thing to become incensed about. (Some have argued, however, that even a small loss is important because that loss, say 1%, occurs year after year. That means we should use the present value of 1% of domestic sales, so $1 at 5% interest for 20 years is worth $2.65.)

Certainly, one can pick different values for the size of the tariff and the elasticity involved, but even doubling them both yields only 8% for *C* + *D*. (The calculation is (.2 x .4) / 2 = 4% for each triangle.) For the vast majority of goods in industrial nations, such figures are unrealistically high. For example, Arnold Harberger's pioneering estimates for the United States showed deadweight losses of less than 1% of GNP. Several factors explain why *C* + *D* is thought to be small. Most industrial nations have only a few tariffs in excess of 10%.[18] Most consumers continue to buy the imported good or its domestic substitute. Thus the shifts in production are only marginal, and the cost of that shift is also marginal. In our first statistical example, that using a tariff of 10%, the combined change in increased domestic production and decreased consumption is only 20%, the price change is just 10% of that, and only half the value of that sum is misallocation as measured by the triangles of deadweight loss *C* + *D*.

It is also fair to say, however, that when countries have quota restrictions, these are likely to have a greater price effect, as we shall see below. Furthermore, in less-developed countries, the costs of tariffs and other protection can run much higher. Some estimates for these countries are: 7% of GDP in Brazil, 3% in Mexico, 6% in Pakistan, 4% in the Philippines, and 5% to 10% in Turkey. (The empirical studies on the subject are usually short-run, however, and apply to rather broad product categories. Elasticities are expected to be higher in the long run and for narrower product categories, so deadweight losses would be higher also.)

to producers and the government. The amount involved in the United States was some $70 billion, or about $1,000 per person, in the early 1990s, a figure that includes some barriers besides tariffs.[19] If some recent cuts in trade barriers are fully implemented, the cost in the year 2005 would be about half that figure.

Such redistribution is one of the least rational of all tax-subsidy schemes. Why should consumers of shoes or chickens be taxed in order to subsidize producers of those goods? If the government had levied a special income tax or a tailored property tax of the same amount on chicken consumers, and voted to use the revenue for a subsidy to producers of that product, it would be in serious trouble. Taxpayers would have two questions: (1) Why should the government subsidize a particular group in the economy? (2) Even given that the subsidy should be granted, why should consumers of the product be the ones to pay it?

For the present, we will accept that the community in its collective wisdom believes that a certain industry must be encouraged and will question only the way in which that encouragement is to be paid for. If a community were able to think through the issue, it might decide that any such subsidy should come from general revenues, where, at least, questions about fairness, collectibility, and economic distortions have already been asked. It is, unfortunately, often difficult to know the ultimate incidence of any tax, but it is likely that with a tariff the consumer of the good is the one who suffers, at least in the short to medium run. Many tariffs (and other import restrictions), particularly in the industrial nations, are almost undoubtedly *regressive* in their effect on incomes, taxing low-income people to support groups higher on the income ladder. This occurs because in industrial countries the heavily protected goods include food, clothing, and cars, situations analyzed at far greater length in succeeding chapters. The Federal Reserve Bank of New York has calculated that tariffs, quotas, and VERs on clothing, sugar, and autos were the equivalent of a 23% income tax surcharge on families earning below $10,000 per year. This compares to only a 3% tax equivalent for U.S. families earning over $60,000 per year. Alternative World Bank figures suggest that the tax equivalence of protection is 66% on people earning less than $8,000 per year, compared to 5% for those earning over $60,000.[20]

With large amounts of their income spent on heavily protected items, poorer consumers—who in any case may be least able to defend themselves from a tariff because they may lack the information, intellectual skills, and political power to do so—pay a disproportionate toll. Many less-developed countries do have high tariffs on luxury goods, with Volvos and Mercedes paying tariffs equivalent to two or three times their cost at the ports, but they, too, often tend to have much in their tariff structure that is regressive.

Thoughtful readers might also ask whether the tariff taxes the people who benefit from it. Road and gasoline taxes, for instance, are designed to tax road users who gain from highway maintenance, and as a whole the tax does succeed in achieving that end, and in that sense is fair. But a tariff on poultry does not tax those who benefit. Consumers of chicken, prevented from buying abroad more cheaply, appear to gain little from having a few more people employed in a rural area hundreds of miles away. While the community may have decided that it is a public good to have chicken farmers, such a benefit, however dubious, is enjoyed by all. Arguably the consumers of chicken should not be asked to pay a disproportionate share of the costs.

Cost-Raising Effects

In the standard neoclassical diagram, the deadweight loss triangles are necessarily small and the costs of tariffs therefore low. In two types of situations, however, costs are greater than the little triangles C and D.

THE X-INEFFICIENCY EFFECT

The assumptions of our model to this point have been that all firms operate at their lowest costs, even when they are protected by a tariff. Presumably this occurs because sufficient competition remains to drive the poorly performing firms out of business or to force executive changes to eliminate inefficient management. We know, however, from the works of management economists such as Herbert Simon, winner of the 1978 Nobel Prize in Economics, that managers develop goals quite separate from those of the businesses' owners and tend toward performances that are satisfactory rather than profit-maximizing. In a protected environment, managers can generate returns satisfactory to their owners without performing optimally, and their owners remain unaware of potential greater returns. The economist Harvey Leibenstein has distinguished between a theoretically optimal performance level and the actual performance level, the latter inefficient to an unknown or X degree that he calls X-inefficiency. Leibenstein connects such X-inefficiency to the strength of oligopoly power, arguing that it is less likely under greater competition.[*]

---

[*] The "X" in X-inefficiency was taken by Leibenstein from Tolstoy's *War and Peace*: "Two armies may be identical in every observable respect—manpower, armaments, cavalry, provisions—yet, one army, in possession of an intangible X-factor, will soundly defeat the other." To make Leibenstein's argument properly, we need to show not only that competition is absent from the marketplace, but also that owners allow their managers to use their capital inefficiently and further that no corporate raider will enter to force management to operate efficiently. We are, in essence, requiring that ownership (or equity) markets be imperfect, as well as the goods markets of which Leibenstein speaks.

The implications of the X-inefficiency argument for welfare are much greater than those of the deadweight loss. Protected firms can afford to be X-inefficient up to the value of the tariff, at which point they would suffer import competition. Under such a situation, costs rise to the level P_d in Figure 4.1, so it is not just triangles C and D, but also areas A and B that are losses. In this case, the resources that A and B represent are drawn into the protected industry, but the output does not increase because of the inefficient way it is run. Suppose a country's corn is grown on farms run by overseers who note that with the higher prices of corn their owners' returns have risen, so they begin to add elegant accommodations to their houses, hire many relatives who do very little, and spend much more time on non-productive activities. Costs could rise as far as the domestic price including the tariff, which would turn all of A and B into costs. On a general equilibrium diagram, X-inefficiency of this nature would appear as a shrinking inward of the production possibility frontier.

Nothing in the standard neoclassical theory of international trade says that industries at a comparative disadvantage are run inefficiently. Indeed, neoclassical theory assumes that all firms, given sufficient competition, are run efficiently. Those who have read the literature on protected industries are struck again and again at how inefficient many of these industries actually are. The discussions in the previous chapters of the automobile industry's adoption of many Japanese planning techniques demonstrate one of numerous examples of how international competition promotes not just resource reallocation, but more efficient (X-efficient, to use Leibenstein's term) use of resources where they are already employed. In the words of Mancur Olson, "tariffs can encourage, and free trade prevent, institutional sclerosis among manufacturers or any enterprises that have international competition."[21] Estimates of losses due to X-inefficiency in the United States run as high as 2% of GNP, higher than the deadweight loss.[22] Much X-inefficiency is not deadweight loss because the higher costs and organizational slack can often be seen as a gain to the managers and workers in the form of plush company cars and clubs, a quieter life, and so forth.

It should be noted that when trade barriers are reduced, the resulting increase in the efficiency of firms that have to face competition from imports is not just from the actual imports themselves. The competition may be potential, as in the contestable market model, with foreign entrepreneurs always ready to enter a market but only doing so when a domestic firm lets itself go slack.[23] Some recent studies suggest that the gains from free trade's tendency to increase competition can be large—one estimate is gains of 29% more than in traditional accounting for the EU, 30% for North America, and 13% for Japan.[24]

SPECIALIZATION EFFECTS

The specialization effects noted in the previous chapter, whether scale, industrial concentration, experience, or product specialization, all involve decreasing costs. In these models the more an industry specializes, the greater the decline in average costs. By preventing trade, tariffs in an importing country can block the attainment of plant and industrial scale, intraindustrial specialization, and the accumulation of experience in an exporter. That in effect keeps the potential decline in costs in the exporter from occurring. In such instances world price levels could have fallen, but because of the barriers they did not. We could then view P_w, the world price in Figure 4.1, as higher than it needs to be.*

Effects on Economic Growth

In combination, several of the effects discussed thus far are likely to reduce the rate of economic growth. Lower trade means less competition (both potential and actual), with a reduced spur to efficiency.[25] If efficiency declines because of protection, then more resources must be used per unit of output and, very likely, economic growth will decline. Growth will also presumably be reduced if domestic inputs that must be used because of the protection are lower in quality or higher in price, or if economies of scale are not realized. It might also be negatively affected by the reduction in innovation and lessened knowledge about technical advances and production methods. If oldline manufacturing industries with a poor record of technical change obtain most of the protection, that, too, can have an adverse influence on growth. F.M. Scherer has pointed out that firms that obtain trade barriers tend to make large cuts in their research and development expenditures.[26] Diversion of entrepreneurial effort undoubtedly goes on behind the trade barriers, as firms are attracted to produce items with the greatest protection and lobby to keep or increase the barriers. The system rewards political skill and connections, not skill in running a company efficiently. Finally, trade barriers may restrict investment, especially foreign direct investment that carries with it better technology and management.[27]

Table 4.2 shows World Bank data indicating that less-developed countries with high trade barriers ("strongly inward-oriented") pay a penalty in reduced growth.

---

* An additional complication with even larger losses inflicted on the community can be introduced. The failure to allow the potential trading partner to specialize will prevent the tariff-levying nation from specializing itself in an export product with declining costs, due either to retaliatory tariffs or insufficient incentive to trade.

Table 4.2

TRADE ORIENTATION AND ANNUAL REAL GDP GROWTH PER
CAPITA IN THE LESS-DEVELOPED COUNTRIES, 1963-1992 (%)

	1963-73	*1974-85*	*1986-92*
Strongly Outward Oriented	6.8	8.0	7.5
Moderately Outward Oriented	4.8	4.3	4.8
Moderately Inward Oriented	3.8	4.4	2.4
Strongly Inward Oriented	1.6	2.3	2.5

Sources: World Development Report 1987, 84, for the figures for 1963-73, calculated by the
authors from the Bank's graphical presentation and therefore approximate. For 1974-85
and 1986-92, IMF, *World Economic Outlook 1993* (Washington, 1993), 76.

A number of recent studies find a strong relationship between trade openness and economic growth.[28] In an influential paper, Jeffrey Sachs and
Andrew Warner defined open economies as not having high tariffs or NTBs,
not being socialist planned systems, not having state export monopolies, and
having exchange rates not far from what the market would dictate. They
found that less-developed countries with more open economies grew by 4.5%
per year in the 1970s and 1980s, compared to only 0.7% per year in the closed
economies. For developed industrial economies, the figures were 2.3%
growth in the open ones and 0.7% in the closed. Another study, by Jeffrey
Frankel and David Romer, also finds a robust correlation between trade and
economic growth. It implies that raising the share of exports plus imports in
the GDP by one percentage point increases income per capita by 2% or more.
Sebastian Edwards reports for the 93 countries in his data set that during the
period 1980-90 the countries with lower openness to trade (as measured by
nine alternative indexes of trade policy) consistently had slower growth in
productivity. Finally, a study reported by the U.S. Council of Economic
Advisors covers the period from 1960 to 1985. It indicates that within a 123-
country sample, a one percentage point increase in openness was associated
with a 0.34 percentage point annual increase in real per capita income. Not
all international economists agree that these relationships are a true reflection
of cause and effect, but many do, including the authors of this book.*

* Among the reasons for doubt: the strongly outward-oriented countries of Table 4.2 are few in
number, and of these, South Korea (and also Taiwan and Japan before it, neither included in
the study) was well known for using a strategy of government aid to strengthen export industries as part of its outward-oriented policy. Thus, outward orientation does not necessarily
mean immediate trade liberalization, and the reductions in these countries' trade barriers was
gradual. Moreover, the correlation between outward orientation and growth is strong only
when market conditions are favorable and weakens considerably in periods of recession; and
the difference in performance is not very great between the moderately outward-oriented and
the moderately inward-oriented. In addition, the poorer a country, the less well openness to

The Incidence of Tariffs: Pass-Through, Rents, Lobbying

PASS-THROUGH

Tariffs on imports have a way of coming around to penalize exports in a so-called *pass-through effect*. There are two possible macroeconomic mechanisms, either or both of which can be at work.

(1) As tariffs cause imports to fall, less foreign exchange is needed to purchase them and the demand for foreign currency declines. The domestic currency will thus rise in value on the foreign exchange market.[*] Exporters find that their foreign-currency earnings purchase less domestic currency and therefore they suffer. Looking back at Figure 4.1, the reduction in spending on foreign exchange is equal to area $F + G$, which is the value at the world price P_w of the fall in imports $Q_1Q_2 + Q_3Q_4$. (Imports also are affected, becoming more attractive than before since the currency appreciation makes them appear cheaper. Even the initial effect of the tariff on imports can thus be eroded.) Econometric work for the United States indicates that a 15% across-the-board tariff would appreciate the dollar by 7%, cutting the initial improvement in the trade balance by about one-half.[29]

(2) The pass-through effect is also felt as tariffs cause the price level to rise. Importers pass on their higher costs to buyers, and industrial buyers pass those costs on in the form of higher prices. For example, products using steel have risen in price following restrictions on the import of steel into many countries. To the extent that steel competes for factors of production with non-tradeable goods and services, then the tariff will raise the price of these as well. Consumers, hit directly or indirectly, include the inflationary price increases in their wage and salary demands. Everybody tries to pass the tax to someone else. The only group that is powerless to pass the costs on further are the exporters, who have to sell at world prices and swallow those costs. In essence, a tax on imports becomes a tax on exports. Studies cited by the World Bank indicate that for a wide range of developing countries, 43% to

---

trade works as an engine of growth. To become a successful exporter in any reasonable space of time, a country must have already developed some minimal industrial base and possess some minimal degree of technical skills. Among the skeptics are fine economists such as David Evans, Gerald Helleiner, Howard Pack, Francisco Rodriguez, Dani Rodrik, Hans Singer, and Nicholas Stern. For a critique, see Francisco Rodriguez and Dani Rodrik, "Trade Policy and Economic Growth: A Sceptic's Guide to the Cross-National Evidence," NBER Working Paper No. 7081, 1999. Most if not all of the skeptics would, however, agree that economic performance in the strongly inward-oriented economies has been especially weak.

[*] This analysis applies if exchange rates are floating. If they are fixed, the fall in imports will affect the balance of trade by generating a trade surplus but will not change the exchange rate. If, however, the currency is revalued to eliminate the trade surplus (or foreigners devalue to eliminate their deficits, or both), the analysis is the same as under floating rates.

95% of an increase in protection against imports is passed on to become a tax on exports. Studies in Australia suggest that protection that raises prices by 5% eventually raises labor costs by 4.4%. In this case, more than 80% of a tariff increase is converted into a tax on exports.[30] Although the effects might not be as obvious in a large nation like the United States, tariffs do tend to push up the price level.

The converse point, that inflation is moderated when trade is free, is well illustrated by U.S. experience in the 1990s. Unemployment has been low and the economy has been booming, but inflation has stayed very modest in part because the availability of imports puts a lid on price increases.

TARIFFS AND ECONOMIC RENT

One way to look at the losers and beneficiaries of the income redistribution that accompanies a tariff is with the concept of *economic rent*. Rent arises because factors are limited in supply. Take the example of the corn and soybean lands and assume that the supplies of labor and capital are perfectly elastic. In that case all the gains from a tariff will go to the owners of land, with the rent of the land producing corn rising with the tariff. In Figure 4.1, the land already producing corn receives an increase in rent consisting of the rectangle *A*. That land that must be converted receives varying amounts of rent, depending on the difference between the return it generated with soybeans and the higher return it generates with corn. This amounts to triangle *B*.[*]

With higher values on corn land, farmers can presumably now sell that land for more money, charge tenants higher rents, or borrow more against the land. In their own costing, they should regard the *opportunity cost* of that land as higher by the amount of potential rent they could receive. As new farmers move in to replace the old ones, they pay a fully competitive value for the land, and thus stand to lose if the tariff disappears.[†] The winners are those who had the land when the tariff rose (unexpectedly). When farmers complain about losing protection, it does not mean that the farmers are presently benefiting from the rent, for they may well have borrowed on the higher value or bought the land with the expectation of the corn rent included. What it means is that farmers erred in their judgment of the land's value.

We can extend the concept of rent beyond land to any factor with a vertical supply curve—in a relevant price range over a relevant period. A rent

---

[*] Technically, each acre of land, which has a vertical supply curve, receives the rent. If there were 1,000 acres between Q_2 and Q_3 of Figure 4.1, then the first acre converted would have a rent just short of the amount of the tariff and the last would have little rent at all.

[†] The naive buyer would pay for the present value of the future corn crops, including the tariff. More sophisticated buyers might discount the value of the land if they believed that the tariff would fall.

limited in time or limited to a certain range of prices is called a *quasi-rent*. Typical quasi-rents involved in trade are the wages and salaries employees receive in excess of what they could get outside the firm or industry in which they are working. Such quasi-rents may accrue in particular to people with industrially specialized skills or knowledge and to workers with seniority. Capital in fixed form (which is, in the short run, all of it) and not easily transferred to other uses (which is to say much of it) often earns considerably more than it could in its second-best use. A reduction in the price of that capital will thus not cause it to leave the industry. Owners of machinery, let us say of corn-planting equipment, are not going to find it easy to convert the machines to other forms of capital, say, to soybean planters (plausible) or to silos full of soybeans (impossible). These quasi-rent-takers also benefit from the tariff and suffer from its removal.

In practice, rent-seeking costs of trade policy (including all forms of trade distortion that are profitable for the recipient, not just tariffs) are not likely to exceed an upper limit of 1-2% of GDP in any advanced country. Estimates for some less-developed countries are very much greater, however, as much as 25% to 40% for Kenya and India.[31]

THE LOBBYING EFFECT

As tariffs and, more particularly, other import restrictions have surged to prominence once more, many firms have turned their energies from meeting the competition to lobbying for barriers against that competition. Gordon Tullock has argued that firms waste considerable amounts of their scarce resources in attempts to secure protection or to prevent others from obtaining it, and that these rent-seeking costs should also be included in an analysis of protection.[32] Figure 4.2 illustrates this idea with a *lobbying curve*. The curve starts at some positive tariff because the legislature may be willing to grant an industry a degree of protection even if it undertakes no lobbying at all. The cost of lobbying will rise as an industry receives a greater amount of protection. Next, we draw a benefit-from-the-tariff curve. This curve is assumed to rise, showing more and more benefits received by an industry until the tariff increases to the point that it prohibits imports altogether. Any further rise is an *excess tariff*, yielding no further benefits. The expectation is that the industry will

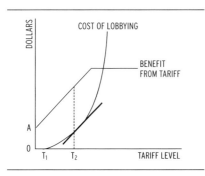

Figure 4.2
LOBBYING CURVE

157

HOW HIGH COULD RENT-SEEKING COSTS BE?

At worst the costs of rent-seeking and defending against losses could conceivably be as much as all of the producer surplus that might be gained ($A + B$) plus all of the consumer surplus that might be lost ($A + B + C + R + D$) in Figure 4.1. But they are unlikely to be that high because consumers are hard to organize. Each individual consumer may lose only a little even though the community as a whole loses considerably. Thus, consumers are not likely to devote as much to lobbying against trade barriers as producers do to lobbying for them. In any case, there is often a perception that the producer has the inside track. If a brother-in-law of the country's president owns a cement company, then that country's consumer lobby might reasonably decide there is little hope of reducing protection on cement. Jagdish Bhagwati calls this, aptly, the brother-in-law theorem.[33]

expend funds for lobbying up to a tariff level T_2, at which point the marginal cost of bringing about an increase in the tariff is equal to the marginal benefit of the increase, thus maximizing the gains.

Such costs of lobbying used to be small by comparison with the size of international trade—they were probably less than $300 million per year for the United States in the early 1980s, only 0.1% of the total value of all U.S. trade, though they appear to have risen in recent years. They are a diversion of resources away from other, presumably more socially useful, purposes.[*] Furthermore, those figures do not include any adverse political consequences abroad, nor do they reflect the damage that can arise from the harassment of trading partners as the legislature responds to the lobbying.

A firm or industry must make a rational decision as to how much effort to put into lobbying for a tariff. Figure 4.2 pictures lobbying costs and the benefits of lobbying, and suggests that firms will stop pressing for higher tariffs when the cost of lobbying exceeds the probable benefit. Finally, lobbying may have to be undertaken by advocates of freer trade as well, either as a defense against protectionist interests or to deflect their losses to others. When competitive lobbying by both producers and consumers becomes the norm, then the costs of this activity can increase greatly.[34]

Once import restrictions are in place, lobbying may intensify because protected interests become vested. Farmers borrow against their more valuable land, plants are built, workers and managers are higher paid and have skills more specific to the firm, professionals and retailers move to one-company

---

[*] The lobbying costs are not, however, deadweight losses because the revenues devoted to them are passed on to a wide range of recipients—the salaries of the lobbyists themselves, restaurant bills, advertising expenses, and the like.

Figure 4.3
THE TERMS-OF-TRADE EFFECT OF A TARIFF

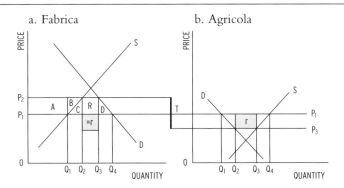

towns, all garnering their share of the income generated from the rent.[35] When the government considers lowering the tariff, the beneficiaries fight even harder to keep the tariff because their very livelihoods are at stake. At this point, the tariff is not just a bonus, as it was in the beginning. An increase in the intensity of lobbying even though protection is falling is called a *magnification effect*.[36]

Before becoming too sympathetic with the people who lose from a decline in protection, however, we must remember that, like any other business people, they had to assess whether the economic conditions prevailing at the time of investment would continue, or perhaps whether they could keep lobbying the government to make them continue. If they erred, it was a business error, like those made by millions of other people who do not expect the government to ride to their rescue.

The Terms-of-Trade Effect and the Optimal Tariff or Tax

The terms of trade are the prices (in physical terms) at which nations exchange goods, for example, the number of bushels of wheat for barrels of oil. A large nation trading with a small country can sometimes force the smaller one to lower its prices by reducing the demand for its exports. In essence, that may force the small country to pay all or part of the tariff the large one levies. This could then change the calculation of net benefits for the larger nation, which could count part of the tariff revenue as a real gain, not just an income transfer. We analyze this in partial equilibrium. (Appendix 4.1 to this chapter shows the analysis in general equilibrium with offer curves.)

The terms-of-trade effect with demand and supply curves uses the same tools employed earlier for showing transportation costs. The price line connects two countries' prices, with a kink in it as in Figure 2.10. If we say

Figure 4.4
A LARGE TERMS-OF-TRADE EFFECT

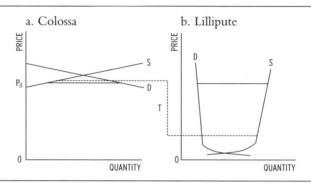

a. Colossa   b. Lillipute

that the reason for the crook in the line is a tariff, not transportation costs, we can attribute all the changes in welfare to the tariff. Figure 4.3 is similar, differing only in showing the tariff revenue as a kink in the price line indicated by *T*. What happens in essence is that a tariff placed on a good by Fabrica causes adjustments in both countries, such that the Agricolan producers lower their price. In so doing, Agricolans lose less of their market in Fabrica, and we find a splitting of the effects of the tariff between the two countries, just as occurred with transportation costs.

An important difference remains: one nation gets all the revenue. The price Fabrican importers pay for wheat from Agricola, not including the tariff, has fallen from P_1 to P_3, so Fabrica receives revenue equivalent to the tariff times the new volume of imports, or $T \times (Q_2Q_3)$. Given the slopes in our diagrams, about half of the revenue comes from higher prices domestically (P_1P_2), and the other half from lower Agricolan prices (by P_1P_3). The loss to Agricola is rectangle *r* in Figure 4.3b, equivalent to the small box under the rectangle *R* in Figure 4.3a. Now, if the revenue Agricola pays to Fabrica exceeds Fabrica's loss from the tariff, that is, if $r > C + D$, it would be to Fabrica's advantage to levy a tariff. Of course, it would not be to the world's advantage because Agricola is stuck paying the costs to offset Fabrica's deadweight losses.

The more inelastic Agricola's curves and the more elastic Fabrica's, the greater Agricola's absorption of the costs of the tariffs. Suppose we consider two nations that are quite different in size—Colossa and Lillipute. Colossa's big, flexible market gives it very high elasticities of demand and supply, as shown in Figure 4.4a, such that small changes in price call forth large changes in the quantity imported. Lillipute, however, has an economy based largely on the export of a primary product to Colossa. Domestic demand is a small percentage of Lillipute's production, while supply, particularly in the short run, is highly inelastic. Figure 4.4b shows that even at very low prices

Lillipute would be exporting about the same amount as at high prices, and domestic consumption would increase very little.

In the situation just described, Lillipute ends up paying virtually all of the tariff. Lillipute has to sell to Colossa because it cannot cut back production or divert much to the home market. What is more, it has to cut prices to sell because Colossa is very price-sensitive and will quit purchasing from Lillipute, making the good itself or doing without, unless Lilliputian exporters absorb the cost of the tariff. In Figure 4.4, the volume of products shipped from Lillipute to Colossa is almost unchanged. Indeed, the change is so small that it hardly affects the Colossan price at all and barely shows on Figure 4.4a. (P_d presumably does rise a bit because the quantity imported into Colossa has fallen slightly.) Thus, all but the smallest part of the tariff, T, is absorbed by Lillipute.

Such a situation would be typical of many small nations facing large developed countries or groups of developed countries. Examples include Fiji's sugar exports to the European Union or the Dominican Republic's to the United States, New Zealand's lamb exports to Europe, and Sri Lanka's tea exports to Britain.[*]

Some have argued that the terms-of-trade effect of a tariff on imports could be used as a policy. An importing nation could deliberately force down prices from the exporter in order to end up ahead. Indeed, if the shift in the terms of trade were great enough to offset the loss in trade volume, the importer *would* be in a better position. Presumably, then, a country could calculate an *optimum tariff* level for its welfare, wherein any greater rise in tariffs would reduce a country's consumption by more than it would gain from prices. The U.S. economy is so large that its optimum tariff would be relatively high, at least in the short run.[37] Such optimum tariffs, despite their technical validity, overlook the likelihood that one tariff to improve the terms of trade will beget another in retaliation. The risk of a trade war is high, understandably, because the gain in welfare to the country imposing the tariff is a loss in welfare to its victim. Economists who model possible strategies for a country facing a tariff imposed from abroad for such terms-of-trade purposes usually recommend a "tit-for-tat" strategy: a response identical to the opponent's move. Such retaliation might be called a *bargaining tariff*, discussed again in Chapter 6.

Beyond retaliation, a further difficulty with using a terms-of-trade tariff or export tax as a weapon is that there is generally little practical knowledge concerning the elasticities of the export and import demand and supply curves, with politicians picking the numbers that suit what they want to do.

---

[*] The terms-of-trade effect may have been known as long ago as ancient Rome, whose officials chose to levy a 25% tariff in the Red Sea and Palmyra, where luxury products were entering the Empire, rather than apply the standard rate of 12.5%. See Conybeare, *Trade Wars*, 88, 90.

Without exact knowledge of both short-run and long-run effects, the manipulation of tariffs or taxes to obtain a terms-of-trade effect is both senseless and dangerous. In fact, there is little to indicate that the United States employs a terms-of-trade strategy to increase its welfare at the expense of other countries. For example, U.S. optimum tariff policy would presumably dictate high duties on primary product imports and stiff taxes on high-technology exports. Nothing of the sort is done. U.S. tariffs on primary product imports are especially low, and export tariffs are constitutionally prohibited.

EXPORT TARIFFS

Export tariffs are less common than tariffs on imports, but they are employed, especially in the less-developed countries. (As just noted, they are prohibited by the U.S. Constitution, Article I, Section 9, which states: "No Tax or Duty shall be laid on Articles exported from any State," and they were abolished by Britain in 1842, by France in 1857, and by Prussia in 1865.)

Export tariffs are a mirror image of import tariffs and are often employed to obtain a terms-of-trade effect. They can be analyzed by means of diagrams like those in Figure 4.3.

Figure 4.5

THE ECONOMIC EFFECTS OF AN EXPORT TAX

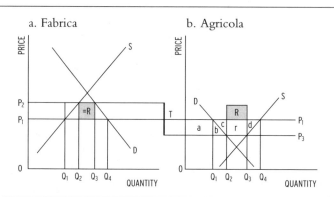

Say Agricola levies an export tax T on its wheat exports, as shown in Figure 4.5b. Exports would fall from Q_1Q_4 to Q_2Q_3. The price per unit would fall in the exporter to P_3, but it would rise in Fabrica, the importer (Figure 4.5a), to P_2. The export tariff T charged on exports Q_2Q_3 will yield Agricola's government a revenue of $r + R$. A portion of that revenue, box R, would come at the expense of consumers in Fabrica because import prices were forced up in that country. Agricola's welfare could conceivably rise because of the tax. Consider the welfare effects in that country: because the price has fallen, producers lose surplus equal to $a+b+c+r+d$. Consumer surplus rises by $a + b$. The government collects export tax revenue of $r+R$. The two a's, b's, and r's cancel one another, being both gains and losses. There is a deadweight loss of $c + d$ and a gain in government revenue of R. The export tax is advantageous for Agricola if the government revenue obtained at Fabrica's expense exceeds its own deadweight losses, that is, if $R > c + d$.

As with an import tariff, it is possible to calculate an optimum export tariff to improve the exporting country's terms of trade. The risks of retaliation are similar, unless a commodity is so important (oil, for example) that trading partners control their urge to hit back. Enormous gains, as all the world knows, followed from the export taxation employed by Saudi Arabia and other oil-producing states. Numerous other countries have employed export tariffs when they believed they had some ability to affect the terms of trade, for example, Ghana on cocoa, Bolivia and Malaysia on tin, Chile on nitrates, Argentina on almost all its commodity exports. At other times, they have been used to encourage local processing: Norway and Sweden on forest products to encourage local woodworking and papermaking; India on hides to foster local tanning, and so on.

QUOTAS AND THEIR ECONOMIC EFFECTS

A Brief Description

Quotas are protectionist devices closely related to tariffs. Rather than using taxes to limit imports, a government sets a limit to the quantity of the good that can be imported during the year. (Occasionally, quotas are also placed on exports, a topic addressed at the end of this section.) The quota might be defined by volume (for example, 10,000 VCRs) or, less commonly, by value ($1 million worth of VCRs). Usually, the government issues licenses that must be presented upon importing the good.

Quotas essentially were invented during World War I; they had been very uncommon before that and were again little used in the 1920s. France resurrected them in 1930-31 during the Great Depression, largely for protection of its farmers and for defense against low-price Japanese imports, which could not be excluded by high tariffs because of prior tariff agreements. By 1934, more than half the items on which France charged tariffs were subject also to the new quota limitations. These limits were strict, with many goods subject to quotas of less than half the quantities formerly imported. French actions were copied by others, including Nazi Germany, and by the end of the 1930s the situation had grown so serious that the term "free trade" came temporarily to mean trade unhindered by quotas, even though the tariffs paid might be quite high.

Vigorous and successful attempts were made by the industrial countries in the period after World War II to end quotas on manufactured goods. But they remained common in agriculture everywhere and in the less-developed countries they are frequently imposed on all sorts of commodities.* In accord with changing international rules on this instrument, many countries have replaced their outright quotas with *tariff-rate quotas* (TRQs). Under this system, imports within a quota amount are subject to a tariff while further imports above the quota are subject to a high (and sometimes prohibitive) tariff, with effects similar to a normal quota, as examined later in this section.

Analysis of Quotas

The diagram to show a quota is almost identical to the figure for a tariff. Indeed, we simply duplicate the earlier Figure 4.1 as Figure 4.6. The difference is that we will not levy a tariff and say instead that the amount Q_2Q_3 is the quota. The diagram still looks the same, though, because any time the quantity of a good is artificially restricted, its price rises. Because imports have fallen from the prequota Q_1Q_4 to Q_2Q_3, the price rises until the quantity demanded once again equals the quantity supplied, which is at Q_3. At that quantity the price is P_d. There is no tariff, but we disagree with the U.S. congressman who recently stated on national television that he would not support new tariffs because these were a tax, but he would support new quotas, since they would not raise prices. On the contrary, if you make something more scarce, its price goes up.

Figure 4.6

THE REVENUE
EFFECT OF A QUOTA

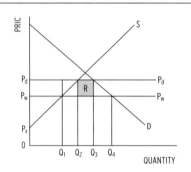

WHO GETS THE REVENUE EFFECT?

With the price at P_d because of the quota at Q_2Q_3, almost all the effects (on production, on consumption, the subsidy and consumer tax aspects, the

---

* Recently, for example, Taiwan required import permits for over 2,000 items and 242 product categories were banned. Brazil once had thousands of quotas (many being phased out in the 1990s), while India still has a huge number.

welfare shifts and deadweight losses, the results for efficiency, the terms of trade, pass-through, and lobbying) are the same as they are for a tariff. The one exception is the revenue effect. No tariff is paid, so who gets the revenue shown by area *R*? The answer is seldom certain under a quota, but here are some possibilities.

1. The government could in effect obtain area *R* by holding an auction of the quotas. That would, in effect, be a type of tariff. Australia, New Zealand, India, Brazil, and some other South American countries have tried this method occasionally, but there is still a potential for difficulty if the bidders collude. The respected Institute for International Economics in Washington, D.C., has called for the auctioning of all U.S. quotas so that the public would obtain the revenue. Its estimate is that quota auctions would yield about $7 billion per year to the U.S. government.[38] Importers usually decry auctions as "unethical," and often argue that their high overhead would allow fly-by-night competitors to underbid them at the auction. Opposition of this sort halted a U.S. plan to auction its quotas on textiles and clothing starting in 1994.[39]

2. The license itself may become a source of political corruption. The officer in charge of deciding who gets the import license has, in essence, a piece of paper worth the difference between the world price and the domestic price, and will be sorely tempted to accept favors from those seeking the license, just as those who covet them will be sorely tempted to bribe the official. Corruption in the granting of licenses is frequently a serious problem in developing countries where the salaries are low and the potential gains high. In some nations, the corruption is institutionalized and the government assigns posts in the office issuing the licenses as a reward to those it favors. (Ironically, however, a well-placed bribe might be much smaller in amount than the producer and consumer lobbying costs under a fair system presided over by honest officials—it is difficult for a crooked officer to take bids for bribes without being discovered.)

3. The U.S. experience has been that the importer gets a share of the quota for nothing and so garners the revenue effect. Note that the revenue is not necessary to stimulate the importers to make the effort; their effort would be the same with a tariff that yielded government revenue equal to rectangle R. It is hard to see why importers should have any special right to this form of subsidy. The case of the American quota restrictions on imported oil during the period 1954-73 is the most notorious example. Oil interests, fearful of cheap Arab oil, persuaded President Eisenhower (and his next three successors) that the American oil industry had to have quotas. So to "reduce American dependence on foreign oil," a quota on imports was declared under the Defense Act. As a result, the U.S. price of a barrel of oil was boosted by about 62%. Oil companies were given import licenses according to 1953

Figure 4.7
DIFFERING RESPONSES OF TARIFF
AND QUOTA TO AN INCREASE IN DEMAND

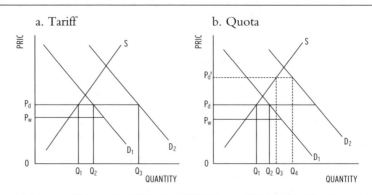

import shares. Americans today are still affected by this long-gone policy. It resulted in much heavier use of domestic supplies than would otherwise have been the case, meaning less security should domestic reserves have to be relied on in some emergency,

4. Foreigners may capture part of the revenue by raising export prices, which could occur if a foreign producer or exporting firm was a monopoly.[40] More commonly, foreigners capture the revenue when the quota is bargained with the foreign nation under the so-called voluntary export restraints, discussed below.

QUOTAS ARE RIGID

Another reason why economists frown on quotas, and believe nations' leaders should also oppose them, involves their rigidity. (That is also an explanation as to why management and unions that are seeking protection prefer quotas to tariffs.)

Quotas are by their very nature fixed. They limit imports to a specific quantity no matter what the foreigner chooses to do about price. Compare Figure 4.7a, showing a tariff, to Figure 4.7b, which portrays a quota. Figure 4.7a shows demand rising to D_2. Even though the tariff of P_wP_d still prevails, the quantity imported rises from Q_1Q_2 to Q_1Q_3. Given the ability of the world to keep supplying at P_w (we assume that the world supply curve is horizontal at price P_w), the price does not rise. Under quotas, however, the quantity of imports cannot increase when demand rises. Figure 4.7b shows the new level of imports, Q_3Q_4, as equal to the quota of Q_1Q_2; the rise in quantity sold has been entirely provided from domestic sources. As a consequence, the price rises to P_d'.

The same result occurs when the domestic supply curve shifts upward and to the left, due, say, to increased wages or a developing scarcity of raw materials. Under a tariff, imports would rise as domestic supply fell off, but under a quota, imports would not rise; the consequence would be an increase in price under a quota, while there would be no increase under a tariff. (The diagram is just a variation on Figures 4.7a and 4.7b and the reader is encouraged to sketch it.)*

A third variation occurs if world prices decrease. Under a tariff, domestic prices will fall by the amount of the decline in world prices. Under a quota, the domestic price cannot fall and the revenue effect, *R*, increases—it goes to whoever is fortunate enough to capture it. Domestic demand and supply conditions remain unchanged because imports are fixed. Thus those benefiting from protection prefer the certainty of quotas. It is far better for them if foreigners are unable to cut their prices in the face of a quota, as they can do with a tariff. It is also better for them that any consumer preference for imported goods cannot lead to a rise in imports.

QUOTAS ENHANCE MONOPOLY POWER

Figure 4.8

TRADE POLICES MONOPOLY POWER, EVEN WITH A TARIFF

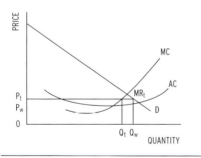

When additional competition is revented by a quota, then any latent or real monopoly position can be exploited and the stimulus to higher efficiency that stems from competition is lost. This case can be made diagrammatically.[41] Say that, as in Figure 4.8, a domestic firm would be a monopoly in the absence of international trade. The firm's market power is exhibited by the downward slope of the demand curve facing it. This firm is not a monopoly in the presence of foreign trade, however, because consumers can buy imports at a price of P_t. That price P_t is the world trade price P_w plus a tariff of $P_w P_t$. Because customers can buy abroad any quantity they want at a price P_t, no one will pay the domestic firm more than that. Therefore $P_t MR_t$ is a horizontal demand curve for the firm's product, and $P_t MR_t$ is the marginal revenue curve for the firm as well. The firm produces where marginal cost

---

* A decrease in demand (leftward shift in the demand curve) or increase in supply (rightward shift in the supply curve) would have the opposite effect. In these cases a tariff is more restrictive than an originally equivalent quota because the unchanged quota would allow more imports at a lower price.

(*MC*) equals marginal revenue (*MR*), or Q_t. The remainder of the country's demand, Q_tQ_w, is supplied from imports. Even if demand were less than shown in the figure, so that the domestic monopoly supplied the entire market and there were no imports at all, that firm could still not charge a price higher than P_t because if it tried, buyers would turn to imports.

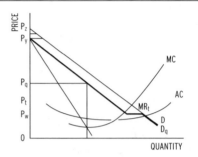

Figure 4.9

WITH QUOTAS POTENTIAL
MONOPOLY POWER BECOMES REAL

Now see the changes introduced by a quota. Let us establish a quota equal to Q_tQ_w on the quantity of imports. At the very top of the demand curve, shown in Figure 4.9, if the domestic firm attempted to charge the high price P_z, consumers would not buy it at all because the small quantity demanded at that price could be supplied from imports. Importers would buy at the low world price P_w and sell at a price that would always undercut P_z. Now what if the domestic firm cut its price a little, to P_y? In that case, there would still be enough imports to meet the entire demand because the horizontal distance over to the demand curve at P_y is just equal to the quantity allowed in under the quota. Any lower price, however, will mean a greater quantity is demanded but no more imports can get by the quota. In effect, starting at P_y the domestic demand curve is moved to the left by the amount of the quota. The leftward shift of the demand curve will continue down to the price level below which the importer cannot go, P_w. At any price below P_w, the domestic firm captures all the demand. The new demand curve shifted by the quota is D_q, shown as the heaviest line.

The end result is that if the same quantity of imports that flowed in under a tariff, Q_tQ_w on Figure 4.8, is brought in under a quota, then consumers' welfare will be worsened. See how that is so. The new demand curve D_q on Figure 4.9, shifted leftward by the amount of the quota, will have an associated marginal revenue curve, MR_q, located as microeconomics tells us halfway between the vertical axis and the demand curve at any price. We know that the profits of a firm are maximized where $MC = MR$. Thus the firm will maximize its profits with a price P_q far higher than it had been under a tariff (P_t). The associated reduction in output will presumably mean lower employment as well. The latent monopoly power, controlled under a tariff, was allowed to emerge into actual monopoly power when the tariff was converted into a quota. (The corollary of this is that converting quotas into equivalent tariffs would predictably have beneficial results for the public, though not, of course, for the firms receiving the protection.)[42] Quotas thus encourage cost inflation by raising prices, and because costs increase, they also reduce the nation's ability to produce, having thus an adverse supply-side effect also.

QUOTAS PRESENT OPERATIONAL DIFFICULTIES

Quotas are difficult to administer and are very hard to allocate. If, for instance, a country decides to let in 1,000 cameras a year, importers would rush to bring in the cameras at the beginning of the quota period to sell them at the high domestic price. The tiny U.S. peanut quota was administered in this way. Almost all foreign peanuts entered the country soon after the beginning of the fiscal year. To counter this seemingly irrational pattern, governments normally issue licenses, most often on the basis of past performance. If imports in 1998 were 10 million cameras and the government wants to cut that figure to 8 million in 1999, then it just issues an order that all firms importing cameras in 1999 can import 80% of their 1998 figure in that year. This method freezes the patterns of trade, lessening competition, and does not allow new and cheaper sources of supply to enter the market. Nonetheless, it is very common. (One possibility for avoiding the problem is to save a part of the quota, say 10%, for new applicants. Even so, the old producers will have a vested position, and will be much more protected under the quota than they would have been under a tariff allowing in an equivalent quantity of imports.)

Furthermore, quotas beget quotas and become ever more complicated. U.S. quantity limitations on steel, for instance, encouraged foreign exporters to shift from supplying inexpensive cold-rolled sheet to supplying specialty steels, which brings producers more revenue per ton. U.S. specialty steel producers had not pressed for a quota previously, because it was the big suppliers, with their ancient open hearths, who were being hurt by imports. When the foreign producers moved upscale, however, the specialty producers were forced to demand quotas of their own. Textile manufacturers faced the same problem as foreign producers turned to supplying goods that had a high profit margin per item, areas that had traditionally been the industrial countries' strongest. The sugar quota has begotten quotas on syrups and on candies. Producers of these items, suffering from the higher costs of the protected sugar, find themselves undercut by imports that use cheap sugar. It is like trying to stem a flood tide: the force of the water is akin to the pressures wrought by comparative advantage; the quotas are sandbags thrown in its way, diverting the flow, saving a firm here or a group of jobs there, but passing the flood on to some other spot, which tries to find sandbags of its own.

When all these objections to quotas are combined with the many effects of the blockages of imports discussed in the tariff section, it seems clear enough that import quotas are inimical to the public interest.

What Happens When Tariffs and Quotas Are Combined?

Sometimes a good is protected by tariffs and quotas at the same time. When they are, one of the two will be the binding restraint and the other will have no effect in limiting trade. Say a quota binds, that is, it is the instrument that causes imports to be what they are. Then the tariff on that good collects revenue but it doesn't by itself limit trade flows. Conversely, the tariff may be the binding restraint, high enough so that imports are below what is permitted by the quota. The quota then has no effect.[43]

From the general idea that a tariff can be combined with a quota has emerged a hybrid instrument called a tariff-rate quota or TRQ. TRQs have become much more common because wily governments have found a way to respond to international efforts to reduce the use of quotas. TRQs give a way to stay within trade agreements but get the same effect on imports as a regular quota while raising some tariff revenue at the same time.

Under TRQs, a quota is established within which goods are charged a low tariff. After the quota is filled, additional goods can still come in, but they must pay a high tariff. Very often the above-quota tariff is so steep as to prevent additional imports altogether, in which case the outcome closely resembles the quotas that they are replacing.

This case of a TRQ coming very close to a regular quota is shown in Figure 4.10. A tariff-rate quota is established, with a moderate in-quota rate of 20%. See how the domestic price P_d is 20% higher than the world price P_w. If any amount could be imported after paying this tariff, then a quantity Q_1Q_3 would be imported. But only a quantity Q_1Q_2 is allowed at the 20% rate; under the tariff-rate quota, imports greater than quantity Q_1Q_2 must pay an above-quota

Figure 4.10

A TARIFF-RATE QUOTA WITH A
PROHIBITIVE (EXCESS) TARIFF

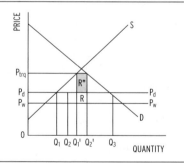

tariff of 200%. A tariff that high is excess; it will prohibit any additional imports. With imports of only Q_1Q_2, the market will force the price to rise, to the point where the imports fill the gap between the supply curve and the demand curve. This is at price P_{trq}, where the quantity of imports is $Q_1'Q_2'$ $= Q_1Q_2$.

The outcome is like a regular quota, with the limited amount imported the binding constraint and prices rising due to that limitation just as in Figure 4.6. The main difference is in the revenue effect. If the rise in price had been due entirely to the tariff, the government would have collected revenue of $R^* + R$. But with the TRQ, the tariff is only P_wP_d. So the government collects only R as its revenue ($Q_1'Q_2' \times P_wP_d$). The remainder of the revenue effect, the shaded area R^*, falls into private hands just as the whole area $R^* + R$ does with a regular quota.

If, however, the above-quota tariff is *below* the level that would prohibit further imports, then the diagram has a different appearance, as in Figure 4.11. Once again, the low in-quota tariff of P_wP_t (say 15%) permits imports limited to the quantity Q_1Q_2. More can be imported at the above-quota tariff P_{trq} (60%). At any price above P_t, buyers will first prefer to exhaust the amount permitted in under the low tariff, so the demand curve for any price above P_t will be shifted to the left by the amount Q_1Q_2. The result is that with an above-quota tariff P_wP_{trq}, there will be imports $Q_1Q_2 = Q_1'Q_2'$ at the low tariff P_wP_t and Q_3Q_1' at the higher tariff.

Figure 4.11

A TARIFF-RATE QUOTA WITH A TARIFF THAT IS NOT PROHIBITIVE (EXCESS)

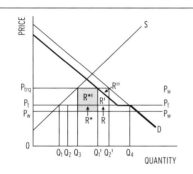

The revenue effect of this TRQ is the total amount imported times the amount by which the price increased, or $Q_3Q_2' \times P_wP_{trq}$, in Figure 4.11 equal to the area $R^* + R^{*'} + R'' + R' + R$. Some of this revenue goes to the government. The government's tariff revenue will be area $R = Q_1'Q_2' \times P_wP_t$ on the in-quota imports plus area $R^* + R^{*'} = Q_3Q_1' \times P_wP_{trq}$ on the above-quota imports, or $R + R^* + R^{*'}$ in total. But not all of the revenue effect goes to the government. Because private interests were able to bring in some in-quota imports ($Q_1Q_2 = Q_1'Q_2'$) at price P_t and sell these imports at price P_{trq}, they would garner a part of the revenue effect. Their gain would be $R' + R''$, which is equal to $Q_1'Q_2' \times P_tP_{trq}$.

Producers will thus prefer a TRQ to a tariff because they obtain some of the revenue effect, $R' + R''$, while governments and economists will prefer TRQs to quotas because the public gains some tariff revenue, $R + R^* + R^{*'}$.

171

Export Quotas And Prohibitions

Quotas on exports and even complete prohibitions of exports have been enforced at certain times and places. The fine word "sycophant," meaning "one who curries favor," has to do with the prohibition of all exports except olive oil by ancient Athens. In Greek *sykon phainein* means fig shower: one who curried favor by showing to officials the illegal exports of figs. Britain prohibited grain exports except under license for over two centuries (1177 to 1394) and also restricted machinery exports (so as to protect its technological lead) until 1842. The Ottoman Empire maintained for many years an entire prohibition of exports; its imports were paid for by cash transactions only. Japan, as is well known, banned almost *all* contact with the outside world for over two centuries, from 1636. Trade was limited to a Dutch ship that touched annually at Nagasaki. The situation was little changed until after Commodore Perry's visits of 1853 and 1854.

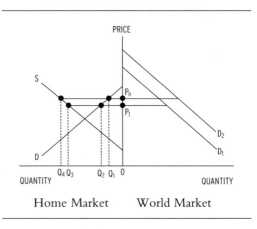

Figure 4.12

EXPORT QUOTAS TO KEEP DOWN DOMESTIC PRICES

Home Market   World Market

On occasion, quotas on exports are imposed for the same reason as export tariffs—to glean a terms-of-trade effect by forcing up the price in importing countries. OPEC's restriction of oil exports is a famous case. Another reason for export quotas is that for domestic political reasons a government may want to keep prices low for consumers at home. (Embargoes on trade with rival nations are another matter, and are taken up in Chapter 8.)

An export quota to reduce domestic prices is shown in Figure 4.12. Here, assume that government decides that rising world demand, seen on the right-hand side of the diagram as a movement from D_1 to D_2, has pulled the home price, shown on the Y-axis, up to a level higher than desired. If export quotas are imposed, and these reduce the quantity exported from Q_1Q_4 to Q_2Q_3, then the market price will decline from P_h to P_l. Consumers gain, while producers lose.

One celebrated case involved the quota placed on U.S. exports of soybeans by President Nixon in the early 1970s. Though this quota lasted only three months, it wrecked America's reputation as a reliable supplier of that product, especially in Japan, which is a major importer. Brazil was the biggest gainer. The U.S. action gave Brazilian farmers the boost they needed and soybeans became a major export of that country, the industry financed heavily by the Japanese. For over two decades the United States restricted the export of oil from Alaska (the ban lifted in 1996) and it still restricts the export of timber from federal lands. The timber prohibition is intended to force Asia (mainly Japan and South Korea) to buy planks instead, though the main result has been a boom in log exports from countries such as Indonesia. There are also procedures in place to control the export of scrap metal from the United States.

Other examples of export quotas include long-standing controls on Thai rice exports to keep Thailand's rice price low and temporary bans on the export of Indian tea and Brazilian rice, corn, and cotton. Ironically, soybeans were also covered for a time by a Brazilian ban, perhaps reflecting a lesson not learned from the U.S. experience. (The Brazilian restraints, associated with the inflation in that country, were lifted in 1988.)[44]

VOLUNTARY EXPORT RESTRAINTS

A *voluntary export restraint,* or VER, is a special kind of quota set on the export of a good to a given country. It is for all intents and purposes an import quota, except that, at least technically, it is administered by the exporter, and not all of the effects are exactly the same.* The United States invented VERs in 1935-36, when U.S. and Japanese producers negotiated limits on Japan's exports of cotton textiles to the United States. (Apparently both governments consented to this private arrangement between producers. The argument has been made that the traditional Japanese practice of avoiding confrontation through compromise was reflected by this first VER.)[45] But voluntary restraints were little used until the 1970s, when they came into sudden prominence. They have since become a major form of protection, at their apex affecting about 15% of world trade.[46]

The somewhat unusual roots of voluntary export restraints lie in the legal systems and treaty obligations of industrial countries that have made other trade barriers harder to employ. Numerous international agreements effectively hinder the raising of tariffs. Furthermore, developments in international trade law have discouraged quotas, especially for manufactured products. To avoid these constraints, protectionists have relied on persuading the

---

* Sometimes VERs are called *voluntary restraint agreements* (VRAs) or *voluntary export restraint agreements* (VERAs), when the parties sign a formal agreement. Government-to-government agreements involving no industry participation in the bargaining and administration are sometimes called *orderly marketing arrangements* (OMAs). In the United States there is a legal distinction between OMAs and VERs, but the difference is unimportant both theoretically and practically.

exporting country *voluntarily* to limit its exports. Of course, an exporting country may well view this as a bad idea, but the importing nation can threaten to establish quotas or raise tariffs at a later date, even if that does mean breaking a treaty or other obligation. These are sovereign nations, after all, and cannot be sued (without their permission) in any court.

Politics contributed greatly to the rise of VERs. Internally, the U.S. legal system makes it difficult to impose quotas or tariffs without involving Congress, something clearly intended by the Constitutional Fathers. If the administration were to go through Congress, it would lose control over the policy and action would be slower. With a VER, however, the administration can decide how much it will try to persuade the other nation to cut down exports.* The executive can continue to talk free trade while negotiating a VER and then can claim that the outcome was not protectionism but an agreement.

From the exporter's point of view, some VERs are voluntary in name only, akin to the outlaw voluntarily putting up his hands when the sheriff is pointing a gun at him. Faced with a choice of dealing with a U.S. administration or the U.S. Congress, foreign nations would rather deal with the administration as the better of two bad choices because Congress has the reputation of being the major source of protectionist sentiment. VERs tend to discriminate against the poor and powerless because countries with a substantial capacity to retaliate are less likely to be challenged. Other VERs may be welcomed by exporter and importer alike as a way to cartelize an industry with government permission and encouragement. A major advantage to the foreign exporter is that in both cases the revenue effect from the quota is usually distributed to the exporter, as explored in the next section. Government in the exporting country gains certainty, and possibly even some control over industry.

These considerations help to explain why VERs proliferated worldwide. In textiles, the Multi-Fiber Arrangement controls textile and clothing exports from the less-developed countries. World trade in steel has been greatly suppressed through their use, and VERs have been common in automobile and electronic goods trade. (All of these are discussed in the next chapter.) At their time of greatest use in the late 1980s and early 1990s, there were more than 250 VERs in place, about 80% of them negotiated between governments and the rest industry-with-government or involving industry-with-industry limits. Government-to-government VERs are by far the most common because their policing is usually more effective.[47]

---

* Such problems are less important in parliamentary systems, where policy coordination is usually better, but can occur when the government is a minority government or when a prime minister wants to handle policy outside the normal legislative channels. There is nothing in a VER that would *require* the British Prime Minister to consult either with parliament or with cabinet before finishing the negotiations.

WHO USES VERS AND WHO IS HIT BY THEM?

Of the known VERs, about half affected imports to the European Union and a quarter were placed on imports to the United States. The greatest impact was in textiles and clothing, steel, autos, and agriculture. Japan has only a tiny number, almost all involving various sorts of textiles from China, Korea, and Pakistan. About three quarters of all VERs have been aimed at less-developed countries, Japan, and Eastern Europe. Recently, about a third of Japan's exports to Europe and the United States were covered by some 70 arrangements. (Japan has often defused demands for VERs by investment abroad, as when it has built auto plants in the United States in response to protectionist pressures against car imports.)[48] Other unknown VERs may exist, involving agreements between private industries or between a government in one country and an industry in another.[49]

Analysis of VERs

When negotiations for a VER get under way, that itself will have an effect. An expected future VER might cause exporters to increase their shipments in an effort to get them in before it is implemented, or it might cause them to decrease shipments in an attempt to persuade the importer that the problem is disappearing. A decrease is more likely if exporters are collusive and act together and if the threats are dire.[50]

Many consequences of a VER are identical to those of a quota. The revenue effect is an exception. It goes to the exporter. (Only if buyers in the importing country were monopsonistic would they be able to extract much of this revenue.) The most common outcome of negotiations is for the government in the exporting nation to agree to issue export licenses to its companies, as is done in Taiwan or Hong Kong. The revenue may accrue to private companies if the licenses to export are given away, as is most frequently true. After a VER with the U.S. covering automobiles, for instance, Japanese car exporters just raised the price of their cars to the higher American price (by some 13-20%). The revenue may accrue to the exporters' government if it auctions off the licenses in a competitive market. If the bidding is rigged, the revenue will be shared in some proportion by government and producers.

In several Asian countries, including Korea, Malaysia, Taiwan, Hong Kong, and Singapore, the struggle to obtain some of the export licenses has become a major factor in politics and economics. The recipients are typically chosen by allocating part of the quotas according to prior market share and the rest as a reward to firms that are doing best in exports to unrestricted

markets. The allocation is run like a con-
test that rewards good performance.[51]
(Often, license holders must use at least
half of their allocation and see to it that
most of what they do not use is used by
others.) In South Korea and Taiwan, the
quota rights cannot be transferred. In
Hong Kong where over 1,000 quota brokers manage the transactions, they can be
sold. It is curious how a government like
that of the United States, which lectures
less-developed countries on the importance of a free-enterprise economy, has
fostered the growth of cartels and state
control abroad to further American
protectionism.

Because many VERs involve an element
of market-sharing and collusion, exporting nations can certainly gain from them
at the expense of the importers that
imposed them. A gain can occur because the revenue obtained from the
higher price charged, all of which is profit, more than offsets the profits lost
because of the smaller volume allowed. Figure 4.13, yet another variation on
our basic tariff diagram, shows how this can be so. The two rectangles labeled
F and G represent the revenue lost to the exporter when complying with the
VER—the old volume of exports, Q_1Q_4, minus the new volume Q_2Q_3 times
the old price, P_x. The compensation for going along with a VER is the
revenue rectangle, R. Michel Kostecki estimates that transfers of revenues
associated with VERs totaled $27 billion a year in the 1980s.[52] Here the
capture of revenue from the higher price is greater than the loss in revenues
because sales volume has declined; that is, $F + G < R$ as shown in the figure.
There is an unambiguous gain to exporting firms, as well as to producers in
the importing country. The profits of both can rise, with consumers footing
the bill—a bill that has been estimated to be about the same as if a U.S. tariff
of about 25% had been placed on all U.S. imports.[53]

Even if the increase in price is a smaller portion of the export price, as in
Figure 4.14, it is still quite possible that the exporter will gain more profits
than it loses. Here R is much smaller than $F + G$, but remember that R is
pure gain while the revenues shown by areas F and G include all the
exporter's production costs as well as profit. Under competitive conditions in
world trade, the profit component of $F + G$ would be normal profit only,
likely to be just a fraction of the total area involved. The addition to profits

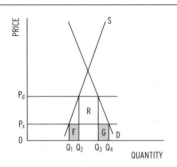

Figure 4.13

VER FAVORING EXPORTER

Note: Under tariffs, the revenue
effect R goes to the government,
while under a VER it goes to the
foreign exporter. But the exporter loses sales revenue of $F + G$.
If R is larger than $F + G$, the
exporter is surely better off.

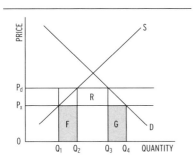

Figure 4.14

FOREIGN FIRMS MIGHT
GAIN EVEN WHEN F + G > R

from the capture of *R* could easily exceed the loss of normal profit as total revenue declines.

Though calculating the gain or loss can be complex and even impossible because of inadequacies in data covering foreign firms, a general principle is clear. The outcome will depend on the elasticities involved. If, for instance, the United States negotiated a VER with Canada on nickel, it would surely be to Canada's great gain, since the U.S. supply of nickel is highly inelastic (there is none being mined) and the demand, because it is an ingredient in other products like stainless steel, is also highly inelastic. Prices would rise greatly, as in Figure 4.13 rather than 4.14.

Even if a VER brings an exporting country profits sufficient to offset the loss as sales volume falls, losses of other kinds to that country may still ensue. Growth in exports will be curtailed, economies of scale and effects of learning will be lost, and the spur of competition from new firms challenging the old in export markets will diminish. On the other hand, it is conceivable that the revenues transferred to a restrained country because of a VER might be plowed back into investment and technical improvement, leaving that country in a better competitive position than before.

Still, the significant chance that exporters' profits will rise possesses undoubted allure. To some large extent, therefore, a VER creates interest groups abroad for its perpetuation. Firms that can rely on getting their piece of the quota may avoid vigorous price competition, may lose their competitive edge, and may instead work very hard on the lobbying or corruption involved in obtaining a large quota. When it is suggested that quotas be dropped, many of these firms may oppose that plan, in a sense because their comparative advantage has been in developing the connections needed to get the quotas. How, for example, could the complex VERs with Japan on steel and cars have evolved without considerable Japanese help? Foreign lobbyists support domestic ones, with perhaps a more protectionist result than if only domestic lobbyists were at work. Large, established foreign firms use the VER procedure to exclude newcomers and small firms, raising their enthusiasm for the arrangement.[54] Smaller nations awarded an unusually large quota, for foreign policy reasons perhaps, might also end up supporting the VER in order to retain their artificially large share of the market.

Several other outcomes of a VER are possible or probable. As prices rise, the market share of exporting countries not included under the restraints is likely to increase. A terms-of-trade effect may occur, with world prices falling because exports are reduced. If that is so, an even greater incentive is created for other exporters not restrained under the VER to divert shipments to the export market where prices have risen. (For example, in the late 1970s Japan was the source of 90% of U.S. imports of color TVs, but then a VER was negotiated. This caused the Japanese market share to fall to 50%; the slack was not taken up by U.S. producers but by those of Korea and Taiwan. These countries as well then had to be included in the restraint.) Exporters also may attempt to evade the VER by laundering their shipments through uncovered countries, which may be reasonably easy if the product concerned is homogeneous and its place of origin difficult to identify—cheap shoes and clothing, for example. Circumvention may also be possible if a nation facing a VER has plants in other countries from which the goods can be shipped without being subject to control. The more easily these can be started up, the less effective the VER will be. The European Union has recently been concerned that its VERs with Japan could be circumvented if the Japanese raise their exports to Europe from their U.S. plants.

AN ADMINISTRATION MIGHT EVEN DESIRE A POROUS VER

A Machiavellian might argue that a porous VER could give the appearance of protection to a legislature and the public, while actually approximating free trade conditions. In this reading the administration might advocate a VER as much to defuse protectionist pressure as to promote it. The administration could rightly claim that a VER had been negotiated, but could then be rather slow in adding new countries to it or rather lax in policing it. Prices would perhaps rise little, if at all.

Even a Machiavellian might on occasion be fooled, however. A VER that was set at the current level of imports could still result in higher prices if potential monopoly power were converted into actual monopoly power, as discussed in our earlier treatment of quotas.

For the importing country that imposed the VER in the first place, other features stand out. Because it is the outcome of negotiations, the VER is unlikely to provoke retaliation by the exporting nation. Offsetting this major advantage, however, is the expensive loss of the revenue effect, estimated to be about $5 billion in the United States when the greatest number of VERs were in effect.[55] Nothing comes back even from the income tax, as would happen if domestic firms protected by a quota garnered the revenue effect. When a foreign firm sells at a high price under a VER, it keeps the gains.

This litany of adverse consequences explains why many economists believe that international surveillance and regulation of VERs should have the highest priority in trade negotiations. Some limits have recently been placed on VERs, as we shall see in Chapter 6. But ways have been found to retain them and new ones are still being negotiated. A U.S.-Russian VER dating from February 1999 is designed to cut back Russian steel exports to the United States to 79% below the 1998 figure. They are likely to be with us for a long time yet.[*]

Conclusion: Where We Go from Here

Tariffs, quotas, TRQs, and VERs are the most familiar of the interferences with trade. They are far from the only distortions to trade, however. Politicians, in league with business people, have become increasingly innovative, finding other, less familiar means to interfere with trade flows. In the major countries, the most successful users of the old and new tools of protection against foreign competition have included the producers of textiles and clothing, steel, autos, and agriculture. The next chapter examines a variety of other less familiar distortions to trade and then looks at the industries that have been most successful in using the weapons in the armory of protectionism.

---

[*] A very new idea, a sort of mirror image to a VER, is a *voluntary import expansion*. Perhaps countries such as South Korea and Taiwan, with large trade surpluses, could be pressured "voluntarily" to raise their level of imports, thus diminishing these surpluses and increasing the exports of trading partners such as the EU and United States. There have even been attempts to get *voluntary import restraint agreements*, particularly in U.S. wood and wood-product exports to Japan. The idea was to limit price rises in the United States along the lines of the Nixon export quota on soybeans discussed earlier.

APPENDIX: THE TERMS-OF-TRADE EFFECT IN GENERAL EQUILIBRIUM

To examine the terms-of-trade effect in a more general setting, it is convenient to use the offer curves developed in Chapter 2. Offer curves allow us not only to see clearly that a large country can affect the world price level, but also to examine the effects of the retaliation that may follow.

In Figure 4.15, *0F* is the offer curve for Fabrica under free trade conditions, while *0A* is the offer curve for Agricola. The equilibrium terms of trade is *0E*. If Fabrica puts a tariff on wheat imports, that will have the effect of moving (distorting) its original offer curve *0F*. Why this is so can be seen at any point on the curve, such as *X*. Here Fabrica was formerly willing to trade *0W* cloth for *WX* wheat. Now, however, Fabrica is willing to give up *0W* cloth only if it obtains the greater quantity *WY* wheat, if *XY* wheat is collected by government as a tariff. Here the tariff rate is *XY/WX*, a rate that looks to be on the order of 33%. Point *Y* is one point on a new tariff-distorted offer curve *0F'*.

We can find other new points in the same manner. Take any other position on the original Fabrican offer curve *0F*, for example at *X'*. Then calculate *X'Y'/W'X' = XY/WX*. This and other such calculations yield a series of new points that lie on an offer curve *0F'*. The new Fabrican offer curve's intersection with the Agricolan offer curve gives a new equilibrium terms of trade *0E'*. The end result is that Fabrica finds its imported wheat is cheaper, and its exported cloth is more expensive, than was true before it imposed the tariff.

As is explained in the text, when a country can affect world prices, there is

Figure 4.15

A TARIFF SHIFTS THE TERMS OF TRADE

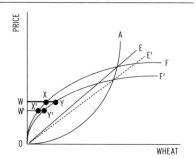

Note: Because a tariff displaces the importing country's offer curve, it may be possible to shift the terms of trade in favor of that country (in the figure from *0E* to *0E'*).

the possibility that it can improve its welfare by means of a tariff that shifts the terms of trade in its favor. (Note how at the new equilibrium Fabrica gives up considerably less cloth to get only a little less wheat.) This gain in welfare is to Fabrica only, however, and is a loss of welfare to Agricola, which finds that its wheat buys less cloth than before. This is why Agricolan retaliation would be very likely, with Agricola raising its own tariffs to recapture the lost welfare.

The results of retaliation are shown in Figure 4.16. Take the case of an imaginary struggle between the United States and the EU. Figure 4.16a shows the EU's offer curve shifted downward as a tariff is imposed by the EU members against imports from the United States. This improves the EU's terms of trade, as shown.

Figure 4.16
A TRADE WAR SHOWN WITH OFFER CURVES

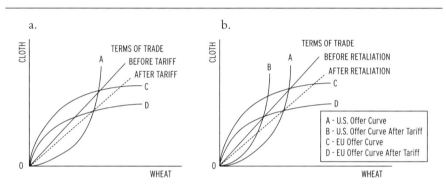

Note: An attempt to move the terms of trade in one's favor may beget a retaliatory tariff, with the terms of trade much as before but with a substantial reduction in the overall level of trade.

In Figure 4.16b, however, the United States retaliates, putting a tariff on EU cloth and thus shifting its own offer curve upward. The terms of trade return to their original relationship. In that sense the retaliation is justified, but total trade is much reduced.

VOCABULARY AND CONCEPTS

Ad valorem duty	Pass-through effect
Consumer surplus	Producer surplus
Consumer tax equivalent	Producers' subsidy effect
Consumption effect	Production effect
Deadweight loss (consumer and producer)	Redistribution effect
Economic rent (from protection)	Revenue effect
Export quotas	Specialization effects
Export taxes	Specific duty
Import effect	Tariffs
Import quotas	Tariff-rate quotas (TRQs)
Incidence of tariffs	Terms-of-trade effect
Lobbying effect	Uniform tariffs
Nominal and effective tariffs	Voluntary export restraints (VERs)
Optimal tariff	X-inefficiency effect

QUESTIONS

1. Explain what a tariff is, and distinguish *ad valorem* from specific duties. Which is harder to administer? Which is best for consumers?
2. "The arguments over categorization are ultimately very sad, as fine and often silly distinctions come to affect much that is serious and important." Comment.
3. "The decision as to where to manufacture or assemble a product is related not to the nominal tariff, but to the effective tariff." Explain what an effective tariff is and explain the statement.
4. How are effective tariffs measured?
5. Explain, using demand and supply curves, the gains and losses from instituting a tariff. Show the production effect, the consumption effect, the import effect, the change in consumer and producer surpluses, the revenue effect, and the consumers' and producers' deadweight losses. Explain briefly the deadweight losses.
6. Deadweight losses probably are not very high. Explain why this is so.
7. Even if deadweight losses are not high, tariffs could cause a considerable loss in efficiency. What other kinds of efficiency losses are there?
8. Even if deadweight losses are not high, we still have major questions about the redistribution effect and the party taxed. Explain why they are important.
9. "Ultimately, tariffs are paid by exporters." Explain.
10. What is the terms-of-trade effect? How is it related to the rather esoteric concept of an optimal tariff? Demonstrate with a diagram.
11. What is the nature of demand and supply between two countries that would cause a tariff to be absorbed by the exporting nation?

12. What is a rent and how do tariffs produce it?

13. Demonstrate, using a diagram, that it is rational for producers to seek rents, and indicate at what point they should stop paying to secure them.

14. Explain how the effects of a quota differ from those of a tariff.

15. Economists dislike quotas far more than tariffs. Discuss why, covering the issues of rent (from the revenue effect), rigidity, monopoly power, and administration.

16. Why are many quotas being replaced by tariff-rate quotas, and how do the two differ from one another?

17. Explain what VERS are and why they became so popular. How do they differ from quotas?

18. Sometimes the exporter is eager to have a VER. Under what circumstances would this occur?

NOTES

1. As suggested by Douglas A. Irwin, "Changes in U.S. Tariffs: The Role of Import Prices and Commercial Policies," *American Economic Review* 88, 4 (September 1998): 1015-26.

2. See D.D. Humphrey, *The U.S. and the Common Market* (New York: Praeger, 1964).

3. USITC, *The Year in Trade 1993* (Washington, 1994), 15.

4. Anne O. Krueger, "Trade Policy and Economic Development: How We Learn," *American Economic Review* 87, 1 (March 1997): 1-22.

5. Gary Clyde Hufbauer and Kimberly Ann Elliott, *Measuring the Costs of Protection in the United States* (Washington: Institute for International Economics, 1994), 46-77.

6. See the *Wall Street Journal*, February 17, 25, 1989.

7. Ibid., May 17, 1993.

8. The sewing kit and opera set stories are from ibid., September 27, 1988. The tale of the girls' ski jackets is from James Bovard, "The Customs Service's Fickle Philosophy," ibid., July 31, 1991. Some of the anecdotes in the box were reported in the *Christian Science Monitor*, July 15, 1983.

9. The history and analysis are covered thoroughly by W.M. Corden, *The Theory of Protection* (Oxford: Oxford University Press, 1971), 35-40, 245-49.

10. The tale is from Humphrey, *The U.S. and the Common Market*.

11. See Peter Kenen, *The International Economy* (Englewood Cliffs, N.J.: Prentice-Hall, 1985), 183-84.

12. For some of these, see Emmanuel Opoku Awuku, "How Do the Results of the Uruguay Round Affect the North-South Trade?" *Journal of World Trade* 28, 2 (April 1994): 75, citing E. Mayo.

13. "The Uruguay Round: Winners and Winners," *World Bank Policy Research Bulletin* 6, 1 (January-February 1995): 3.

14. There is an analytical study by Stephen S. Golub and J.M. Finger, "The Processing of Primary Commodities: Effects of Developed-Country Tariff Escalation and Developing-Country Export Taxation," *Journal of Political Economy* 87, 3 (1979): 559-77.

15. Based on 1970s data and quoted in the Brandt Commission Report, *North-South: A Programme for Survival* (London: Pan Books, 1980), 141-42.

16. World Bank, *World Development Report 1990*, 125.

17. *The Economist*, July 25, 1998.

18. See ibid., September 23, 1989.

19. Hufbauer and Elliott, *Measuring the Costs of Protection*.

20. See "The Consumer Cost of U.S. Trade Restraints," *Federal Reserve Bank of New York Quarterly Review* 10, 2 (Summer 1985): 1-12; for the World Bank figures, a citation in *The Economist*, September 13, 1986, 15.

21. Mancur Olson, "The Political Economy of Comparative Growth Rates," paper presented at the Cliometrics Conference, University of Chicago, May 1978, 92. A recent volume that emphasizes the role of competition in promoting more productive and innovative business behavior is Michael Porter, *The Competitive Advantage of Nations* (New York: Free Press, 1990).

22. One interesting test is reported by Walter Primeaux, "An Assessment of X-Efficiency Gained Through Competition," *Review of Economics and Statistics* 59 (February 1977): 105-08.

23. Thomas J. Schoenbaum, "The Theory of Contestable Markets in International Trade," *Journal of World Trade* 30, 3 (June 1996): 161-90.

24. T.T. Nguyen and R.M. Wigle, "Trade Liberalisation with Increased Competition: The Large and the Small of It," *European Economic Review* 26 (1992): 17-36, esp. Table 3.

25. Schoenbaum, "The Theory of Contestable Markets."

26. F.M. Scherer, *International High-Technology Competition* (Cambridge, Mass.: Harvard University Press, 1992). Some of the points in the paragraph are made by W. Max Corden, *Protection and Liberalization: A Review of Analytical Issues*, IMF Occasional Paper 54 (Washington: IMF, 1987), 14-15. The negative effects of protection on economic growth are explored further by Bernhard Heitger, "Import Protection and Export Performance," *Weltwirtschaftliches Archiv* 123, 2 (1987): 249-61.

27. See *International Economic Review*, November/December 1997.

28. See Jeffrey D. Sachs and Andrew Warner, "Economic Reform and the Process of Global Integration,"*Brookings Papers on Economic Activity* 1 (1995): 1-118; Jeffrey Frankel and David Romer, "Trade and Growth: An Empirical Investigation," NBER Working Paper No. 5476, 1996; Sebastian Edwards, "Openness, Productivity and Growth: What Do We Really Know," *Economic Journal* 108, 447 (March 1998): 383-98; Jeffrey A. Frankel and David Romer, "Does Trade Cause Growth?" *American Economic Review* 89, 3 (June 1999): 379-99; *Economic Report of the President 1998* (Washington: Council of Economic Advisors, 1998), 238.

29. See work of David Morrison reported in *The Economist*, January 31, 1987. For a recent study of how changes in currency values affect prices, see Pinelopi Koujianou Goldberg and Michael M. Knetter, "Goods Prices and Exchange Rates: What Have We Learned?" *Journal of Economic Literature* 35, 3 (September 1997): 1243-72.

30. See Kenneth Clements and Larry Sjaastad, *How Protection Taxes Exporters* (London: Trade Policy Research Centre, 1985), and the discussion of this work in *The Economist*, May 25, 1985, 69.

31. Stephen P. Magee, "The Political Economy of Trade Policy," in David Greenaway and L. Alan Winters, *Surveys in International Trade* (Oxford: Basil Blackwell, 1994), 143, 156.

32. They are called Tullock Costs by some economists. See Gordon Tullock, "The Welfare Costs of Tariffs, Monopolies, and Theft," *Western Economic Journal* 5 (June 1967): 224-32.

33. See Jagdish Bhagwati, *Protectionism* (Cambridge, Mass.: MIT Press, 1988), 103-04. Other sources used for our analysis of rent-seeking are Robert E. Baldwin and T. Scott Thompson, "Responding to Trade-Distorting Policies of Other Countries," *American Economic Review* 74, 2 (May 1984): 271-76; Magee, "The Political Economy of Trade Policy"; Stephen P. Magee, William A. Brock, and Leslie Young, *Black Hole Tariffs and Endogenous Policy Theory: Political Economy in General Equilibrium* (Cambridge: Cambridge University Press, 1989); Neil Vousden, *The Economics of Trade Protection* (Cambridge: Cambridge University Press, 1990).

34. See John T. Wenders, "On Perfect Rent Dissipation," *American Economic Review* 77, 3 (June 1987): 456-59.

35. For comments on which firms lobby hardest, see Stefanie Lenway, Randall Morck, and Bernard Yeung, "Rent Seeking, Protectionism and Innovation in the American Steel Industry," *Economic Journal* 106, 435 (March 1996): 410-21.

36. Magee, "The Political Economy of Trade Policy," 153.

37. The evidence is noted by W.M. Corden, *Trade Policy and Economic Welfare* (Oxford: Oxford University Press, 1974), 182-84, citing Arnold Harberger, M.E. Kreinen, J.E. Floyd, Giorgio Basevia, and Franklin V. Walker.

38. See C. Fred Bergsten, Kimberly Ann Elliott, Jeffrey J. Schott, and Wendy E. Takacs, *Auction Quotas and United States Trade Policy* (Washington: Institute for International Economics, 1987). For a discussion of how such auctions might work in the presence of monopoly power, see Wendy E. Takacs, "Economic Aspects of Quota License Auctions," *Journal of World Trade* 22, 6 (December 1988): 39-51.

39. *Wall Street Journal*, March 3, 16, 1994.

40. The variations brought about in the presence of monopolies or oligopolies of producers of export goods, exporters of these goods, and importing firms are detailed by Elhanan Helpman and Paul R. Krugman, *Trade Policy and Market Structure* (Cambridge, Mass.: MIT Press, 1989), esp. ch. 3; Bergsten et al., *Auction Quotas and United States Trade Policy*, Appendix A, 185-203.

41. This proof is provided in the appendices to various editions of the Lindert and Lindert and Kindleberger text, *International Economics* (Homewood, Ill.: Richard D. Irwin).

42. See Corden, *Trade Policy and Economic Welfare*, 202-03.

43. Margaret Kelly and Anne Kenny McGuirk, *Issues and Developments in International Trade Policy* (Washington: IMF, 1992), 100.

44. USITC, *Operation of the Trade Agreements Program, 40th Report*, 1988, 133; *The Economist*, September 9, 1989.

45. See Kent Jones, "Voluntary Export Restraint: Political Economy, History and the Role of the GATT," *Journal of World Trade* 23, 3 (June 1989): 129.

46. Michel M. Kostecki, "Marketing Strategies and Voluntary Export Restraints," *Journal of World Trade* 25, 4 (August 1991): 87-99.

47. The total number of VERS was reported by Margaret Kelly, Naheed Kirmani, Miranda Xafa, Clemens Boonekamp, and Peter Winglee, *Issues and Developments in International Trade Policy*, IMF Occasional Paper No. 63 (Washington: IMF, December 1988), 1-2. The percentage is from Kostecki, "Marketing Strategies and Voluntary Export Restraints."

48. Bruce A. Blonigen and Robert C. Feenstra, "Protectionist Threats and Foreign Direct Investment," in Feenstra, ed., *The Effects of U.S. Trade Protection and Promotion Policies* (Chicago: University of Chicago Press, 1997), 55-80.

49. For the numbers, see Kelly and McGuirk, *Issues and Developments in International Trade Policy*, 24, 117; Magee, "The Political Economy of Trade Policy," 162; Clemens F.J. Boonekamp, "Voluntary Export Restraints," *Finance and Development* 24, 4 (December 1987): 2-5. Boonekamp's analysis of VERS is also used at several subsequent points in the text.

50. L. Alan Winters, "VERS and Expectations: Extensions and Evidence," *Economic Journal* 104, 422 (January 1994): 113-23.

51. World Bank, *The East Asian Miracle: Economic Growth and Public Policy* (New York: Oxford University Press, 1993), 98.

52. For the Kostecki estimate, see Boonekamp, "Voluntary Export Restraints." The year was 1984.

53. Magee, "The Political Economy of Trade Policy," 163.

54. Ibid.

55. The $5 billion estimate is from Robert E. Baldwin, "U.S. Trade Policy: Recent Changes and Future U.S. Interests," *AEA Papers and Proceedings* 79, 2 (May 1989): 132.

Chapter Five

The Face of
Modern Protectionism

OBJECTIVES

OVERALL OBJECTIVE   To demonstrate that it is not just tariffs, quotas, TRQs, and VERs, but a broad array of subsidies, laws, rules, and institutions that distort trade, acting as barriers to the free import of goods and services and as stimulants to exporting.

MORE SPECIFICALLY
  • To identify and expound on distortions to trade—subsidies on production, exports, and imports; taxes with implications for trade; administrative protection; technical, health, safety, and environmental standards; and restrictions on trade in services.
  • To show the techniques for measuring the distortions to trade.
  • To convey a sense of the way in which firms use such laws for their own benefit, emphasizing the industries and sectors most famous for success in obtaining trade barriers.

....

Tariffs, quotas, TRQs, and VERs are the most familiar of the distortions to trade. Trade today is affected by many other distortions, however, including subsidies and taxes of various kinds that stimulate exports or discourage imports, and a wide variety of less familiar non-tariff barriers (NTBs) applied to imports at the border and non-tariff measures (NTMs, a broader term including administrative, health, safety, and environmental standards that may sometimes distort trade). Of the hundreds of different sorts of existing distortions to trade, many have little effect on trade flows and can therefore be safely ignored here. Some, however, are an important part of the international economic environment and warrant description. The first part of this chapter looks at these devices and how the amount of protection they provide might be compared. (Blessedly, with the exception of subsidies, they do not require much additional economic analysis.) The chapter then concludes with a review of the industries, including textiles and clothing, steel, autos, and agriculture, that have had the most success in engineering trade distortions in all their forms for their own benefit.

SUBSIDY AND TAX ISSUES

Subsidies and taxes interfere with free-market pricing and can introduce distortions to comparative advantage. These distortions take several forms.

Subsidies to Production

If a nation decides that the public welfare requires the maintenance of an aircraft industry or a shoe industry, would it not be better just to subsidize it directly, rather than blocking imports of the product? Furthermore, if comparative advantage is influenced by economies of scale, industrial concentration, experience, and product specialization, then perhaps a government might conclude that subsidies as part of an industrial strategy will provide a head start. These propositions can be analyzed by means of the familiar tariff effect diagram, Figure 4.1, modified here in Figure 5.1 to show a subsidy.[1]

With no barriers to imports, goods enter the country at the world price P_w. Domestic production at that price is Q_1 while imports are Q_1Q_4. Now assume that the government pays a direct subsidy of P_wP_d per unit produced by domestic firms. In first-year economics, students learn that a sales-type *tax* shifts the supply curve vertically upward, because suppliers would continue to act as they did before the tax only if the full amount of the tax were paid to them in the form of higher prices. Conversely, a per-unit *subsidy* shifts the supply curve vertically downward, reflecting that a supplier would be willing to market a

Figure 5.1

A PER-UNIT SUBSIDY
PAID ON PRODUCTION

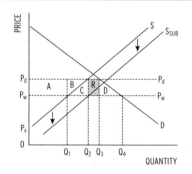

Note: A direct subsidy amounting to the difference between S and S_{SUB} shifts the supply curve, leaving the domestic price at world price levels, avoiding both the revenue (R) effect and consumer deadweight loss effect (D).

given amount of a good at the former price less the amount of the subsidy. Using this standard analysis, a subsidy equal to $P_w P_d$ per unit would shift the supply curve in Figure 5.1 from S to S_{SUB}.

This case has been designed so that the quantity of output rises because of the per-unit subsidy $P_w P_d$ by exactly the same amount, from Q_1 to Q_2, as would have been true in the presence of a tariff $P_w P_d$. See how with a price of P_w domestic firms with their new supply curve S_{SUB} would produce a quantity Q_2. We can then compare the various costs of a subsidy to the costs of a tariff, given that domestic industry is stimulated to exactly the same degree. The total cost of the subsidy is the subsidy per unit $P_w P_d$ times the number of units, Q_2, which is equal to the area of the rectangle $A + B + C$. That, we recall, is just enough to cause producers to raise their output to Q_2 rather than remaining at Q_1; they respond just as if the price were P_d, even though it remains at P_w.

Because consumers continue to pay the price P_w, there is no tariff revenue generated (R) or consumer deadweight loss (D). The net loss for the economy is only triangle C, the producer deadweight loss. As taxpayers, consumers must pay $A + B + C$. If a tariff had been in place, consumers would have paid $A + B + C + R$, but R represents revenue to the government so taxes could be lower or government services could be increased. Therefore, the main difference between a subsidy and a tariff is that the portion of consumer surplus shown by triangle D, lost under a tariff, is restored. If a quota were in place instead of a tariff, then the damage to society would be greater and to that extent more benefits would flow from using subsidies instead. With a quota the revenue effect R will usually go to the importers lucky enough to have a license to import. Consumers lose C, D and R. If a VER is used rather than a quota, the outcome is more dramatic and a subsidy, therefore, even more advantageous: C, D, and R continue to be losses, but in this case the revenue effect R will most likely be captured by the foreign exporters.

The taxes to pay for the subsidy could certainly carry welfare costs of their own, as explained in the accompanying box on costs associated with the tax collection. One would not, therefore, want to insist that a given subsidy *must* carry fewer distortions than a tariff or a quota. The tax system currently in use would have to be examined with care to see if its distortions might not be larger than those carried by the protectionist tools. It is highly unlikely, however, that the tax systems of the United States, the EU, and Japan are nearly so distortionary as is trade protectionism.

The main reason economists favor subsidies over tariffs, quotas, TRQs, and VERs is actually a different one: the subsidies are visible. The legislature and the press review the government's budget frequently. Both the incidence of taxes and the effects of subsidies come under consideration in a normal legislative process, however unsatisfactory it may seem. Tariffs, quotas, and

TAX COLLECTIONS CARRY WELFARE COSTS OF THEIR OWN

An income tax with high marginal rates can, by reducing incentives, affect the amount of effort expended. A sales-type tax introduces distortions of its own, because the tax introduces a wedge between prices and costs. Consumers would be willing to pay for one additional unit of output more than the cost to society of producing that additional unit. In the 1960s and early 1970s, economists believed that the distortions caused by taxes were relatively modest, but later the pendulum swung far in the other direction. A common view of the 1980s was that taxes had large effects on economic behavior. The more recent view is that labor supply is *not* very sensitive to tax policy, and especially that moderate tax increases will not lead to a severe decline in work effort in any but the world's highest-tax countries, of which the United States is not one. In any case, there is a type of tax that theoretically can avoid these difficulties: the lump-sum progressive levy on income that tax experts suggest would eliminate the distortions accompanying standard income and sales-type taxes. Lump-sum progressive taxes have proved difficult to implement, however, both administratively and for political reasons.

VERs tend to escape scrutiny, however, perhaps for very long periods of time. In general, economists do not approve of subsidies, but at least they are less damaging than tariffs and quotas as long as the tax system carries fewer distortions than does the protection (which is very likely). Even if the tax system is poorly constructed, the subsidies will receive much more frequent critical review. Consequently, there is less danger that they will fossilize into permanent features.

In spite of the advantages of subsidies, politicians will often decide not to adopt them. The costs of the subsidy will be in the national budget, financed by an unpalatable tax increase or an unwelcome rise in the budget deficit, whereas the costs of a tariff or quota are not in the budget at all. Legislatures may thus shun subsidies, even though economists would note that the public very probably bears a *greater* burden with tariffs, but especially with quotas and VERs.

As we shall see in Chapter 7, when subsidies are paid they can give rise to considerable international controversy. Such payments on output, which is then exported, often violate the laws of the importing country, and the resulting penalties are legal under the rules of international trade. There is widespread disagreement on just what does and does not constitute a subsidy. Included in these grey areas are regional development grants (Britain, France, Italy), tax holidays and concessions (France, Italy), accelerated depreciation

(France, Germany, Japan, the United States), cheap loans (Germany, Italy, Japan), enhanced unemployment compensation for seasonal industries (Canada), and cheap government-controlled prices for natural resources (Canada, Mexico). An international consensus on the meaning of the word "subsidy" has yet to be attained.

Subsidies on Exports Only

Instead of subsidies paid on production, a government could pay the subsidy on exports only. This strategy has quite different results, as seen in Figure 5.2.

Figure 5.2

ANALYZING AN EXPORT SUBSIDY

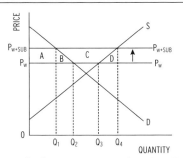

Say a country has an advantage in the production of computers, so that exports Q_2Q_3 are occurring at a world price (P_w) that is slightly above the no-trade equilibrium price. Assume the country is a small one, so that the world demand for its exported computers is perfectly elastic, at a price P_w. What if the country now pays an export subsidy of $100 on each computer produced? That would raise the amount received per unit by computer manufacturers to the price P_w plus the amount of the subsidy, or $P_{w + \text{SUB}}$.

Note: A subsidy on exports only raises P_w to $P_{w + \text{SUB}}$. Consumers lose $A + B$, producers gain $A + B + C$, and the subsidy costs the government $B + C + D$. The result is a net loss of triangles $B + D$.

Suppliers will then raise the quantity they export from the old amount Q_2Q_3 to the new and higher Q_1Q_4. They will not sell at home for a price any less than $P_{w + \text{SUB}}$ per computer, because with world demand elastic, they could always earn that amount from their international sales. Since the domestic price will thus rise, domestic demand will decrease to Q_1.[*]

In welfare terms, there is a rise in producer surplus of $A + B + C$. Consumer surplus falls by $A + B$. The cost to the government is the amount

---

[*] In a free market, a backflow of imports would result, with foreigners re-exporting computers acquired at price P_w and selling them in the country of origin for the higher price $P_{w + \text{SUB}}$. To prevent this backflow it will be necessary to erect barriers against their importation. It should also be noted that an export subsidy, by increasing the quantity of exports, could lead to a fall in price in importing countries. This would be an export subsidy's *terms-of-trade effect*, opposite to that of a tariff.

IMPORT SUBSIDIES

Figure 5.3

AN IMPORT SUBSIDY

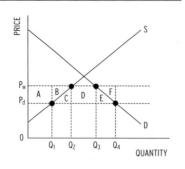

Subsidies on imports are also employed, particularly by less-developed countries. Their effects are the opposite of subsidies on exports. In Figure 5.3 we show a subsidy on rice imported into "Penuristan." When the subsidy of $P_w P_d$ per unit is paid, the domestic price falls to P_d, below the world price P_w. The quantity produced domestically is reduced by $Q_1 Q_2$, while consumption increases from Q_3 to Q_4. Imports thus rise from $Q_2 Q_3$ to $Q_1 Q_4$. The cost of the subsidy to the government is the price per unit $P_w P_d$ times the quantity imported $Q_1 Q_4$, or the area $B + C + D + E + F$.

Now consider the welfare implications. Buyers gain consumer surplus equal to area $A + B + C + D + E$. Local farmers lose producer surplus $A + B$. The government loses $B + C + D + E + F$. Netting the gains against the losses reveals a deadweight loss consisting of the triangles $B + F$.

of the subsidy on each unit (the distance from P_w to $P_{w + \text{SUB}}$) times the quantity exported ($Q_1 Q_4$). This yields a rectangle $B + C + D$. Against the gain of $A + B + C$ there are losses of $A + B$ and $B + C + D$. Netting these reveals a loss to society of the triangles B and D. The area D is a loss because foreigners are obtaining the country's computers at a price below the social (resource) costs of producing them. The other triangle, B, can be seen first as lost consumer surplus because the price has risen; second as a rise in producer surplus; and third as part of the government subsidy, which is a cost. Thus, two losses weigh in the balance against one gain, the net result being that triangle B is lost.

If an export subsidy is sufficiently large, it could conceivably turn an importer into an exporter. Glance back at Figure 5.2. If the world price had started out at a price below where domestic supply and demand curves cross, the country would have been an importer. An export subsidy that pushed the price up above the crossing point would make the country into an exporter. That is what has happened in the EU for some agricultural commodities.

The World Trade Organization (WTO), which umpires the international rules on trade, holds that subsidies paid on exports of manufactured goods are illegal for developed countries and that an importing country can countervail them with penalty duties when they are detected. They are still commonly found in agriculture, however, and less-developed countries have been able to employ export subsidies more freely.

The subject of subsidies to industry, either generally or on exports, has rapidly achieved new status as the possibilities for a strategic trade policy have been perceived and understood. That topic is considered in Chapter 7.

Subsidies on Export Credit

Export credit subsidies involve low-cost credit advances to the buyers of a country's exports. The major industrial countries all have agencies granting export credits to overseas buyers: Britain's Export Credit Guarantee Department, Germany's Hermes and Kreditanstalt für Wiederaufbau, France's Coface and Banque Française du Commerce Extérieur, Canada's Export Development Corporation, the Export-Import Bank of Japan, and the Export-Import (Exim) Bank of the United States.[2]

A source of trade distortion arose from the financing of exports by these agencies because the rate of interest charged to borrowers was well below the

---

HOW THE U.S. EXPORT-IMPORT BANK WORKS

The U.S. Exim Bank illustrates how these agencies work in practice. The Bank was founded in 1934, intended to finance trade between the United States and the Soviet Union. That plan did not succeed because the Soviets made no use of the new institution. But the Exim Bank survived.

The Exim Bank does nothing to assist imports, and thus its name is a misnomer. Its main function is to borrow from the U.S. Treasury and then lend the proceeds to foreign buyers of U.S. exports. A study by the U.S. Treasury has estimated that two-thirds of U.S. exports financed by the Exim Bank would probably not have been made without the financing. The proportion of U.S. exports financed in this way is actually quite small, only about 3%. Most U.S. exports are financed by commercial banks. Other countries' agencies finance a much greater proportion of their exports, ranging from Germany's 6% to France's 23% and Japan's 51%.[3]

The Exim Bank, and the foreign agencies as well, now also insure against the risk of non-payment by buyers. It was once widely believed that government export insurance was justified because private insurance was expensive and limited in coverage. More recently, economists have argued that these gaps are not market failures, but instead reflect high risks and difficulties in identifying these risks on a worldwide basis. If so, then the government export insurance also represents an element of subsidy on exports.

---

market rates they would have had to pay for commercial loans. In the late 1970s, a credit war broke out among the major developed countries, with their agencies competing to cut the rates they charged on export credits. Rates reached 25-30% below market rates.

As long ago as 1980, governments tried to establish consensus rates for export credit, but these agreements tended to break down with competition emerging once again. Later, the agreements were policed more strictly and the rates were kept closer to market levels. Emphasis then turned to subsidizing the credit portion of foreign aid to less-developed countries when the credit is part of a package that also includes government grants of aid. The latest agreement dates from 1995. Under its terms, subsidized export credit is permitted only for the group of less-developed countries and when commercial finance is not available.

But why should a government provide *any* export credit at all? The justification for it is market failure, with credit from government filling a gap in what is available commercially. Critics note the increased scale and sophistication of international banking today. They ask why governments are making loans that commercial interests will not make. If the private reluctance to lend is a sign of high risks and difficulties in identifying these risks (as noted in the box above), then the government export credits, even at market rates, contain an element of subsidy on exports. Critics also maintain that any one country's export credit agency is partly a defense against what other countries do. They have one and so must we, if only to negotiate it away in due course.

The wisdom of ever subsidizing export credits at all is certainly questionable. A subsidy means transferring income from industrial-country taxpayers (not necessarily rich) to buyers (not necessarily poor) in foreign countries and to the domestic exporters who benefit from the subsidies. It also allows the subsidized firms to transfer resources away from unsubsidized firms, including other exporters. Even when part of a foreign aid package, the subsidized credits do not seem an optimal way to deliver aid to the poor.

Taxes Can Distort Trade

Internal tax systems can distort trade in ways comparable to subsidies.[4] The main potential distortion is caused by value-added taxation (VAT). Almost all industrial countries (excepting only Australia, Switzerland, and the United States), plus many less-developed countries, use the VAT system of indirect taxes. (In Canada it is called the goods and services tax, or GST.) VAT is collected on the value added by the firm being taxed. This is determined by subtracting the money value of purchases from other firms from the money value of sales, the remainder equaling the value added. The rate of tax ranges from Japan's 3% to over 20% in a few countries. VATs typically collect 12-30% of a country's total revenue.

Unless an adjustment is made, trade distortion would occur whenever trade takes place between a country with a high VAT and another with a lower one or none at all. For example, if a good includes a high VAT but is then exported, it would be at a disadvantage in countries charging a lower VAT or none at all. For that reason it is usual to rebate this tax at the border. For symmetry, it is also usual to charge the same amount of tax on imports of the same good. If that were not done, imports from countries with no VAT or a policy of rebating the VAT on its exports would have an advantage over domestic production. Charging the VAT on imports equalizes the price of imports with the price of goods produced domestically.*

In general, if imports were not charged the same VAT that domestic producers must pay, they would receive an advantage against domestic production and more would be imported. If the tax were not rebated on exports, exporters (which cannot pass the tax on to foreign buyers in competitive markets) would bear the loss and would reduce their exports. The tax mechanism would distort trade patterns.

In most cases, that procedure is used and taxation by means of VAT does not distort trade flows. However, if the adjustments are not made, or if they are exaggerated, then VAT can have a substantial effect on trade. For some years Brazil used a scheme of over-rebates, rebating *more* than the initial amount of the tax. The over-rebates, of 11%, were eventually abandoned in the face of heavy international pressure. Japan's VAT is subtraction-style, differing from the usual VAT in that a firm can take a tax credit for purchases from businesses exempt from paying VAT even though no tax was actually paid on the purchase. (There are many exempt businesses in Japan.) That creates a clear incentive for Japanese firms to purchase from other Japanese businesses rather than from importers who do not receive the credit.[5]

There are many other, lesser-known ways that domestic taxation can be used to distort trade. For years the United States has allowed its exporting firms to establish off-shore subsidiaries in tax havens such as the Bahamas and the Cayman Islands. Profits on the exports can be assigned to these subsidiaries, exempting them from taxation. The Canadian government forbids Canadian businesses that advertise in non-Canadian magazines from deducting any of the cost (or more than half the cost after 1999) of the advertising as a business expense when calculating their taxes. This is a major reason why U.S. magazine publishers do not have "split-runs," that is, Canadian editions

---

* This is a clear example of bias in favor of producers. The fairness principle used to justify the charging of VAT on imports is never mentioned when subsidies are used. When domestic production is subsidized, imports are never eligible to receive them, nor do manufacturers have to rebate production subsidies at the border when goods are exported. Logic would seem to compel such treatment, but there would be no advantage in this for producers, and so this extension to the practice is not made.

of U.S. magazines.[6] Another tax issue recently came to light in South Korea. Korean taxpayers must indicate on their tax returns the make of the autos they own. Taxpayers are said to believe that tax audits will be used against buyers of imported cars, and indeed audits are believed to have occurred for this reason. (Korea says it has halted the practice.)[7]

ADMINISTRATIVE PROTECTION

Around the world, most countries have adopted certain laws and regulations that serve in one way or another to protect the domestic market against imports. In this section we examine a number of cases of administrative protection that do not appear to involve technical, health, safety, or environmental considerations (which cases are treated later in the chapter). Many of these measures can come very close to outright harassment of trading partners.

Marks of Origin

Perhaps most widespread and least objectionable of the administrative measures are the mark-of-origin requirements. Under these, imports must have a label announcing where the good was made, as in the familiar "Made in USA," "Made in Canada," "Made in the Republic of Korea." These labels do give information, but they are also presumably intended to stir patriotic feelings, allow citizens to bypass products from foreign parts, and promote the consumption of goods made at home. Certainly the very first such requirement, the British Merchandise Marks Act of 1887, had this effect.[8] It revealed a large amount of German imports and alarmed the British public, even though the imports were simply the counterpart of the very high level of British exports of the time. At the least, requiring an import to be printed or stamped with "Made in Spain," "Hecho en España," "Fabriqué en Espagne," and so on can increase the cost of some goods substantially.

From time to time, attempts are made to toy with these requirements.* In 1994, the American Automobile Labeling Act required every new car to carry a window sticker naming any country producing more than 15% of the car's parts, the proportion made in the United States or Canada, and the origin of the engine and transmission. Under this Act, Canada counts as part

---

* We believe that the hoary old story that the city of Usa, Japan, took to stamping its products "Made in USA" to profit from the requirement is mythical, and a libel at that. First, the goods involved would immediately have been spotted by customs because they would have been unloaded at U.S. ports, obviously imports with illegal markings. Second, and much more suspiciously, the *Times Atlas of the World* shows Usa to be a small place, in Japan's far south on Kyushu, not a port, and not served by a railway.

of the United States but Mexico does not, an unusual geopolitical stroke presumably made because many more "U.S." cars are made in Canada than in Mexico. (The sticker also does not reveal the value of the labor added at foreign-owned U.S. auto plants. If it did, it would show that U.S.-made Honda Accords have 82% U.S. content compared to the figure of just 50% actually stated.)

A major attempt was made to get around the U.S. mark-of-origin requirement in 1997. If a charge led by New Balance Shoes had succeeded, the Federal Trade Commission would have allowed "Made in USA" to be used if the U.S. content was only as much as 75% compared to the "all or virtually all" (98%) currently in force. Companies outsourcing more and more of their production obviously do not like the labeling results. In December 1997, the FTC decided to keep the standard as it had been.

Red Tape and Delay

Many administrative regulations involving red tape and delay appear to serve clearly protectionist purposes. France's administrative treatment of Japanese cars is a case in point. To limit the Japanese market share, the French government first altered the quota on permitted imports from yearly to monthly, making compliance more difficult. Next, the ministry in charge of issuing certificates of approval for new models started to delay issuance, including in the delay models to which the changes had only been cosmetic. Approval that formerly took two months slowed to six months or more; in effect, customs had trapped thousands of Japanese cars on the docks by following the rules exactly. In the 1980s, Canadian customs adopted the same general approach, checking every Japanese car at Vancouver in order to pry from the Japanese a "voluntary" agreement to limit exports.

Brazilians have become adept at erecting administrative barriers. Their Operation Tortoise was a slowdown by customs that very effectively blocked imports through long delays at the ports. Taiwan has held up imports while a large, often indeterminate, number of approvals are affixed to the shipping documents. Officials are said to show great zeal in ferreting out minor discrepancies in documents, which when found cause long delays.

Perhaps the most famous of all the cases of red tape and delay for a protectionist purpose was the treatment meted out by the French to Japanese video cassette recorders, probably to force the hapless (but efficient) Japanese exporters to agree to a VER. The French authorities ordered in 1982 that all VCRs entering the Republic must come to the customs station at Poitiers, near Tours. The Poitiers customs house was tiny, with a staff of four later enlarged to eight. Of high significance, it had very few berths for ships—none, in fact, because Poitiers is far inland! It did, however, have plenty of parking for the bonded trucks in which the VCRs were transfered from the ports.

At the same time, the French announced that all documents covering trade had to be in French rather than the English and German that were commonly used. All documentation was carefully examined, each container was opened, and serial numbers were checked. Some machines were taken apart to ascertain whether they had in fact been built in Japan and not somewhere else. The instructions were examined to ensure that they were in French. Some 64,000 VCRs had cleared customs per month before the new rules; that number fell to less than 10,000, with the excess marooned for months in bonded warehouses at Poitiers. The French government eventually lifted the Poitiers restrictions in exchange for a tight VER and a decision by Japanese Victor to produce some machines in France. Poitiers-type policies need not be implemented every day. Exporters are likely to remember for a long time an impact as stunning as this.*

Government Buying Policies

Many countries give limited or total preference to domestic producers where government purchases are concerned.[9] Though it is difficult to gather information on such practices, they are pervasive. Federal and national governments, states (in the United States, Germany, Australia), provinces (in Canada, Italy), counties (in the United States, Great Britain), departments (in France), cities, wards, and even school boards frequently have rules that require preferential buying.† The procedures for announcing contracts, bidding, and finally drawing up agreements tend to favor insiders, mostly nationals, because the instructions are deliberately unclear, complex, and difficult for outsiders to follow. Because the public sector of any modern economy is much larger than it was a half-century ago, the overall impact of preferential government buying is probably much greater than it used to be.

U.S. GOVERNMENT PREFERENCES

An excellent example of protection through the use of preferential buying policies is the U.S. federal government's Buy American Act dating from 1933. The Buy American Act requires the federal government to place contracts with U.S. firms rather than with foreigners whenever the U.S. price

---

* The combative former U.S. Speaker of the House, Newt Gingrich, appears to have followed this case closely. He has suggested the following plan for negotiating trade issues with Japan: order all Japanese cars to enter the United States at Seattle; assign seven customs inspectors to the job of clearing them and send two of the inspectors on vacation; tell the Japanese that their auto problem will end when the trade negotiations are successful.

† Note that even if one were to track down every example of preferential legislation, the full magnitude of the problem would still not be exposed because officials and agencies frequently buy at home through habit even when not required to do so.

does not exceed that of the import by more than 6%, or 12% in depressed areas of high unemployment, or 50% for goods purchased by the Department of Defense. There is a Buy American provision for ball bearings used by the military, for steel in U.S. highway and bridge construction and repair, for heavy-duty electrical equipment as long as the cost disadvantage in doing so is no greater than 25%, and for purchases for the U.S. stockpile of strategic commodities when this is possible. The buying rules also allow for retaliation against countries whose governments discriminate in their purchases.

A similar kind of law applies to ocean freight. The Ship American Act was applied first to military cargo in 1904. It has been widely extended, and requires that three-quarters of all U.S. government cargoes (foreign aid, subsidized grain, oil for the U.S. strategic reserve), and all military cargoes, must go in U.S.-flag ships.[10] The charges on these shipments are roughly twice as much as on foreign-flag ships, while the price per ton-mile for U.S.-flag tankers shipping oil for the U.S. strategic petroleum reserve is about four times more than the charter price for tankers at international rates. Presently, one-third of the revenue of U.S. shipping companies exists only because of these Ship American provisions.

A growing area of U.S. preferential buying involves state and municipal governments. Thirty-seven U.S. states have their own Buy American laws. There is a suspicion that these laws are often not enforced very vigorously, but it is striking how few states are without them. Local governments do the same thing. Among all these Buy American cases we have a favorite: in the early 1990s the town of Greece, New York, near Rochester, patriotically chose to buy a John Deere earthmover priced at $55,000 instead of a Komatsu at $40,000, only to discover that the Deere was made in Japan while the Komatsu was made in Illinois. (Town officials could console themselves a little because the Deere's motor was made in Des Moines.)

EUROPEAN AND JAPANESE GOVERNMENT PREFERENCES

Historically, government buying policies with a protective intent have also been very common, and even more sternly enforced, in Europe and Japan. For many years, few government contracts of any kind were put out to open bidding. Governments and publicly owned firms for the most part invited bids only from domestic concerns, or invited contract offers just a short time before they were awarded. Little information was provided with the bid invitation, so that insiders had a distinct advantage in bidding. European governments have been especially reluctant to allow U.S. firms to supply telecommunications equipment.[11]

In Japan, for decades *single tendering* was the rule, meaning that government would approach a single supplier with a contract proposal, there being no competitive bidding process. When foreign bidding was allowed, information on technical requirements was often only released in Japanese and, sometimes the requirements were as thick as a desktop dictionary. The replies had to be in Japanese as well. Translating the documents was a lengthy and costly process. The buying policies of the EU governments are estimated to have raised procurement costs (that is, subsidized domestic firms) by about 10%.[12]

Japanese public construction has been especially contentious, in particular a rule that foreign firms must have contracting experience in Japan to qualify as bidders. Because no contracts were ever issued to foreign firms, obtaining such experience was impossible. After long negotiations, the Japanese government has yielded somewhat, yet many Japanese public works projects remain closed and foreigners continue to complain.[13]

THE PROCUREMENT CODE

Through international negotiation, a procurement code has been negotiated. Under the first version of this code, which took effect in 1981, the national governments that signed agreed to provide open procurement through competitive bidding for any government purchases valued above about $180,000 and to give at least 40 days' notice of the bidding. A revised code (1994, taking effect in 1996) extended coverage to services, to construction, to some states and localities in some countries, and to certain public utilities, including federal ones in the United States.[14]

Much government procurement, however, is still outside the code. There are only 12 signatories (though the EU counts as one of the 12). Even for signers, about three-quarters of government purchases are too small to qualify for inclusion. Several countries have deliberately kept their contracts small so as to circumvent the regulations and have excluded specific sectors—certain EU government utilities, such as post offices and telephones, mass transit, and highway building generally, and for small and minority business in the United States. The code's application to construction is limited to large projects worth $6.5 million or more.

Cabotage Laws

In maritime shipping and air transport, preferences are carried much further. In this realm the preferences apply to all traffic, not just to government shipments. The topic is called *cabotage*, meaning carriage by sea from port to port within a nation's waters, or from airport to airport in a nation's airspace.* Cabotage laws are common around the world.

---

* This interesting word came into English from the Spanish *cabo*, or cape; a mariner who sails from Cape Finisterre to Cape Ortegal is engaged in cabotage, or coastal shipping in Spanish waters. The ancestors of John and Sebastian Cabot, the transatlantic explorers, must have made much shorter voyages than did their famous descendants.

CABOTAGE IN MARITIME TRADE

In the United States, the first cabotage rules date from 1817. The present law for shipping, the Jones Act of 1920, requires that all ships used in domestic trade (that is, in traffic between American ports) must be built in U.S. shipyards, manned by American crews, and owned and registered in the United States.[15] Construction costs for U.S.-flag shipping are high, perhaps three times more than for ships built in a Japanese or Korean yard. Operating costs are even higher, with an American seaman's wage six times that of a Taiwanese, for example. Because of the Jones Act, heavy goods that could be shipped to the west coast, such as steel from Pennsylvania, cannot compete with Japanese or Korean steel; west coast lumber cannot compete with Canadian lumber in the U.S. Northeast; and Corpus Christi, Texas, cannot serve as the port for Monterrey, Mexico, as geography would otherwise dictate, for goods coming from other U.S. ports.

The Passenger Services Act of 1886 is similar legislation for cruise ships, explaining why foreign cruise ships cannot take you from Bar Harbor, Maine, to New York, and why Seattle has hardly any cruise ship traffic to Alaska while Vancouver in British Columbia has many sailings. U.S. maritime interests have been so generous in their support of these laws that "three of the past five chairmen of the House Merchant Marine Subcommittee have been indicted for criminal links to the maritime industry.... (A fourth chairman was indicted for other reasons.)"

Other countries have their own versions of such laws. Australia's has the result that it costs more to ship a ton of freight from Melbourne to Fremantle than it does to ship the same ton from Melbourne to California. In Japan, where coastal shipping is a cartel and new ships cannot be constructed unless old ones are taken out of service, it costs more to ship cargo from Yokohama to Hokkaido than it does from Yokohama to Los Angeles.

So far it has been impossible to liberalize the maritime trade laws, and in 1996 the United States pulled out of the negotiations to do so. Talks on the subject will start again in 2000.

PREFERENCES IN AIR TRAFFIC

Almost universally, airlines do not have the right to pick up and discharge passengers in another country. Air Canada can take Canadian passengers to Chicago, but it cannot fly passengers to Chicago, pick up more passengers, and fly on to New York with a mixed load including people that boarded in Chicago. Similarly, no American carrier can enter the Canadian market other than to fly people from Canada to another country.

In some cases, governments have negotiated such landing rights but disputes about them arise anyway. An ongoing one is between the United States and Japan. Under an agreement dating back to 1952, two U.S. airlines (United and Northwest) have the right to fly to Japanese airports, pick up passengers, and fly them elsewhere. JAL had similar "beyond rights" from New York City with a mandatory stop at San Francisco. The Japanese now protest that many more people board U.S. aircraft in Japan than they do Japanese aircraft in the United States, and they demand a change in the arrangement.[16]

Even country-to-country flights are strictly controlled by the need to allocate landing slots at busy airports. The allocation provides a convenient way to give preferences to domestic carriers and to discriminate against foreign airlines. Landing rights are carefully hoarded, to be traded off from time to time with another country to gain one's own access to that country's airports. All the while, air travelers may pay extortionately for their passage when competition is reduced or eliminated by these means.

Miscellaneous Prohibitions on Private Purchases

More rarely, prohibitions may be enforced in the private sector. In Canada, many provinces have their own "Buy Provincial" legislation controlling private as well as public buyers. Quebec and British Columbia require that fish caught there be processed there. Doctors from other provinces cannot easily practice in Quebec. Allowable truck lengths differ. Until 1992, beer could be marketed only in the province where it was brewed.[17] An oil company in Alberta cannot even have some items brought in from neighboring British Columbia and may have to restrict its hiring to provincial residents. Similarly, the province-owned utility companies are required to give preference to local manufacturers, which means that most provinces have a wire and cable producer. While restricting domestic trade, such laws also restrict international trade. (Barriers to interstate commerce in the United States would, of course, be unconstitutional.)

South Korea has had a number of national "frugality" campaigns that many observers interpret as protectionism against imports. The campaigns attempted to convince the public not to buy imported big-ticket items (such as the foreign autos that also triggered the tax audits mentioned earlier in the chapter).

DOMESTIC CONTENT LEGISLATION

Domestic (or local) content legislation requires a certain proportion of domestic inputs to be contained in imported products if a penalty is to be avoided.[18] Such laws have been relatively common worldwide, even though international trade regulations now frown on them.* Among the several countries that have recently applied them to automobile production are Australia, with an 85% requirement, South Africa, 66%, the Scandinavian countries, 60%, Mexico, 60% (reduced to 36%, 1990), and Spain, 55%. In the United States, bills have passed the House (but have not been enacted) to require some minimum domestic content in U.S. cars. The latest of these would have established a sliding scale: for the first 100,000 cars sold, the company making them would have to ensure that they were 10% American made, 20% for 200,000, and up to 90% for over 900,000 cars. In effect, the bill was a ploy by domestic labor to import foreign entrepreneurs (who would be forced to establish domestic production to avoid the law) rather than foreign products.

The EU adopted domestic content requirements of 35-45% for many electronic products and for ball bearings; integrated circuits must be "diffused" (that is, given their memories) in Europe or heavy duties apply. Mexico's economy has been widely affected by such laws. Many of the nearly 30 other countries with domestic content requirements are not industrialized, however, and these countries' laws are usually not designed to protect a long-established industry.

Analytically, domestic content legislation would be expected to increase the demand for domestic inputs and raise the cost of the final output. It is not, however, easy to predict the overall outcome, and there have been few detailed studies. Pressure for such laws appears to be strongest when barriers to entry make the expansion of production difficult, for then economic rents are more likely to accrue to the firms and factors providing the local content.[19]

Most economists, along with a growing body of trade law, oppose the idea. But attempts to ignore the advice and evade the law are common enough. Recently, the U.S. Congress imposed an assessment on cigarettes if a minimum of 75% domestic tobacco was not used in them. It disguised the intent by calling the levy a "budget deficit assessment." After a challenge under international trade law, the United States agreed to modify it.[20]

TECHNICAL, HEALTH, SAFETY, AND ENVIRONMENTAL STANDARDS

All would agree that standards to ensure technical uniformity, health and safety, and protection for the environment are reasonable public policy. Moreover, the demand for such standards is undoubtedly income elastic,

---

* Under a recent international agreement, they are supposed to be phased out over seven years (shorter for the developed countries). Rooting them all out is likely to be quite a job.

increasing as incomes rise. Many such standards are obviously desirable in their own right: barriers to importing fruits, plants, and animals as a safeguard against the spread of disease; hygienic requirements in food production; and safety standards for vehicles and other machinery. Even though technical, health, and safety regulations are not border barriers, as they are enforced on all producers, not just foreigners, the anecdotal evidence is legion that they sometimes go further, toward bias against imports or even their complete exclusion. It is not always easy to separate a genuine public purpose from a protectionist intent.[21] An international Technical Barriers to Trade Agreement explicitly allows for protection of the environment and safety, and requires that these barriers not serve as disguised protectionism.[22] Enforcement is extremely difficult, however, because a protectionist intent is hard to show.

Technical, Health, and Safety Standards

Even at their most justifiable, the standards are fully capable of distorting trade. Long-established differences in the threading of nuts (a metric or non-metric pitch, clockwise or counterclockwise rotation), pole instead of knife-type electrical connections, 110-120 volts or 220-240, steering wheels on the left rather than the right, and dissimilar railway gauges all give rise to under-standable, reasonable, but different national standards. Though innocent enough, such regulations are often quite inconvenient for exporters.

In some cases the choice of a technical standard is likely to have major effects on national leadership in the production of a given item. Europe fought hard to set the standards for high-definition television sets. It lost in 1993. The U.S. Federal Communications Commission (FCC) recently ruled that the Japanese standards for high-definition TV will not be approved by the United States because that would make obsolete many U.S. TVs. Cellular phone makers vie around the world to ensure that government standards are favorable to their own product and unfavorable to others. Europe has moved to implement mobile phone technical standards that would not be compatible with U.S. equipment. The United States objects, arguing that businesses should agree on harmonized world standards without government dictate.[23]

The problem of standards is pervasive in agriculture and forestry, where the outcome often means exclusion. The United Nations has noted that Latin American exports are subject to almost 400 U.S. trade barriers related to standards; about 100 similar Japanese barriers exist, along with some 300 erected by the EU. Many fruits, plants, woods, and meats are excluded. These regulations may sound wholly reasonable in their aim to prevent the spread of plant and animal diseases, such as oak wilt or foot-and-mouth disease, or to prevent mad cow disease in humans. But when the number of restrictions is so large, the suspicion grows that some of them are difficult to justify and mainly protective in intent.

The familiar U.S. and Canadian safety standards on automobiles (and also on tractors and electrical equipment), justifiable as they may be, effectively prevent the importation of many foreign makes and models. Bringing cars into conformity can be prohibitively expensive for companies whose North American markets are small. Even fuel efficiency standards can have a protective design. The U.S. CAFE (Corporate Average Fuel Economy) standards are fleetwide, imposing a tax on the whole output of all models a company makes if the fleet averages less than 27.5 miles per gallon.* U.S. manufacturers can meet this standard because they produce small cars as well as big ones, while European producers (Volvo, BMW, Mercedes) typically cannot. (A higher gasoline tax would have avoided this problem.) Similar issues can arise anywhere. In Switzerland, for example, the standard size for some kitchen appliances is five centimeters less than the requirement in the rest of Europe. Prices for these small Swiss washers, dryers, and dishwashers—not surprisingly, given the diseconomies of scale—are high, 45% above the European average.[24]

Table 5.1 presents some of the outstanding cases involving technical, health, and safety standards during recent years. (Many of these cases have now been solved, incidentally.) They are just the tip of the iceberg; thousands of similar measures never get any publicity.

The rich variety of such measures certainly suggests that some of the regulations are protectionist in intent. In addition, frequent changes in the rules, and apparently tiny modifications that suddenly exclude imports, would seem to confirm such suspicions.

The news is not all bad, however. The EU and the United States, both of which from time immemorial insisted on their own testing in many fields ranging from electric razors and appliances to pharmaceuticals and tele-communications equipment, agreed in 1997 to accept each other's test results. This Mutual Recognition Agreement (MRA) is making trade in thousands of items much easier than before.[25] Other recent agreements with the EU have solved disputes on veterinary standards and approval of meat-packing plants, which led to EU bans on imports of U.S. pork in 1990 and beef in 1991. The solution involved mutual acceptance of standards. Japan has also become much more willing than formerly to accept foreign standards and test results.

---

* The penalty for not meeting the CAFE standard is $5 for each 0.1 mpg the fleet falls below the standard times the number of vehicles produced.

Table 5.1

NOTEWORTHY RECENT USES OF STANDARDS TO BLOCK TRADE

Product	Exported From	Exported To	Barrier	Comment
Poultry	United States	EU	Special chilling required	Most EU producers already used the required method; U.S. producers did not.
Snails	Everywhere	France	Rigorous veterinary checks	Only one customs post with proper equipment in Jura region where the industry was located, and that one off the beaten track.
Small lobsters	Canada	United States	Complete ban on imports	Said to promote conservation; implied Canadian incompetence to manage their lobster beds.
Fish	Other EU Countries	France	Rigorous health checks	Took so long the fish rotted. Had nothing to do with health. Used to appease angry French fishermen.
Meat	World	United States	Closer inspection	Resulted in ban on imports from 14 countries, some in Europe where no charges of unsafe or unsanitary practice were made.
Meat	United States	EU	Ban on wood in packing houses	No evidence that use of wood is unsafe.
Meat	United States	EU	Ban on beef and pork imports	Poor hygiene claimed. U.S. said its standards were equivalent; bills in Congress to ban EU meat.
Meat	Canada	United States	Some states put embargo on pork	Dubious claim that Canadian hogs were fed with prohibited chemicals.
Forklift trucks	Germany	France	Brake pedals must be on left, battery must be 60 volt	German forklifts had pedal on right and 50-volt battery.

Product				
Scotch, bourbon	France	U.S., Britain	Advertising banned	No ban on cognac or wine ads.
Beer	Germany	Everywhere	Ban on "adulteration"	German brewers use traditional methods, foreigners don't.
Light beer	Italy	Everywhere	Complete ban on sale	Protects wine industry.
Hammers	Germany	Britain	Had to be stamped with maker's name	Justified because hammers are "dangerous goods."
Non-fizzy mineral water	Germany	Everywhere	Complete ban on sale	Germany argued that the bubbles in the fizzy kind (which German firms specialize in) kill bacteria.
Margarine	Belgium	Everywhere	Royal decree that it be packaged as cubes	Imported margarine was packaged in sticks or as round balls.
Cars	Japan	Everywhere	Mirrors had to be specially designed	Large expense for firms that sold only a few hundred cars in Japan.
Telecom equipment	Japan	Everywhere	Strict standards for tying into local grid	Kept Nippon Telephone & Telegraph from buying imported equipment.
Tennis balls	Japan	United States	Imports from Dunlop stopped	Safety concern about high pressure in cans.
Skis	Japan	Everywhere	Ban on imports	Not suited to unique Japanese snow.
Metal bats	Japan	United States	Could not obtain safety certification	Dangerous to softball and baseball players.

Who Makes the Decisions? How Strong Must the Evidence Be?

Some of the disputes on technical, health, and safety matters involve a more difficult and contentious question. Given that countries can ban imports for health and safety reasons as long as they also ban domestic production of the same product, how strong must the evidence be? Can the decision be based on uninformed public opinion, or must it be based on firm scientific evidence?

This question of what happens when a ban is not based on scientific evidence and acts to exclude imports has grown into a major dispute between the United States (and Canada) and the EU. The main area of dispute concerns growth hormones.[26] About 90% of U.S. beef production is routinely treated with such hormones, and the same hormones are used in every major meat-producing country outside of Europe. No scientific evidence exists to show that growth hormones do any harm at the doses employed, and both the World Health Organization and the UN Food and Agriculture Organization have declared them to be safe—with the three main hormones used making up only a fraction of what people ingest when they eat other foods or what the human body produces by itself.

There had been a bad case back in 1980, when Italian farmers marketed meat with very high hormone concentrations that did cause a health problem. That is a major reason why many European consumers object to *all* hormones in meat. An EU ban on meat from livestock treated with growth hormones dates from 1989, and was renewed in 1994. The ban applies even when no traces of the hormone can be detected by scientific means. It has significantly cut beef exports to the EU. U.S. sales, which must be certified as hormone-free, were under 2% of U.S. beef sales to Japan in 1998. The EU would not agree to submit the dispute to an international panel of scientists, presumably because it believed it would not win, especially since scientific bodies in the EU had already concluded that no health hazard exists. In 1996 the United States took this growth hormone dispute to the new World Trade Organization (WTO), where it was supported by Argentina, Canada, Chile, and New Zealand, which also use growth homones. Notice that this case does not involve labeling the meat's country of origin so buyers could avoid it if they wanted to, but a complete ban. Many economists believe that labeling is superior to a ban. If the evidence is that growth hormones are *not* dangerous, then consumers can decide for themselves what sort of meat they want to buy.[27]

A WTO panel ruled against the EU in August 1997 and the appellate body upheld this in January 1998. The EU was allowed to continue studying the risks for 15 more months, but in early 1999—continuing to claim that the hormones may have long-term effects science has not discovered—it announced it would not be meeting the deadline.[28] The United States, angry

at the flouting of the WTO decisions, announced it would be levying retaliatory tariffs of 100% on about $300 million in goods (mostly foods, such as
truffles and paté, and also motorcycles) from the EU. At that point the EU
announced it had found hormone residue in hormone-free beef and said it
would block *all* U.S. beef, trotting out a report that one of the six growth
hormones used in U.S. beef is a carcinogen. The U.S. replied blisteringly that
the study was not proper science and that the World Health Orgnization had
again certified the hormone in question as safe only three months before.[29]
This science-versus-opinion question is thus still ongoing.*

Indeed, it has been expanded. In 1997, the EU decided that genetically
modified foods had to be labeled as such. Here was science versus opinion
once again. The United States, Canada, and other exporters of everything
from tomatoes to soybeans insist that genetic engineering causes no loss of
nutritional value, is not toxic, does not cause allergies—in short, causes no
harm whatsoever. But it does convey a variety of benefits, such as faster
growth and (especially in corn) resistance to worms. The exporters to the EU
argue that mandatory labels play on popular prejudice, cause discrimination,
and are not easily enforced because the usual practice is to mix modified and
non-modified crops. EU politicians say the public's right to know trumps the
economics of the issue.[30]

All the cases discussed in this section reflect the unexpected difficulties that
may lie in wait for an unwary exporter. Even when a solution is found, an
exporter cannot know what the next barrier will be or where it might arise.
Indeed such difficulties are spreading as developing countries begin to adopt
their own rules, which are sometimes based on those enforced in their major
developed-country trading partners.

Trade Barriers Based on Environmental Concerns

International trade law allows countries to take "measures necessary to
protect" public morals, human, animal, or plant life, or to conserve natural
resources as long as the measures apply to domestic production as well as
to imports.[31] Tens of thousands of environmental regulations now exist
all around the world, and by now virtually every country has them, at least
on paper.

---

* Similar opinion-versus-science disputes simmer with the EU concerning hormones to boost
milk production and health-based poultry inspection, and with Japan concerning the safety of
imported apples. The EU has actually found that BST (bovine somatotropin), which increases
milk production, is safe, but it still opposes it presumably because of its effect in raising milk
production. (The EU subsidizes milk output so more milk is a drug on the market, as we used
to say.)

Protecting the environment is, as all would agree, a worthy cause. We must begin by noting, however, that numerous examples of trade protectionism under the guise of saving the environment have come to light. Those who support a cleaner environment will want to be alert to the possibility that motives are not always pure.

Here are several examples. Denmark banned beer and soft drink sales in all but the returnable glass bottles used by Danish bottlers. Ontario put a 10¢ environmental tax on aluminum beer cans so its brewers, which favor bottles, would face less competition from U.S. imported beer that comes largely in cans. Similarly, Germany put a deposit on plastic bottles (often imported) but not the glass bottles preferred by Germany's own bottlers. Shopkeepers often did not want to go to the trouble of dealing with the imported plastics. German legislation required all sellers to take back the packaging their goods came in and carmakers to recycle their cars when they were junked. Because of the logistics involved, recycling is much harder on Japanese importers than on EU producers. The Japanese had to shift their auto manufacturing to Germany or ship their junk all the way back to Japan.

The United States banned tuna imports from Canada to conserve the species, but somehow neglected to limit its own tuna catch. Not to be behindhand, Canada limited exports of herring and salmon, again for conservation, but failed to put limits on its own fishing industry. In both cases international panels found that the restrictions were not meant for conservation but were protectionist. Thailand seemed to be taking a principled stand when it recently banned cigarette imports in the name of good health. But another panel called by the United States ruled against the Thais. Though, as the panel noted, imports can be banned for health reasons, Thailand was still permitting the sale of domestically produced cigarettes. The government-owned Thai Tobacco Monopoly was being protected, not the lungs of consumers. Many of these laws have been modified or abolished, but they show how easy it is to use environmental concerns to justify trade protectionism.

IMPOSING ENVIRONMENTAL LAWS ON OTHERS

Both legally and morally, many questions arise when just one country or group of countries tries to make other countries follow its own environmental bans. Under the rules of international trade, international agreements can protect human, animal, or plant life or health so long as they are not a disguised restriction on international trade and the regulations apply to domestic producers as well as foreign ones. International treaties that exclude some imports for environmental reasons date back to the beginning of the century.[*]

---

[*] The first was an international import ban on white phosphorus matches, agreed on in 1906 because the white phosphorus caused a loathsome occupational disease.

Species decline or extinction was an early concern. Regulations against sealing and the hunting of sea otters date from 1911. A Convention on Trade in Endangered Species (CITES), dating from 1975, banned the trade in ivory, rhinoceros horn and tiger bones (the demand for which stems from supposed physiological effects and led to much poaching), rare turtle shells, and other animal products where extinction is an issue. The convention instituted a permit system for trade in endangered species. A 1986 treaty stopped commercial whaling. The Montreal Convention of 1987 and its successors prohibit imports of ozone-killing CFCs (chlorofluorocarbons), the import of products containing CFCs, and imports of goods produced with, though not containing, CFCs. A Basel Convention on movements of hazardous waste was signed in 1989, banning waste shipments to non-signatory countries.

WHAT IF COUNTRIES DISAGREE ABOUT ENVIRONMENTAL QUESTIONS?

The question is much more difficult when countries disagree about the need for environmental action. It is not really surprising that people would have different views on how much environmental protection is appropriate. Differences in climate, prevailing winds, existing pollution, economic needs, risk preferences, and population density might all play a role in differing choices.[32] A problem arises for international trade when one country decides to sanction another's environmental laxity by restricting trade with it.

The case for one country enforcing trade barriers against another appears strongest when that country is directly affected by the actions of the other, which will neither stop the practice nor pay compensation. Transboundary pollution, such as smoke, polluted rivers, and acid rain, is a case in point. It seems weakest when the harm only has effect in the polluting country itself.[33]

In between are cases where the harm is elsewhere, perhaps affecting international waters not under the jurisdiction of the importing country and with no direct effect on it. Can trade barriers be used then? Logically, one would want to have a high standard of proof that a threat to an ecosystem or species is very significant, with the greater the harm, the more the justification for trade restrictions. In general, the better course would seem to be an international agreement, or eco-labeling, or education, or financial aid to get the conduct stopped, rather than trade restriction in such ambiguous and intrusive circumstances.[34]

A fine example of the dilemma involved is the ongoing tuna/dolphin case. A U.S. law of July 1991 banned the import of fish from countries that allow large-scale driftnet fishing. Driftnet fishing for tuna kills dolphins. Mexico thereupon objected that international trade law does not allow such restriction because the fishing was not going on in U.S. waters. More pointedly, Mexico argued that it should not have to give up an efficient method of fishing that does not threaten dolphins' existence—the dolphin is not an endangered species—just because Americans have a dolphin fetish. It added that driftnet fishing provides poor people with cheap protein and gives some export earnings as well.[35]

Eventually an international panel ruled in Mexico's favor, finding that "in principle it is not possible" under the rules of international trade "to make access to one's own market dependent on the domestic environmental policies of the exporting country."[36] That interpretation meant that unilateral trade restrictions could not be used against the environmental practices of other countries. Environmentalists were outraged. (People are free to organize boycotts of tuna for any reason they please, by the way.)* The U.S. Congress responded by passing even stronger trade restrictions on dolphin-unsafe tuna fishing, and later by refusing to negotiate an international agreement to put official observers on fishing boats to monitor fishing practices—even though President Clinton and President Zedillo supported such an agreement.†

The state of trade law in this area remains controversial. International agreements to restrict trade for environmental reasons are permitted, but unilateral bans on trade are not.

POSSIBLE DANGERS FROM A GREENING OF TRADE LAW

More heat is certain to be generated on the question of trade barriers for environmental purposes. Many "Greens" appear to favor trade restrictions as a way to force other countries to support environmental agreements. For example, a ban on wood imported from countries that do not use sustainable logging practices would force them to do so and halt the forest destruction

---

* The U.S. driftnet fishing law also bans imports from third countries that have bought the tuna from the country that did the fishing. Another U.S. law protects sea turtles from shrimp fishermen. About 80 countries face an embargo on their exports to the United States of several different fish products if they do not adopt turtle excluder devices on the nets carried by their trawlers. An international trade law panel recently ruled that the United States had breached trade law by banning shrimp imports from countries that use nets that trap turtles (India, Malaysia, Pakistan, Thailand) in the absence of a negotiated agreement on the issue. See *The Economist*, October 17, 1998. Similarly, threats are being made against countries, including Iceland and Norway, that have indicated they might resume whaling. Under its environmental laws the United States would be compelled to impose a trade ban on fish imports from them, and perhaps on countries that import whale products from these two countries.

† The United States is vulnerable to similar action. An EU rule bans trade in fur caught in leg traps. The United States (with Canada) has protested the rule as a violation of trade law, taking the opposite side from that adopted in the tuna/dolphin dispute. The EU opposed the U.S. tuna restrictions, and so switched sides as well. See Robert E. Hudec, "Comment," in Michael Bruno and Boris Pleskovic, eds., *World Bank Annual Conference on Development Economics 1996* (Washington: World Bank, 1997): 344-45.

that is a cause of global warming. Trade barriers also avoid the problem that arises when imports involving environmental harm reduce the profits of "clean" domestic firms and make it harder for them to conform to the law.

There is a danger, however, that environmental clauses in trade laws could play into the hands of protectionists, ending up costing the public more than the benefits they deliver. Where are the limits?[37] For example, if the Central African Republic failed to preserve okapis and gorillas, would trade barriers be used against its goods? What if China generates electricity with dirty coal? Could other countries then establish trade barriers against products that use this electricity in their manufacture? What about precautionary barriers

THE POLLUTION-HAVEN HYPOTHESIS

A pollution-haven hypothesis has arisen suggesting that unless something is done, dirty industries will move to poor countries.[38] Their poverty will keep them from protecting their environment, which will give them a comparative advantage in industries that pollute. Competition from firms that do not have to meet strict environmental standards will undermine environmental standards in other countries. To stop these developments, inhibiting their trade may appear easier politically than bribing them or working out international quotas would be.

Yet, few data exist to show that poor countries are becoming a haven for polluting industries. The costs of controlling pollution in the rich countries have not been large enough to make much of a difference. Abatement costs in U.S. manufacturing, including fines, is only 0.8% of the value of shipments, and though that is up from 0.3% in the early 1970s, it is still quite low.[39] When multinational firms establish themselves in less-developed countries, they often use the same technology as at home; that is cheaper than developing new technologies. In any case, multinationals are not the biggest polluters. The greatest offenders are usually small companies. Furthermore, political and economic uncertainties in the LDCs have discouraged investment of all kinds. No significant movement of polluting industries to poor countries has set in as yet. Anecdotal evidence indicates that Ireland has tried to attract some polluting industries, depending on its windy, rainy, oceanographic setting to keep the environment clean. (Such action could be rational if self-cleansing is greater.[40]) Some U.S. furniture-makers have moved to Mexico to avoid California's air-quality laws, and other movements have been made by producers of asbestos, arsenic trioxide, benzidine-based dyes, some pesticides, nonferrous metal processing, and some organic chemicals. The moves seem to have been of little consequence.[41] No doubt, however, a potential does exist for polluting industries to move to more hospitable countries to escape environmental regulation.

against goods that *might* cause harm? Obviously, a great door could swing closed in world trade if the protectionists and environmentalists could persuade each other to ally on these issues.

SOLUTIONS?

Clearly, a way must be found to make informed decisions on the reasonability of environmental measures and to expose and defeat those environmental measures that are in fact protectionist. An improved dispute settlement process would be helpful in mediating cases where trade goals conflict with environmental goals. Already the World Trade Organization has established a Committee on Trade and the Environment to discuss the use of trade measures for environmental protection. (The WTO is opening up its dispute settlement mechanism to allow environmental organizations to attend hearings and submit legal briefs, which was formerly not allowed.[42])

Clear warnings on labels ("eco-labeling"), which are fully legal under international trade rules, ought to solve many issues. The WTO has explicitly approved eco-labeling and has called for more such programs as a better way to handle the problem than trade restrictions. It is noteworthy that the tuna/dolphin case was in a sense settled by market forces because "dolphin-safe" labels and advertising calling attention to them have made it difficult to sell "unsafe" tuna. With labeling, consumers in effect can vote, and they may even be willing to pay premium prices to support a cause.* Another possible avenue is for environmentally minded people and their governments to fund the operations of lobbies and pressure groups that could advocate environmental improvement in polluting countries. They could also lobby multinational firms to agree to abide by the same environmental standards wherever they operate.

Yet there probably should be some scope for trade barriers in support of environmental treaties, just as trade sanctions are used for unacceptable political behavior (see Chapter 9). Moreover, negotiated agreements with trading partners to raise their level of environmental protection would help because it would remove a major argument used by protectionists in environmental clothing. Some less-developed countries such as Brazil and India have been especially critical of what they view as unwarranted environmental policing.

---

* The United States has done less with labeling than have Germany with its Blue Angel policy, Canada with its environmental choice programs, and Scandinavia through the efforts of the Nordic Council. There is opposition to labeling in the business community, however, and it is reasonable to believe that some international body should regulate and police it for scientific factuality and truthfulness. See Daniel C. Esty, *Greening the GATT: Trade, Environment and the Future* (Washington: Institute for International Economics, 1994), 134, 171, 252; *Christian Science Monitor*, July 10, 1996.

They argue that they are being asked to bear costs that are due mostly to growth in the developed countries. They believe that the main cause of the problem is the failure of these countries to force producers and consumers to pay the costs of their pollution, which stems from a resource-intensive and consumption-oriented lifestyle. Subsidies to them, not trade barriers against them, is their view of the proper course. However reasonable such arguments are, they also involve some political blundering of their own, perhaps based on inadequate appreciation of how strong the forces for environmental advance have become in the developed countries and the necessity to placate these forces.[43]

A WTO environmental body, or even a separate organization (a "Global Environmental Organization"), that could judge issues of trade and the environment and facilitate negotiation of international agreements, such as the driftnet fishing law, might be considered. A new body could be instructed to review trade measures designed to protect the environment, deciding

---

LOWER TRADE BARRIERS MAY IMPROVE THE ENVIRONMENT

There are reasons for hoping that lowering trade barriers may bring environmental improvement. Freer international trade means that less-developed countries will be able to make and export more textiles, clothing, steel, and other manufactures whose trade is now controlled by barriers. These products are likely to cause less harm to nature than is caused by pesticides and clear-cutting. Opening trade would also be expected to raise national incomes, and richer countries clearly both desire and can afford a cleaner environment. Some pollutant emissions, for example, suspended particles, decrease as income rises at all levels of income. Others, including major ones such as sulfur dioxide and smoke, rise with income when income is low but then turn down at an income level of about $5,000 per capita.[44] (Carbon dioxide and carbon monoxide emissions, among others, clearly *rise* as income grows, however, and must await a change in attitudes to bring them down.)

A major environmental improvement would likely follow freer trade in agriculture. The heavily protected farmers of Europe and Japan use extraordinary amounts of fertilizer in their agricultural production. Not nearly so much is needed to produce agricultural commodities in the countries that have the comparative advantage. Arguably, certain trade restrictions could be quite counterproductive. Environmentalists, for example, could succeed in banning timber imports to stop the clearing of rain forests. But the ban likely would result in a reduction in the value of the forests that produce the timber, which settlers then might clear at an even faster pace than before in order to farm—and perhaps export the resulting crops.

whether they are appropriate or protectionism in disguise, and negotiating who should pay the costs.

HOW CAN DISTORTIONS TO TRADE BE COMPARED?

As the first part of this chapter demonstrates, the array of distortions to trade is vast. Robert Baldwin's influential book of three decades ago enumerated hundreds of different non-tariff barriers (NTBs) and non-tariff measures (NTMs) of all kinds.[45] There are now more than there were and a current publication of the World Trade Organization, *Inventories of Non-Tariff Measures*, attempts to catalogue them on an annual basis. They are becoming ever more visible as the average rate of tariffs drops through international negotiations and as quotas and VERs are more carefully policed.

Given the great diversity of all the various distortions to trade, a major task has been to find a method for obtaining some common denominator that allows comparisons to be made of their strength and incidence. Such attempts at measurement are necessary to carry out trade negotiations, but complete agreement has not been reached on what methods to use.

Several such measures have weaknesses.[46] A *frequency index* measures the percentage of tariff classifications covered by NTBs, but this does not reveal the importance or restrictiveness of the NTBs. A *trade coverage ratio* is the percentage of import value covered by NTBs. For example, recently almost 19% of all non-fuel imports were covered by non-tariff measures, with the figure much higher for iron and steel (53%), textiles (39%), clothing (63%), and motor vehicles (55%). Such information is useful but not fully adequate because a very strict NTB will suppress imports, perhaps even to nothing.

Instead of these, international negotiators have been using a method that calculates an effective rate of assistance on the individual goods in international trade.[47] The plan builds on the calculation of effective protection presented in Chapter 4. It starts from the proposition that distortions to trade will affect either a price or, if a subsidy or similar measure is employed, a cost. Many NTBs and NTMs raise the prices of traded goods, just as do tariffs and quotas. Distortions with a subsidy element lower the prices of traded goods. Calculating an effective rate of assistance is tantamount to estimating the degree to which a barrier or subsidy changes prices. To be sure, our method for finding tariff equivalents is rough and much more sophisticated methods are available—but that is a graduate-level topic.[48]

Figure 5.4 shows a typical calculation in the form of bar graphs. An investigator needs to know the world price of the item, the domestic price of the item including the estimated price-boosting effect of any trade distortion, the cost of inputs used to produce the item without inclusion of any subsidy

Figure 5.4

CALCULATING THE EFFECTIVE
RATE OF ASSISTANCE

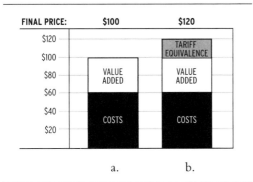

a.   b.

Figure 5.5

ALLOWING FOR SUBSIDIES
AND INPUT TAXES IN
CALCULATING THE ERA

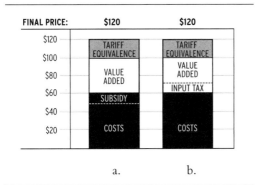

a.   b.

element, and this same cost including any subsidy. The bar on the left presents no measurement problem. In this case there is no protection and no subsidy; the final price of $100 is made up of $60 in input costs and $40 of value added. The effective rate of assistance (ERA) is zero.

The bar on the right introduces a difference. One or more trade barriers are in place. A tariff equivalence has to be calculated. Here, because the price of the item has been raised by $20 to $120, the tariff equivalence is $20. The ERA can then be calculated. It is the total value added, including any trade distortion, minus the value added under free trade, expressed as a percentage of the value added under free trade. In the example, the total value added including the tariff equivalence of $20 is $40 + $20 = $60; while the value added under free trade, without inclusion of the distortion, is $40. The ERA would thus be (60 − 40) / 40 = 50%. This method is related to the one we used to calculate the effective tariff on strung pearls in the last chapter.

Figure 5.5a introduces greater complexity in the form of an input subsidy, or some measure equivalent to a subsidy, that reduces input prices by $10. We assume that measures with a tariff equivalence of $20 are still in place and that the final output is still sold for $120.* In this example, the ERA now amounts to the value added including the effects of the distortions, here the free trade value added plus the tariff equivalence plus the effect of the subsidy, all of that

---

* If the subsidy reduces the price of the final output, the example must be altered accordingly. We leave it to the reader to work through such an example.

expressed as a percentage of the free trade value added, or (70 − 40) / 40 = 75%. Finally, Figure 5.5b shows taxes, tariffs, or other NTBs on *inputs* giving a tariff equivalence of $10, along with an unchanged output tariff equivalence of $20 and final price of $120. In this case, the ERA is less; the producer is penalized by the taxation of inputs. The total distortion is only $10; the complete ERA calculation is (50 − 40) / 40 = 25%.

Through methods such as these, economists work to find acceptable ways to assess the effects and intensities of distortions to trade. The method shown is not the only one available, but it is understandable and results in a single percentage figure that can be used to make comparisons.

PLAYING THE PROTECTIONIST INSTRUMENTS

Here we look at some of the industries and sectors (autos, steel, textiles and clothing, agriculture, and many services) that have achieved the greatest success in establishing barriers to trade, consider the interplay of economics and politics that has led to the barriers, describe their nature, and examine some of the costs involved.

Automobiles

U.S., Canadian, and European automobile producers have been important players in the battle for protection. All have used VERs against Japanese car exporters. The U.S. VER with Japan is highly interesting. Negotiated in 1981, it was extended annually, rising from an original 1.68 million Japanese cars per year to 2.3 million from 1985 to 1991, and then falling to 1.65 million per year for 1992 and 1993, when the VER expired.[49]

Just as economic theory predicts, car prices rose in the United States, by 1985 up by 6-12% for American-made autos and by 15-25% for imports from Japan.[50] The price boost for Japanese cars was greater because, logically, Japanese manufacturers switched to better equipped and larger models to take advantage of the scarcity value.

The VER had further impacts. The higher prices sucked in more imports from countries not covered by the VER. The Japanese share of the market fell, from 22.6% in 1982 to 17.5% in 1984, but some large part of the higher consumer costs, estimated at $6.6 billion per year, flowed to the Japanese— estimates run from $750 million per year to $2.2 billion.[51] A tariff, remember, would have prevented this loss of the revenue effect. An increase in the profits of the major Japanese automakers allowed them to improve their competitiveness.

Another response to the VER was local production by the Japanese inside the trade barriers. (Local production also reduces transport costs, which was another reason for undertaking it.) Table 5.2 shows the location, ownership, start-up date, and capacity of these plants in the United States and Canada (which have free trade in cars). These operations are called *transplants* in the industry's jargon. Notice that all the transplants were established during the time of the auto VER.

Table 5.2

JAPANESE-OWNED OR JOINT AUTO ENTERPRISES

Place	Participants and Start-up Date	Annual Production Capacity
Marysville and East Liberty, Ohio	Honda, 1982 and 1989	608,000
Georgetown, Kentucky	Toyota, 1988	420,000
Smyrna, Tennessee	Nissan, 1983	300,000
Normal, Illinois	Mitsubishi, 1988	240,000
Flat Rock, Michigan (AutoAlliance)	Ford/Mazda, 1987	240,000
Fremont, California (NUMMI)	GM/Toyota, 1984	220,000
Lafayette, Indiana (SIA)	Subaru/Isuzu, 1989	180,000
Ingersoll, Ontario (CAMI)	GM/Suzuki, 1989	120,000
Alliston, Ontario	Honda, 1986	120,000
Cambridge, Ontario	Toyota, 1988	85,000

Note: In addition to engaging in joint ventures, U.S. companies now import cars built abroad and sell them under an American name. These are "captives" in the jargon.
Source: Ward's Automotive Yearbook, 1997, 108.

Output of Japanese cars made in U.S. plants reached 14% of the U.S. market by 1990, compared to 18% coming in as imports. To the degree that the VER forced production in the United States that would not have occurred otherwise, the result is a decline in the efficiency of production. But by the early 1990s, the Japanese appear to have quite effectively protected themselves against the car VER by this large move to transplant production to North America.[52]

During the time of the VER, there was substantial improvement in the quality of many cars made by U.S. producers. Douglas Nelson, a careful student of this development, believes that it was due to competitive pressure from the transplants and continuing imports, not to the protection. The turnaround involved a reduction in employment by U.S. automakers that advocates of protection said they wanted to avoid.[53]

A fascinating aspect of the auto VER was that the U.S. government eventually ceased to demand its renewal, and the formal VER expired on March 31, 1985. But the Japanese announced that they would maintain export limits anyway, outside any agreement with the United States. Thus this one VER became truly and uniquely voluntary. Economists suggested that the unilateral limits were continued, first, because that made good political sense in appeasing congressional protectionists, second, because they could prop up the prices of Japanese cars and hence the profits made on them, and, finally, because swings in demand were dampened by the market guarantee. (In Japan the ministry in charge of allocating export permits granted a very limited share of the VER to some of the smaller firms, which froze out potential new competitors but pleased the big companies.[54])

Then, as transplant production grew in the late 1980s and as car sales dropped in the early 1990s recession, the limit of 2.3 million cars ceased to bind. So the U.S. government and U.S. car producers became interested again, and under pressure from them in 1992 the Japanese lowered the ceiling to 1.65 million cars. The figure still did not bind, however, because the U.S. recession continued, a high yen discouraged Japanese exports, and transplant production increased—which is why the export limits were dropped.[55]

Canada and Europe also have had auto VERs with Japan, with results similar to those in the United States. Canada's has ended, while the European limit of 1.1 million cars survives, though it will probably disappear in 2000. The European VER is much more generous than the national quotas that until 1994 limited imports from Japan to just 3,000 cars in Italy and to 3% of the market in France.[56]) In Canada and Europe, imports of larger, higher-priced Japanese cars grew relative to smaller and cheaper ones. In Europe, the Japanese moved toward production inside the protected market, with three plants in Britain and others elsewhere. Europe, in an aggressive move, brought these plants under its VER, something the United States never did.

Steel

In the 1980s and 1990s, the U.S. steel industry (which has to face less than 5% of U.S. imports by value) has been responsible for almost half (46%) of the nation's trade actions against imports.[57] The United States engineered a huge voluntary restraint arrangement, as the steel VER was named, in 1982. Eventually, imports from about 30 countries were covered. Steel prices rose by 20-40%, bringing distress to firms that used steel as an input. President Bush allowed the steel VER to expire in 1992, reflecting two developments. First, steel users organized to oppose the protection. In this they were led by

Caterpillar Tractor, America's single largest user of steel. Second, minimills using scrap steel and electricity as their fuel and having no need for expensive coke ovens and blast furnaces made the market much more competitive, real prices of minimill steel falling about 40% over the past 20 years. Minimill steel has risen to over 40% of all U.S. capacity, with one reason for its growth being the higher price for steel caused by the VER.[58] These developments reduced the political influence of large integrated producers.

Regrouping, big steel has continued to pursue barriers to trade. Its enthusiasm for barriers increased in 1997-98 because Asia's economic crisis caused currency devaluations, which made foreign steel cheaper. Imports from Japan and Korea rose substantially. Brazil went through much the same experience, and Brazilian steel made inroads as well. Russia's economic problems caused that country to sell more steel abroad and added to the pressure.[59] Even the U.S. minimills surged, because competitive pressures on steel prices lowered the cost of the scrap steel that minimills use as their input. U.S. big steel went back on the attack.

In February 1999, Russia avoided new duties of 71% to 218%, depending on the type of steel, by agreeing to a VER that will limit steel imports from Russia to 750,000 tons henceforth, compared to 3.5 million tons in 1998. A month later (March 1999), in a stunning vote of 289 to 141—just one short of the two-thirds needed to overturn an expected presidential veto—the House of Representatives voted to scale back U.S. steel imports. This Visclosky Bill, named for Peter Visclosky of Indiana, would instruct the administration to decide whether to use quotas, tariffs, or voluntary agreements to achieve such a reduction, which could approach 30%. In passing the bill, the House members ignored the opposition of both the Republican leadership and a White House warning that the measure would violate world trade agreements.[60] They also ignored the fact that higher U.S. steel prices would serve to further encourage minimill output to the detriment of the big steel they are trying to protect.

Europe has controlled imports of steel even more drastically, limiting them to 10% of consumption by means of a VER.

Textiles and Clothing: The Multi-Fiber Arrangement (MFA)

Textiles and clothing are heavily protected in the United States, Canada, and Europe. This industry employs a great many workers and has had a record of very effective lobbying. In the United States, it has considerable political power based in the congressional delegation representing the southern states, where the industry is now concentrated, and political weakness on the part of the mostly Asian countries that are affected by this American protectionism. The success in keeping foreign competition at bay has been astonishing.[61] The

221

main tools for doing so are high tariffs combined with a mammoth global system that in effect combines quotas and VERs. This Multi-Fiber Arrangement (MFA) is distinctive for being directed not at all countries, but only at the less-developed ones and Japan. It covers half of all world trade in textiles and clothing.

The effect is major because textiles and clothing make up 10% of world trade in manufactures, and a quarter of poor-country manufactured exports. In numerous poor countries, textiles and clothing together are the largest non-agricultural export and provider of employment. It appears that these countries have a healthy comparative advantage in the many lines of production where low labor costs are crucial and quick delivery is not important.

The MFA was first cobbled together in 1974, the name indicating that it applies to fiber made from cotton, wool, and synthetics. It grew to labyrinthine complexity of over 20,000 separate rules encompassing about 3,000 bilateral quotas on different countries and products within the arrangement. For example, in 1998 U.S. textile quotas were in place against about 1,200 individual items from 47 countries.[62] For years, the Pacific island of Guam was subject to U.S. quotas under the MFA, which was hard for Guamians to tolerate since Guam has been a U.S. territory since 1899. (Angry lobbying and large campaign contributions ensued, and the rules against Guam were finally dropped during the Clinton administration.) Recently, the EU had about 400 quotas within 27 country agreements. Nor is there respite in the smaller developed countries. Australia, Canada, and Scandinavia have relatively stringent protection as well, all involving bilateral agreements. These agreements freeze market shares, and unused quotas may not be transferred among countries. The enormous complexity creates uncertainties that undoubtedly have their worst effect on small suppliers with limited expertise and on potential exporters who are discouraged from attempting to expand to overseas markets.

Each agreement covers a wide range of individual products, such as types of shirts and underwear, with over 100 separate limits facing some countries. The American Textile Manufacturers Institute is a major player in allocating U.S. quotas by country and by product, and most of the Institute's recommendations have been accepted.[63]

The effect on consumers is higher prices for clothing, curtains, bedding, towels, rugs, and so forth. The cost for consumers in the United States is equivalent to a tariff of approximately 25%. The figure is about the same in Canada.[64] The impact is regressive because these products take a higher proportion of the income of the poor. The worst effects are felt by the relatively powerless less-developed countries. It is believed that poor-country textile and clothing exports would be about twice as large if the MFA did not exist. (To be sure, the MFA looks better if one assumes that national protection would have been even worse without it.)

The MFA begets a universe of legal and enforcement problems. The United States sends "jump teams" of customs agents who search through factories in foreign countries with the countries' permission, though China and some 10 others will not allow the visits.[65] The teams look for avoidance of the rules, as when clothing coming from Hong Kong was actually made in China.* Hong Kong's computer surveillance of clothing exports to the United States has become quite sophisticated. In prominent factories, computers are attached to the desks of women sewers recording the work so that the charge cannot be made that the work was done in China.[66]

The MFA's mass of impenetrable detail means that even when imports would otherwise be permitted, great uncertainty faces exporters.[67] Quota sublimits may be hit long before the nation's quota is reached. When a quota is filled for a particular garment from a country, imports that arrive from the fulfilled country have to be put into a bonded warehouse until January 1 of the next year. Sometimes the goods are then shipped back to the country of origin or sold at a discount. Recently, a U.S. government computer error caused the publication of information that the quota on Chinese-made cotton coats was still open. When the error was discovered, the quota was immediately closed, and importers who acted on the incorrect information suffered serious loss when they had to renege on their contracts.

The effects on exporting countries can differ greatly according to circumstances. In some cases firms gain because the rents they obtain from selling their products at a higher price in protected markets is more beneficial than the loss in exports.[68] Frequently, the agencies that administer the quotas are captured by existing exporters, who usually work to reduce the quota share that goes to new firms.[69] China in particular has had hard treatment in its agreements with the United States. In 1994, an amendment cut the permitted growth of clothing imports to zero for 1994 and just 1% for 1995 and 1996. A new four-year U.S.–China textile agreement of 1997 cut China's access to the U.S. market by 2.6%.[70]

THE PLAN TO END THE MFA

On January 1, 1995, following negotiations that led up to the foundation of the World Trade Organization, a new Agreement on Textiles and Clothing (ATC) was implemented.[71] Under the ATC, it is intended that the MFA quotas will be phased out in four stages over a 10-year period, with a commitment that they will end entirely in 2005.

---

* If you are of a mind, incidentally, you can fly to Hong Kong, get a new suit made, and import it outside of the quota, which does not apply to garments bought for personal use—which some U.S. trade negotiators dealing with MFA issues recently did. *Rushford Report* (October 1998).

Importing countries will determine the order in which products are liberalized. Because the ATC includes product lines that have not been subject to quotas (a little over a third of textile and clothing imports), results have so far been meager. During the first period of the phase-out, which ended in January 1998, the only products covered were items such as seat belts and umbrellas, which did not have quotas anyway. Phase Two, which will end in January 2002, liberalizes trade in such items as handkerchiefs, hosiery, and baby clothes. Serious phasing out will not begin until 2002, but by 2005 there would still be quotas on pants, suits, blouses, coats, and other items making up 89% of the clothing now subject to quotas.

China in particular is disadvantaged. It will not get any benefit from the ATC unless and until it joins the World Trade Organization. Indeed, the ATC rules concerning country of origin have been changed to work directly against China. It used to be that when fabrics were woven in one country and cut to size, dyed, printed, or finished in another country, they counted against the country quota where the processing activities were done. Now, however, they count against the quota of the weaving country.

We remain somewhat skeptical on the question of whether the MFA restrictions will disappear entirely in 2005. The industry has shown persistence and zeal in its struggle for barriers. Even though it did not mount a strong campaign to defeat the WTO phase-out (which some observers attributed to political decline), that phase-out will take so long that regrouping could occur.* Ingenuity could result in new barriers down the road, perhaps involving environmental penalties and tariffs on cheap labor. Textile and clothing tariffs will stay high in any case, dropping only from an average of 15.5% to 12.1% during the course of the ATC. At the end of the process, over 25% of such imports will still be subject to tariffs exceeding 15%.[72] We suspect that there is plenty of life left in the developed countries' protectionist textile and clothing lobbies.

Agriculture

Agriculture is heavily protected in many countries.[73] It has to be as long as governments want to boost prices and incomes for farmers. If governments did not restrict imports, they would flood in as a response to the high prices, overwhelming governments' ability to assist farmers by purchasing

---

* One harbinger: for a time the industry succeeded in persuading the U.S. government to leave the system of quotas in place even though the quotas would be expanded until they did not bind. This left the possibility that they could be tightened again in or after 2005. Adverse attention caused the government to drop this plan in July 1998. See *Rushford Report* (January 1998 and August 1998).

Figure 5.6
METHODS USED TO SUPPORT AGRICULTURE

a. Price Support

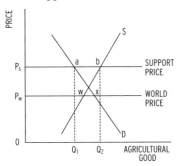

b. Output Restriction

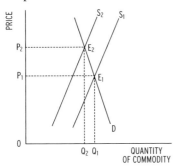

c. Deficiency Payment

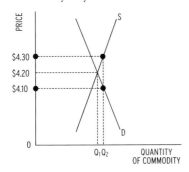

commodities.* As a result, countries with a comparative advantage in agriculture suffer from loss of markets. Among the major losers from trade barriers in farming are Argentina, Canada, Australia, and New Zealand.

THE MAIN MEANS FOR ASSISTING FARMERS

The three main methods used to support farmers, illustrated in Figure 5.6, all have impacts on international trade. The distortions are sometimes dire.

Price supports require the government to purchase output to raise price. The higher price would attract foreign suppliers and make the program unworkable unless imports are restricted. Also, the surplus *ab* may be disposed of on international markets, lowering prices on these markets. Output restriction reduces supply, which raises prices. Unless imports are restricted, they would flood in and wreck the plan. Deficiency payments mean more production by a country's farmers and hence lower prices for commodities, making imports less profitable and so decreasing them.

In Figure 5.6a, the government pays a support price P_s, which is above the world price P_w. It has to buy a quantity Q_1Q_2, equal to the excess supply *ab* at price P_s, to keep the price that high. Before the support price was implemented, the country was an importer, importing the quantity *wx* as shown. The government, unwilling to

---

* Under the rules of international trade, quotas to exclude agricultural imports were given very permissive treatment from 1955. The rules exemption for agriculture was instigated by the United States, which, unthinkingly, did not see the massive distortions to trade that would result.

buy enough of world output to keep the price high, must restrict imports or else they will flow in. Foreign suppliers lose the market share wx that they formerly possessed. That is not all the bad news for foreigners. The surplus ab acquired by the government cannot be put on the home market, for that would depress prices back to their old level. The government being unwilling to throw it away, it will probably try to sell it abroad at whatever the market will bear. Thus the world price P_w will probably decline, further damaging countries with a comparative advantage.

Output restriction is illustrated in Figure 5.6b. Here the government pays or orders farmers to reduce the supply of a commodity, usually by taking land out of production or sometimes by enforcing some stated limit on domestic output. The supply curve moves leftward, from S_1 to S_2, causing a shift in the equilibrium from E_1 to E_2 and therefore a rise in price from P_1 to P_2. The higher price would obviously cause imports to flow in, meaning that imports have to be restricted to keep the scheme afloat.

A deficiency payment is shown in Figure 5.6c. The government buys nothing, but it does pay farmers the difference between the market price and some target price, here $4.30 a bushel. Farmers will produce a quantity Q_2 rather than the quantity Q_1 that they would have produced in the absence of payment. That extra production drives the price down to $4.10 per bushel, for that is what buyers will pay for that quantity. The effect is felt by potential importers because the price they would receive is lower. This market is now less attractive to them. (Deficiency payments do not, however, require a direct limit on imports, and for that reason they are less trade-distorting than are price supports and output restriction.)

By these methods, the EU, Japan, the United States, Canada, and many other countries assist their farmers. The generosity reflects the political influence of the agricultural sector but it is often justified to the public with arguments such as keeping the land tidy and establishing self-sufficiency in food production.

Notice that if governments decide to enhance farmers' income by means of grants, such grants would not depend on the amount produced and would thus not directly affect the amount of foreign trade. Grants are not, however, the standard method of assisting farmers. One reason is psychological: farmers view the grants as handouts. Another is economic: rich and successful farmers stand to gain much more from a system based on production than they would from a system based on grants to individual farmers.

The amount of assistance in agriculture is measured as a producer subsidy equivalent (PSE), which is the value of the assistance divided by the total return to farmers. So if $100 is the total value received by farmers and $30 of that is the result of government action to boost prices or transfer resources, then the PSE is 30%. PSEs in the 1990s ranged from 30% in the United States to 45% in Canada, 49% in the EU, 66% in Japan, and 80% in Switzerland.[74] (Programs that lower the cost of inputs used by farmers are not included in these calculations.)

Several results are evident. Price supports and output restriction involve high costs to consumers because the price of agricultural commodities is pushed up. The proportion of income spent by U.S. consumers on food, beverages, and tobacco is 13.1%. In Japan, the figure is 20.4%, in Germany 22.5%, in Britain 21.1%.[75] The difference is not due to any great difference in per capita income. It is because, compared to the United States, the EU and Japan are more avid users of measures that increase price.

EU AGRICULTURE

For many years, the standard method for aiding farmers in the EU was price supports, as shown in Figure 5.6a above. Under the Common Agricultural Policy, or CAP, the EU bought output to maintain price. The prices paid were in general about 40% more than world prices, meaning that about 40% of farmers' income came from EU government programs. Surplus stocks were the inevitable result of the government purchases. About a quarter of EU farmland produces nothing but these surplus commodities, called "mountains" (or, with wine, a "lake").*

There are two major consequences for international trade. First, imports have to be restricted or they would flow in and disrupt the price support program. The restriction was originally in the form of quotas, while now it is very high tariffs. The second outcome is that the EU tries to be rid of these surpluses. Many schemes were tried domestically. For some years, about one-third of all table wine production was turned into industrial alcohol. Butter was used for axle grease, in soap, in paint, and as a processed cooking oil. On occasion the butter was fed to cows, which then, of course, produced more butter. Some has simply been thrown away, and some has been donated as aid. Such schemes were never enough, and so the EU ended up exporting much of the surpluses at what the market would bear, lowering prices in export markets below what they would otherwise have been. These sales were, of course, at a loss; the loss is tantamount to an export subsidy.

International trade rules prohibited such subsidies if they led to the acquisition of "more than an equitable share of world trade," but the EU largely ignored the clause, with the result that the region, without a comparative advantage in agriculture, became in the mid-1980s the world's largest exporter of farm commodities. By 1988 its share of world farm exports

---

* The mountain of cereal grains reached 27 million tons in 1993; butter piled up to a total of 1.2 million tons; the wine lake overflowed at 740 million liters.

reached 36%. Indeed, in many farm products the EU turned itself from a substantial importer into an exporter, as Table 5.3 shows. In sugar, for example, the EU produced 82% of its own consumption in 1968-69, but by 1988-89 it was producing a surplus 24% greater than its needs, which it exported at cheap prices, becoming the world's largest exporter. The EU also reached the number-one position as exporter of dairy products, poultry, eggs, and veal, vied with Argentina for the number-two position as a beef exporter, and was number three in wheat. It had been a net importer of sugar, dairy products, and beef as late as 1974.

The situation was very disruptive for world trade. The subsidized exports were sold in foreign markets in competition with domestic production and the exports of other countries. The prices received by local farmers in the countries that import the EU surplus, and by other exporters that face the new competition from the EU, were forced down, and both groups lost market share. This, of course, was damage in addition to that caused from the lost markets in the EU itself, where imports were sharply restricted by trade barriers.

Table 5.3

AVERAGE DEGREE OF EU
SELF-SUFFICIENCY

Commodity	1968-69	1988-89
Wheat	94	123
Maize	45	95
Sugar	82	124

Source: Margaret Kelly and Anne Kenny McGuirk, *Issues and Developments in International Trade Policy* (Washington: International Monetary Fund, 1992), 139.

The United States retaliated to try to hang on to its own export markets. The U.S. Export Enhancement Program subsidizes agricultural exports, particularly of wheat, to targeted countries. The EEP probably ran up the costs for the EU's CAP and so made it more likely that the EU would negotiate to change the situation. But it also made the situation worse for the innocent bystanders (especially Argentina, Canada, Australia, New Zealand, and Uruguay) that were damaged even more than before and could not afford to follow this expensive tactic.

In 1995, the EU completed a three-year reform that cut prices and compensated farmers for their losses by means of direct payments.[76] Cereal farmers who took land out of production were compensated with set-aside payments. The result has been a great fall in the surpluses, but they still exist and still distort trade. Moreover, it is fully possible that surplus stockpiles will rise again and further EU exports will ensue unless prices are cut further, but a 1999 attempt to do so failed completely. (On top of that is a fairness problem—80% of EU farm aid goes to the richest 20% of the farmers.)

Thus, the EU still spends a very large part of its total budget—about 50%—on farming, meaning that admitting new members from agricultural Eastern Europe into the EU would be very expensive, raising the CAP's costs by at least 30%.[77] That makes it doubtful that new members will in fact be added until the CAP is reformed in a major way—which is too bad because some of the countries in Eastern Europe have a comparative advantage in agriculture. They now lose substantially and would gain from exporting, while the EU would benefit from lower food prices. Worse, EU farm policy remains a major obstacle to future negotiations on lowering world trade barriers.

JAPAN'S AGRICULTURE

Japan uses a system of price supports (Figure 5.6a) to assist its farmers, who are politically powerful because of the electoral system. As a result, it imposes severe restraints on imports, formerly by means of quotas, now with very high tariffs. Strict limits on sugar imports help to raise the domestic selling price to about five times the world price; meat is three times more expensive than world prices, and some cuts of steak sell in Japan for 10 times the price in U.S. supermarkets; wheat sells for nearly 11 times the world price.

Rice presents the greatest problem. This is Japan's most important crop, as much for its political and emotional mystique as for its economics.[78] Farmers currently are paid 10 times the world price and consumers, who are expensively subsidized, pay four to six times the price in a California supermarket. Because of the high prices for farmers, about 5% of the land in the Tokyo city limits is farmland.

The usual reason given by Japanese politicians for the quotas—that an island nation is ensuring food security—seems to be widely accepted by the public. Yet the security argument is not very tenable.* Food security is not the same as food self-sufficiency. A war or boycott that cut off imported food would also presumably cut off imported petroleum-based fertilizers, without which Japanese agriculture could not feed the country. The alternative of stockpiling food against future emergencies is not practiced. Stockpiles of food could be purchased cheaply on world markets, and could be enlarged or diminished as the international situation dictated.[79]

The argument is often made in Japan that Japanese consumers prefer the taste of their own rice to the taste of imported rice. This is clearly not an argument in favor of trade barriers. If it is true, then barriers are not needed, and if it is false, then free trade would be an improvement for consumers.

The Japanese government is willing to go far to protect its rice farmers. There was a persuasive demonstration in the 1994 crisis when emergency

---

* The same argument, subject to the same weaknesses, is used by Switzerland, the Scandinavian countries, South Korea, and Saudi Arabia, among others.

imports of foreign rice were permitted because of a cold, rainy growing season the previous year.[80] A 580% tariff was applied, bringing the price up to the $15 per pound for Japanese rice. To prevent consumers from deciding they liked a particular type of foreign rice, the imported rice, by government dictate, had to be blended with Japanese rice. The proportions chosen were 30% Japanese, 50% Californian, Chinese, and Australian, and 20% Thai. The blend could not be properly steamed, while California rice is steamable. When the rule was later changed, all foreign rice could be sold separately except Californian, which had to be mixed with other American rice. The policy appeared to be flagrant discrimination designed to prevent California rice from gaining a place in the market.

It would be to Japan's benefit if it were to rid itself of agricultural protection. Foreigners then could not use it as an argument for trade barriers against Japanese manufactured goods. Yet, when international negotiators agreed to move from quotas to very high tariffs in agriculture, Japan was able to obtain a six-year moratorium in return for agreeing to a minimum access for foreign rice, starting at 4% of consumption in 1994 and rising to 8% in 2000.*

U.S. AGRICULTURE

In the United States, government programs are not as important as they are in the EU and Japan, but into the early 1990s they were still providing some 30% of farmers' incomes. The barriers with the greatest effect are those on cotton, peanuts, dairy products (butter, milk, cheese), meat, and above all, sugar, including syrup and sugar-containing items. All protect a price-support program in one form or another.

Until recently, the quota for upland cotton was tiny, 28,000 bales or about 0.002% of the market. When the quota was "tariffied," the tariff was set at a very restrictive 16.77¢ per pound. Peanuts are a similar case. Domestic output is strictly controlled by its own quota, which is allocated by farm and supervised by (it seems a joke but it is not) federal inspectors acting as a "peanut police." That required protection against imports, which for decades was subject to a tiny quota on imports, established in 1953, of 775 metric tons, or about two imported peanuts per person per year. When this was tariffied, the rate chosen was 193%, falling to 164%. The 44,000 U.S. licensed peanut growers, about one-third of them absentees, profit greatly. Butter and cheese also faced very restrictive quotas, limiting imports to about 0.06% of U.S. butter production and about 2% of U.S. cheese production. Milk and cream imports were also limited by quota to only 1.5 million gallons. These quotas allowed in approximately one teaspoon of foreign ice cream per person and

---

* South Korea is in the same situation. It has agreed to open its rice market, starting at 1% in 1995 and rising to 4% by 2005.

one pound of foreign cheese. They have now been succeeded by high tariffs: 10% + $1 per lb. for butter and 10-20% + $0.70-$1.20 per lb. for cheese, for example.

Meat was for many years subject to quotas, with VERs agreed to by foreign exporters to keep the quotas from being tightened further. In 1995, in a negotiated agreement the United States ended its meat quota, substituting a tariff-rate quota (TRQ) of 31.1% that sets in after 1,448 million pounds, falling to 26.4% over six years. (The in-quota tariff is low, 2¢ per lb.)

U.S. sugar protection is of long standing. A system of quotas imposed by country and based on historical performance was in effect from 1982, and under that system U.S. imports fell 70% between 1982 and 1987. Following a challenge by Australia in 1989, the quotas were replaced by a two-tier tariff-rate quota under which a limited quantity enters at a low rate (1.7¢ per lb.) while the over-quota tariff permits additional imports at 19¢ per lb. The over-quota tariff is very high given that world prices are often around 4¢ to 8¢ a pound, so the new system is equivalent to the old quotas.

U.S. sugar protection has a negative effect because sugar cane can be grown efficiently in at least 100 countries, some of them very poor and whose alternatives for exporting other items are equally poor. In the Dominican Republic, for example, sales to the United States have plunged to one-fifth their old level. There and on a number of Caribbean islands that have a comparative advantage in sugar, significant unemployment has been the result.[*] The U.S. scheme is believed to have forced down the world sugar price by a fifth to a third, a terms-of-trade effect caused by the U.S. protection.[81]

The high U.S. price of about 21¢ per pound represents a tremendous lobbying success for the 12,600 strongly united U.S. sugar producers. Clearly, numbers and their votes alone could hardly explain such success. Organization and regional influence can explain it, though—by occupation, sugar producers are the third largest contributor of funds in American politics, behind only lawyers and doctors.[82] It is estimated that U.S. growers glean over $260,000 per grower from this system, with the biggest producers collecting the biggest benefits (an average of $1.6 million per producer in Florida). The only reason the country is not swamped with domestically produced sugar is that production costs are high.[†] Meanwhile, U.S. families

---

[*] Even so, it is important for countries that have a guaranteed share of the U.S. market to sell the permitted amount at the high U.S. price. Otherwise they would be throwing money away. That explains why some countries have actually imported sugar in order to export it again to the United States. Examples include St. Kitts-Nevis and Guyana. See *South* (September/October 1991).

[†] Because of the trade barriers and the resulting high sugar price, it has become profitable to manufacture sweetener from corn. High-fructose corn sweetener (HFCS) has become a major product in the Midwest.

pay about $100 extra per year for their sugar. If an outspoken statement may be permitted, the U.S. sugar regime is scandalous and should be scrapped.

ATTEMPTS TO CONTROL THE SITUATION

International negotiations to reduce the need to exclude agricultural imports and lower the barriers have been going on for years. Some modest successes were registered in the mid-1990s, lessening but not eliminating the problem which still stands as one of the greatest in trade relations. The nature of the agreements and their deficiencies are addressed in the next chapter.

Protection in Services

Services, the invisibles that include banking, transport, travel, and insurance, are growing steadily as a percentage of domestic economic activity, having now reached over 60% of developed-country GDP and about two-thirds of all employment. But services amount to only about 26% of world trade.* This relatively low figure is due to a wide variety of non-tariff barriers to trade in services. In defense of some of the protective measures, there is no doubt that politicians often consider services to be quite intrusive from a cultural and political point of view, and few people anywhere would agree to have them completely in foreign hands. Radio, television, and domestic airlines are cases in point, with foreign operation seldom permitted, even in the United States.

Other services, however, are kept off limits to foreigners even though free trade would appear to give cheaper access to information processing, professional services, finance, and technology. For example, foreign insurance, banking, data processing, telephone operation, and computer hardware and software are sometimes excluded, even when foreigners have an obviously large comparative advantage in them. Among the services where protectionism is currently most common are the following.

Insurance. Numerous countries have laws directed against foreign insurance. A few nations (India, for one) do not allow any underwriting of any kind. Life insurance seldom crosses national boundaries, and fire and auto insurance are often limited. All exports from and imports to some countries must have insurance from domestic underwriters. About two dozen countries allow foreigners to write coverage only if the type of insurance the foreigner is providing is not available locally.

Banking. Laws that discriminate against foreign banks are commonplace. New entrants from abroad may be prohibited from going into retail banking

---

* The United States is the largest services exporter, with 17% of the world total. The next five are France (with half the U.S. total), Italy, Britain, Japan, and Germany.

and the proportion of foreign shareholding in a country's banks may be limited to some figure such as 25%.

Shipping. Liner codes fix market share and rates. These, plus other laws, often require that your country's exports must go in your ships. Australia's law mandates that 40% must do so. In Japan, the traditional ship-Japanese practice is a custom rather than a law, but Japanese ships nevertheless carry over 50% of Japanese exports even though in recent years they have charged some 35% more than market rates. The U.S. "Ship American" provisions and Jones Act have already been reviewed earlier in this chapter. Even stationary objects at sea or on the shore share in the endemic maritime protectionism. Britain prohibits foreigners from the design and construction of oil-drilling platforms. Taiwan will not allow foreign ownership of container facilities at the ports.

Professional services (accounting, legal services, and so forth). Such services face considerable discrimination. Frequently, foreign lawyers are not permitted to practice and foreign accounting firms face discrimination. In numerous cases accountants practicing their skills must possess a local degree, or accreditation, or be supervised by local auditors.

TV, advertising, and films. An EU television directive of 1989 reserves a majority of TV time for European-made programs and films. The EU taxes audio and videotapes, with the revenue going to EU artists to compensate them for illicit copying. France puts an 11% tax on movie admissions to subsidize the French film industry. In Canada, Argentina, and Australia, broadcasts of commercials of foreign origin are restricted on television and radio. Similar regulations abound. It can certainly be argued that such rules do protect the national culture and domestic actors, musicians, and performers, but just as surely they also protect the local advertising and film industries.

Computers. In some countries, companies that use computers must do some or all of their data processing in that country. The result is that comparative advantage in data processing cannot be fully utilized, and companies such as American Express cannot completely centralize their processing of travelers' checks and credit cards.

ADVANCES IN TRADE IN SERVICES

After years of negotiation, a rather weak General Agreement on Trade in Services (GATS) was agreeed to in 1994. It proved contentious, with strong opposition especially from Brazil and India.[*] A number of separate areas were

---

[*] Some less-developed countries, however, have become important exporters of services. South Korea, Singapore, Hong Kong, and Mexico are all in the world's top 20 exporters. They do not side with most of the other Third World countries.

omitted from the GATS, including financial services, information techology, telecommunications, shipping, and airlines. All became the subject of separate negotiations, as examined in the next chapter.

Opponents of reform have yet to appreciate fully that concessions in this area could be exchanged for freer trade in manufactured goods and agricultural commodities. One hopes that the less-developed countries will come to understand that if they wish to capture the world's low-wage manufacturing, because that is where their comparative advantage lies, then they ought to allow countries with a comparative advantage in services to trade these. Eventually more persuasive to such countries might be the argument that poor services in such areas as banking and telephones can clearly damage the prospects for exporting manufactured goods. At the same time, it is fair to say that developed-country governments have not generally been very sympathetic toward measures for maintaining cultural independence. A greater degree of tolerance, for example, in attitudes toward TV and radio regulation, would increase the chances for a compromise settlement.

One intractable problem with any reform is that freer trade in services will require more foreign staff. The increases in immigration, even if temporary, may be troublesome. Would Korean construction workers be very welcome in Britain or the United States? Probably not, even though the exchange of labor-intensive services for capital-intensive services makes just as much sense as the similar trade in goods and would enhance welfare. All in all, a comprehensive agreement on trade in services has been difficult to achieve, and this sector remains laced with barriers to trade.

CONCLUSION

As Chapter 1 noted, the very existence of nation-states with their various laws, regulations, and taxes creates the field of international economics. Nowhere is this clearer than in the observation of non-tariff barriers and subsidies. As these, in all their rich and sometimes rather opaque forms, have come to take precedence over the traditional tariffs, a developing pattern of policy has become apparent.[83] (1) Trade distortions have become considerably less open, less visible, and less easy to quantify. (2) They have generally become more subject to administrative discretion and less like firm rules. (3) They have included a great deal more discrimination against individual countries or groups of countries, thus representing a retreat from multilateralism and equal treatment. (4) More and more, the distortions to trade have been on a sectoral basis rather than representing a coherent national policy. The barriers and subsidies are granted to some industries but not others according to the balance of political power within a country. Autos or textiles and clothing or steel or computers and microchips or agriculture may shelter behind high barriers while others must face the competition. The lack of openness, the discretionary nature, the discrimination, and the absence of clear knowledge of what industry will be next are inhibiting for trade because they increase risk.

In all this we are dealing with governments' policies toward trade. Every government is conscious, at least to some extent, that its various laws affect its commerce with foreign countries. The struggle to achieve reasonably integrated and consistent approaches toward these laws is one of the most difficult tasks facing a modern government. It is to this subject that we turn in the following chapter.

VOCABULARY AND CONCEPTS

Administrative protection
Buy American Act
Cabotage laws
Domestic content legislation
ERA (effective rate of assistance)
Exim Bank
Export credit subsidies
Government buying policies
NTBS, NTMS

Single tendering
Ship American Act
Subsidies to exports
Subsidies to imports
Subsidies to production
Technical, health, safety, and
 environmental standards
VAT

QUESTIONS

1. What is a non-tariff barrier? Why have they become more important in recent years?
2. Subsidies in general are superior to tariffs and quotas, but not as common. Explain why they are superior, and why they are not used so much.
3. What differences are there in the analysis of subsidies to production, to exports, and to imports?
4. What are subsidies on export credit? Why are such subsidies used so much? What kinds of international agreements restrict their use?
5. How can government buying policies inhibit trade? Give examples from the United States, Canada, and Japan. What kinds of international controls exist to cover such problems?
6. "The reason foreign firms have trouble getting government contracts is that they don't produce local votes." True in part, but what are other reasons for the difficulties?

7. "A nation has a sovereign right to protect its citizens against what they consider to be unhealthy food, regardless of whether it interferes with trade." Comment.

8. "Health, technical, safety, and environmental regulations are a necessary function of national governments; applying to domestic producers and importers alike, they cannot possibly be considered import barriers." True, false, or misleading?

9. Under what circumstances do you feel a country should restrict imports because of the environmental damage their manufacture causes?

10. How are NTBs measured? What is the difference between a tariff equivalent and an effective rate of assistance? How does the ERA compare with an effective tariff?

11. Why does government support of farmers have repercussions on the international trade in agricultural commodities?

12. The United States has been pressing heavily for freer trade in services. Is trade in services really so restricted?

NOTES

1. Diagramming production and export subsidies is discussed in Erna van Duren, "An Economic Analysis of Countervailing Duties," *Journal of World Trade* 25, 1 (February 1991): 91-105.

2. This section relies in particular on all recent editions of the U.S. International Trade Commission (USITC), *The Year in Trade*, and the coverage in the *International Economic Review*.

3. *Christian Science Monitor*, March 17, 1995.

4. See Vito Tanzi, *Taxation in an Integrating World* (Washington: Brookings Institution, 1995).

5. Gilbert E. Metcalf, "Value-Added Taxation: A Tax Whose Time Has Come," *Journal of Economic Perspectives* 9, 1 (Winter 1995): 128.

6. *The Economist*, February 27, 1999; *Wall Street Journal*, May 27, 1999.

7. See *International Economic Review* (October 1994).

8. Rondo Cameron, *A Concise Economic History of the World* (Oxford: Oxford University Press), 281.

9. Much of the information in this section is from the annual issues of USITC, *The Year in Trade*.

10. Neela Mukherjee, "Multilateral Trade Negotiations and Trade Barriers in Service Trade: A Case Study of U.S. Shipping Services," *Journal of World Trade* 26, 6 (October 1992): 52.

11. USITC, *The Year in Trade 1994*, 78.

12. Cited in Jacques Pelkmans, "Liberalization of Product Markets in the European Community," in Herbert Giersch, ed., *Free Trade in the World Economy: Towards an Opening of Markets* (Boulder, Colo.: Westview Press, 1987).

13. USITC, *The Year in Trade 1993*, 93.

14. *International Economic Review* (June 1994); USITC, *The Year in Trade 1993*, 51.

15. Gary Clyde Hufbauer and Kimberly Ann Elliott, *Measuring the Costs of Protection in the United States* (Washington: Institute for International Economics, 1994), 83. There are details in James Bovard, "Torpedo Shipping Protectionism," *Wall Street Journal*, November 26, 1991.

16. *The Economist*, February 8, 1997.

17. *International Economic Review* (July 1994).

18. The classic article is Gene M. Grossman, "The Theory of Domestic Content Protection and Content Preference," *Quarterly Journal of Economics* 96, 4 (November 1981): 583-603.

19. See Stanislaw Wellisz and Ronald Findlay, "The State and the Invisible Hand," *World Bank Research Observer* 3, 1 (January 1988): 59-80.

20. USITC, *The Year in Trade 1994*, 16.

21. For details, see recent issues of USITC, *The Year in Trade*, and coverage in *The Economist* and the *Wall Street Journal*.

22. USITC, *The Year in Trade 1993*, 11.

23. See Joanne Guth, "The U.S.-EU Third-Generation Mobile Phone Technology Debate: Who's Calling the Shots on Standards?" *International Economic Review* (January/February 1999): 9-10.

24. *The Economist*, November 28, 1992.

25. USITC, *The Year in Trade 1997*, 95; *The Economist*, May 24, 1997.

26. Materials from this section are from recent issues of the *International Economic Review* and USITC, *The Year in Trade*; *Wall Street Journal*, April 22, 1999; and *The Economist*, May 15, 1999.

27. See T.N. Srinivasn and Jagdish Bhagwati, "Trade and the Environment: Does Environmental Diversity Detract from the Case for Free Trade?" Yale Economic Growth Center Discussion Paper No. 721, January 1995, 59.

28. *New York Times*, March 23, 1999.

29. *Wall Street Journal*, May 5, 1999; *The Economist*, May 8, 1999.

30. *The Economist*, May 1, 1999.

31. Material in this section is drawn from Kym Anderson and Richard Blockhurst, eds., *The Greening of World Trade Issues* (Ann Arbor: University of Michigan Press, 1992); Jagdish Bhagwati and Robert E. Hudec, eds., *Fair Trade and Harmonization: Prerequisites for Free Trade?*, Vol. 1, *Economic Analysis*, and Vol. 2, *Legal Analysis* (Cambridge, Mass.: MIT Press, 1996); Steve Charnovitz, "Exploring the Environmental Exceptions in GATT Article XX," *Journal of World Trade* 25, 5 (October 1991): 37-55; Steve Charnovitz, "Environmentalism Confronts GATT Rules," *Journal of World Trade* 27, 2 (April 1993): 37-53; Steve Charnovitz, "The World Trade Organization and Social Issues," *Journal of World Trade* 28, 5 (October 1994): 17-33; Daniel C. Esty, *Greening the GATT: Trade, Environment, and the Future* (Washington: Institute for International Economics, 1994); Hilary F. French, "Reconciling Trade and the Environment," in Lester R. Brown, ed., *State of the World 1993* (New York: Norton, 1993); Adam B. Jaffe, Steven R. Peterson, and Paul R. Portney, "Environmental Regulation and the Competitiveness of U.S. Manufacturing: What Does the Evidence Tell Us?" *Journal of Economic Literature* 33, 1 (March 1995); David Palmeter, "Environment and Trade: Much Ado About Little?" *Journal of World Trade* 27, 3 (June 1993): 55-70; Vinod Rege, "GATT Law and Environment-Related Issues Affecting the Trade of Developing Countries," *Journal of World Trade* 28, 3 (June 1994): 95-169; Srinivasn and Bhagwati, "Trade and the Environment"; "Trade Liberalization and Pollution in Manufacturing," *International Economic Review* (March 1995).

32. Esty, *Greening the GATT*, 106.

33. Ibid., 123, 126.

34. Ibid., 124-25.

35. Ibid., 188, 190.

36. *Wall Street Journal*, February 12, 1992. The tuna/dolphin dispute, involving several separate cases and numerous countries besides Mexico and the United States, receives regular coverage in the *International Economic Review* (see, e.g., the issues of June 1994 and November 1994), and annually in USITC, *The Year in Trade* (see especially *1996,* 106). Also see Esty, *Greening the GATT*, pp. 29-32.

37. These questions are asked in the special section on the environment in *The Economist*, May 30, 1992.

38. Two surveys of the subject are Adam B. Jaffe, Steven R. Peterson, and Paul R. Portney, "Environmental Regulation and the Competitiveness of U.S. Manufacturing: What Does the Evidence Tell Us?" *Journal of Economic Literature* 33, 1 (March 1995): 132-63; Maureen L. Cropper and Wallace E. Oates, "Environmental Economics: A Survey," *Journal of Economic Literature* 30 (June 1992): 675-740. Also see H. Jeffrey Leonard, *Pollution and the Struggle for the World Product* (Cambridge: Cambridge University Press, 1988).

39. "Trade Liberalization and Pollution in Manufacturing," *International Economic Review* (March 1995). The cost figures are for 1992. Abatement costs are higher, between 1.5 and 2% for paper, chemicals, coal and petroleum, and primary metals. They are higher yet when all costs of pollution control, including government costs, are included: 0.88% of GDP in 1972, rising to 2.32% in 1992. See Jaffe, Peterson, and Portney, "Environmental Regulation and the Competitiveness of U.S. Manufacturing," 140.

40. "Trade Liberalization and Pollution in Manufacturing," *International Economic Review* (March 1995).

41. Ibid.; Srinivasn and Bhagwati, "Trade and the Environment," 28.

42. *The Economist*, October 3, 1998.

43. This paragraph draws heavily on Esty, *Greening the GATT*, 5-6, 159-61, 163-64, 181-83.

44. Gene Grossman and Alan Krueger, "Environmental Impacts of a North American Free Trade Area," NBER Working Paper No. 3914, 1992.

45. See Robert E. Baldwin, *Non-tariff Distortions of International Trade* (Washington: Brookings Institution, 1970).

46. See Margaret Kelly and Anne Kenny McGuirk, *Issues and Developments in International Trade Policy* (Washington: International Monetary Fund, 1992), 13-14, 99, 116.

47. For a survey of empirical methods, see Sam Laird and Alexander Yeats, *Quantitative Methods for Trade-Barrier Analysis* (New York: New York University Press, 1990). The example used is from *The Economist*, March 5, 1988.

48. See, for example, J.E. Anderson and J.P. Neary, "A New Approach to Evaluating Trade Policy," *Review of Economic Studies* 63, 1 (1996): 107-25.

49. For details, see Hufbauer and Elliott, *Measuring the Costs of Protection*, 2, 97. A good survey of the auto VER is Douglas R. Nelson, "The Political Economy of U.S. Automobile Protection," in Anne O. Krueger, ed., *The Political Economy of American Trade Policy* (Chicago: University of Chicago Press, 1996), 133-91; also see Nelson's "Making Sense of the Automobile Voluntary Export Restraints: Economics, Politics, and the Political Economy of Protection," NBER Working Paper No. 4746, 1994. For a recent quantitative analysis, see Steven Berry, James Levinsohn, and Ariel Pakes, "Voluntary Export Restraints on Automobiles: Evaluating a Trade Policy," *American Economic Review* 83, 3 (June 1999): 400-30.

50. See Kelly and McGuirk, *Issues and Developments in International Trade Policy*, 101. For a higher cost estimate, see Charles Collyns and Steven Dunaway, "The Cost of Trade Restraints," *IMF Staff Papers* (March 1987): 150-75.

51. See Collyns and Dunaway, "The Cost of Trade Restraints."

52. James Levinsohn, "Carwars: Trying to Make Sense of U.S.-Japan Trade Frictions in the Automobile and Automobile Parts Market," in Robert C. Feenstra, ed., *The Effects of U.S. Trade Protection and Promotion Policies* (Chicago: University of Chicago Press, 1997), 11-32.

53. Anne O. Krueger, "Conclusions," in Krueger, ed., *The Political Economy of American Trade Policy*, 426.

54. Richard N. Cooper, "Comment," in Krueger, ed., *The Political Economy of American Trade Policy*, 195.

55. Hufbauer and Elliott, *Measuring the Costs of Protection*, 2, 97.

56. *Wall Street Journal*, March 3, 1994.

57. Ibid., March 27, 1998.

58. See Michael O. Moore, "Steel Protection in the 1980s: The Waning Influence of Big Steel," in Krueger, ed., *The Political Economy of American Trade Policy*, 73-125; *Wall Street Journal*, March 19, 1999.

59. *Wall Street Journal*, March 10, 1999.

60. See Alison Mitchell, "By a Wide Margin, House Votes Steel Import Curbs," *New York Times*, March 18, 1999.

61. J. Michael Finger, "The MFA Paradox: More Protection and More Trade," in Krueger, ed., *The Political Economy of American Trade Policy*, 197-259.

62. *Rushford Report* (January 1998); USITC, *The Year in Trade 1997*, 148.

63. Finger, "The MFA Paradox."

64. Kelly and McGuirk, *Issues and Developments in International Trade Policy*, 101-02.

65. *Wall Street Journal*, January 10, 1994

66. *Rushford Report* (October 1998).

67. *Rushford Report* (February 1998); Sri Ram Khanna, *International Trade in Textiles: MFA Quotas and a Developing Exporting Country* (New Delhi, 1991).

68. Yongzheng Yang, "The Impact of MFA Phasing Out on World Clothing and Textile Markets," *Journal of Development Studies* 30, 3 (April 1994): 892-915.

69. Khanna, *International Trade in Textiles*.

70. USITC, *The Year in Trade 1996*, 109; *Wall Street Journal*, February 3, 1997; *International Economic Review* (February/March 1997).

71. See Sanjoy Bagchi, "The Integration of the Textile Trade into GATT," *Journal of World Trade* 28, 6 (December 1994): 31-42; Niels Blokker and Jan Deelstra, "Towards a Termination of the Multi-Fibre Arrangement," *Journal of World Trade* 28, 5 (October 1994): 97-118; *Rushford Report* (February 1998); USITC, *The Year in Trade 1993*, 9-11; *1995*, 82; *1997*, 146-48.

72. Richard Harmsen, "The Uruguay Round: A Boon for the World Economy," *Finance and Development* 32, 1 (March 1995): 24-26.

73. A good survey is Fred H. Sanderson, ed., *Agricultural Protection in the Industrialized World* (Washington: Resources for the Future, 1990).

74. *The Economist*, August 24, 1991, December 12, 1992.

75. Charles Yuji Horioka, "Japan's Consumption and Saving in International Perspective," *Economic Development and Cultural Change* 42, 2 (January 1994): 304-05, citing OECD data.

76. For book-length studies, see Giovanni Anania, ed., *Agricultural Trade Conflicts and GATT: New Dimensions in U.S.-European Agricultural Trade Relations* (Boulder, Colo.: Westview Press, 1994); C. Falmer et al., *The Common Agricultural Policy Beyond the MacSharry Reform* (Amsterdam: Elsevier, 1995); Brian Gardner, *European*

Agriculture: Policies, Production, and Trade (London: Routledge, 1996); K.A. Ingersent, ed., *The Reform of the Common Agricultural Policy* (London: Macmillan, 1998); Alan Swinbank, *Farm Policy and Trade Conflict: The Uruguay Round and CAP Reform* (Ann Arbor: University of Michigan Press, 1996). See also *The Economist*, January 20, 1996, September 6, 1997.

77. *The Economist*, February 20, 1999.

78. *National Geographic* 185, 5 (May 1994): 69.

79. See Kelly and McGuirk, *Issues and Developments in International Trade Policy*, 57.

80. For the 1994 crisis, see *Wall Street Journal*, June 1, September 2, 1994.

81. Brent Borrell and Ronald C. Duncan, "A Survey of the Costs of World Sugar Policies," *World Bank Research Observer* 7, 2 (July 1992): 171-94. At one point the reduction in the world price caused by the U.S. sugar protection was estimated to be as much as 48%.

82. *The Economist*, December 12, 1992.

83. See W.M. Corden, *The Revival of Protection*, Group of 30 Occasional Paper No. 14, 1984.

Chapter Six

The Political Economy
of Trade Barriers

OBJECTIVES

OVERALL OBJECTIVE   To set the present context of trade policy by exploring its history and some of its political economy, and by scrutinizing the litany
of arguments for restricting trade.

MORE SPECIFICALLY
- To develop through historical discussion an understanding of American
  trade policy, the forces that drive it, and why American legislation is so
  important to any progress in trade discussions.
- To understand the purposes and role of the new WTO and the GATT that
  came before it.
- To identify the key issues facing world trade negotiators.
- To show why it is that despite protectionism's lack of economic ratio-
  nality, protectionist interests are so powerful.
- To appreciate the arguments for trade barriers and the specific rebuttals
  concerning:
    » preference for domestic production as a personal value,
    » preservation of jobs and easing dislocation,
    » prevention of foreign sweatshops,
    » reduction of the trade deficit,
    » trade barriers as devices for bargaining,
    » development of infant industries, and
    » maintenance of the national defense.

Trade barriers almost always arise out of public policy. They come about because governments conceive them, impose them, and enforce them. The debate on whether to raise or lower the barriers is a central feature of the day-to-day activity of national executives and legislatures around the world, continuing a centuries-old tradition of prominence for polices on international trade. Costs and benefits rain out from these decisions, sometimes as a gentle shower, sometimes in thunderous storm. This chapter considers the relationship between public policy and trade barriers.

A SHORT HISTORY OF TRADE POLICY

Tracing the history of public policy toward trade barriers, even if briefly, is a useful exercise because, over and over, countries have returned to the same issues, and often enough have made the same mistakes. Knowledge of past trade policies can lead to more informed policy choices in the future. American law and policy is key to understanding what can or cannot be done internationally. However idiosyncratic its laws may appear to people in other countries, everyone interested in trade policy must have an acquaintance with them.

Tariffs were originally designed for revenue, with little thought being given to their protective effects. The United States, for example, used a modest tariff of 5% as its earliest and almost its only source of revenue.[*] Other sources of revenue proved difficult to generate. George Washington's admin-istration had to face a Whiskey Rebellion when it tried to tax the domestic output of that product.

Only in the late eighteenth and early nineteenth centuries were the pro-tective effects of tariffs recognized and employed. In England, the repeal of the Corn Laws (the English called grain "corn" in those days) was based on the recognition that farming interests were being protected and industry was being discriminated against by these tariffs on imported grain.[†] In the United States, Alexander Hamilton, the first Secretary of the Treasury, recommended protective tariffs to develop infant industries. Use of these infant-industry tariffs raised the U.S. tariff rate to an average 12.5% at the outbreak of the War of 1812 and to about double that after the war.

---

[*] Under the U.S. Articles of Confederation, even tariff revenue was unavailable because unani-mous agreement of the states was necessary for major legislation to be adopted. Two attempts were made, but opposition from Rhode Island in 1781 and New York in 1783 caused tariff initiatives to fail. Under Article 2 of the U.S. Constitution, Congress received the power to regulate and tax trade.

[†] The Corn Laws favoring landowners had been first enacted by Charles II in 1663. The group united in opposition to the Corn Laws was called the "Manchester School." The name lives on as one of Britain's leading journals of economics.

The South depended on imported goods, however, and managed to block really substantial protective tariffs favored by the North until the Civil War—with one exception, the short-lived "Tariff of Abominations" of 1828. This high tariff so angered the South that one state (South Carolina) threatened to secede, forcing a new tariff law that cut tariffs by two-thirds a scant four years later. At the time of the Civil War, the Confederate States of America continued the South's traditional opposition to the protective tariff by making it unconstitutional to protect any specific industry with a tariff.

The ascendancy of northern manufacturing interests after the Civil War ushered in a long period of high tariffs. Shortly before passage of the Sherman Act, the Congress raised tariffs greatly—no doubt partly as a payoff to industry for accepting the first antitrust restraint.[1] With the Tariff of 1897, protection reached an average level of 57%. Across the Atlantic, German industrialists and economists were successfully advocating the protection of infant industries by tariffs, asking how Germany could ever develop industries in the face of floods of low-priced British manufactures. Thus, by the end of the nineteenth century the use of the protective tariff was well established.

World War I gave tariffs an additional boost, one reason being that the war caused most trade agreements to be canceled.[2] Britain, which had had virtually free trade since the 1840s, turned to tariffs as a means to finance its skyrocketing war costs. The United States, which in 1913 had lowered its tariffs (to 29%), found that World War I had stimulated new, burgeoning industries in chemicals and pharmaceuticals. When it ended, these war babies demanded protection against imports, and in 1921 the Republicans, long the high-tariff party, were back in office and ready to help.

The world began to slide into greater protectionism, with numerous countries choosing higher tariffs if only for bargaining purposes during the negotiations to replace the pre-war trade agreements. In the United States a curious bargain was struck in Congress. American agriculture had changed much during the war years; high prices due to European demand and increased mechanization had expanded output greatly. As European agriculture began to recover, there was a sharp drop in grain prices, causing severe dislocation. To aid the farmers, Congress first increased duties on agricultural imports. This was, however, a futile task because there were so few imports anyway. The tariffs were largely "excess tariffs." Figure 6.1 shows the United States with low wheat imports; the world price P_w is barely below the non-trade equilibrium price of P_{nt}. A tariff of P_wP_t cannot improve the price of agricultural goods beyond P_{nt}. Moreover, there is no revenue once imports fall to zero at P_{nt}. Hence the part of the tariff $P_{nt}P_t$ that lies above the equilibrium point is an excess tariff.

Like consecutive life sentences, a high tariff is not necessarily more effective than a moderate one. Once the tariff is high enough to exclude all imports (P_{nt}), anything higher is an excess tariff.

Farm states received their largely useless protection in 1921; the next year the manufacturing interests claimed their part of the bargain, and the farm bloc voted for high duties on manufactured goods, the so-called Fordney-McCumber Tariff named after its legislative sponsors. Unfortunately for the farmers, the high tariffs on manufacturing were not excess tariffs and thus had a large impact on price. The farmers had traded

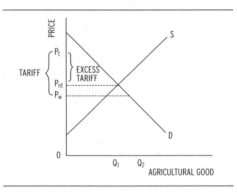

Figure 6.1

AN EXCESS TARIFF

something for nothing. In Europe, revenue tariffs of the war years turned into protective tariffs. Fear of competitive devaluations (a justified fear in many cases) and a rise in economic isolationism encouraged more protectionist tariff policies. In Canada, protectionist interests grew stronger as well.

By the end of the 1920s many people of foresight felt that the tariff situation was out of hand. Some farm senators realized that, in fact, tariffs were not doing them any good. Surely the time had come to lower them. There was, however, no mechanism for negotiating reductions. American tariff policy was securely in the hands of Congress; the President could promise a nation that the legislature would be asked to cut tariffs, but the legislators would not necessarily comply. It was not like a parliament, which would always agree to the cabinet's wishes or force a new election through a no-confidence vote.

The Smoot-Hawley Tariff

President Herbert Hoover had protectionist inclinations, and before his election he had argued that the United States should confine its imports to items that could not be produced domestically.[3] Hoover asked Congress in April of 1929 for a revision of the tariff, seemingly to decrease manufacturing duties somewhat and to increase agricultural ones. The world waited for that decline in manufacturing tariffs. The House of Representatives, in which revenue bills must always first be introduced, voted through a bill sponsored by Representative Willis C. Hawley of Oregon with higher agricultural tariffs and more moderate manufacturing protection. But month after month in the Senate, where the rules on amendments were looser, new tariffs were tacked on under the leadership of the arch-conservative Reed Smoot of Utah. Eventually they totaled 800 items in all fields, at rates that averaged 59.1%, the highest ever in the United States and nearly twice the 1913 figure.* These developments were the less defensible since the United States was running a balance of trade *surplus* at the time.

Meanwhile, the Great Depression had begun, but Hoover suggested no changes in the Smoot-Hawley legislation.† On June 13, 1930, after many months of congressional logrolling, the bill passed the Senate by a close vote of 44-42, passed in the House a day later by 245-177, and sat on Hoover's desk for just three days.[4] Just over a thousand economists, a great majority of the membership of the American Economics Association, sent the President a statement that the bill not only would fail to help agriculture but would certainly invite retaliation by foreign governments on American exports.

To the dismay of the thousand and to the shock of world leaders, who had been hoping to stimulate their economies by exporting more to the United States, President Hoover signed the bill anyway. The psychological effect was immediate and immense, further weakening business confidence abroad. Precisely those evil results predicted for the bill came to pass. Many of the tariffs were excess tariffs in that only part of the increase was enough to halt all trade; the remainder accomplished nothing except to anger foreigners.‡

The United States obviously did not expect such heavy retaliation, but it was sharp and rapid.[5] Twelve large trading countries replied with their own heavy tariffs. Spain, for example, showed how a small and poor country might resist anyway, knowing it would bear the costs. It broke its trade treaty with the United States and imposed very high tariffs, including a prohibitive one on autos; the Swiss public boycotted American products. Italy announced it would buy no more from the United States than the United States did from Italy; Belgium, the Netherlands, Denmark, Sweden, and Norway negotiated as a bloc to increase their leverage. Some countries moved toward clientage: Germany granted trading concessions to the Balkan countries, while Britain and France moved toward imperial preferences for their colonies and dominions.

---

* In another sense, tariffs had been higher during the nineteenth century because there were fewer duty-free imports.

† By tradition the first name on a bill is its chief sponsor in the originating house of the legislature. Thus "Hawley-Smoot" would be the correct name, and it is preferred by some. Senator Smoot was a commanding figure, however, and so "Smoot-Hawley" was and remains the more familiar term.

‡ The bill made provision for an "equalizing tariff" (Section 336) under which the tariff would make the foreign cost of production plus the tariff for an item equal to the domestic production cost. Under this clause there were 101 cases leading to 29 increased tariffs until the section lapsed after 1941. But because so many tariffs were excess, Section 336 could also be used to lower tariffs, which happened 25 times. See J. Michael Finger and Ann Harrison, "The MFA Paradox: More Protection and More Trade?" in Anne O. Krueger, ed., *The Political Economy of American Trade Policy* (Chicago: University of Chicago Press, 1996), 203.

Canada's retaliation was striking.[6] In May 1930, a month before Smoot-Hawley was passed, Canada had fired a warning shot across U.S. bows by establishing new duties on 16 products involving about 30% of all U.S. merchandise exports to Canada. A month after Smoot-Hawley was enacted, Canadian voters elected a new Conservative government, the only Conservative majority between 1911 and 1958. This government was intent on retaliation, rapidly hit 125 U.S. export items with higher tariffs, and actively cajoled Britain to grant imperial trade preferences.

World trade spiraled downward. The total imports of 75 countries had been almost $3 billion per month at the start of 1929. They fell below $2 billion in June 1930, below $1 billion in July 1931, and fetched up at about half a billion dollars in March 1933.[7] In volume terms, the total exports of the United States declined more than those of any other major nation and were only 53% of their 1929 volume in the year 1932. (Note that the volume of trade fell less than did its value because prices also declined. The price reductions in themselves served to increase trade barriers, however, because most tariffs of the time, including those under Smoot-Hawley, were specific rather than *ad valorem*.) Perhaps three-quarters of the collapse in trade must be attributed to the income effects of the Great Depression.[8] As output and income fell around the world, countries imported less, which meant their

REVISIONIST VIEWS OF THE SMOOT-HAWLEY TARIFF

Central though the Smoot-Hawley Tariff has been considered by economists who study the Great Depression, it is possible to exaggerate its importance, and a revisionist scholarship has appeared.[9] The new duties covered only about a third of all imports, and the duty increases in percentage terms (20% to an average of 47%) were somewhat smaller than they had been in the 1922 Fordney-McCumber Tariff. The further rise in the average rate of duty to 59.1% was due to the combination of specific tariffs and a decline in prices. Moreover, it can be argued (and John Maynard Keynes did so) that by cutting imports the tariff switched consumer purchases toward domestic production and increased the incentive to invest in domestic industries. But that interpretation neglects the negative effect on production and investment because exports were cut.

In spite of the revisionism, no one doubts that Smoot-Hawley, coming as it did just at the onset of the Depression, gave rise to bitter hostility and had a stunning psychological impact. The major lesson from Smoot-Hawley is that trade wars provoked by protection can cause a meltdown of world trade, that reductions in trade can make depressions worse, and that the political results can be doleful.

trading partners exported less, which meant their output (exports being part of output) and incomes fell further. Even so, these income effects were related to trade because of the psychological impact of Smoot-Hawley on world investment. This was surely America's second "Tariff of Abominations."

Perhaps most portentous were the abhorrent political ramifications of the rise of barriers and the decline of trade. In Japan, the 23 percentage-point rise in the average tariff on Japanese goods tended to undercut the liberals in the Japanese government and spurred the supremacy of militaristic nationalism. In Germany, the important steel, chemical, and electrical industries turned to the Nazi Party's protectionist Ostpolitik and rearmament strategies. Hitler, chosen chancellor in 1933 after a strong electoral showing, was a protectionist who found his ideas on trade validated by the barriers rising around the world.

A Turn in Trade Policy

When the Roosevelt administration assumed office in 1933, after an election that saw both Senator Smoot and Representative Hawley defeated by large majorities, it took rapid though belated steps to undo the harm. The result was the Reciprocal Trade Agreements Act of 1934, which has formed the basis for all subsequent American trade policy.* With the RTA Act, the United States began a process that, where tariffs are concerned, has not ceased. Several key parts of the act still survive.

1. The word "reciprocal" pointed to a main feature. Tariff cuts were made by the United States only in return for tariff cuts by trading partners. During its long life, the RTA Act was renewed 11 times, and eventually it covered 54 countries. The idea that mutual concessions would generate double gains, with increased imports benefiting consumers while increased exports benefited producers, was and remains a powerful one. Reciprocity also has an appearance of fairness, with each side appearing to give up something. The principle of reciprocity is still central to trade negotiations.

2. Congress gave the President *prior* authorization to cut tariffs on an item-by-item basis. This provision avoided the earlier problem of the executive branch being unable to negotiate for fear that Congress would not agree. The principle was continued under the trade acts of 1962, 1974, and 1988; the

---

* Roosevelt's Secretary of State, Cordell Hull of Tennessee, was the leader in promoting the RTA Act. Hull was a committed believer in the idea that international trade promotes peace, as countries see that their prosperity depends on good relations with their trading partners. Hull frequently told the story of two Tennessee neighbors, Jenkins and Jones, who feuded until Jenkins's mule went lame and Jones ran short of corn. After Jenkins rented a mule from Jones and paid him in corn, they became fast friends. It is a powerful idea (though admittedly in 1914 Germany was a major trading partner of Britain, Belgium, and Russia). See Finger and Harrison, "The MFA Paradox," 208.

President retained the power to negotiate tariff reductions in a big package. The Smoot-Hawley Tariff was thus the last time in U.S. history that Congress initiated an entire trade bill without delegating its power to the President. The situation did not develop so favorably in the European Community (EC, or European Common Market), where for a long time each member nation bargained separately, with no central authority authorized to carry out trade negotiations. In recent years, however, negotiations have been undertaken collectively by the European Union (EU), which succeeded the EC.

3. All tariff concessions were to be made on a non-discriminatory basis. If the United States cut a tariff to one nation, it would cut them to all. This provision is known in diplomatic language as the *most-favored-nation* clause, or MFN. Even in 1934, it was a very old principle of tariff legislation. It had developed initially in Europe in the fifteenth and sixteenth centuries and had become common in trade pacts because no country wanted to be left behind. The first treaty ever signed by the United States, with France in 1778, embodied the principle of conditional MFN treatment—the United States guaranteed MFN treatment for France if France guaranteed the same thing to the United States.

For a brief period early in this century the United States departed from this tradition, but the provisions proved unworkable.* The problems of defining and enforcing separate tariffs for each of the thousands of product classifications were compounded greatly by multiplying all these by the number of countries in the world. Hence the 1922 (Fordney–McCumber) tariff re-established the MFN principle that was retained in the RTA.

A major exception from MFN treatment is permitted under the rules for free trade areas, customs unions, and common markets, such as the EU, whose member countries can lower tariffs among themselves without granting the same privilege to outsiders. A second exception to the MFN provision is political in nature, made after World War II when the Communist bloc refused to enter into negotiations on tariffs. Rather than grant the Communists something for nothing, the United States and some other countries exempted them from the new tariff levels. A country denied MFN treatment by the United States finds that it faces the old Smoot-Hawley rates. Russia and Ukraine received MFN treatment only in 1992, while China's eligibility must be reviewed every year.

A final and more recent exception to MFN treatment is the Generalized System of Preferences, or GSP, which allows for duty-free entry of many

---

* Weaseling out of MFN commitments is an old tradition. The most famous dodge of all times was the German tariff of 1905 on cattle. The Germans wanted to give Switzerland a discriminatory rate without affecting the rate given to other countries. Hence, this wording was adopted: "The [favorable] tariff shall apply to dappled mountain cattle or brown cattle reared at a spot at least 300 meters above sea level, and which have at least one month's grazing each year at a spot at least 800 meters above sea level."

goods from the less-developed countries. Crucially for modern trade, however, MFN does not apply to non-tarrif barriers. The rapid rise of these barriers has spelled trouble both for the LDCs and for small manufacturing countries, neither of which have much bargaining power to retaliate against discriminatory practices. See the accompanying box for further details.

THE GSP FOR LESS-DEVELOPED COUNTRIES

Since the 1970s the less-developed countries have been granted special tariff preferences by the developed countries. Many of the former Communist countries have recently been made eligible for the same treatment. This Generalized System of Preferences (GSP) is constantly held up as a major concession by the rich nations to the poor ones. The EU first offered GSP in 1971; the United States in 1976. A form of GSP is now run by some 27 industrial and other rich countries. In the United States, over 4,000 products from more than 130 countries are covered, with about $16 billion in imports (2% of the total) coming in duty-free under the program.[10]

By boosting the returns on exports from the LDCs, the GSP increased trade and thereby has probably contributed to faster economic growth. In general, however, GSP has been a disappointment. All the GSPs have time limits; they are not permanent, and renewal always involves a battle. (In 1997 the U.S. law expired, and until it was renewed retroactively in August normal tariffs were collected.) The rich countries unilaterally reserved the right to exclude items or remove the preferences and have frequently done so. For example, the United States has always excluded textiles, clothing, shoes, and some electronic goods and steel, all of which are products of interest in the LDCs. Other exclusions apply when imports rise over certain trigger levels. Furthermore, under U.S. law since 1985 the President is permitted to graduate a country when it reaches an income level of $8,500 per capita. (This seems reasonable. When it becomes rich, a country deserves more normal treatment and full incorporation into the regular trading system.) Taiwan, South Korea, Hong Kong, and Singapore are four of the graduates.

Politics (including insurgencies, oil issues, and trade disputes) can lead to cancellation of the preferences. Clauses in the U.S. law allow the President to end the preferences if a beneficiary fails to provide reasonable access to its markets and require recipients to assure "internationally recognized worker rights," including trade unions and "acceptable" conditions of work. GSP can also be denied for non-cooperation with drug policies and failure to protect intellectual property rights. Among the countries that have lost their U.S. GSP treatment for these reasons are Burma/Myanmar, the Central African Republic, Chile, Mauritania, Nicaragua, Paraguay, Romania, and Sudan. The AFL-CIO files numerous petitions to remove GSP preferences for these reasons.

The EU and Japanese GSP schemes differ from U.S. GSP in having many tariff-rate quotas (TRQs). Duty-free entry is allowed up to a certain quantity with a higher tariff beyond that figure, as analyzed in Chapter 4.

Probably the great attention devoted to GSP has been a mistake. It gives the developed countries a sense that they are generous, and it convinces the LDCs they have received a concession. But making the LDCs full partners in world trade and proceeding with general tariff cuts would have been even better. In that case, the many exceptions and limits would not have been possible because most-favored-nation treatment would have applied.

Progress in Cutting Tariffs

Progress in implementing reciprocal tariff cuts was slow at first. In 1934, the world was so mired in the Great Depression that tariff cuts were hardly enough to stimulate much export-led growth anywhere. World War II followed, imposing its own restrictions on trade, so that most of the major negotiations came in the postwar period. By 1962, however, in the presence of 54 reciprocal agreements with other countries, the average tariff level in the United States had fallen from a 1934 figure of about 53¢ per dollar to only 11¢. About half of the fall was due to the RTC negotiations. The other half was due to the fact that most U.S. tariffs at the time were specific duties such as "10¢ per widget." As already noted, rising prices lessen the impact of any specific duty, and the inflation that occurred in those years was about as effective as trade negotiations in bringing down the level of tariffs.[11]

The General Agreement on Tariffs and Trade (GATT)

The century's most favorable development in the struggle to reduce tariffs came after World War II with the formation of an organization called the General Agreement on Tariffs and Trade (GATT).[12] GATT lasted for almost half a century until it was succeeded by the new World Trade Organization (WTO) in 1996. It was a powerful force in furthering the goal of tariff reduction and in encouraging trade.

GATT had an unusual origin. In 1944 at the Bretton Woods Conference in New Hampshire, it was decided to establish an International Trade Organization (ITO) to accompany the International Monetary Fund and the World Bank that were established at the same time. The ITO was intended to liberalize protection once World War II had ended. A charter signed at Havana in 1947 formulated rules for the ITO, and the organization was to have real teeth to enforce those rules. Unlike the other organizations created by Bretton Woods, however, the ITO failed to gain approval, largely because the U.S. Congress did not ratify the Havana Charter. Congress withheld its consent for several reasons, but mostly because of fear that other countries would not abide by the various rules of the ITO.

An agency had already been established, however, to set the ITO on its way. This Interim Committee of the ITO was authorized by an administrative working agreement called the General Agreement on Tariffs and Trade. GATT thus did not require U.S. congressional ratification. Attempts were later made in Congress to ratify it, but these never succeeded. GATT nonetheless remained in existence, its headquarters in Geneva, Switzerland, because the need for it was seen and appreciated. Despite its small staff (only about 350, compared to the 6,000 or so employed by the World Bank) and small budget (some $40 million), it was an international agency of great significance.[*]

THE GATT'S INFLUENCE ON WORLD TRADE

GATT grew from 23 original member nations to well over 100 in the 1990s, with nearly 90% of world trade conducted among the member nations. On joining, members had to agree to a number of rules, though significantly, GATT had no power whatsoever to enforce these rules. Enforcement was in the hands of the members, who were empowered to retaliate against a wrongdoer. Among the GATT rules, all still in force under the successor WTO, were the following.

1. With tariffs, the most-favored-nation principle had to be extended to all members. As already noted, allowable exceptions to MFN treatment are the reduced tariffs for less-developed countries under the GSP program and the permission to members of customs unions to lower tariffs among themselves.

2. GATT prohibited quotas, with two exceptions. One was for less-developed countries that needed temporarily to defend their balance of payments. The other was that countries with price support programs were permitted to impose quotas against agricultural imports. Because of this clause, the GATT had little effect on farming. (Even though other quotas were illegal under the GATT rules, the prohibition against them was violated often enough.)

3. Members agreed to consult on trade problems at meetings of the GATT Council of Representatives and to submit their disputes to GATT panels. Before the mid-1980s, only two or three panel decisions per year had been the usual total, with 52 panels giving a ruling between the time of GATT's foundation in the late 1940s to mid-1986. After that, much more use was made of the mechanism. A good many GATT panels were successful in healing trade disputes. The successes were limited, however, with many major areas of friction never making it to GATT, as when a voluntary restraint was negotiated. Other disputes could not be settled because GATT panel decisions

---

[*] GATT personnel carried identity cards and Swiss work permits that bore the name Interim Committee of the ITO.

had to be implemented by consensus. A party to a dispute could engage in delay or even ignore a ruling. Among the panel reports adopted between 1986 and 1992, more than two-thirds were not satisfactorily implemented or were postponed. The lack of any power to enforce decisions was an embarrassing one.

4. GATT promoted agreements to "bind" tariffs. When a tariff is bound, the nation imposing it agrees not to raise it unilaterally. In time, most developed-country tariffs came to be bound, as is shown in Table 6.1. Less-developed countries bound far fewer of their tariffs, often only one-fifth or one-quarter of them.

Table 6.1

TARIFF BINDINGS,
PERCENTAGE OF ALL TARIFFS

United States	98
Canada	96
Japan	91
EU	88
Australia	12
All developed countries	82

Source: Margaret Kelly and Anne Kenny McGuirk, *Issues and Developments in International Trade Policy* (Washington: International Monetary Fund, 1992), 115.

5. For a long time, political sensitivity inhibited GATT's ability to search for violations of its rules and publish the information. This changed in 1989, when a Trade Policy Review Mechanism was put in place. Member countries of GATT (continued under the later WTO) make reports on their existing barriers, after which a commentary is issued. About a dozen countries a year are reviewed.[13]

THE GATT ROUNDS OF TRADE NEGOTIATIONS

The most impressive activity of GATT was its sponsorship of conferences or rounds of multilateral trade negotiation. Eight rounds took place, and another is currently planned under the WTO (a preliminary meeting was held in Seattle in late 1999). Table 6.2 gives the details.

The tariff reductions were phased in over several years. For example, the Kennedy Round, which cut tariffs to an average *ad valorem* level of 10.3%, became fully effective on January 1, 1972, while the Tokyo Round became fully effective on January 1, 1987. The reductions were partly spoiled by the rise of many other sorts of obstacles already described in Chapters 4 and 5, but they nonetheless stand as an impressive monument to the efforts of the GATT negotiators.

Until the Uruguay Round, the most disappointing results were in agriculture, which for many years has been a very difficult trade issue. Another disappointment is (and continues to be) that tariff peaks still exist, rising above the relatively low duties on most products. The average rate may be low, but the peaks can distort trade significantly in the sectors where they apply.

Table 6.2

GATT ROUNDS OF TRADE NEGOTIATIONS

Name of Round	Dates	Number of Participants	Tariff Cut (%)
Geneva	1947	23	
Annecy, France	1949	13	
Torquay, England	1951	38	73
Geneva	1956	26	
Dillon Round	1960-61	26	
Kennedy Round	1964-67	62	35
Tokyo Round	1973-79	99	33
Uruguay Round	1986-93	125	40

Source: Economic Report of the President 1995 (Washington: Council of Economic Advisors, 1995), 205.

Finally, tariffs continued high in many less-developed countries, often five to ten times more on average than the tariffs found in the developed countries.

The first six GATT rounds focused almost entirely on tariff reduction, but starting with the Tokyo Round attention turned to questions such as regularizing valuation for tariff purposes, attacking obstacles imposed by means of rules and appeal procedures, opening up government purchases, bringing the problem of subsidies for exports under control, and including trade in services in the negotiations.

THE URUGUAY ROUND AND
THE WORLD TRADE ORGANIZATION

During the early 1980s there was a long debate on the desirability of a new GATT round of trade talks. The most enthusiastic supporters were the United States, which wanted to control the problems in agriculture, services, and high-tech products, and Japan, which wanted to put a rein on the rapidly growing worldwide protection against its manufactured goods. At Punta del Este, Uruguay, the GATT membership in 1986 finally agreed to a new Uruguay Round of negotiations that began in 1987. The Uruguay Round (which in spite of its name was mostly hammered out in Geneva) was by far the broadest ever undertaken, with many aspects of international trade being considered that had never before been taken up in a GATT round. At one time 15 separate groups of negotiations were under way. The issues were very much interlinked, with progress in one area contingent on progress in others, which is why the membership had to achieve a big package deal that proved very difficult to negotiate. By contrast to the earlier GATT rounds, the Uruguay Round was surrounded by much less secrecy and was conducted by much bigger delegations. At a major Uruguay Round meeting held at Brussels in December 1990 there were over 300 official representatives from the United States alone, with another 600 or so industry and congressional observers and lobbyists in the U.S. entourage.

The negotiations took seven years to complete and the agreement will not be fully implemented until 2005, meaning 17 years from start to finish. By the time the Uruguay Round treaty was signed at Marrakesh, Morocco, 125 countries were participating in the negotiations.[14] That treaty occupies 424 pages plus over 20,000 pages of country commitments.[15]

FAST-TRACK: AVOIDING U.S. CONGRESSIONAL MEDDLING

A major lesson of the Smoot-Hawley Tariff was the danger that Congress would meddle in trade policy with amendments that raised barriers. The experience that one member would support a tariff of interest to another member in return for that member's support for another barrier was too vivid to ignore. The Reciprocal Trade Agreements Act of 1934 accordingly granted the President prior authority to cut tariffs, as did the Trade Expansion Act of 1962. The problem later negotiators faced was that the various non-tariff barriers could not be so easily defined as tariffs and it was unclear just what Congress should authorize ahead of time. Thus the principle of the fast-track: Congress would give the President negotiating authority and deed away its right to amend the resulting agreement.

For example, the Trade Reform Act of 1974 enabled the United States to enter the Tokyo Round negotiations. The President received the authority to reduce tariffs by 60% on most items over a 10-year period, and the ability of Congress to obstruct an agreement was limited by giving that body only 60 legislative days to veto the presidential action with the only options being to vote "yes" or "no."

The 1988 Omnibus Trade Act allowed Presidents Bush and Clinton to negotiate in the Uruguay Round. The Act lengthened the fast-track to 90 days, with no-amendment consideration of the results if these results were submitted to Congress before May 31, 1991. A two-year extension was provided for unless Congress blocked it by majority vote, and extension proved to be necessary when the 1991 deadline was reached without an agreement yet in sight. Attempts to block the extension failed, and the Uruguay Round was ratified on the mandated up-or-down vote.[*]

---

[*] U.S. ratification was halted for a time by the tariff cuts in the Uruguay Round. The predicted loss of $12 billion in tariff revenue over five years clashed with congressional budget rules. Thus, the administration had to come up with the revenue from numerous obscure sources, which was difficult, and required a 60-vote budget rule waiver in the Senate—all this in spite of clear evidence that future tax revenues would rise as trade increased and incomes grew. According to testimony at the time, the Uruguay Round tariff cuts would produce $3 in new government revenue from taxes for every $1 lost from tariff cuts.

The sequel has been theatrical. When the fast-track provisions expired in 1993, President Clinton, along with most economists, called for its renewal. They have been calling ever since. An attempt at renewal was abandoned in 1994, and others failed in 1997 and 1998. After the 1997 failure the vocabulary changed to "renewal of traditional trading authority." The main reason fast-track has failed is because of resistance from a "blue-green coalition" (blues opposed because they believe that labor rights should be protected, greens because they believe trade law is not strong enough on the environment), plus antitrade proclivities of some in both the Republican and the Democratic parties.[16] By 1999, Congress was even proposing "check-in rights," meaning that a vote would be required *before* the President would be permitted to sign a new trade agreement.[17] As a result, the Clinton administration has virtually given up the attempt to resuscitate fast-track and plans to undertake a new round of trade negotiations without it. But it remains essential that any bill to ratify new results must come up for a vote on a reasonable schedule and that amendments be limited in some way.[18]

The Attack on Barriers in the Uruguay Round Agreement

The scope of the Uruguay Round is broad. The main areas of the original agreement are discussed below, though we postpone treatment of a few aspects until these areas are reached later in the book. Certain other topics were left as loose ends, and these are considered later in this chapter.

TARIFFS

Industrial countries agreed to cut their tariffs 40% in five equal annual steps of eight percentage points ending in the year 2000.[19] That exceeded the original goal of a 33% cut. Under the "zero-for-zero" agreement, tariffs are being eliminated in a number of sectors, including beer, whiskey, and brandy, construction equipment, farm equipment, furniture, medical equipment, paper, pharmaceuticals, and toys, some at once, some in five years, some in 10 years, and will be greatly reduced in several other sectors (chemicals, wood, aluminum). The percentage of goods

Table 6.3

LDC TARIFFS (%) AND
THE URUGUAY ROUND

	Before	*After*
Argentina	38	31
Brazil	41	27
Chile	35	25
Colombia	44	35
India	71	32
South Korea	18	8
Malaysia	10	9
Sri Lanka	29	28
Thailand	36	28
Venezuela	50	31

Source: IMF Survey, November 14, 1994.

entering duty-free will go from 20% to 44% when all cuts are complete. The average tariff on manufactures (weighted by the importance of the trade in each category) will have fallen from 6.3% to 3.8%. Developed-country tariffs will not exceed 5% except for textiles and clothing, leather, footwear and other leather and rubber products, and transport equipment. Less-developed countries are reducing their tariffs significantly, many by more than the developed countries, as seen in Table 6.3. They are also increasing their bindings of tariffs.

Table 6.4

TARIFF ESCALATION: TARIFF RATES ON
DEVELOPED-COUNTRY IMPORTS FROM LDCS (%)

	Raw Materials	*Semi-Manufactures*	*Finished Products*
Pre-Uruguay Round	2.1	5.4	9.1
Post-Uruguay Round	0.8	2.8	6.2
Percentage-Point Reduction	1.3	2.6	2.9

Source: Norman S. Fieleke, "The Uruguay Round of Trade Negotiations: An Overview," *New England Economic Review* (May/June 1995): 3.

There are still remaining problems. Tariff escalation against processed commodities, discussed in Chapter 4 and harmful to the LDCs, still exists, as Table 6.4 shows. There are still tariff peaks and high rates in the LDCs that await further treatment.

QUOTAS AND VERS

The Uruguay Round aims to phase out quotas and VERs, with special attention to reducing the heavy protection in textiles, clothing, and agricultural commodities. All are subjected to *tariffication*—that is, tariffs and tariff-rate quotas (TRQs) are being substituted for quotas. It will take years, however, to convert the textile and clothing quotas to tariffs, as explained in Chapter 5. Moreover, tariffs in these areas will be very high. (Note that converting quotas to their tariff equivalents, even if no lowering were undertaken, would immediately increase government revenue, some of which could be used to aid workers and firms harmed by imports.) Future VERs against the signatory WTO members are prohibited unless they come under new rules concerning so-called dumping and safeguards discussed in this chapter and the next.[20] Existing VERs not in these categories were eliminated at the start of 1999 with the exception of one grandfathered VER for each member that will be allowed to extend to 2000. They can still be used against non-members, however, and they can be retained for a time if a non-member joins the WTO.

AGRICULTURE

Agricultural trade is only about 13% of all merchandise trade, a declining figure. But the issue of trade barriers in agriculture, necessary because of farm price support programs as discussed in Chapter 5, almost wrecked the Uruguay Round.[21] The EU initially refused to move far on the issue as countries with a comparative advantage in agriculture insisted that support for agriculture be uncoupled from production and that the subsidized exports be stopped. After years of debate, a great compromise was finally proposed by GATT Director-General, Arthur Dunkel. The EU agreed to reduce the volume of its subsidized exports by 21% from a 1986–90 base over six years, less than the 24% of the Dunkel draft but still a substantial figure. U.S. negotiators agreed not to count direct payment to farmers as production subsidies to be assessed against the 21% reduction in subsidized exports. The way seemed clear for the EU to cut back on its price supports and move to a new system of direct income payments less directly connected to production. (U.S. deficiency payments to farmers would not be counted as subsidies either.)

EU farmers, particularly in France, reached extremes of opposition. It was an "agricultural Munich," said Jacques Chirac of the neo-Gaullists.[22] French farmers sprayed manure on roads and politicians, burned foreign sheep alive, and dumped dirt and planted crops in crucial places such as the Champs Elysées in Paris. But eventually France and the EU agreed to the compromise.* It included the following features:

A *market access agreement* requires all countries to convert their agricultural quotas to tariffs or TRQs and then bind them. The developed countries must reduce their tariffs by 6% per year on average over 6 years, 1995–2000, for a total average reduction of 36%, with a minimum 15% reduction for each product. Signers agreed to a minimum access provision of 5% of the domestic market in 2000 (rising from 3% in 1995), meaning that a minimum of 5% of consumption will be imports. A safeguard is provided for, with a tariff-rate quota allowed if there is a surge in imports or if the price of imports falls below a reference price. The tariff rises as the price changes or as imports surge.

Less-developed countries must tariffy, then reduce their tariffs by 2.4% per year over the 10 years from 1995–2004, for a total reduction of 24%. A minimum access provision of 3% of the domestic market in 1995 and 5% in 2004 is provided. The poorest of the LDCs will not be required to make a reduction, though they will have to bind their tariffs.

---

* The United States agreed to a "peace clause" whereby it would not use trade law to object to compromises reached in the agriculture negotiations even if they would otherwise break trade law.

Special import access rules were negotiated in specific cases for "developing-country dietary staples." A minimum access of 1% of domestic access had to be allowed initially, rising by 0.25% per year to 2% in 1998 and 4% in 2004. The rule applies, for example, to South Korea's rice market. Japan was also allowed to have the special rule for rice, rising from 4% of the market in 1995 to 8% in 2000. After that, the market would be open but a high declining tariff would apply. In effect, Japan and South Korea will lift their rice bans. (Thailand is likely to be the biggest gainer.)

The liberalization of trade in agriculture is limited because countries tariffied based on tariff equivalents in the years 1986-88, a time of high protection—actually, the highest that could have been picked. In any case, most countries appear to have used high-range estimates. The EU and other European countries were the worst offenders. The EU's bound tariffs on sugar and milk are nearly 300%, over 100% for milk and cheese, over 150% for wheat, 125% for some beef, 826% (!) for offal. But others have chosen high duties, too. U.S. tariffs for milk and sugar are about 200%. The Canadian tariffication resulted in duties of 286% for chicken, 188% for eggs, 273% for yogurt, and the TRQs for dairy products have over-quota tariffs as high as 300%. All of these are prohibitive rates.[23]

The *domestic support agreement* reduces subsidies to agriculture. Developed countries agreed to lower domestic subsidies by a total of 20% over the six years 1995-2000 from a 1986-88 base period. For LDCs, the reduction is 13.3% over 10 years, 1995-2004. The poorest LDCs need not reduce, though they must cap or bind their level of support. Programs to limit production, direct payments to farmers, and deficiency payments of the U.S. type are excluded from the calculations. So are support programs that contribute less than 5% to an item's value (10% for LDCs).

An *export subsidies agreement* requires a reduction of 36% in the value of export subsidies and 21% in the volume of goods benefiting from such subsidies by 2000 compared to a base of 1986-90. The reductions have to apply to each product group and are not just an average. For LDCs, the percentages are 23% and 14% for 10 years, 1995-2004. The poorest LDCs are exempt. "Backloading" was insisted on by the EU. This allows some large sales from surplus stocks early in the period, with the agreement biting more severely in later years.

TRIPS AND TRIMS

TRIPS are *trade-related aspects of intellectual property*. New rules had to be adopted by the developed countries no later than 1996, by less-developed countries no later than 2000, and by the poorest LDCs no later than 2006. Patents have to be protected for 20 years and copyrights for 50. The patent and copyright protection will be especially important for developed-country pharmaceuticals, agricultural chemicals, and computer software. (Canadian makers of generic drugs complained bitterly about the extension.)

TRIMS are *trade-related investment measures*. Various practices that discriminate against foreign firms, such as domestic content laws, export requirements, trade-balancing requirements in which the firms are required to export in order to import, and limiting access to foreign exchange to what a firm earns from exporting, are being phased out. Their elimination is over two years (to January 1, 1997) for the developed countries, five years for the LDCs (on January 1, 2000), and seven years for the poorest LDCs (January 1, 2002).[24] Brazil, Egypt, India, and the Philippines led spirited opposition to this measure but lost. A much-needed item, an agreement to limit or eliminate the bidding over tax holidays and reductions used to lure production from one country to another, has not been achieved as yet.

The World Trade Organization (WTO)

The most imposing outcome of the Uruguay Round by far was the establishment of the World Trade Organization, or WTO, as a successor to the GATT.* The WTO opened for business on January 1, 1995, and during the following year GATT and the WTO coexisted legally so as to ensure a smooth transition.[25] The WTO occupies the GATT headquarters at Geneva, Switzerland, and is about the same size as the old GATT secretariat. It is not part of the United Nations system. There is a one-country one-vote procedure (though the EU has as many votes as it has members). The idea of one vote per member attracted much adverse attention in the large countries, but no voting in GATT had been undertaken since the late 1950s and consensus continues to be the normal method for decision-making in the WTO as it was under GATT. Amendments require a two-thirds vote and waivers a three-quarters majority.

THE WTO MEMBERSHIP

In 1999, there were 134 WTO members.[26] Numerous GATT non-members have applied for membership, including Albania, Algeria, Armenia, Azerbaijan, Belarus, Cambodia, China, Croatia, Estonia, Georgia, Iran, Jordan, Kazakhstan, Lithuania, Macedonia, Moldova, Nepal, Oman, Russia, Saudi Arabia, Sudan, Taiwan, Ukraine, Uzbekistan, Vietnam, and Yemen. The non-members not applying are Afghanistan, Iraq, Iran, Liberia, Libya, North

---

* Originally the name was to be the Multilateral Trade Organization (MTO), but Canada proposed a name change in 1990. The negotiations were scheduled to conclude in December 1990, but several deadlines were missed.

THE ARGUMENT THAT THE WTO IS "WORLD GOVERNMENT"

Much ink has been spilled arguing that the WTO constitutes a move toward world government that will supersede national law. Some legislators in the United States were particularly exercised about this charge, even though the U.S. itself had pushed for many years for an international trade body with more teeth. It is hard to make the case that the WTO has dangerous supernational power, however. Its panel decisions and agreements do not have legal force in the United States, and when U.S. legislation contravenes WTO rules it is up to Congress to decide what to do. The implementing treaty states "No provision … that is inconsistent with any law of the United States shall have effect." (If a panel decision is adverse and no compensation is made, the winner is authorized to retaliate, of course.)[27] Should the WTO pursue a U.S. state as a defendant, the U.S. government has agreed to negotiate on that state's behalf. If it felt sufficiently aggrieved, the United States, like any other member, could simply withdraw after giving six months' notice. This was not enough for Senator Dole, who pushed through a law to make it politically easier to withdraw. That law has created a panel of five federal judges who will review WTO decisions and rulings adverse to the United States. If the panel decides the WTO has "exceeded its authority" three times in five years, a congressional vote to withdraw is permitted. (The President has veto power.)[28]

Korea, Somalia, Yemen, and Yugoslavia (Serbia and Montenegro), which lost its membership when the old Yugoslavia broke up.

Russia's entry has been delayed because it will not agree to eschew barriers contrary to WTO rules. Russian tariffs have risen higher than before (now a trade-weighted average of 14%) because they have become an important source of revenue. It also requires many import licenses, pays subsidies, and has customs irregularities and "rough and ready" standards, testing, and labeling.[29]

Difficult problems have delayed China's entry. Importers must have a government license to import anything into China, joint ventures require Chinese partners with a majority holding and are subject to rules such as exporting a minimum amount and buying local components, and no foreigners can engage in distribution or transportation or banking. Disputes surround whether China will be treated as a developed country or as an LDC. The United States insists on the former, which would mean a rapid run-down of aid to state-operated enterprises. Many U.S. members of Congress oppose membership because they demand linkage between entry, human rights, workers' rights, and weapons proliferation. A Gephardt bill would require the President to have congressional approval before supporting China's admission. (A major result of China's membership would be an end to the annual spat over MFN treatment—members get MFN treatment automatically. The debates on this topic have grown so discordant that the U.S. administration has given up using the term "most-favored-nation," fearing the public will believe, mistakenly, that favoritism is involved. The new term is "normal trading relations.")

In 1999, China offered a better deal than most anyone expected in its attempt to gain WTO entry.[30] But the U.S. government (to which the offer was made, for that is where the greatest opposition has been) turned down Premier Zhu Rongji's offer. The United States may have been taken by surprise by the scope of the Chinese proffer. Under the deal, tariffs on priority items would have fallen far, to an average of only 7%, and China offered zero tariffs within a few years on information and technology items and an end to quotas on citrus, meat, and wheat. Over three years, foreign firms could have trading and distribution rights. The service concessions were broad as well. Within five years, foreign banks could open anywhere and deal with anybody. The restriction on the number of foreign insurance companies would be lifted at once. The movie industry would be thrown open and foreign participation up to 49% of ownership would be allowed in telecommunications. It was a brave offer because in the short run it had the potential to cause as many as 11 million workers to have to change their jobs.

But the United States wanted more, including consumer finance for car purchases, favorable access to the securities industry, extension of quotas on textiles and clothing to 2010, and better terms on protocol issues such as labor rights and the environment. Observers fear that the Chinese opposition to liberalized trade would cause some of the handsome concessions to be retracted.[31]

THE DIRECTOR-GENERAL

The choice of the first Director-General of the WTO involved a struggle. The EU candidate (supported by many former colonies in Africa, the Caribbean, and the Pacific) was Italy's Renato Ruggiero, trade minister in three Italian governments and a director of Fiat. He had supported the harsh Italian rules on Japanese auto imports and his candidacy was opposed, even disparaged, by the United States.[32] The U.S. candidate, Carlos Salinas of Mexico, withdrew when his brother was involved in a political murder. The Japanese candidate was Kim Chul Su, South Korea's trade minister. In a consolation prize, he was appointed (perhaps unnecessarily) as fourth assistant director-general. Ruggiero won the job and performed creditably, though according to reports he had to agree to serve only four years with an understanding that the next director-general would not be a European.[33]

So it transpired, but when Ruggiero left office in 1999 the struggle was renewed.[34] Two candidates emerged to succeed him, Supachai Panitchpakdi, Thailand's Deputy Prime Minister, and Michael Moore, a former Prime Minister of New Zealand. Deadlock ensued, with the United States and Europe supporting Moore, and Japan and many less-developed countries, including those of Southeast Asia and Mexico, supporting Panitchpakdi. When Ruggiero departed at the end of April 1999, the choice had still not been made. "WTO Paralyzed by Leadership Crisis" was the Associated Press headline.[35] The matter is important. A strong director-general is essential in refereeing negotiations, arranging compromises, and ensuring that the rules will be followed. The task is formidable. (A solution of sorts was eventually reached. Moore and Panitchpakdi are to split the six-year term, with Moore going first from September 1999.)

DISPUTE SETTLEMENT

As we have seen, the dispute settlement process of GATT was undermined because panel decisions had to be adopted by consensus. A country that did not accept a panel's decision would thus block it, and retaliation by an offended party was not authorized. The Uruguay Round brought a great advance on this unsatisfactory state of affairs in which any country, including the defendant, had veto power.

The WTO dispute settlement mechanism is now far more automatic.[36] First, any member with a dispute can request consultations with any other member. If there is no settlement in 60 days, the plaintiff can ask for a decision from the seven-member Dispute Settlement Board (DSB). Panel members are drawn from a lengthy list of international trade-law experts. Panel reports must be completed within six months and are automatically adopted unless there is a unanimous consensus not to or there is an appeal. Decisions of the DSB must be by consensus. There is an appellate body to review the DSB findings, with all parts of the process occupying no more than 15 months. If a losing defendant does not accede, the winning plaintiff can demand compensation. If that is not forthcoming, the winner can impose sanctions such as suspending concessions previously granted and raising duties. Cross-retaliation is permitted, meaning that the winner can take back benefits and impose duties in sectors unrelated to the dispute (and so adding considerable clout to a panel ruling).

By 1998, there had been 115 requests for consultations within the dispute settlement process regarding 80 separate matters.[37] There have been nine appeals.[38] This is a heavier caseload than under the preceding GATT, a sign that members see the situation as improved. The first case taken up by a WTO panel was in April 1995, when Venezuela, joined by Brazil, charged the

United States with unfairly restricting gasoline imports. (Venezuela ships to the U.S. east coast, where reformulated gasoline was required, even though U.S. refineries did not have to produce the clean gas.)[39] Venezuela eventually won its case. The United States also lost the first case actually decided, a Hong Kong complaint concerning U.S. quota limits on wool shirts.

One case beyond all others, however, has cast doubt on the ultimate workability of the dispute settlement mechanism. This is the now-famous banana case. In 1993 the EU instituted a special banana regime for the island republics and territories of the East Caribbean, all former colonies of EU members Britain, France, and the Netherlands. The regime involves favoritism for bananas imported to the EU from these former colonies and discrimination against Latin American bananas. The actual mechanism was a tariff-rate quota (TRQ) permitting Latin America to export two million tonnes with a tariff of 20% while additional fruit had to pay 170%. The EU bought off some of the Latin American complainants with quotas of their own, but the United States (whose Chiquita brand is a major loser) then took up the case and, joined by Guatemala, Honduras, and Mexico, asked for a GATT panel. The Caribbean island countries and the EU protested that ending the favoritism would cause severe economic damage. (Indeed, islands such as St. Lucia and Dominica send 90% of their bananas to EU markets.) The United States and its Latin allies replied that the EU could change its rules and provide aid if only it wanted to. They also pointed out that the TRQs mainly benefit well-off distributors, not poor Caribbean farmers. Only $150 million of the $2 billion cost paid by EU consumers goes to growers.[40]

The GATT panel made its portentous decision in 1994, finding that the EU banana regime was inconsistent with WTO rules. But the EU blocked the decision, which, we recall, was possible under the old rules.[41] In 1996, the United States and its allies (now including Ecuador) asked the WTO to take the case, which it did. The WTO panel ruled against the EU in 1997. The EU appealed, but the WTO appeals body also found against it and gave the EU 15 months to modify its plan.[42]

That began a new phase in which the EU proposed modifications (for the most part, slightly enlarged quotas under its TRQs) for non-Caribbean exporters) that were never thought to be sufficient by the United States, its Latin allies, or the WTO. It became startlingly apparent that there was no judgment mechanism to decide when and whether modifications in response to a dispute settlement decision were sufficiently great. The United States threatened retaliation with 100% duties on 16 EU products worth $520 billion, picked strategically to punish the countries whose former colonies were involved. Then in April 1999 a WTO panel ruled one more time against the EU, the fifth negative ruling when all the WTO and GATT panels and appeals are counted.[43] This ruling authorized the United States to impose the 100%

tariffs, though it reduced the amount involved to $191 billion. It was the first such authorization in WTO history.

Quite obviously the banana case has uncovered a major flaw in the WTO dispute settlement process. The ability of the EU to evade and avoid not one but several panel decisions showed that the WTO was not able to enforce its rules. That problem urgently needs fixing. Perhaps an arbitrator should be added to ascertain when and if a panel decision has been complied with.

Expected Gains

Various estimates predict that the Uruguay Round will increase world trade in a range from 9% to 24%, the lower figures using an assumption of perfect competition and constant returns to scale and the highest assuming monopolistic competition and increasing returns to scale.[44] A frequently cited estimate is that world income will grow by $510 billion per year assuming monopolistic competition, increasing returns to scale, dynamic as well as static gains from trade, and calculating the gains as of the year 2005.[45] Other studies predict gains ranging from $96 billion to $274 billion per year. The lower estimates are due to omission of gains from ending the MFA in textiles and clothing and protecting intellectual property, not counting the dynamic gains from economies of scale and the effect of more trade in increasing saving and investment, and estimating the gains using as a base the world economy in 1992.[46]

The greatest gains will be reaped by the developed countries because they gave up the most protection. The less-developed countries gave up less and thus will gain less. Sub-Saharan Africa is the only area expected to lose (though only slightly), mainly because food prices will rise as developed countries reduce their subsidies.

Later Agreements on Postponed Issues

Agreement could not be reached on a number of Uruguay Round issues that had to be postponed. Work on these has been proceeding for some years.

SERVICES

A rather weak General Agreement on Trade in Services (GATS) was negotiated in 1994, as noted in Chapter 5.[47] The GATS was conducted on a sector-by-sector basis, unlike the goods trade negotiations, which were across the board. One result was good progress in some areas and none whatsoever in others (water and air transport, postal services, basic telecommunications, education, health, and social services, for example) where vested interests were strong. Some countries did not sign on at all. One central feature was that the dispute settlement mechanism was extended to services, although as of 1998 only 6% of the uses of the mechanism were in this area. Another feature, but a weak one, was that most-favored-nation treatment was adopted as an obligation. MFN had not applied previously in services. But countries were permitted to exempt certain sectors from MFN, and most took advantage of this clause. The United States exempted transport services; the EU exempted audio-visual service, transport, and insurance.

But negotiations continued and there has been significant advance. A Financial Services Agreement was concluded in December 1997 (after two extensions). As a result, most-favored-nation treatment was extended to financial services; 100% foreign ownership of banks is now permitted by 59 countries; 44 countries permit foreign ownership of securities firms; and 52 countries have allowed broad foreign access to insurance markets. Also, following a breakdown in 1996, a Telecommunications Agreement involving 69 countries was negotiated in February 1997. It took effect in 1998. Monopoly telecommunications operators charge high prices and often possess limited technology. The agreement opens this sector to greater foreign competition among the signatories. In particular, North America, the EU, and Japan will allow foreign firms to acquire stakes in domestic firms. Finally, an Information Technology Agreement dates from March 1997. It involves 43 countries that agreed to eliminate tariffs by the year 2000 on computers, software, semiconductors, and telecommunications products such as fax machines, modems, pagers, and scientific instruments.[48]

More talks will be needed to clarify the GATS exceptions to most-favored-nation treatment in services. New negotiations will undoubtedly continue on a sectoral basis rather than across the board. For example, cabotage negotiations are stalled and talks will not resume until 2000. An agreement to end shipbuilding subsidies by the United States, the EU, Japan, Norway, and South Korea (which produce 80% of the world's ships) failed in 1996 when the U.S. House passed amendments that were inconsistent with the agreement. The other countries ratified it, but it will not enter into force until the U.S. does so as well.[49] Much work is needed on government procurement of services, the code for which applies to just 12 countries (though the whole EU counts as just one of them).

The Future for the WTO

Major problems clouding the WTO's future include such areas as environment and labor standards (strongly opposed by LDCs) and national laws and regulations on competition. The question is which of these reflect different comparative advantage and which involve competitive distortions that ought to be negotiated away. Another problem is what to do about regional trading agreements. Are they building blocks or stumbling blocks? After a fine start the dispute settlement mechanism is now in doubt because of the banana case.

The most worrisome development is that trade barriers are gaining more support politically in many countries. In the United States, unions have been shifting their support to trade barriers, business lobbies that might be expected to support free trade have turned uncommonly quiet, Republicans and Democrats both have been distancing themselves from free trade, and Senator Patrick Moynihan has been led to remark that the old free-trade political coalition is shattered.[50]

These weaknesses led many to doubt that any new round of world trade talks would be held for many years to come. But in spite of the worrying prospects, President Clinton, together with other trade-minded leaders, pushed forward anyway, and the WTO membership agreed to begin new negotiations with a conclave at Seattle in November 1999 and with negotiations to follow at Geneva early in 2000.[51] Proposed names are the Seattle Round, New Millennium Round, and Clinton Round. The agenda includes agriculture, a further reduction in tariffs on manufactured goods, investment, competition policy, "GATS 2000" to enlarge the services agreement, and labor and environmental standards. It remained to be seen how questions such as the disarray of the dispute settlement mechanism, the headlessness of the WTO, the rise of protectionist sentiment, and the unwillingness of the U.S. Congress to grant fast-track negotiating powers will affect these plans.

WHY DO COUNTRIES PERSIST IN PROTECTIONISM? THE POLITICAL BASE OF TRADE BARRIERS

The argument underlying the theory of comparative advantage is very strong, as Chapter 2 demonstrated. Barriers to trade lead to a less efficient use of the factors of production, as was argued in Chapter 4, with resulting restrictions on consumption and choice. Yet many people support trade barriers, and we must ask why they do so. The answers explored below are fourfold. (1) Most people do not understand trade theory and are largely unaware of how they are being hurt by barriers. (2) Those who might be hurt, or fancy themselves as being hurt, may be rational in seeking protection. (3) Politically strong industries, particularly those with a regional base, are able to use the state's powers to their own benefit, yet pass their actions off as legitimate by appeals to national interest. (4) A varied group of arguments exists under which some barriers to trade can be considered more or less legitimate and valuable tools. The traditional case is examined in this chapter. Newer arguments justifying trade barriers on the grounds of unfair foreign practices and strategic necessity are considered and critiqued in Chapters 7 and 8.

On the Understanding of Theory

However elegant, the theory of trade is not particularly accessible to the average citizen. J.Q. Public recognizes taxes as a burden and is reasonably astute when it comes to tax and expenditure issues, but J.Q. is quite at a loss when the government action increases the cost of goods without taxing them. For that matter, even extremely well-informed citizens with training in economics will often have difficulty in estimating the actual effect on prices of some given barrier to trade.

As we have seen, protection raises the price of a product on the domestic market such that additional income goes directly from buyer to producer. Imagine the public outcry if Congress voted a tax of $100 on every family of four to be paid to 12,000 U.S. sugar growers. Yet in effect that is exactly what has been done by means of trade barriers, with hardly a peep from the public.

Trade theory, moreover, cannot absolutely say that freer trade will improve welfare because of the difficulty of measuring welfare effects. Advocates of free trade are in the difficult position of having to defend their case against any conceivable objection, often theoretical ones with no empirical content. The theory, too, is rather vague on how displaced resources are going to be re-employed. However strong and however practical, no theory can give the certainty some citizens demand—and that applies to biology, geology, and physics as well. "What you have is a theory," sneers the speaker. "What I have is 10,000 unemployed workers." In essence, the level of economic knowledge is not sufficiently advanced. Politicians will listen to economists only if the voters are listening as well, but, too often, deafness reigns.

Elements of Political Economy

The political case for protection is almost always stronger than the case for freer trade because the benefits of freer trade are spread thinly across the entire population, while the drawbacks are concentrated heavily on a narrow segment. Mr. and Mrs. J.Q. Public are not going to fight hard over a tariff that adds an extra $2 on a pair of shoes. Even if they recognize that trade barriers do involve a cost for them, they have to figure out how to influence the governmental process, and do that for less than the few dollars each year it will cost them in higher shoe prices. The shoe companies and employees have their invested capital and their jobs at stake; particularly in areas where one-industry towns prevail, the local banks and shopkeepers find their interests affected also. Because they stand to lose major amounts of money, the narrowly based industries organize effective political actions. The box on page 269 discusses which industries can best organize to do so.

What happens, of course, is that 100 or 1,000 cases come up, each with the same pattern, until Mr. and Mrs. Public find themselves paying hundreds or even thousands of dollars; they have been nickeled and dimed to death. At no point did it ever appear worthwhile to fight, yet the accumulated process has caused serious economic damage.

When a move toward trade barriers is made that harms a group with some political power, it is less likely to be successful. Manufacturers of machinery may be able to out-lobby the ball-bearing industry if the latter demands barriers; the damage to the machinery manufacturers is immediate and obvious. Computer manufacturers may eventually prevail when microchip makers demand protection; here, too, the consequences are obvious. All too often, however, the harm is so spread out among the consuming public that neither the political will nor the ability to resist is sufficiently great.

An out-and-out appeal to transfer income from a large majority to a minority is unlikely in itself to be successful. Normally it must be glossed over with some appeal to legitimacy—protecting national workers, the evils of foreign sweatshops, national defense, and so forth. The smallness of the loss combined with the psychic pleasure of supporting national workers or striking a blow against foreign sweatshops may be enough to quiet opposition. One of the reasons we hear so much of fairness and level playing fields in the discussion of tariffs is to give a sense of legitimacy to what otherwise would appear to be a strictly economic, money-grabbing activity.[52] Here and in the next two chapters, we will address some legitimate arguments made by economists that justify interference with the international market. But very frequently when industries receive protection in modern industrial countries, the reasons used to justify it bear little resemblance to economists' arguments for barriers.[53]

The long and short of it is that sectoral interests often determine trade policy, and sectoral interest may well not be the same as national interest. Furthermore, national interest may not correspond with international or global interest. Would that these all coincided. That they often do not is the central issue of political economy.

On Rents

Both the labor and the capital in a protected industry benefit from the trade barriers. Both now have more security and higher revenues, which can be divided between them.

As Chapter 4 showed, the increased producer surplus is in some senses a rent. But note that the principal benefactors are usually those who hold the resources when protection is established, particularly if they acquired the resources before the possibility of the trade barriers was anticipated; it is they

VOTING PRESSURES TO BRING TRADE BARRIERS

Modeling by economists has attempted to identify which interest groups can bring the greatest pressure on legislatures.[54] A significant statistical fit links the presence of protection with the size of an industry's labor force (called the "adding machine" model), the labor-output ratio in an industry, voting strength and political contributions, the industry trend in employment ("job losses"), the poverty of the workers involved (the "equity" model), the profitability of the industry, the share of imports in an industry's markets and declines in these markets, and geographical dispersion of the industry.

Generally, the greater the number of workers involved and the wider the spread of an industry, the more successful it is in obtaining protection. Governments typically work hardest to avoid harm to the largest numbers. The tariff history of an industry makes a difference—a long history of barriers seems to smooth the way. The bargaining strength of the countries producing the imported goods also counts for something, with greater ease in excluding imports if they come from small countries with little bargaining power. It helps if there is no division in the industry (as with big steel wanting barriers and minimills ranged against them). Finally, good organization and lobbying make a difference. Models embodying these assumptions often predict the height of trade barriers reasonably well, though there are as yet many unanswered questions.

Robert E. Baldwin posits that a legislator will be more likely to vote for protectionist positions (1) the higher the percentage of voters in a constituency working in industries threatened by imports, and the larger their campaign contributions; (2) the lower the percentage of voters who work in industries producing goods for export or in industries that use protected goods as inputs and the smaller their contributions; (3) the more protectionist is the legislator's political party and the chief executive; (4) if there is no damaging political trade-off in a bill; and (5) the fairer the protection appears, for example, if it aids low-income workers with low skills rather than the privileged, or if it retaliates against blatantly unfair foreign trading practices.[55]

The idea that protection often adheres to the industries with the largest number of workers connects nicely to the factor-proportions arguments of Chapter 3. Recall that trade brings a higher return to the factors of production that are relatively abundant, that is, the ones that produce what is exported, and a lower return to the scarce factors of production producing what is imported. The industries clamoring for protection because they face intense foreign competition may most likely be the industries employing intensively the country's scarce factor of production. Imports will then be injurious to that scarce factor. The tariffs that protect a labor-intensive industry when a country's scarce factor is labor will raise the return to labor and lower it for land and capital. This argument, propounded by Wolfgang Stolper and Paul Samuelson and named after them the Stolper-Samuelson theorem, is that protection benefits the scarce factor at the expense of the abundant one.

who collected the windfall. Take the notorious case of the U.S. establishment of quotas on imported oil (in 1954), which effectively kept domestic oil prices one-third higher than international prices. We would expect that the price of all oil-producing lands would increase. Domestic oil refineries, producing a higher-priced product, would also rise in value.

The risks of doing business will decrease as foreign competition is lessened. Lenders to the newly protected industry, who previously had demanded higher interest rates will reduce their rates as the risks decline. Similarly, employees may previously have been nervous about committing themselves to an uncertain future. They thus demanded a compensating wages or bene-fits package, but with the quota they find themselves more secure. Those already employed continue to enjoy higher-than-market wages. Only the previous riskiness brought this boon, but the employees do not rush to refund their "extra" pay.

Some economists believe that the original owners walk off with the rent and subsequent owners buy at market prices. In this case the original owners would sell off their properties to investors who may be unaware of the impor-tance of protection in keeping industry revenues high and risks low. That view assumes that the investors and workers coming into a protected indus-try are naive, unwittingly taking the risk that the protective measures will disappear. Surely, however, investors, and hopefully employees, are not so naive when they commit themselves to other risky projects, for example, opening a business in a small mining town, developing a pharmaceutical drug that is not yet approved and may never be, or going to work on a distant pipeline project. *Any* investment or employment decision must take into account the possibility that the firm or industry will have a limited life.

The logical conclusion is that no compensation need be paid to losers when trade restrictions are removed. *If* investors and employees had enough information to calculate, however notionally, the risks of being in a protected industry, then they have *already been paid* enough to "fold their tents and silently steal away" when the trade barriers vanish. If they failed to act on information, they are stupid. If information was available and they failed to get it, they are lazy. If information was not even remotely available, then they are merely unlucky.

With this theoretical (and philosophical) background, we turn to examine the common arguments for protection.

THE ARGUMENTS FOR TRADE BARRIERS

The arguments favoring trade barriers are highly diverse and run the gamut from the intensely theoretical to popular folklore. The remainder of this chapter covers the traditional arguments, all of which have been around for most of this century at least. Chapter 7 moves on to consider how the traditional arguments have broadened to include legal restrictions against a number of so-called unfair trade practices. Finally, Chapter 8 takes up the new case for the national management of trade.

Domestic Production as a "Good"

Many people think of domestic production as being a kind of public good. Like a flag, a currency, a national symbol, and a world-champion sporting team or individual, having a domestic steel industry or producing one's own sugar or defending jobs against foreign attack confers some kind of emotional satisfaction.

Certainly many public opinion polls indicate that people are increasingly attracted to protectionist policies. Whereas polling data in the mid-1970s found only a quarter of Americans surveyed favored keeping foreign-made goods out of the country, that figure was up to 40% in answer to the same question in 1980 and over 50% in the mid-1980s. Now it is even higher. A *Los Angeles Times* poll in 1996 asked whether imports should be restricted to protect American industry and jobs, or unrestricted to permit the widest choices and lowest prices. The response: 63% favored restriction, 28% didn't. The *Wall Street Journal* found similar results in 1998 when it asked whether trade is bad for the economy because cheap imports hurt wages and jobs (yes, 58%), or good because it creates foreign demand for U.S. goods and leads to economic growth and jobs (yes, 32%). Ten percent said they were not sure.[56]

All this must be taken with a grain of salt. If higher prices, less choice, and retaliation by foreign countries are included in the questions, the favorable opinion of trade barriers drops radically, to 26-28% support according to pollster Daniel Yankelovich.[57]

Nonetheless many people do appear to have a "tribal" preference for products made at home. Data to this effect are available. In 1985, 22% of Americans polled said they purposely sought out U.S.-made goods, while by the start of the 1990s that number had reached 39%.[58] In democracies, legislatures reflect opinion, and the votes in the U.S. Congress reflect a recent erosion of support for free trade. The U.S. implementing legislation for the Tokyo Round of 1979 passed by votes of 395-7 in the House and 90-4 in the Senate; the Uruguay Round implementing legislation passed in 1994 by much smaller margins of 288-146 in the House and 76-24 in the Senate; while the implementing legislation for the North American Free Trade Area passed by only 234-200 in the House and 61-38 in the Senate.[59]

Economists have tended to view personal preferences as none of their business as long as they are voluntary, with their attitude much the same as

---

DISTURBING PSYCHOLOGICAL FACTORS APPEAR IN SOME POLLS

The answers to certain polling questions seem especially meaningful, suggesting that disturbing psychological factors must be at work. Recent polling data indicate that the public's preference for barriers to save American jobs is about 10 percentage points higher when imports from Japan are mentioned as the cause of the job loss rather than just imports in general. Over 80% of the U.S. population would prefer slower growth in both Japan and the United States to faster growth in both countries, if with the faster growth Japan were to take an economic lead.[60] Psychology rather than economics must be at work here. The reasoning must include a fear of losing first place, jealousy of the good foreign performance, and perhaps some element of racism.

---

toward the lawyer who cuts his or her own firewood because that activity is viewed as recreation. The high opportunity costs can be seen as balanced by the high perceived benefits of exercise in the out-of-doors. Thus discriminatory decisions to buy American, buy British, or buy Japanese, when voluntary ones based on tastes, have usually been thought to be off limits to policy. Economists in their role as policy advisers do not have to accept a prejudice against foreign goods (or foreigners themselves) as a given, however. They can treat it as the product of ignorance that should be excised by education, exhortation to do otherwise for the national good, and government promotion policies, perhaps even including import subsidies.

The view held by many economists that voluntary individual choices should be respected loses its innocence when governments by means of trade barriers *impose* a prejudice against foreign goods on their citizens. There is a gray area between individual choice and imposed barriers, however. For example, the Korean government apparently encouraged buy-Korean thinking, and the Japan Federation of Cement Users Cooperatives, with the government looking on, advised members not to use imported cement. The Korean case was a serious one: during much of 1990 an anti-import campaign was being waged, and though Korean newspapers reported it as a grassroots protest against conspicuous consumerism, it seemed to be sponsored by the government.[61] Alertness is called for when "free choice" is actually a government protectionist policy in disguise.

The Loss of Jobs

The models of trade presented to this point do not explicitly treat unemployment. An industry in an industrial country that is under pressure due to low wages abroad is in fact under attack due to high wages at home. If its labor force did not have other opportunities for employment (or for comfortable leisure), workers could not demand the high wages. That is the fundamental insight of comparative advantage. If capital did not have other uses, it would not be so expensive, and the same is true of land. But not every displaced worker has another opportunity. Some, with very poor alternative occupations, receive high wages nonetheless. Wages are set to attract the *marginal* worker,* and usually that point forms the basis for the wage structure, with increments for seniority and additional skills. The increments for seniority are at least partially means for attracting workers on the margin, who come because they have a future in the company. If a plant closes, those workers who are young and better educated, and who had been attracted to their jobs by wages slightly above those elsewhere, will find nearly equivalent work. Some, when driven into the market for a job search, may even find better work. Other workers will find rather poorer substitutes, and yet others, particularly the older and less skilled, may find nothing at all.

Our trade models handle this situation poorly because they assume—or apparently assume—a full employment situation in which all released resources can be re-employed. If, however, some resources are never re-employed, or must be employed in residual low-productivity occupations, then the loss for the economy can be substantially greater. It was thinking of this sort that led Walter Mondale during the 1984 presidential campaign to ask "What do we want our kids to do? Sweep up around Japanese computers?"

Recent empirical research does indeed lend some support to the position that re-employment may be difficult for some factors displaced by trade. The jobs lost would mostly be in blue-collar manufacturing while the gains would largely be in the service sector—professional, managerial, marketing, and clerical. Whether the individuals who lose the blue-collar jobs are the ones who could fill the service jobs is a troublesome question and open to doubt. Is this the Achilles' heel of trade theory? Since that theory is an enduring one, we should investigate more closely.

1. If we can show that the motivation of the older workers was economically rational, taken with adequate knowledge of risk, we may conclude that the economy has already paid them their full compensation. Suppose that workers were informed that their firm might close in the next decade. Indeed, we might even suppose the odds were known. The youngest workers would, of course, leave, and the oldest workers would stay. The middle-aged workers would have to calculate their costs of finding other employment— perhaps a lower wage, retraining, moving, or a longer commute—against the value of staying on. If they stay, then they have taken their loss at that point.

---

* "Marginal" in its economic meaning, not in the sense that the worker is marginally needed, but in the sense that the worker is the one most likely to find a job somewhere else.

2. Keeping workers employed through ensuring that the plants stay open is an expensive proposition. If the government tries to keep the plant open, it finds that the plant still needs the younger workers and needs regular infusions of capital, such that the cost per job saved, particularly per job saved *of those who would not find another job*, is normally very high. As the next section shows, in the United States such costs run from around $90,000 to over $1 million *per job per year*. In these cases, the figures are averaged over all additional employment, not just those who would otherwise be unemployed, a figure rather difficult to derive. Notional or not, the number who would remain jobless is unlikely to be more than one-third of the workers, so the cost of keeping those jobs could be triple the figures cited above.

THE HIGH COST OF RETAINING JOBS THROUGH PROTECTION

Whatever the cost to the individuals who would lose jobs except for the trade barriers, protection as a method for keeping them employed is much more costly for society. That is so because those who could find other work stay employed in their old jobs producing high-price products and because new capital that could be more productively employed elsewhere is attracted into the protected industry. Studies by economists in this area often present cost estimates so high that on first reading they appear to be misprints. They are not misprints.

Economists have made a number of studies, principally in the United States and usually on an industry-by-industry basis, that examine the cost of one job saved for one year through protection. The first of these studies to achieve wide attention was carried out in the early 1980s at Washington University, St. Louis. More recently, a major research project was published by the Institute for International Economics in Washington, D.C. Its authors, Gary Hufbauer and Kimberly Ann Elliott, have brought together numerous estimates of protection costs in various U.S. industries.[62] Table 6.5 summarizes the data for the 21 highly protected sectors of the U.S. economy shown in Column A, representing somewhat less than half the total losses from American protection.

The figures in Table 6.5 are obtained by estimating how much the tariffs (or tariff equivalents, if quotas or voluntary export restraints are the device) shown in Column B raised the price of the product. Recall that a $1 tariff will not increase prices by $1 if foreign producers cut their price. Then a calculation is made of the annual extra cost to consumers from the protection. This is obtained by multiplying the price increase by the annual consumption of the protected product from both imports and domestic production (basically $A + B + C + R$ of Figure 4.1. Next an estimate is made of the

Table 6.5

THE HIGH COST OF SAVING U.S. JOBS
THROUGH PROTECTION, 1990

A Product	B Tariff or Tariff Equiv. (%)	C Jobs Saved by Protection	D Consumer Loss per Job Saved ($)	E Avg. Annual Change in Emplmt. (%)
Apparel	48.0	152,583	138,666	− 1.59
Ball bearings	11.0	146	438,356	3.71
Benzenoid chemicals	9.0	216	> 1,000,000	0.40
Canned tuna	12.5	390	187,189	− 3.79
Ceramic articles	11.0	418	244,019	− 4.48
Ceramic tiles	19.0	347	400,576	2.48
Costume jewelry	9.0	1,067	96,532	− 1.75
Dairy products	50.0	2,378	497,897	0.19
Frozen orange juice	30.0	609	461,412	0.53
Glassware	11.0	1,477	180,095	− 0.55
Luggage	16.5	226	933,628	− 2.00
Machine tools	46.6	1,556	348,329	− 2.09
Maritime shipping	85.0	4,411	415,325	n.a.
Peanuts	50.0	397	136,020	negl.
Polyethylene resin	12.0	298	590,604	4.90
Rubber footwear	20.0	1,701	122,281	− 3.90
Softwood lumber	6.5	605	758,678	− 5.10
Sugar	66.0	2,261	600,177	− 2.53
Textiles	23.4	16,203	202,061	− 0.38
Women's footwear	10.0	3,702	101,567	− 5.90
Women's handbags	13.5	773	191,462	− 9.20
		(Weighted average		− 1.14)

Source: Gary Clyde Hufbauer and Kimberly Ann Elliott, *Measuring the Costs of Protection in the United States* (Washington: Institute for International Economics, 1994), 4-5, 8-9, 12-13, as interpreted by the authors. In a supplementary table (p. 20), Hufbauer and Elliott calculate the consumer loss per job saved in semiconductors at $525,619, for steel $835,351, for a binding VER on autos at > $1,000,000, and also > $1,000,000 for a reclassification of minivans and sports utility vehicles as trucks.

induced increases in employment caused by the higher domestic output resulting from protection (shown in Column C). Note that the numbers are relatively small, being greatest in textiles and apparel (totaling about 170,000) but ranging down to only a few hundred in a number of industries. Then the cost to consumers is divided by the number of jobs saved by the protection, yielding the annual cost to the consuming public per job saved in the industry as shown in Column D.*

These results usually come as a shock to those unaware of how large the costs are. In all cases, the figures are well above average wages in the industry concerned. Some of the figures are stratospheric. Even the lowest of the figures, $96,000 annually for a job saved in costume jewelry, is over three times the actual wages paid per production worker in that industry. This does not appear to be a very good bargain for the public. The figures drive home the point that maintaining jobs by means of protection is an expensive proposition, and it would be much cheaper if the taxpayers paid the workers in these industries their old wage or more just to stay home!

The figures in Table 6.5 are lower than they might be because they do not include some other costs of protection that are more general in nature. These include the adverse effects on management efficiency, reduced scale economies, less learning, sluggishness in adopting new techniques, and slower growth. All are ignored in this analysis; if they could be calculated, they would raise the cost per job saved higher yet. (On the other side of the coin, adjustment costs involved in transferring workers out of these industries if they were *not* protected are also ignored. But these adjustment costs are short run, whereas the costs of protection are continuous.)

EVEN WITH BARRIERS, JOBS ARE LOST

Ironically, the ability of protection to save jobs over time is poor. This is because of economic responses on the part of both consumers and producers. On the demand side, higher prices lead consumers to search for substitutes, and after some initial expansion in the domestic share of the market, a portion of the gains is lost. (This represents the old Marshallian rule that demand becomes more elastic in the long run.) On the supply side, the cause of the job loss is likely to be factor substitution. Labor, especially less-skilled labor, is a relatively expensive factor in the United States. Whatever the market price of the finished product, protection or no, management will see advantages in shifting factor proportions away from the expensive factor when it is possible to do so. The higher profits after protection may even be the catalyst for this decision. Thus capital and technology substitute for labor in the

---

* It should be pointed out that the range of estimates for the costs of protection in a given U.S. industry is wide, often by as much as 50% or more from highest to lowest. See the range cited by Robert C. Feenstra, "How Costly is Protectionism?" *Journal of Economic Perspectives* 6, 3 (Summer 1992): 163. Though the estimates vary and fewer studies have been made in countries other than the United States, the conclusion that protection is very expensive per job retained is apparently universal. A forthcoming study by Patrick Messerlin gives a European Union figure of $215,000 per job saved in 22 protected sectors (cited in *The Economist*, May 22, 1999).

industries where labor is an important share of costs, and thus even during a period of protection, employment in the protected industry is likely to fall anyway. It did in fact fall in most of the cases shown in Column E of Table 6.5, with a weighted average reduction of 1.14%.

Interestingly, then, industries after being granted protection have on the whole continued to adjust to changed economic circumstances, at least where their labor force is concerned. In effect, even with the very high cost of the protection to consumers, many jobs were lost, no doubt at a slower rate than in a free market, but lost in large numbers nonetheless.

Cheap Labor: The Fallacies of the Low Wages Argument

The aspect of employment loss from trade that generates the greatest concern with the general public—and is a wellspring of protectionist sentiment—is the fear of competition from cheap labor abroad. Generations of managers, voters, and legislators have harbored this fear, which holds that a developed country's industry is at a disadvantage when competing against foreigners who pay very low wages to the workers they employ. As we have seen, the Smoot-Hawley Tariff had a section that embodied this argument, as did its predecessor, the Fordney-McCumber Tariff. Its designers attempted to craft an "equalizing" or "scientific" tariff to equalize all costs of production between the United States and its trading partners. Had the U.S. government followed the law literally, there would have been no trade at all. In the 1920s the United States actually sent delegations abroad to try to assess foreign costs so as to recommend an equalizing tariff. As can be imagined, foreign governments and manufacturers were not particularly receptive to these delegations. Where cheap labor is concerned, the idea has not gone away. Some politicians including Pat Buchanan and Ross Perot, still support an equalizing or scientific tariff.

Undeniably, there is a large differential between hourly wages paid in the United States, Western Europe, and Japan and wages paid in less-developed countries. Even in a major industry such as steel or autos, the wage gap can sometimes be as much as eight or ten times, or even more. Table 6.6 shows recent averages for labor costs in manufacturing.

Proponents of the cheap labor argument use the data on low wages abroad to make two claims, both of which appear persuasive to much of the public. First, goods manufactured by the cheap labor will so undersell domestic output that domestic producers cannot compete; and second, domestic firms will be motivated to transfer their operations overseas so they, too, can employ cheap labor. Unemployment mounts at home.

The argument contains grave weaknesses, however, some of which can be clarified by the theory of comparative advantage, others of which can be

Table 6.6

AVERAGE HOURLY WAGE IN MANUFACTURING,
SELECTED COUNTRIES, 1996 (INCLUDES WAGES,
FRINGE BENEFITS, AND LABOR TAXES)

Germany	$31.87	Hong Kong	$5.14
Japan	$21.04	Mexico	$1.50
United States	$17.74	Thailand*	$0.71
Britain	$14.19	Philippines*	$0.68
Singapore	$8.32	China*	$0.54
South Korea	$8.23	Sri Lanka	$0.48

Source: U.S. Bureau of Labor Statistics, reported by Stephen Golub, "Does Trade with Low-Wage Countries Hurt American Workers?" in Federal Reserve Bank of Philadelphia, *Business Review* (March-April 1998): 4; *Wall Street Journal*, September 30, 1994, for those marked with an asterisk.

addressed on political and pragmatic grounds. Consider first this question: if indeed cheap labor is all-powerful in the marketplace, then how is it possible that a rich country can *export* anything at all in competition with the low-wage rates? How can the United States and Japan, with their expensive labor, be the world's first-and second-ranking exporters? Why is Germany third, even though its wages are so very high? The answers in Chapters 2 and 3 are enlarged upon here.

FALLACY #1: CHEAP LABOR MAY NOT BE PRODUCTIVE LABOR

Even in a rich country's labor-intensive industries, the labor may be sufficiently productive so that the high productivity offsets the high wages. A simple example will show this. What if wages in some developed country's industry are six times higher per person per hour than they are in poor Poveria? If productivity in terms of output per worker in this rich country's industry is less than six times higher, then Poveria will have the advantage; but if productivity is *greater* than six times more per worker, then the rich country will have the advantage. Its "unit labor costs" will be *lower* than in Poveria, not higher, and its large wage gap is offset by an even larger productivity gap. Evidence bears this out, with average unit labor costs in manufacturing lower in the United States than in a number of apparently low-wage countries including India, the Philippines, and Malaysia.[63]

Productivity differences have many causes, including complementary physical capital, superior education, training, and skill levels, and more advanced technology. But the reasons may be even more basic, as when the low-wage labor is illiterate, or malnourished, or sickly, or unused to factory methods.

The observer must not miss that the low-wage workers of poor Poveria, or middle-income Thailand or Malaysia, may themselves view with substantial alarm the competitive strength of countries where capital is relatively cheap, where technology is relatively more advanced, where the stock of natural resources is large, and where labor is well educated and highly skilled.

Of course, some given industry may find that cheap foreign labor is sufficiently productive so that by comparison its own unit labor costs are indeed high and foreign competition gives problems. But there are other fallacies in the argument.

FALLACY #2: THE NUMBER OF JOBS IS NOT FIXED

The cheap labor argument often implies that protecting specific jobs also protects the total number of jobs, that workers put out of work end up unemployed, on welfare, or "sweeping up around Japanese computers." In this view the total number of jobs is fixed, and a job gained by a foreigner is a job lost to us. The total number of jobs is not fixed, however, and labor that loses employment in one occupation can be transferred to other uses. The damage done by low wages is not general but specific to labor-intensive industries where labor costs are high relative to productivity.

For two reasons, increased international trade should cause more jobs to open up. First, as a country follows its comparative advantage, employment will increase in its export sector, and the higher demand in that sector should pull up wages there. (In most countries, average pay in the export sector is higher than it is for the labor force generally.) Second, international trade usually has positive effects on economic growth, so trade increases income. The higher income levels will promote the demand for non-traded goods and especially for services, which as a whole are income-elastic and which in many cases do not and cannot face foreign competition. In the United States of the late 1990s, real national income was the highest in history; in 40 years average weekly earnings in the private sector have grown and never fallen; real wage growth (2.6% in 1998) was the strongest since the early 1970s and in four decades has only been exceeded in 1959, 1962, 1965, and 1972; and unemployment was lower than it had been since the late 1960s.[64] Whatever damage is caused by cheap foreign labor, the U.S. data show that it certainly does not damage the majority of the population.

A remarkably large part of the labor force in every country is naturally protected against imports because transport of services is costly or impossible. Table 6.7 illustrates this widespread insulation against foreign competition. In 1998, total U.S. employment outside of agriculture was 125.8 million people. Of this total, those employed in the service jobs shown in the table were subject to very little competition from imports.

The 106.6 million jobs in Table 6.7 make up 85% of the 126 million total, and that 85% is substantially protected from foreign competition. This naturally protected service sector is actually expanding; the figure was a lower 80% in 1989, 78% in 1984, and 76% back in 1976. It is true that foreign firms are increasingly being allowed to compete in sectors such as construction, banking, motels, insurance, airlines, and department stores. But such competition would not weaken the claim of natural protection because the immigration laws require that these firms hire mostly American workers and not foreigners. At worst, some high management or technical positions would be lost. The natural protection remains intact. (It is true that huge illegal flows of immigrants might alter this picture, but that case is a far different one from claiming protection because of cheap labor abroad.)

The only segments of the non-farm labor force that do not benefit from natural protection, then, appear to be manufacturing and mining.[*] The remaining 15% of the labor force in these sectors, however, includes those workers employed in industries that produce for export, a figure that is well above one-third of manufacturing jobs.

Table 6.7

U.S. SERVICE EMPLOYMENT BY SECTOR, 1998 (MILLIONS)

Construction	6.0
Transport, public utilities	6.6
Wholesale, retail trade	29.3
Finance, insurance, real estate	7.3
Other services	37.5
Government (federal, state, local)	*19.9*
Total	106.6

Source: Bureau of Statistics, U.S. Department of Labor, reported in *Economic Report of the President 1999* (Washington: Council of Economic Advisors, 1999), 380-81.

FALLACY #3: FOREIGNERS ARE GIVEN REASONS TO RETALIATE

In a developed country it is a dangerous game to protect the labor-intensive industries harmed by low wages abroad. Keeping out the labor-intensive products of foreigners is an open invitation for them to limit imports of the developed country's own capital-intensive or high-technology products. Such trade war strategies are no solution—though they could and probably would benefit the owners and workers in the rich countries' labor-intensive industries, and the higher-tech, more capital-intensive industries of the less-developed countries.

---

[*] Even some mining and manufacturing employment is naturally protected when the product is low in value, transport costs are high, and availability is general—coal or dirt, for example.

In short, protection against cheap labor is unnecessary as far as the vast majority of American jobs is concerned. Even if such protection were attempted, it would jeopardize the large export sector that would surely be retaliated against. It would not be possible to erect barriers against cheap foreign labor without other countries raising their own barriers against what they see as cheap physical and human capital, cheap natural resources, and high-tech advantages.

The Sweatshop Argument: Core Labor Standards and Child Labor

Sometimes the cheap labor argument is made in another way. It is highly immoral, many would say, to purchase imported goods made by sweatshop labor working under substandard conditions. This human rights argument carries considerable influence, and laws to protect against goods produced by child labor or in countries that discriminate against union labor have been enacted by a number of countries.

CORE LABOR STANDARDS

The import of products made by slave labor and prison labor is prohibited by many countries.* Some now go beyond this to call for core labor standards, in the want of which barriers would be erected. "Denial of worker rights" has been a cause of U.S. trade action since 1988. Among countries that have lost tariff exemptions because they were held to have denied these rights are Burma/Myanmar, the Central African Republic, Chile, Liberia, Nicaragua, Paraguay, and Romania.

The rights most often discussed are freedom to join unions and engage in collective bargaining. Some activists call for higher minimum wages, shorter workdays, and better working conditions in cheap labor countries. Though many less-developed countries believe this is a disguised form of protectionism, the U.S. Congress has directed the President to seek a working party on labor standards within the WTO (an idea also supported by France, though subject to substantial opposition elsewhere). The UN's International Labor Organization has had an ongoing study since 1994 of how to integrate social welfare and trade. Currently there is considerable debate on the addition of strong labor standards to existing new trade pacts. For example, before the North American Free Trade Agreement was passed, political pressure led to a side agreement on labor cooperation. (This does not set common minimum standards, but it does support principles of organizing and collective

---

* The import to the United States of goods made by "convict, forced, or indentured labor" was prohibited by the Smoot-Hawley Act of 1930. The clause has had importance in several recent cases, including a charge that China has exported goods produced with forced labor in penitentiaries, labor camps, and re-education centers.

281

bargaining, and provides that in case of dispute over whether a country is fully enforcing its labor laws, binding arbitration and penalties are provided.)[65] The subject is sure to figure in the new round of WTO trade negotiations in 1999-2000.

Many economists would not accept the proposition that poor countries should have to enforce the labor standards of rich countries to escape trade barriers. These economists would argue that the workers in the plants of developing countries are there because they have considered that the balance of costs and benefits is more favorable than it is in other occupations, such as subsistence agriculture or petty trade. While by rich-country standards conditions may be bad, or even very bad, they ask us to compare the situation in an LDC factory or farm producing for export with conditions elsewhere in the country, which are worse.

If the market is operating reasonably, these people have chosen to work in whatever circumstances and at whatever wages they accept because to the best of their knowledge they cannot do better. Our great-grandmothers and great-grandfathers made much the same choice. If an importing country were to restrict trade because of labor's poor conditions or low pay, the demand for labor would fall in the low-wage country. Predictably, this would cause wages to decline still further in that country or would result in unemployment if wages did not fall—in either case, not what the supporters of better labor conditions wanted.

These concerns point toward alternative policies, for example, encouraging the establishment of labor standards through such organizations as the International Labor Organization. Codes of conduct could be adopted by multinational firms and audited by independent organizations. Perhaps multinational firms could be persuaded to use the same labor standards wherever they operate.[66] The labeling of goods produced under such codes would allow consumers to make a choice and would avoid the use of trade law that might be manipulated by protectionist interests.[67]

CHILD LABOR

The International Labor Organization estimates that 250 million children between the ages of 5 and 14 are at work, about half full-time and half part-time. Of the total, 61% are in Asia, 32% in Africa (making up 40% of all children, the highest percentage), and 7% in Latin America. Some country figures include 42% in Kenya, 30% in Bangladesh, 25% in Haiti, 24% in Turkey, and 10-17% in Pakistan, Brazil, India, China, and Indonesia. The estimate for Mexico is 7%.[68]

Everyone agrees that a very bad hand has been dealt to children in many poor countries. The question is what to do about it. Many humanitarian groups, including students on college and university campuses, have taken up the cause. One policy response has been a call for a ban on the import of goods made by child labor, and Senator Tom Harkin of Iowa has sponsored such a bill in the U.S. Senate. Less draconian has been the expanded use of labeling. The outcry against child labor in making rugs and carpets has led to the voluntary "Rugmark" label certifying that no child labor was used in production. Labeling is now being widely advocated for other products as well. A barrage of negative publicity about Kathy Lee Gifford's line of clothing sold at Wal-Mart led in 1997 to a voluntary pact among several companies to eliminate child labor.[69]

Yet, a number of considerations turn what some believe is a black-and-white case into a shade of gray. First is the possibility that blocking trade in goods produced by child labor might make people poorer. Working children in many cases provide some income for poor families. Oxfam says that in Bangladesh, American pressure on firms has caused 30,000 to 50,000 children to lose jobs in the textile industry over a two-year period, but many of these children didn't go back to school but found work in local non-export industries. Second is the certainty that around the world, child labor is used much more in domestic production (90-95% of it) than it is in producing for international trade. Blocking trade in items produced by child labor would therefore put only a small dent in the problem.

It would seem that economic development is the only sure way to improve the situation.[70] With development, adult wages would rise by enough to offset the lost income if children do not work. With development, schools could be improved so that parents will want their children to go to school rather than work. Multinational firms might provide education, meals, and medical care in the workplace. Rich countries might make direct grants to children and to education so that the economic motive for child labor is reduced. Yet it is evident that in the rich countries, particularly the United States, recent years have seen declining rather than increasing support for these purposes. Here, indeed, is a dilemma.

On their part, poor countries may find that improved regulations on child labor are necessary to offset protectionist sentiments in the developed countries as well as of benefit to the children, if the regulations are well-designed. (China, for example, has recently enacted new legislation in this area.)

It is hard to find agreement, but many participants in this debate would surely agree on one thing. Banning trade in goods produced by child labor and leaving it at that, with no further effort to improve the lot of the children, would not help most children who work, might harm some of them, and would convey its main benefit to protectionist interests who would benefit from the trade barriers.

A Legitimate Side to the Job Loss and Cheap Labor Arguments

The last two sections have considered the arguments that international trade is unfair in that it will lead to job losses, with the main cause being cheap foreign labor against which high-paid labor cannot compete. As seen, these arguments have grave weaknesses. Why should labor costs represent unfairness any more than a tropical climate does? If a rich country complains that "Poveria has cheap labor, which is unfair to us," then why shouldn't Greenland complain that "California can grow oranges much more cheaply than we can, which is unfair to us." It is a reasonable question, and points to the fact that at least in this sense trade is always fundamentally unfair—something makes it possible for someone else to produce a good more cheaply than we can.[71]

Yet arguments about cheap labor do have a legitimate side. In developed countries, manufacturing jobs in industries with low skill requirements will be under heavy competitive pressure from cheap labor costs abroad, and workers in these industries may well be forced to find new employment. If these workers are unskilled, uneducated, and untrainable, the jobs open to them may pay less than the jobs they have just lost. If that is the case, public policy may have an important remedial role to play—a topic taken up in Chapter 8.

Cheap labor and job losses are the most common justifications for trade barriers, but there are others, which are taken up below and in the next two chapters.

Protection as a Device for Bargaining?

High protectionist barriers can be made to serve as a trade-off for bargaining purposes. This, it is said, is a reason for having them. The argument is very similar to the debates surrounding disarmament. Once you are disarmed, you lose the means to bring pressure on some adversary, who may then be less likely to disarm than before. This argument is probably correct in principle, but there are also a number of points to consider.

1. Little or no unilateral reduction in protection will then take place, just as little unilateral disarmament ever occurs. Since the argument often seems to be applied to some possible future bargain, the action taken at any present moment is limited, and the harm from the trade barriers outweighs the gains from the bargain.

2. Nothing is wrong with large unilateral decreases in protection. It has been done before—Britain in the nineteenth century, the United States in the 1840s and again in 1913, Australia and New Zealand in the 1980s, India, China, and Argentina in the 1990s. The results are not as good as they would be if the rest of the world cut protection, but they do increase welfare. What is more, they might increase welfare far more than some small multilateral

decline in the future, for which the bargaining tariff is preserved. To repeat a vivid question first asked by Frederick Bastiat in the nineteenth century, should a country put big rocks in its harbors because other countries have rocky coastlines? Is not the very existence of the foreign rocks punishment enough for the foreigners? The question is not only vivid, but fair.

3. The argument is equally able to justify increasing protection, for that course will presumably enhance one's bargaining power. It is actually quite common for countries to boost their tariffs in anticipation of negotiating new trade agreements. That could be very dangerous, however, in a world where retaliation is possible and trade wars can occur. Economists estimate that a full-blown trade war, if it were conducted with quotas and if it involved several rounds of retaliation, could reduce output in the United States and the EU by as much as 20%. Not only would exports decline, but the tendency toward higher prices (assuming unchanged monetary policy) would boost interest rates and depress output even outside the foreign trade sector.[72]

In the end a trade negotiator may simply have to accept that trade negotiations are to some extent based on a false theory of implicit mercantilism, that exports are a good thing and imports are bad. In that case a negotiator's most successful ploy could well be to gain the support of a country's exporters to offset the opposition of producers facing import competition. This may be a key bargaining tactic for maintaining free trade.[73] But economists do not have to keep silent about the flaw in the logic.

The Infant-Industry Argument

The infant-industry argument for protection was propounded by Alexander Hamilton, George Washington's Secretary of the Treasury, in his *Report on Manufactures* of 1791. It was further developed by Germany's Friedrich List in his *Das nationale System der politischen Œkonomie* of 1841. Both Hamilton and List directed their arguments against the massive preeminence of British manufacturing during this period. They emphasized that when an industry is small in scale, new, and inexperienced, its products will naturally be expensive, and it may be unable to compete with a well-developed foreign industry. If the infant is protected, that will allow new firms to operate, to acquire the knowledge needed to train their labor and move down their learning curves, to accumulate capital (since capital markets may themselves be in their infancy), and to improve production processes. When these goals are attained, the infant industry tariff can be removed, as it will no longer be necessary.

In technical terms, trade barriers to protect infant industries are expected temporarily to put a country on a lower indifference curve because imports are made more expensive, but these barriers are erected in the expectation that eventually the production possibility curve will shift outward far enough to more than recover the lost ground.[74] Crucial to the argument is that eventually the whole world gains—both the country that develops the infant and the rest of the world that imports products from it if the industry grows up to have a comparative advantage.

In recent history, infant-industry protection has been employed heavily by Japan; Canada and Australia were important supporters of the argument and still are to some extent. The theory is especially popular in less-developed countries such as Brazil, South Korea, and Taiwan, all of which have used it with enthusiasm (and with tariff rates much higher than the United States and Germany employed in the nineteenth century).[75] It has even been resurrected for autos, steel, and other industries where some pioneer nation has less modern equipment than do latecomers, or where an industry has become less competitive behind protective barriers. With the barriers now lower, the industry believes that if it were given a breathing space to adjust, it would again become competitive. (This last case might be called a pseudo-infant or senescent industry.) These arguments are now often included in making the case for a strategic trade policy, a subject we consider in Chapter 8.

For many years, the infant-industry argument was recognized as an interference with free trade that could increase welfare. But there are also a number of serious problems with the position that must be considered.[76]

1. It is all too easy to extend infant-industry protection to firms that have little or no chance of ever growing up. The literature on development is rife with examples of steel mills, automobile assembly plants, and petrochemical complexes built in nations whose markets, under any conceivable circumstances, could not support such operations for many years to come. General import substitution of this sort as a development strategy has been much criticized in recent years because of the rather indiscriminate approach to choosing protected industries.

2. Protection may be very hard to eliminate even if the infant grows up. The labor, management, and capital in the industry will lose if the protection is removed, no matter how successful the industry has become. The higher incomes earned by protected industries can finance a substantial amount of political activity to ensure that the trade barriers are retained. Points (1) and (2) together are the "Mill Test," named after John Stuart Mill, who emphasized that the protection must eventually be dispensed with for the argument to work.

3. Those who bear the costs of infant-industry protection do not particularly benefit from it. Even if the protection is removed after an industry grows up, there has still been a cost paid by the country's consumers. Only if the industry eventually has sufficient earnings to repay consumers for their initial sacrifice can the protection be said to have succeeded. The repayment (presumably through the tax system) would have to be with interest, of course,

because forgone interest would also figure in the real opportunity cost of the protection. This is the "Bastable Test," named after Charles F. Bastable, who stressed that the costs must be paid back to justify the action. It should be noted that this is a high hurdle because the cost of production has to fall below the world level by enough to make the payments.[77] Also if it takes five or 10 years to bring production costs below world levels then the interest costs would be high—and the longer the public outlay lasts, the greater these interest costs would be.* The Bastable Test is rather academic, however, as any such repayment is rarely if ever made.

4. Recently, economists have become more wary of the infant-industry argument on the ground that no need for protection exists if capital markets are working well. Entrepreneurs, realizing that with a few years of experience they could bring costs down to the levels of their international competitors, would finance a few years of money-losing operations. There is nothing strange in a new enterprise losing money in its initial years. Such new enterprises may be units of larger firms, receiving their financing through the parent firm. Others may finance themselves through sales of shares and a limited amount of bank credit. Basically, financiers need only to anticipate future earnings high enough to cover the cost of using capital for a number of years without a return. (Witness the patient shareholders of Amazon.com, which has yet to make money but has had no problem in borrowing.)

Because an adequate capital market undercuts the need for infant-industry protection, believers in that case must therefore argue that the capital system is imperfect. Banks may be biased against new entrepreneurs and are reluctant to invest in human capital and technology, which make poor collateral. But that argument applies to any new entrepreneur. Why should the banks be prejudiced just against those who want to make substitutes for imports? Moreover, capital markets include not only banks, but involve the large internal capital markets of conglomerate firms and holding companies, stock markets, and bond markets. Firms that face competition from imports may be a special case only in the sense that they can appeal for infant-industry protection, whereas firms that face domestic competition cannot. Furthermore, their chances of obtaining barriers may be better than their chances for obtaining loans from the credit markets. If private investors make a mistake, they must suffer the consequences, but if government officials make a mistake, they lose other people's money.

In all this, perhaps a less costly alternative solution would be for government to reform capital markets and help disseminate information rather than

---

* If the going interest rate is 5%, the annual gain needed to compensate for the loss from infant-industry protection over five years would have to be 28% more than the mean annual loss. For 10 years it would be 63% more. See Douglas A. Irwin, *Against the Tide* (Princeton, N.J.: Princeton University Press, 1996), 133.

resort to protection. Yet it must also be admitted that in some less-developed countries, it may be cheaper and more effective to provide infant-industry protection than to reform the capital markets. Even an argument that is often abused may occasionally be correct.

5. Finally, on both political and economic grounds many economists would prefer an infant-industry subsidy to a tariff. (John Stuart Mill himself eventually came around to this point of view.) A subsidy can achieve the same end without raising prices for consumers, so the market for the infant industry's goods will thus be wider. (The Bastable argument still applies, however. The infant industry should repay the taxpayer, for example, by paying a bounty to the government and thus cutting tax bills.) Moreover, a subsidy is fitting if the country as a whole benefits from having the industry. Above all, a subsidy is likely to receive frequent review from the legislature, annually in many countries, so there is more chance that it will eventually be ended. Even then, a subsidy to infant industries may discriminate against the firms that export, attracting resources away from them and to the infants. It may be better to direct the subsidies toward education or infrastructure development so as to keep incentives uniform throughout the economy.

The National Defense Argument

It is said that protection must be made available to industries manufacturing such products as aircraft, firearms, ships, electronics, ocular glass, ball bearings, petroleum, and the like. If foreign competition were to ruin these industries, so the argument runs, a country would find its national defense compromised. The national defense argument dates back at least to Adam Smith and his *Wealth of Nations*, and it has always had a certain logical appeal. But there are also strong objections. As with infant industries, subsidies for this purpose are much to be preferred because a legislature can assess exactly how much is being spent and has an annual opportunity to reconsider its policies. A subsidy is also called for because defense is clearly the responsibility of all, not just the consumer of the protected good.

An annual review seems especially valuable because claims to protection based on defense can test credulity. Everyone wants to be considered valuable for national defense, and at various times and places, claims for protection on that ground have been made by the watch industry, by candle makers (emergency lighting), by textile manufacturers (uniforms) and clothespin makers (*clean* uniforms), and by toothpick makers (good dental hygiene for the troops, of course). Japan, with its small defense establishment, has nonetheless used the argument to prevent imports by Nippon Telephone & Telegraph of many parts for communications satellites. Characteristic language for making the defense case was recently used by the President of the American Footwear Industry's trade association. He argued that:

In the event of war or other national emergency, it is highly unlikely that the domestic footwear industry could provide sufficient footwear for the military and civilian population.... We won't be able to wait for ships to deliver shoes from Taiwan or Korea or Brazil or Eastern Europe.... Improper footwear can lead to needless casualties and turn sure victory into possible defeat.

Patriotism may not be solely the last refuge of the scoundrel, to paraphrase Dr. Samuel Johnson. In that refuge may also be found industries feeling the pinch of foreign competition.*

Even so, the argument once had some merit. Presumably it still does in some countries such as Israel, where sudden boycotts could have an impact on small arms and ammunition supplies, tanks, aircraft, and the like. Similarly, some Middle Eastern members of OPEC are perhaps acting reasonably in using the defense argument to justify protection of domestic food production in expectation that denial of access to sufficient food supply might someday be used as a weapon against them.

In the United States, under Section 232 of the Trade Act of 1962 the President can impose (or private firms can petition for) protection on the grounds that a product is necessary for the national security.[78] The Secretary of Commerce must report and the President must decide within 90 days. Neither unfair foreign practices nor substantial injury from trade have to be shown. Used before 1986 only to allow oil import quotas, this clause surfaces from time to time. In that year the machine tool industry made sufficient progress with it so that the Reagan administration negotiated a VER with Japan to limit imports. More recently, efforts to use the argument have been made by producers of ball bearings, petroleum, refined uranium, plastic injection molding machinery, industrial gears, and ceramic semiconductors. None of these cases succeeded, and there has been no case since 1994.

When a major country such as the United States bases part of its trade policy on the defense argument, logic is strained or trampled in most cases. It is hard to conceive of a modern war so serious that it halts international trade. Dependence on some vital imported item can certainly be worrisome, but if the item is available from a number of competing and geographically dispersed sources, the concern should presumably be reduced. This, together with some stockpiling of equipment and materials, should give adequate security. In any case, the greater interdependence fostered by open trade might encourage less violent solutions to political differences.

---

* "Why, a moral truth is a hollow tooth / Which must be propped with gold." Edgar Lee Masters, "Sexsmith the Dentist," in *Spoon River Anthology* (New York: Macmillan, 1963) [1914].

Relief from Temporary Disruption

Free trade can and often does bring nasty surprises for producers that cannot remotely be connected to any inefficiencies or mistakes on their part. A sharp devaluation in some other country's exchange rate due to a capital crisis (Mexico, Brazil, Southeast Asia) or a decline in home markets caused by politics or economic recession (Russia, Japan) could lead foreign competitors to increase their exports very suddenly. As these shipments pour in, firms in an industry may find themselves under sudden pressure they did not expect. Profits plunge, bankruptcy threatens. The crisis may blow over in a year or two, but in the meantime the industry might be destroyed. The private capital markets might give a temporary transfusion, of course, extending credit to injured firms if a surge of imports is believed to be temporary and the firm is expected to survive. But these capital markets did not expect the crisis either, the surge of imports may be of uncertain duration, and the firm's survival may be in question. Alternatives for their funds being many, caution costs the markets nothing. Some firms may go under, not having had time to assess the situation and plan for adjustment either by fighting back or by running themselves down. They are victims, as it were, of free trade. Arguably, a short period of assistance might bring enough relief from the temporary disruption so that a beleaguered firm will survive and thrive again.

Many would say that market systems require adjustment all the time, so why should firms hurt by imports be granted any special perquisites? But this neglects the probability that protectionist trade barriers might be obtained through lobbying if the cause of the disruption is imports, whereas other causes of disruption must simply be borne.

Since the days of GATT, this logic has been persuasive and countries have been permitted to take temporary safeguard or escape clause action to guard against sudden disruption from imports.[79] Most countries' safeguard measures are essentially similar. In the United States, under Section 201 of the Trade Act (and hence called "Section 201 cases" in the jargon), the U.S. International Trade Commission is asked to make a finding that temporary protection is justified.[*] The President is then empowered to impose a tariff or a tariff-rate quota, negotiate a voluntary export restraint agreement (which remains permitted as part of safeguards), establish an adjustment assistance program (which could be financed by using the tariff revenue from the safeguard), or take no action at all. If barriers are imposed, they are limited to a maximum period, including one extension, of eight years.

Before 1974, a firm claiming protection under the escape clause had to show that it was being injured by imports coming in because of a trade

---

[*] The U.S. ITC dates from 1916. Its six members are appointed by the President to terms of nine years. According to law, not more than three members may come from the "same political party," which means that the ITC often has members who are political independents.

concession and that these imports were the "major cause" (interpreted to mean the cause of over half) of the harm. After 1974, proof that the imports were due to a trade concession was no longer required, and the words "substantial cause" replaced "major cause." Even so, the harm was not easy to prove, and the President has discretion to overturn an ITC recommendation. (Congress, by resolution, can require the President to act, though this power has never been used.)[80] Moreover, the Trade Act of 1988 introduced yet another obstacle: an industry granted relief is required to present a plan describing how it proposes to become competitive again.

On top of that, discrimination was not permitted under the GATT rules—safeguard duties had to apply on a most-favored-nation basis to all trading partners. Also under the GATT rules, governments that took safeguard action had to offer compensation in other areas, say by reducing a barrier elsewhere, and the compensation had to be paid at once. These restrictions had the effect of keeping governments from pursuing safeguards and making them unattractive to private firms as well. That explains why safeguard action has been taken by the United States only four times since 1983. (But one of these, a safeguard for the heavy motorcycles produced by Harley-Davidson, proved to be a great success. A declining tariff-rate quota was imposed in 1983.* Harley reorganized and improved its product, and eventually announced that it did not need the last year of the five years of protection provided, so the TRQ was ended in 1987.)

CHANGES IN THE URUGUAY ROUND

In the Uruguay Round, trade law on safeguards was standardized for the WTO members (four years with one permitted extension of four more years, as in the United States). It was also made more attractive. Now the compensation does not have to be paid for the first three years. In addition, the safeguards, with approval of a new Safeguards Committee, can be selective rather than general, though the selective safeguards must end after just four years.[†]

Yet safeguard action remains very rare. For example, in 1998-99 there were only two U.S. measures in force, a TRQ on broom corn and a TRQ on Australian and New Zealand lamb.[81] The lamb TRQ is low but declining (9% to 6% to 3% to zero) on imports up to 1998 levels and high but declining on imports above 1998 levels (40%, 32%, 24%, zero). The standards of proof are

---

* The quantity of imports allowed in under the quota (15,000) paid no tariff; after that number a 45% duty was charged in the first year, declining in steps to 10% in the fifth year and zero in the year after that.

† There are special rules for safeguards employed against less-developed countries. They cannot be used against any single LDC whose share of the market is 3% or less or against any group of LDCs whose market share is 9% or less. LDCs can also apply safeguards of their own for two years longer than can developed countries, or 10 years in all.

still strict, however, and other forms of protection are easier to pursue. In spite of the rarity, numerous economists believe that they are a reasonable short-run policy response to temporary import surges—and that both economists and politicians should call attention to the Uruguay Round improvements and push for their greater use in place of more permanent and damaging protectionism.

CONCLUSION

This chapter has discussed the traditional reasoning used to justify trade barriers. That reasoning in a few cases is reasonably convincing, though for the most part we have seen that protection inflicts costs on society greater than the benefits delivered to the firms and factors that shelter behind the walls.

The next chapter continues in this same vein by examining the barriers that legislatures around the world have erected against a relatively new sort of economic crime, "unfair trade practices." What these practices are is now of central importance to international trade, and the attack on them through legislative and judicial action has become a major contributor to increased trade barriers.

VOCABULARY AND CONCEPTS

Bastable Test
Core labor standards
Dispute settlement panels
Equalizing tariff
Excess tariff
Fast-track
GATS (General Agreement on Trade in Services)
GATT (General Agreement on Tariffs and Trade)
GSP (Generalized System of Preferences)
Infant-industry argument
ITO (International Trade Organization)
Kennedy Round
Mill Test
MFN (most-favored-nation)

Reciprocal Trade Acts
Safeguard (Escape clause)
Scientific Tariff
Smoot-Hawley Tariff
Sweatshop argument
Tariff bindings
Tariff of Abominations
Tariffication
Tariffs for revenue
Tokyo Round
TRIPS and TRIMS
Uruguay Round
WTO (World Trade Organization)

QUESTIONS

1. "The United States had low tariffs only so long as strong export interests had influence and recognized how tariffs hurt them." Show the validity of this statement, using evidence from American history.
2. What did the Smoot-Hawley Tariff show about Congress and about the limitations of American legislation?
3. Why must the world always wait for the U.S. Congress to pass a trade bill in order to have trade negotiations?
4. A number of key features of American tariff policy today emerged in the Reciprocal Trade Act of 1934. What are they? In particular, how did the RTA handle the problem of Congress having the last word?
5. What was GATT and why was it formed?
6. State briefly the main features of the GATT agreement.
7. "GATT had no teeth, but the WTO is stronger." Debate, discussing the strengths and weaknesses of GATT and the WTO.
8. What was the Uruguay Round and what were its results?
9. Discuss the issue of "fast-track" negotiation.
10. Given that economists have demonstrated time and time again the costs of trade barriers, why do they persist? That is, what are the political-economic factors that drive their persistence?
11. Brown and Hogendorn argue that protection produces rents, but critical questions remain about who collects them. Explain.
12. It appears to be very expensive to maintain employment through restricting trade. Why? Give some examples and explain why it is so expensive.
13. In most cases, it would be cheaper to retire workers displaced by imports than to keep them working in protected industries. Why?
14. Frequently the extent of adjustment required due to trade liberalization is over-estimated because the model people have in mind is one of interfactoral, rather than intrafactoral, competition (that is, inter-, rather than intraindustrial trade). Why should it make a difference? (See also Chapter 3.)
15. What are the arguments to support protection of infant industries? How well do they fit with ideas in Chapter 3? Why are Brown and Hogendorn leery of them?
16. "With well-functioning capital markets, no need exists for protection." Explain in the context of the infant-industry argument.
17. A footnote suggests that moral truths are hollow and used as glosses for underlying economic advantages. The comment is cynical, but at least partially correct. Explain why.
18. Discuss critically the cheap labor and sweatshop arguments.
19. The national defense argument is much overused. Why?
20. What are the Mill Test and the Bastable Test? What is their current relevance?
21. There may be some reason for temporary trade barriers. Why might that be so, and what improvements were made in the Uruguay Round that will increase their use?

NOTES

1. F.M. Scherer, *Competition Policies for an Integrated World Economy* (Washington: Brookings Institution, 1994), 21-22.

2. John A.C. Conybeare, *Trade Wars* (New York: Columbia University Press, 1987), 241.

3. Judith A. McDonald, Anthony Patrick O'Brien, and Colleen M. Callahan, "Trade Wars: Canada's Reaction to the Smoot-Hawley Tariff," *Journal of Economic History* 57, 4 (December 1997): 802-26.

4. Ibid.

5. The retaliation is catalogued by Joseph M. Jones, Jr., *Tariff Retaliation: Repercussions of the Hawley-Smoot Bill* (Philadelphia, 1934). See especially Conybeare, *Trade Wars*, 247.

6. McDonald, O'Brien, and Callahan, "Trade Wars."

7. See the work of Charles P. Kindleberger, especially *The World in Depression, 1929-1939* (Berkeley: University of California Press, 1973).

8. See Douglas A. Irwin, "The Smoot-Hawley Tariff: A Quantitative Assessment," *Review of Economics and* 80 (May 1998): 326-34.

9. Ibid.; Barry Eichengreen, "The Political Economy of the Smoot-Hawley Tariff," NBER Working Paper No. 2001, August 1986.

10. USITC, *The Year in Trade 1997*, 141-43.

11. Douglas A. Irwin, "Changes in U.S. Tariffs: The Role of Import Prices and Commercial Policies," *American Economic Review* 88 (September 1998): 1015-26; Don D. Humphrey, *The U.S. and the Common Market* (New York, 1962).

12. Some of the details in this section are from Margaret Kelly, Naheed Kirmani, Miranda Xafa, Clemens Boonekamp, and Peter Winglee, *Issues and Developments in International Trade Policy*, IMF Occasional Paper

No. 63 (Washington: IMF, December 1988), 139; recent issues of the USITC's *The Year in Trade*; frequent articles in the *International Economic Review*, *The Economist*, and the *Wall Street Journal*.

13. The reviews can be found on the Web at http://www.wto.org/wto/reviews/tpr.htm

14. *International Economic Review*, September 1995, which contains a complete annual schedule of the steps taken under the Uruguay Round agreement.

15. For discussion and analysis see Jagdish Bhagwati, ed., *The Uruguay Round and Beyond: Essays in Honor of Arthur Dunkel* (Ann Arbor: University of Michigan Press, 1998); Ernest H. Preeg, *Traders in a Brave New World: The Uruguay Round and the Future of the International Trading System* (Chicago: University of Chicago Press, 1995); Jeffrey J. Schott with Johanna W. Buurman, *The Uruguay Round: An Assessment* (Washington: Institute of International Economics, 1994); John Whalley, *The Trading System After the Uruguay Round* (Washington: Institute for International Economics, 1996).

16. *Wall Street Journal*, September 13, 1994; *The Economist*, September 20, 1997, October 3, 1998.

17. *Rushford Report*, February 1999.

18. Craig Van Grasstek, "Is the Fast Track Really Necessary?" *Journal of World* 31, 2 (April 1997): 97-124. For a recent detailed study, see Jeffrey J. Schott, ed., *Restarting the Fast Track* (Washington: Institute for International Economics, 1998).

19. Among many sources, see Norman S. Fieleke, "The Uruguay Round of Trade Negotiations: An Overview," and "The Uruguay Round of Trade Negotiations: Industrial and Geographic Effects in the United States," *New England Economic Review* (May/June 1995); and all recent issues of USITC, *The Year in Trade*.

20. See George D. Holliday, "The Uruguay Round's Agreement on Safeguards," *Journal of World Trade* 29, 3 (June 1995): 155-60.

21. See Giovanni Anania, ed., *Agricultural Trade Conflicts and GATT: New Dimensions in U.S.-European Agricultural Trade Relations* (Boulder, Colo.: Westview Press, 1994); C. Falmer et al., *The Common Agricultural Policy Beyond the MacSharry Reform* (Amsterdam: Elsevier, 1995); Brian Gardner, *European Agriculture: Policies, Production, and Trade* (London: Routledge, 1996); Timothy E. Josling, *Agriculture in the GATT* (Basingstoke: Macmillan, 1996); Josling, *Agricultural Trade Policy: Completing the Reform* (Washington: Institute for International Economics, 1998); Will Martin and L. Alan Winters, *The Uruguay Round and the Developing Countries* (Cambridge: Cambridge University Press, 1996); Alan Swinbank, *Farm Policy and Trade Conflict: The Uruguay Round and CAP Reform* (Ann Arbor: University of Michigan Press, 1996).

22. *The Economist*, June 26, 1993.

23. USITC, *The Year in Trade 1996*, 88; *1997*, 86; *The Economist*, May 22, 1999; David Orden, "Agricultural Interest Groups and the North American Free Trade Agreement," in Krueger, ed., *The Political Economy of American Trade Policy*, 335-82; Merlinda D. Ingco, "Agricultural Trade Liberalization in the Uruguay Round: One Step Forward, One Step Back?" *World Bank Development Brief* No. 49 (March 1995). The sugar tariff is higher than stated by Ingco because it is specific and world sugar prices have been declining.

24. USITC, *The Year in Trade 1993*, 12, 49-50; Fieleke, "The Uruguay Round of Trade Negotiations," 9.

25. Gabrielle Marceau, "Transition from GATT to WTO: A Most Pragmatic Operation," *Journal of World Trade* 29, 4 (August 1995): 147-63.

26. The latest WTO membership list can be found at: http://www.wto.org/wto/about/organsn6.htm

27. Council of Economic Advisors, *Economic Report of the President 1995* (Washington: 1995): 213; *The Economist*, November 26, 1994; USITC, *The Year in Trade 1994*, 8.

28. Edwin Vermulst and Bart Driessen, "An Overview of the WTO Dispute Settlement System and Its Relationship with the Uruguay Round Agreements," *Journal of World Trade* 12, 1 (March 1995): 131-61; *The Economist*, November 26, 1994; USITC, *The Year in Trade 1994*, 8-9.

29. *International Economic Review*, May/June 1997, January/February 1998.

30. *Wall Street Journal*, April 13, 20, 23, 1999.

31. Ibid., April 23, 1999.

32. *The Economist*, June 18, 1994, March 25, 1995.

33. Ibid, March 25, 1995.

34. *New York Times*, April 8, 1999

35. AP, May 3, 1999.

36. A good account is Norio Komuro, "The WTO Dispute Settlement Mechanism: Coverage and Procedures of the WTO Understanding," *Journal of World Trade* 29, 4 (August 1995): 5-95. USITC, *The Year in Trade*, contains comprehensive information.

37. Up-to-date and authoritative information on disputes and appeals can be found at: http://www.wto.org/wto/dispute/bulletin.htm

38. USITC, *The Year in Trade 1997*, 6, 31-39.

39. *Wall Street Journal*, April 11, 1995.

40. *The Economist*, April 10, 1999; Joseph A. McMahon, "The EC Banana Regime, the WTO Rulings and the ACP," *Journal of World Trade* 32, 4 (1998): 101-14.

41. *International Economic Review*, November/December 1998, 3-5.

42. Ibid; USITC, *The Year in Trade 1997*, 99-100.

43. *The Economist*, April 10, 1999; *Wall Street Journal*, April 7, April 20, 1999.

44. Fieleke, "The Uruguay Round of Trade Negotiations," 12-13.

45. Glenn Harrison, Thomas Rutherford, and David Tarr, "Quantifying the Outcome of the Uruguay Round," *Finance and Development* 32, 4 (December 1995): 38-41.

46. See IMF, *World Economic Outlook 1994* (Washington, 1994): 83-87, citing GATT Secretariat, *An Analysis of the Uruguay Round Agreement, with Particular Emphasis on Aspects of Interest to Developing Countries,* MTN. TNC/W/W122, Geneva, November 1993; Ian Goldin, Odin Knudsen, and Dominique van der Mensbrugghe, *Trade Liberalization: Global Economic Implications* (Washington, 1993); T. Nguyen, C. Perroni, and R. Wigle, "An Evaluation of the Draft Final Act of the Uruguay Round," *Economic Journal* 103 (November 1993): 1540-49; OECD, *Assessing the Effects of the Uruguay Round*, Trade Policy Issues 2 (Paris, 1993).

47. See André Sapir, "The General Agreement on Trade in Services: From 1994 to the Year 2000," *Journal of World Trade* 33, 1 (February 1999): 51-66, and Bernard Hoekman, "Assessing the General Agreement on Trade in Services," in Martin and Winters, eds., *The Uruguay Round and the Developing Economies.*

48. *Economic Report to the President 1998*, 225-26; USITC, *The Year in Trade 1997*, 18, 25; *Wall Street Journal*, March 3, 1997; *The Economist*, February 22, 1997; Sapir, "The General Agreement on Trade in Services," 59.

49. *International Economic Review*, October/November 1996.

50. *Rushford Report*, April 1999.

51. *The Economist*, May 8, 1999.

52. Interested students might start with the first three chapters of Bruno S. Frey, *International Political Economics* (Oxford: Basil Blackwell Publishers, 1984).

53. Anne O. Krueger, "Introduction," in Krueger, ed., *The Political Economy of American Trade Policy*, 1.

54. These types of models and their testing are discussed in Robert E. Baldwin, "Trade Policies in Developed Countries," in Ronald W. Jones and Peter B. Kenen, eds., *Handbook of International Economics*, vol. 1 (Amsterdam: Elsevier, 1984), 573-582; Baldwin, *The Political Economy of U.S. Import Policy* (Cambridge, Mass.: MIT Press, 1985); Krueger, ed., *The Political Economy of American Trade Policy.*

55. See Baldwin, *The Political Economy of U.S. Import Policy*, 40-41.

56. *Wall Street Journal*, December 10, 1998.

57. Daniel Yankelovich, "A Widening Expert/Public Opinion Gap," *Challenge* 35, 3 (May/June 1992): 22.

58. *Christian Science Monitor*, February 3, 1992.

59. Craig Van Grasstek, "Is the Fast Track Really Necessary?" *Journal of World Trade* 31, 2 (April 1997): 97-124

60. *Wall Street Journal*/NBC News polling data reported in the *Wall Street Journal*, 1990. For a report of an experiment in this regard, see Robert Reich, "We Need a Strategic Trade Policy," *Challenge* 33, 4 (July/August 1990): 41.

61. *International Economic Review*, January 1991.

62. See Gary Clyde Hufbauer and Kimberly Ann Elliott, *Measuring the Costs of Protection in the United States* (Washington: Institute for International Economics, 1994). An earlier study is Gary Clyde Hufbauer, Diane T. Berliner, and Kimberly Ann Elliott, *Trade Protection in the United States: 31 Case Studies* (Washington: Institute for International Economics, 1986). For the Washington University study, see Center for the Study of American Business Working Paper No. 80, and a version of this paper, Michael C. Munger, "The Costs of Protection," *Challenge* 26, 6 (January/February 1984): 54-58. A comprehensive survey is Robert C. Feenstra, ed., *The Effects of U.S. Trade Protection and Promotion Policies* (Chicago: University of Chicago Press, 1995).

63. Stephen S. Golub, "Are International Labor Standards Needed to Prevent Social Dumping?" *Finance and Development* (December 1997): 20-23.

64. Bureau of Statistics, U.S. Department of Labor, reported in *Economic Report of the President 1999* (Washington: Council of Economic Advisors, 1999), 376, 382.

65. *Economic Report of the President 1995* (Washington: Council of Economic Advisors, 1995), 250.

66. Golub, "Are International Labor Standards Needed?" 20-23.

67. See *The Economist*, February 27, 1999.

68. *Wall Street Journal*, November 12, 1996.

69. Ibid., April 10, 1997; *Christian Science Monitor*, April 14, 1997.

70. Alan B. Krueger, "International Labor Standards and Trade," *Annual World Bank Conference on Development Economics 1996* (Washington: World Bank, 1996), 281-302.

71. This is the message in Jagdish Bhagwati and Robert E. Hudec, eds., *Fair Trade and Harmonization: Prerequisites for Free Trade?* 2 vols. (Cambridge, Mass.: MIT Press, 1996), which provides thorough analysis of whether conditions must be similar for free trade to be beneficial.

72. See *The Economist*, January 31, 1987.

73. Paul Krugman, "What Should Trade Negotiators Negotiate About?" *Journal of Economic Literature* 35, 1 (March 1997): 113-20.

74. William R. Cline, *International Economic Policy in the 1990s* (Cambridge, Mass.: MIT Press, 1994), 63-65.

75. Tibor Scitovsky, "Tariffs," *The New Palgrave Dictionary of Economics*, vol. 4 (London: Macmillan, 1987), 587.

76. The classic debunking is by Robert E. Baldwin, "The Case Against Infant-Industry Tariff Protection," *Journal of Political Economy* 77, 3 (May/June 1969): 295-305.

77. Cline, *International Economic Policy in the 1990s*, 63-65.

78. USITC, *The Year in Trade 1997*, 145-46.

79. For this section we utilized all recent issues of USITC, *The Year in Trade*; George D. Holliday, "The Uruguay Round's Agreement on Safeguards," *Journal of World Trade* 29, 3 (June 1995): 155-60; P. Kleen, "The Safeguard Issue in the Uruguay Round—A Comprehensive Approach," *Journal of World Trade* 23, 5 (October 1989): 73-85.

80. See Baldwin, *Political Economy of U.S. Import Policy*, 35-36.

81. USITC, *The Year in Trade 1997*, 127.

Chapter Seven

Unfair Trade Practices

OBJECTIVES

OVERALL OBJECTIVE   To examine closely unfair trade practices, demonstrating that the laws, not the practices, are unfair.

MORE SPECIFICALLY
- To define what dumping is, explain the antidumping laws, and analyze the changes brought about by the Uruguay Round.
- To discuss the strength of the economic arguments against dumping.
- To explain the biases and arbitrariness that exist in American dumping and countervailing duty legislation and practice.
- To define what subsidies are and which ones can be countervailed, showing how law has expanded its definitions and how the Uruguay Round changed the situation.
- To evaluate the more aggressive crowbar provisions of the U.S. trade act.

....

This chapter analyzes the emergence and central position of so-called unfair trade practices in modern international trade. Tariffs declined and controls were placed on quotas and VERS in the GATT rounds of trade negotiations. As a result, new significance has come to these once-obscure protective measures that allow tariffs to be imposed in special circumstances involving alleged unfairness. The economic logic for banning these practices is weak, however. The most acceptable defense for them, prevention of predatory pricing, seldom has anything to do with the unfair practice laws. Yet from a political point of view the question of unfair trade practices is a burning one. If the people who are hurt by imports believe, and can convince others, that the source of the harm is an illegitimate tactic by foreigners—say, sales at unfair low prices or government subsidies to the exporter—then they can gain political support for trade barriers even if these barriers are very costly for consumers.

The often-heard call for a level playing field is part of this appeal. The laws described below are pushed by a sense that it is unjust for people to be injured by the unfair practice. No matter that such practices are for the most part entirely legal when done by one's own firms within the country, when done by foreigners they just do not appear fair. That setting is perfect for protectionists, who, defending their own interests, are able to use fairness arguments to great effect. Indeed, those responsible for these laws have won a great battle in convincing congresses and parliaments that the practices they legislate against really are unfair and deserve to be attacked. In fact, as this chapter shows, the laws and their administration are highly arbitrary, serving to harass foreign exporters in ways that should embarrass the citizens and taxpayers. The balance of the chapter explores what these practices are and how the laws against them have become central to protectionist strategy.

The unfair practice laws are technical in nature, developed more by lawyers in legislatures and judges in courts than by economists, and their evolvement is dominated by a rather small community of legal experts.[1] The warning issued by Paul Krugman is apt: "Economists pronounce on legal matters at their peril; law, even international trade law, is a discipline all its own, with a jargon just as impenetrable to us as ours is to them."[2] The laws include antidumping duties against what is called *dumping*, countervailing duties against foreign subsidies, and measures in response to violations of trade agreements. All of them treat foreign firms more harshly than domestic ones, providing an effective means at least to harass foreign competitors and at most to erect a significant barrier to imports.

Firms seeking limits to imports have good reason to favor the unfair trade practice approach as compared to the safeguards discussed in the preceding chapter. Being a product of the law and the courts, they are more respectable than ordinary barriers. The laws are very legalistic; for example, in the United States the President has no discretion to interfere in the process and the penalties are mandatory. They can be used in discriminatory fashion against single countries (and in theory, even against each plant of a given firm) or groups of countries in a coordinated assault. They require no compensation to be paid to foreigners. They have the major effect of creating uncertainty that will inhibit trade. Furthermore, the unfair trade practice laws do not allow matters of foreign policy or of harm to domestic consumers—including domestic firms using the sanctioned import as an input to production—to be taken into account. These users are considered irrelevant. No wonder the laws concerning unfair trade practices have become so popular among those who want to wall off world trade.

DUMPING

The first of the unfair trade practices is dumping, the idea that foreigners will unfairly undersell domestic firms and that penalties should be imposed to raise their prices to a fair level.[3] Few words in economics sound quite so horrid as "dumping," and even those who do not know what it means could hardly be expected to defend anything apparently so nasty. The issue goes back to the late eighteenth-century concern that Britain's exporters would swamp the United States with cheap goods. Canada introduced the first antidumping law in 1904, reacting to the possibility of predatory tactics by U.S. firms—they might lower their prices, drive Canadian firms out of business, and then raise their prices in Canada to monopoly levels, or so the argument went. The first U.S. legislation of 1916 was also aimed at predatory behavior by foreign firms.

Predatory Dumping

Predatory dumping is a potentially serious problem, and most economists find it easy to recommend harsh treatment if and when such cases are found. Predatory dumping is akin to the domestic practice of carrying on a price war, cutting prices, perhaps to below marginal cost, with the intent of driving competitors out of the industry. The predator presumably then raises its prices to a high level to extract monopoly returns. Such warlike tactics seldom if ever find support among economists, whether they are perpetrated by a firm in domestic operations or in foreign trade.

It is questionable, however, how common the practice is in international trade. Even domestically, its existence is dubious in goods trade (though it is more likely in a service such as airlines trying to discourage competitors).[4] The problem is that once a potential monopolist drives out its competitors and establishes its monopoly price, new competitors re-enter. A predatory firm would have to decide that the costs of driving existing competitors out of business can be made up by the high price charged between the time old competitors are driven out and new ones appear. That is a difficult case to prove either theoretically or historically.[5] Furthermore, the predatory firm would have to have international, not just national, monopoly power in order to justify the tactic, or else imports would flow in as prices were raised.

Virtually every economist doubts whether such behavior is at all common in international trade.[6] At one end of a short spectrum, data suggest there may be a few examples. One recent study concluded that predatory dumping might possibly have occurred in 5% of cases, but probably did not.[7] At the other end of the spectrum, some authorities doubt whether a single authenticated instance exists of a foreign predatory dumper acquiring monopoly power in a major trading country and then extracting monopoly rents.

301

According to dumping specialist N. David Palmeter, in not one of the 767 affirmative antidumping determinations reached by Australia, Canada, the EU, and the United States in a seven-year period of the 1980s was there even a hint of predatory pricing.[8]

Many business people nonetheless believe that predatory dumping does occur, and occasionally an academic case is made that predation is not intended to drive competitors out of the industry but merely to deter them from planned market expansion or new investment or new product development.[*] If judicious price-cutting can lower a rival's profit expectations, one's own profits could be protected.

Perhaps so, and therefore perhaps antidumping law aimed at predatory behavior is a useful supplement to antitrust law aimed at predation. (U.S. antitrust law cannot hit foreign exporters; it applies only to firms located within the country—a practice generally followed by other countries as well.) But the present situation is that there is absolutely no requirement under the dumping laws even to hint at predatory behavior. As noted, under the original 1916 U.S. antidumping statute, predatory intent had to be shown. That was dropped in the 1921 version of the law, which also made the antidumping process administrative rather than judicial.[9] With that law dumping was redefined to include far less obviously damaging behavior by foreign firms. (The new U.S. interpretation of 1921 is said to have been designed to protect against imports of German chemicals after the Versailles Treaty threatened Americans with increased imports as Germany attempted to pay war reparations.) The present dumping law is so far removed from predation that dumping charges have actually been brought against foreign exporters that have held less than 1% of the market. It is plain that monopoly power is more likely to be furthered by dumping duties than by the predatory practice of foreigners. Notwithstanding all the above, however, if and when predatory practice is found it deserves attack on the ground that the results would distort world efficiency.

Quite to the contrary, however, almost all of the behavior covered by current dumping law penalizes foreigners for doing what honest and prudent domestic business people do with complete legality all the time. Not only that, but the definition of what constitutes dumping has been greatly enlarged over the years. The inherent bias against foreigners in the law and the broadening definition of the crime are intensified because the importing country serves as prosecutor, judge, jury, and jailer.

---

* Some of the newer game-theory approaches suggest some situations in which modified predation might be useful. Even so, industrial organization specialists remain largely skeptical. For development of a game-theory model, see Jean Tirole, *The Theory of Industrial Organization* (Cambridge, Mass.: MIT Press, 1990).

The Primary Definition of Dumping: Export Sales Below the Home Price

Under the 1921 U.S. legislation and around the world, dumping is defined as sales in an export market at prices below those charged in the exporter's home market.[10] If a Japanese firm that sells at home and also exports charges $100 in Japan and $90 in the United States for the same good, then that firm has dumped.* Ordinarily, cases are not brought if the dumping occurs only occasionally and for short periods. Such "sporadic dumping" is common under conditions of temporary overstock and resembles the clearance sales held by department stores or the short-term loss-leader tactics used by firms to break into new markets. The antidumping statutes refer to dumping over an "extended time," usually defined as six months.

The same practice carried on for a longer period is known as persistent dumping and can be sanctioned under the dumping laws. Even at the outset it is clear that these laws exhibit analytical oddity. First, notice that "reverse dumping," as when Mercedes or BMW charges higher prices in its export markets than it does at home in Germany, is perfectly legal and done all the time. Second, economists would find it hard to agree that export sales below the home price are such a bad thing. Take the extreme case where the exporter is a monopoly at home and a competitor in its export market. If costs are the same in the two markets, then the exporter will certainly want to dump. The damage, so one would think, is not the dumping in the export market, but the monopoly pricing that harms consumers in the *home* market.

Take an example: the recent minivan case of the early 1990s. The Big Three U.S. automakers charged Toyota and Mazda with dumping minivans. It was not surprising that the price of Japanese vans in Japan was higher than the price of these same vans in the United States, however. There is a near-monopoly situation in Japan because no competing U.S. van has its steering wheel on the right for the driving to the left that the Japanese do. Dumping was found, so to avoid large penalties the Japanese producers rapidly raised their prices. Now those Americans who still want to buy a Japanese van get to pay the same monopoly price the Japanese must pay.

Consider the problem as a technical one involving dissimilar demand in two markets. A profit-maximizing firm will have a motive to engage in dumping if the demand curve facing the firm is placed differently in these markets. The difference in shape, and hence in elasticity, may be due to

---

* According to a recent interpretation, if home market sales (e.g., in Japan by a Japanese firm) are less than 5% of sales in the export market (e.g., the United States), then the sales price in a single third-country export market (e.g., Germany) can be used as a proxy for the home price as long as those sales are over 5% of those in the U.S. market. Some convictions have recently been obtained in the United States under this new interpretation. See *Wall Street Journal*, December 9, 1993.

variations in tastes, habits, national traits, levels of income, or degree of competition in the two markets. Trade does not equalize prices, perhaps because of monopoly power, or transport costs, or trade barriers.

In Figures 7.1a and 7.1b, we see two different demand curves, D_a and D_b facing Watanabe Electronics, a large Tokyo firm with markets for its product in both Japan and the United States. The downward slope indicates that the firm has some degree of market power in each market. Each demand curve has an associated curve for marginal revenue, MR_a and MR_b. The marginal cost curves MC_a and MC_b are drawn on the assumption that marginal costs are the same in each market.

Figure 7.1

WHY A FIRM WOULD WANT TO CHARGE A
HIGHER PRICE AT HOME THAN ABROAD

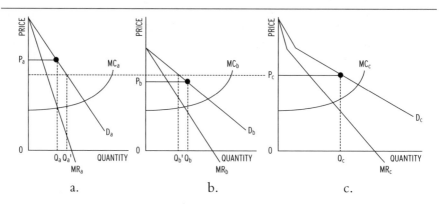

a.   b.   c.

Note: A firm with two separate national markets can often maximize profits if it keeps the prices different. The *MC* curve is the same in all three diagrams, but the demand and *MR* curves differ. The firm maximizes profit in 7.1a at a price of P_a and in 7.1b at a price of P_b. If 7.1b represents the United States, then Americans pay a lower price, but the foreign exporter would be guilty of dumping. Forced to charge the same price in both markets, the firm combines demand curves as in 7.1c, and charges the same price in both markets, P_c.

The managers of the firm must now decide what price to charge in each market. A moment's reflection will show that profits will be maximized (where $MC = MR$) if two different prices are charged. In Figure 7.1a, which is Watanabe's home market, marginal cost equals marginal revenue ($MC_a = MR_a$) at a price P_a and quantity Q_a. This price is significantly higher than in Figure 7.1b, the export market, where the profit-maximizing price is P_b (and the quantity is Q_b). In effect, a higher price is charged in the home market where demand is less elastic. Under WTO rules, as we have seen, this is dumping.

Thus, it is easy to appreciate why dumping is carried out—it is a profit-maximizing strategy. It is also understandable why many companies might choose to adopt an equal price strategy anyway. The exporter accused of dumping can avoid the charges by equalizing the prices in the two markets. The better part of valor may be a flat pricing strategy.

The results of a decision to charge the same price in the two markets is a bit curious, as seen in Figure 7.1c. If Watanabe Electronics considers the combined demand in the two markets, the resulting demand curve D_c is the horizontal addition of D_a and D_b. Similarly, the combined marginal revenue curve MR_c is the horizontal addition of MR_a and MR_b. Given the unchanged marginal cost curve MC_c, the price charged in the combined market will be P_c because that price will maximize profits if the markets are treated as one. Look carefully at the diagrams: the result of eliminating dumping is a lower price in Watanabe's home market (Japan) and a higher price in the export market (the United States). The single price P_c would result in a quantity Q_c. Of this quantity, an increased amount (Q_a') will be sold in the home market and a smaller quantity (Q_b') in the export market.

Doubtless, the idea of charging a higher price at home than abroad in export markets does, in these latter markets, seem to violate the producers' sense of fair play. It is not usually explained why persistent dumping is thought to be so bad if a foreign firm is just matching a domestic competitor's price (a fully adequate defense for a *domestic* firm charged with price discrimination), or if it is charging more at home because it has a greater degree of monopoly power there. Is it sensible to claim that the importer, too, should pay higher monopoly prices for the product? Differential pricing among markets is *not* illegal if done by domestic firms. Senior citizens and student discounts, lower prices for new magazine subscribers, brand-name products sold for higher prices than the same unbranded product, loss leaders to get you into the store and to experience the product are all quite legal in *domestic* trade. Indeed, they are everyday business practice.

Furthermore, though the word "dumping" sounds very naughty indeed, the practice does benefit consumers by bringing lower prices. The thought crosses the economist's mind (though with little effect on the business community) that if a foreigner wants to charge us lower prices than are charged at home, then such generosity might even be welcomed! Chapter 4 demonstrated that an import at a lower price brings net benefits to society because the gains to consumers from the import outweigh the loss to producers. If a country could gain in real income because of the sales of cheap dumped goods, it could presumably devote part of its gains to compensating losers and still be better off as a whole. But under present political conditions the abandonment of the antidumping laws, rather than being welcomed, would probably unleash yet more protectionist sentiment.

The Secondary Definition of Dumping: Sales in Export Markets at Prices Below Average Cost

What if you are an exporter with *low* prices at home compared to the price you charge in your export markets, or perhaps with few or no sales at home and you sell only in the export market. It would seem that no dumping charge is then possible, but this is not correct. A secondary or cost definition of dumping, invented by the United States in 1974, was adopted with little or no debate and entered the laws of the other major countries by about 1980. If there are no home prices to work with, then a fair home price (called "normal value") is constructed from data on cost. The cost definition used is full short-run average cost, including variable and fixed costs plus an allowance for selling costs, general and administrative costs, and a margin for profit.* If an exporter sells at a price in the United States below that constructed cost, then it is guilty of dumping. Under this cost definition, dumping occurs in the export market even if sales below constructed cost are occurring in the firm's home market as well.

THE COST DEFINITION IS ESPECIALLY IMPORTANT IN A RECESSION

This cost definition is a powerful weapon in a recession. First-year economics courses for decades have covered the shutdown rule, the idea that it would not make sense to shut down your firm unless prices fall below average variable costs. Many firms make losses in a recession, sometimes billion-dollar losses, but they continue to produce because that minimizes their loss. Under the dumping laws, however, a foreign exporting firm is not permitted to sell at below average total cost, and thus behavior that is common for domestic firms in recessions is illegal if the firms are foreign ones attempting to export to a country with an antidumping law. This helps to explain why the number of dumping cases soars in a recession. Firms not only *want* trade barriers then, but dumping is easier to prove.[11] Note that a result is that in recessions, when the price of imports would otherwise fall, they may not, to the disadvantage of firms using imported inputs.[12]

DUMPING TO DECREASE A FIRM'S COSTS OF PRODUCTION

Another reason why a foreign firm may choose to sell in an export market at a price lower than average cost is that the foreign firm may be restricting output in a protected home market and selling at high prices there. Then, as a regular practice it might decide to dump (that is, sell at a lower price in its

---

* Note the difference with what constitutes unfairness under the U.S. antitrust laws. Here it is sale below *marginal* cost that is accepted as evidence of predatory activity.

export market) so as to move down its cost curve (and perhaps its learning curve as well, which has the same effect). The lower costs could bring increased profits in the high-price home market. The tactic could pay as long as sales in the export market are made at a price equal to or above the firm's marginal cost, even if below its average total cost. Essentially, the argument is that a firm can use more of its capacity, driving costs down and pushing profits up, if it sells below cost in an export market.

The logic of this case is explored in Figure 7.2. In the diagram, the average cost of production is already covered at home in the domestic market, where the firm has some

Figure 7.2

PROFITS MAY BE ENHANCED BY EXPORT SALES AT PRICES BELOW AVERAGE COST

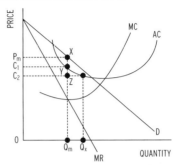

Note: A firm could keep its monopoly price in the home market at P_m, but lower its costs from C_1 to C_2 by selling extra production of $Q_m Q_x$ at marginal cost to an export market. Profit would increase.

degree of monopoly power, buttressed perhaps by protection. The quantity produced is equal to Q_m; the price is P_m. Cost per unit is C_1. Profit is $C_1 P_m XY$.

This firm has an opportunity available to it if it dumps in its export markets. What if the firm were to increase its output, say to Q_x, selling the increase $Q_m Q_x$ in an export market? The firm might sell these exports at a price just high enough to cover the marginal cost of the additional output $Q_m Q_x$. Note that the increased output allows the firm to bring down its average costs from C_1 to C_2. That fall in average cost serves to raise profits in the protected home market by $C_2 C_1 YZ$.

In any price-discrimination situation, the discriminating firm must keep its markets apart; otherwise buyers in the cheap market will resell in the expensive one. Alternatively, competing sellers in the cheap market will sell in the expensive one and also reap the value of the market separation; such competitive selling will move the markets toward a single price. Only if the discriminator's home market is protected against reimports or imports from the foreign market can the discrimination strategy succeed.

A number of comments are in order. In such a situation there is certainly an argument that the *foreign* government in the *exporting* country should strengthen its antitrust laws and reduce its trade barriers so that its own consumers will benefit. The first-best solution would be for the importing country's government to encourage the exporter's government to make the exporter's home market competitive.

If this fails, the importing country can console itself that by receiving the dumped goods it is benefiting from the lower prices, and the standard trade model predicts that the benefits will outweigh the costs to producers harmed by the imports. The foreign exporter, rather than staying up its cost curve, is willing to move down it and share the benefits with consumers abroad. Predatory behavior is not occurring in this case. Firms in the importing country will not like the result, of course, but even they will have to admit that if conditions in the exporter's domestic market had been more competitive, costs there would *already* have been lower.

The cost definition turns up in a few other arguments charging that dumping occurs. Firms are said to cross-subsidize, for example, by pricing TV sets below cost and making it up by selling high-profit items to people who come into the TV shop. Firms are also accused of dumping when they give temporary specials on goods to encourage consumers to try them out to discover their benefits. After buyers find they like the products, the firms raise the costs. This is technically dumping, although such practices are normal for domestic firms. The question arises why, if the practice is permitted for domestic firms, it should be prohibited for foreign firms. Is this a level playing field?

THE COST DEFINITION AND NON-MARKET (COMMUNIST) ECONOMIES

The cost definition of dumping is more difficult when the dumping charge is against a centrally planned or transition economy, where there are no market prices by which the cost of production can be determined or where these prices are not an accurate reflection of costs. It might be thought that because market prices are not used, dumping charges on the cost definition would not be possible. But this underestimates the ingenuity of the law's administrators, who have found a way—pioneered by the United States.

The first method used by the Department of Commerce to establish costs in such a situation was to examine the price of a like product in a comparable economy with a free market. Cooperation of a producer of the like product had to be obtained, however, and that dried up when the data furnished by a Finnish steel company in a 1982 case against steel from non-market Romania was used in 1984 to prosecute the Finnish company.

The Department of Commerce thereupon moved to a second method, reconstructing the costs of production from the costs of the factor inputs in similar market economies. For an example, consider the remarkable case of Polish golf carts. Melex golf carts were a popular item on golf courses, used even at the President's Camp David retreat. Melex was accused of dumping by selling below cost during a period that extended from 1975 to 1980. The Commerce Department reconstructed the Mielec, Poland, production cost of the carts by using Spanish costs as a proxy. It challenges the imagination to discover what Spain and Poland have in common that would make their costs similar. Perhaps they just drew the name from a hat. In any case, the attempt was made to estimate what it would have cost to produce the carts if the Polish firm were transplanted to the plains of Castile. Then the cost in Spanish pesetas was converted to dollars to get the proxy for the American price. (Only a small amount of dumping was actually found, incidentally, but this case was still being litigated in the mid-1990s, with Melex appealing an adverse decision concerning duties owed from the late seventies.) In the 1990s, Poland was still being treated as if it were Communist, with prices in Thailand, South Africa, and Malaysia used as proxies in a steel dumping case with a 62% duty levied.

For all the uncertainty in this method, its use against non-market economies became standard under the 1988 Trade Act. It has been employed in many recent actions against China, where production costs were established by estimating what they would have been if the product had been produced elsewhere. For Chinese paint brushes, 27% dumping was found by using a Sri Lankan firm as the surrogate. In steel wire nails, Korea was the surrogate; in wax candles, it was Malaysia and the Republic of Guinea; for steel, Pakistan; for menthol, Paraguay; for porcelain-on-steel cooking ware, it was a weighted figure for Japan, Canada, Switzerland, Germany, the Netherlands, and France. Because labor costs in all these other countries are higher than China's, the results seem irrelevant and the method badly flawed. In any case, inefficiency in non-market economies may mean greater-than-usual factor use that, when valued at market prices, might mean dumping would always exist if any exports at all were sold. In all this it should be noted that an accused country cannot know which surrogate will be selected and is not told until after the case begins.

The issue continues to simmer because China demands that its treatment as a non-market economy in antidumping cases be ended in five years (2003), while the United States wants to continue using proxies in the foreseeable future. (The EU and Australia have dropped their non-market dumping methods, by the way.)[13] Economists smiled a little when they heard that China's first antidumping duties, levied in 1998, were against U.S. and Canadian newsprint makers whose costs were constructed for them. The U.S. companies were hit with 79% duties. Turnabout is fair play.[14]

New Interpretations

New interpretations of what constitutes dumping have emerged. In the past, the rules said nothing about the dumping of components subject to an antidumping duty, such as for inputs in foreign-owned screwdriver assembly plants. The European Union from 1987 moved to attack such *input dumping* to such plants, and the United States followed suit in 1988.[15] These are called anticircumvention criteria because they keep the dumping duties on components from being circumvented. An extended U.S. interpretation of input dumping allowed the antidumping laws to cover imports from third countries that use components subject to an antidumping duty as inputs (diversionary input dumping, so-called). This is the "D'Amato Law" named for defeated New York Senator Alphonse D'Amato. The anticircumvention rules were not in the final Uruguay Round agreement on dumping. The United States and the EU are maintaining their policies anyway, and the WTO is calling for further negotiations. In yet another new twist, when the Japanese firm Jujo Paper was accused of dumping it reacted by trying to get Japanese competitors to raise prices in the U.S. market. It was thereupon accused of price fixing by the U.S. antitrust authorities.[16]

The repeated extensions to what constitutes dumping—from the original definition of predatory practice to the price definition to the cost definition to input dumping—appears to justify the observation by J. Michael Finger that dumping has become anything you can persuade the government to act against. "Trouble-making diplomacy, stupid economics, and unprincipled law," he grumps. Jagdish Bhagwati adds that the mechanism gives every appearance of having been captured by sophisticated protectionists.[17]

Tracing a Dumping Case under U.S. Law

This section traces a dumping case under U.S. law. Keep in mind three points: (1) The process is complex. If two slightly different steel products are allegedly being dumped by five separate countries, then 10 separate cases are adjudicated independently and can result in 10 different antidumping duties.[18] (2) If dumping is found, a penalty tariff equal to the dumping margin (the price difference between the exporter's home price or constructed cost and the price in the United States) will be placed on the exporter's goods. (3) A case against a foreign exporter can be halted at any time if that firm makes a price undertaking, that is, it agrees to charge a higher price in return for dropping a complaint. If that sounds like a cartel to fix prices, so be it.

The charge. Dumping cases usually begin with a petition from several American firms to the Department of Commerce and the International Trade Commission. (After Uruguay Round changes, petitioners must represent at least half of the firms expressing an opinion, or at least 25% of the domestic production of the product, and with the burden of proof for establishing this shifted from the defendant to the government bringing the charge. The total amount of imports from the dumping country must be at least 3% of total imports—this import share requirement is odd because in a heavily protected industry an importing country might have a tiny market share that is still a big share of imports.) A foreign country is named in the petition, with some basic evidence to back the charge. Nearly all dumping petitions are accepted. (Alternatively, the Department of Commerce can initiate the charge.) All foreign firms from that country now stand accused, including new ones that couldn't possibly have dumped, even though only one or two firms might actually be guilty.

Those firms that can afford to make a defense will want to contact an American law firm at this time, because dumping is easy to prove under the present rules and not mounting a challenge is risky. The defense is likely to be expensive, involving not just attorneys but also an accountant and perhaps an economist and a computer programmer, all of whom can expect to work long hours over an extended period. A routine antidumping investigation can easily cost the investigated firm $100,000, and the average case brings a bill for $200,000 to $300,000.[19] Such costs are more than enough to ruin a small exporting firm even if it is found not guilty, and it is no wonder that so many firms just surrender by raising their price or halting their exports altogether. A *big* case, such as the one against foreign steel producers that ended with major duties against 19 countries in January 1993, can cost a foreign exporter from $500,000 to $3 million just for the American attorneys. (The legal system that has developed around these laws is a bonanza for specialized counsel and their specialized economic consultants.)

Analysts now speak of two patterns for the filing of charges—outcome filers and process filers. Outcome filers, greatly in the majority, aim for a favorable outcome with an antidumping duty, while process filers aim to get benefits from the mere act of filing, which harasses and inflicts costs on foreign competitors.[20] Either way, the cost and disruption to an innocent party can be great.

Even the very hint of a dumping charge can have a chilling effect and lead foreigners to raise their prices and restrict their exports. Data indicate that on average imports fall 18% in the first year after proceedings are initiated as skittish foreigners worry about their risk of losing.[21] Large corporations with significant budgets for a legal staff versed in these matters have come to see this aspect of the antidumping statutes as a useful means to annoy and impose costs on their competition. It is surely no coincidence that J.M. Finger's research has revealed that big, concentrated industries are responsible for bringing the greater proportion of dumping complaints, but that these

311

complaints succeed less frequently by comparison with complaints made by smaller firms. They still pursue the tactic, knowing that the growth of imports usually declines following a complaint.[22]

WHAT IS AN AMERICAN FIRM?

With the globalization of trade, dumping cases can be difficult. Under American law, only U.S. companies are eligible to bring charges. But what is a U.S. company? In case law, though not by statute, it is when half or more of a product is made in the United States. A Japanese firm's U.S. subsidiary, Brother Industries USA, makes portable electric typewriters in the United States. In 1993 it won a dumping case against Smith-Corona, a U.S. company that makes its typewriters in Singapore.

The investigation. The timetable is strict. The Department of Commerce has 160 days to make a preliminary determination and 75 more for to a final determination.* Its practice is to investigate some firms, but not all, and then to assign the weighted average dumping margin for the firms investigated to the firms not investigated. A questionnaire is distributed to the chosen firms, allowing 30 calendar days for completion. It is in English, usually about 100 pages long, or 220 pages in the recent case against Norwegian fish farmers. (Imagine getting a 220-page questionnaire in *Norwegian* due in 30 days.) It demands data on home prices adjusted to from–the-factory value, U.S. retail prices, packaging, shipping, selling, and distribution costs, duties on inputs, U.S. duties, and value added in the United States. Price and cost data must be submitted in hard copy and computer-readable form.

If a reply is not received, or if the reply is found wanting, then "best information available" will be used. This is the original information supplied by the accusers, leading some to say it is actually the worst information available. In a sample of cases studied by Robert Baldwin and Michael Moore, when best information available is used the average dumping margin and therefore the penalty tariff is 67%, compared to 28% under the questionnaire method. No doubt some foreign firms fail to reply because they are guilty, but others do not do so because the requirements are onerous.

The injury. The dumping laws require that American firms have to have been "materially injured" by the dumped imports, not "seriously injured" as in antitrust cases. Following a 1984 amendment of the trade law, a threat of material injury suffices. (The EU has also shifted to a "threat of harm" interpretation.) Within 45 days, a preliminary finding to that effect must be

---

* A preliminary adverse finding often results in a deposit being collected. Although it is refundable if reversed in the final decision, small firms often stop shipments altogether at this point.

TWO NOTEWORTHY INVESTIGATIONS: ACRYLIC SWEATERS AND CUT FLOWERS

How dumping charges are actually investigated can be illustrated with two cases, acrylic sweaters and cut flowers.[23]

Ninety million sweaters a year are (or used to be) imported into the United States from Hong Kong, Korea, and Taiwan. Four Hong Kong producers were investigated out of hundreds. One refused to cooperate, two were found not to be dumping, and one was found to be dumping. A 5.86% duty was imposed, followed immediately by the same duty on the hundreds of other Hong Kong sweater producers that were *not* investigated.

Hundreds of Taiwanese firms, some of them very small, were asked in this same investigation to fill out quickly a 100-page questionnaire. The average firm was asked to provide over 200,000 bits of information. In the end a 21.84% duty was imposed on the firms not investigated. This was atop the high barriers on sweaters that already existed.

Dumping charges against foreign growers of cut flowers are common. Nine times in 13 years, American flower growers brought antidumping charges against Colombian rose growers. Of the eight previous charges, only one had succeeded. The president of one company in Bogota wrote in a plaintive letter to the *Wall Street Journal* that he had to bring nearly three tons of cost and sales records along with his entire administrative staff to Miami to answer questions because U.S. agents would not visit his headquarters for safety reasons. Ten questionnaires were involved. Information had to be segregated by variety (of which there were nearly 100), by stem length (there were five), distribution channel (four different ones), terms of sale (two types), and type of packing (several). Software consultants had to be hired. Every single transaction had to be checked to provide a monthly average price. Deadlines were inflexible.

made by the U.S. International Trade Commission, with 45 more days before a final determination.

Though the injury test could be an important qualifier, the law is very weak. To show harm, the authorities can cumulate small quantities of dumped goods from several different countries, a far cry from proof of predatory practice.[24] In determining injury, another questionnaire is used, this one sent to American firms. Scientific sampling is not done, the information is not verified, and there is no external check on accuracy. Often it is enough to show a price-suppressing effect that keeps prices below the figure they might otherwise have reached. Of course, *all* imports and all *domestic* competition tend to keep prices below what could have been reached. The ease of showing injury explains why between 1980 and 1997, only 12% of the claims were rejected at the preliminary level.[25]

When the ITC decides on injury, tie votes go in favor of the party asking for protection, a rule unique in parliamentary and judicial procedure; elsewhere, tie votes are lost, not won (ITC votes are often 3-3). No account is taken of the injury to the public or to companies that use the imported product as an input. They have no standing to protest even if they can prove that the harm to them is demonstrably greater than the injury to those charging dumping.*

The measurement. How the dumping is actually measured adds greatly to the impact of the laws, which are biased against foreign exporters to a considerable degree. The biases make it easier to find that dumping has occurred. (In some cases the Uruguay Round mitigated the biases, but not by much, because the Uruguay Round changes to dumping rules were a movement closer to existing U.S. procedures rather than away from them, and in any case the United States and the EU were strongly opposed to liberalizing the antidumping regime.)[26]

First bias. The Commerce Department takes the U.S. sale price for a product—say, Brazilian orange juice. It subtracts from that U.S. price transport costs and tariffs, for these are not counted. For example, the United States has a 40% tariff on orange juice, so 40% is subtracted from the U.S. sale price of Brazilian orange juice. It then compares the resulting adjusted U.S. price to Brazil's home market price. If the U.S. price is lower, dumping has occurred and importers of the juice are lawbreakers. It does not matter that with transport costs and tariffs Brazilian orange juice actually sells for much more in the United States than in Brazil. This is not considered.

Second bias. Say an investigation finds that during the period studied (usually six months) some foreign sales in the U.S. have been *above* the price in the home market. In assessing the dumping margin, any degree of pricing above home market prices is simply ignored and not counted with sales at below U.S. prices.

Third bias. To find the dumping margin *individual* sales prices in the U.S. market are compared to the *average* foreign price over a six-month period. For example, an exporter sells at $100 in its home market this month and $200

---

* It does not matter whether, as with cement, Florida's costs rose by $100 million a year; or whether anti-friction bearings, which American exporters incorporate in their products, rose in cost 120-150% because of antidumping duties; or whether a 63% antidumping duty on flat panel computer screens proved prohibitive for companies making laptop computers in the United States. In this latter case, a small company, Optical Imaging Systems, was the only U.S. maker of laptop computer screens when in 1992 it won punitive 63% duties on the screens. As a result, Apple, Compaq, and IBM threatened to move laptop manufacturing overseas. Fortunately, Optical Imaging Systems requested that the duty be lifted in 1993. Its business connections to Apple are said to have played a part in the request. See Susan E. Smith, "Input Tariffs as a Way to Deal with Dumping," *New England Economic Review* (November/December 1993): 46-47; James Bovard, "The Myth of Fair Trade," *Policy Analysis* No. 164 (November 1, 1991): 2-8.

next month. It sells at the same prices in the United States. The average home price is $150; dumping is found on the $100 sale in the export market, while the $200 price is ignored.[27] (In a Uruguay Round change, the comparison must be home market average to export market average, except that if a regional variation is found, for example, sales in the Middle West at $200 and in California at $100, or if a pattern of pricing varies significantly over time, then dumping can be found even if domestic firms price the same way. The new law also contains a statement that the average-to-average method will be used "during the investigation phase." That leaves the loophole that the old method might be used for subsequent reviews to recalculate dumping margins.)[28]

Fourth bias. Say the Department of Commerce finds that some of the exporter's home market sales have been made at below the firm's estimated average cost of production. These low-price sales are considered as being not in the "ordinary course of trade" and they are also disregarded in determining whether dumping has occurred. Because sales in the home market at prices below average cost are not counted while export sales prices include *all* sales no matter what the cost, the probability increases that dumping has occurred and the dumping margin is larger. It may also reduce the number of available home market prices so as to require that costs be constructed and the cost definition of dumping be used, as noted in the next bias below.[29]

Fifth bias. If the cost definition of dumping is used, the cost is constructed, that is, estimated, by the investigators. As already mentioned, the practice is to use "best information available," which usually means the information supplied by the accusers when the charge is made. When the costs of the foreign exporter are constructed, the chances of dumping are raised by the method used. It used to be that an extra 10% was added on for selling, general, and administrative expenses, plus a fixed 8% profit margin on top of that. These added figures tended to raise the constructed cost of production in the home market and gave a high likelihood that your price would be below your cost. For example, the average rate of profit in the United States has in recent years been only 5% to 6%. No law forces domestic firms to earn an 8% profit or to incur 10% sales expenses. (In the Uruguay Round, some changes were made: "best information available" should not mean a firm has to adopt a new computer system, and if the firm's information is not perfect it will not automatically be rejected. Governments are now required to check the best information available against independent sources when practicable. Each of these points reverses previous practice. The sales expenses and profit allowances should not be fixed percentages, but should be based on actual data and sales in the "ordinary course of trade," primarily from information on the exporter's sales costs and profit on the "same category of products." As with the ordinary course of trade defined in the fourth bias, the allowance for profit must exclude the losses on any sales below cost. This is hardly explicable except as a means to boost profit in the calculation, and would be criminal if a firm actually reported its profits this way.)[30]

Sixth bias. Say the cost definition is used, that costs are constructed, and an exporter has considerable research and development costs for new products. Full recovery of R&D spending is usually assumed to be necessary within the first year, rather than the several years customary for big-ticket durables in domestic trade. This makes it easier to show that foreigners are selling below cost.[31] No law forces domestic firms to recover R&D costs quickly. (In a Uruguay Round change, firms that have just started up are temporarily exempted from the rule of sales below cost, although the start-up period is not clearly defined.)

Seventh bias. Dumping duties are imposed even though the dumping margin is very small. (The *de minimis* rule defining how much it had to be was formerly as tiny as 0.5%, but the Uruguay Round raised the figure to 2%.) When tiny amounts of dumping still attract charges, the benefit for the accuser is not the margin itself but that importers are exposed to an open-ended liability that may last for years. Far down the road, perhaps four or five or even 10 years in the future, the first temporary finding will become a permanent finding as Commerce goes back and completes a thorough transaction-by-transaction comparison. All that time, importers have been paying a deposit to the government to import the goods. Perhaps the permanent finding will show lower dumping and some of the deposit will be returned. But perhaps it will show *greater* dumping, increasing the liability for imports made several years before, and with no theoretical upper limit. Even the mere charge is therefore damaging, as exporters may not want to run the risk involved. Thus, very small preliminary duties can be a large barrier to trade because of the uncertainty they cause.

Eighth bias. Say you are a Japanese exporter. You know distribution costs in Japan are high (many more Mom and Pop stores than in the United States) but you also hope that these sales and distribution costs can be subtracted to get the price used in calculating dumping. Not so, however. Foreign firms can subtract sales and distribution costs only up to the amount of these costs in the U.S. market.

Ninth bias. With floating foreign exchange rates, if the rate changes but an exporter does not alter the price, then dumping has occurred. Say a good is priced at ¥120 in Japan and $1 in the United States, with the foreign exchange rate ¥120 = $1. Now say the dollar depreciates (yen appreciates) from ¥120 to ¥100 = $1. The good is priced at ¥120 in Japan, but that is now equal to $1.20. Unless the exporter immediately raises the dollar price in the export market to $1.20, whatever the consequences for the firm's market share, or consumer resistance to price change, or the menu costs of making a change, or whether many inputs to the exported good were produced in countries where the currency did not appreciate—no matter, it is a case of dumping. Countries with volatile foreign exchange rates have indeed been especially vulnerable to dumping charges. A similar problem occurs when an exporting country has a seriously overvalued foreign exchange rate, its value kept artificially high by government exchange controls. Say Penuristan's penuri at 50 to 1 U.S. dollar is sharply overvalued, and that if there were a free market the exchange rate would be more like 100:1. Then if a Penuristan exporter sold an item in the United States at $1 and sold the same item at home for 100 penuris, it would be easy to prove dumping if the overvalued official rate were chosen to make the conversion. At the official rate, 100 penuris is $2, so the home price in the exporting country is higher than the price in the export market. In fact, official rates *are* used by the United States in making the comparison, even if the exporter was not able to obtain this rate at home and thus did not really dump. (In a Uruguay Round change, exchange rate movements do not have to be reflected immediately. Now an exporter has 60 days to reflect an exchange rate change in a price change.)

The Antidumping Duty

After all this, if both dumping and injury are shown, the Department of Commerce then applies an antidumping duty equal to the amount of dumping. The duties are often 8-10 times more than regular tariff rates. The 1990-95 U.S. average was 57%. The largest duty in place in 1997, on super-computers from Japan's NEC, was 454%.[32] The levy stays in effect until the guilty firm shows it has stopped dumping. That can be done in either of two ways: by showing no sales at all for three years or no dumping for two years at annual reviews. These reviews cost some $50,000, so $100,000 would be the fee to show no dumping, a considerable expense for a small exporter. (In a Uruguay Round advance, a "sunset provision" was adopted. The duties must end after five years unless there is a review, and the burden of proof is on the government to prove that the duty should be kept in place. The first U.S. sunset reviews started in mid-1998.)[*]

Dumping Charges Have Become Very Common

Antidumping law used to be just a minor sidelight. Of 371 dumping investigations conducted under U.S. law between 1955 and 1968, only 12 resulted in duties—and no other country uses dumping law as much as the United States.[33] Now, however, half to three-quarters of the cases are successful in either obtaining a duty or forcing a change in the foreigner's price, although

---

[*] Canada had already (in 1984) adopted a five-year sunset law that caused the number of antidumping duties to fall considerably from 1989.

even unsuccessful ones play a part in inhibiting imports because foreigners must worry about making a defense. (The success rate over 10 years to 1997 is 64% in the United States, 63% in Canada, and 60% in the EU.)[34] About 20 antidumping duties are imposed every year in the United States, and at the start of 1998 there were 309 (including suspensions, meaning an agreement by a foreigner to desist from dumping) in effect against 56 countries. Many are directed against China, Brazil, South Korea, Japan, and the EU; over half the U.S. duties hit less-developed countries and "transition" economies such as Russia and Poland.

Table 7.1

ANTIDUMPING DUTIES IN FORCE IN MAJOR USERS (START OF 1997)

U.S.	311	Australia	47
EU	153	Turkey	37
Canada	96	South Africa	31
Mexico	95	Argentina	30

Source: WTO data cited in *The Economist*, November 8, 1997. Brazil and India are other major users.

Buyers of acrylic sweaters, aspirin, bicycles, cement, codfish, computers, computer disks, cooking utensils, flowers, martial arts uniforms, mirrors, photograph albums, radios, shingles, telephones, TVs, and nearly 300 other products are purchasing something protected by a dumping order. They can last a long time, too: the earliest dates from 1968 (titanium sponge from Russia), and quite a few have been in force since the 1970s.[35]

The steel industry is a constant user of dumping law, often bringing sweeping charges against dozens of producers of a variety of steel products, sometimes as many as 70 at a time. (Metals represented 45% of all U.S. cases in the decade to 1997.)[36] In the latest steel cases during 1999, dumping margins of 25-67% were announced against Japanese steel and 50-71% against Brazilian steel. These were "lockout rates," and if enforced for any length of time they will stop imports from these countries. Russia, as seen in Chapter 4, accepted a VER with a six-month's moratorium on exports of hot rolled steel and a 1999 rollback in its exports to 22% of its 1998 shipments, rather than suffer the 70-217% antidumping duties that would have halted Russian steel exports entirely. This episode presumably taught Russians a lot about the virtues of free markets.[37]

When other major users of antidumping duties—the EU, Canada, and Australia in particular—are included, the number of cases has grown into the thousands (nearly 200 against the United States in the period 1987-97, by the way).[38] In early 1998, worldwide there were 538 duties in effect outside the United States.[39] Table 7.1 shows the number of antidumping duties outstanding in the major users a year before that (start of 1997).

It is notable that dumping laws are spreading rapidly. Only eight countries had such laws in 1980, but 53 had them in 1992. Many less-developed countries, including Argentina, Brazil, China (first use in 1998), and Mexico, and Eastern European nations such as Poland and Hungary, are emulating the richer countries in moving toward use of their own new laws.[40] This may prove difficult for them because dumping law is so complex that less-developed countries are less likely to be able to administer successfully their laws, which is no hindrance to developed countries.[41] Japan also has a dumping law, but almost never uses it; its first major antidumping duties were levied in January 1993, against Chinese steelmaking materials.

Antidumping duties are an effective barrier. Eventually (after three or four years) import quantities into the United States fall by about 40%.[42] The fall is greater (73%) when the antidumping duty is high, and smaller (16%) when it is low. Even when a case is lost, imports fall (by an average of 3.2%), reflecting prudent self-protection on the part of the seller. Another ramification is that foreign exporters not subject to the antidumping duty may find they can raise their prices in the protected market, too. Cases lead to collusion and price-fixing with foreign firms whether the duties are imposed or not. In an eight-industry survey, the minimum cost to U.S. consumers of creating a new job with antidumping duties was $113,800.[43]

It is, however, fair to note that a powerful company intent on obtaining trade barriers has reasons to lobby for methods other than antidumping duties. The protection is often limited because only a subset of all foreign exporters is penalized. The exporters not convicted will probably increase their shipments, with the diversion greater the higher is the antidumping duty. Politically strong firms realize that in a dumping case, lobbying will be of limited utility—the case being part of a judicial process, not a legislative one—and so they may prefer to pursue other barriers. The other side of the coin is that industries becoming politically weaker may turn to the dumping laws. Finally, even a big win will involve considerable costs of litigation to the victor that have to be weighed in the balance.[44]

What To Do About Dumping?

The antidumping rules have become a major new source of protectionist pressures. About the only real argument in their favor is that predatory behavior cannot be policed by antitrust laws alone because the antitrust laws do not apply to foreign exporters located outside the country. Whether this is an important justification is doubtful, given that predatory strategies are so rare and implausible in international trade.[45]

The contention caused by these rules has grown exponentially. The chief EU negotiator in the Uruguay Round declared that the changes in dumping law aroused passions like no other issue, which is remarkable since passions were so very high in other areas, such as agriculture. Indeed, the Uruguay

Round helped only a little, and it is not even clear whether the WTO will require countries to refund antidumping duties if they are found to violate the changed rules.[46] David Palmeter is surely correct when he says that dumping law is haunted by "mind-numbing, eye-glazing technicalities."[47] Many economists, including the authors, believe that the dumping laws should be abandoned as expensive and capricious barriers to trade. Perhaps the last word should go to James Bovard, who writes, "The dumping law is the Big Lie of modern foreign trade policy. Instead of openly raising tariffs, governments create convoluted trade laws that allow them to convict almost all foreign companies and yet deny that they are subverting free trade."[48]

SUBSIDIES

Government subsidies distort international trade when exports from foreign firms receiving the subsidies but without a comparative advantage harm domestic firms that *have* a comparative advantage. The amounts involved differ greatly from country to country, as Table 7.2 shows. Note the higher figures for much of Europe and the low ones for the United States and Japan.* (The percentages one sees reported are perhaps not always completely trustworthy because countries are reluctant to make themselves vulnerable to charges of unfair trade.)

There is a clear sense, strong among business-people, that subsidies abroad are unfair to domestic producers even though for consumers the subsidy is like a gift. Subsidies are often part of the national trade policies discussed in the next chapter, which adds to the heat. Yet there is also a realization that some subsidies may counter distortions in an economy, poor transportation, for

Table 7.2

INDUSTRIAL SUBSIDIES,
PERCENTAGE OF GDP

Sweden	7.5	Canada	2.6
Belgium	4.4	Italy	2.6
Norway	3.9	Great Britain	1.9
France	2.9	Germany	1.8
Netherlands	2.9	Japan	1.0
Denmark	2.8	U.S.	0.5
Austria	2.7		

Source: Margaret Kelly and Anne Kenny McGuirk, *Issues and Developments in International Trade Policy* (Washington: International Monetary Fund, 1992), 122. The figures are for the 1980s.

---

* These figures do not include soft loans by government at low interest rates, tax concessions, or government purchase of stock, all of which raise the subsidy element, sometimes considerably. The United States would itself seem open to the charge of subsidization if the definition used were broader. The U.S. has investment tax credits, R&D tax credits, and accelerated depreciation allowances in its tax laws, maintains policies that provide cheap water, grazing land, and mineral rights in the West, and cheap food when deficiency payments to farmers reduce market

example, and for this reason they are not opposed as enthusiastically as is dumping. Observers generally agree that the Uruguay Round agreement on subsidies has fewer flaws than the one on dumping.[49]

Unlike dumping action, which is aimed at firms, countervailing duties are aimed at countries that subsidize. A countervailing duty (CVD), which is a charge equal to the amount of the subsidy, is the remedy for this unfair trade practice. (CVDs are usually much lower than antidumping duties—by about two-thirds.) The U.S. President has no discretion to interfere with the course of the law on the matter. That tends to increase the popularity of countervailing duties in the business community and also makes it possible to apply pressure on governments, perhaps leading to voluntary reductions in exports. (But such duties are not a perfect protectionist device; like antidumping duties, they may cause imports to flow in from countries not hit with penalties.)

It used to be that almost all CVDs were imposed by the United States, 281 from 1980 to 1986 compared to just seven in the EU, where the law was not as broad, and just one in Japan, where it was and remains virtually a dead letter. A few more cases occurred in Canada and Australia, but many other countries, including Austria, Norway, Sweden, and Switzerland, never imposed countervailing duties at all.[50] Recently, however, the number of cases in the rest of the world has expanded to the point that their total number is now greater than those imposed by the United States.[51] In many countries, the number of investigations and new countervailing duties have undergone a massive increase. There were a little more than 200 U.S. subsidy investigations in the four decades from 1934 to 1974, and of those only 41 resulted in CVDs .[52] But in the decade of the 1980s, there were about double that number of U.S. cases, about two-thirds against less-developed countries.[53] Fifty-nine U.S. duties were in place at the start of 1998, some dating back to the 1970s. The modern high was reached in 1995, when 106 CVDs were in effect at the start of the year.[54]

What Can Be Countervailed? Export, Production, and R&D Subsidies

Explicit export subsidies are generally illegal, both to the World Trade Organization and to the United States under U.S. laws dating back to 1897 and now mostly based on the Tariff Act of 1930. There are two exceptions.

---

prices. Companies are allowed to patent a claim for land by showing that there are resources on it. The land can be bought at $2.50 to $5 per acre, and then they pay no royalties when the resources are mined on it. The federal charge per cow for grazing on federal land averaged $1.20 per month between 1965 and 1992, whereas the comparable private charge was $11.20. Timber from federal lands (under rules dating from 1897) is sold for less than it takes to prepare the timber for sale, particularly the cost of road-building. The loss was $195 billion in 1995. (See *The Economist*, December 13, 1997.) Similarly, Japan formerly made wide use of low-interest government loans in some sectors, and many countries still do so.

One is agriculture, where export subsidies are permitted if they do not result in an increased share of world trade for the country paying the subsidy. The other is export subsidies paid by less-developed countries. The WTO recognizes that such subsidies are a legitimate tool of development and does not outlaw their use by countries at a low level of per capita national income (under $1,000). Countervailing duties may be imposed against them, but only when material injury in the home market is shown. Injury in third markets elsewhere is not a sufficient cause to trigger a penalty. These poor countries must, however, phase out export subsidies based on the use of domestic rather than imported inputs by the year 2003.[55]

The situation is more tortuous when subsidies are paid on domestic production only and not on exports. Arguably such domestic subsidies do cheapen production and make exports more likely, though they also may do nothing more than correct for some economic distortion or even smooth the path to an industry's complete close-down. The old GATT rules were not very clear, and national laws varied considerably. In the United States under a trade law amendment of 1922, the granting of domestic subsidies to a selected industry or group of industries can be countervailed.

In the Uruguay Round agreement, a traffic light analogy was followed, with subsidies divided into prohibited (red light), permitted but actionable (yellow light), and non-actionable (green light). Green-light subsidies can be challenged if they have serious effects on a domestic industry, however.[56] *Red-light subsidies* are those on exports contingent on export performance and on using locally produced goods. *Yellow-light actionable subsidies* are production subsidies making up 5% or more of the cost of the product or covering the loss of making the product, or routine or periodic alterations to a product. Adverse effects must be demonstrated. *Green-light non-actionable subsidies* include job training, general tax cuts, aid for research and development up to 75% of industrial research costs and 50% of "precompetitive development activity" up to the first non-commercial prototype, aid to disadvantaged regions if generally available, and aid to lessen environmental consequences up to 20% of the costs of doing so. Noncommercial research to enlarge general and scientific knowledge isn't actionable at all.

How Is a Subsidy Countervailed?

In the United States, the procedure for obtaining a countervailing duty is much like that for dumping. Private firms in an industry directly affected make the complaints. Self-initiation of a case by the Department of Commerce has been permitted since 1979, but that power is rarely used. Following the complaint, Commerce is responsible for determining whether a subsidy is being paid on exports or on production, and how large it is. (The Treasury had this task before 1979 but was much less interested in such questions.) The U.S. International Trade Commission must then determine whether there is material injury to U.S. firms.* Duties used to be imposed even if no harm or injury was shown to have occurred—a very protectionist bias. The WTO now has a material injury criterion, but injury still does not have to be shown in subsidy cases against non-members of the WTO. Where they are concerned, the law states broadly that any benefit from the subsidy can be countervailed. All that needs to be proved is that a subsidy exists, not that the subsidy has an effect on trade. In the United States, as in antidumping law, injury is defined as to the producer, not to downstream firms or consumers that buy the product. Countervailing duties against subsidies are imposed without any consideration at all of what would happen in using industries.

To economists, the proper action would be to estimate the effect on exports of any given subsidy, as this is the degree to which the subsidy distorts trade. Doing so is easiest for export subsidies, more difficult for subsidies on domestic production. Estimating the trade-distorting effects of the latter would require that the domestic subsidy be converted to an equivalent export subsidy and the effect on exports estimated. Under U.S. law and the WTO rules, however, that is not necessary.

As with antidumping law, there is a sunset clause of five years on countervailing duties. The case for a CVD must either be made again or the duty lifted after that period of time.

THE INTENT OF THE SUBSIDY

In many respects, no account needs to be taken of the intent of subsidies. Some are designed to allow the controlled winding down of a declining industry. Say a subsidy is paid to a firm to persuade it to tear down one plant a year for three years and so put itself out of business. This subsidy is countervailable under trade law, although it is fair to say that action of this sort has been rare.

Other subsidies may be intended to compensate for government regulations such as above-market minimum wage laws, overvalued foreign exchange rates, or export taxes of various sorts. Consider a U.S. case against Thailand. A countervailing duty was imposed against imports of rice from that country after various subsidies were found, including some price support, mortgage assistance, discounts to rice millers, and government assistance to

---

* As with the U.S. dumping laws, there is a strict timetable after the filing of a petition: 45 days for the International Trade Commission's preliminary finding, 40 more days for the Department of Commerce, 75 more days to Commerce's final determination, and 45 more days for the ITC final determination. For the time limits applying to subsidy investigations, see J. Michael Finger and Tracy Murray, "Policing Unfair Imports: The United States Example," *Journal of World Trade* 24, 4 (August 1990): 42.

cooperatives. But at the same time Thailand was collecting a large export tax that was over five times as high as the subsidy. (At the time the United States was paying large export subsidies to its own rice farmers. The U.S. program was transferring over $1 million per year to the average American grower, while the Thai program was transferring about $100 to the average Thai farmer per year before payment of the export tax.) Similarly, Argentine wool growers were hit by a U.S. countervailing duty after a finding of a 6% subsidy, even though a 17% export tax was charged and even though U.S. wool growers got direct government payments that boosted the return to wool growing by about 50%.[57]

Only subsidies that increase market share in export markets at the expense of other producers are a clear distortion to trade; the others can be considered as desirable corrections for market failure. Yet all production subsidies are treated alike under trade law.

The Growing List of What Can Be Countervailed

A number of difficult issues have arisen concerning subsidies. The following cases have arisen in the United States, but the debates have occurred widely in countries that employ antisubsidy laws.

1. What about cheap access to a government-owned resource? For example, cheap oil made available from a government's national oil company might lead to lower prices than otherwise for Mexican manufactured goods or Saudi Arabian petrochemicals. Other examples might include access to cheap water or other natural resource inputs. A major case has involved Canadian provinces, which own more than 90% of Canada's timber. Historically the provinces charged low prices (or stumpage fees) to Canadian timber companies for cutting rights on government land. Was this a counter-vailable subsidy? Yes, and a duty was levied by the United States in 1986.

2. What about a related case where the subsidy is paid not on the product itself, but on some input? An example of such an "upstream" subsidy might be subsidized steel used by an unsubsidized automaker. Until 1984 counter-vailing duties were not applied, but under the U.S. Trade Act of that year, upstream subsidies were brought under the law and an unsubsidized product can now be penalized if some principal input is subsidized.

3. What if harm to domestic firms flows from production in a third country that embodies subsidized parts imported from a second country? Yes, countervailable under the 1988 Trade Act.

4. What about parts imported for a foreign-owned screwdriver plant if the imported product was covered by a countervailing duty. Yes, that, too, can be penalized according to the 1988 Trade Act.

5. What about a subsidy by a consortium of nations rather than by an individual country, for example, the EU's Airbus program? Not countervailable by the United States until the 1988 trade law allowed action to be taken. We return to the Airbus dispute in the next chapter.

6. What if the subsidy is paid on an item that is leased rather than sold? Yes, sometimes now countervailable under the 1988 trade law, in which a clause backed by Boeing and McDonnell-Douglas made it possible to challenge leases that were equivalent to sales. Such leases are most common in the aircraft industry.

7. What if the product subsidized by another country is not imported at all, with the effects felt only in third-country export markets or in the markets of the country paying the subsidy, so that the subsidy therefore harms one's exporting firms rather than firms that compete with subsidized imports? In that case countervailing duties would deliver no benefits. Under international trade law, it is possible to bring complaints about the effects of subsidies in overseas markets to a WTO panel.

The Concept of General Availability

All these cases have extended the reach of the laws against subsidies. But in one important area—when governments give assistance to all industries or a large group of industries—the scope of the law has been limited. For example, several European countries pay wage subsidies to promote employment, Japan subsidizes firms' R&D to stimulate technical change, and Canada provides health care that in the United States is provided by private firms. Under a provision in the WTO rules, such subsidies cannot be countervailed.

It is understood that if a subsidy is generally available to all industries, then it will distort trade less than will a subsidy to a specific industry or group of industries. The reason is that a generally available subsidy, received by all, tends to appreciate the country's currency. The subsidy makes all exports cheaper to foreign buyers, meaning that the demand for the exporting country's currency will rise, thus pushing up the value of that currency. The appreciation will in turn mean that the country's exports appear more expensive than before to foreign buyers, thus reducing the initial effect of the subsidy. (This case is akin to the pass-through effect of an across-the-board tariff, which also appreciates the currency, as seen in Chapter 4.) Imports benefiting from generally available subsidies are therefore less reasonable targets for countervailing duties than are imports produced by industries that receive specific subsidies. Since 1986, however, the United States has applied a new concept of "de facto specificity" when it finds a few dominant users of a widely available subsidy, and cases employing this definition have now been prosecuted.

In the Uruguay Round, regional development subsidies were classified as generally available. Before that agreement, under U.S. law (since 1973) these could be attacked, as when a Canadian subsidy to the Michelin tire company persuading it to build a plant in Nova Scotia, was deemed sufficient to trigger a penalty.

THREE U.S.-CANADIAN CASES: DAIRY PRODUCTS, TIMBER, WHEAT

Three subsidy cases involving the United States and Canada show why subsidies and countervails can be contentious, and how long they can last.

In the dairy products case, the U.S. protested the marketing board system wherein Canadian producers of dairy products for export can acquire their raw material, milk, at prices well below what domestic producers pay. The U.S. challenge complained that the dual price system was tantamount to an export subsidy and an attempt to escape the WTO rules requiring that these be reduced.[58]

The softwood lumber case was the longest, spanning 15 years, and the most acrimonious.[59] In 1982-83, the U.S. Department of Commerce decided that the low stumpage fee charged by the provinces to the Canadian timber companies was a subsidy but not a specific one. Thus, since the subsidy was generally available no countervailing duty could be levied. In 1986, it reversed the decision and levied a duty. Canada retaliated, but then agreed to impose a 15% export tax. (Canada kept the revenue effect of nearly half a billion U.S. dollars.) Then in 1991 Canada, noting the decline in its share of the U.S. lumber market and that some provinces had raised their stumpage charges, withdrew its export tax.

The drama then began all over again. Antisubsidy action was initiated, unusually, by the U.S. administration itself, and a countervailing duty was levied. Americans wondered why their lumber prices were rising so sharply, the Canadian government reacted with anger, and the dispute returned to full boil. A dispute settlement panel and an appeals panel (part of the U.S.-Canada Free Trade Agreement and not the GATT/WTO mechanism) both ruled against the United States. Duties on softwood lumber imports were eliminated and the duties already collected were to be returned. The United States called for an extraordinary challenge. The prospect of trade war was suddenly averted when in 1996 a five-year pact was agreed on. It involved a VER that reduced softwood lumber exports from Canada and a U.S. promise not to take further subsidy or dumping action or other recourse to trade law during the life of the agreement. The agreement allows more Canadian lumber to enter if U.S. demand rises, but the additional lumber is subject to a Canadian export tax. Once again, Americans wonder why their lumber prices are so high; once again, Canadians fumed—they were forced to accept the VER because otherwise they would have been hit by CVDs. Economists, worrying about the precedents, shook their heads.

U.S. complaints against subsidized Canadian wheat turned on the existence of transportation subsidies, which the U.S. claims are an illegal export subsidy. (Canada says it is a legal domestic subsidy.) Canada's century-old rail subsidy plan paid part of the freight charge from the wheat's point of origin to a port. The amount involved was 51% of the freight charge from Saskatchewan to Vancouver. The United States argued that this subsidy was ruining U.S. export markets, particularly in Mexico where the U.S. market share fell from 75% in earlier years to 14% in 1992. Also, the United States complained that cheap Canadian wheat was raising the cost of U.S. deficiency payments to farmers.[60] The U.S. retaliated with wheat subsidies of its own under the Export Enhancement Program. Canada ended its transport subsidy in 1995 (compensating farmers with a lump sum of U.S. $1.2 billion to owners of farmland). The amount involved in the last year of the scheme was 51% of the freight charge from Saskatchewan to Vancouver.

The Future for Subsidies in International Trade

The United States would like to redefine a subsidy as any government action that delivers a benefit. That would include such things as a favorable decision under antitrust law or government insurance against changes in foreign exchange rates. The EU and most other countries want to use a definition that covers only an actual transfer of resources from government. In none of these cases is it clear how the antisubsidy portions of trade law will evolve. The subject is returned to in the next chapter, where national trade policies involving subsidies are examined.

From all the complications one salient point does emerge. The current heavy use of subsidies may to some significant extent interfere with comparative advantage.

OTHER UNFAIR TRADE PRACTICES

The unfair trade practice laws govern a number of other international transactions as well. Like the dumping and subsidy regulations, these laws have become more important as the average level of tariffs has fallen.

Intellectual Property

Intellectual property, largely in the form of patents and copyrights, has extraordinary importance in such areas of trade as computer software, biotechnology, and pharmaceuticals. Worldwide, commerce in counterfeit goods involving pirated knowledge is now estimated to be as much as 3-6% of world trade. Most of the purloining has occurred in the less-developed countries.

The TRIPs (trade-related intellectual properties) agreement was part of the Uruguay Round, and it was reviewed in Chapter 6. This provided for safeguard of patents for 20 years and copyrights on sound recordings for 50 years. Computer software obtained the same status as literary works, and compulsory licensing procedures were controlled. India proved to be an especially tough negotiator; it managed to obtain a 10-year grace period for the less-developed countries—meaning, for example, that India's pharmaceutical firms could go on producing counterfeit drugs for a significant amount of time.

In the United States, the enforcement mechanism for intellectual property disputes is Section 337 of the U.S. Tariff Act of 1930. Under its terms, goods can be excluded if they involve patent violations, false labeling, or infringement of copyrights and trademarks. Cases can be brought by means of private complaints to the International Trade Commission or by the ITC on its own. There were 50 exclusion orders under Section 337 in effect at the start of 1998, mostly concerning patents and most (about 80%) aimed at less-developed countries.[61] The biggest case involved 31 Chinese factories that were producing copies of American CDs, videotapes, and software. The United States was close to massive retaliation in early 1995. An agreement was reached in that year but fell apart. U.S. sanctions were again threatened in 1996 (and China promised to retaliate with 100% tariffs on a range of products) until a compromise was achieved on the day in June when U.S. sanctions were to have come into force. About half of Chinese CD factories (15 of them) have now been closed by the authorities and new ones have been prohibited.[62]

A major area of concern has been how to handle violations when the resulting counterfeited item or technology does not involve imports. U.S. law allows barriers against other goods as retaliation, so-called cross-retaliation. The U.S. argument is that if cross-retaliation is not permitted, very little leverage exists against those who steal intellectual property. Many countries, especially less developed ones against which most charges arise, fear that cross-retaliation is a very blunt weapon. The Uruguay Round established that cross-retaliation could be used if a favorable decision is obtained from a dispute settlement panel. For non-members of the WTO, a panel decision is not needed, and this explains the threat of cross-retaliation against China.

The Crowbar: Violation of Trade Agreements (Section 301)

Major attention has focused on laws that attempt to open up foreign markets closed to U.S. exports by attacking imports from the offending countries.

Under Section 301 of the Trade Act of 1974 the U.S. Trade Representative is required to take action if a foreign government violates a trade agreement; the legislation gives discretionary authority to retaliate if a trade policy is judged to be unreasonable or discriminatory in excluding U.S. goods from a foreign market.[63] Note that this so-called "crowbar" protects exports, not imports. The 301 actions are issue-oriented: EU oilseeds protection, Korean insurance restrictions, China's pirating of intellectual property, and so forth. Crowbar exclusions have proved to be extremely contentious. They are noteworthy in that they deviate considerably from approved WTO procedures for settling disputes. They violate most-favored-nation agreements by discriminating among countries. They also usually impose high tariffs with 100% *ad valorem* a common figure, thus violating undertakings to bind tariff rates. As such they are highly visible and controversial.*

USING THE CROWBAR

The Trade Representative usually initiates action, but the process may also begin by private petition. If a finding for action is made, then steps must be taken within 30 days, or in 180 days if the Trade Representative determines that delay is desirable or substantial progress is ocurring. The action terminates automatically in four years unless a case for extension is made.

There were very few uses of Section 301 until 1986, with the President taking action in only two of 40 cases. Since then this part of trade law has become much more important, with 48 more investigations by the start of 1992. Some of the 1996-99 301 cases were:

- EU enlargement to include Austria, Finland, and Sweden, whose tariffs were in some cases lower than the EU standard rates;
- the famous banana and growth hormone cases with the EU;
- the photographic film made by Japan's Fuji;
- Korean imports of beef and pork;
- Japan auto parts;
- Chinese pirating of intellectual property;
- Japanese market access to agriculture products;
- EU export subsidies on dairy products;
- EU subsidies for wheat gluten;
- Korean barriers to auto imports.

---

* There is also a Section 406 of U.S. trade law covering disruption by imports from Communist countries. The 406 mechanism works much like the safeguard or escape clause (Section 201), explaining the rarity of its use and why the 301 crowbar has more recently been employed against China. The last use of 406 was a 1992 petition, later withdrawn by the petitioner, for barriers against Chinese oscillating fans.

In some respects, the 301 approach has been a success. The United States does indeed have a great deal of leverage in trade negotiations because it is such a large importer. A country often will prefer to yield in a trade dispute rather than risk attack with the 301 crowbar. Arguably, it works best when it is not used, and is worth retaining for its deterrent effect. In the 77 cases between 1975 and 1990, actual duties were imposed in only about 10% of the cases and victory was achieved in about a third of them.[64] Results were uncertain in 55% of the cases. The success rate was greater, 68%, against Japan and South Korea. Foreign counter-retaliation has been even rarer.

Yet the device has proved inflammatory. One problem is the Super 301 provisions, explored in the accompanying box. Another is the hypocrisy.[65] The United States pursued Canada on beer even though there are many U.S. state regulations on imported beer. It pursued Japan on oranges even though the United States has 40% tariffs on Brazilian orange juice. The 301 case against Korea's beef import restrictions was in spite of U.S. beef quotas of its own; the case against Japanese leather import quotas was despite U.S. leather tariffs of 40%; the 301 action on shoes against Taiwan, Brazil, and Korea left intact U.S. shoe tariffs ranging as high as 67%; the 301 case against Fuji film is based on Fuji's large market share in Japan even though Kodak has about the same market share in the United States. (In a recent agreement, Kodak and China agreed that Kodak would be the only foreign film producer allowed to operate in China. Imported Fuji film has to pay a 40% tariff. This is more anti-competitive than anything Fuji was charged with under 301.[66]) Many U.S. 301 cases have been against agricultural export subsidies, which the United States uses itself. Also, 301 action has been used to boost U.S. tobacco and cigarette exports.

An additional 301 problem has become widely recognized. To some considerable extent the United States has ceased to discuss giving up its own barriers and uses sheer economic power to force trading partners to remove barriers of their own. The tool does work to force open foreign markets, but the link between lower foreign trade barriers and lower U.S. barriers has been severed. "Might makes right" seems to be the apt description. Another difficulty is that the 301 approach, when successful, opens up foreign markets only to the United States, but not to others. These other innocent parties, many no doubt weaker and unable to bring their own leverage to bear, are left out.

The United States has agreed to use the WTO dispute settlement mechanism rather than impose 301 crowbar penalties where WTO members are involved.[67] After that, however, it can be used if the United States wins a case and the defendant doesn't give in, or when it is dissatisfied with the outcome. In areas outside the Uruguay Round and the WTO, it is in full use, against China, for example, or in still unsettled areas such as government procurement.

THE CONTROVERSIAL SUPER 301 PROVISIONS

The 1988 trade bill contained new Super 301 provisions written by Richard Gephardt that proved even more controversial than 301 itself. Under Super 301, in effect in 1989 and 1990, a country's entire set of trade practices could be attacked. It required the President to compile a hit list of trade offenders, with the countries being named and their unfair practices being announced. It differed from regular 301 by having a very rigid timetable. The Super 301 clock starts running on March 31 with the publication by the U.S. Trade Representative of the "National Trade Estimate Report on Foreign Trade Barriers," or NTE Report.* Based on that list, the administration designates "priority foreign country practices" by September 30, beginning a 21-day period of preliminary negotiations followed by a formal complaint. The President's Trade Representative is required to negotiate with foreign countries to end the problems; success is judged not by elimination of the practice but by an increase in exports over three years. If no agreement can be reached, the Trade Representative has to decide whether to impose penalties. (As with the regular 301 law, Super 301 can also be initiated by private petition.)

The first countries named as trade offenders were Japan, Brazil, and India. The responses of the indicted countries differed greatly. Japan and Brazil rapidly made concessions on each of their named issues and they were dropped from the list. The EU, certainly a candidate for listing in many areas, announced that if this were done it would bring a GATT case and would retaliate immediately. Though the issues were all relatively minor, the Super 301 listing attracted worldwide attention (and caused considerable foreign resentment). Congress treated this procedure as the centerpiece of its new toughness on trade.

When the Super 301 provisions expired at the end of 1990, the charges against India were simply dropped. The expiration was greeted with a sigh of relief around the world. But then in 1994, Congress having granted the President discretionary power to do so, Super 301 was revived by executive order for two years, until 1996, and then for another two years, through 1997.[68] There were few uses; only Korea was named in 1997. But then there was an apparent change of strategy. The President renewed Super 301 once more in April 1999, but this time cases were announced almost immediately against the EU, South Korea, India, Canada, and Argentina.[69] The new strategy seemed to be to use Super 301 at the time the United States requests a WTO dispute settlement panel. It seems a means to combine a threat of action with a call for a panel.

---

* Who says trade negotiators have no sense of humor? Often within 24 hours, Canada publishes its *Register of United States Barriers to Trade*, while the EU counters a few days later with its own listing, *Report on United States Trade and Investment Barriers—Problems in Doing Business with the U.S.* Both are patterned after the U.S. original and present unfair U.S. practices.

CONCLUSION

The laws concerning unfair trade practices are an appeal for a level playing field. Yet they possess substantial disadvantages. They diminish the flexibility with which governments address trade issues. Overly legalistic and overly rigid, discriminatory and creating great uncertainty, they focus on punishment rather than cooperation. In so doing they present private firms with excellent opportunities to harass their competition and bring pressure on their own governments. At best, this system of procedural protection tends to break down or be counterproductive in big cases against foreigners with substantial bargaining power, while biting sharply where retaliatory power is weak.

More broadly, these laws fail to take into account the entire playing field, instead looking only at a few sections of it. Our understanding of comparative advantage is that making one product (item A) artificially cheap, for example, by means of a subsidy, will make others artificially costly. Item A attracts factors of production from the manufacture of items B and C, driving up their production costs. If item A is an export, then exports of it will rise, and if B and C are also imported, then imports of them will rise. If A is also imported, then the subsidy will cause less of it to be imported. If B and C are export items, then their export will be discouraged. For every producer abroad who competes with item A and squirms over the subsidy to A, there should be a foreign producer of item B who has less to fear from competition and who may now even export B to the country that subsidizes A because the costs of the subsidy have put domestic producers of B at a disadvantage. The playing field has been dug down in some places by the subsidies, but bumps appear elsewhere. The favors granted to one set of producers act as a tax on another set. Overall, the field remains much more level than those concerned about unfair practices care to admit, but efficiency declines and energies are directed toward obtaining government favors.

Unfair trade practice legislation lies at the heart of modern protectionist strategies. Together with the more traditional approaches, these laws will certainly be used by firms seeking trade barriers against imports. The most that can be said for these laws is that they may serve as a useful deterrent against countries intent on predatory practice or on employing some of the national trade policies of the sort examined in the next chapter.[70] The worst that can be said about them is that they verge on an immoral use of legal authority, harassing perfectly legitimate exporters with ever more complicated and expensive legal proceedings. A thorough re-examination is overdue, and the Uruguay Round failed to provide enough change.

VOCABULARY AND CONCEPTS

Antidumping duty
Countervailing duty
The crowbar
De minimis clauses
Dumping
General availability

Injury
Intellectual property
Level playing field
Persistent dumping
Predatory dumping
Price discrimination

Red, yellow, and green
  lights
Section 301
Sporadic dumping
Super 301

QUESTIONS

1. Examine what dumping is, using both the primary and secondary definitions.
2. Why might firms engage in dumping? Is there a difference between persistent dumping (for price discrimination reasons) and predatory dumping? Why should we object to persistent dumping? What evidence is there for predatory dumping?
3. Argue, using the American antidumping laws as a case in point, that what is most unfair about unfair trade practices is the law, not the practices.
4. When or why should we, as consumers, want to impose antidumping duties?
5. What improvements in dumping legislation were made in the Uruguay Round?
6. "Anyone can sympathize with a company that has seen its market drop sharply because a foreign government is subsidizing exports. That does indeed seem unjust. But in practice it is usually quite the other way around, as the scope of what constitutes a subsidy or a countervailable subsidy expands from the obvious and conspicuous to the obscure and nebulous." Explain.
7. Why do subsidies resemble traffic lights under international trade law?
8. If subsidies and persistent dumping are so unfair, why don't countries ban them internally? After all, American states and Canadian provinces certainly subsidize some industries and penalize others, and firms often charge different prices in different areas.
9. Are crowbar provisions good or bad?
10. How does Super 301 differ from regular 301 cases, and why do foreigners so dislike this provision of U.S. trade law.
11. "A level playing field is an appealing but deceptive image. Short of making all nations' laws exactly the same, there will always be bumps. What is important is to get on with the game and to realize it is not the foreigner our complaints hurt but our fellow citizens." Explain.
12. Is the principal problem with unfair trade practice law its poor economics or its ultimate unjustness? (Adam Smith was, after all, a professor of moral philosophy, so the question is economic.)

NOTES

1. Robert E. Cumby and Theodore H. Moran, "Testing Models of the Trade Policy Process: Antidumping and the 'New Issues'," in Robert C. Feenstra, ed., *The Effects of U.S. Trade Protection and Promotion Policies* (Chicago: University of Chicago Press, 1997), 161-90.

2. Paul Krugman, "What Should Trade Negotiators Negotiate About?" *Journal of Economic Literature* 35, 1 (March 1997): 113-120.

3. An outstanding and up-to-date survey is Jorge Miranda, Raúl A. Torres, and Mario Ruiz, "The International Use of Anti-dumping: 1987-1997," *Journal of World Trade* 32, 5 (October 1998): 5-71. For this section, in addition to the sources cited below we used Richard Boltuck and Robert E. Litan, eds., *Down in the Dumps* (Washington: Brookings Institution, 1991) especially the chapters by Tracy Murray and N. David Palmeter; J. Michael Finger, *Antidumping: How It Works and Who Gets Hurt* (Ann Arbor: University of Michigan Press, 1993); J. Michael Finger, "Dumping and Antidumping: The Rhetoric and the Reality of Protection in Industrial Countries," *World Bank Research Observer* 7, 2 (July 1992): 121-43; John H. Jackson and Edwin A. Vermulst, eds., *Antidumping Law and Practice* (Ann Arbor: University of Michigan Press, 1989), especially essays by Alan V. Deardorff and Gary N. Horlick; Martin Jerge, "Foreign Multinational Corporations and U.S. Antidumping Law," *Journal of World Trade* 28, 4 (August 1994): 67-82; Angelos Pangratis and Edwin Vermulst, "Injury in Anti-Dumping Proceedings—The Need to Look Beyond the Uruguay Round Results," *Journal of World Trade* 28, 5 (October 1994): 61-96. The *Journal of World Trade* contains frequent articles, and Greg Rushford's *Rushford Report*, a newsletter from Washington, D.C., is a mine of useful information by a skeptical observer who knows how to dig for facts.

All U.S. dumping duties are listed in USITC, *The Year in Trade*. Those who want to read a defense of dumping law could try Greg Mastel, *Antidumping Laws and the U.S. Economy* (Armonk, N.Y.: M.E. Sharpe, 1998).

4. For an examination of classic cases, see John McGee, "Predatory Price Cutting: The Standard Oil (N.J.) Case," *Journal of Law and Economics*, (1958): 137-69; Isaac R. Mark and L. Vernon Smith, "In Search of Predatory Pricing," *Journal of Political Economy* 93 (April 1985): 320-45; Roland Koller, "The Myth of Predatory Pricing: An Empirical Study," and Kenneth Elzinga, "Predatory Pricing: The Case of the Gunpowder Trust," both in Yale Brozen, ed., *The Competitive Economy: Selected Readings* (Morristown, N.J.: General Learning Press, 1975).

5. For example, no one has ever won the treble damages available in American antitrust law in a private suit if predatory practice is proven. See Gary N. Horlick and Geoffrey D. Oliver, "Antidumping and Countervailing Duty Law Provisions of the Omnibus Trade and Competitiveness Act of 1988," *Journal of World Trade* 23, 3, (June 1989):5-49.

6. See David G. Tarr, "Does Protection Really Protect?" *Regulation* (November/December 1985): 29-34.

7. Patrick A. Messerlin and Geoffrey Reed, "Antidumping Policies in the United States and the European Community," *Economic Journal* 105, 433 (November 1995): 1568-69.

8. N. David Palmeter, "The Antidumping Emperor," *Journal of World Trade* 22, 4 (August 1988): 6. The years were 1980 to 1986.

9. Robert W. Staiger and Frank A. Wolak, "Differences in the Uses and Effects of Antidumping Law across Import Sources," in Anne O. Krueger, ed., *The Political*

Economy of American Trade Policy (Chicago: University of Chicago Press, 1996): 385-417; Cumby and Moran, "Testing Models of the Trade Policy Process."

10. The rules can be found in the USITC's "Antidumping and Countervailing Duty Handbook."

11. The problem can perhaps be exaggerated. D.G. Tarr's work, cited by R.E. Baldwin, "Trade Policies in Developed Countries," in Ronald W. Jones and Peter B. Kenen, *Handbook of International Economics*, vol. 1 (Amsterdam: Elsevier, 1984), 606, turned up no evidence in the steel industry that cyclical dumping during recessions was being resorted to in the United States, the EU, and Japan.

12. C. Fred Bergsten and Marcus Noland, *Reconcilable Differences? United States-Japan Economic Conflict* (Washington: Institute for International Economics, 1993), 70.

13. *Wall Street Journal*, April 20, 1999.

14. *Rushford Report*, September 1998.

15. For this section, see Gary Clyde Hufbauer and Kimberly Ann Elliott, *Measuring the Costs of Protection in the United States* (Washington: Institute for International Economics, 1994), 113-14; Norio Komuro, "U.S. Anti-Circumvention Measures and GATT Rules," *Journal of World Trade* 28, 3 (June 1994): 5-49, esp. 36; Gary N. Horlick and Eleanor C. Shea, "The World Trade Organization Antidumping Agreement," *Journal of World Trade* 29, 1 (February 1995): 5-31; and Ivo Van Bael, "EEC Anti-Dumping Law and Procedure Revisited," *Journal of World Trade* 24, 2 (April 1990): 5-23.

16. *Rushford Report* (August 1998).

17. For the comments, see Finger, *Antidumping*; Finger, "Dumping and Antidumping," 135, 141; Jagdish Bhagwati, "Free Trade: Old and New Challenges," *Economic Journal* 104, 423 (March 1994): 239.

18. A point made by Michael O. Moore, "Steel Protection in the 1980s: The Waning Influence of Big Steel?" in Krueger, *The Political Economy of American Trade Policy*, 73-125.

19. Michael Ryan, "Court of International Trade Judges, Binational Panelists, and Judicial Review of U.S. Antidumping and Countervailing Duty Policies," *Journal of World Trade* 30, 6 (December 1996): 119; IMF, *World Economic Outlook, 1988*, 93.

20. Robert W. Staiger and Frank A. Wolak, "Differences in the Uses and Effects of Antidumping Law across Import Sources," in Krueger, *The Political Economy of American Trade Policy*, 385-417.

21. See Messerlin and Reed, "Antidumping Policies in the United States and the European Community," 1565-75; Bernard M. Hoekman and Michael Leidy, "Dumping, Antidumping and Emergency Protection," *Journal of World Trade* 23, 5 (October 1989): 33, 36, citing work of Patrick Messerlin.

22. Work of J.M. Finger cited by R.E. Baldwin, "Trade Policies in Developed Countries," in Jones and Kenen, *Handbook of International Economics*, vol. 1, 606.

23. Details are from James Bovard, "The Myth of Fair Trade," *Policy Analysis* 164, (November 1, 1991): 2-8; *Wall Street Journal*, October 21, 1994.

24. Pietro S. Navola, *Regulating Unfair Trade* (Washington: Brookings Institution, 1993).

25. Federal Reserve Bank of New York, *Current Issues* 4, 8 (August 1998):4.

26. Good summaries of the changes can be found in David Palmeter, "United States Implementation of the Uruguay Round Antidumping Code," *Journal of World Trade* 29, 3 (June 1995): 39-82; Gary N. Horlick and Eleanor C. Shea, "The World Trade Organization Antidumping Agreement," *Journal of World Trade* 29, 1 (February 1995): 5-31.

27. From Palmeter, "United States Implementation."

28. The point is made by David Palmeter, "A Commentary on the WTO Anti-Dumping Code," *Journal of World Trade* 30, 4 (August 1996): 43-69.

29. Robert E. Cumby and Theodore H. Moran, "Testing Models of the Trade Policy Process: Antidumping and the 'New Issues'," in Robert C. Feenstra, ed., *The Effects of U.S. Trade Protection and Promotion Policies* (Chicago: University of Chicago Press, 1997), 161-90.

30. The point is Palmeter's, from "A Commentary on the WTO Anti-Dumping Code."

31. Gary N. Horlick, "How the GATT Became Protectionist: An Analysis of the Uruguay Round Draft Final Antidumping Code," *Journal of World Trade* 27, 5 (October 1993): 5-17.

32. *The Economist*, November 7, 1998.

33. See Gary Clyde Hufbauer and Kimberly Ann Elliott, *Measuring the Costs of Protection in the United States* (Washington: Institute for International Economics, 1994), 113-14.

34. Miranda, Torres, and Ruiz, "The International Use of Antidumping", 50.

35. USITC, *The Year in Trade 1997*, 183-89; Hufbauer and Elliott, *Measuring the Costs of Protection*, 113-14.

36. Miranda, Torres, and Ruiz, "The International Use of Antidumping," 18.

37. See *Rushford Report*, March 1999.

38. See Miranda, Torres, and Ruiz, "The International Use of Antidumping."

39. Federal Reserve Bank of New York, *Current Issues* 4, 8 (August 1998): 1.

40. Malcolm D. Rowat, "Protectionist Tilts in Antidumping Legislation of Developed Countries and the LDC Response: Is the 'Race to the Bottom' Inevitable?" *Journal of World Trade* 24, 6 (December 1990): 1-29.

41. Messerlin and Reed, "Antidumping Policies in the United States and the European Community," 1573-74.

42. The data here are from ibid.; Hoekman and Leidy, "Dumping, Antidumping and Emergency Protection."

43. Keith B. Anderson, "Antidumping Laws in the United States: Use and Welfare Consequences," *Journal of World Trade* 27, 2 (April 1993): 99-115.

44. Moore, "Steel Protection in the 1980s," 73-125.

45. This is the argument of Gunnar Niels and Adriaan ten Kate, "Trusting Antitrust to Dump Antidumping," *Journal of World Trade* 31, 6 (December 1997): 29-43.

46. Edwin Vermulst and Norio Komuro, "Anti-Dumping Disputes in the GATT/WTO—Navigating Dire Straits," *Journal of World Trade* 31, 1 (February 1997): 5-44.

47. Palmeter, "A Commentary on the WTO Anti-Dumping Code."

48. *Wall Street Journal*, December 9, 1993.

49. Howard P. Marvel and Edward John Ray, "Countervailing Duties," *Economic Journal* 105, 433 (November 1995): 1576-93.

50. See Hufbauer and Erb, *Subsidies in International Trade*, esp. ch. 3.

51. Marvel and Ray, "Countervailing Duties," 1590.

52. Hufbauer and Elliott, *Measuring the Costs of Protection*, 113.

53. J. Michael Finger and Tracy Murray, "Policing Unfair Imports: The United States Example," *Journal of World Trade* 24, 4 (August 1990): 52-53; USITC, *The Year in Trade 1997*, 191-92.

54. USITC, *The Year in Trade 1997*, 191-92; *1994*, 187.

55. See George Kleinfeld and David Kaye, "Red Light, Green Light?" *Journal of World Trade* 28, 6 (December 1994): 43-63; *International Economic Review*, September 1995 and November/December 1997.

56. Kleinfeld and Kaye, "Red Light, Green Light?"; USITC, *The Year in Trade 1993*, 17-18, 183-85; *1994*, 5-6, 73-75, 187; *International Economic Review*, September 1995.

57. The rice and wool cases are from Bovard, "The Myth of Fair Trade," 9-10.

58. USITC, *The Year in Trade 1997*, 85-89.

59. For the details, see Gilbert Gagné, "The Canada-U.S. Softwood Lumber Dispute: An Assessment after 15 Years," *Journal of World Trade* 33, 1 (February 1999): 67-86; Joseph Kalt, "Precedent and Legal Argument: Do They Matter to the Political Economy of the Lumber Dispute," in Krueger, ed., *The Political Economy of American Trade Policy*, 261-88; USITC, *The Year in Trade 1995*, 47; *1996*, 88-89; *International Economic Review*, October 1991; *Wall Street Journal*, March 6, 1992.

60. USITC, *The Year in Trade 1993*, 87-88; *1994*, 73; *1995*, 48; *Wall Street Journal*, August 2, 1994.

61. USITC, *The Year in Trade 1997*, 193-98.

62. *The Economist*, June 22, 1996.

63. A thorough 301 review is in each issue of USITC, *The Year in Trade*. Also see Jagdish Bhagwati, "Explaining Section 301," Appendix IV of his *The World Trading System at Risk* (Princeton, N.J.: Princeton University Press, 1991); Jagdish Bhagwati, "Departures from Multilateralism: Regionalism and Aggressive Unilateralism," *Economic Journal* 100, 403 (December 1990): 1304-17; Jagdish Bhagwati and Hugh T. Patrick, eds., *Aggressive Internationalism: America's 301 Trade Policy and the World Trading System* (Ann Arbor: University of Michigan Press, 1990).

64. *The Economist*, March 12, 1994.

65. Most of this paragraph is from James Bovard, "A U.S. History of Trade Hypocrisy," *Wall Street Journal*, March 8, 1994.

66. *Rushford Report*, May 1998.

67. *Economic Report of the President 1995* (Washington: Council of Economic Advisors, 1995), 211.

68. *Wall Street Journal*, March 4, 1994; USITC, *The Year in Trade 1997*, 130.

69. *Wall Street Journal*, May 3, 1999; AP, May 2, 1999.

70. See Robert E. Baldwin and T. Scott Thompson, "Responding to Trade-Distorting Policies of Other Countries," *American Economic Review* 74, 2 (May 1984): 271-76.

Chapter Eight

National Trade Policies

OBJECTIVES

OVERALL OBJECTIVE   To examine national trade policies as strategies in three areas: gaining certain competitive advantages by promoting chosen industries, furthering adjustment to trade through adjustment assistance, and employing trade warfare.

MORE SPECIFICALLY
- To examine managed trade (trade targeting) and analyze the tactics involved.
- To evaluate whether strategic trade policy can be or is effective in overcoming imperfect knowledge and reaping externalities from learning, scale, or agglomeration.
- To examine the degree to which Japanese national trade policy comports with a strategic trade policy.
- To consider the harm to those who lose from trade and assess the effectiveness and wisdom of a vigorous trade adjustment strategy.
- To probe the effectiveness of trade sanctions in achieving political ends.

Much of trade policy is piecemeal in nature, involving barriers and subsidies to make politically powerful industries more profitable, keep beleaguered industries afloat, or allow governments to maintain high agricultural support prices. Beyond these essentially reactive approaches are national trade policies that in one way or another are expected to yield a better outcome for their users than would result from laissez-faire. The designs have somewhat different goals and carry various names. *Managed trade* is a broad term that involves a country's government pressuring a foreign government to raise its imports.

Strategic trade is a policy of picking winners, with governments acting to subsidize or otherwise assist industries they expect to succeed in international markets—a policy generally believed to be used by Japan and lately by a number of other Asian countries. *Trade adjustment assistance* is government help to firms and workers that are downsizing because of pressure from imports. *Economic sanctions* are means governments use to influence foreign political, economic, or military behavior. This chapter examines these national trade policies.

MANAGED TRADE

The typical managed trade tactic involves some sort of pressure on a foreign exporter. Examples include export targets agreed to by the exporter and the importer, and "voluntary import expansions" (VIEs) by the countries being hit by the managed trade policy. Governments carry out managed trade by setting targets using *temporary quantitative indicators* (TQIs) to find how successful they have been. Managed trade is a unilateral policy in that it is intended to benefit the country imposing it, not anyone else, with third parties often objecting that any gains bypass them. The tactic came to prominence in the United States during the late 1980s and early 1990s, particularly in relations with Japan. Clinton administration proponents included Laura d'Andrea Tyson, chair of the Council of Economic Advisors, and Mickey Kantor, the U.S. Trade Representative.

Semiconductors (Microchips) as an Example of Managed Trade

Semiconductors (microchips) are an outstanding example of managed trade.[1] The original five-year VER to assist U.S. chip makers had two main thrusts. First, the Japanese agreed to limit exports and maintain a fixed price minimum in the American market. But Japan found that to boost prices, as required by the VER, it had to arrange a fall in exports to third countries as well as to the United States. It did so by imposing voluntary export controls according to the previous market share of its exporters. The output restraint, coupled with heavy demand from a healthy U.S. economy in 1988, led to chip shortages and a quadrupling of prices. The resulting large profits led to much more R&D spending by Japanese firms, strengthening their new predominance in the industry. But chip prices did not rise in Japan, giving manufacturers that used them an advantage. Meanwhile, U.S. computer and software firms had to pay higher prices for the chips they installed, and U.S.

consumers found their computers and other chip-using products cost more.*

Then came another development. The high chip prices led to new competition from Korea, whose production was not covered by the VER. Korean sales rose 80% from 1988 to 1989. By the start of 1993 Korea claimed 20% of the world market, most of that seized from the Japanese, and ranked second to Japan in the U.S. market. All in all, the whole episode seemed to demonstrate how *not* to design a trade strategy. The agreement was effectively a tax on chip users imposed to aid a few chip makers. (The superior policy of subsidizing the industry would have kept the Japanese from getting higher profits and the Koreans from being attracted into the market.)

When the first semiconductor VER expired in 1991, only a few producers lamented its passing. It was succeeded one day later by a new five-year agreement that did not contain the export restrictions. Japanese chip makers only agreed to collect and make available cost-of-production data to facilitate dumping charges if chips are sold below production costs.

The second aspect of the semiconductor VER with Japan was pure managed trade. The Japanese manufacturers agreed to allow foreign firms a market share in Japan of 20% by 1991, compared to the 1986 figure of 9%. Though they did not reach the target by the deadline, it was repeated in the 1991 VER renewal. The 20% guarantee caused endless trouble because for a long time that share failed to go above 14% and because the Japanese insisted it was a target, not a guarantee. By 1996, the situation was changed, with the foreign share having risen to 30.6%. Japan announced it was unwilling to renew the 1991 agreement. Japan also opposed the 1991 clause requiring firms to maintain and make available in 14 days price and cost data in the format used in U.S. antidumping cases. The United States insisted on continued government involvement. In August 1996 an agreement was reached that allowed both sides to claim victory. The industry, rather than the government, now collects the data, but the governments continue to maintain a consultative mechanism.[2]

Recently, the United States has regained some momentum in the chip market, taking the lead in the development and production of advanced microprocessors; these processing chips are much more sophisticated and profitable than run-of-the-mill chips. A number of joint development agreements have been achieved by U.S. and Japanese chip makers. The collaboration, plus the better U.S. performance, may have defused the U.S.-Japan microchip battle to a degree. Ironically, the share of U.S. producers in

---

* The EU found the 1986 VER highly objectionable, because prices were raised there, too, and complained to the GATT. A GATT panel in 1988 found in favor of this EU complaint that the worldwide export restraints of the semiconductor VER were illegal under GATT rules, which barred export quotas. Japan responded by agreeing in 1989 not to control chip prices on exports to or production in third countries. The United States was thus the only market in which the penalty of higher prices was being paid.

the U.S. market has changed little: Korea's is up from a little over 10% in 1990 to over 40% in 1997; Japan's is down from about 80% to a little over 30%; and the United States has held at under 10% in both years.[3]

SOME OTHER USES OF MANAGED TRADE

Other U.S. demands on Japan for managed trade with voluntary import expansions and quantitative indicators have included glass, car parts, medical equipment, telecommunications equipment, paper and paper products, machine tools, and insurance. For example, a 1992 agreement obligated the Japanese to raise their imports of U.S. paper and paper products and provided for monitoring of the agreement, though without mentioning a specific level of imports.[4] A recent example is Motorola cellular phones. To favor Motorola, the United States has demanded specific market-opening as well as numerical targets. Basically, the demand was that the Japanese ensure the installation of a Motorola-compatible network instead of the non-compatible system that had been put in first.

Managed trade has also inspired considerable interest in the EU, where the idea is being used to force foreign firms to invest in Europe if they want to sell there.

A FALL IN ENTHUSIASM FOR MANAGED TRADE

Many economists object to managed trade policy. Among their several complaints is that the most powerful lobbies rather than the most deserving will obtain the support of government in dealing with their complaints about foreigners. Any established minimum numerical figure for imports is arbitrary, depending on the strength of the parties involved. The country imposing managed trade leaves itself open to the same tactic. It tends to cartelize markets and, because it discriminates, targeting violates WTO rules. A side effect of targeting is that it increases the amount of government involvement in the economy of both the exporter and the importer, where mechanisms have to be established to enforce any agreement, thus increasing the politicization of trade. By the mid-1990s it was apparent that managed trade had produced little benefit, and the new U.S. Trade Representative, Charlene Barshevsky, was a less enthusiastic proponent than her predecessor.

STRATEGIC TRADE POLICY

Strategic trade policy describes collaboration and co-operation among businesses and governments to alter more quickly than the market would the existing pattern of comparative advantage. The tools for doing so usually involve a combination of subsidies and home-market protection by means of tariffs, quotas, VERs, and so forth to accelerate the development of some chosen industry. The subject has caused considerable stir among international economists, and at least theoretically represents a new intellectual challenge to the proponents of free trade.

Elements of strategic planning by governments date back to the nineteenth century, when Germany began a long campaign to acquire export industries. The stratagem has, however, come to be associated primarily with Japan since the 1950s, and later with South Korea and Taiwan, which closely followed Japanese policy. (The next major section concentrates on Japan's use of strategic trade policy.) An increasing number of Asian countries, including Malaysia and Indonesia, have similar policies, and elsewhere Brazil, France, and others have stressed these methods.[5] In the United States, economists who advocate a U.S. strategic trade policy have recently received considerable publicity.[6] Some Democrats have taken up the theme to suggest national measures to increase research and development expenditures and otherwise assist certain targeted industries. Republicans generally oppose.

The economics of strategic trade policy involve new departures from the traditional trade debates explored in Chapters 5-7. Four main rationales supposedly support strategic policies: imperfections in knowledge, the existence of external economies, the need to achieve learning and scale effects, and the capture of profits (rents) from foreign competitors in imperfect markets. Each of these arguments is examined in turn.[7] The strategic policies can be defensive (to battle the trade barriers of and export promotions of others) or offensive, involving an aggressive strategy to capture markets.

Strategic trade policy contrasts with the idea of national industrial policies involving government participation in an effort to raise productivity generally by means of educational reform, infrastructure improvement, and R&D efforts. Such industrial policies are not specifically designed to affect international trade and are not surveyed here beyond a brief examination of R&D measures that do impact trade flows.

Imperfect Knowledge

For convenience, most classroom economic models assume that the producers and consumers are well informed. Consumers know what products are available to meet their needs and producers know what consumers want. Knowledge, however, is not evenly distributed over the short run, something the text looks at more closely in Chapter 19. A great deal of business behavior consists of finding out what can be made, discovering what consumers want, and trying to inform or persuade consumers that what the business has made is something they want. Normally, firms spend a great deal of energy in seeking information, then try to profit from what they have learned. A major role of the firm is, in fact, the provision and distribution of information.

Every country recognizes, however, that governments have an important role in providing information that would be difficult to generate privately. It may be that it is simply too hard for the private sector to keep its knowledge private enough to collect revenue, a problem characteristic of much software and digitized information bases. Or it may be that the public deems the information of such importance that it does not want to charge for it—as with much public health information. Is there something particularly difficult about foreign markets that the private sector cannot solve, justifying a role for the government to provide free information?

The simplistic argument goes this way: foreign markets are so different from domestic markets that they are very expensive to enter. Small firms, in particular, do not know the basics of exporting or marketing in foreign countries. They are prone to make egregious mistakes in language, such as the pen advertised in Spanish that was supposed to say that one would not be embarrassed by a leaky pen, but it came out that one would not be made pregnant (the meaning of *embarazar* in Spanish). They may fail to meet foreign customs requirements or idiosyncrasies, or find that their product doesn't meet some unexpected requirement.

There is undoubtedly something to this argument. Only 1% of American firms account for 85% of American manufactured goods exports, and small firms are rarely active in exporting. To remedy this supposed problem, governments provide enormous amounts of information about exporting and the characteristics of foreign markets. As noted earlier, they even make available cheap credit. Of course, they rarely provide much information to help importers, even though any increase in trade increases the country's welfare.

A note of caution, however. The enormous increase in international trade in the latter half of the twentieth century was not likely the effect of governments' providing more information. Firms do internationally what they do domestically—they seek markets and products and try to analyze needs and potentialities. Yes, international markets may on the whole be more complicated and expensive to enter than domestic ones, but the barriers are hardly insuperable. Indeed, firms can make stupid errors at home too. It was an Ontario firm that advertised to the Quebec market that it had a terrifying pen when it wanted to say its pen was terrific.

EXPORT TRADING COMPANIES

Numerous countries, most of Europe and Japan, for example, allow individual firms to band together in export trading companies financed by a parent bank, the company then marketing their products. Such companies are exempt from antitrust action. They have been particularly successful in Japan, where there are 8,000 of them, called *sogo shosha* or "general trading companies." The largest are C. Itoh, Sumitomo, Marubeni, Mitsui, and Mitsubishi. The nine biggest of these companies are responsible for over half of Japan's total trade. They advise and manage in the areas of transport, marketing, finance, and distribution, breaking down knowledge barriers that might otherwise keep small firms out of exporting and maintaining a far-flung Japanese presence around the world.

The United States is far behind in such activities, though there has been some progress. Under the Export Trading Company Act of 1982, the old Glass-Steagall Act of 1932 that prohibited banks from engaging in trade was partially repealed. U.S. banks are now allowed to participate in foreign trade, with bank holding companies permitted to invest a maximum of 5% of their capital and surplus, not to exceed $10 million, in an export trading company (ETC). Recently there were some 60 of these ETCs. The U.S. design appears to resemble the Brazilian and South Korean arrangements most closely. Their particular value lies in persuading small firms to enter exporting.

The U.S. law is provides less flexibility and a far smaller financial base than the Japanese *sogo shosha* have. Furthermore, some argue that the emphasis on quick profits in the United States, together with the tight management control traditional in banking, has denied U.S. ETCs the fast flexibility combined with patience that are needed in this game. The U.S. Department of Justice has claimed that most ETCs have been formed to ensure against vertical antitrust suits. In any case, growth of the U.S. ETCs since 1982 has been slow, and they still account for only a small fraction of U.S. exports.

GOVERNMENT TRADE PROMOTION: THE CASE OF JETRO

Governments also promote international trade by means of various agencies that deal in information. Although most countries have one or more agencies for doing so, the Japan External Trade Organization (JETRO) is by far the best known and most successful.[8] Dating from the 1950s, JETRO is modeled on a British original that lasted only a few years. It carries out general overseas market research, arranges participation in trade fairs and exhibitions, and does public relations work for Japan's trade as a whole. It also manages major programs to coordinate technical cooperation, joint research, and joint production. To the extent that trade promotion is a public good, this is useful and cost-effective. Originally, JETRO was of special importance to small and medium-size exporting firms, but it is now a major promoter of *imports* as part of Japan's campaign to change its image of closed markets. It hosts "export to Japan" seminars, sponsors trade fairs and exhibits of its own, and maintains an ombudsman to whom foreign firms can complain about bad treatment. It supplies data on customs procedures and trade financing both in Japan and overseas, and now even trains interns from other countries, mostly less-developed ones.

Hong Kong, Korea, China, and other countries now have their own versions of JETRO. The Korean Trade-Investment Promotion Agency has offices all over the world. Atypically, the Hong-Kong Trade and Development Agency charges user fees. Some say this means higher quality in the agency concerned.[9]

The United States, long backward in this area, has made great strides in the Clinton administration, led by the late Commerce Secretary Ron Brown. U.S. spending on this activity is still well below that of its competitors per dollar of GDP: 60% of Japan's and Germany's, less than half of Britain's, 18% of France's. Nevertheless, a TPCC (Trade Promotion Co-operation Council) now co-ordinates the activities of 19 separate government agencies. Fifteen one-stop centers called United States Export Assistance Centers bring together information from the Commerce Department, the Exim Bank, the Small Business Administration, the Agency for International Development, and (coming soon) the Department of Agriculture. The Exim Bank is quite active in the program: it helps small firms' exporting with credit insurance and working capital loans. Exim now has an 800 number for exporters. There is still much duplication of effort and information availability is far below that provided by JETRO, but a good start has at last been made.[10]

External Economies

Other arguments for strategic trade are more controversial. The existence of external economies, or spillovers, is one such. If R&D spending is the key to obtaining comparative advantage in a product, then the existence of external economies may mean that government subsidies to support the R&D are called for. A free market would lead to appropriate levels of private spending on this activity only if externalities did not exist or if they could be completely appropriated by the firm undertaking the expenditure. One illustration might involve a firm's willingness to pay. It may believe that the expensive R&D would soon become available to competitors if personnel with knowledge of it were hired away by those competitors. Another example might involve other firms disassembling and copying products embodying the new technology without otherwise paying for the R&D. The benefits might then be so reduced by this leakage of knowledge to others that the firm will not proceed with the R&D spending in the first place. A very similar argument is older and has been used to justify training subsidies: skilled labor might be trained at great expense, but then the cost of the training is lost to competitors who hire away the skilled labor.

Thus, where R&D is a key to new comparative advantage but diffusion of the resulting knowledge to others who did not pay cuts the benefits severely, it may make sense for government to subsidize the activity to offset the market failure. Conceivably, a government subsidy could improve the whole world's welfare because new products might not become established, or processes adopted, if the R&D is not undertaken. The existence of distinct geographical concentrations of high-tech industries in a number of countries is advanced as evidence that a head start in R&D is important.

Though this argument for a strategic trade policy is persuasive within its bounds, it is also limited. One difficulty is that neither government nor firms are able to assess at the start which level of subsidization is optimal. Firms would presumably lobby for the maximum access to this open public trough. (In the United States, economists favoring an interventionist U.S. strategic trade policy with subsidized R&D have been restrained: Paul Krugman has suggested only about $10 billion be spent on such subsidies.)[11] Another problem is that foreigners would still be able to appropriate the new knowledge as easily as before—in the end, a country's subsidies may do no more than establish a new comparative advantage somewhere abroad. An argument might actually be made that a country could improve its position in international trade by carrying on *less* R&D and appropriating what it needs from the countries with a comparative advantage in that activity. Finally, a substitute for subsidies might be to permit research consortia of a country's own producers, or even an international group, to pursue joint projects. In the United States, the antitrust laws would have to be relaxed further to allow more of this, even though some steps have been taken since a change in the law in 1984. Further relaxation might be as effective as a subsidy while being much less expensive for the public purse.[*]

Realizing the Effects of Learning and Scale

Chapter 3 emphasized the growing importance of learning and scale economies as explanations for changing comparative advantage. The country that appreciates these possibilities might decide that a small initial push provided by subsidies, or through protection of the domestic market against imports, might be the impetus for competitive strength in some new industry. This proposition is really an old one in a new guise—it is the infant industry argument in modern dress. Though the language is changed, and though the reasons why the infant needs support are altered to emphasize learning and

---

[*] A more theoretical argument has arisen concerning uncertainty. If some line of activity is especially subject to risk, then investment in that activity may be unduly discouraged unless it is subsidized. Newbery and Stiglitz argue that strategic intervention may be justified under these conditions. Dixit replies that incorporation of insurance markets in the Newbery-Stiglitz model would tilt the balance against government intervention. See D.M.G. Newbery and J. Stiglitz, "Pareto Inferior Trade," *Review of Economic Studies* 51, 1 (1984): 1-12, and A.K. Dixit, "Trade and Insurance with Moral Hazard," *Journal of International Economics* 23 (1987): 201-20.

U.S. EFFORTS TO INCREASE R&D

The United States used to do little to support non-military R&D spending. That situation is changing. One move has been to loosen the antitrust penalties against firms that carry out joint research projects. A beginning was made with the National Cooperative Research Act of 1984. This act allows joint research ventures of a pre-proprietary nature, permitting firms to pool R&D resources and exempting them from the triple damages provisions of the antitrust laws. In a private suit, only actual damages can now be awarded. One outcome has been USCAR (United States Council for Automotive Research), a Ford-GM-Chrysler project established in 1992 to carry out joint work on electric cars and electronics control programs and to develop improved plastics and other composite materials for use in automobile bodies. Another was the joint research on the PowerPC microchip undertaken by IBM, Apple, and Motorola.

A further loosening of the antitrust laws to cover joint *production* ventures took place in 1993. In that year, a new law removed the triple damages provision from production in joint ventures if the courts find that the competitive climate (including foreign competition) warrants the removal. The joint ventures' production must be in the United States for the new rule to apply. It remains the case, however, that joint manufacturing and marketing in the United States continues to run up against the antitrust laws. It remains easier for U.S. firms to collaborate with foreign ones than with each other.*

Going beyond antitrust exemption, the government has moved toward new forms of cooperation and collaboration. Sematech, dating from 1987, is a public-private consortium supported by the U.S. Defense Department to improve microchip technology. The U.S. government and the private chip makers each agreed to supply half the money.

The Clinton administration expanded the Commerce Department's National Institute of Standards and Technology, including NIST's Manufacturing Technology Centers, and has promoted development of dual-use (civilian and military) technology. The Advanced Technology Program supports with NIST grants the development of civilian technologies. Recently it has focused on car-making technologies, chemical catalysts, materials processing, digital data storage, and advanced refrigeration. The High Performance Computing and Communications Program (pushed by Al Gore) is an interagency program for computer development. PGNV, Partnership for a New Generation of Vehicles, is between the government and the Big Three automakers to develop fuel efficiency and

---

* Not all economists favor these relaxations of the antitrust laws to permit more joint research and production. The doubters warn that the joint projects may lead to price rigging for the products involved, and that incentives to introduce innovations may be fatally compromised if oligopolistic firms fear to upset the status quo. These economists warn that innovation usually brings most benefits when competitive rivalry is strong.

emissions control. (USCAR, mentioned earlier, is another agreement.) The Flat-Panel Display Initiative is a Defense Department effort to help develop a domestic flat-panel display industry, obtain funding for research, and promote exports. National laboratories are encouraged to use their talents for joint R&D with private firms; the Argonne National Laboratory has spun off about 30 companies to commercialize its research; Sandia National Labs in New Mexico, the nuclear weapons installation, now has 95 joint projects with private firms.[12]

less orthodox scale economies, the logic is the same. A dynamic exporting industry might arise out of the subsidies or protection.*

The usual objections apply. Why would the private capital markets not be able to see these possibilities as well as or better than government does, and why would it not make loans available? Such a "private subsidy," repaid with interest from the later profits of the firm receiving the loan, would meet the market test and avoid the burden on the government's budget. If protection is used rather than subsidies, then all the standard complaints surface. These complaints include higher costs for consumers and producers who use the protected product as an input, the X-inefficiency if firms lose the spur of competition, and the scale diseconomies if the domestic market for the new product is small. The targeting of some attractive industries, computers by Brazil, for example, while plausible on the surface, might simply reveal the importance of local co-operation between computer designers and microchip makers, which are non-existent in Brazil.

THE ASIAN MODEL

Strategic policies based on the advantages of learning and scale have been important in a number of Asian economies such as South Korea, Taiwan, Singapore, Malaysia, and Thailand. Of course, there are many differences among the countries that emphasize learning and scale. The general idea is always much the same, however, and in stylized form is as follows: success in one industry leads to growth in related industries, as new methods in the one have effects on others where processes are related.[13] The concept of clustering, taken from Alfred Marshall as discussed in Chapter 3, is part of this concept. A push that leads to a cluster of firms could reduce transaction costs, improve the flow of information and the diffusion of ideas, attract new start-up firms, and give extra motivation because of the proximity of rivals. Government's role is to support the clustering of related firms and to ensure

---

* Hardly ever noticed in the debates over this proposition is that *international* subsidies to promote learning and scale in countries that otherwise possess the most suitable factor proportions might be the best policy of all, with the world financing the resulting increase in global welfare. As is obvious, such proposals are at present utopian.

that competition is maintained and rent-seeking controlled by harnessing the rivalry among these firms. Government has to focus on providing education and training, for the clustering will not take place without supporting human resources and scientific infrastructure. The investment of multinational firms can contribute and should be supported.

Economists who believe that government failures are always greater than market failures will not be approving of this view of the Asian model. But plenty of evidence does indicate that emphasis on learning and scale has been an important part of East Asian economic success.[14]

Strategic Trade Policy to Capture Rents

An intriguing argument for a strategic trade policy is that governments could use subsidies to enable domestic firms to capture part or all of the economic rents being earned by imperfect competitors abroad. This argument is new and has relevance for the ongoing dispute between Boeing in the United States and Airbus in the EU.

Assume that just *two firms* are the world's only manufacturers of some good. A capture of oligopolistic rents would be a possibility if a firm in country A finds a way to lower its production costs. It could then charge a lower price and thus expand at the expense of a firm in country B, which would contract its operations as the demand for its output shrinks. The profits for the firm in country A rise, first, because of the fall in costs, and second, because its share of the market has increased. One way to push country B's firm into this position would be for A's government to pay a subsidy to the firm in A. That would be the equivalent of lowering the firm's costs and would start the process. A's government would expect the profits earned by the home firm to be larger than the subsidies paid to start the ball rolling. (If this were *not* the case, the gambit would have failed.) The strategy, when successful, would ordinarily be predatory on A's part, the gains to A coming at B's expense.* The gains would be even greater if the subsidy allowed more learning and scale effects; but if learning and scale were important, then country B would lose even more than otherwise.

To achieve its aims, the strategy would have to fulfill a number of conditions. (1) It would have to be credible. If the firm in B does not believe a subsidy will actually be paid after all, or will be paid only for a short time,

---

* These gains would not necessarily accrue just to the owners and managers of the one firm, and the factors employed there. Taxes could be used to distribute the gains to the public. It is conceivable that the fall in prices to consumers made possible by A's subsidy, plus the rents captured from B, would in the long run sum to a greater amount than the cost of the subsidy and the rents lost to B. That would raise *world* welfare rather than welfare in country A alone. One would not want to count on that, however.

it may not contract its output, and thus no capture of rents will result. (2) The subsidy ought not to be paid to firms in a highly competitive industry, for then there will be few foreign profits to capture. An industry with high capital requirements forming a substantial barrier to entry (aircraft?) would seem much better suited for the strategy. Similarly, subsidies paid to declining industries might just stave off foreign competitors for a time but result in no advances at their expense. (3) The best outcome for the strategy would be if foreign rivals had many other production alternatives, for then foreign output would fall considerably as prices declined. It would also be most advantageous if the home firm moved rapidly down steep cost and learning curves as its output increased. (This implies, in turn, a disadvantage if any factor inputs are fixed or limited in supply because factor prices would rise as output increased.)

EUROPEAN AIRBUS SUBSIDIES AS AN EXAMPLE OF A RENT-CAPTURING STRATEGY

The Airbus consortium in the EU is apparently an excellent example of a rent-capturing strategy. The Airbus passenger aircraft, actually several different wide-bodied models, has received massive subsidies from European governments. There are no other European producers of wide-bodied commercial aircraft; no Japanese producers; and McDonnell-Douglas in the United States has now merged with Boeing. If the Airbus subsidies could convince Boeing *not to produce* some new model, then Airbus might capture the economic rents that Boeing otherwise would have earned.

Paul Krugman illustrates this with a matrix of strategic possibilities, which we show below as Figure 8.1.[15]

The letters p and P signify a decision has been made to go ahead with production by Airbus and Boeing respectively, while the letters n and N indicate no production will be undertaken by the two firms. In row P, Boeing will produce; in row N it will not. In column p Airbus will produce; in column n it will not. The lower left number in any quadrant is Boeing's profit; the upper right number is Airbus's profit.

Figure 8.1

A KRUGMAN MATRIX OF
STRATEGIC POSSIBILITIES

Consider first the upper right quadrant. If Boeing produces a new model commercial aircraft, but Airbus does not, Boeing would expect to earn profits equal to 100 while Airbus would get nothing. The situation is reversed in the lower left: if Airbus proceeds while Boeing does not, the 100 goes to Airbus and Boeing gets the zero. If *neither* produces the new model aircraft, as in the lower right quadrant, *both* get a zero. If, on the contrary, *both* produce, then both will make losses (−5) as in the upper left quadrant.

Now alter this example so that the governments sponsoring Airbus make subsidies available, with an amount (+10) paid either on output or on export. In Figure 8.2, we see that this decision changes the outcome. Now even if Boeing undertakes to produce in competition with Airbus, it will suffer a loss of

Figure 8.2

A STRATEGIC SUBSIDY SUCCEEDS IN CAPTURING THE MARKET

	Airbus	
	p	n
	5	0
P	−5	100
	110	0
N	0	0

(Boeing — rows P and N)

−5 (upper left quadrant), whereas Airbus will make a profit of 5. Boeing, certain that Airbus will produce whatever it does, and equally certain that it will thus make a loss, may decide it has no hope in the long run of lasting out such a situation and may withdraw from the competition. If so, the Airbus subsidy of +10 has been well worth it to the governments concerned because we see in the lower left quadrant that Airbus captures all the rents, leaving it with 110, a fine return on the governments' money.

A number of studies, however, have not lent much empirical support to the concept of rent capture as a means to increase a country's welfare, and Krugman himself has been highly critical of many policy suggestions purportedly based on his idea. Most of the studies on the issue show that losses from price distortion and X-inefficiency that accompany the subsidies usually outweigh the gains from the increased rents.[16]

DETAILS OF THE AIRBUS DISPUTE

The real-life events surrounding the Airbus dispute are, as usual, more convoluted than the model.[17] Airbus Industrie is owned jointly by Aerospatiale of France (38%), Germany's Daimler-Chrysler Aerospace (38%), British Aerospace (20%), and CASA of Spain (4%). The amount of the subsidies Airbus received from EU governments is a closely guarded secret. But subsidies in the form of cheap loans with no set timetable for repayment and some of the loans written off probably covered 70-90% of development costs.[18] The United States, asserting that the subsidies allowed Airbus to cut its prices by at least 10%, demanded a reduction to 25% of development costs, while the EU offered 45%.

Airbus had charges of its own. It claimed that Boeing receives large indirect support from U.S. government military contracts and space research for NASA. (It seems an implausible argument. Aviation experts doubt whether military work has much carryover to civilian wide-body jets. If anything, where it exists the flow of technology may be in the other direction. Furthermore, the space subsidies are for basic research only and are freely available to all.)

In any case, a compromise was reached in 1992.[19] Development subsidies were limited to 33% with repayment over 17 years for aircraft of 100 seats or more. (The subsidies are still real because private credit would cost much more.) Production subsidies were prohibited. The United States said it would limit indirect support through defense and NASA contracts that could be seen as subsidies for commercial jet production. The agreement did not end the dispute, however. The United States claims the subsidies to Airbus exceed the limits and is asking for a WTO panel. Airbus claims that the U.S. government has continued its indirect subsidies and that the Boeing McDonnell-Douglas merger was anticompetitive.[20] (The specific EU objection was to the 20-year Boeing contract with Delta and American to acquire only Boeing aircraft.) The EU said it would have its antitrust authorities rule on the merger and levy fines, with the potential fine being 10% of turnover or $4 billion. In July 1997, Boeing backed down, agreeing to make no new deals and not to enforce the ones already signed in order to get the EU approval of the merger.[21]

New relevance was added to the Boeing/Airbus dispute in 1998-99 as the two companies' plans came into direct conflict. With Airbus considering production of the A3XX for the 600-seat super jumbo market, Boeing retreated, shelving its own plans for the jumbo 747XX. In the small airliner market, the Airbus A318 announced in April 1999 would compete directly with the planned Boeing 717, a McDonnell-Douglas design that Boeing acquired in the merger: "100-seat Airbus clouds outlook for Boeing 717" said the headline in the *Wall Street Journal.*[22]

Defense Against Predatory Subsidies

The discussion above concerns policies designed to seize rents at the expense of firms in other nations. For countries facing active policies of this sort, it is necessary to consider how to reply. A major aim for the victims would be to convince the perpetrator that a predatory strategy is dangerous and uncertain in its result.

A government could retaliate with its own subsidies to the firms harmed by the foreign strategy or could impose protection against the subsidized product. Controlled repetitive experiments using the mathematical theory of games indicate that a tit-for-tat strategy may in fact be the most effective means of replying.[23] In this view, a clearly delineated announcement of plain and predictable steps that will be taken against a predatory strategy would have the greatest effect in discouraging such behavior. Tit-for-tat does not start a battle, requires a response to provocations, and in the end is forgiving of a country that abandons its original predatory plan. It never wins in the sense of capturing the rents of others, but it does encourage co-operation and general avoidance of conflict.

Intriguingly, this rule-based retaliation against subsidies, which we criticized in Chapter 7 as inflexible and dangerous, might be better than a discretionary policy because it would be a more dependable deterrent. The United States already has used tit-for-tat replies to a degree. Some uses of the countervailing duty laws against subsidies can be so seen, and are effective, though these duties do not affect subsidies that result in the seizure of markets in third countries. Further U.S. rejoinders to the strategic designs of others include the subsidies paid on agricultural exports and the cheap export credits made available by the U.S. Export-Import Bank. Replies do not have to be limited to the area of trade: a far wider arena offers itself. The retaliation might concern the defense umbrella, or the maintenance of foreign exchange rates (encouragement by the U.S. authorities of dollar depreciation, for example, which would make the subsidized foreign good appear more expensive to Americans). Removal of foreign aid is another possibility, while cultural, educational, and technical exchanges could also be pressed into service as bargaining chips. The possibilities are large. Yet even when defensive strategies to deter the predatory policies of others are logically sound, they must be handled with the utmost care to keep them from becoming the tools of special interests. It would be better by far to adopt a multilateral approach under WTO auspices. WTO rules to control aggressive strategic trade initiatives would seem clearly called for.

Reasons for Rejecting an Activist Policy

To this point in the discussion an active strategic trade policy has been pre-sented as a more or less reasonable use of public policy. Yet many economists are nonetheless most reluctant to recommend such action. It all seems to reflect a conundrum: laypersons seem to believe that free trade is optimal in theory but not in practice, while among economists the belief seems to be that free trade is suboptimal in theory but optimal in practice.[24] The objec-tions by economists, including ourselves, are twofold. The action would be incalculably costly, and it would be subject to political manipulation.

THE HIDDEN COSTS OF AN ACTIVE POLICY

Opponents of an active strategy warn that governments are not competent to make the necessary choices because the knowledge of the hidden costs involved is far too limited. They point to the difficulty of even identifying above-normal profits in the first place: how to distinguish these from returns that compensate for risky past investments is not easy. They note the possibility that subsidies might attract other entrants into the *domestic* market, leading to open-ended expense for the government. What about the cost to domestic consumers if export subsidies divert production away from the home market, they ask. What about the rise in factor costs as greater production in the subsidized industry draws resources from other industries? Would not that raise costs in these other industries? Might not the budget deficits or higher taxes resulting from the subsidies be more damaging than any good that would flow from an active strategy? The unknown size of all of these are indeed a cause for queasiness.[25]

THE POLITICAL DANGERS OF AN ACTIVE POLICY

Worse yet, claim the critics, an active policy runs a high risk of dangerous confrontation and political corruption. Why assume the subsidies would act as a deterrent, rather than assuming they would provoke a new type of trade war as foreigners re-retaliate? That is, after all, the very warning that economists issue whenever they analyze the optimum tariff strategies discussed earlier. And what about the politics of the situation? Would not an active policy be a wedge for self-interest in the business community? Like a Moses leading his flock, any trade evangelist promising subsidies will at once have an enormous following among business people. Does anyone believe that small industries would be more likely to get the subsidies than big ones? Does anyone doubt that on occasion a subsidy would be made available just before an election in some closely contested state or province, whether or not the industry involved fits the model very well? Arguably the politics of strategic trade intervention would cause a supported industry to spread out across the country, thereby gaining political strength but avoiding the benefits of conglomeration that have accrued to Boston's Route 128, California's Silicon Valley, North Carolina's Golden Triangle, and so forth. With politicians holding the purse-strings being major gainers from an active strategy, what is to control its size? And if a program *did* grow to large size, how would it be ended if it did not work as expected?

The problem thus amounts to comparing the benefits of successful deterrence to the costs, many hidden, of the same policy. We certainly cannot judge this issue: information is far too limited at present to permit a conclusive answer. We admit, however, to intense concern that these debates will be turned to serve the purposes of the self-interested.

JAPANESE USE OF A NATIONAL TRADE STRATEGY

Among all the world's countries, Japan is considered by the public and by many business people to be the most effective user of a national trade strategy.[26] Chalmers Johnson has called Japan a mercantilist "developmental state." Other authors have characterized the Japanese economy as a "noncapitalist market system" and "network capitalism."[27] Great myths have grown up: Japan has erected impenetrable trade barriers; behind these barriers it develops an industry, takes over that industry worldwide, then lifts the protection and moves on to take over yet another industry. This section considers the accuracy of the claims.

MITI's Strategy

To a considerable degree, even the claim that Japan has an explicit national strategy is now a myth as well, but some truth does attach to it and once did so even more strongly. As Japan began to recover in the 1950s from World War II, its new and powerful Ministry of International Trade and Industry (MITI) instituted a policy of encouraging industrial winners that could succeed in international trade. Who the winners would be was obvious enough at the time. Initially, very low labor costs provided the advantage. Later, scale-based development involving heavy capital investment could focus on industries easy to identify from sales trends in the United States and Western Europe. The Ministry of Finance guided scarce credit—at below market rates—to large firms in the favored sectors. MITI's advice was usually respected. It employed the best graduates of the best universities, and the bureaucrats who retired from the ministry at a relatively young age often obtained top posts in the very firms MITI was attempting to persuade.

A tight system of quotas, covering about 60% of imports until 1960, reserved internal markets for favored firms, paving the way for their efforts in international trade. The higher prices paid by consumers—Japan's TVs sold for two and one-half times more in that country than the same Japanese sets sold in the United States, for example—served as a sort of tax to promote investment and development as the profits were reinvested. The government permitted cartels and gave the firms favorable tax treatment, both of which stimulated profits that eventually financed massive marketing expenditures and heavy R&D spending. The R&D was supplemented by modest government subsidies, including cheap loans. At the time technology was borrowed wholesale. The guidance is thought to have been important in the 1950s for steel and shipbuilding; in machine tools, some electronic goods, and perhaps autos in the 1960s; and for high-tech electronic goods in the 1970s. Japan's economic growth, as the whole world knows, set records. (Note that few

356

people suggested the Bastable test be applied to this modern version of the infant industry argument. There was no explicit recompense to the public for money transferred to the favored industries.)[28]

It is, all in all, a pretty picture of a successful trade strategy, and it is probably even true that the strategy was partly responsible for the success. At the very least, as Kozo Yamamura notes, the importance of the strategy cannot be *disproved*, so giving encouragement to those who favor national trade strategies. As so often, however, the lessons are not really that clear, and the importance of the government's guidance is debatable. Japan, with its educated and highly motivated labor, much of it available for industrialization because it was employed in low-productivity agriculture, its energetic and innovative managers, and its very high national rates of saving and investment, would surely have enjoyed rapid growth anyway, even if those first-rate MITI officials had never gone to college.[29]

AN EXAGGERATED VIEW OF MITI?

As early as the 1970s, the government lost its ability to allocate loans as the private capital market grew and as prosperous companies found retained earnings sufficed for their financial needs. MITI guidance and industrial cartelization appeared to deter the technical breakthroughs that come from the competitive, and even duplicative, R&D efforts made by adversaries. It became difficult to identify obvious winners. Worse, experience revealed that many early choices had been poor. Steel had few external economies, its targeting did not result in much capture of foreigners' rents, and the profits realized in this industry were well below the Japanese average. In the end it was rapidly overrun by Korean and other competition. Shipbuilding did well only for a relatively short time. Petrochemicals and aluminum were industries of choice, but the energy crisis made it impossible for Japan to compete against countries with lower energy costs. Above all, major developments of the 1970s and 1980s that improved Japan's competitive ability had little to do with the government. These developments were important, as seen earlier in the book. They included focusing on market segments to obtain in-plant scale economies, flexible factories using CAD/CAM techniques, and just-in-time production and delivery. Japan's automobile industry provides an excellent example of such developments, yet it was very low on the list of MITI priorities.

Some observers argue that Japanese industrial assistance is not at all well correlated with the industries that actually succeeded. The case is made in Table 8.1, which shows numerical ranking in change in output in percent per year together with the ranks for various forms of government assistance.[30] Clearly, the government was picking a lot of losers as well as winners.

Table 8.1

GROWTH AND ASSISTANCE, 1955-1990, BY RANK ORDER

Industry	Change in Output	Cheap Loans	Net Transfers	Trade Protection	Tax Relief
Electrical machinery	1	8	9	8	8
General machinery	2	12	4	11	8
Transport equipment	3	7	11	4	8
Fabricated metal	4	10	6	12	7
Oil and coal	5	2	13	7	3
Precision instruments	6	13	10	6	8
Ceramics, stone, glass	7	5	8	9	3
Pulp and paper	8	6	5	10	13
Chemicals	9	3	7	5	3
Basic metals	10	4	2	3	6
Processed food	11	9	12	1	12
Mining	12	1	1	13	1
Textiles	13	11	3	2	2

Source: Richard Beason and David Weinstein, "Growth, Economics of Scale, and Targeting in Japan (1955-90)," Harvard Institute of Economic Research Discussion Paper No. 1644, 1994. In the last four columns, 1 means the most assistance and 13 the least. Cheap loans are those subsidized by government. Net transfers includes direct subsidies minus taxes. Trade protection is defined as effective protection.

CHANGES IN MITI STRATEGY

MITI's winner-picking strategy is now almost gone, with little survival of targeting.[31] Government still employs subsidies, but these are directed toward assisting broad-based technologies. Four areas now receiving aid are (1) large-scale R&D for super/hypersonic transport propulsion; (2) next-generation developments such as basic technology for carbohydrates in industry; (3) energy research, including superconductivity in power generation and coal liquefaction; and (4) R&D for high-definition TV and automatic translating telephones. In pursuit of technological goals, Japan's Science and Technology Agency funds basic research at research labs and universities.

The subsidies remain modest, however, and as a percent of GDP are only slightly higher than the U.S. figure, as seen in Chapter 7. Probably more significant than the government money has been the encouragement of joint public-private research projects to promote technological advance in these areas. The government activities are important, but they are also a far cry from the old policy of widespread targeting plus protection.

Japanese Institutions that May Hinder Imports

The perception of Japan as a nation using a national trade strategy survives and thrives. A major charge is that certain Japanese institutions act as implicit barriers to imports, an unorthodox kind of protectionism. The existence of the institutions does not imply that they were deliberately designed to restrict imports, only that they have this effect. (A few economists and many politicians and business people *do* believe that deliberateness is involved.) The institutions most frequently mentioned are the fragmented distribution system, the high cost of moving goods through the ports and on to their final markets, and the close ties amounting to vertical integration among producers of final products and suppliers of their inputs. There is considerable disagreement over how high these non-standard barriers to trade are, and the differences in opinion on how much imports would increase if their effect were eliminated vary widely—Gary Saxonhouse holds to a figure below 10%, while Peter Petri suggests as much as 100%.[32]

THE DISTRIBUTION SYSTEM

One allegation of an implicit barrier to imports involves Japan's complex and fragmented distribution system. That country has one store or shop for every 80 people, double the ratio for North America and the EU.[33] Approximately 80% of Japan's wholesale establishments employ fewer than 10 workers. These feed a huge number of small Mom-and-Pop stores, which make up about 40% of all stores and in part are an employment system for retirees who otherwise face a penurious social security system. The retirees are often set up in their stores by their former employers. Tax advantages help to perpetuate the system: income tax is 10 percentage points lower for small shops and they are exempted from paying the 3% value-added tax.[34] That has left Japan with a huge number of retail shops, 1.6 million compared to the 1.5 million of the United States, which has two times the population and 25 times the area. The situation fits the tastes of Japanese housewives, who have little storage space in their homes and because of traffic congestion mostly walk to the shops daily—and may be quite reasonable in these circumstances.[35] But distribution costs are raised substantially.

Moreover, Japanese law allows small shopkeepers some say in the granting of site permits for supermarkets. For a long time these permits often took three years to acquire, and sometimes as much as seven or even 10 years. One result is that Japan's largest retailers account for a relatively small percentage of total retail sales. Because the large stores import proportionally much more than the small shops, imports are penalized. Furthermore, price-fixing is common, sales involving mark-downs are rare, coupons in newspapers are not legal, and many stores will stock only the goods of the manufacturers that set them up. The right to return unsold goods to the manufacturer for a cash rebate plus exceedingly generous credit advances to wholesalers and retailers both contribute further to high distribution costs. In addition, sole import licenses have heretofore been legal under Japanese law. It appears that these practices are mostly responsible for the high retail price of goods in Japanese stores, prices that average almost half again more for a large market basket of goods and services than in the United States.

Foreigners have long urged the Japanese government to take steps to improve the cumbersome distribution system, and that country has committed itself to a reform, making several moves in the early 1990s.[36] The government agreed on a large-store approval process that would last 18 months at maximum and not require approval from small store owners. (But permission still has to come from local government committees, which include many small store owners in their membership.) Big stores were redefined in 1994 to be over 1,000 square meters instead of 500.* Also, Japan's laws allowing resale price maintenance were repealed. The growth of chain stores, malls, and catalog shopping will all open markets for importers. But the distribution system is still fragmented and still hurts imports, while the Japanese Fair Trade Commission, which could act to police the situation, remains rather ineffectual.

The design of the distribution system puts a premium on long-term relations with suppliers. The system can be difficult for foreigners to break into. Entry can be difficult for the Japanese, too; in some years bankruptcies among firms have run six times higher than in the United States. This suggests that the distribution system is not designed as a trade barrier, as some would have it, but is simply an institutional fact of life.

HIGH DISTRIBUTION COSTS FOR IMPORTS

Distribution costs for Japan's imports are especially high. Getting the goods into the country usually means shipment through a port, which is very expensive. The ports are operated as a cartel by the Japanese Harbor Transportation Authority, which mediates between shipping companies and the very strong dock workers' unions. The JHTA administers a "prior consultation system" that includes all parties except foreigners and requires agreement on virtually all operational matters. Foreigners are not licensed to operate their own terminals. All cargo—even that in standardized containers—must be weighed and measured by sworn measurers. Sunday work is prohibited (though

---

* But in North America 1,000 square meters is still quite small. Author JSH's Shaw's Supermarket in Waterville, Maine, measures about 5,000 square meters, and author WBB in Winnipeg, Manitoba, no doubt shops in a bigger store yet.

permitted temporarily in some periods).* Even after the goods are ready for shipment at the dock gate, distribution costs are rather extreme. If Japanese costs for land, construction, overland container shipment, and warehouse rental costs are all measured by an index number of 100, the comparable U.S. costs are 8, 73, 19, and 20, respectively.

KEIRETSU RELATIONSHIPS AS TRADE BARRIERS

Keiretsu means "system" in Japanese.[37] The term is used in a number of ways, but here it means tight relationships between manufacturers, their suppliers, and their distributors and retailers, with the manufacturers being the dominant player.[38] While such administered channel relationships are common enough in the West, the Japanese ones are extremely tight, and some 40 industrial groups have them.[39] Such relationships are most important in autos, steel, and electronics, and include firms such as Hitachi, Toshiba, Nissan, Toyota, and Nippon Steel.[40] Some economists and many foreign business people view the tightness of the *keiretsu*-administered channels as collusive behavior serving to close the market against imports. Robert Lawrence's recent work does indicate that they hold down imports to a degree, sometimes by as much as half.[41] One result for Japanese consumers is much higher domestic prices. The flat-glass industry, in which distributors tied to three big suppliers control 97% of the market, would not handle foreign glass. (In a 1994 agreement, the suppliers announced to dealers that they are free to buy foreign glass and will certify that they no longer discriminate.)[42]

A major case has been brought by the United States to the WTO against Japan's *keiretsu* system.[43] It involved Fuji film's distribution through small stores, which are under tight control, while government discourages large outlets, keeping Kodak's market share at only about 10%. It started as a 301 "crowbar," and then was handed on to a WTO dispute settlement panel. The case was perhaps doomed in advance, because WTO rules seem hardly to touch competition policy and much was involved beyond *keiretsu* behavior. (In the case, the United States also cited horizontal practices, such as price-fixing and group boycotts, and vertical ones, such as resale price maintenance

---

* In April 1997, the U.S. Federal Maritime Commission started charging a $100,000 retaliatory fee whenever a ship belonging to one of Japan's three largest shipping companies docks in a U.S. port. The Japanese shipping firms refused to pay, and a few weeks later the Federal Maritime Commission voted to bar Japanese vessels from unloading. The dispute was settled in October in what appeared a model use of retaliatory strategy. The United States depended on allies in Japan, especially the shipping companies disgusted with the stranglehold on the ports held by the JHTA. The Japanese government agreed to create a system wherein foreign shippers can negotiate directly with stevedores instead of the JHTA. For all that, the costs of bringing goods through the ports are still very high. For details see *International Economic Review*, July 1997; *The Economist*, January 11, 1997; *Wall Street Journal*, September 5, October 20, 1997.

and tied contracts. It was not typical for such a wide variety of issues to be included in a single dispute.) The Japanese had a good argument that they could make in reply: Fuji's 15–16% market share in the United States, where Kodak dominates, is not that much greater than Kodak's 10% market share in Japan. The WTO rejected the U.S. claim of Japanese protectionism-by-*Keiretsu*, noting that it relied on rather old evidence and was not very convincing in attacking vertical distribution alliances. The WTO panel rejected all 21 portions of the U.S. complaint. Kodak is now said to be asking for antidumping duties and other unilateral action. The Kodak/Fuji dispute was the first time Japan carried out its repeated warning that it would not enter a bilateral negotiation and would instead fight the charge in a WTO panel.

In an independent move dating from 1992, the U.S. antitrust authorities announced that they might prosecute U.S. branches of Japanese firms if some action in Japan (by *keiretsu*, for example) would be illegal if done in the United States. This extraterritorial application of U.S. antitrust laws drew heavy foreign fire as well as opposition within the Bush administration, and the proposal was eventually withdrawn. A better idea by far would be joint U.S.-Japanese antitrust action in both countries.[44]

Keiretsu relationships, however, may not be trade barriers at all. Supporters of the "*keiretsu* as protectionism" argument cite the high percentage of Japanese automobile subcontracting as evidence, yet worldwide the automobile industry has been moving away from vertical integration to subcontracting; and most observers would hold that subcontracting is a looser arrangement than vertical integration. In any country, administered channels are legal and accepted means of doing business, so long as they do not lead to monopoly, because such channels make good sense and keep down costs. Indeed, evidence exists that manufacturers in vertical *keiretsu* have better export performance than firms that buy their inputs at arm's length. Furthermore, argue the critics, if comparative advantage is improved by a *keiretsu* arrangement with domestic suppliers, then it is understandable that inputs produced domestically will predominate over imports. In this view, countries lacking a network of mutually supporting, vertically related firms in close proximity to one another should go about encouraging their formation rather than harassing countries that have already achieved it.

In some respects, Western firms are following this advice, with supplier alliances now common and with some reports that they work better than the original Japanese model because supplier independence may encourage innovation. Japanese firms have held their *keiretsu* partners to very thin margins, so these partners may have little ability to conduct independent R&D activity. Western arrangements have typically protected supplier margins and make it possible to conduct more R&D. Motorola, Philips Electronics, and Marks & Spencer are all examples of Western adaptation of the favorable aspects of *keiretsu* practice.[45]

Rather clearly, this is an area where economists should discriminate more between the actions of *keiretsu* that improve efficiency and those that involve collusion and exclude outsiders. The Japanese government appears to agree. It is strengthening its Fair Trade Commission, which is acquiring more powers to levy fines and is now bringing some criminal charges even though it brought only one in the 17 years before 1991. But weakness in Japanese antitrust enforcement is still pronounced, with sectors such as paper, glass, and car parts still largely closed and with significant bid-rigging in construction.[46]

Two Disputes Reveal the Extremes: Car Parts and Cars

Japan's trading partners have recently been making much of implicit trade barriers while pressuring Japan to mend its ways. Two of these disputes with the United States, car parts and cars, represent a spectrum with two extremes even though the products involved—car parts and cars—seem so similar. The argument here is that one of the cases, car parts, is a rather clear case of implicit Japanese protectionism, while the other case, cars, represents embarrassing exaggeration by U.S. exporters. The main lesson of these disputes is the inadvisability of making broad judgments about implicit barriers. Each ought to be investigated on its merits.

HIDDEN PROTECTION: THE CAR PARTS DISPUTE

The car parts dispute reveals a systemic design so exclusionary to imports that it is hard to avoid the conclusion that it is intentional.[47] Japan's car inspection rules require inspection three years after manufacture and then every other year in an inspection garage certified by the Ministry of Transport. The inspection is pervasive and bringing a car up to standard is very expensive (often $1,000 or more). Repairs to certain areas such as the drive train, brakes, steering, engine, transmission, and shock absorbers must be made at these garages. Many of them are owned by manufacturers, auto dealers, or parts makers, and it is hard for new garages to obtain certification. The rules require that the parts be supplied from an approved critical parts list. Unlisted parts cannot be installed, and the list is not publicly available. Directions on how to get *on* the list are not available either. Such parts are therefore costly in Japan—$600 to change the front shock absorbers for example, compared to $250 in the United States—and average a little more than double parts prices in the United States.

The United States argued that this tough system of auto inspection discriminates against foreign parts makers because the auto inspection stations are controlled by the Japanese auto companies or their approved suppliers. The Japanese reply that they do not want their standards undermined, though given the circumstances of the case, that argument seemed rather threadbare.

The auto parts dispute led to a three-year voluntary agreement in 1992 that called for Japanese automakers to increase their use of U.S. parts. This was a voluntary import expansion, or VIE. The Japanese would not extend the voluntary agreement on parts, which expired on March 31, 1995, but they did consent to a 1995 pact on autos and parts that made changes in the system. In it the Japanese agreed to review their motor vehicle inspection system and remove shock absorbers, struts, power steering systems, and trailer hitches from the list of critical parts that can be provided only by designated repair garages. The government also promised to begin a process permitting non-certified garages to make inspections, and agreed to write letters to the garages informing them "that motor vehicle inspections and other regulatory requirements ... will not discriminate against vehicles equipped with foreign or 'nongenuine' parts." Finally, Japanese carmakers agreed voluntarily to raise their purchases of U.S.-made parts by $6 billion for their U.S. plants and $2 billion for their plants in Japan.

SUBSTANTIAL EXAGGERATION: THE CAR DISPUTE

Autos are an excellent example of how exaggerated the case against Japanese barriers to imports can become (as opposed to car parts, which are a very different story).[48] U.S. auto executives argue that the playing field is not level because U.S. cars are kept out of Japan by hidden trade barriers. It is true that the U.S. share of Japan's car market is tiny (0.5%). It is true that until 1980, Japanese car dealers, about 40% of them actually owned or partly owned by the manufacturers, could not handle the cars of other manufacturers. It is also true that in 1995, just 20% of Japanese dealerships handled imports (and only 7% handled imports of U.S. cars) compared to 94% of dealers handling imports in the United States. (It is perfectly legal for U.S. dealers to refuse to handle foreign makes, by the way.) It is true, as well, that Japan's rules require the U.S. red warning lights be changed to amber and that changes must be made to mirrors. Finally, high land prices make it hard for foreigners to establish dealerships.

But in the light of other facts, the charges of Japanese auto protectionism seem greatly exaggerated. The markup charged by foreign sellers is high, often about 40%. U.S. cars are mostly big, few having engines of less than two liters, a size that makes up about 80% of the Japanese market, and American cars get relatively low mileage for a country such as Japan where gasoline is very expensive. U.S. vehicles are on average larger than Japanese ones; many Japanese roads are narrow and so are parking spots. Garages are small. Japanese license plates will not fit in U.S. holders; U.S. makers do not offer retractable mirrors, needed to keep the mirrors from being knocked off in narrow passageways; speedometers are in miles per hour and not kilometers; and there is a notable lack of American dealerships. In one survey, inadequate servicing was cited by 60% of potential Japanese buyers of U.S. cars. U.S. cars in Japan are often sold with English-language manuals. (European automakers have acted on most of these problems.) Above all, Japan, like Britain, drives on the left. Not until January 1993 did any U.S. car, truck, or van maker place the wheel on the right, where the Japanese need it to be.*

This picture should not be misunderstood. It is not one of blundering, inept American car companies. At root is another issue. American car companies are not seriously interested in selling a lot of cars in Japan. They are unlikely to make any money in that tough market and are sticking to a "skimming" strategy where they will sell only to people with very special wants or needs. The unique skills or assets of American car companies are not of particular use in Japan. It is disingenuous, of course, for them to argue that Japan should buy more American cars, but that isn't because they are inept. Instead they are trying to portray the Japanese as highly protectionist, principally as a way of giving legitimacy to their own demands for protection against foreign autos. The car companies would do better to argue against Japanese agricultural protection. If that were ended, they would sell more of their cars to American ranchers than they would ever sell if the purported Japanese automobile protection were somehow ended.

Eventually the United States demanded that car dealers in Japan be forced to handle more American cars.[49] Japan replied that its government has no business forcing private firms to alter their behavior and that if it offered a voluntary target, this would be interpreted by the United States as a commitment. Japan also insisted that it got no credit for the exports of cars from Japanese plants in the United States to Japan—Honda in 1994 exported more cars to Japan than did the Big Three automakers. Negotiations broke down because Japan would not agree to numerically managed trade and the U.S. would not compromise on its demand for a voluntary import expansion. Under the Section 301 crowbar law, the United States in May 1995 announced it would impose tariffs of 100% on 13 of the highest-price (over $33,000) models, including the Lexus, Acura Legend, Mitsubishi Diamante, Mazda Millenia, and Infiniti.

The high-profile tariffs were not imposed because of an agreement struck a few hours before the June 1995 deadline. In that agreement, which included auto parts as well as the cars themselves, the Japanese government promised

---

* The first U.S. company to move the wheel was Chrysler on its exported Jeep Cherokees; the Neon and Grand Cherokee followed in 1996. A right-hand Ford Probe and a Ford Mondeo (from Europe) came in 1994, a Taurus in 1996, an Explorer after that. No right-hand cars came from GM until 1996; now there are a Chevrolet Cavalier sold under the Toyota name and a Saturn. In mid-1995, when the dispute was very hot, there were just three U.S. models with right-hand drive on sale compared to 154 European models. Two interesting facts: the U.S. market share in Great Britain (0.6%) is almost identical to that in Japan (0.5%), and Japan sells 167 models and versions with left-hand drive in the United States.

to encourage dealers to carry imports the way American companies commonly do. This will be especially helpful because of the high land costs. The United States dropped its demand for numerical targets and for a Japanese government guarantee of "voluntary" commitments by the Japanese firms. It seems clear that these results were a tiny outcome for such a grand dispute—but rightly so, for the charge that the low sales of American cars in Japan are proof of a tilted playing field does not seem serious.

Japan's National Trade Strategy: A Summary

In short, the Japanese did indeed employ a national trade strategy involving both protectionism and subsidies. But contrary to widespread perception, Japan's orthodox trade barriers are low, except in agriculture, and government subsidies are modest. These tools belong to Japan's past, an era of infant industries when winners were easy to pick, and they play a much less important role today when picking winners is not nearly so obvious. Thus the country most often cited for government activism in trade does not now provide very persuasive evidence of this case.

Now, however, the thrust of foreign complaints has turned toward criticism of various institutional structures and practices that are said to act as implicit trade barriers. The evidence is mixed, but it is clear that in some areas, such as the distribution of imported goods, it would be advantageous to both Japanese consumers and foreign exporters if reforms were made. Admitting that sometimes exaggeration is involved, it is in Japan's interest to move toward more open competitive practices if only to defuse foreign hostility. But pressure to that end is far better done internationally through negotiations on competition policy than by means of bilateral threats.

ADJUSTING TO TRADE AS A NATIONAL STRATEGY

The national strategies discussed thus far have been either active ones designed to pick winners and seize rents or reactive defensive ones to deter the policies of others. At this point we take up a national strategy very different in both its outlook and its implications: government adjustment assistance to help industries through the transitions that may be imposed on them by international trade.

At base, this strategy involves an admission. At least in the short run, free international trade is likely to impose costs on those employed in industries that do not have a comparative advantage. The models discussed in earlier chapters certainly suggest this. Paul Samuelson's factor price equalization theorem (Chapter 3) states that imports of goods containing a country's scarce factor will tend to lower, relatively or absolutely, the returns to that factor. The Stolper-Samuelson theorem holds that removal of trade barriers harms the scarce factor. One likely possibility is that large concentrated industries may have been earning rents that were shared with workers, and then international competition eroded the rents.[50]

Plenty of evidence does indicate that less educated and less skilled workers have done poorly in terms of wage gains compared to educated and skilled labor.[51] In the past two decades the real earnings of the top fifth of American men increased about 25% while the real earnings of the bottom fifth fell about 10%. The fall for the bottom tenth of American men was almost 20%. In that period, the wage margin for college-educated labor compared to those with just a high school education or less increased from a little over 30% to about 70%. The pattern indicates a shift in demand and supply against unskilled labor that lowered wages. The situation is similar, though not so pronounced, in Canada and Britain. In much of the rest of Europe, wage inequality has not increased but unemployment has, reflecting less flexibility in European labor markets. Various institutional factors, such as stronger labor unions, high minimum wages, and generous welfare benefits, all mean that a decline in labor demand causes unemployment to mount more than it causes wages to decrease.

Few economists doubt that the *major* reason for the declining fortunes of less-educated and less-skilled labor is what is called biased technical change. New technology requires better educated workers and some technology, such as computers, results in the replacement of low-skill workers. The evidence is the fall in the ratio of unskilled to skilled labor in almost every manufacturing subsector of every advanced economy, whether or not the industries involved compete against imports or receive low pay.

But *some* of the pressure on wages is, by wide agreement, caused by the pressures of imports on the demand for low-wage labor. The existing estimates concerning the role of imports run along a spectrum from only about 5% of the widened gap to about half of it. But there is something of a consensus that international trade with cheap labor countries is responsible for perhaps 15%, though not much more, of the decline in demand for unskilled and less-educated labor.

The two main means for investigating the role of imports in causing harm to some workers, the factor content approach and the price change approach, differ considerably.[52] The figure of some 15% emerges from both types of modeling, which given the difference in the methods raises confidence that the results are reasonably accurate.

The factor content approach involves estimating the changes in factor endowments resulting from imports. That is, the investigator asks how much labor would have been required to produce domestically the goods that are imported from low-wage countries. For example, assume that 10 imported toys could have been produced by five unskilled U.S. workers. That means the imports of 10 toys reduced the demand for U.S. unskilled labor by five workers. With assumptions about demand and supply elasticities of labor, the effect of international trade on earnings can be calculated.

The other commonly used method is to search for a decline in the prices of imported goods made with unskilled labor, which could be seen as the source of changes in employment. This is directly in the tradition of the Heckscher-Ohlin model, which suggests that for trade to have dragged down relative earnings for the less skilled, then the prices of unskilled labor-intensive imports must have fallen. In this view, an initial push from imports causes a fall in demand for the domestically produced product, thus a fall in the price of that product, a decline in labor demand, and hence a reduction in worker earnings.

Chapter 6 explained that wage gaps caused by pressure from imports do not normally persist. Exports create better jobs than those that were protected, with a standard rule of thumb in the United States that $1 billion of new exports means 20,000 new jobs, jobs that pay 12% more (U.S. ITC estimate) to 17% more (Congressional Budget Office estimate) on average than other jobs. Moreover, as income rises, more jobs will be created in the non-traded service sector. Some people charge that service-sector jobs are inferior, but pay in service-sector jobs has been rising, with average pay in U.S. service-sector jobs now at 96% of the pay in goods-producing jobs.[53]

Transition Costs

The problem, therefore, is not a long-run one. But what about the short-run costs of transition? It takes time because the adjustment process is not instantaneous, and during the time it takes to play out there may be substantial costs.

The transition costs would be most serious whenever there are downward rigidities in real wages and prices so that markets do not adjust rapidly (which, as seen above, is more true of Europe than of North America). Where there are market rigidities, unemployment may develop in the affected industry along with excess capacity in plant and equipment that might be long

Figure 8.3

ADJUSTMENT MAY BE COSTLY

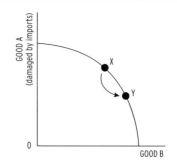

Note: If resources cannot be transferred easily from point X, involving much prodction of the good A damaged by imports, to point Y, the country may remain inside its production possibility curve for some time.

lasting. The market will in time bring adjustments, as in Figure 8.3, where an economy does move from good *A* (facing damaging competition from imports) to good or service *B*. The problem is that the economy may dip temporarily below its production possibility curve before climbing back to it as the adjustment occurs. The process will be slower and more costly if information is imperfect, if transactions costs are high, and if the downward rigidities of prices and wages are long lasting.

The transition costs will be even more damaging if *hysteresis* in unemployment is present. Hysteresis is the concept that the longer a worker is out of a job, the more likely it is that the worker will *stay* jobless.* One may become an outsider whose commitment to work becomes suspect, and whose skills may be eroding due to lack of use. In effect, hysteresis means that high unemployment might remain high.

Specific Costs of Adjusting to Trade Flows

Unfortunately, even if the transition is relatively smooth and rapid, trade may inflict other costs on individuals working in the industry damaged by the competition from imports. These costs take several forms. Perhaps most important is the sudden obsolescence of specific skills and the loss of seniority. In figure 8.4 curve *EE* shows the normal path of earnings for workers in a given industry, rising, though at a slowing rate, as age increases. Curve *OO*, the opportunity wage in the worker's next-best alternative occupation, behaves differently. It falls with age as opportunities diminish. (Though as shown, it might have started at a point higher than *EE* if young workers pick jobs partly because of future earn-

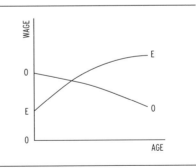

Figure 8.4

WAGES AND OPPORTUNITY COSTS OVER WORKING LIFE

ings prospects.) The gap between the two curves shows the sacrifice if trade results in loss of jobs. The gap will be greater yet if time and money have to be devoted to retraining and the acquisition of new skills. Note too that as workers age they become tied to their industries and their skills become more specialized. They earn more money, as the curve *EE* shows. Their ability to earn high pay elsewhere, however, usually declines, so *OO* shows falling opportunity cost.

---

* The word is taken from the physical sciences. It is used, for example, to describe the persistence for a time of an electromagnetic field even after the electricity is shut off. Edmund Phelps of Columbia University first applied the term "hysteresis" to unemployment.

The problem is made acute in the United States because workers who shift jobs do not carry their health-care insurance with them.* In *any* country they may have to make a geographical shift, possibly with high moving costs, take a capital loss on their housing, and suffer a breakup of family and social ties. (If the causes of the increased trade are of the factor-proportions, interindustrial type, then the newly unemployed workers may have to make greater shifts in occupation and location than is usual when unemployment occurs, because a whole industry may be affected rather than just a firm. If the trade is intraindustrial, the adjustments need not be so severe.) The older the worker, the worse the loss, due to the likelihood that age brings more local ties, a greater stake in the pension plan, and higher seniority in a present job, but reduced opportunities in alternative occupations. In part, this will be due to age discrimination, and in part to the specific nature of the skills possessed by experienced workers. The costs will also be higher in smaller towns, because the local job pool and the local housing market will both be smaller, with more difficulty in finding alternative employment and a greater capital loss in selling one's house.

The greatest adverse impact for individual workers will be in beleaguered industries where wages, for historical reasons, are far above the national average. Perhaps the high wages are a result of an earlier but now eroded productivity advantage, or perhaps the result of protection, with strong labor unions able to extract a share of the gains from the firms in the industry. In this case, there is every chance that alternative employment will be at a lower, possibly much lower, wage. In communities dependent on a single firm or industry, the damage can spread more widely, to merchants and anyone else selling goods and services to the now-distressed workers, and decreased property tax collections from the damaged firm or industry might be passed on to all owners of property, who must make up the difference. For workers and communities, there is no easy way to insure against all this or to recover quickly. A stockholder can rapidly adjust shareholdings to avoid or reduce losses, but for a worker or for a town, the problems are likely to be less tractable.

All these costs lead to a number of conclusions. First, a reduction in protection and a shift to freer trade are likely to be more acceptable politically if they are gradual. Letting attrition do the work is likely to be less painful than adjusting all at once. Second, these costs explain why multilateral tariff reductions are better than unilateral ones. When trading partners also cut their barriers, there will be a sharper stimulus for export industries to expand, thus reducing the dislocation costs. Finally, the costs will be reduced if the removal

---

* The United States is the only major industrial nation without government-provided health insurance. When workers or employees in that country lose their jobs, their options are either private insurance (at much higher rates) or no insurance at all. The costs of U.S. adjustment therefore exceed those of its major trading partners.

of protection comes during a period of economic growth and not in the middle of a recession when jobs are scarcer everywhere.

But the costs explain one more thing as well. Unlike the "normal" unemployed, those who lose their jobs because of the impact of imports are free to seek tariffs and quotas from congresses and parliaments. Those who stand to lose from the protection—consumers, foreign countries with a comparative advantage in some protected product, potential exporters to those foreign countries—are less well organized and carry less influence. This raises the risk that the affected industries may lobby for and succeed in obtaining trade barriers from compliant legislatures, where politicians note the complaints from their home district. Of course, the barriers attract new resources into the industry, penalize consumers and exporters, and restrict the gains from trade.

Trade Adjustment Assistance

In this view, a government program of trade adjustment assistance (TAA) can compensate those with power to do harm, in effect buying them off and simultaneously acting as a caution signal that the aided industry is a declining one. One significant reason why protectionist pressures have intensified worldwide is lack of attention to well-designed programs of trade adjustment assistance. To many, this is a missing link in modern trade policy.

Fortunately, the numbers of workers dislocated by imports are quite limited compared to those who change jobs for other reasons—perhaps only 5-10% of those changing jobs in the United States—and thus a program aimed at those impacted by trade would bring much less budgetary stress.[54] In any case, budgetary costs are of less concern because trade barriers are so expensive for consumers. A generous TAA program could easily be financed for a tenth of the cost inflicted by trade barriers. Moreover, an economy following its comparative advantage will be a richer economy, with increased tax collections that can help to finance adjustment assistance.

U.S. EXPERIENCE WITH TAA

Up to the time of writing, the United States has never had an effective TAA program. TAA was first introduced in the Trade Expansion Act of 1962. For many years, the program did little more than grant workers displaced by imports an extension of unemployment benefits for one year on top of the six months of normal compensation (which is still the chief benefit). The downside of making cash payments the centerpiece of TAA is that the extended compensation takes away the motive to find new work quickly.

The politicization of TAA was noteworthy. Auto workers and steel workers received the lion's share of the benefits; politically unimportant industries received little. Conservatives generally opposed spending for this purpose, and with deep budget cuts after the election of President Reagan, Congress just managed to keep TAA alive, a shadow of its old self, its funding only 5% of its former figure. For a time in 1985-86 it was even allowed to expire.*

Useful parts of the program, such as job search allowances to help dislocated workers find new jobs, relocation allowances to assist them in moving, and training to help them acquire new skills were neglected. In the years 1977-84, only 5% of assisted workers enrolled in retraining programs, only 2% completed the training, and only 0.3% found jobs that used their new training. Training did eventually receive greater emphasis, with 22% of the 108,843 workers certified for TAA in 1997 taking it. But only 0.3% were granted a job search allowance, and only 0.6% a relocation allowance.[55] A special TAA program for workers displaced by the North American Free Trade Agreement, called NAFTA Transitional Adjustment Assistance and dating from 1994, shares the same problem. Of the 54,757 workers certified in 1997, a very small 7% received training, 0.6% job search assistance, and 0.3% a relocation allowance.†

It would appear that economists who supported NAFTA erred in their failure to strengthen TAA in a major way when the agreement was made.

The position of TAA in the United States is presently an uncomfortable one. The Clinton administration would prefer to see a substantial extension of assistance to include other programs for workers whose jobs are cut because of technical change, military conversion, and the like. In one area the administration has succeeded.[56] With the passage of the Workforce Investment Act in 1998, individual training accounts allow unemployed workers to seek training at any eligible training provider. New local centers allow job

---

* Funding for TAA always presents budgetary problems, especially given the political opposition to it on the part of fiscal conservatives. An across-the-board import fee of 0.15% was included in the 1988 Trade Act, the first time that U.S. tariff revenue was ever to have been devoted to trade adjustment. That caused a great deal of trouble, however, because a tariff increase would have broken U.S. commitments to bind tariffs at their present level. U.S. trading partners refused to accept this violation of GATT rules, even though from economists' point of view the cause was a good one. The 1988 Trade Act had ordered the President to implement the fee anyway, if after two years the GATT had not made a rules change. In the end President Bush did not do so, which was permissible if he found that collecting the fee was against the national interest. Congress did not try to overturn the ruling. (At least once in the United States, under the National Wool Act of 1954, tariff revenue was transferred directly to producers to persuade farmers to accept the lowered tariffs on wool that clothing manufacturers had lobbied for. Up to 70% of the lower duties were to be used to compensate farmers for the lessened amount of protection. The Roth-Moynihan Bill that did not pass in 1985 would have funded trade adjustment assistance with a 1% tariff on all imports, much larger than the 0.15% figure in the 1988 act.)

† It appears that the NAFTA-TAA eligibility requirements are being interpreted quite loosely to bring aid to workers who lose jobs from various causes. This may tend to overstate the number of workers who have lost their jobs because of NAFTA. But some firms apparently do not apply for assistance because they do not want to be accused of shipping jobs to Mexico. The Clinton administration would like to merge regular TAA and NAFTA-TAA.

DECLINING CONFIDENCE IN TRAINING

Retraining of displaced workers seems obviously beneficial, but among economists it has fallen into some disrepute: A study of U.S. retraining by James Heckman of the University of Chicago found that there was no effect at all on the later earnings of trainees under 21 years of age, a poor result. (The record was better for women and adults.)[57] A recent experiment showed one group of unemployed that received just job-search assistance did as well as another group that received training. Unfortunately, U.S. experience with government training programs has been replicated around the world. Too often the training does little to fit workers for new jobs. Managerial, professional, administrative support, clerical, and other service jobs are clearly areas where employment gains will occur. The retraining of steel or textile workers for these positions (writing computer programs, for example) is likely to encounter difficulties. Elderly people and minorities are harder to train, and the training does not work if the economy is bad.

A long look will have to be taken at the low-skill unemployed, especially those raised in an environment where schools, learning, and skill acquisition have not been emphasized. Such workers may be exceptionally difficult to train. A broader focus on improved basic education may be needed, perhaps with massive remedial education together with a vigorous full-employment policy.

Critics say the training does so little to fit workers for new jobs that it should be ended. Some call for it to be superseded by insurance so that unemployed workers who take a job at lower pay can be compensated for doing so. This is called wage insurance. The compensation could be half the difference between the old wage and the new one, and it could be capped at perhaps $10,000.[58]

counseling, sign–up for training, and registration for unemployment benefits all at the same time, and provide data on training providers and job openings (America's Job Bank)—a major advance.[59] National certification of most worker skills would increase the portability of training. To this end, the Clinton administration's National Skills Standards Act provides a framework for encouraging the development of national standards—but so far it is a framework only.

Conservatives remain deeply skeptical of the effectiveness of TAA and have opposed most of these steps. Thus, a little improved TAA program barely slips by each budget cycle, renewed for a few months only to face cancellation once again. After a nine-month extension of funding expired on June 30, 1999, the program was forced to limp along on funds diverted from other sources. A one–year renewal was still being debated in the Congress at the time of writing.

TRADE SANCTIONS

A national trade strategy can go well beyond the ideas discussed thus far and in its broadest definition can include trade sanctions for political and military purposes.[60] Countries usually carry out trade sanctions to triumph in an armed conflict, to destabilize foreign governments without military force, or to achieve some specific purpose such as the abandonment of racial discrimination (South Africa, Rhodesia) or poor environmental practices (whaling, killing of dolphins and sea turtles).

Obvious examples of trade sanctions accompanying military action are World Wars I and II. Earlier major instances include the British and French countermoves of embargo and blockade during the Napoleonic Wars, Thomas Jefferson's embargo strategy that started in 1806 and lasted until the end of the War of 1812, and the federal blockade during the American Civil War.

In the twentieth century, sanctions have frequently served as means to destabilize or achieve specific goals. They were employed 115 times world-wide between the start of World War I in 1914 and 1990, with a success rate, defined as a desired change in policy, of about 35%. The League of Nations treated Italy to an embargo on strategic goods to protest Mussolini's invasion of Ethiopia, which was unsuccessful because too many fascist or near-fascist countries refused to cooperate. Japan was similarly served during its period of aggression in China and Indochina. This had a powerful effect after the United States embargoed shipments of oil, iron, steel, and rubber shortly after the Japanese army occupied French Indochina in September 1940. At the time of the embargo, there was only a six-month supply of oil available in Japan.[61] But the sanctions backfired by increasing Japanese militancy—the government made plans to obtain the resources it needed by acquiring a "Greater East Asia Co-Prosperity Sphere" and began to plot a carrier attack on Pearl Harbor.[62] Fascist Spain was embargoed during part of the period when Generalissimo Franco was in power, though with little practical effect beyond ensuring that Spain would remain rather poor.

The GATT agreement had a clause, repeated in the WTO rules, allowing trade sanctions in the interest of national security. The U.S. measures include trade embargoes or restrictions aimed at Cambodia (during the rule of the Khmer Rouge, repealed in 1992), Castro's Cuba (dating from shortly after the fall of Batista in 1959, and strengthened in 1992 and 1996), Iran (in 1996 due to accusations of support for terrorism), Saddam Hussein's Iraq (from 1990 because of the invasion of Kuwait), Qadaffi's Libya (imposed by the United States in 1986, and by the UN in 1992 after the downing of Pan Am flight 103), Kim Il-Sung's North Korea (for a half-century, the longest lasting of them all), Vietnam (lifted in 1994 after 19 years), Nicaragua (removed after the 1990 electoral defeat of the Sandinistas), and South Africa late in the era of apartheid rule (ended after Nelson Mandela's election in

1994). Outstanding cases from the Cold War against the Soviet Union include the American grain embargo and Pipeline War to protest the Soviet policies concerning Poland and the U.S.S.R.'s invasion of Afghanistan.

In the 1990s the use of trade sanctions has grown rapidly, with 50 cases up to 1998—nearly half the total from 1914 to 1990.[63] Much in the news during the 1990s has been a trade embargo against Serbia for its various aggressions in Bosnia and Kosovo. Imposed initially in 1992, later relaxed in 1996, then reimposed in 1999, this particular embargo is being enforced by many countries, including the United States and Canada. Food and humanitarian supplies are exempted from its terms. U.S. sanctions were imposed automatically against Pakistan and India following their spring 1998 nuclear tests. Both being poor countries, there was an outcry and the sanctions were lifted within a few months.

Judging the Effectiveness of Trade Sanctions

The net effectiveness of a sanctions strategy is the loss of income suffered by the "enemy" minus the loss of income to the imposer. The effect is greatest when one country identifies imports vital to the economy of another, hence inelastic in demand, that are either completely unavailable domestically or are inadequate in supply even when the enemy economy is at maximum output of these vital goods. Call these goods "impossible to supply," or ITS goods.

The counter-strategies open to the enemy will be to buy the proscribed ITS goods from neutral countries (but no doubt at a higher price, so raising costs to the enemy); or possibly to buy illegally from the country or countries conducting the trade sanctions in laundered transactions through a neutral; or, best of all, acquiring a patron who will take up the slack even if at high cost.

The potential for success in dealing with an enemy is highest in the following circumstances:

- When goals are modest. A small and powerless country as the enemy of a country important in international trade and a single issue not of overwhelming concern to the enemy offer the greatest chance of success.
- When the imports of the enemy economy contain a high proportion of ITS goods. Again, the smaller the enemy's economy, the more likely this will be.
- When a high proportion of world output of the ITS goods are produced by the country enforcing the trade embargo and its allies. Sanctions are especially effective if directed at a former friend that has no patron to bail it out.
- When there is a large terms-of-trade effect. Thus, if the enemy buys its ITS imports from neutrals, a substantial price rise will follow, and if the

enemy diverts its exports to these neutrals, their price will fall sharply. It is also desirable that the expenses of transshipment (by means of blockade runners, smugglers, or launderers) raise the cost of imports considerably and reduce greatly the revenues from exports.

- When there is low slippage. The allies must maintain a united front, the blockade ought not to be leaky, laundering should be difficult, and smuggling hard. Blockade-running and smuggling into the Confederacy in the U.S. Civil War and the willingness of many countries—much of Europe, Canada, Japan, South Korea, and Taiwan—to continue trade with Nicaragua in the face of a U.S. embargo are both excellent examples of high slippage. Small, landlocked countries have special problems in arranging adequate slippage. When India blockaded Nepal in 1989 over a trade dispute, that Himalayan kingdom was immediately in serious trouble because India could easily police most points of entry. In 1986, South Africa's blockade forced little Lesotho (which it completely surrounds) to submit to its list of demands in just three weeks.

- When the economic development of the enemy is at a low level. This is a major advantage. A poor, developing country is likely to suffer more heavily than a rich one for several of the reasons just cited. (1) Its imports will probably contain a high percentage of ITS goods. (2) There are likely to be more vital bottlenecks to the smooth running of the economy, including electricity, roads, railroads, and communications. If a boycott covers the main bearings to hydroelectric facilities, and a bearing fails in a poor country, that may knock out the whole electrical grid. (3) A country at a low level of development will probably experience foreign exchange shortages, often meaning that payments to agents, neutral suppliers, smugglers, launderers, and the like are more difficult. If the enemy is not in a position to pay very large sums for ITS goods, then neutral sources of supply may be less sympathetic because their effort will be less profitable. (4) There is an inadequate technical base, making it difficult for local industries to substitute domestic capital goods for imported capital. (5) Often the demand for a poor country's primary product exports is likely to be inelastic. Diverting these products to neutrals will thus result in a significant fall in price. (6) Above all, a poor country is likely to be less flexible in reallocating its resources from one use to another.

- When the costs of trade sanctions are low for the country pursuing the strategy. This is most advantageous, but if this is not so—if, for example, harm to domestic producers and exporters becomes more and more apparent—then domestic political opposition will grow rapidly. The U.S. embargo before and during the War of 1812 was so damaging to the business community in New England that that region virtually exited from the war. As discussed below, the opposition of U.S. farmers to the grain embargo against the Soviet Union grew so formidable that the embargo had to be dropped.

In summary, the existence and control over ITS imports are critical to a strategy of trade sanctions. Encouraging slippage and developing domestic substitutes are the counter-strategy. To make sanctions effective, it is essential either to bring into an alliance or to bring under control all major suppliers of vital ITS goods to the enemy. For that reason alone, embargoes by *one country* against another are likely to be ineffective.

THE ROLE OF TIME

In judging whether sanctions are likely to succeed or fail, the role of time is important. Generally, the passage of time allows the enemy to adjust to the shortage by stockpiling, arranging more slippage, and adjusting production in the home country. Thus results may be best when the time span of the action is short and the impact is large. Surprise is obviously helpful in such cases— your enemy has no time to plan adjustments. A good example of a short, sharp strategy was President Jimmy Carter's protest against the Soviet invasion of Afghanistan, when exports connected with the Moscow Olympic Games of 1980 were prohibited. The ban could not be overcome in the time available.

In general, the role of time is ambiguous. Time is on the sanctioning country's side if its enemy simply cannot adjust in a satisfactory way. Then the sanctions will pinch more the longer they last. Perhaps more often, however, it is worse for the sanctioning country when the time span of the action is long. Various benefits of more time to the enemy are clear. Consider first capital goods. A spare parts industry for embargoed capital goods can, and very often actually does, spring up. Even the imported capital goods themselves, not just the spare parts, can become domestic manufactures, though of course at some extra cost that might be very great. If primary product natural resources are embargoed, then domestic production can be increased by tapping old reserves more intensively and by locating and developing new reserves. If that is not possible, then substitutes in supply can be obtained through research.

A main lesson is that our enemies may surprise us with their technical ability. The nitrate embargo against Germany at the outset of World War I is the outstanding example of a surprising response. In the first decade of the twentieth century, the rich nitrate deposits in the Atacama Desert of Chile and the guano islands of Peru were essential for the manufacture of explosives. War machines around the world were dependent on nitrate exports from these countries, which comprised over two-thirds of the world nitrate market just before the outbreak of World War I. Britain's Royal Navy halted all exports of the essential material to Germany. With German artillery firing more shells during the Battle of the Marne in September 1914 than in the whole of the Franco-Prussian War of 1870-71, it was expected that the Wehrmacht would run out of ammunition by the start of 1915. But smart German chemists upset the embargo strategy. At the Oppau plant of the German firm Badische Anilin und Sodafabrik (BASF), a technical break-through by Carl Bosch led to the availability of synthetic nitrates drawn from nitrogen in the air. Germany never lacked for nitrates.[64]

Similar cases include U.S. development of synthetic rubber production after the fall of Southeast Asia in 1942, German production of gasoline from coal in World War II, Biafran "backyard stills" that converted petroleum to gasoline in the Nigerian civil war, and even beet sugar, developed by Napoleon's chemists in response to the British blockade and so keeping French morale high through more than a decade of British blockade.

Alternatively, production might be redesigned to minimize the use of an embargoed input, as in German economizing on ball-bearing use after the massive bombing of their ball-bearing capital, Schweinfurt, in 1943. Economizing and technical improvement explain how even though just four blockade-running steamers managed to get through to Germany in 1942-43, their 8,000 tons of rubber were enough to support a year's synthetic rubber production. Only *one* blockade runner got through in 1944, which never-theless covered German needs for rubber, tungsten, and tin for an entire year.[65]

Pitfalls of Trade Sanctions

Though more use has been made of trade sanctions in recent years, the pit-falls of using them have also become more apparent. This section looks at these pitfalls, using for illustration the experience gained from various recent episodes. The negative side to sanctions has undoubtedly cooled some of the ardor for this harsh policy tool.

TOO MUCH HARM FOR THE INNOCENT? THE EMBARGO OF IRAQ

Under UN auspices, trade sanctions against Iraq were imposed on August 6, 1991, four days after that country invaded and occupied Kuwait. They applied both to exports (mostly oil) and imports.

It was estimated that within five months Iraq's GDP had been cut in half, with most of the effect due to the four million barrels per day of lost oil exports.[66] Iraq's loss of imports was painful to its citizens—too painful, some would say, with a major increase in child mortality and a decrease in health in the Iraqi population.[67] It soon became apparent that Saddam Hussein was fully prepared to countenance the suffering of his own people, which could be used as a propaganda weapon, while available supplies of food, medicine, and other goods could be maintained for the army and government officials. The innocent have paid a heavy price, unfortunately added atop the discomfort of living in a dictatorship; the guilty have suffered little. The sanctions are still in place at the time of writing in 1999, though Iraq is now permitted to export some oil if it uses the revenue to purchase food, medicine, and other non-military goods. The Iraqi case provides an extended test of whether sanctions can in the end alter a country's policy of aggression, and if they do, whether the suffering of innocent victims of the policy is justified by that outcome.

TOO MUCH HARM FOR YOUR OWN EXPORTERS? THE U.S. GRAIN EMBARGO OF THE U.S.S.R. AND HIGH-TECH EXPORTS

Obviously, a country must be careful in sanctioning exports to an enemy. The harm from halting the exports can be both severe and localized. One famous case stemming from Soviet intervention in Afghanistan resulted in a U.S. grain embargo against the Soviet Union, announced by President Carter in January 1980. The U.S. government believed that the grain embargo would be an effective use of sanctions because the U.S.S.R. was suffering at the time from highly erratic grain production due to its underlying economic inefficiencies in agriculture.

The embargo was not a success, however. Although there was a large reduction in exports from the United States, Canada and Argentina raised their own exports enough to make up for the shortfall. U.S. farmers were incensed by the policy and applied enormous political pressure in an attempt to get it reversed. They succeeded. In April 1981, the newly elected President Reagan suddenly lifted the embargo. Thousands of farmers believe to this day that the downturn of American farming that set in during the 1980s can be traced directly to the shift in markets that occurred at the time the shipments were halted. (This judgment is not very credible, by the way. The real harm to exports came later, from the strong dollar and large export subsidies paid by the Common Market countries.)

Similar to the grain embargo, though on a much larger and more protracted scale, are restrictions on high-tech exports such as powerful computers and software with military applications, encryption technology, fiber-optic telecommunications equipment, radars, and the like. For many years, from 1949 until 1994, there was a COCOM (Allied Coordinating Committee for Strategic Export Control), made up of all the NATO nations minus Spain and Iceland, plus Japan and Australia. This organization drew up rules for what constituted strategic equipment banned for export. A large amount of American trade with the Soviet Union, as much as 40% in 1988, required an export license under the COCOM regulations. COCOM's demise did not end controls on the export of strategic goods, though periodic revisions (the last in June 1999) have substantially cut the coverage and streamlined the issue of permits. The United States maintains a long list of controlled items for countries that support international terrorism, and in general the U.S. control measures are stricter and more labyrinthine than those of other countries, but they have also become much more ad hoc and patchwork in nature than formerly. Firms whose exports are restricted complain bitterly, making the point that competitors in countries with easier rules will get the business.

TOO MUCH HARM TO YOUR FOREIGN RELATIONS?
THE PIPELINE WAR, HELMS-BURTON, IRAN, AND LIBYA

A sanctions strategy may anger allies and so be counterproductive. Two prominent examples are the Pipeline War begun by the United States in response to Soviet intervention in Afghanistan (and the troubles in Poland) and the Helms-Burton Law concerning foreign economic relations with Cuba.

The Pipeline War involved the large Siberian natural gas pipeline project that connected the Soviet Union with the Western European gas grid. The Soviets needed imported equipment to build this line. Important U.S. items included in the project were General Electric rotors and nozzles for turbines, and compressors from Dresser Technology. President Reagan embargoed the shipment of these items in December 1981.

At once a major loophole developed: a French nationalized firm, Alsthom-Atlantique, had a license to build the GE rotors and moved to supply them. President Reagan closed the loophole with a stern executive decree stating that European firms with an American controlling interest or firms that had a licensing agreement with U.S. firms were prohibited from delivering the listed products. The list was soon expanded to include oil and gas equipment even where contracts had already been signed. About seven subsidiaries and 13 licensees were affected by the regulations, which made them subject to a $100,000 fine per item shipped or a prison term of 10 years for their executives. This extraterritorial application of U.S. law incensed its European allies, which argued that the gas purchase was their own business and no one else's. They quickly dusted off their long-standing laws forbidding a foreign government from dictating commercial policy to a national firm and in 1982 issued a series of direct orders to such firms to ignore the American ban. Checkmated, the United States in November 1982 abruptly lifted the poorly designed sanctions. The application of U.S. law against European manufacturing and engineering firms, retroactively and outside U.S. territory, seemed certain to be taken as a threat to national sovereignty, and so it was.

Extraterritoriality (the enforcement of a country's laws outside its own boundaries) and the anger of friends are also themes of U.S. trade policy toward Cuba. Between 1963 and 1975, U.S. law prohibited not only U.S. firms, but also the foreign subsidiaries of these firms, from trading with Cuba. Foreign countries reacted coldly; some required subsidiaries operating within their borders to ignore the law, much like the Pipeline War described above. To defuse the growing dispute, Congress repealed the law. But then in 1992, mainly because of the political situation in south Florida, U.S. law was tightened to prohibit trade by foreign subsidiaries. The new law also prohibited ships from moving cargo to or from U.S. ports for six months after a call in Cuba. Britain rapidly issued a blocking order stating that Britain, not the United States, would determine whether British companies would trade with Cuba. Many other countries, including Canada and much of Latin America, protested that the move violated their sovereignty.[68]

Without giving an inch, in March 1996 the United States upped the ante by passing the Helms–Burton Act, named for Senator Jesse Helms of North Carolina and Representative Dan Burton of Indiana. Drawn up after two anti-Castro planes were shot down off the Cuban coast and officially named the "Libertad Act," this law was aimed at foreign firms trading with Cuba. It was thus yet another extraterritorial measure. Helms–Burton bars the sale in the United States of products that contain Cuban components or ingredients, including sugar. It also allows U.S. citizens to sue foreign companies that benefit from property confiscated during and after the Cuban revolution, and bars from entry to the United States executives of firms doing extensive business in Cuba.

As a result of the law, a number of foreign firms divested their holdings in Cuba, deciding that the costs of possible litigation were greater than the costs of the sunk capital in Cuba. Investment in Cuba has clearly been reduced, with the number of joint ventures falling from 74 in 1994 to 42 in 1996. There has been a marked decline in investment by bigger firms, which probably consider themselves vulnerable to potential litigation

But there was a considerable downside for the United States.[69] Canada and the EU have objected very strenuously. Indeed, there was worldwide condemnation of Helms–Burton, with several countries considering blocking laws that could prevent companies from testifying or providing information. A Canadian law of 1997 allows Canadian firms sued in the United States to countersue in Canada against Canadian subsidiaries of U.S. corporations, and also provides that Canada will not recognize U.S. court rulings issued under Helms–Burton.* Even so, Canada has probably cut its investment in Cuba.

---

* In a fine joke, a "Godfrey-Milliken Bill" named for its parliamentary sponsors would permit Canadians to sue in Canadian courts for return of Loyalist property seized by the United States in the Revolutionary War. See Christopher Moore, "Helms-Burton Meet Godfrey-Milliken," *The Beaver*, February/March 1997, 52-53.

Meanwhile, the EU brought a complaint to the WTO, to which the United States responded by announcing it would boycott the proceedings of this panel.

Fortunately, there is a safety valve in Helms–Burton. The President is empowered to issue periodic waivers to the rules concerning lawsuits against foreign companies. President Clinton, who did not favor the bill in the first place though he did sign it, kept peace with America's friends by using this waiver power twice. (The visa denials provision cannot be suspended.) Use of the waiver persuaded the EU to postpone its WTO case and to agree to develop a system to block European firms from acquiring expropriated property. Economists have complained about the vagueness and confusion engendered by the law and its unpredictability. Political scientists have emphasized the damage in foreign relations with allies.

Similar, though less acrimonious than the Cuban imbroglio, has been the Iran and Libya Sanctions Act of 1996.* It continues embargoes against Iran and Libya, with the President allowed to choose the imported products that can be banned, but it also has extraterritorial provisions that have offended allies. These provisions require U.S. sanctions on foreign companies that invest over $40 million per year in the oil and gas industries of the two countries. The President must impose two of six sanctions on any company that does so, two of which are denial of access to loans from U.S. banks and a ban on access to American goods and technology that must be sold under license.

When the Belgian Firm TOTAL decided to invest in developing an Iranian oil field, the U.S. moved to use the law. But the EU vowed to retaliate and threatened WTO action. The Clinton administration found a way to back down in 1998, having been given cover when an agreement was signed with the EU withdrawing its case from the WTO and the United States promising to waive sanctions against firms that invest in energy projects in Iran or Libya.[70]

TOO MUCH FRAGMENTATION: REGIONAL
AND LOCAL GOVERNMENT USE OF SANCTIONS

In some countries, particularly the United States and Canada but also some others such as Switzerland, regional and local governments have been attempting sanctions policies of their own. Proponents of these local policies no doubt always feel strongly about the issues involved, but the fragmentation to national trade policy that ensues undoubtedly adds complexity and unpredictability to already difficult issues.

Recently, for example, the states of New York and Pennsylvania had sanctions against companies that invested in Northern Ireland; Ann Arbor,

---

* By executive order in May 1995, President Clinton had already banned U.S. trade with Iran, including all imports, all exports except humanitarian items such as donated medicine and food, and all investment.

Los Angeles, and the state of Massachusetts against dealings with Myanmar/ Burma; Berkeley and Oakland, California, against Nigeria; and Dade County, Florida, against Cuba. About 30 cities, including Seattle, San Francisco, and Boulder, Colorado, in the United States, Toronto, Montreal, and Vancouver in Canada, and Geneva in Switzerland, have passed resolutions defending the right of city governments to engage in such activities.[71]

Limiting Sanctions

In recent years, the U.S. Congress has increasingly been inclined to adopt trade boycotts even when they are porous and accomplish little. They are an easy way to take the moral high ground, and if not too much trade is prevented, they can be politically attractive. The whole process is selective in the extreme. For example, the United States never discouraged trade with the vicious dictatorships of Duvalier in Haiti, Somoza in Nicaragua, Idi Amin in Uganda, and dozens of others, nor does it do anything to suppress cigarette exports with their proven ability to kill their buyers.

Perhaps a change is occurring, with the Clinton administration clearly tired of the adverse consequences of a sanctions strategy that it does not fully support in the first place. A bill to limit the use of sanctions was in the U.S. Congress in 1998 and again in 1999. President Clinton proposes cost–benefit analysis to judge the effectiveness of proposed sanctions, an annual review of all sanctions in place, an automatic two-year sunset clause, and a major effort to redesign sanctions policy to minimize damage to one's own interests. Economists everywhere would likely lead the applause if this were done.

VOCABULARY AND CONCEPTS

Airbus	*Keiretsu*	Trade adjustment
Car and car parts disputes	Managed trade	assistance
COCOM	MITI	Trade sanctions
Helms–Burton law	Pipeline War	VIES
JETRO	Strategic trade policy	

QUESTIONS

1. Explain the case for the government acting as a visible hand, choosing which industry to promote and thereby gaining scale or learning advantages.
2. Explain why Brown and Hogendorn remain skeptical of government's effectiveness, despite the theoretical considerations.

3. The rent-capture argument is on the surface a strong one, yet it is hard to find good examples. Why is that?

4. To what extent is the charge correct that unusual barriers to trade block imports to Japan?

5. Debate the pros and cons of the *keiretsu* form of organization.

5. "Trade adjustment assistance is only a second-best choice. In some senses it is unfair, and in many instances it is ineffective." Explain what the statement means and comment on what a better choice might be.

6. There was considerable talk in Canada before the signing of the Free Trade Agreement that Canada would establish a trade adjustment system second to none, yet nothing has been done. Given the experience of the United States and other countries, what might be the problems in establishing such a system, and why might the government (and opposition for that matter) let it fall low in their priorities?

6. Does the United States have an adequate adjustment assistance program?

7. Given the "Brown-Hogendorn Requirements" for successful trade warfare, would you say that the embargo against [whatever country we are now embargoing—say Serbia] will work? Why or why not?

8. Discuss the extraterritoriality problem, noting why it is so contentious and explaining the major cases.

NOTES

1. For details, see Kenneth Flamm, *Mismanaged Trade?: Strategic Policy and the Semiconductor Industry* (Washington: Brookings Institution, 1996); Laura D'Andrea Tyson, *Who's Bashing Whom? Trade Conflict in High-Technology Industries* (Washington: Institute for International Economics, 1992), ch. 4; Michael G. Borrus, *Competing for Control: America's Stake in Microelectronics* (Cambridge, Mass.: Harper Business, 1988); Kenneth Flamm, *Creating the Computer: Government, Industry, and High Technology* (Washington: Brookings Institution, 1988); Michel M. Kostecki, "Electronics Trade Policies in the 1980s," *Journal of World Trade* 23, 1 (February 1989): 17-35; Michael Borrus, Laura D'Andrea Tyson, and John Zysman, "Creating Advantage: How Government Policies Shape International Trade in the Semiconductor Industry," in Paul R. Krugman, ed., *Strategic Trade Policy and the New International Economics* (Cambridge, Mass.: MIT Press, 1986).

2. *International Economic Review,* September 1996.

3. *The Economist,* November 1, 1997.

4. USITC, *The Year in Trade 1992,* 62.

5. See Dominick Salvatore, ed., *National Trade Policies* (New York: Greenwood Press, 1992), which is a description of the strategic trade policies of 22 trading nations. Also see Gene M. Grossman, "Promoting New Industrial Activities: A Survey of Recent Arguments and Evidence," *OECD Economic Studies* 14 (Spring 1990): 87-125.

6. Examples of support in the 1990s for such a U.S. policy include Robert Kuttner, *The End of Laissez-Faire: National Purpose and the Global Economy after the Cold War* (New York: Alfred A. Knopf, 1991); Robert

Reich, *The Work of Nations: Preparing Our-selves for 21st Century Capitalism* (New York: Alfred A. Knopf, 1991); Tyson, *Who's Bashing Whom?* Reich served as Secretary of Labor in the Clinton administration; Tyson was chair of the Council of Economic Advisors.

7. The first academic studies involving these arguments for strategic trade date from the early 1980s. James A. Brander and Barbara J. Spencer were early in this field, with their "Tariff Protection and Imperfect Competition," in H. Kierkowski, ed., *Monopolistic Competition in International Trade* (Oxford: Oxford University Press, 1984). Krugman, ed., *Strategic Trade Policy and the New International Economics*, is a good introduction. Essays by Brander, "Rationales for Strategic Trade and Industrial Policy," and Spencer, "What Should Trade Policy Target?" are included in the volume, as is a skeptical evaluation of the concept by Gene M. Grossman, "Strategic Export Promotion: A Critique." Also skeptical is Jagdish Bhagwati, *The World Trading System at Risk* (Princeton, N.J.: Princeton University Press, 1991). An important work is Robert Z. Lawrence and Charles L. Schultze, eds., *An American Trade Strategy: Options for the 1990s* (Washington: Brookings Institution, 1990). Essays by Rudiger Dornbusch and Laura D'Andrea Tyson are favorably inclined toward managed trade; the view taken by Anne O. Krueger in "Free Trade Is the Best Policy" is different. Robert E. Baldwin agrees. He asks, "Are Economists' Traditional Trade Policy Views Still Valid?" *Journal of Economic Literature* 30, 2 (June 1992): 804-29, and his answer is basically "yes." For empirical work on the success of the policies, see Paul Krugman and Alasdair Smith, eds., *Empirical Studies of Strategic Trade Policy* (Chicago: University of Chicago Press, 1994). Other useful works on the subject are Elhanan Helpman and Paul R. Krugman, *Market Structure and Foreign Trade* (Cambridge, Mass.: MIT Press, 1985); Helpman and Krugman, *Trade Policy and Market Structure* (Cambridge, Mass.: MIT Press, 1989); H.V.

Milner and D.B. Yoffie, "Between Free Trade and Protectionism: Strategic Trade Policy and a Theory of Corporate Trade Demands," *International Organization* 43 (1989): 239-72; Robert M. Stern, ed., *U.S. Trade Policies in a Changing World Economy* (Cambridge, Mass.: MIT Press, 1987), esp. the essays by Paul Krugman, Alan Deardorff and Robert Stern, and Avinash Dixit. A technical approach is John McMillan, *Game Theory in International Economics* (New York: Harwood Academic Publishers, 1986).

8. See Terutomo Ozawa and Mitsuaki Sato, "JETRO, Japan's Adaptive Innovation in the Organization of Trade," *Journal of World Trade* 23, 4 (August 1989): 18-24.

9. *The Economist*, February 1, 1997.

10. Ibid.; TPCC, *The National Export Strategy*, October 1966.

11. See William R. Cline, *International Economic Policy in the 1990s* (Cambridge, Mass.: MIT Press, 1994), 66.

12. George Kleinfeld and David Kaye, "Red Light, Green Light?" *Journal of World Trade* 28, 6 (December 1994): 43-63; *Christian Science Monitor*, May 11, 1993.

13. This is, more or less, the model as depicted by Michael E. Porter, *The Competitive Advantage of Nations* (New York: Free Press, 1990).

14. The subject is a staple of development economics, and a number of important works are available on the emphasis on learning and scale in Asia. See, in particular, World Bank, *The East Asian Miracle: Economic Growth and Public Policy* (New York: Oxford University Press, 1993). Japan is included in the study. Other works include Shirley W.Y. Kuo, *The Taiwan Economy in Transition* (Boulder, Colo.: Westview Press, 1983); David Lim, "Explaining the Growth Performances of Asian Developing Economies," *Economic Development and Cultural Change* 42, 4 (July 1994): 829-44; Harry T. Oshima, "The Transition from an Agricultural to an Industrial Economy in East Asia," *Economic Development and*

Cultural Change 34, 6 (1986): 783-809; Peter A. Petri, "Korea's Export Niche: Origins and Prospects," *World Development* 16, 1 (January 1988): 47-63; Anthony M. Tang and James S. Worley, eds., "Why Does Overcrowded, Resource-Poor East Asia Succeed—Lessons for the LDCs?" a special issue of *Economic Development and Cultural Change* 36, 3 (April 1988) that includes a useful article by Paul W. Kuznets, "An East Asian Model of Economic Development: Japan, Taiwan, and South Korea," S11-S43; Ezra Vogel, *The Four Little Dragons: The Spread of Industrialization in East Asia* (Cambridge, Mass., 1991); Robert Wade, *Governing the Market: Economic Theory and the Role of Government in East Asian Industrialization* (Princeton, N.J.: Princeton University Press, 1991); Peter G. Warr, ed., *The Thai Economy in Transition* (Cambridge: Cambridge University Press, 1993). There are special sections in *The Economist*, November 16, 1991, and October 10, 1992.

15. The example is taken from Paul R. Krugman, "Is Free Trade Passé?" *Economic Perspectives* 1, 2 (Fall 1987): 131-44.

16. Ten studies are surveyed by J. David Richardson, "Empirical Research on Trade Liberalization with Imperfect Competition: A Survey," *OECD Economic Studies* 12 (Spring 1989): 8-44. Krugman's comments are in Paul Krugman, *Peddling Prosperity* (New York: W.W. Norton, 1994), 245-67.

17. See Steven McGuire, *Airbus Industrie: Conflict and Cooperation in U.S.-EC Trade Relations* (London: Macmillan, 1997); John Olienyk and Robert Carbaugh, "Competition in the World Jetliner Industry," *Challenge* 42, 4 (July-August 1999): 60-81; Richard Pomfret, "The New Trade Theories, Rent-Snatching, and Jet Aircraft," *The World Economy* 14 (1991): 269-77; *The Economist*, July 8, 1995.

18. Olienyk and Carbaugh, "Competition in the World Jetliner Industry," 67.

19. *The Economist*, March 27, 1999; USITC, *The Year in Trade 1992*, 50-51; 1993, 30.

20. *Wall Street Journal*, April 28, 1997.

21. *The Economist*, May 17, 1997, July 26, 1997.

22. *Wall Street Journal*, April 20, 1999. The aviation journal *Air International* gives frequent coverage to the new designs. See especially the April 1998 issue.

23. For the background to this research, which amounts to a type of "prisoners' dilemma," see Thomas Schelling, *The Strategy of Conflict* (Cambridge, Mass.: Harvard University Press, 1960); Howard Raiffa, *The Art and Science of Negotiation* (Cambridge, Mass.: Belknap Press, 1982). The experiments referred to in the text were conducted by Robert Axelrod. See the review of the work in J. David Richardson, "The New Political Economy of Trade Policy," in Krugman, ed., *Strategic Trade Policy*.

24. Rachel McCulloch, "The Optimality of Free Trade: Science or Religion?" *American Economic Review* 83, 2 (May 1993): 367-71, and see Paul Krugman, "Does the New Trade Theory Require a New Trade Policy," *World Economy* 15 (July 1992): 423-42.

25. See Peter A.G. van Bergeijk and Dick L. Kabel, "Strategic Trade Theories and Trade Policy," *Journal of World Trade* 27, 6 (December 1993): 175-86.

26. There is a wealth of material on which to draw. Recent studies include C. Fred Bergsten and Marcus Noland, *Reconcilable Differences? United States-Japan Economic Conflict* (Washington: Institute for International Economics, 1993); Scott Callon, *Divided Sun: MITI and the Breakdown of Japanese High-tech Industrial Policy, 1975-1993* (Stanford, Calif.: Stanford University Press, 1995); Stephen D. Cohen, *An Ocean Apart: Explaining Three Decades of U.S.-Japanese Trade Frictions* (Westport, Conn.: Praeger, 1998); Mark Fruin, *The Japanese Enterprise System: Competitive Strategies and Cooperative Structures* (Oxford: Oxford University Press, 1992); Takatoshi Ito,

"Japan's Economy Needs Structural Change," *Finance and Development* (June 1997): 16-19; Chalmers A. Johnson, *MITI and the Japanese Miracle: The Growth of Industrial Policy, 1925-1975* (Stanford, Calif.: Stanford University Press, 1982); Paul Krugman, ed., *Trade With Japan: Has the Door Opened Wider?* (Chicago: University of Chicago Press, 1991); Robert Z. Lawrence, "Efficient or Exclusionist? The Import Behavior of Japanese Corporate Groups," *Brookings Papers on Economic Activity* 1 (1991): 311-41; Edward J. Lincoln, *Japan's Unequal Trade* (Washington: Brookings Institution, 1990); Okabe Mitsuaki, ed., *The Structure of the Japanese Economy: Changes on the Domestic and International Fronts* (New York, 1995); Pietro S. Navola, Regulating Unfair Trade (Washington: Brookings Institution, 1993); D.I. Okimoto, *Between MITI and the Market: Japanese Industrial Policy for High Technology* (Stanford, Calif.: Stanford University Press, 1989); Clyde Prestowitz, *Trading Places: How We Allowed Japan to Take the Lead* (New York: Basic Books, 1988); Gary R. Saxonhouse, "What Does Japanese Trade Structure Tell Us About Japanese Trade Policy," *Journal of Economic Perspectives* 7, 3 (Summer 1993): 21-43; Michael Smitka, ed., *Japanese Prewar Growth: Lessons for Development Theory?* (New York: Garland, 1998); Mark Tilton, *Restrained Trade: Cartels in Japan's Basic Materials Industries* (Ithaca, N.Y.: Cornell University Press, 1996); Tyson, *Who's Bashing Whom?*; Robert M. Uriu, *Troubled Industries: Confronting Economic Change in Japan* (Ithaca, N.Y.: Cornell University Press, 1996); articles in the *Atlantic Monthly* by James Fallows, 1989; and numerous articles in *The Economist, Wall Street Journal, New York Times,* and *International Economic Review,* as well as all recent editions of USITC, *The Year in Trade,* annual.

27. Following Bergsten and Noland, *Reconcilable Differences? United States-Japan Economic Conflict,* 7.

28. McCulloch, "The Optimality of Free Trade."

29. Paraphrasing Kozo Yamamura, "Caveat Emptor: The Industrial Policy of Japan," in Krugman, ed., *Strategic Trade Policy,* 201.

30. Richard Beason and David Weinstein, "Growth, Economics of Scale, and Targeting in Japan (1955-90)," Harvard Institute of Economic Research Discussion Paper No. 1644, 1994. Also see the table in Ali M. El-Agraa, "U.K. Competitiveness Policy versus Japanese Industrial Policy," *Economic Journal* 107, 444 (September 1997): 1509.

31. El-Agraa, "U.K. Competitiveness Policy versus Japanese Industrial Policy," 1504-17.

32. Bergsten and Noland, *Reconcilable Differences? United States-Japan Economic Conflict,* 188; Margaret Kelly and Anne Kenny McGuirk, *Issues and Developments in International Trade Policy* (Washington, 1992), 23.

33. *Christian Science Monitor,* May 18, 1994.

34. See David E. Weinstein, "Foreign Direct Investment and *Keiretsu*: Rethinking U.S. and Japanese Policy," in Robert C. Feenstra, ed., *The Effects of U.S. Trade Protection and Promotion Policies* (Chicago: University of Chicago Press, 1997), 81-116.

35. "Update on Japan's Distribution System," *International Economic Review,* August 1993.

36. *The Economist,* January 11, 1997, and October 29, 1994.

37. For the *keiretsu,* in addition to the sources cited below, see P.A. Geroski, "Vertical Relations Between Firms and Industrial Policy," *Economic Journal* 102, 410 (January 1992): 138-47; Lawrence, "Efficient or Exclusionist?"

38. Wilson B. Brown, "Firm-like Behaviour in Markets," in Martin Carter, Mark Casson, and Vivek Suneja, eds., *The Economics of Marketing* (Cheltenham: Edward Elgar, forthcoming).

39. See Weinstein, "Foreign Direct Investment and Keiretsu."

40. For analysis of the advantageous relationship between automobile producers and parts suppliers, see Michael J. Smitka, *Subcontracting in the Japanese Automotive Industry* (New York: Columbia University Press, 1991).

41. Robert Z. Lawrence, "Japan's Different Trade Regime: An Analysis with Particular Reference to Keiretsu," *Journal of Economic Perspectives* 7, 3 (Summer 1993): 3-19, esp. 13-16. Also see Bergsten and Noland, *Reconcilable Differences? United States-Japan Economic Conflict*, 74-75, 182-83.

42. See *International Economic Review*, March 1995

43. *The Economist*, June 22, 1996; *Wall Street Journal*, May 24, June 1, 1996, December 8, 1997; *International Economic Review*, February/March 1997.

44. Bergsten and Noland, *Reconcilable Differences? United States-Japan Economic Conflict*, 78, 214. For discussions of extraterritorial application of antitrust law and much more concerning market structure and trade, see F.M. Scherer, *Competition Policies for an Integrated World Economy* (Washington: Brookings Institution, 1994); Edward M. Graham and J. David Richardson, eds., *Global Competition Policy* (Washington: Institute for International Economics, 1997); Einar Hope, ed., *Competition and Trade Policies: Coherence or Conflict?* (London: Routledge, 1998).

45. *Wall Street Journal*, December 12, 1995.

46. *The Economist*, October 23, 1993; Bergsten and Noland, *Reconcilable Differences? United States-Japan Economic Conflict*, 78.

47. *International Economic Review*, July 1995; Bergsten and Noland, *Reconcilable Differences? United States-Japan Economic Conflict*, 185.

48. See Associated Press story, February 8, 1994.

49. For the dispute and the subsequent agreement, see *International Economic Review*, July 1995; *The Economist*, April 22, July 1, 1995; *Wall Street Journal*, April 19, April 20, August 24, 1995; *Christian Science Monitor*, April 28, November 13, 1995.

50. Gary Burtless, "International Trade and the Rise in Earnings Inequality," *Journal of Economic Literature* 33 (June 1995): 806.

51. For details, see David A. Brauer and Susan Hickox, "Explaining the Growing Inequality in Wages Across Skill Levels," *Federal Reserve Bank of New York Economic Policy Review* 1, 1 (January 1995): 61-72; Richard B. Freeman, "Are Your Wages Set in Beijing?" *Journal of Economic Perspectives* 9, 3 (Summer 1995): 15-32; Chinhui Juhn and Kevin M. Murphy, "Inequality in Labor Market Outcomes: Contrasting the 1980s and Earlier Decades," *Federal Reserve Bank of New York Economic Policy Review* 1, 1 (January 1995): 26-32; J. David Richardson, "Income Inequality and Trade: How to Think, What to Conclude," *Journal of Economic Perspectives* 9, 3 (Summer 1995): 33-55.

52. The effect of international trade on wages is a major research topic. We consulted the following: Freeman, "Are Your Wages Set in Beijing?"; Robert Z. Lawrence, "U.S. Wage Trends in the 1980s: The Role of International Factors," *Federal Reserve Bank of New York Economic Policy Review* 1, 1 (January 1995): 18-25; Robert Z. Lawrence and Matthew Slaughter, "International Trade and American Wages in the 1980s: Giant Sucking Sound or Small Hiccup," *Brookings Papers on Economic Activity, Microeconomics* (1993): 161-226; Edward E. Leamer, "Wage Inequality from International Competition and Technological Change: Theory and Country Experience," *American Economic Review Papers and Proceedings* (May 1996): 309-11; Jeffery Sachs and Howard Shatz, "Trade and Jobs in U.S. Manufacturing," *Brookings Papers on Economic Activity* 1 (1994): 1-84; Adrian Wood, "How Trade Hurt Unskilled Workers," *Journal of Economic Perspectives* 9, 3 (Summer 1995): 57-80; Adrian Wood, *North-South Trade, Employment and Inequality* (Oxford: Clarendon Press, 1994).

53. Max Dupuy and Mark E. Schweitzer, "Are Service-Sector Jobs Inferior?" Federal Reserve Bank of Cleveland *Economic Commentary*, February 1, 1994.

54. A figure of 5% is cited by Charles F. Stone and Isabel V. Sawhill, "Trade's Impact on U.S. Jobs," *Challenge* 30, 4 (September/October 1987): 12-18.

55. An annual statistical update on how many are aided and how is in USITC, *The Year in Trade*. See the 1997 issue, 128-29.

56. See Council of Economic Advisors, *Economic Report of the President 1999* (Washington, 1999), 127-29.

57. *The Economist*, April 6, 1996.

58. See Gary Burtless, Robert Lawrence, Robert Litan, and Robert Shapiro, *Globaphobia* (Washington: Brookings Institution, 1998); *The Economist*, October 3, 1998; *Rushford Report*, May 1998.

59. You can see for yourself at http://www.ajb.dni.us/

60. For many details and points of analysis in this section we relied on Gary Clyde Hufbauer, Jeffrey J. Schott, and Kimberly Ann Elliott, *Economic Sanctions Reconsidered: History and Current Policy* and the companion *Supplemental Case Histories,* 2nd ed. (Washington: Institute for International Economics, 1990), and on an update by Elliott and Hufbauer, "Same Song, Same Refrain? Economic Sanctions in the 1990's," *American Economic Review* 89, 2 (May 1999): 403-08. Also H. Peter Gray and Roy E. Licklider, "International Trade Warfare: Economic and Political Strategic Considerations," *European Journal of Political Economy* 1, 4 (1985): 563-83; Makio Miyagawa, *Do Economic Sanctions Work?* (New York: St. Martin's Press, 1993); Y. Wu, *Economic Warfare* (New York: Macmillan, 1952).

61. Norman Polmar and Thomas B. Allen, *World War II: America at War 1941-1945* (New York: Random House, 1991).

62. See Robert W. McGee, "Trade Embargoes, Sanctions and Blockades," *Journal of World Trade* 32, 4 (August 1998): 139-44.

63. Elliott and Hufbauer, "Same Song, Same Refrain? Economic Sanctions in the 1990's," 404.

64. For details, see Gerd Hardach, T*he First World War, 1914-1918* (Berkeley: University of California Press, 1977), 31, 59, 266, 268-71.

65. Gerhard L. Weinberg, *The World At Arms* (New York: Cambridge University Press, 1994), 400-01.

66. *Christian Science Monitor*, April 10, 1991.

67. For this case, see McGee, "Trade Embargoes, Sanctions and Blockades," 141.

68. *International Economic Review*, December 1992.

69. Our thanks to Professor Kenneth A. Rodman of Colby College for information from his yet-unpublished paper on the topic.

70. *Wall Street Journal*, May 19, September 9, 1998; USITC, *The Year in Trade 1997*, 100.

71. *Public Citizen* 19, 3 (May/June 1999).

Chapter Nine

Economic Integration

OBJECTIVES

OVERALL OBJECTIVE   To evaluate whether preferential trade agreements (PTAs) improve world welfare, or even the welfare of their participants, examining in theory and practice what leads to high benefits and what leads to high costs.

MORE SPECIFICALLY
- To show what kinds of PTAs exist in theory, law, and actuality.
- To show what makes a PTA trade-creating or trade-diverting.
- To assess the economic effects of the European Union, the North American Free Trade Agreement, and numerous arrangements involving developing countries, exploring why they do or do not work.
- To look at foreign trade zones as partial moves toward freer trade.

....

Economic integration is the process of joining together two or more countries into a closer economic union than each has with the rest of the world.[1] Typically, economic integration begins with a preferential arrangement in which tariffs and non-tariff barriers are abolished among the nations involved, but not with the rest of the world. Economic integration, however, can also involve freedom of resource movement, common economic policies, even a common money. Both in theory and in practice, integration raises important economic issues that can cause surprises.

THE TYPES OF ECONOMIC INTEGRATION

Economic integration is hardly new, with some agreements dating back to the Middle Ages and even before. Chapter 4 noted that internal tolls and tariffs were once common, with their abolition (United States, 1789; Austria, 1775; France, 1790; Prussia, 1816) serving as important steps in nation-building.

The first great move to economic integration among a group of independent nations was the German *Zollverein* (customs union) of 1834. Dozens of separate national territories existed in what is now Germany; only in 1871 were they unified politically under Bismarck. Before that, each government enforced its own separate tariffs. Follow a wagonload of goods from Paris, France, to Warsaw, then in Russia, in the year 1830. If the wagon master takes the straightest road, he will face customs at the following borders: Kingdom of Prussia (Rhine Province), Duchy of Nassau, Prussian enclave of Wetzlar, Grand Duchy of Hesse, Electoral Hesse, then three tiny Thuringian statelets so obscure they are not named on any of our historical atlases, then Prussia's province of Saxony, then the Kingdom of Saxony, and once more into Prussia, the fourth time the wagon master has had to pass Prussian customs.[2] Every stop meant delay and red tape, though it is true that most of these states allowed the wagon to transit without paying duty or allowed a *drawback* (refund) when it left the country concerned. Prussia, however, was notorious for its *transit duties*—a payment to allow goods to cross its territory. (Transit duties were abolished by the Barcelona Treaty of 1921.) The *Zollverein* brought complete internal free trade to most of the region.* It greatly increased trade, transformed these once-impoverished economies, and understandably received an ecstatic welcome from the German population.

When GATT was established, a portentous decision was taken to allow preferential trading arrangements as one of only two permitted exceptions to the rule that most-favored-nation treatment must be applied to tariffs. (The other exception is that tariffs can be lowered or abolished by rich countries in favor of poor ones.) The rule continues under the WTO. But the right to give preferences was subject to two restrictions: (1) the agreement must not "on the whole" result in barriers that are more restrictive to outside exporters than the barriers that had existed before; and (2) trade barriers must be eliminated on "substantially all trade" among the members of an agreement within "a reasonable length of time." The clear meaning of the second restriction is that though countries can *eliminate* their barriers against the other members, they *cannot* under the rules of international trade cut them by less than 100% for

---

* Several states in north Germany stayed out for a decade or two, while the last holdouts, the free cities of Hamburg and Bremen, were not included until the German Empire was formed in 1871. The exclusion of Austria was a major component in the struggle between Austria and Prussia for predominance in Central Europe.

more than a transitional period. Yet these rules have in practice not had much importance. The quoted passages, "on the whole," "substantially all," and "reasonable length of time," have provided wide latitude for arrangements to do much as they please, and neither GATT nor the WTO has ever formally objected to a single agreement.[3]

Examples of economic integration under the GATT (and now the WTO) rules began to appear in the 1950s. Once rare, they have now proliferated, with well over a hundred arrangements of various types having been formed by the mid-1990s, and with 76 in existence at that time.[4] (It may seem odd that 180-odd countries could have as many as 76 preferential trade agreements, but that is easily explained. Many arrangements overlap and most are bilateral rather than multilateral. Only about 30 are "important.") The fastest growth in PTAs has been in the 1990s, which have seen the formation of over half of them—for reasons not always altogether laudable, as we shall see.

Preferential Trade Agreements:
Free Trade Areas, Customs Unions, and Common Markets

In general, economic integration involves preferential trade agreements, or PTAs. There are important differences in the types of PTAs, however. In a *free trade area*, the members eliminate their tariffs against one another, but maintain their own national protective barriers against outsiders. In Figure 9.1a, each country has its own trade barriers, their strength indicated by the thickness of the circles. In 9.1b, a free trade area has been formed, with internal free trade but the same old barriers against the rest of the world. The members need supplementary regulations dealing with country-of-origin rules; otherwise, goods will be shipped

Figure 9.1

FORMING A FREE TRADE AREA

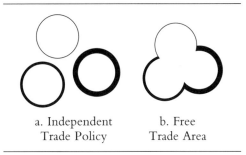

a. Independent
Trade Policy

b. Free
Trade Area

from the outside into the lowest-tariff nation and then exported to members with higher tariffs. Such rules will ordinarily specify how much value must be added in the low-tariff country to qualify the good for onward shipment to other members at a zero rate. This, of course, creates economic inefficiencies by encouraging processing within the low-tariff country.

For many years, the best-known free trade area was the European Free Trade Association (EFTA) made up of the European countries that did not join the original Common Market. EFTA is now a shadow of its former self because so many of its members eventually entered the EU. It now consists of just Switzerland, Liechtenstein, Iceland, and Norway.* The outstanding example at present is NAFTA, the North American Free Trade Agreement among Canada, Mexico, and the United States. MERCOSUR (Mercado Comun del Sur) in South America (Argentina, Brazil, Paraguay, Uruguay) is another well-known example.

A *customs union* is more ambitious. Instead of the differences in protection against outsiders that characterize a free trade area, a customs union has a common external tariff against goods entering any of the members from the outside. Figures 9.2a and 9.2b illustrate the change from three independent tariff structures to that of a customs union with a common external tariff that is approxi-

Figure 9.2

A "COMMON EXTERNAL TARIFF"
DISTINGUISHES A CUSTOMS UNION

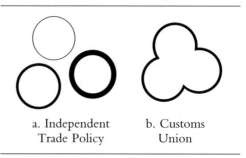

a. Independent
Trade Policy

b. Customs
Union

mately the average of the countries' rates before the union. The European Union started as a customs union. (Note that the term "customs union" was once used more broadly to mean any preferential trade agreement, and many writers use the term in the old way. In this book, customs unions have their more specific meaning.)

A *common market* is a customs union but carries the additional provision that capital and labor move freely within it. The original European Common Market, later called the European Community (EC), was the most famous of the common markets, but it took years for the term to be fully justified. Only after reforms adopted in 1992 did the members enlarge upon free trade to include free movement of workers and capital, as when Italian workers take jobs in Germany and German capital flows to Italy. The EC then became a true common market.

Finally, *economic union* goes beyond a common market to include fixed exchange rates among the members' currencies and requirements for monetary and fiscal policies to support the stability of these rates. A union may go even further by adopting a common currency. In addition, an economic union will usually involve coordinated public policies for the transfer of revenues from richer to poorer areas, for agricultural policy, and so on. In the 1990s the EC took steps that moved it toward full union and changed its name

---

* In 1994 EFTA (minus Switzerland and Lichtenstein which opted out of the arrangement) joined the EU in forming a European Economic Area. This is a free trade area in that the separate EFTA members retain their individual national barriers against outsiders.

to European Union or EU. In 2002, some of the membership will end their own currencies in favor of the new money, known as the euro, but other members will not be using the euro, at least not at first. The European Union will not be a fully accurate name for a number of years yet.

THE GREAT DEBATE:
TRADE CREATION OR TRADE DIVERSION

For many years, economists believed that any economic integration would be beneficial. Free trade was the optimum, and free trade areas and customs unions represented a movement toward free trade. Therefore, the integration must increase welfare. Well into the twentieth century, an adequate theory did not exist to explain the economic impact of integration. Few questioned the conclusion that it was a good thing, but in fact no one had made a rigorous study of the subject and the literature covering it was scant.

Then came a striking theoretical development, in 1950, when Jacob Viner showed in his book, *The Customs Union Issue,* that the standard opinion was not necessarily correct and that under certain circumstances economic integration could result in a reduction of welfare.* Viner's conclusion illustrates what came to be known as the paradox of the second best. This paradox, first put in print by Richard Lipsey and Kelvin J. Lancaster of the London School of Economics, states that although a first-best course of action *must* optimize welfare, the second-best course of action may *not* increase welfare (something like jumping 99% of the way across a canyon).

Table 9.1
NO CUSTOMS UNION, 200% TARIFF IN X

	in X	*in Y*	*in Z*
Cost of wheat	$2.00	$1.50	$1.00
Tariff in X	———	$3.00	$2.00
Price in X	$2.00	$4.50	$3.00

How can this be so? All along, people had assumed that integration would allow lower-priced imports from a trading partner to replace higher-priced domestic output, thus increasing welfare. Viner showed this could indeed be the case, as is demonstrated in modified form in Table 9.1. Case 1 presents the price of wheat in three countries, X, Y, and Z. To protect its domestic producers, X has a tariff of 200%. At that tariff, not even Z, with its low

---

* Notice that Viner used the term customs union in its general sense of a preferential trade area.

production cost of $1, can compete in X with X's $2 wheat. Assuming constant production costs for the present, it is certain that all of X's wheat is purchased at home.

Now X forges a customs union with Y, as Table 9.2 shows. The union lowers Y's price to consumers in X, so that they shift their purchases to Y, leaving X's farmers to grow something else. Assuming full employment, X is clearly better off producing something else and importing wheat from Y, the low-cost producer.

Table 9.2

AFTER CUSTOMS UNION, 200% TARIFF IN X

	in X	*in Y*	*in Z*
Cost of wheat	$2.00	$1.50	$1.00
Tariff in X	——	——	$2.00
Price in X	$2.00	$1.50	$3.00

Viner called this type of arrangement a "trade-creating customs union," and so it is, with trade in wheat replacing domestic production. Today we would speak of it as being a customs union that had only a trade-creation effect. Of course, X would have been even better off if Z had been included in the customs union, but the welfare of X is nevertheless improved, while the welfare of Z is unaffected.

Table 9.3

NO CUSTOMS UNION, 90% TARIFF IN X

	in X	*in Y*	*in Z*
Cost of wheat	$2.00	$1.50	$1.00
Tariff in X	——	$1.35	$0.90
Price in X	$2.00	$2.85	$1.90

Consider, however, that this case is only one possibility, and that the result would be very different if the level of the tariff is changed. In Tables 9.3 and 9.4, substitute a 90% tariff for the 200% tariff.

Before the customs union, the cheapest wheat in X was that imported from Z, hence X's farmers did not grow wheat and Z enjoyed X's wheat market. With the signing of a customs union with Y, however, a curious thing occurs: Y's price to X's consumers falls below Z's, so that X *diverts* its trade from Z, the lowest-cost supplier, to Y, a higher-cost supplier. People in X may think they are getting wheat more cheaply—the price for them is down 40¢ per

Table 9.4

AFTER CUSTOMS UNION, 90% TARIFF IN X

	in X	*in Y*	*in Z*
Cost of wheat	$2.00	$1.50	$1.00
Tariff in X	——	——	$0.90
Price in X	$2.00	$1.50	$1.90

bushel from the $1.90 they used to pay for imports from Z. But they have forgotten that their government was collecting 90¢ per bushel in tariff revenue, 50¢ of which is now lost and 40¢ of which goes to the consumer. The world has seen wheat that cost $1 supplanted by wheat that uses up $1.50 in resources. Viner called this a "trade-diverting customs union," in which trade has been diverted from a more efficient to a less efficient producer.

Diagramming Trade Creation and Trade Diversion

Later research concentrated on further explorations of trade creation and trade diversion.[5] Viner had focused attention on changes in production, but diagrammatical analysis soon made it apparent that the effects of a customs union could be more complex. The partial equilibrium model of the gains from trade and harm from tariffs illuminates this issue.

Figure 9.3 illustrates the customs union effect. It shows country X's demand and supply curves and the price of wheat imported from Y and Z. Country X has increasing costs, as indicated by the positively sloped supply curve. For illustrative clarity, Y and Z have constant costs. (Perhaps that is because they are large countries unaffected by trade with X, or perhaps it is just that the diagram gets very messy without this assumption.) P_z is the price of Z's wheat before a tariff, and P_y is Y's wheat price. The tariff, a specific duty amounting to T, can be added to both P_z and P_y, giving $P_z + T$ and $P_y + T$.

With no tariff at all, M_1 is produced in country X, M_6 is consumed, and M_1M_6 is imported. There will be no imports from Y, and in fact very little production in X. After the tariff, country Z with its price $P_z + T$ is still the lowest-cost supplier. X's production expands to M_3 and its consumption declines to M_4, these being the usual effects of a tariff.

Now a customs union opens between X and Y. The price of Y's wheat falls to P_y, below $P_z + T$, and trade is thus diverted to Y. The lower price and greater quantity traded lead to a gain in consumers' surplus, which is the triangular area above the price but below the demand curve. The triangle of consumers' surplus has expanded to an area larger by $A + B + C + D$, because the price has fallen and the quantity has increased.

Figure 9.3
A TRADE-DIVERTING CUSTOMS UNION

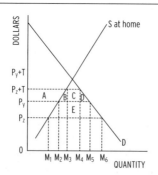

Note: P_y is the price of the good from the partner country and P_z from the outsider. The gain from the customs union is $B + D$, the elimination of some deadweight loss. The loss to the customs union is the higher costs from producing in the partner country, or E. Under the conditions of a great difference in cost between partner and outsider ($P_y > P_z$), a high tariff ($P_z + T$), and inelastic demand and supply curves, B and D are small and E is large.

But this is not an unadulterated gain for society. Country X's own domestic producers are harmed by the lower price; their producers' surplus is reduced by area A. Tariff revenue is also down. Country X had been collecting tariffs on its imports, but does so no longer on the imports from Y, its fellow member in the customs union. This lost tariff revenue is equal to areas $C + E$, which is found by multiplying the tariff T by the quantity of imports M_3M_4. C is redistributed to consumers, but not E, which must be used to pay Y's higher costs. In short, there is a welfare gain comprising $A + B + C + D$, and a welfare loss to society of $A + C + E$.

The net result is determined by comparing the little triangles B and D to the rectangle E. If B and D are larger than E, then gains in consumer surplus outweigh lost producers' surplus and lost tariff revenue. The customs union thus creates more trade than it diverts; it enhances welfare. But the reverse case, with E larger than $B + D$, shows reduced welfare in a customs union that is on balance trade-diverting. In Figure 9.3, trade diversion obviously predominates, with $B + D$ smaller in size than area E. Rectangle E represents not only country X's loss, but world loss. It shows the additional resources used in producing wheat in Y; or, to use the numbers given earlier, the 50¢ per bushel additional cost for Y's wheat.

By contrast, Figure 9.4 shows a trade-creating customs union. Again, the gain in consumers' surplus is $A + B + C + D$. Again the lost producers' surplus is A; again tariff revenue falls by $C + E$. But here the net gain is great because triangles $B + D$ are far larger than area E. Trade creation predominates; trade diversion is minor; welfare is enhanced.

Make careful note of the two main characteristics of the figure that cause $B + D$ to exceed E, so giving rise to trade creation. (1) The supply and demand curves are highly elastic. The extra flatness of these elastic curves will, if price falls, cut domestic output sharply and also increase consumption greatly, thereby raising imports by a substantial amount. See in Figure 9.4

398

Figure 9.4
A TRADE-CREATING CUSTOMS UNION

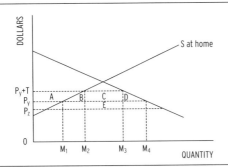

Note: As in Figure 9.3, the partner country has a price (cost) of P_y and the outside country P_z; the tariff is P_z + T. Because the demand and supply in the home country are highly elastic, and the fall in price large, B and D are large. Because there is not much difference between the price in country Y and country Z, E is small. The customs union creates more trade than it destroys.

how imports rise substantially after a customs union, from M_2M_3 to M_1M_4. The larger volume of trade increases consumer surplus. The flatter curves serve to raise the size of B and D. (2) The price in the home country X differs greatly from its partner in the customs union, Y; and at the same time the difference is small between the partner's price P_y and the price P_z in the lowest-cost non-member in the outside world, Z. Note in Figure 9.4 that Y's price is indeed close to Z's price, so that little trade diversion is possible.

A General Tariff Reduction Beats a PTA: The Cooper-Massell Demonstration

C.A. Cooper and B.F. Massell have demonstrated, using Viner-type diagramming, that a general tariff reduction will have better effects on welfare than will forming a customs union.[6] The tariff can be set at the level that will generate the same amount of trade creation that a customs union will. In Figure 9.5, the tariff on Z's goods is set so that the price of imports from Z is P_z + T', the same as the price P_y that Y's goods would have cost if a PTA had been formed with Y. The imports from Z will generate tariff revenue, while if there had been a PTA the imports from Y would not have done so. See how imports from country Z at tariff P_z + T' would mean imports of M_2M_5 times a tariff T' (the distance from P_z to P_z + T'), giving a rectangle of tariff revenue equal to FEG. Since the quantity of imports from Z is the same as would have come from Y if there had been a PTA, there is no trade diversion. Lowering the tariff against all countries including Z would cause consumer surplus to rise by $A + B + C + D$, producer surplus to fall by A, and tariff revenue to go up from $C + E$ to $F + E + G$, rising rather than disappearing as it would have if a customs union had been formed.

Figure 9.5 also serves to illustrate that if a PTA is formed with country Y, trade creation can always be made to predominate by lowering the tariff against low-cost producer Z. A country participating in economic integration

Figure 9.5

A GENERAL TARIFF REDUCTION BEATS A PTA

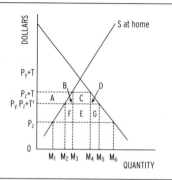

Note: A general tariff reduction beats a PTA because the tariff can be set at the level that would give the same amount of imports from the cheapest producer Z that would have come from the PTA partner, Y. The same amount of trade is created either way, but the country collects tariff revenue so its welfare is enhanced.

needs only to lower its tariff against outsiders to leave the total amount of trade unchanged. In that case trade diversion would not occur and the PTA, by eliminating all internal tariffs, would be unambiguously beneficial. This "Kemp-Wan proposition," named for its formulators, has unfortunately had little practical effect.[7] The problem is that countries engaging in integration hardly ever make an effort to adjust their external tariff to avoid trade diversion. Note that free trade areas would find it easiest to follow the Kemp-Wan logic, because individual members could decide to lower their own barriers to offset any trade diversion. The members of a customs union must have a common external tariff, so the entire membership would have to support its reduction. Furthermore, a customs union might require its most liberal members to *raise* their barriers to the common level, increasing the chances for trade diversion.

Further Conclusions on Trade Creation versus Trade Diversion

Important conclusions emerge from the analysis of trade creation and diversion. The first is that the larger the customs union, the less possible is trade diversion. This is reasonable because if all countries were to be in the same customs union there could be no trade diversion whatever. The unpleasant corollary, however, is that the larger the customs union, the greater the harm to those left outside it. Consider the circumstances of the last nation in the world left out of a "World Economic Community". If this pariah is to trade at all, and is being underpriced because of competitors' tariff-free privileges, it will have to cut prices to absorb the tariff. (If it were country Z, for example, it would have to lower its price to be competitive with Y, thus absorbing most of the tariff.) This explains the urgency with which outsiders pursue membership in large arrangements: Eastern Europe and Turkey to enter the EU, for example, Mexico's sudden desire to join the

U.S.-Canada Free Trade Agreement, and so on. Even so, every successful joiner passes along the problem of being an outsider to the remaining non-member nations, which now have to face a larger customs union than before.

A second theoretical conclusion is that the WTO rule requiring 100% elimination of trade barriers among member countries actually increases the danger of trade diversion. A permanent partial cut would deliver a smaller advantage to the member countries, so less trade would be diverted. In this view, the WTO rule is too strict.[8]

DYNAMIC EFFECTS OF ECONOMIC INTEGRATION

So far we have examined preferential arrangements only in terms of their static effects—as if the production possibility curves of the member nations were unchanged by the integration. It is likely, however, that economic integration will also have *dynamic* effects that serve to push out the production possibility curves of the members. The dynamic effects usually cited are in two categories, both of which would increase production possibilities:

1. *Competition effects.* These include higher levels of investment that reduce costs, improved marketing, greater productive efficiency, reduced supernormal profit, and the spur to the adoption of new technologies.
2. *Scale effects.* A larger market means that industries can realize scale economies through exporting to other members, which is not possible in a smaller market.*

The dynamic effects of economic integration are often called on to buttress the arguments in favor of such action. As the discussion below indicates, the most successful examples of integration include a number of cases where dynamic effects have far outweighed any negative static effects from trade diversion. In these cases, impressive economic growth was generated by the ultimately improving impact of competition and the development of scale economies. It would be odd indeed to complain about an arrangement that caused a diversion of 10% of trade if the same union had produced sufficient economic growth to generate a doubling or tripling of total trade.

For example, the old pattern of multinational firms setting up national subsidiaries in the various markets of Europe changed considerably after the

---

* Economists sometimes overlook a point made by political scientists. PTAs make it less necessary to have a large domestic market to glean the benefits of scale economies. That means, in turn, that small independent countries are more viable economically if they can be integrated with other countries' markets. Economic integration is therefore perhaps more likely to lead to political fragmentation than the reverse. For this case, see *The Economist*, April 29, 1995, citing work of Alberto Alesina and Enrico Spolaore.

formation of the original European Common Market. Thereafter, it became standard practice for multinational firms to design and produce goods in one center for the entire Common Market, allowing for greater productive efficiency on a community-wide scale. In all the members, other firms, formerly sheltered from the winds of trade, were forced to cut costs and become more efficient in both production and organization in order to maintain their market share and profit margin. Nicholas Owen's research suggests that dynamic effects based largely on scale economies resulted in an increment of some 3-6% of GDP for the original six members.[9]

Such arguments about the dynamics of integration are, however, subject to certain difficulties: one must show that the customs union was *necessary* to have the dynamic consequences. All the results categorized under "competition effects" can be achieved with unilateral cuts in tariffs and NTBs. If a country wants the bracing wind of international competition, all it has to do is cut its import barriers. If every one of the present members had wanted more competition, they could have had it immediately by simply lowering their tariffs to all outsiders. Such a mutual lowering of tariffs would also have provided the opportunities for scale economies, albeit with more international competition. In the specific case of the growth in the original European Common Market, one sails into treacherous statistical waters in ascribing the dynamism and growth of its members to the customs union itself. The nations were already growing in 1956 before the Common Market was formed; Sweden and Switzerland, outside the market, grew just as rapidly. We are rather inclined to accept the dynamic arguments as being generally valid, but admit to uncertainty about attempts to quantify them. It is not at all clear by how much the growth induced by the economic integration expanded trade, nor is it easy to say if that extra boost to growth overcame the sometimes very substantial trade diversion that accompanied the Common Market's agricultural policies.

Dynamic Effects Are Not Necessarily Positive

Not all dynamic effects of economic integration are necessarily positive. Consider first the scale effects. What if economies of scale are important but external tariffs are high? With the now-larger market allowing for scale economies, new industries might become established behind the protective walls at costs low enough to capture markets from importers. Yet these producers would not have survived without the trade barriers. This is known as the *trade suppression* that might follow from economic integration, and will be most likely when the external barriers are steep.

Then consider that economic integration may increase regional disparities within member countries. Say the new dynamism within a union has a more favorable effect in some members than in others. In many unions, cultural and linguistic barriers to migration prevent labor's easy movement from declining regions to more prosperous ones. Thus, in the EU when Germany prospers but Greece does not, there is little movement of Greeks to Germany. In the United States, people who need jobs are far more likely to move from one state to another, explaining why unemployment rates are much more similar among the states than they are among the countries of Europe.

In general, if the resources freed by new imports into a member cannot find new employment elsewhere because of labor market inflexibilities or ill-judged economic policies, that would have to weigh against the trade creation of a PTA.[10]

The Long Term: A Common Currency

Perhaps the single most important dynamic advantage of economic integra-tion may come in the long term if the members move to economic union involving a common currency. The advantages of monetary unification are wholly obvious, and the United States is often used as the best example. A single currency is highly desirable for safety and convenience. There is no necessity for foreign exchange transactions or for maintaining numerous separate currencies and central banks. There is no risk of fluctuations in rates and no need for a forward market in currencies. Any American knows how advantageous it is that a dollar is a dollar in New York, in Chicago, and in Los Angeles. For example, travelers in the United States with $1,000 in U.S. currency never need to exchange it at all and incur no costs for commissions. But those same travelers in (pre-euro) Europe with $1,000 in U.S. currency, if they exchange their money in each of the 15 EU countries would lose over half of it to commissions (see Chapter 18).

Trade in the world's customs unions and free trade areas would indeed be much simpler, cheaper, and convenient if the currencies were unified. There is, however, a significant downside. If member countries adopt a common currency, then they must give up exchange rate changes and separate monetary policy as tools of economic management, leaving only fiscal policy or no policy at all. Monetary union among the countries engaged in economic integration has been rare, with a few limited exceptions such as most of the island countries of the Caribbean. But 11 members of the EU are adopting the euro as their sole currency on January 1, 2002, in a huge advance for the concept of monetary union. Keeping separate floating currencies is the proper prescription if countries wish to pursue independent fiscal and monetary policies for the fight against inflation and unemployment, and when they want to maintain an image of political independence.

A CHECKLIST OF CONDITIONS
FOR WELFARE IMPROVEMENT

The following is a checklist of the static and dynamic conditions that will generally determine when a regional trade arrangement will be most successful in raising the welfare of its members.[11] Success will predictably be greatest when the following twelve conditions are met.

1. If the elasticity of demand in the member countries is high, a cut in the barriers against fellow members of the arrangement will lower price and cause a large increase in consumption. Much additional trade is generated. The result will be more positive the higher the duties were in the first place.

2. If the elasticity of supply in the member countries is high, production within the arrangement will rise rapidly to take the place of the former imports from non-members when a demand increase occurs because of the fall in tariffs.

3. If low-cost producers of any given good also belong to the arrangement, then there will be only a small sacrifice in shifting trade from non-members to members. It follows that the larger the area involved, the better for the participants, for then the chances are greater that low-cost producers will be among the membership, so lessening the trade diversion.

4. If countries already conduct a large proportion of their trade with one another before integration takes place among them, then there is bound to be little trade diversion when a union is created.

5. If the member countries import only a small percentage of their consumption, then diversion of trade to a higher-cost source within the arrangement will make little difference.

6. When countries forming an arrangement had very low tariffs to start with, or very high ones, the chances for trade diversion are lessened. When tariffs were very low, the diversion will be slight when they are dropped altogether. If they were very high, there was little trade to divert because the high tariffs suppressed it.

7. If in negotiating a customs union, the external tariff against outsiders is more or less an average of the previous rates existing in the member countries, then the dispersion of tariffs is likely to be reduced. This is an advantage. When very high and very low tariffs exist together, incentives become skewed toward and away from the industries concerned. A smaller variation in tariffs means comparative advantage has a greater chance to work.

8. If the union is so large that its external tariff can affect the world market for an imported item, then it may be able to manipulate the tariff to alter the terms of trade in its favor. If a large union results in a shift of members' demand away from non-members' exports, the non-members may have to cut their prices if they wish to continue exporting. The union might also be

able to obtain a terms-of-trade effect with exports if export taxes are standardized. Note that in these situations any gain to the welfare of the membership is automatically a loss in welfare to outsiders.

9. Arrangements among countries with very different factor proportions will tend to stimulate trade along Heckscher-Ohlin lines. Countries will specialize and trade the items that have the right factor proportions. On the contrary, countries with similar factor proportions will see less trade creation when trade occurs because of Heckscher-Ohlin principles.

10. If trade is instead based on decreasing costs due to traditional scale economies, in-plant economies from specialization, learning curves, and the like, then much of it will be intraindustrial. In that case, the growth of trade will be greater when incomes are high and the integrated market is large.[12] Intraindustrial trade tends to be less disruptive for the economies of the members. There will be fewer cases of entire industries having to go out of business. (One reason why trade expanded in the original European Common Market to a far greater degree than it did in EFTA is that the Common Market, with its high average income levels and its large market, could support substantially more intraindustrial trade.)

11. If the economic growth of the members is rapid, then adjustment to free trade within an arrangement will be easier. "A rising tide lifts all boats." Wealthy countries can afford regional development funds and trade adjustment assistance to cope with the temporary damage that may be caused by imports.

12. Outward-oriented economic policies in such areas as foreign exchange rates and government regulation give a greater chance that trade will increase as barriers are lowered. On the contrary, overvalued foreign exchange rates, price-fixing by strong vested interests, and corrupt governments can hinder the effectiveness of trade liberalization.

THE MAJOR EXAMPLES OF ECONOMIC INTEGRATION

Of the many existing PTAs, only a few are of world-class status. These are discussed below.

The European Union

The European Union is the most famous example of modern integration.[13] The connection between political and economic unity was not lost on the public officials of Western Europe and America who sought to rebuild the Western world after the World War II. These leaders did not want a divided Europe to continue. Rather, they envisioned a Europe united politically, economically, and militarily, a Europe that would no longer fight with itself but would be strong enough to resist the threats from the Soviet Union and from homegrown radicalism. The first and most practical step would be to create a customs union. Not only did a customs union make economic sense, it would force the countries into regular political consultation. The tolerance of the United States toward some of the excesses of the resulting union must be understood in this broader political context. A mixture of lofty ideals and hard economic and political realities can produce some unusual reactions.

The European Economic Community (EEC), often called the Common Market, was established by the Treaty of Rome in March of 1957. It began operating in 1958. Originally there were six nations: France, West Germany, Italy, Belgium, the Netherlands, and Luxembourg. Its forerunners were a 1948 customs union among the last three of these nations—the Benelux union—and industrial free trade in coal and steel—the ECSC or European Coal and Steel Community of 1951. The EEC rapidly cut tariffs on industrial goods and established in 1968 a common external tariff somewhat lower than the weighted averages of the then-existing European tariffs. By contrast, agricultural policy developed slowly and painfully, and not until the mid-1960s did agricultural commodities flow freely.[*]

The Six became The Nine when Britain, Denmark, and Ireland joined in 1977. Greece made it The Ten in 1981, Spain and Portugal advanced the number to 12 in 1986, and the present number, 15, was reached when Austria, Finland, and Sweden joined in 1995. (The addition of the latter three countries led to a major dispute with the United States, just as had the earlier addition of Spain and Portugal. The reason was that some tariffs in the new members went up to reach the EU's common level.[†] Eventually a settlement was reached involving hundreds of compensatory tariff reductions on other goods to make up for the increases.)

Along the way, the name "European Community"—implying a goal of ultimate political unity—replaced the original name EEC or the more colloquial Common Market in the speech of those who shared the goal of union. After that came the adoption of the usage "European Union" which is now generally accepted.

The results were spectacular. Trade among the nations that comprised The Twelve was only 34.5% of their total trade in 1960, but that figure had grown

---

[*] The external tariff raised German and Benelux barriers, because these countries originally had relatively low tariffs, and lowered the high French and Italian tariffs. The effect on outsiders was very different, depending on whether they traded more with the former four countries or the latter two.

[†] For example, the EU duty on semiconductors was 14% compared to zero in Finland and Austria and only 2.3% in Sweden. Duties also rose on chemicals, plastics, electronics, precision equipment, and agricultural commodities. See *The Economist*, February 4, 1995.

to 60.4% by 1990, making up over one-fifth of all world trade. (Such statistics are a useful indicator of whether economic integration has worked to increase trade among the members. By this test, the EU's performance has been superb, far surpassing any other of the world's free trade areas and customs unions. Keep in mind, however, that an increase in intraregional trade is not necessarily the same as a welfare increase, because trade diversion may have occurred.)

ADVANCES TOWARD UNION

The EU has been keen not only to end tariffs but to end other forms of protection and subsidies as well. This has led it to try to harmonize tax systems, to turn subsidies and a number of other powers over to the EU executive, and to standardize products, labeling, health, and safety requirements. EU ministers meeting in Brussels now fix farm prices and set the fishing rules for all the members. The EU Commission manages antitrust policies, regulates aid to industries, and conducts much of the bargaining in international trade negotiations. A value-added tax (VAT) has been adopted by all the members, and the rates are now closer to harmony than they once were. Great progress has been made in reducing non-tariff barriers to trade among the members, including the difficult issues of health and safety standards, labeling, and administrative regulations. Even the size of trucks is now standardized, so that goods do not have to be transshipped or put into especially small vehicles to move from one nation to the other. Thus, heavy European trucks have been causing annoyance in many of England's small towns. Although this may be a burden, there are many balancing benefits. NTB eliminations mean, for instance, that a lathe or radio made in England can be sold without modification in any of the member countries. Quotas and VERs are now EU-wide, rather than being separately administered by the member countries as was formerly true. No antidumping duties are levied by one member against another.

Many reforms leading to a single market were scheduled to take effect at the end of 1992, and although the target was not hit, the term "1992" became part of the language of those who study the EU. Among the 1992 single-market reforms were the following:[14]

1. The EU simplified border crossing, eliminating its customs checks at borders at the start of 1993. The days of truckers filling out dozens of documents at borders are done. Passport checks are gone except for Britain, Ireland, and Denmark.
2. The regulations on truck transport that prohibited foreign trucks from carrying goods from point to point within a country, and which caused a third of all foreign trucks to travel empty on their return home, disappeared, reducing distribution costs by perhaps 10-15%.

3. Product health and safety standards are being subjected to mutual recognition and so will no longer create an internal barrier. This development will be significant for exporters to the EU. For example, goods allowed into Portugal will then be allowed into Germany as well, so exporters should benefit.

4. Public procurement has been made more competitive among the members, with the EU Commission taking more control of this problem.

5. All controls on capital movements are gone; financial services such as banking and insurance are opened up to free trade with branches and agencies able to open anywhere; and professionals (lawyers, accountants, and so forth) are able to practice anywhere within the union. Students can now attend universities in other member countries as a matter of right.

Large R&D and infrastructure subsidies, which many business people apparently believed would be part of "1992," were not included in the final plan.

THE SINGLE CURRENCY (EUROPEAN MONETARY UNION)

In the most major advance since the formation of the Common Market, a single currency area was begun on January 1, 1999, among 11 of the 15 EU members, with actual euro notes to circulate in place of the various national currencies from January 1, 2002. The plan for European Monetary Union, or EMU, had been set in place by the Maastricht Treaty of 1991, with the details finally agreed on in 1995. To control the new currency and manage EU monetary policy, a new European central bank has been established. Its headquarters are in Frankfurt's Eurotower. This book's treatment of the euro is in Chapter 18.

TRADE CREATION AND TRADE DIVERSION IN THE EUROPEAN UNION

The extent of the trade creation and trade diversion that resulted from the founding of the EU is a subject of considerable importance. In manufacturing, the model that emphasizes trade creation seems to fit the case best. EU members have economies that are competitive with one another, so substitution among commodities is easy and demand curves are flat. Mass production techniques that allow large increases in output with little or no rise in costs lead to an elastic supply. Incomes are high and the market was large right from the start, so intraindustrial trade creation was vigorous, especially in chemicals, machinery, fuels, and transportation equipment. Trade diversion in industry was unlikely to be very important because many of the industries in the EU were already cost-competitive with the rest of the world (meaning there would be no trade to divert) or were close to it (meaning only a small loss in diversion) at the time the market was established. This analysis suggests that trade-creation effects have dominated in manufacturing.

By contrast, agriculture in the EU appears to approach the heavy trade diversion model of Figure 9.3.[15] In the main, the lowest-cost producer within the union is by no means the *world's* lowest-cost producer. This certainly applies to grains, dairy products, and meat. Demand is relatively inelastic for many agricultural commodities such as grain and meat. Supply is also inelastic in the short run, as production is difficult to increase or cut back during the life cycle of animals or during a crop year. Substantial trade diversion is thus likely, especially from the United States, Canada, New Zealand, Australia, and Argentina. The major impact in the EU appears to be felt by Britain and Germany, both of which formerly imported a great proportion of their food supplies from the cheapest sources overseas but now must import from high-cost sources within the EU.

A wide range of empirical estimates has appeared in the literature on the EU, generally supporting the conclusion that considerable trade creation has occurred in manufacturing and considerable trade diversion in agriculture. The overall balance between creation and diversion is still being debated; a survey by Richard Pomfret states that the empirical work on the overall outcome is not conclusive one way or the other.[16] Some limited evidence also indicates that there has been a positive terms-of-trade effect for the EU as foreign suppliers had to cut prices because of the higher trade barriers that some members put in place when the common external tariff was adopted. A fair conclusion is that welfare gains on standard analysis are not exceptionally large, but that extended modeling that considers increased competition, greater product variety, economies of scale, and other dynamic effects supports a conclusion of great gains.[17]

NEW MEMBERS?

Further new EU memberships are being negotiated. Early applications from Cyprus, Malta, and Turkey are still pending, and talks have been conducted with and applications made by or imminent from Estonia, Latvia, Lithuania, Poland, Hungary, Slovenia, Slovakia, Bulgaria, and Romania. Even if all goes well, however, entry from this list is going to be difficult until the EU modifies its Common Agricultural Policy, for farming is important in almost all of these countries. Expensive support for agriculture in the prospective new members could cost as much as $50 billion a year. An alternative would be to admit new members but not make them eligible for the expensive budget items.

Trade agreements are already in force establishing free trade areas between the EU and Turkey (since January 1, 1996, its full membership apparently blocked by Greece), with Estonia, Latvia, and Lithuania to be fully complete in 1999 and much of the rest of Eastern Europe to have full effect by 2003.

Free Trade Agreements in North America

NAFTA is the most famous of present-day free trade agreements. It had its start in a U.S.-Canada Free Trade Agreement of 1987, which was expanded to include Mexico in 1994. NAFTA was controversial and remains so in all three countries. It tends to be a litmus test of views toward all trade and barriers to it.

THE HISTORICAL BACKGROUND: U.S.-CANADA FREE TRADE

Free trade between the United States and Canada was one of the original ideas for economic integration. An agreement was actually reached in 1854, eliminating barriers against natural products. But the United States terminated it in 1866, partly out of pique against what it took to be too much British sympathy with the Confederate States in the Civil War, partly because high tariffs were politically back in fashion at that time. Another attempt to integrate was defeated in the U.S. Senate in 1874. In 1891 an election was lost in Canada by a government that supported free trade, and a replay took place in 1911 when the United States and Canada were set to sign a free trade agreement. (It was in itself not a treaty but an agreement to pass concurrent legislation allowing almost all goods free access to the other country.) The Canadians had dissolved Parliament and were facing an election, with all signs favorable for the bill's passage. But south of the border, an over-enthusiastic U.S. congressional leader suggested that the agreement would be the first step in annexing Canada. In a memorable campaign, Prime Minister Wilfrid Laurier's Liberal government was turned out of office; "no truck or trade with the Yankees" was the battle cry that carried the day for his opponents. The new government never passed the necessary legislation.

A later attempt by President Franklin D. Roosevelt and Prime Minister Mackenzie King foundered in the uncertainties of the Great Depression. The failure of these attempts diverted Canadian development policy back to a strategy of attracting American branch-plant manufacturing through levying high tariffs. After World War II, Canada, like other developed nations, lowered its tariffs, but like Australia and New Zealand it cut them less than did the United States and Europe.[18]

The high level of already-existing trade meant that a U.S.-Canada FTA probably would not divert very much trade. Furthermore, the similar economic structure and high income levels of the two countries meant that intraindustrial trade should eventually expand significantly.[19] The signs were auspicious.

CLOSE CONNECTIONS ALREADY EXISTED BEFORE THE PACT

Canada and the United States were already very closely linked when negotiations for the free trade agreement began in 1986. Even before the agreement, Canada sent more than three-quarters of its merchandise exports to its southern neighbor, representing about 22.5% of Canadian GDP. On the U.S. side, imports from Canada in most years exceeded those from any other country. (Japan is always close, and in some years has held the first-place position.) Canada was the largest foreign supplier of natural gas to the United States, the second-largest of oil (Mexico is first), and a major source of electric power. Meanwhile, about 70% of Canada's imports were from the United States, accounting for 21% of all U.S. exports, nearly twice as much as the number-two buyer of U.S. exports, Japan. Ontario alone imported more U.S. goods than did Germany, France, and Italy combined. Trade (exports plus imports) between Canada and the United States was and remains by far the largest bilateral trade in the world, $321 billion in 1997 compared to U.S.-Japanese trade of $190 billion. About three-quarters of U.S. and Canadian trade (70% of U.S. exports to Canada and 80% of Canadian exports to the United States in 1988) already entered each other's markets duty free. For all that, Canada had rather high tariffs for a developed country, about double those of the United States, and a wide and growing range of non-tariff barriers applied to imports into both countries.

THE U.S.-CANADA FTA OF 1987

Renewed negotiations for a free trade area between Canada and the United States began in 1986. Clearly, the talks grew from fears that exclusionary trading blocs, such as the enlarged EU, might be developing abroad. After some melodramatic moments, including a walkout by Canadian negotiators, agreement came on October 3, 1987, one day before the U.S. congressional grant of authority to negotiate a pact was to expire.[20] Formal signature by President Reagan and Prime Minister Mulroney came on January 2, 1988.

THE OPPOSITION

In the United States there was limited opposition, concentrated mostly among the lumber, fishing, and potato interests of Maine and the west coast. These foes were overwhelmed in Congress, which ratified the agreement by a wide margin during 1988. In Canada, however, emotions ran high. After Prime Minister Mulroney signed the treaty, the Canadian Senate, in a nearly unprecedented step, blocked its ratification. That Senate is not elected, and its honorific members, appointed by the Prime Minister whenever one of the 104 seats falls vacant, serve to age 75 unless they choose to retire. Never before had the Senate refused its assent to a bill passed by Parliament, but on U.S.-Canadian free trade, it did so. That led to a national election in November 1988, after a campaign that was focused principally on the trade issue.

The sources of the political opposition in Canada were varied. By region, the greatest aversion was in Ontario, which had the largest share of Canada's protected manufacturing. By political party, the Liberals (who might well have struck a similar agreement had they been in power) caved in to that party's nationalist left, now opposed to free trade, and argued that any such development would be a U.S. victory. Other Canadian opposition to the agreement came from industries in which protection had traditionally been high, such as electronic goods, shoes, and publishing; most labor unions (often splitting from their employers); many intellectuals; and parts of the media, including the *Toronto Star* and the Canadian Broadcasting Corporation.

Five objections were most frequently voiced by those who opposed the agreement. (1) Canada is almost as rich as the United States, so ran the argument. Why risk the dislocations that can accompany the small-country role in a free trade arrangement? (But then, as has been demonstrated, the growth of protectionism is a risk, too, and the establishment of a free trade area served to avoid it.) (2) Canada gave up too much. The rules on dumping and subsidy were not strict enough; the guarantee on energy went too far. These are discussed below. (3) The treaty was a trap on cultural grounds. Canadian values would be altered unfavorably by the presence of giant American corporations and their increased advertising. Canada's liberal unemployment insurance, its public health-care program, its special insurance arrangements, and much else would be jeopardized as illegal subsidies. ("Wouldn't happen," said most economists. These subsidies are "generally available," not easy to attack under the rules of international trade, and not countervailable under current U.S. practice.) (4) Increased trade with the United States would aid the Americans in achieving some of their unworthy international aims, an argument representing an underlying current of anti-Americanism present in Canada since the War of 1812. (5) The Americans would abuse the agreement, which, considering the stance of U.S. law, jurisprudence, and administrative action, was a plausible argument, and therefore Canada would be better off to negotiate in multilateral arrangements rather than bilaterally with a much more powerful neighbor.

The election was the most bitter in recent Canadian history, but the Conservative supporters of the FTA were victorious, allowing another parliamentary ratification, persuading the Senate to withdraw its objections, and permitting the agreement to go into effect as scheduled on January 1, 1989. Many Canadians still believe that the best part of the U.S.-Canada FTA is that it can be abrogated—either country can withdraw from it by giving six months' notice.

CONTENT OF THE AGREEMENT

The 300-page agreement established a free trade area, not a customs union. The different tariffs of the two countries stayed in place against outsiders. The agreement was sweeping and its technical details were innovative. All tariffs were eliminated in a 10-year period to 1998. Some went at once, others were reduced by 20% of their original amount per year in each of the five years after the implementation of the agreement. (Four hundred tariffs were eliminated faster than indicated by the original schedule.) Finally, yet other tariffs—those on the most sensitive items, including steel, many agricultural commodities, processed fish, pleasure boats, textiles, and wood products—fell by 10% of their original amount per year over 10 years. Virtually all quotas were eliminated at once. To qualify for preferential treatment, it was agreed that goods must be of North American origin. Three ways are open to meet this test. First, a good can be wholly made in North America. Second, it can be sufficiently modified in the production process so that it becomes subject to a different tariff classification. Finally, as with autos, it qualifies if 50% of production costs are North American. Government contracts are open for bidding by nationals of both countries if they exceed a quite small figure of $25,000. The clauses freeing the trade in services and giving equal treatment in both Canada and the United States to the firms of the other country are the most liberal in the world. Both governments promised not to impose restrictions on free trade in energy.

Several exceptions were written into the agreement, some reasonable, some embarrassing. Transport, telecommunications, legal and medical services, and child care were excluded wholly or in part. Escape clause (safeguard) rules remained mostly intact. Free trade did not apply to Canadian fresh fish and poultry, beer, and logs produced in both countries. The Jones Act restricting shipping between American ports to U.S.-flag ships remained in force; so do some restrictive rules on trucking. The notorious U.S. sugar protection still applies. Most of these exceptions were the result of bargaining: if you keep the Jones Act, we won't let your trucks pick up and deliver in Canada. All these matters are treated outside the FTA, with several disputes having gone to WTO.

Much labor went into the construction of the mechanisms for settling disputes under the FTA. Disputes are taken up by a Canada-U.S. Trade Commission, which oversees the operation of the agreement and attempts to resolve problems. If the Commission cannot agree, controversies are submitted to binding arbitration by five-member dispute settlement panels, with two members chosen by each country and a fifth by the Commission or by the other four arbitrators.

It proved impossible to forge the same mechanism for dumping and subsidy disputes, however. *Non-binding* arbitration panels were adopted for these disputes. Even so, such disputes have mostly been resolved in a satisfactory way. Most of the panels convened so far have involved agricultural issues. Once an opinion has been released, it is possible to appeal to an extraordinary challenge committee for a quasi-judicial decision. Each country appoints one judge, and these two select a third. All in all, the binational nature of the tribunals and attached arbitration panels has had a major role in keeping disputes within the FTA from boiling over into politics.

ONGOING DISPUTES

Trade problems between the United States and Canada persist, of course. The disputes concerning softwood lumber, wheat, marketing boards for dairy products, and the so-called split-run magazines that are basically the U.S. magazines with Canadian ads have already been discussed elsewhere.

Another major dispute is a general one on trade barriers in agriculture. When the World Trade Organization opened for business on January 1, 1995, Canada imposed TRQs with high over-quota tariffs on many U.S. dairy, poultry, and egg products. This contravened the part of the FTA on the elimination of tariffs for U.S. exporters of these items by 1998. Canada argued that the WTO rules on converting its quotas to TRQs superseded its commitments to the United States under the free trade agreement. Some of the tariffs are very high, 240-300% on butter, eggs, and cheese, for example. The United States invoked the FTA's dispute settlement process but the panel found for Canada, deciding an article in the agreement provided for replacement of the FTA obligation by a WTO commitment. Canadian consumers and American producers continue to suffer.[21]

Another dispute concerns the domestic content of Hondas produced in Canada. The domestic content rule is that to qualify as made in Canada, 50% of the value of the car must be produced there. U.S. customs says the cars don't meet the test, while Canada (and Honda) say they do.

PREDICTED GAINS FROM THE FTA-CANADA

Economists expected Canada to realize significant scale economies because the American market is 10 times larger than the Canadian. The scale economies were expected to be proportionally greater for British Columbia, Alberta, Saskatchewan, Manitoba, and the Atlantic Provinces because the "Canadian customs union" up to the time of the FTA was a significant tradediverter as far as these provinces were concerned. Canada also stood to benefit from the effects of greater competition in the inefficient segments of manufacturing.

Another reason to expect rewards for Canada involves the small-country rule of Chapter 2. Recall that when trade is freed, one expects the prices in the trading partners to move furthest in the smallest country, which has less influence over the now-unified market. Thus the small country has the advantage of being able to trade at prices close to the large country's original prices, with the potential to glean the greater gains.

Moreover, tariffs were already much lower than in the past, so the necessary adjustments to free trade would not be wrenching. Finally, the expectation was that most of the growth in trade brought about by the agreement would be intraindustrial, so labor displacement would be even more limited. Finally, Canada was buying insurance against a rise of protectionism in the United States. Without the FTA, Canadian firms would have faced difficulties in planning their long-term investment strategies when they were unable to predict what protective measures might be taken next in their largest foreign market. (One reason business interests were generally supportive is that they retained their unhappy memory of the 1970s when Britain joined the Common Market, leaving Canada on the outside.)

The problem Canada had before the FTA was an inefficient manufacturing sector, with Canadian labor productivity (output per worker hour) sharply below the American.[22] The cause of the lower productivity was almost undoubtedly the small product runs and unspecialized production of tariff-protected Canadian industry, as Chapter 3 described. Many economists felt that a decrease in protection, allowing Canadian industries to produce in a more focused way in a continental or world market, would increase manufacturing productivity by over 20%.[23]

One study, based on surveys of manufacturing plants, showed that Canadian costs were 25% more than American costs, despite the fact that wages were 20% below American wages.[24] Scale economies in some industries were also severely constrained by the small Canadian markets.[25] The binationalization of the automotive industry, following the 1965 Automobiles Pact between the U.S. and Canada, had indeed resulted in large increases in Canadian productivity, which in some cases surpassed American productivity in similar plants.[26] Economists anticipated that Canadian productivity would rise sharply with the introduction of NAFTA agreements. But did it?

The answer appears to be that it did. A recent study by the University of Toronto's Daniel Trefler demonstrates that productivity increases were substantial, although not in the 20% range. Trefler factored out long-term industry trends, American productivity trends, and macroeconomic fluctuations. He concludes that the loss in protection accounts for productivity gains of 0.6% a year for those industries that had been moderately protected (about 4% in total over the 1989–96 span he studied), and 1.5% (11% in total during the period) for more heavily protected firms.[27] Since Canadian multifactor (capital and labor) productivity grew only a little above 0.6% a year during that time period and these figures are *in addition to the long-term trends*, the contribution from the industries affected by the tariff cuts was substantial. This result is consistent with the sharp increase in trade, much of it intraindustrial, and much of that in the industries that were previously protected more heavily.

The results of freer trade have been lost in a more general discussion about Canadian manufacturing productivity. Productivity, particularly when it deals with that of capital as well as labor (multifactoral), is difficult enough to measure domestically, but problems compound for international comparisons. Those who tend to be skeptical of the benefit of the free trade arrangements are comforted by those figures that show poor growth in productivity.[28] The newer figures noted above, however, suggest that free trade did indeed do what it was expected to do—cause productivity to rise in protected industries. Moreover, the high percentage of intraindustrial trade and the growth of trade as a percentage of GDP indicates that many firms were quite successful in establishing export markets.*

PREDICTED GAINS FROM THE FTA–UNITED STATES

For the United States, the predicted advantages were far more limited. The U.S. market was already more than adequate to promote economies of scale, and the United States was the large country, subject to the rule that large countries are likely to gain less from preferential trade agreements.

ECONOMIC RESULTS OF THE FTA

It is exceedingly difficult to separate the overall effects of the FTA from all the other determinants of macroeconomic performance. Arguably, the agreement has helped. Both U.S. and Canadian economic growth (GDP per capita) has exceeded European and Japanese growth for several years. Inflation is low in both countries. Unemployment is well under European levels (though higher in Canada than in the United States). Intraregional exports as a percentage of the total exports of the United States and Canada rose from 26.5% in 1960 to

---

* Some, particularly an economist for one of Canada's leading banks, have argued that the low Canadian dollar stimulates exports and hinders imports, thus increasing the competitiveness of Canadian manufacturing even though its productivity is low. (As Chapter 15 argues, that is what *any* price level or exchange rate change is supposed to do.) The problem with the argument, however, is that manufactured exports have risen sharply as a percentage of Canadian exports, meaning that they are more competitive with *non-manufacturing* industries. This means that manufactured exports have risen in productivity against the non-manufactured goods.

34.0% in 1990 and 36.3% in 1997. Canadian trade (imports and exports) rose from 60% to 80% of GDP, and the rise in Canadian exports of manufactured goods to the United States has been pronounced. On the U.S. side of the border, several cities, especially Buffalo, New York, were experiencing a new prosperity from the additional commercial activity. Scholars believe that the FTA has also had a significant impact on international corporate mergers and acquisition activity. Some plants or firms with broad product lines and production on both sides of the border have been rationalized, with output concentrated at one spot instead of two or more. That has meant the shut-down of some plants, but it has also meant higher productivity and exports from those that remain open. It is fair to say, however, that the impact of free trade has been considerably exceeded by more general macroeconomic forces, such as the early 1990s recessions in both countries and the differing monetary and exchange rate policies in the two partners (examined in this book's second part).

NAFTA

The movement to enlarge U.S.-Canada free trade to include Mexico in a North American Free Trade Agreement involved the greatest political strug-gle over trade of the last several decades. It was a close-run thing and is still on the political front burner.

THE U.S. VIEW OF NAFTA

Before the 1980s, Mexico was determinedly protectionist, showing no interest in any trade arrangement with the United States, but its interest rose, bringing to the fore discussion of free trade. The talk turned increasingly bitter within the United States. All the living presidents at the time—Nixon, Ford, Carter, Reagan, Bush, and Clinton—supported NAFTA, and so did all the living Nobel prize-winning U.S. economists along with the great majority of their less-distinguished brethren. Politically, the original impetus came from Presidents Reagan and Bush. President Clinton and Vice-President Gore had to brave considerable Democratic Party opposition and the hostility of many trade unions, including the AFL-CIO. Environmentalists and labor rights activists joined in, as is discussed below. On the other side of the political spectrum, there was intransigence on the part of some Republicans, such as Pat Buchanan, and independent Ross Perot (NAFTA would make a "giant sucking sound" as jobs flowed to Mexico, opined the prickly Perot, though he was unexpectedly upended in a famous debate by the supposedly wooden Al Gore).

Economists predicted only limited effects on the United States because Mexico's economy is relatively small, only about 4% the size of the U.S.

THE MAQUILADORA PROGRAM

U.S. plants had been able to move to Mexico's *maquiladora* zone for many years. (The name came from the toll that millers collected in Spanish colonial days for processing someone else's grain.) The *maquiladora* zone along the border had been in existence since 1965, and liberal rules were in place by the mid-1980s.[29] The initial idea sprang from an attempt to do something about the high unemployment in border areas following the end of seasonal farm work. Originally, a strip 12 miles deep was designated all along the border from Mexicali in Baja California to Matamoros opposite Brownsville, Texas. Later (from 1972) it became possible to obtain the same status in the interior, where labor was even cheaper. The inland activity subject to the special rules was no more than one-fifth what it grew to be along the border, however, mostly due to transport problems.

Under the scheme, Mexico's restrictive investment rules do not apply, and duty-free access is permitted for imported raw materials and semi-finished goods, as well as for plant equipment. Business boomed in assembly plants, most of which are U.S.-owned. Garments, electronics, woodworking, plastics, and especially autos and auto parts predominate. The most important centers are Ciudad Juarez, Tijuana, and Nogales. When the products are exported back to the United States, they benefit because U.S. tariffs were already low, U.S. tariff law allowed for duty only on the value added in Mexico, and the program called GSP (which all other major countries have as well) had already eliminated duties on many goods anyway. The *maquilas* became Mexico's second-largest earner of foreign exchange in 1986, ranking behind only oil, and eventually they supplied almost half of Mexico's exports to the United States.

Mexican criticism of the *maquiladoras* has been intense. It is said that their simple assembly tasks and the preponderance of women in the workforce are clues to their low impact on the economy; that they purchase very few other inputs locally; that they pay low taxes and are footloose industries that would quickly move elsewhere if wages rose; and that they represent closer control of the Mexican economy by the *estadounidenses* to the north. All the charges are true to some degree. Yet the *maquilas* pay wages 30% to 50% higher than in other Mexican industry, and their unwillingness to purchase local inputs is partly due to quality problems that would not have lasted forever.

The *maquiladoras* have plenty of detractors in the United States as well, with their arguments the same as those advanced against NAFTA itself. They take U.S. jobs; they avoid health and safety regulations for labor; and the labor works long hours for low pay.

A major change in the *maquiladora* program is being made because of NAFTA. After the year 2000, duty-free imports of inputs from non-members of the free trade area will no longer be permitted. *Maquiladoras* will be like any other industry.

economy—but with larger consequences in the states of the Southwest. They did note, however, that a more prosperous Mexico would be a reduced source of immigration to the United States.

All the opponents feared that U.S. firms would move to Mexico in search of the longer working hours (a six-day week is allowed), the less strict health and safety standards, and especially the low wages, 20% of the U.S. figure and well below the wages of the major Asian exporters, such as South Korea, Taiwan, and Hong Kong. (The U.S.-Canada Free Trade Agreement had not raised these fears because labor costs in Canada are much the same as in the United States.) Opposition from industry emanated from lower-tech segments of steel, textiles, and agriculture.

Supporters pointed out that the low-wage U.S. jobs would be lost anyway, going to other cheap-labor countries if not to Mexico, and that U.S. jobs would be created from new exports (mainly of higher-tech products) to replace those lost to new imports. Still, economists and union leaders missed a chance to emphasize that low-skill, low-paid U.S. labor would undoubtedly suffer somewhat even though the country would gain, so raising the need for trade adjustment assistance for displaced workers. (A TAA-NAFTA program was adopted, but with all the flaws of the regular TAA program, as discussed in the previous chapter.)

The job-loss argument ("giant sucking sound"), with U.S. plants moving to Mexico for the cheap labor, was greatly exaggerated during the NAFTA debates. First, the overwhelming majority of companies would not chase cheap labor because of the problem of low productivity, discussed in Chapter 6. Cheap labor is not cheap after all when its low productivity is taken into account. Even when the cheap labor was sufficiently productive to give it an advantage, companies that wanted to go to Mexico in search of it had actually been able to do so for many years before because of that country's unusual *maquiladora* system, explored in the box on the preceding page.

THE MEXICAN VIEW

For NAFTA to come about, there had to be a tremendous change in the Mexican government's attitude; the idea would once have been unthinkable. Mexico was an intellectual center of so-called dependency theory—the belief that trade is an inadequate means to development, or even is counter-productive—and politics reflected that fact.[30] Free trade would make Mexico a "backwash" area, so it was argued, with little chance to break away from primary product exports, raw materials processing, and labor-intensive manufacturing. This belief lay behind numerous long-standing deviations from international trade rules. Mexico banned U.S. service imports in many fields. Its export quota requirements often mandated that 50% of a foreign firm's output had to be exported. Its Mexican domestic content requirements (36% Mexican materials for cars, for example) and its market limitations (American cars were limited to 20% of the Mexican market and car engines under 1.8 liters were simply prohibited) were other high barriers to trade. It maintained strict limits on repatriation of profit and other controls over capital movements. It established an extensive structure of producer subsidies. It had many quotas, and its tariffs averaged 2.5 times higher than those of the United States.

Many of these rules were well outside those permitted under the rules of international trade, explaining why Mexico refused to join GATT until 1986. Even as late as 1987, former President de la Madrid stated that free trade with the United States was not a possibility. But de la Madrid's successor, President Salinas, saw the harm that such rules caused and threw strong support to a free trade agreement. He backed the support with major efforts to reform Mexican trade law. A major influence in the negotiations was the Mexican belief that NAFTA would act as a guarantee to Mexico that it would not be shut out of the large American market by some future rising tide of protectionism. Mexico would also stand to gain from an arrangement because of the small-country rule.

In the end, Mexican opinion shifted toward free trade, even though almost all its restrictive rules would have to be scrapped. It was always certain that protected Mexican industries and the workers in them would have to make much greater adjustments to freer trade than was true of U.S. or Canadian firms—but with the compensation that far more jobs were sure to be created in Mexico by that country's participation in NAFTA than was true of the other two members.

THE CANADIAN VIEW

Mexican–Canadian trade is small, only 5% of that between Mexico and the United States. Less than 0.5% of Canada's total exports go to Mexico compared to over 75% going to the United States and any economic gains to Canada would be small, which explains the rather lukewarm Canadian reception to NAFTA. (Some Canadians feared that the auto plants located in that country might move south to Mexico if complete free trade were adopted.) From a political point of view the major advantage to Canadian membership was insurance that it would be a participant in rule-making, such as determining what rules of origin would apply, and perhaps in enlisting Mexico's help to reduce the unpredictability of U.S. trade law.

THE ENVIRONMENTAL DEBATE

Environmentalists, allying themselves with protectionists, decried Mexico's lower level of regulation, and it was undeniable that enforcement was weaker in that country. The low standards of regulation would, it was argued, cause U.S. factories to move to Mexico. Some environmentalists (especially the Sierra Club and Greenpeace) and state attorneys-general argued that NAFTA would give Mexico the right to challenge the strict U.S. regulations. That was true—WTO rules do indeed permit challenges by Mexico or any other country—but any such challenge must be based on an absence of scientific evidence justifying a trade barrier. The WTO explicitly allows countries to enact stricter standards if they are scientifically based, and states and cities may do so as well. The burden of proof is on the challenger when a claim is made that a standard is not scientifically based. Nothing prevents laws against unsafe food or unsafe products. Mexico (or Canada, for that matter) would have to make and win a case on the absence of evidence, just as is true of similar U.S. actions against the EU and Japan. On its part, Mexico insisted that it had no intention to become a dumping ground for pollutants. Its 1988 law has standards similar to those of the United States, and enforcement has improved since 1990. Higher Mexican income will make it possible to enforce tougher laws.

In spite of these points in mitigation, it was true that the situation could get worse before it got better, with deleterious effects on those who live north of the border. President Clinton thus called for environmental measures to be added to NAFTA as a side agreement.

The measures agreed on represented a significant broadening of the treaty. (1) A North American Development Bank was established to make loans for cleanup in border areas. (2) A U.S.-Mexican Border Environment Cooperation Commission was established, the world's most advanced environmental reform in a trade treaty. Charges can be brought to this three-nation commission by any interested party, and teeth are provided if a finding is adverse. Any two of the three members can call for investigations of persistent abuse, with fines of $20 million on the government found guilty. As a last resort, tariffs can be passed consonant with the abuse.

A recent NBER study is optimistic. It finds that NAFTA will probably cause Mexico to reduce production of chemicals, rubber, and plastics, all "dirty" items, because that country does not have a comparative advantage in these products. Taking their place will be more agricultural production and labor-intensive manufacturing, both relatively cleaner. According to the study some of the improvement will be offset by much larger production of electrical equipment in Mexico, which is dirty, but the net effect would be a (rather small) decline in toxic emissions. The study suggests that the movement of some U.S. firms to Mexico, going on for some years because of the *maquiladora* program, has not included industries that are especially polluting. It identifies the causation as mainly associated with lower costs for unskilled labor. The authors note that pollution abatement costs for the average U.S. manufacturing firm are 1.4% of value added, far less than the difference made by lower labor costs for labor-intensive industries.[31]

THE AGREEMENT

The negotiators reached agreement in August 1992 and President Bush signed it the following December. The newly elected President Clinton called for revisions on the environment, which were added during the following year. Ratification involved the 90-day fast-track procedure that President Clinton lost soon thereafter. The vote in the U.S. House of Representatives on November 17, 1993, was the key vote: 234-200 in favor. NAFTA came into being at the start of 1994. The main provisions are as follows:[32]

1. *Withdrawal.* The abrogation rules are the same as in the U.S.-Canada FTA: countries can withdraw from NAFTA on six months' notice.

2. *Tariffs.* About half of the existing tariffs were phased out immediately, 15% more go over five years, and the remainder will be removed over 10 years or 15 years (to the end of 2008) on imports in the so-called sensitive industries. Textiles, glassware, citrus fruits, sugar, watches, footwear, luggage, and some steel and electronic products are on the U.S. sensitive list. The period allowed before tariffs are eliminated is longer than permitted in the U.S.-Canada FTA, where the final phase-out occurred on January 1, 1998.

3. *Unusual Mexican barriers.* Most of the unusual Mexican barriers to trade in goods, services, and investment discussed above were dropped. Mexico will keep its state monopoly on exploration for oil (by Pemex, the national oil company).

4. *Agriculture.* Barriers are to go over 15 years, a condition that is much more liberal than the new WTO rules. But Canada won its case that the WTO rule changes superseded the NAFTA schedule, so agriculture remains an area of contention. There are agricultural safeguards permitting temporary barriers to be reerected if imports reach some trigger level.

5. *Rules of origin.* Rules of origin remain controversial. The domestic content (made in North America) rule for cars to qualify as made in Mexico is 62.5%, higher than the 50% in the U.S.-Canada FTA. In textiles the rule of origin is more Byzantine: the clothing must be sewed in North America from fabric made in North America from yarn made in North America.[33] Such rules will probably lead to trade diversion. Also, textile/clothing quotas can be reimposed temporarily if imports cause serious damage.

6. *Services.* Transportation restrictions were much reduced on a schedule mostly complete by 1999. But the truck agreement to allow U.S. and Mexican trucks free access and roaming rights in the six Mexican and four U.S. border states is still not implemented. The intellectual property agreement is considered a fine reform, a model for other PTAs.

7. *Dispute settlement.* A dispute settlement procedure and provision for panels in dumping and subsidy cases were introduced. In effect, the dumping and subsidy agreements gave access to the mechanism that already existed under the U.S.-Canada agreement. Major disputes have arisen over tomatoes

(settled by setting a reference price that Mexican suppliers won't undercut under U.S. antidumping law), avocados (a U.S. ban dating from 1914 covered the whole country even though its justification, fruit fly infestation, is a danger in only a few states—the ban was partially lifted in 1997), and trucking (the United States continues to postpone access for Mexican trucks for safety reasons).

8. *Other side agreements.* In addition to the environmental side agreement struck before the treaty went into effect, two other side agreements were included after the election of President Clinton. Trinational commissions were established to consider labor standards and emergency action in case of trade surges. The labor standards commission examines coercion of unions, child labor, prison labor, enforcement of minimum wage laws, and the like. The side agreement on import surges creates an early warning mechanism to identify sectors where damage from imports is likely. If severe harm *does* ensue to U.S. workers, a temporary restoration (called a snapback) of tariffs to pre-NAFTA levels can be made for three years.

THE IMPACT OF NAFTA: EARLY EVIDENCE

It was rather silly for NAFTA's critics to claim that its major impact would occur right away because the Mexican economy is so small and because the phase-in of tariff cuts is over 15 years for the most sensitive products. U.S.-Mexican trade has certainly increased, from a total (exports plus imports) of $63 billion in 1991 to $177 billion in 1997. Mexico is now the second-largest market for U.S. exports, having replaced Japan in second place in 1997, and third, behind Japan, which is second, as a source of U.S. imports. (Canada is first in both categories.) Of U.S. exports to Mexico, 29.1% involves production sharing between U.S. and Mexican plants, and that is true of 40.4% of all U.S. imports from Mexico.[34]

After NAFTA came into force, the American trade surplus with Mexico turned into a deficit.[35] This has been used—unfairly—by NAFTA's critics as evidence against it. It is an unfair claim because the deficit reflects not the effect of NAFTA but the major depreciation of the peso in 1994-95, with a low value continuing to the present (nine per U.S. dollar in 1999 compared to just four per dollar in the early nineties). The fall of the peso had various causes, as is explored in Chapter 18, but the free trade agreement was not one of them. The depreciation of the peso stimulated manufacturing in the *maquiladoras* because it lowered the cost of producing in Mexico. Auto parts and electronics benefited especially. As part of the peso crisis, Mexico raised tariffs significantly in 1995, on 500 items, though of course not against its NAFTA partners.* If Canada and the United States had been hit by the tariff

---

* It was able to do so even where its tariffs were bound because over several years Mexican tariffs had fallen below their bound rates. *The Economist*, October 18, 1997.

increase, their exports to Mexico would have fallen much more than they did. The peso collapse had another effect. It rendered obsolete much work scholars had spent on estimating the number of jobs that would be created in exporting and lost through the competition of imports. It emphasized yet again the difficulty of predicting the results of a PTA with any accuracy.

The most thorough accounting of the impact of NAFTA so far is a report issued in 1997 by the U.S. Trade Representative.[36] It confirms that NAFTA has had much greater impact on Mexico than on the United States and Canada, and states that the agreement has had modest positive effects on U.S. exports and income and a more positive effect on Mexico. The number of workers who have had to change their jobs in the United States is small compared to the number dislocated for other reasons, such as technological change. (Overall U.S. unemployment at the time of writing was, as noted in the previous chapter, lower than at any point since the late 1960s.) There has been no great flood of plants to Mexico; U.S. investment in that country has averaged under 0.5% of U.S. firms' total spending on plant and equipment since 1994.[37] It will of course take many years to assess the full effects of NAFTA, but at present a conclusion of modest gains seems justified.

NAFTA'S EXPANSION DELAYED

Many expected that NAFTA would rapidly be expanded, with Chile first in line. Talks began in July 1995, soon after the NAFTA start-up. Congressional opposition developed in the United States. There were demands for tighter environmental and labor rules, for elimination of the dumping and subsidy dispute settlement mechanism where Chile was concerned, and for some sort of rule to prevent currency depreciation, which (as Mexico showed) can upset trade relations.[38] In the end President Clinton lost his fast-track negotiating authority, which has still not been regained. Chile announced it would not negotiate specific steps until that happens, so the talks are on hold. In the meantime, Chile has negotiated a separate free trade agreement with Canada.

Numerous Caribbean island-nations agreed in 1994 to seek NAFTA membership as well, but they, too, are unlikely to achieve it unless and until the U.S. President regains fast-track authority. A U.S. bill to grant these nations parity of treatment has several times failed to receive congressional assent.

OTHER IMPORTANT PTAS

Several of the world's many preferential trade agreements are important because of their innovative particulars or because they are large in size.

THE AUSTRALIA-NEW ZEALAND AGREEMENT

An antipodal arrangement, the Australia-New Zealand Closer Economic Relations Trade Agreement (ANZCERTA), is important because of its comprehensiveness and its openness. Following its start in 1983, tariffs were completely eliminated in 1987, and all quota restrictions were removed in 1990. Subsidies on exports within the area have been abolished, as have antidumping rules. Technical, health, and safety standards are harmonized, and equal access has been given to government contracts. This is one of the few arrangements to liberalize its protection against outsiders at the same time that the internal barriers were being torn down. The chances of trade diversion are accordingly lessened. Intraregional exports as a percentage of the total exports of Australia and New Zealand are still (1997) a very low 10.5%, however.

ASSOCIATION OF SOUTHEAST ASIAN NATIONS

The Association of Southeast Asian Nations (ASEAN) was founded in 1967 by Indonesia, Malaysia, the Philippines, Singapore, Thailand, Brunei from 1984, and Burma/Myanmar from 1997. ASEAN has announced that Cambodia, Laos, and Vietnam will eventually be allowed to join. This group only agreed to move to a free trade area (with its own name, Asian Free Trade Area or AFTA) in 1993, the process to take 15 years. There are many problems, including the desire of Indonesia and the Philippines to move slowly, the existence of many NTBs, and the existence of high tariffs in some countries (Indonesia) and low ones in others—Singapore tariffs are virtually zero. Strict rules of origin to qualify for preferences (50% of a given product's value added must be local) limit the benefits yet further. The recent serious slowdown in the Asian economies has lessened the impetus for immediate free trade, the argument being that beleaguered industries should not have to face additional pressures during bad times.

MERCOSUR

MERCOSUR (Mercado Comun del Sur), the "Southern Market" composed of Argentina, Brazil, Paraguay, Uruguay, started up in 1991 as a free trade area.* In 1995 it moved to customs union status with a common external tariff at 11 different levels ranging up to 20%. The customs union involved a tariff reduction by Brazil and a rise by the others. About 90% of all goods now move duty-free within MERCOSUR, including virtually all goods except cars and sugar between Argentina and Brazil. Remaining intra-market tariffs are scheduled for

---

* Brazilians speak Portuguese. There the arrangement is known as MERCOSUL.

elimination in 2006. Since 1996 there has been a new MERCOSUR/Chile FTA, as Chile sought another union instead of NAFTA. Bolivia has also signed on with MERCOSUR/Bolivia free trade. Brazil is pushing for a South American Free Trade Area, or SAFTA, by 2005, and negotiations are scheduled for a MERCOSUR-EU free trade area.

Unlike NAFTA, MERCOSUR has made little progress in attempting to cover services, intellectual property, or government procurement.[39] The dispute settlement mechanism is primitive and little tested. There are many remaining NTBs, including import licenses, and about 300 products, including many high-tech items, still have their own separate external tariffs (as in a free trade area). MERCOSUR has been somewhat disrupted by the recent economic problems in the Southern Cone. Brazil's inflation rate is much higher than Argentina's. Argentina's "statistical tax" on all imports included those from MERCOSUR. Brazil's crisis led that country suddenly to impose quotas on auto imports, cutting shipments by half. (Within MERCOSUR, many cars are made in Argentina and shipped to Brazil.) Later, Brazil abolished the quotas on MERCOSUR imports, but by then damage had been done. Border controls still mean a lot of red tape and currency regulations still exist in Brazil. That country responded to a large 1997 trade deficit by limiting import credits. Firms purchasing goods on less than 180 days' credit have to purchase the foreign exchange when the goods are delivered. Brazil's 1999 devaluation of its currency caused substantial dislocation in Argentina, whose peso is pegged to the dollar. For a time exports from the latter to Brazil fell by nearly a quarter and imports surged.

Most economists believe that MERCOSUR has caused more trade creation than trade diversion.[40] But Alexander Yeats notes that the fastest-growing trade has been in cars, buses, agricultural machinery, and other capital-intensive products that are not competitive internationally. Yeats argues that there has been considerable trade diversion in MERCOSUR.[41] A special concern for the membership is that such diversion would reduce access to high-technology imports from advanced industrial countries, thus limiting opportunities for technical improvement and perhaps limiting growth.[42] For all that, intra-market trade has grown from only $4 billion in 1990 to $18 billion in 1997—though trade was falling in 1998-99 because of recessions in Brazil and Argentina.[43]

THE CENTRAL EUROPEAN FREE TRADE AREA

A Central European Free Trade Area (CEFTA) was established in 1993 by the Czech Republic, Hungary, Poland, and Slovakia.* By means of bilateral free trade agreements, CEFTA benefits were later extended to Slovenia, Bulgaria, and

---

* All these were former members of the Communist bloc's own PTA known as COMECON, the Council for Mutual Economic Assistance. It was also known by the initials CMEA. COMECON included the Soviet Union, six Communist countries of Eastern Europe (but not Albania and Yugoslavia), Mongolia, Cuba, and Vietnam. The wave of reform that swept over the old Soviet Union and Eastern Europe in 1989-91 brought the death of COMECON and considerable

Romania. Tariffs among the members are to be eliminated by the year 2001, and all members have free trade agreements with the EU, although their agricultural commodities remain excluded, their textiles for 10 years, and their steel for five years. Most imports from anywhere into these eastern countries are now free of controls except for tariffs. Intra-CEFTA trade is actually quite small, less than 10% of total trade for all countries except the Czech Republic and Slovakia.

ARAB FREE TRADE AREA

An Arab Free Trade Area (AFTA), was launched at the start of 1998, aiming for removal of trade barriers by 2008. It consists of 18 of the 22 members of the Arab League. But intra-AFTA exports are now only 7% of all exports.[44]

VERY LARGE PTAS

Preferential trade agreements are not just growing in number. Plans for them are also growing in size. The trend has led to a reaction, with some economists questioning whether the trend is healthy. The major plans for new very large areas include the following:

Asia-Pacific Economic Cooperation

An Asia-Pacific Economic Cooperation (APEC) agreement has set a goal of free trade by 2010 for the developed-country participants and 2020 for the developing-country ones.[45] The signatories are Australia, Brunei, Canada, Chile, China, Hong Kong, Indonesia, Japan, Malaysia, Mexico, New Zealand, Philippines, Papua New Guinea, Singapore, South Korea, Taiwan, Thailand, and the United States. Which countries are in which group is not fully established, nor is "free and open trade" fully defined. There is a long way to go, because tariffs average 40% in some countries. Services are not mentioned either. At present, APEC seems to be moving more toward unilateral liberalization rather than toward becoming a PTA.

Free Trade Area of the Americas

There is a framework agreement to work toward free trade among virtually all the Latin American and Caribbean countries and the United States and

---

disintegration of the trade of the former Communist countries. Even today, there are still considerable barriers, even among the states that once made up the U.S.S.R. (Russia and Belarus did, however, establish a free trade agreement in 1994.) New countries such as Armenia, Azerbaijan, Georgia, Estonia, Latvia, Lithuania, Kazakhstan, Kyrgyzstan, and Ukraine rapidly redirected their trade away from Russia and to the outside world. Not only trade with Russia but trade among the old republics of the U.S.S.R. has also fallen substantially.

Canada.[46] The political leaders of every country of the Americas except Cuba have agreed in principle to a Free Trade Area of the Americas (FTAA) to start in 2005 and to be implemented in the 10 years that follow. The FTAA would coexist with present arrangements such as NAFTA and MERCOSUR. Suggested by President Bush in 1990, this vast proposal was originally known as "Enterprise for the Americas". (Twenty years ago the idea would have been vilified by that region's leaders as Yankee imperialism.) Because only about 13% of U.S. trade is currently with Latin America, there is presumably some significant chance of trade diversion.

Transatlantic Free Trade Area

A Transatlantic Free Trade Area or TAFTA between NAFTA and the EU has been suggested, originally by Canada. Major difficulties lie in the way, including the EU's Common Agricultural Policy and high tariffs on textiles, cars, electronics, and paper products, as well as considerable remaining tariff escalation. Although a "New Trans-Atlantic Agenda" was established to cooperate in moving toward free trade, the TAFTA is presently considered to be a premature idea.[47]

Trade Diversion and Regional Integration

The danger of extensive regional integration is that trade diversion will become substantial, harming not only outside countries but the people within the PTAs themselves. Whether serious trade diversion occurs depends principally on the size of the external trade barriers. Politically, too, successful PTAs may undermine the support for multilateral reductions in barriers. For example, if you own factories in Mexico and the United States as an advantageous consequence of NAFTA, then with multilateral free trade you might find you have to close your Mexican factories because other sources of supply are now cheaper.[48]

There would be less reason to worry if a PTA always meant that all members would adopt the lowest tariffs of any single member. Unfortunately, however, they may often be easiest to negotiate when they result in a *higher* tariff against non-members, and competitive pressures from non-members may result in quick rises in unbound tariffs against them. Both tendencies increase the danger of trade diversion. Also, they may be easier to forge when some threatened sectors are excluded.[49] Large and hostile regional free trade blocs peering at one another over forbidding external barriers hardly seems optimal. Trade wars are worse when the many rather than the few are involved, and the dangers would seem intensified in a world consisting of a few very large PTAS.[50] Furthermore, severe difficulties might face the small countries left out of a regional arrangement.

The danger inherent in the growth of large regional integration arrangements is that substantial trade diversion is possible or even likely.[51] It is generally agreed that trading blocs are less trade diverting if they are small, and also that there will be no diversion if one bloc grows so large as to encompass the entire world. Following this logic, a small number of very large blocs might cause the greatest amount of trade-diversion. Two or three large blocs focused around Europe, the United States, and Japan might be the worst case.[52]

Following Paul Krugman, a number of economists downplay the problem, arguing that arrangements among neighboring countries will usually be less trade-diverting because the natural protection of transport costs causes such countries to trade more with one another. "Natural zones" are less trade-diverting because so much trade goes on among the neighbors anyway. In this reading, "unnatural" free trade areas among members located very far away from each other would be more likely to cause trade diversion.[53]

Fred Bergsten's view of the Krugman position is cautious. The effect of geographical propinquity has been diminished by reductions in transport and distribution costs, he notes. A great deal of trade is *not* among neighbors; trade diversion is the *goal* of numerous arrangements.[54] Many neighbors (in Africa, South Asia, and Latin America) trade little with one another in any case. It can be added that trade bargaining may become much harder when it is between large blocs. The countries within the blocs may have had a difficult time in coming to an internal decision among themselves, with so many carefully balanced compromises that there is little scope to change the position in negotiations with another bloc. A prime example is the agricultural policy of the EU. The internal negotiations leading to that policy have been so hard fought that there is virtually no room for give and take with foreigners—the arduous task of reaching an internal consensus would have to be done all over again. All these considerations point to multilateral free trade as much the best policy.*

Admittedly, some of the talk on large regional preferential arrangements probably contains an element of bluffing to propel forward negotiations within the WTO. Yet no one can be sure whether the large regional blocs would be "halfway houses to global free trade or the battlements from which future trade wars will be fought."[55]

---

* Jagdish Bhagwati and his co-authors go further, and are actively hostile to the concept of the natural free trade area. Several theoretical and practical reasons for this skepticism are discussed in Bhagwati and Arvind Panagariya, eds. *The Economics of Preferential Trade Agreements* (Washington: AEI Press, 1996), ch. 1. Such free trade areas are called "stumbling blocks, not building blocks" in Bhagwati, David Greenaway, and Panagariya, "Trading Preferentially: Theory and Policy," *Economic Journal* 108, 449 (July 1998): 1128-48.

PTAS WITH A RICH PATRON

Mexico is poor and the United States and Canada are rich. NAFTA represents a new trend toward economic integration between less-developed countries and developed countries. Often such PTAs involve "hub-and-spoke" arrangements. Small-country B has an FTA with large-country A and so does small-country C, but spoke-spoke trade between B and C is not liberalized. In such cases the firms in the small countries have trouble competing with the hub's firms, which get duty-free inputs from all spokes. These crisscrossing PTAs with different tariff rates, dubbed "spaghetti bowl" arrangements by Jagdish Bhagwati, are especially common in the agreements of the European Union and the United States.[56]

Such action has a certain "colonial" pattern, as it usually ties the trade of the poorer partner tightly to the metropolitan economy of the "patron." In many cases there will be aid, technical help, and a defense umbrella accompanying the deal, raising the benefits for the poor country. Some of these are one-way patron-client relationships. That is, the less-developed countries involved do not have to extend reciprocal tariff cuts to the patrons. This greatly increases the chance for trade diversion in the poor countries.[57]

The European Spaghetti Bowl

The EU has moved strongly toward many free trade agreements with a wide variety of poor-country partners.[58] The many pacts with Eastern European countries have already been noted. Bilateral agreements involving bilateral preferences exist between the EU and North African, Mediterranean, and Middle Eastern countries. In 1999, the EU signed a new free trade agreement with South Africa and continued talks with Mexico leading toward an FTA. Reports indicate that negotiations between the EU and MERCOSUR may establish an FTA in the not-too-distant future.[59]

THE LOMÉ CONVENTION

The oldest of the EU preferences are those advanced by the EU to the former colonies of its members, the African-Caribbean-Pacific (ACP) states. They are not reciprocal—that is, the ACP states do not have to give free access to EU goods and most do not. The arrangement is called the Lomé Convention, having first been established in Togo's capital, Lomé, in 1976.[60] Renewed several times, it grants lower tariffs and guaranteed access outside quota barriers and VERs to the ACP countries. Since it is not a full-fledged free trade agreement, it has required and has received a waiver from the GATT and WTO rules. The current version is scheduled to expire in February 2000.

The Lomé preferences have had only limited benefits—the margins are slim, trade diversion has predominated, monopsonistic European buyers have captured some of the preferences, and the poorest ACP states have not been flexible enough to take advantage of the arrangement. The EU wants to replace the present arrangement with free trade areas linking Europe to six different regions in which the present roster of ACP states is found. Unfortunately, such FTAs would cause a large loss of tariff revenues to some of the world's poorest countries, and European exporters with monopsony power (for competition among overseas firms is limited in many African markets) might raise their prices to capture the revenue effect. Surely a better step would be a move toward multilateral free trade rather than the more dubious benefits of the EU proposal.[61]

U.S. Free Trade Agreements

The United States has a much smaller number of spaghetti-bowl rich-poor arrangements—with the Caribbean, the Andean countries, and Israel. (Attempts to construct a broad free trade agreement with sub-Saharan Africa have been made several times, but have not yet gained congressional approval.)

THE CBERA

The first of the U.S. agreements is the Caribbean Basin Economic Recovery Act (CBERA), which took effect January 1, 1984. CBERA is the trade portion of the Caribbean Basin Initiative dating from 1982. Originally subject to a time limit, it was renewed permanently in 1990.[62] The long time frame is important for planning investments. CBERA was the first U.S. preferential treatment for an entire geographical area. Its details are explored in the accompanying box. Canada has a similar arrangement with the Caribbean called Caribcan. Neither scheme requires the Caribbean partners to extend the same preferences.

U.S. CBERA DETAILS

All Caribbean territories are included except Cuba and Suriname, which have not qualified for political reasons, and Anguilla, the Cayman Islands, and the Turks and Caicos Islands, which have had tax disagreements with the United States. To acquire duty-free status, an article must be imported directly to the United States from a CBERA territory. Thirty-five percent of the import's appraised value has to be value added in one or more of the beneficiary countries. All U.S. import quotas remain in force, including those on textiles and clothing and the TRQ on sugar, both of which are of interest to the CBERA

---

countries. Sugar is especially important for some islands, and any gains from CBERA have to be weighed against the decline in their cane sugar production to half the level of 20 years ago. Furthermore, U.S. antidumping and counter-vailing duty legislation continues to apply, petroleum and petroleum products do not qualify for preferential treatment, and there is a clause carrying extra safeguards for perishable agricultural commodities.

The result of all the exclusions is that the impact of CBERA has been strictly limited, with only about a third of all member exports to the United States receiving a benefit. While not denying that eventual dynamic effects might develop, it is quite clear that CBERA has been gutted by U.S. protectionist interests.

After NAFTA came into effect, the CBERA countries negotiated to obtain parity of treatment with Mexico. Later they expressed willingness to exchange their CBERA preferences for NAFTA membership. So far neither quest has been successful.

THE ANDEAN TRADE PREFERENCE ACT

An Andean Trade Preference Act (ATPA) was passed by the U.S. Congress in 1991. It established a duty-free arrangement resembling CBERA for Bolivia, Colombia, Ecuador, and Peru. Much the same exclusions apply as they do to the CBERA countries. The act will expire in 10 years, unlike CBERA, which is permanent.

THE U.S.-ISRAEL FREE TRADE AGREEMENT

The remaining U.S. preference agreement took effect in March 1985, when the United States and Israel agreed to eliminate all tariffs against one another in four stages over a 10-year period culminating in 1995.[63] The customs union with Israel might appear not very important on the world stage, but it was the first U.S. bilateral arrangement and it removed virtually all tariff and non-tariff barriers. (Escape clause safeguards, antidumping laws, the regulations against subsidies, and textile protection still apply.) This new union would appear to pose some threat of trade diversion for Israel, with more expensive U.S. exports substituting to some extent for what Israel could buy at cheaper world market prices. From the Israeli point of view, however, that problem is no doubt completely overshadowed by the further evidence of a strong political and economic alliance with the United States. Any costs of diversion are well offset by benefits in other forms, including aid and military support.

The "Colonial" Pattern of These Agreements

These agreements reveal an increasing tendency for rich patrons to cement their poor clients into trading blocs, all discriminating against one another, and with the client states becoming wedded to their privileges. There is some irony in the United States joining in that game, because intransigent opposition to the very similar imperial preferences of the British and French colonial days was a hallmark of U.S. foreign policy for three-quarters of a century.[64] No single patron-client arrangement may have the capacity to do very much damage, but together, by making trade discrimination common-place, they could harm world welfare. The possibility of trade diversion is ever present. At the very least, the growing need to administer different trade laws applying to different countries means a more bloated bureaucracy than before and increased frictions over trade issues. The suspicion arises that many of these patron-client PTAs are subterfuges designed in part to avoid having to lower trade barriers to outsiders.

THE RISK TO A SMALL MEMBER

Small countries run risks when they enter PTAs with rich patrons. True, they enjoy the small-country advantage of being able to trade at the large country's prices. But, alarmingly, the preferences might cause shifts in their economies, which can then cause trouble if the rules are changed or if threats are made to change them. A fine illustration from a century ago has recently attracted the attention of economists and stands as a reminder of the risk run by small members of a PTA involving a large hegemon.[65] The Kingdom of Hawaii faced a dilemma in the days of King Kalakaua (1874-91). By the last quarter of the nineteenth century, the Hawaiian kingdom had advanced remarkably. Its independence was respected by all, it had constitutional government with a credible legislature and judiciary, and property rights were secure. Its surprisingly modern capital city of Honolulu boasted buildings of stone and brick and a streetcar system. And it had a tariff reciprocity treaty with the United States, pushed by King Kalakaua and signed in 1876.

The U.S.-Hawaii reciprocity treaty removed the high U.S. sugar tariff from Hawaiian exports. Since Hawaii had a cost advantage over U.S. states such as Louisiana and Florida, the islands' sugar industry was rapidly developed by foreign planters. But the treaty was a short-term one, expiring in 1883. Hawaii, with its valuable new sugar industry, had much to lose by non-renewal, so the United States could and did demand better terms—which in this case involved a Hawaiian grant of base rights at Pearl Harbor, a concession that had previously been impossible as a political matter. Then, just seven years later, the U.S. Congress passed the McKinley tariff of 1890, which made sugar a duty-free import but gave U.S. producers a 2¢ per pound bounty (as subsidies were then called). On the day the new rate came into force, the U.S. sugar price fell by 38%. Hawaii's exports plummeted, from a total of $13 million in 1890 to $8 million in 1892. The capital invested in the sugar industry was at risk. The American planters, led by Sanford Dole, overthrew the Hawaiian kingdom in a *coup d'état* of January 1893. They wanted U.S. annexation, and they got it in 1898. Now the planters could obtain the U.S. bounty, too. (In the interim, President Dole—yes, there *was* a President Dole after all—and his allies had to settle for a republic.)

The story has general application. The small country might gear up to produce its specialty with costly expansion and upgrading. This capital is in a sense "hostage". One can see a similar process in German–Balkan relations in the Hitler era, with the Balkans becoming more attached to the German economy and less attached to the rest of the world and so more vulnerable to German political pressure. Later, Balkan governments had to make more and greater concessions to keep their entrée to the German market. The lesson is repeated to this day in Canada by opponents of U.S.-Canadian free trade— and these opponents do have a point—small economies have to keep their eyes open.[66]

REGIONAL TRADE ARRANGEMENTS IN THE LDCS

Most examples of economic integration are actually among the less developed countries, not the developed ones, with more of them in Africa and Latin America than elsewhere.[67] The vast majority are obscure.*

---

* The prominent ones are ASEAN, MERCOSUR, and the new Arab Free Trade Area, already discussed. Several others have attracted some notice because of their size or their structure, or their problems. (1) CARICOM (the Caribbean Community) dates from 1973. Its island members formed an FTA in 1991 and plan to have a common external tariff. In July 1994, Caricom leaders agreed to seek full membership in NAFTA and did not accept the NAFTA parity offered by the United States. (2) The CACM (Central American Common Market) dating from 1960 was broken up in 1969 by a war between El Salvador and Honduras, revived from 1986, and achieved free trade in 1996. Trade diversion is believed to have outweighed trade creation, however, with considerable oligopolistic behavior instead of specialization and scale economies. (3) An Andean Group of 1969, consisting of Bolivia, Ecuador, Colombia, Peru, and Venezuela, was formed partly to escape from Brazil's influence. It attained FTA status in 1992 and a customs union with common external tariff in 1994. Large static gains have been claimed, although some authorities state that these gains are exaggerated. (4) SACU, the Southern African Customs Union, is made up of Botswana, Lesotho, Namibia, South Africa, and Swaziland. It is unusual in that the members employ a revenue-sharing formula that allocates a fixed proportion of the union's tariff revenue among its members. This provides over half of Lesotho's government revenue and a third or more of Namibia's and Swaziland's.

Why Arrangements among the LDCs Usually Do Not Perform Well

Most attempts at economic integration among less-developed countries have not performed very well. When the level of industrialization is low, new industries do not spring up easily and when they do they are high in cost so the chances for trade diversion and monopoly creation are increased. Frequently, regional arrangements among poorer countries have quite high external barriers against outsiders, which increases these chances. Moreover, many of the poorest countries still engage in foreign exchange control—their exchange rates are artificial and the signals of comparative advantage register weakly. Finally, some poor-country PTAs seem to involve a degree of shamming. Trade ministers see new opportunities for photo-ops; extra bureaucratic posts give expanded scope for patronage; untrodden avenues open for rewarding supporters and penalizing opponents.

When production already exists in one country but not the others, progress is difficult. The country with the lead typically wants to eliminate trade barriers rapidly; the others obstruct in the hope that they can catch up and grouse when they do not do so; the advance slows. Perhaps more important than the political element, however, is that the economic characteristics of most poor countries do not favor the extensive intraindustrial (and intrafactoral) trade that characterizes developed nations. No wonder Ali El-Agraa says of such PTAs, "the record of achievement is almost blank."[68] Especially in Africa, "negligible trade creation has been the rule, rather than the exception."[69]

A FURTHER LOOK AT THE PROBLEMS OF LDC ARRANGEMENTS

Unfortunately, even though most regional trading arrangements have been formed in the less-developed countries, often these countries cannot meet many of the conditions already discussed earlier in the checklist for welfare improvement.[70] The numbers below are the same as in the checklist, which can be referred to as needed. The comments in parentheses indicate why the conditions may not be met by many arrangements.

1. The elasticity of demand should be high, so that as internal barriers are lowered, trade will be created among the members. (LDC imports often contain a high proportion of essential inputs such as capital goods and oil. Demand may be quite inelastic.)

2. The elasticity of supply should be high, so that as tariffs fall among the members production will rise rapidly to take the place of imports from non-members. (A poor economy is an inflexible one; LDCs have more government controls over economic activity, an inadequate infrastructure of transport and communications, low levels of literacy, education, and so forth. Supply may be inelastic as a result.)

3. Low-cost producers should belong. (Especially in capital-intensive and high-technology manufacturing, LDCs are not the lowest-cost producers. Furthermore, LDC unions often have a rather limited membership.)

4. If countries already conduct a large proportion of their trade with one another, then diversion of trade to a higher-cost source within the union will make little difference. (Many LDCs carry on little trade with their neighbors. Transport to the developed industrial countries is often much easier.)

5. If the member countries import only a small percentage of their consumption, then diversion of trade to a higher-cost source within the arrangement will make little difference. (Some LDCs, including the smaller ones and minerals exporters, import a large share of their consumption.)

6. Tariffs in a middling range may leave the membership most vulnerable to trade diversion. (LDC tariffs are often in a middling range.)

7. The external tariff should be constructed to reduce the dispersion of tariffs. (LDCs' tariffs show great variation; LDC trade arrangements have often adopted high external barriers.)

8. A union, if economically important, may be able to exert a favorable terms-of-trade effect. (LDCs are often economically unimportant; their unions will seldom have this power.)

9. Very different factor proportions will stimulate trade along Heckscher-Ohlin lines. (The economic structure of the LDC members of a union is often quite similar, so trade creation on Heckscher-Ohlin lines does not occur.)

10. Growth in intraindustrial trade may make an arrangement less disruptive. (LDC trade is seldom intraindustrial. Their level of development and income are too low to permit trade creation along intraindustrial lines.)

11. Fast economic growth is advantageous. Wealthy countries can afford regional development funds and trade adjustment assistance. (Economic growth in numerous LDCs has been slow, especially in Africa but also in Latin America and South Asia. Regional development funds and trade adjustment assistance are often unaffordable.)

12. Outward-oriented economic policies will tend to stimulate trade. (Inward-oriented policies are common in the LDCs. Vested interests are strong; corruption may be rampant. LDCs tend to resist reductions in internal barriers; they know some parts of their small industrial base will suffer but that government funds for adjustment will be limited or unavailable. Rules of origin are often very strict. Economies of scale frequently do not appear, largely due to an oligopolistic structure that includes market-sharing and the fact that barriers have often not been reduced sufficiently to generate them.)[71]

THE LESSON FOR THE LDCS

The lesson is that policy-makers must be especially alert to possible trade diversion when preference arrangements are made. None of the above is writ in stone. A strong commitment to free trade can work wonders, and even if static trade diversion predominates an arrangement still might be worthwhile if the dynamic effects—economies of scale in intraunion sales, higher investment, improved marketing, a greater spur to productive efficiency, better management, technical change, an end run around proliferating NTBs in trading partners—are large enough to offset the trade diversion. The greater zeal for open trade in the LDCs and the adherence to free trade arrangements by major players like Mexico, Brazil, and Argentina (in NAFTA and MERCOSUR) may in time begin to change the perception that LDC arrangements work poorly.

FOREIGN TRADE ZONES: LITTLE BITS OF FREE TRADE

If a nation cannot join with others and fears the effect of simply removing tariffs, it has the option of making *part* of its country free of trade barriers. Under WTO rules it is perfectly proper to designate certain geographical areas as zones of free trade, even when the rest of the country is subject to normal tariffs, quotas, and VERs. These are called foreign trade zones (FTZs) or alternatively export processing zones.[72]

Such zones are much used everywhere and have been for many years (the first one was established at Hamburg, Germany, in 1888).* Zones now exist in over 80 countries, including Russia and China, with some 10% of global trade routed through them. They are "isolated, enclosed, and policed" areas, to use the language of the U.S. law, where a country's trade regulations mostly do not apply. If the goods are intended for sale in the country concerned, duties, quotas, and so forth are levied only when the goods cross the boundary of the zone. (Antidumping and countervailing duties cannot be avoided, however. These are still collected when goods arrive in a zone. Laws concerning illegal products or substances continue to apply as well.)

U.S. FTZs

In the United States, FTZs are allowed under an act of 1934. The first one was established at Staten Island in New York. For many years they were typically used for warehousing of goods in transit—imports later re-exported—and for

---

* Long before this time a single ship had been given similar status by the Imperial Russian government. When Tsar Peter the Great opened the new port and capital city of St. Petersburg in 1701, he granted to the first foreign merchant vessel that arrived exemption from Russian tariffs for the rest of its life. Not surprisingly, this wooden ship proved to have an extraordinarily long career, lovingly maintained in good repair by its Dutch owners, keeping to the seas for nearly a century, and, needless to say, calling often at Russian ports. See Fernand Braudel, *The Wheels of Commerce* (New York: Harper and Row, 1979), 241.

inspection, destruction of inferior goods, remarking, and repackaging. For example, it would be embarrassing to import 10,000 pairs of shoes and then, having paid the duty, to find that 50 pairs were defective. Far better to import the shoes into an FTZ and examine the shipment there. No waste would occur when the shoes cross the zone's boundary; no duty will have to be paid on defects.*

But business was slow to develop. By 1970, there were still only eight U.S. zones, and turnover was only about $100 million in value. Several developments increased their attractiveness. Manufacturing inside U.S. FTZs was authorized by the Boggs Amendment of 1950. A Treasury Department ruling in 1980 allowed domestic processing costs incurred in the zones and profits earned there to be free of duty. Thus, tariffs applied only to the imported inputs. Finally, a 1982 amendment allowed the exclusion of overhead costs such as transport and insurance from dutiable value, further reducing the base value on which tariff is collected.[73] Business boomed.

All customs ports of entry are eligible to have an FTZ. Subzones may be established elsewhere at the discretion of the U.S. Foreign Trade Zones Board, which administers the law. Typically, a subzone surrounds a manufacturing plant. The subzones generate much the most activity. Of the merchandise received in 1997, 10% came to zones and 90% to subzones. Petroleum and autos and auto parts are by far the most important products involved. Over two-thirds of the shipments into zones and subzones came from U.S. domestic suppliers.

In total there are 319 active U.S. FTZs and subzones, compared to a total of just 27 in 1975. About 2,900 firms operate in them, employing over 365,000 people. The most in any state is 27, in Texas.[†] Exports used to be the major activity, but now the domestic market is the preferred destination; 90% of the output manufactured in the zones is sold in the United States, and is thus subject to the trade regulations. Only 10% is exported.

---

* A recent application is from the U.S. Department of Energy so that foreign producers of petroleum can store reserves in the United States in the U.S. Strategic Petroleum Reserve. This reserve has excess capacity. Foreign producers would not have to pay duty and the oil could be exported from there. The U.S. government would gain some revenue by charging a storage fee.

† Students researching the activities undertaken in the zones had best be alerted that their managers are tight-lipped about them. (See the comment to that effect in the *Wall Street Journal*, September 30, 1987.) In Maine, author JSH could not persuade the manager of the Bangor zone (No. 58) to reveal the names of any of the firms operating there, even after explaining that all he wanted was some examples for an international economics textbook. Under a new rule, authority to operate an FTZ lapses if it has not been used for five years from the date of approval.

RECENT USES OF THE ZONES

Production in FTZs has several advantages over production outside the zones.[74] (1) Whenever components pay a higher duty than a finished product, which is called a reversed-cascading or inverted tariff structure, a firm can import components, assemble the product in a zone, and then sell the product in the national market, so reducing its tariff liability. Two cases in point: imported parts for TVs are dutiable at double the rates on complete televisions, while with autos, the tariff on parts is as much as four times the tariff on the vehicles themselves. Over two-thirds of the firms responding to a recent survey of the U.S. International Trade Commission said they used the FTZs to lower their tariff bills when tariffs were higher on components than finished products. (2) A firm can delay tariff payments. Ordinarily, the tariff is due within 10 days of the import, but with assembly in an FTZ the tariff is due within 10 days of the good leaving the zone. (3) FTZs help because some customs formalities are streamlined, thus saving time and money when producers use just-in-time inventory management.

OPPOSITION TO THE ZONES

Though the U.S. zones had virtually no adversaries for many years, in the 1980s the opposition to them grew intense. Protectionist interests have severely limited the use of FTZs by producers who use imported sugar or make bicycles or TVs. The Foreign Trade Zones Board in practice applies limits if it believes the inverted tariff structure causing components to have higher duties than finished products was intended by Congress, but it does not do so when it believes that the situation has resulted from trade concessions and negotiations.

Many critics now claim that the absence of duties on imported components fuels U.S. imports. A proposal presently being considered by the Foreign Trade Zones Board is to disallow applications for FTZs that would cause a net increase in imports. The AFL-CIO has called for the *complete abolition* of the U.S. law, or, at minimum, repeal of the portion of it that permits manufacturing in the zones. Critics have charged that liberalizing trade inside the zones may divert attention from illiberal policies outside the zones, a sweeping under the rug that could conceivably do more harm than good. The path to freer trade, even in the innocuous form of a foreign trade zone, here as elsewhere can be a rough one.

China: A Major User

China has been a major user of FTZs, which in that country are called special (or open) economic zones.[75] Possible since 1979, these zones have additional benefits for their users, including favorable tax policies and simplified investment procedures. In 1980 China established four large ones—Zhuhai, Shenzhen (these two near Hong Kong), Shantou in Guangdong, and Xiamen in Fujian opposite Taiwan. The Shenzhen zone, on China's border with Hong Kong, became the most prosperous, accounting for about 15% of China's exports. In 1984, 14 coastal cities were allowed most of the privileges of the SEZs, and in 1988 the entire large island of Hainan was made into a zone. In 1990, part of the city of Shanghai was given even more liberal privileges, while in 1992 SEZ status was extended to 23 inland cities and 13 more along borders.

Like FTZs everywhere, China's zones are walled off by policed boundaries from the rest of China. Joint ventures with foreigners make much use of the zones, their interest stimulated by the important 1992 decision to allow foreign firms and joint ventures to sell their zone-made products within China. Most foreign investment is there, with the country's production of electronics, machinery, and textiles and clothing mainly located in them. Hong Kong firms have invested the most, about two-thirds of the total, with Taiwan second (mostly in Fujian), the United States third, and Japan fourth.

Criticism of China's policy is self-evident. Since these zones have been so successful, it is hard to see exactly why reasonable public policy would not grant the same benefits to the rest of China. The zones have brought prosperity to some regions without touching other regions. Actually, the migration of labor and movement of capital into the zones can be seen as a negative for areas losing the labor and capital. The same comment can be made concerning foreign trade zones everywhere in the world, but it is salient for China because of the poverty and the protection outside the zones.

CONCLUSION

The major message of this chapter derives from both theory and evidence. Economic integration in all its forms may bring substantial benefits. But it will not necessarily do so. A broad body of evidence points to static and dynamic advantages in a wide variety of settings. Against these, the discovery of the trade diversion effect in the 1950s followed by the EU's trade-diverting actions in agriculture and the unremarkable performance of many poor-country PTAs have made economists far more aware of the economic burdens that integration places on non-members and the costs that could be inflicted on the member populations. Finally, the possibility that several great trading blocs will emerge to dominate world trade gives pause to many economists. An outcome where integration leads to even more intense disputes than the present ones is alarming indeed. As so often in economics, the real labor is to separate the wheat from the chaff.

VOCABULARY AND CONCEPTS

ANZCERTA (Australia-New Zealand
 Economic Relations Trade
 Agreement)
ASEAN
Caribbean Basin Economic Recovery
 Act (CBERA)
Common market
Customs union
Economic union
European Free Trade Association (EFTA)
European Union (EU, also EC and EEC)
Free trade area (FTA)
Hub-and-spoke PTAs

Maquiladoras
MERCOSUR
North American Free Trade Agreement
 (NAFTA)
Preferential trade agreements (PTAs)
Spaghetti bowl PTAs
Transatlantic Free Trade Area (TAFTA)
Trade-creating customs union
Trade creation
Trade diversion
Trade-diverting customs union
Trade suppression
U.S.-Canada FTA

QUESTIONS

1. What is the difference between a free trade area and a customs union? An economic union? Use Europe and NAFTA to illustrate your points.
2. For the EU, what was the significance of the single currency for the type of arrangement?
3. Explain, using simple (Viner-type) arithmetic, the concept of trade diversion and trade creation.
4. Show, using diagrams, what causes a customs union to be trade diverting and what causes it to be trade creating.
5. In a customs union, under what circumstance will the importing nation be a net loser? Demonstrate. (Hint: Check the relation of $C + E$ to $B + D$.)
6. In what types of goods has the EU shown trade creation effects more than trade diversion? Vice versa? Why?
7. Can you design a tariff against outsiders that would leave your country better off than it would be in a customs union?
8. Why do customs unions among poor countries seem to work less well? Give examples and show what conditions lessen their chances for success.

9. Where the United States and Canada are concerned, NAFTA is predicated on dynamic gains to specialization, as discussed in Chapter. Explain.

10. Static gains involving elimination of deadweight losses would hardly have been enough for Canada and Mexico to enter an FTA with the United States. Why?

11. Explain and evaluate the pros and cons of NAFTA, including the environmental questions.

12. What might be the problems of world trade if the world becomes divided into large trading blocs?

13. "Like so much else, an FTZ is the product of a nation's rather peculiar laws." Explain why FTZs are formed. Supposing they remained legal, consider what kinds of changes in national laws would lead to fewer of them. (Don't concentrate on regulating FTZs. Think instead of why companies use them.)

NOTES

1. The literature on economic integration has grown exponentially. See Jagdish Bhagwati, David Greenaway, and Arvind Panagariya, "Trading Preferentially: Theory and Policy," *Economic Journal* 108, 449 (July 1998): 1128-48; Jagdish Bhagwati and Arvind Panagariya, eds., *The Economics of Preferential Trade Agreements* (Washington: AEI Press, 1996); Ali M. El-Agraa, *Economic Integration Worldwide* (New York: St. Martin's Press, 1997); Ali M. El-Agraa, *International Economic Integration,* 2nd ed. (Basingstoke: Macmillan, 1988); Ali M. El-Agraa, *The Theory and Measurement of International Economic Integration* (New York: St, Martin's Press, 1989); Jeffrey A. Frankel, ed., *The Regionalization of the World Economy* (Chicago: University of Chicago Press, 1998); Robert C. Hine, "International Economic Integration," in David Greenaway and L. Alan Winters, *Surveys in International Trade* (Oxford: Basil Blackwell, 1994); Takatoshi Ito and Anne Krueger, eds., *Regionalism versus Multilateral Trade Arrangements* (Chicago: University of Chicago Press, 1997); Miroslav Jovanovic, *International Economic Integration* (New York: Routledge, 1992); Edward D. Mansfield, ed., *The Political Economy of Regionalism* (New York: Columbia University Press, 1997); Richard Pomfret, *The Economics of Regional Trading* (Oxford: Clarendon Press, 1997); L. Alan Winters, "Regionalism versus Multilateralism," World Bank Policy Research Working Paper No. 1687, 1996; Ronald J. Wonnacott, "Free-Trade Agreements: For Better or Worse?" *American Economic Review* 86, 2 (May 1996): 62-66.

2. For the journey, see William R. Shepherd, *Historical Atlas,* 8th ed., (New York: Barnes & Noble, 1956), plates 158-59.

3. Norman S. Fieleke, "One Trading World, or Many: The Issue of Regional Trading Blocs," *New England Economic Review* (May/June 1992): 6.

4. There is a comprehensive list in Bhagwati and Panagariya, *The Economics of Preferential Trade Agreements,* 55-73; and see *The Economist,* September 16, December 7, 1995, December 7, 1996.

5. For an analysis of the empirical measurement of trade creation versus trade diversion, see W.M. Corden, "The Costs and Consequences of Protection: A Survey of Empirical Work," in Peter B. Kenen, ed., *International Trade and Finance: Frontiers for Research* (Cambridge: Cambridge University Press, 1975), 51-91.

6. See C.A. Cooper and B.F. Massell, "A New Look at Customs Union Theory," *Economic Journal* 75 (1965): 742-47.

7. The Kemp-Wan proposition was advanced by M.C. Kemp and H. Wan, "An Elementary Proposition Concerning the Formation of Customs Unions," *Journal of International Economics* 6 (1976): 95-98.

8. Jeffrey A. Frankel, Ernesto Stein, and Shang-Jin Wei, "Regional Trading Arrangements: Natural or Supernatural?" *American Economic Review* 86, 2 (May 1996): 52-56.

9. See Nicholas Owen, *Economies of Scale, Competitiveness and Trade Patterns in the European Community* (Oxford, 1983).

10. Victor Bulmer-Thomas, "The Central American Common Market: From Closed to Open Regionalism," *World Development* 26, 2 (February 1998): 313-22.

11. See Augusto de la Torre and Margaret R. Kelly, *Regional Trade Arrangements*, IMF Occasional Paper No. 93 (Washington: IMF, 1992); David Greenaway and Chris Milner, "South-South Trade: Theory, Evidence, and Policy," *World Bank Research Observer* 5, 1 (January 1990); Frank R. Gunter, "Customs Union Theory: Retrospect and Prospect," in David Greenaway et al., eds., *Economic Aspects of Regional Trading Arrangements* (New York: New York University Press, 1989); Corsten Kowalczyk, "Welfare and Customs Unions," NBER Working Paper No. 3476, 1990; Jeffrey J. Schott, "Trading Blocs and the World Trading System," *The World Economy* 14, 1 (March 1991): 1-17; Paul Wonnacott and Mark Lutz, "Is There a Case for Free Trade Areas?" in Jeffrey J. Schott, ed., *Free Trade Areas and U.S. Trade Policy* (Washington: Institute for International Economics, 1989); Constantine V. Vaitsos, "Crisis in Regional Economic Cooperation (Integration) among Developing Countries: A Survey," in Paul Streeten and Richard Jolly, eds., *Recent Issues in World Development* (Oxford: Pergamon, 1981), 279-329.

12. See Greenaway et al., *Economic Aspects of Regional Trading Arrangements*, for the connection between intraindustrial trade and the performance of integration arrangements.

13. In addition to the works cited below, see the general studies of Michael Artis and Norman Lee, eds., *The Economics of the European Union: Policy and Analysis* (Oxford: Oxford University Press, 1994); Enzo Grilli, *The European Community and the Developing Countries* (Cambridge: Cambridge University Press, 1993); Peter B. Kenen, *Economic and Monetary Union in Europe: Moving Beyond Maastricht* (Cambridge: Cambridge University Press, 1995).

14. For a widely quoted accounting of the benefits from the 1992 program, see Paolo Cecchini, *The European Challenge, 1992: The Benefits of a Single Market* (Aldershot: Edward Elgar, 1988). For discussions and debate on the estimates, see Richard Baldwin, "Measurable Dynamic Gains from Trade," *Journal of Political Economy* 100 (February 1992): 162-74; Richard Baldwin, "The Growth Effects of 1992," *Economic Policy* 4, 9 (October 1989): 248-81; Harry Flam, "Product Markets and 1992: Full Integration, Large Gains?" *Journal of Economic Perspectives* 6, 4 (Fall 1992): esp. 24-27, with numerous sources cited there; Hine, "International Economic Integration," 258; M.J. Peck, "Industrial Organization and the Gains from Europe 1992," *Symposium of Europe 1992, Brookings Papers on Economic Activity* 2 (1989): 277-99. For discussions of the economic effects of "1992" on the rest of the world, see Baldwin, "The Growth Effects of 1992"; A. Jacquemin and A. Sapir, *The European Internal Market: Trade and Competition* (Oxford, 1989); André Sapir, "Europe 1992: The External Trade Implications," *International Economic Journal* 6, 1 (Spring 1992): 3; Gary C. Hufbauer, "An Overview," in Hufbauer, *Europe 1992: An American Perspective* (Washington: Institute for International Economics, 1990), 22-23. We often referred to the coverage in *The Economist*. See the issues of July 3, 1993, January 8, October 22, 1994, January 7, 1995.

15. Empirical work emphasizing the trade diversion aspect is noted in Ali El-Agraa, *The Economics of the European Community* (New York: St. Martin's Press, 1980); and the same author's "The European Community," in his *International Economic Integration*.

16. See Richard Pomfret, *Unequal Trade: The Economics of Discriminatory International Trade Policies* (New York: Blackwell Publishers, 1988), esp. 131 and the sources cited in this work. Another study citing many sources is L. Alan Winters and Anthony J. Venables, eds., *European Integration: Trade and Industry* (Cambridge: Cambridge University Press, 1991).

17. Following Hine, "International Economic Integration," 257.

18. See C.P. Stacey, *Canada and the Age of Conflict*, vol. 2 (Toronto: University of Toronto Press, 1981), 169-79.

19. de la Torre and Kelly, *Regional Trade Arrangements*, 21.

20. See the discussions in recent editions of USITC, *The Year in Trade*; Jane Sneddon Little, "At Stake in the U.S.-Canada Free Trade Agreement: Modest Gains or a Significant Setback," *New England Economic Review* (May/June 1988): 3-20; John Whalley with Roderick Hill, eds., *Canada-U.S. Free Trade* (Toronto: University of Toronto Press, 1985); Paul Wonnacott, *The United States and Canada: The Quest for Free Trade: An Examination of Selected Issues* (Washington: Institute for International Economics, 1987); Margaret R. Kelly et al., *International Trade Policy*, IMF Occasional Paper No. 63 (Washington: IMF, 1988), 12; and the coverage in *The Economist*, the *Wall Street Journal*, and the *Globe and Mail* (Toronto).

21. *International Economic Review*, July 1995 and December 1996/January 1997.

22. Paul Wonnacott and Ronald J. Wonnacott, *Free Trade Between the United States and Canada* (Cambridge, Mass.: Harvard University Press, 1967); and these authors' "Free Trade Between the United States and Canada: Fifteen Years Later," *Canadian Public Policy* (1982): 412-27.

23. Ronald J. Wonnacott, *Canada's Trade Options* (Ottawa: Economic Council of Canada, 1975).

24. Donald Daly, J.B.A. Keys, and E.J. Spence, *Scale and Specialization in Canadian Manufacturing* (Ottawa: Queen's Printer for the Economic Council of Canada, 1967).

25. John Baldwin, Paul Gorecki, and J. McVey, "Canada-U.S. Productivity Differences in the Manufacturing Sector: 1970-1979," in Donald G. McFetridge, ed., *Canadian Industry in Transition* (Toronto: University of Toronto Press, 1986); Donald Daly and D.C. MacCharles, *Canadian Manufactured Exports: Constraints and Opportunities* (Montreal: IRPP, 1986).

26. Donald J. Daly, "Canadian Research on the Production Effects of Free Trade: A Summary and Implications for Mexico," working paper for presentation, Schulich School of Business, York University, North York, Ontario, April 1998, 16. This section has drawn heavily from Daly's summary of research.

27. Daniel Trefler, "Quality vs. Quantity," *Report on Business Magazine, Globe and Mail*, July 1999, 87-88.

28. The Canadian productivity problem (if, indeed, there is one) and its measurement and cure (if needed) have been widely debated in recent years. For a summary of the various viewpoints, see *Report on Business Magazine* cited above.

29. See Leslie Sklair, *Assembling for Development: The Maquila Industry in Mexico and the United States* (Boston: Unwin Hyman, 1989); Nigel Harris, "Export Processing in Mexico," *Journal of Development Studies* 27, 1 (October 1990): 122; *International Economic Review*, February/March 1996.

30. For details on Mexico and NAFTA, see Peter M. Garber, ed., *The Mexico-U.S. Free Trade Agreement* (Cambridge, Mass.: MIT Press, 1993); Victor Bulmer-Thomas, ed.,

444

Mexico and the North American Free Trade Agreement: Who Will Benefit?* (New York: St. Martin's Press, 1994).

31. Gene Grossman and Alan Krueger, "Environmental Impacts of a North American Free Trade Agreement," NBER Working Paper No. 3914, 1992.

32. See Gary Clyde Hufbauer, Jeffrey J. Schott, and Philip L. Martin, *NAFTA Briefing Book* (Washington: Institute for International Economics, 1993).

33. James Bovard, "NAFTA's Protectionist Bent," *Wall Street Journal*, July 31, 1992.

34. For this paragraph, see especially *International Economic Review*, April/May 1996, March/April/May 1998.

35. For this paragraph, see *International Economic Review*, April 1995, April/May 1996.

36. USITC, *The Impact of the North American Free Trade Agreement on the U.S. Economy and Industries: A Three-Year Review* (Washington: 1997), esp. xviii, 4-19. Many other sources are cited in USITC, *The Year in Trade 1997*, 61.

37. *The Economist*, July 5, 1997.

38. *International Economic Review*, November 1995.

39. Details are in *The Economist*, October 12, 1996, April 24, 1999.

40. Ibid., October 12, 1996; *Wall Street Journal*, October 23, 1996, April 2, 1997; Claudio Frischtak, Danny M. Leipziger, and John F. Normand, *Industrial Policy in MERCO-SUR: Issues and Lessons* (Washington: World Bank, 1996).

41. Alexander Yeats, "Does Mercosur's Trade Performance Raise Concerns about the Effects of Regional Trade Arrangements?" World Bank Policy Research Working Paper No. 1729, 1997.

42. Michelle Connolly and Jenessa Gunther, "Mercosur: Implications for Growth in Member Countries," Federal Reserve Bank of New York, *Current Issues* 5, 7 (May 1999).

43. *The Economist*, April 24, 1999.

44. *The Economist*, October 10, 1998.

45. See USITC, *The Year in Trade 1997*, 71; *The Economist*, October 18, 1997.

46. *The Economist*, May 27, 1995, October 12, 1996; USITC, *The Year in Trade 1997*, 74; *International Economic Review*, March/April/May 1998. For an earlier book on the subject, see Sidney Weintraub, ed., *Integrating the Americas: Shaping Future Trade Policy* (New Brunswick, N.J.: Transaction Publishers, 1994).

47. *The Economist*, October 18, 1997; Matthew B. Canzoneri, Wilfred Ethier, and Vittorio Grilli, eds., *The New Transatlantic Economy* (Cambridge: Cambridge University Press, 1996).

48. See Philip I. Levy, "A Political-Economic Analysis of Free-Trade Agreements," *American Economic Review* 87, 4 (September 1997): 506-19.

49. Frankel, Stein, and Wei, "Regional Trading Arrangements," 52-56; Gene M. Grossman and Elhanan Helpman, "The Politics of Free-Trade Agreements," *American Economic Review* 85, 4 (September 1995): 667-90.

50. Wonnacott, "Free-Trade Agreements: For Better or Worse?" 62-66.

51. For an exploration of the issues, see Greenaway et al., eds., *Economic Aspects of Regional Trading Arrangements*; Jeffrey J. Schott, "More Free Trade Areas," in Schott, ed., *Free Trade Areas and U.S. Trade Policy*; C. Michael Aho and Sylvia Ostry, "Regional Trading Blocs: Pragmatic or Problematic Policy?" in William Brock and Robert Hormats, eds., *The Global Economy* (New York: W.W. Norton, 1990).

52. See Paul Krugman, "The Move Toward Free Trade Zones," *Federal Reserve Bank of Kansas City Economic Review*, November/December 1991, 11.

53. Ibid., 13; Wonnacott and Lutz, "Is There a Case for Free Trade Areas?" in Schott, 59-84.

54. C. Fred Bergsten, "Commentary: The Move Toward Free Trade Zones," *Federal Reserve Bank of Kansas City Economic Review*, November/December 1991, 27-35.

55. Christian E. Petersen, "Trade Conflict and Resolution Methodologies," *American Economic Review* 82, 2 (May 1992): 65.

56. Wonnacott, "Free-Trade Agreements: For Better or Worse?"; Bhagwati, Greenaway, and Panagariya, "Trading Preferentially: Theory and Policy."

57. For this argument, see Paul Luyten, "Multilateralism Versus Preferential Bilateralism: A European View," in Schott, ed., *Free Trade Areas and U.S. Trade Policy*.

58. For an accounting of the EU's regional agreements, see André Sapir, "Regional Integration in Europe," *Economic Journal* 102, 415 (November 1992): 1492.

59. For the recent EU efforts, see *International Economic Review*, January/February 1999.

60. See Olufemi A. Babarinde, *The Lomé Conventions and Development: An Empirical Assessment* (Aldershot: Avebury, 1994).

61. *The Economist*, April 24, 1999.

62. For this section we have drawn on USITC, *Annual Report on the Impact of the Caribbean Basin Economic Recovery Act on U.S. Industries and Consumers*; Joseph and Gregory K. Schoepfle, "The Impact of the Caribbean Basin Economic Recovery Act on Caribbean Nations' Exports and Development," *Economic Development and Cultural Change* 36, 4 (July 1988): 753-96; Peter D. Whitney, "The CBI: Important Incentives for Trade and Investment," U.S. Department of State Current Policy No. 1065, April 1988; Richard E. Feinberg and Richard Newfarmer, "The Caribbean Basin Initiative: Bold Plan or Empty Promise," in Newfarmer, ed., *From*

Gunboats to Diplomacy (Baltimore: Johns Hopkins University Press, 1984); W. Charles Sawyer and Richard L. Sprinkle, "Caribbean Basin Recovery Act," *Journal of World Trade Law* 18, 5 (1984): 429-36; *International Economic Review*, April and September 1989; all recent editions of USITC, *The Year in Trade*; and personal communications from the Latin America/Caribbean Business Development Center of the U.S. Department of Commerce.

63. See Sidney Weintraub, "A U.S.-Israel Free Trade Area," *Challenge* 28, 3 (1985): 47-50; recent issues of USITC, *The Year in Trade*.

64. For a discussion, see Richard Pomfret, "The Quiet Shift in U.S. Trade Policy," *Challenge* 27, 5 (1984): 61-64.

65. Sumner J. LaCroix and Christopher Grandy, "The Political Instability of Reciprocal Trade and the Overthrow of the Hawaiian Kingdom," *Journal of Economic History* 57, 1 (March 1997): 161-89.

66. John McLaren, "Size, Sunk Costs, and Judge Bowker's Objection to Free Trade," *American Economic Review* 87, 3 (June 1997): 400-20.

67. Greenaway and Milner, "South-South Trade," 56.

68. Ali M. El-Agraa, "Economic Integration," in Enzo Grilli and Dominick Salvatore, eds., *Economic Development* (Westport, Conn.: Greenwood Press, 1994), 228.

69. de la Torre and Kelly, *Regional Trade Arrangements*, 37.

70. We consulted especially Beverly Carl, *Economic Integration Among Developing Nations: Law and Policy* (New York: Greenwood Publishing Group, 1986); Vaitsos, "Crisis in Regional Economic Cooperation (Integration) among Developing Countries."

71. de la Torre and Kelly, *Regional Trade Arrangements*, 37.

72. For surveys and analyses of the zones, see Peter G. Warr, "Export Processing Zones: The Economics of Enclave Manufacturing," *World Bank Research Observer* 4, 1 (January 1989): 65-88; Don Clark, "U.S. Production in Foreign-Trade Zones: Potential for Reducing Tariff Liability," *Journal of World Trade* 22, 6 (December 1988): 107-15; Walter H. Diamond and Dorothy B. Diamond, *Tax-Free Trade Zones of the World* (New York: Matthew Bender & Co., 1977); D.L.U. Jayawardena, "Free Trade Zones," *Journal of World Trade Law* 17, 5 (1983): 427-44; *International Economic Review*, August 1989; *South*, February 1989. The statistics on the U.S. zones are from the 59th *Annual Report of the Foreign Trade Zones Board*. (These annual reports have fallen behind schedule because of funding problems. This latest is for 1997.)

73. See Deborah L. Swenson, "Explaining Domestic Content: Evidence from Japanese and U.S. Automobile Production in the United States," in Robert C. Feenstra, ed., *The Effects of U.S. Trade Protection and Promotion Policies* (Chicago: University of Chicago Press, 1997), 36-37.

74. Ibid.

75. For discussion and analysis, see Michael W. Bell and Kalpana Kochhar, "China: An Evolving Market Economy—A Review of Reform Experience," IMF Working Paper 92/89, November 1992; World Bank, *China: Between Plan and Market*, World Bank Country Study (Washington, 1990); Nicholas R. Lardy, *Foreign Trade and Economic Reform in China, 1978-1990* (Cambridge: Cambridge University Press, 1990); Dwight Perkins, "Completing China's Move to the Market," *Journal of Economic Perspectives* 8, 2 (Spring 1994): 23-46; Richard Pomfret, *Investing in China: Ten Years of the Open Door Policy* (Ames: Iowa State University Press, 1991); *International Economic Review*, July 1994, March/April/May 1998; *The Economist*, October 5, 1991.

Part Two

International Macroeconomics: Saving, Growth, and Finance

Chapter Ten

Saving, Investment, and the Trade Balance

OBJECTIVES

OVERALL OBJECTIVE   To reveal the strength of the patterns of consumption, investment, and production in determining trade imbalances.

MORE SPECIFICALLY
- To show the key national accounts formulas, particularly those dealing with the saving-investment and income-absorption gaps, to demonstrate the relation of trade imbalances to national income.
- To demonstrate that these gaps equal the net financial flows into or out of the country.
- To show that persistent and awkward trade imbalances are usually symptoms of other, generally more deeply rooted, factors associated with savings, investment, and growth.
- To demonstrate that financial flows in themselves may be principal or contributory factors in giving rise to persistent trade imbalances.
- To explore the role of demographics and the role of the government in trade imbalances.

Trade deficits and surpluses are central to international macroeconomic discussions. While in themselves trade imbalances are neither good nor bad, when swollen to unusual levels, they often are the visible signs of troublesome underlying conditions. This chapter examines trade imbalances in the context of national income and expenditures, demonstrating the close connection between patterns of national saving and investment and emerging trade imbalances. It shows how the patterns of income, consumption, saving, and investment are connected to financial flows between countries, examining how deficits or surpluses arise. In so doing, it lays a foundation for the ideas and theories of later chapters.

HOW CAN COUNTRIES HAVE TRADE IMBALANCES?

Popular wisdom suggests that the cure for trade imbalances is to manipulate exports and imports through taxes, subsidies, quotas, and like instruments. When the United States has a trade deficit, for instance, Congress and the President press Japan to lower real or imagined trade barriers, and in decades past they introduced measures to subsidize exports. Others argue that trade deficits arise because of lagging productivity at home or higher productivity abroad and push their favorite schemes for increasing productivity. Thus in 1998 when the Canadian dollar fell to 65 cents (U.S.), people desiring a strong trade surplus to raise the dollar's value argued for lower taxes, presumably (often with the mechanism rather fuzzy) because this would lead to greater productivity. Others argued that more expenditure on education would increase productivity and plumped for that solution. Yet, nothing demonstrated in the first chapters of this book suggests that productivity or trade manipulation, however greatly they may reduce the *volume* of trade and influence what goods are traded, alters the *balance* of trade. The answer to the most fundamental of questions—that of how any nation can develop a trade imbalance—is not in productivity or trade barriers; it lies elsewhere.

The Market at Castoria

Perhaps the best way to understand how a trade balance develops is to consider just two nations. Imagine a situation as in the beginning of the North American fur trade. On a given market week in a place somewhat at the edge of the fur trade country, all the Fabricans and all the Castorians come to a marketplace, each with their packets of trade goods—the Fabricans carrying cloth and the Castorians beaver pelts for the trade. Unfortunately, the Castorian trapping has been poor, so, compared with the previous year, the market has more cloth than pelts. With a greater supply of cloth than pelts, the price of cloth in terms of pelts should fall and the market should clear. No packets of goods should be left in the marketplace at the end of the day. How, then, could there be a deficit or a surplus?

Fabricans are, of course, unhappy about having to bring home fewer pelts. They consider packing up some of their cloth and returning home with it, never offering some of their cloth on the market. But that would be difficult (that is, costly), so they offer the Castorians a deal: they will let the Castorians have all the cloth this year, in exchange for additional pelts *next year*. With expectations of better trapping, the Castorians agree. Furthermore, the Castorians recognize that they do not have to make cloth or substitutes for cloth and can get down to the business of expanding traplines, placing more traps, and building larger canoes. To put the agreement in writing, the Fabricans and the Castorians make pictures of beavers in an account book to show how many beaver skins they owe.

Now consider some observations based on the trading scenario.

1. The market clears in the sense that the marketplace is empty at the end of the day, but promises as well as goods have been exchanged. Fabrica has *lent* cloth to Castoria. Fabrica now has a trade surplus and Castoria a trade deficit.

2. Since prices were not flexible, the market cleared only with promises of more goods to be delivered at another time.

3. Castoria now has more goods available than it actually produced (measured by the prices it traded for). It brought a smaller harvest to the market, but went back with the same amount of cloth. It can therefore use for consumption and investment more than it actually produced. The opposite is true of Fabrica, which produced some bundles of cloth, which it counts in its national income as if it were sold, but for which it has not yet been paid. What Fabrica uses for investing and consuming is therefore less than its output.

4. Fabrica has *invested* the cloth that the Castorians are using. Fabricans have counted the value of that cloth as their income, but, lacking pelts this year, they have not used the income for purchases; accordingly, they have saved income equivalent to the value of the cloth they lent. They could have taken the cloth home and put it in storage, which would have increased inventories (which are also investment), but instead they accepted a promise that Castoria would pay. Next year, the Fabricans expect to receive pelts for that cloth.

5. The Castorians have borrowed the cloth. They are able to spend more than they produced because more cloth is available than otherwise would have been were the Fabricans to have packed it up and taken it home. Castorian consumption and investment is therefore higher than Castorian income.

6. The willingness of the Fabricans to lend and of the Castorians to borrow shows up on the financial statistics (the pictures in the account book), which has credits flowing from Fabrica to Castoria and a matching debit from Castoria to Fabrica. When the Fabrican exporters report their sales to their shareholders, they include the goods they sold, even though they also provided credit, and the sales increase their profits. The amount lent shows up as a trade credit. (In more developed systems, a third party, such as a bank, might have provided the credit.) The Castorian accounts, of course, show the reverse, with sales less than expenditures, lower profits, and borrowed funds.

7. Over a longer period of time, the Castorians and Fabricans would not want their credits and debts to keep mounting, expecting that next year more furs would be available: that is, the market should still clear. If the statistics combined two years and the Fabricans and Castorians were correct in their assessment that the following year would be good for trapping, Castoria could repay Fabrica. To do so, some of its beaver pelts would be used to settle the old promise and would not appear in this year's price-setting bargaining. Castoria would develop a trade surplus and Fabrica a trade deficit. For the two-year period, however, the market would clear completely.*

The basic example provides key insights into underlying realities: that (one-year) markets fail to clear only if the parties offer and accept debt obligations; that these debt and credit arrangements are in fact financial flows; that when those obligations occur, the borrowing nation has more goods and services on hand than it produced, and the lender faces the opposite situation; and that the lender's domestic saving must cover the goods lent abroad and the borrower's domestic saving must fall short of the goods borrowed from abroad. Consider these points now in a more conventional manner.

THE THREE REAL IMBALANCES: IMPORTS-EXPORTS, SAVING-INVESTMENT, AND OUTPUT-ABSORPTION

What a Trade Imbalance Tells about Saving and Investment

In 1996 and 1997, the United States had a trade deficit (including goods, services, and factor income) of somewhat over $110 billion in each year, which was around 12% of exports and 1.4% of GNP.[1] As the example of Castoria shows, the $110 billion says much about other numbers, far more hidden. While the public sees the $110 billion, it is in a sense a shadow upon a screen, a product itself of other figures moving in the background. A trade deficit, like such a shadow, may be projected from several shifting figures more dimly perceived and understood.

The relationships of the Castorian example show much about some shapes behind the screen. And, while it is difficult to be able to marshal the statistical evidence to prove beyond doubt causal relationships, good clues abound. The trade deficit of $110 billion, for instance, indicates that domestic investment exceeds domestic saving by $110 billion, and it shows that what the

---

* In a Walrasian market, there must be perfect speculation (or time arbitrage) between the beginning and the end of the period of time the market represents. If we allow the same speculation between two markets, neither market need clear, but the two together must do so.

United States used for consumption, government, and domestic investment (called absorption) exceeds output Americans generated by $110 billion. And, lastly, it indicates that the United States borrowed from abroad $110 billion more than it lent there.

The relationships of the trade deficits to the other variables are accounting ones. They do not indicate what caused what, showing only that any of these changes must be reflected in changes in the other variables. Many things could be the principal cause of a $110 billion deficit—a decline in income, a decrease in saving, or a decline in the price of exports would suffice. But whatever the cause or the initial shock to the system, the other figures must adjust to it. If imports become cheaper, changes occur in income, savings, investment, and financial flows. Much in the chapters that follow explain the mechanisms by which such changes happen, but to begin, it suffices to explore the accounting and algebraic relationships themselves and to suggest some of the real factors that may underlie trade imbalances.

The Concept of Absorption

When statisticians add up national income figures, they cannot tell whether a given expenditure they have classified as consumption, investment, or government has been spent on imports or not. An automobile, for instance, could be entirely of foreign manufacture, could have imported parts, or could have in its parts imported steel and rubber. Tracing the origins of every piece of every consumption good is impossible. So, after $C + I + G$ is totaled, they subtract imports from the total. That still leaves the expenditure foreigners made on exports uncounted, yet they produced wages and profits, so the statisticians add those. With trade, the formula for GNP is:

(Eq. 10.1) $\qquad C + I + G + (X - M) = \text{GNP}^{*}$

The word "absorption"[2], symbolized with an A, is the short way of referring to $C + I + G$. When absorption is larger than GNP (the nation is *absorbing* more than it produces), it has a trade deficit equal to that excess absorption. When it absorbs less than it produces, it has a trade surplus. Using the symbol Y, meaning income, for GNP, the emerging formula is:

(Eq. 10.2) $\qquad Y - A = X - M$

---

* $X - M$ is put in parentheses simply to identify it; there is no mathematical reason to do so. In all our figures we include net factor payments as imports and net factor receipts as exports, so technically, we must use GNP in the formula.

IRELAND: AN ILLUSTRATIVE CASE

Ireland provides a good example of the relationship of trade to income and absorption because the differences are very great and show easily on diagrams. Figure 10.1 shows Ireland's expenditures by consumption, investment, and government, forming absorption. Any figures in excess of 100% of GNP are matched by a trade deficit in that amount.

Figure 10.1

IRELAND: INCOME, ABSORPTION, AND THE TRADE BALANCE

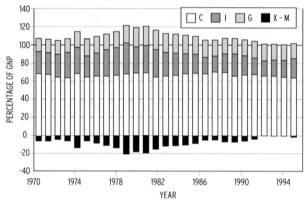

Source: IFS, Ireland: national accounts. Hereafter *IFS*, 1999.

In 1979, the most extreme year, Irish consumption was over 60% of GNP, investment nearly 40%, and government consumption another 21%, bringing the total $C + I + G$ to 121% of AD. $X - M$, of course, was negative by 21%, bringing total expenditure on goods and services down to 100%. By the mid-1990s, however, absorption had declined as a percentage of GNP: investment levels were lower than in the heady days of the late 1980s, and government and household consumption, while still higher in real terms, had not risen as much as GNP rose.

THE RELATIONSHIP OF X − M, S − I, AND Y − A AS A FLOW DIAGRAM

Two flow diagrams capsulize the foregoing discussion. Given a fixed level of output, an increase in absorption due to increases in investment, consumption, or government spending leads to a worsening trade balance, as in *FD* 10.1a, and the opposite, as in *FD* 10.1b.

(FD 10.1a) $Y - A \uparrow \quad \rightarrow \quad (X - M) \downarrow$

(FD 10.1b) $Y - A \downarrow \quad \rightarrow \quad (X - M) \uparrow$

The Saving and Investment Approach

SAVING AND INVESTMENT IN A CLOSED ECONOMY

The Irish example highlights how a saving and investment approach can further an understanding of what has happened. More detail, however, is in order.

Basic national income accounting systems classify all goods and services produced as either consumption or investment—that is, either used up during the year or set aside for future use. The measure of investment is Gross Fixed Capital Formation—which is all the new investments in machinery, plant, housing, roads, and schools, whether built privately or publicly—plus any increase in inventory, known technically as change in stocks. Since to save something from one year to the next requires it to be in physical form, everything else produced in that year has to be consumed.[*]

The income spent on consumption and investment produces wages, salaries, interest, and profits, which in turn are *disposed of* as either consumption or saving. That is, households either use the income to buy goods or they don't use the income at all.[†] This results in a simple accounting identity:

(Eq. 10.3) $\qquad C + I = C + S$

Since the consumption of goods and services produced equals in value the income spent on them, C can drop from both sides of the equation, getting:

(Eq. 10.4) $\qquad I = S$

In this basic model, investment expenditures always equal saving.

---

[*] This is the way the System of National Accounts (SNA) keeps the numbers, about which many economists hold reservations. There are difficult questions of "saving" of services, as in increased education, of "investment" in durable goods, or in knowledge that the SNA has trouble addressing.

[†] For some purposes it is useful to view households as "investing" in appliances and the like, but again we are being quite traditional here (if only because the numbers we find are from traditional sources).

EXPENDITURES AND SAVING AND THE BALANCE OF TRADE

The relation of the balance of trade to domestic saving and investment emerges when imports and exports enter the equation. Expenditures on exports (X) come from outside the country and add income, resembling investment in their effect on demand. Exports include goods and services, with services including payments gained from investments abroad. Expenditures on imports $(M)^*$ act domestically much like saving and are withdrawn from the income stream.[†] Domestic households have the goods to use, but nobody domestically receives any income from them. The formula now has two added elements, X and M, such that:

(Eq. 10.5) $C + I + X = C + S + M$

or (Eq. 10.6) $I + X = S + M$

With the added two variables, it is no longer true that domestic saving has to equal domestic investment. If, for instance, exports exceed imports, then saving will exceed investment. Equation 10.6 can be rearranged as follows:

(Eq. 10.7) $X - M = S - I$

—which is to say that exports exceed imports by the same amount that saving exceeds investment. A trade deficit equals the shortfall of saving; a trade surplus is the excess of saving.

Note that Castoria also experienced a situation in which its domestic use of resources (presumably for consumption and domestic investment) exceeded its production (by the amount of imported cloth). Fabrica undoubtedly saved more than the surplus of cloth it exported, but it used all but the savings matching the cloth exports on various forms of domestic capital formation and inventories. (If it had brought cloth back from the trading market rather than lending cloth to the Castorians, it would have put this in inventory, which would have been a domestic investment.)

Two related flow diagrams help illustrate the relation of $S - I$ to $Y - A$ and $X - M$. Both show that changes in $S - I$ cause changes in A (as consumption and investment or government changes), as well as changes in the trade balance. In the first, either savings falls or investment rises, leading to changes in

---

* Imports include the same categories of goods and services as exports.

† The reader should be warned that it is customary to use M for imports as well as for money supply; the alternative is to use something like Z for imports, which is fine for formulas but in practice it tends to throw some people more than having M occasionally mean something else. If the difference is not sufficiently clear from context, we refer to the money supply as MS.

absorption and to changes in the trade balance. (*S* could fall because government or private consumption expenditures rose, while *I* could rise as private investment rose.)

(FD 10.2a) $(S - I)\downarrow \rightarrow (\overline{Y} - A\uparrow)\downarrow \rightarrow (X - M)\downarrow$

And in its opposite:

(FD 10.2b) $(S - I)\uparrow \rightarrow (\overline{Y} - A\downarrow)\uparrow \rightarrow (X - M)\uparrow$

The fact that the trade deficit makes up the difference between saving and investment should not be taken to mean that the imported goods were necessarily used directly for investment. Imported consumption goods free resources from producing competitive import substitutes such that they can make capital goods. If a country takes 10,000 people off farms to build an irrigation system, it will import the food they would have produced. Imports could be entirely consumption goods, but still be essential for an increase in capital.

Consider again the Irish situation as illustrated in Figure 10.1 to see the relation of saving to absorption. Figure 10.2 shows that during the period of high trade deficits, Ireland was not constraining its consumption, which rose to nearly 70% of GNP, or its government's consumption expenditures, which poked above 20% of GNP, so its savings level fell from around 15-20 % of GNP to only about 10-12% of GNP. With only 10% of GNP in national savings and investment levels around 30%, the trade deficit swelled.

Figure 10.2

IRELAND: CONSUMPTION AND SAVING

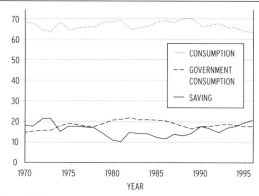

Note: Saving is derived from the formula $I + X - M = S$, that is, domestic saving is equal to all domestic capital formation and inventory accumulation plus whatever trade surplus the country produces, as described in the text.

Consumption was between 65 and 70% of GNP throughout the period, and in the periods of heaviest foreign borrowing showed no slackening. Investment in the 1980s grew much more than saving, causing $S - I$ to fall, which caused absorption to rise because investment rose without consumption falling to match the rise in I. The increase in absorption caused $Y - A$ to fall, in turn causing the trade deficit, as in FD 10.2a. In the 1990s, however, investment declined, pushing $S - I$ into the positive range and bringing a minute trade surplus. Another way to put it, is that Ireland's investment/saving gap fell after 1981.

In contrast to Ireland's sharp rise in investment, the U.S. trade gap in the 1980s is closely linked to a decline in saving. Figure 10.3 expresses the saving gap as $I - S$, to produce a positive figure to describe the size of the gap and the trade gap as the usual $X - M$.

Figure 10.3

THE U.S. TRADE BALANCE AND SAVINGS GAP, 1965-1997

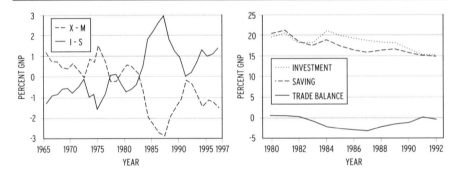

Note: The U.S. trade deficit appears as the mirror image of the saving gap in the left panel. The cause of this relationship is the accounting identity of $X - M$ with $S - I$. The diagram expresses the saving gap as $I - S$, such that any excess of investment over saving is reflected in an excess of imports over exports, as measured on $X - M$. The trade deficit as figured in national accounts often differs somewhat from the figures given in balance-of-payments accounting. The System of National Accounts makes no attempt to reconcile balance-of-payments figures with national account figures.

Source: IFS, 1999.

The right panel examines the savings and investment figures showing that saving declined as a percentage of GNP in the early 1980s and that the trade deficit improved only as investment declined. Unlike what occurred in Ireland, where high levels of investment appear to have caused the trade deficit, the American situation saw lower levels of saving (and therefore higher levels of consumption) lead to the trade deficit. Like Ireland, however, lower levels of investment in the 1990s led to the decline of the trade deficit.

KOREA: A CASE IN POINT

In 1982 and again in 1997, Korea faced major economic crises that came about when investors suddenly reappraised the health of the economy. In 1982, the reappraisal came when Mexico defaulted on loans and investor sentiment consequently turned away from most developing countries. At that point, Korea quickly recovered. In 1997, however, both Korean and foreign investors began to question the health of the Korean banking system itself and made it very difficult for Koreans to borrow abroad. The following diagrams indicate that in 1996 most macroeconomic measurements showed the economy to be healthy, and certainly no worse than it was in 1992.

Figure 10.4

KOREA: SAVINGS, INVESTMENT, AND FOREIGN BORROWING

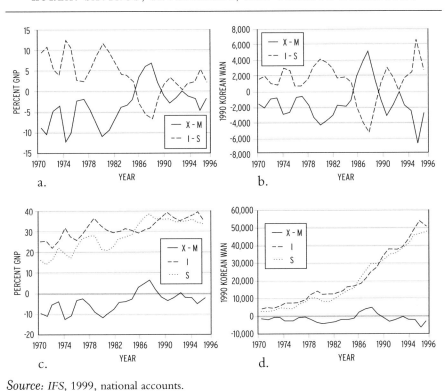

Source: IFS, 1999, national accounts.

461

The upper two panels show how Korea's overly large trade deficit developed in the 1970s, how quickly it was corrected in the 1980s, and how it grew once more in the 1990s. As a percentage of GNP, the Korean trade deficit in 1996 was smaller than it had been for most of the 1970s, but because Korean national income had grown enormously, the trade deficit in real terms was much larger than it had been before.

The two lower panels show the pattern of saving and investment. The sharp turnaround in the trade balance between 1982 and 1990 occurred as savings increased sharply both as a percentage of GNP and in real terms, while investment fell off a bit, to around 30% of GNP. (In real terms, investment continued to rise substantially.) Investment in the 1990s, however, again began to outpace savings, opening up a trade deficit. While Korea managed the trick of increasing savings once, it is highly doubtful that the country could raise the level of savings beyond the extraordinarily high levels it has already achieved.

Government Saving, Investment, and Consumption

To simplify matters, economists often lump government activities with private ones, such that C includes government consumption, I includes government investment, and S includes government saving. Finer analysis can separate out the government's activities.

Adding government expenditures and taxation to the formula is straightforward. G is government expenditure, which, like investment and exports, produces income. To conform to normal statistical categories, consider only that part of government expenditure that is on consumption goods and services, and specify it as Gc.* Government expenditures on investments, such as on roads, bridges, and buildings (in the United States, about 15% of all government expenditure) are included with I—gross fixed capital formation plus change in inventories. To specify that I includes both private and government investment, call it Id, for domestic investment.

T is government taxation and, like saving and imports, is a disposal of income.† Total domestic saving less taxes is now just private saving, labeled Sp.

---

* The $C + I + G$ approach keeps the concepts on a theoretical level. First-year texts argue that an increase in government consumption investment stimulates the economy. In a sense, G is a policy consideration. Most countries' national accounts, however, do not separate government investment from private investment, and give only a figure for government consumption. (The U.S. is the only national account to separate out government investment.) More detailed breakdowns of gross fixed capital formation appear only after some years in the *National Accounts Statistics Yearbook*. The *Government Financial Statistics Yearbook* gives some useful capital numbers, which we have employed here.

† Neither G nor T includes government transfer payments: $10,000 in pension payments given to one person and taken from another is treated as if it were moved directly from the taxpayer

(Eq. 10.8) $Id + X + Gc = Sp + M + T$

Government saving is $T - Gc$, tax revenues minus government consumption expenditures.* Combined with private saving, Equation 10.9 emerges:

(Eq. 10.9) $X - M = Sp + Sg - Id$

This is a very useful relationship. While it shows $X - M$ as the trade balance, the forms moving behind the screen (on the right side of the equation) may be of greater importance. A trade deficit, for instance, might arise from an increase in domestic investment, a fall in private saving, or a fall in government saving. Policy to reduce the deficit would be different in each case, as it might call for a decrease in investment, an increase in private saving, an increase in government saving, or some combination thereof, but in no case does it call for any action directly on exports or imports.

A Decline in Saving Can Cause a Trade Deficit

Korea's and Ireland's trade deficits were closely related to a high level of investment without equivalent domestic saving, but trade deficits can as easily arise because domestic saving falls off sharply. Suppose saving declines (either government or private) *and* national income doesn't change:

(FD 10.3) $S\downarrow - I \rightarrow (X - M)\downarrow$

Since a decline in S means an increase in C, then A, absorption, has also risen, so:

(FD 10.4) $Y - A\uparrow \rightarrow (X - M)\downarrow$

THE UNITED STATES AS AN EXAMPLE OF DECLINE IN SAVING

A number of economists have cited the increasing government deficits as causing the severe balance-of-trade problems of the 1980s.[3] The basis for the

---

to the recipient and does not appear as T or G. As the first chapter noted, the vast increase in government expenditure has not been on goods and services, but on transfers, so T, or the taxes net of transfers is considerably lower than all government tax receipts (or R); just as G, government expenditures on goods and services, is much lower than gross government expenditures, including transfers, (or E). In this case we are concerned only with taxes and government, net of transfers.

* A government deficit includes some expenditures that are capital formation. These are not consumption expenditures, and therefore are part of government saving, so it is possible for a government to have a deficit, and be a net saver, just as it is possible for a household to end up farther in debt, even though it saved a great deal and put it into a new house.

argument is the relation of government deficits to the trade deficits. A refinement of Figure 10.3, Figure 10.5 shows how in the 1970s U.S. private saving tended to offset government dissaving, leaving a small trade surplus. After 1980, however, private saving failed to rise to cover the increased government dissaving, producing the deficit, and then itself began to fall.

Figure 10.5

U.S. PRIVATE AND GOVERNMENT SAVING,
INVESTMENT, AND TRADE DEFICIT

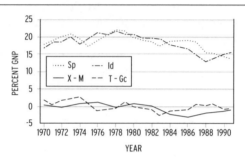

Source: IFS, 1999; *Government Financial Statistics Yearbook* (for taxation).

Until the mid–1980s, American private saving was about 20% of GNP. Government saving $(T - Gc)$[4] was negative during most of the period. It fell especially sharply after the Reagan tax cuts took effect. Notice how the slopes of $T - Gc$ and $X - M$ are close in the early 1980s. As governments, principally state ones, improved their balance sheets in the late 1980s, private saving continued to fall. The trade deficit did not worsen because domestic investment also fell off sharply.

In the case of the United States, it appears that until the late 1980s changes in government saving were most significant, as represented in a flow diagram.

(FD 10.5) $(Sg\downarrow + Sp - I)\downarrow \rightarrow (X - M)\downarrow$

If the cut in taxes led to higher consumption, then:

(FD 10.6) $C\uparrow \rightarrow (Y - A\uparrow) \rightarrow (X - M)\downarrow$

Trade Imbalances and Their Effect on S – I

To this point, discussion has centered on the idea that it is powerful domestic factors, which drive the trade balance. Yet, however dramatic the analogy,

$X - M$ is more than a shadow on a screen, and we have something to gain by shifting the scene, putting $X - M$ behind the screen and $S - I$ in front. Changes in $X - M$ also cause changes in $Y - A$ and $S - I$. How could $X - M$ influence $S - I$?

1. A decrease in the value of exports lowers income. As people try to maintain some semblance of their old spending levels, they decrease saving far more than they decrease consumption.

2. An increase in the price of imports, particularly of imports with inelastic demand curves such as food and fuels, may cause people to dig into savings so that they can buy both the imports and also the domestic goods they were accustomed to buying.

3. A decrease in the price of exports in itself may cause the government deficit to rise, either because (a) total tax revenues are down or, more specifically, (b) much tax revenue derives directly from exports.

4. Misapplied Keynesian methods (expanding an economy when in fact there was little true unemployment) might be partially to blame for the deficit. If the government realizes that income has fallen and tries to stimulate the economy through fiscal means, and prices rise, rather than incomes, then the trade deficit will also rise.

FINANCIAL MARKETS: BORROWING AND LENDING

The Market for Funds and National Income Aggregates

In financial terminology, funds refers to claims on resources offered on a market. A household receiving an income of $10,000 more than it spends on goods and services has a claim on the economy it has chosen not to exercise and instead has lent the excess to others for their use. Loosely, people refer to this as money, but it does not fit the economic definition of money. It is not the same as savings either, as explained below.

The path from domestic saving and investment to the lending and borrowing of funds is not as straightforward as it may at first appear. Certainly, what a country borrows from abroad should turn up as borrowed funds, but what is the mechanism? The mechanism would be simple enough if all savings were placed in the financial markets and all investments made from borrowed funds. In that case, income minus consumption would equal savings for any household, firm, or government in the country. Some of these units would produce surplus funds to be lent while others would borrow from the market, and the net saving would equal the difference between what is borrowed and what is lent.

Figure 10.6

SOURCES OF FUNDS FOR FINANCIAL MARKETS

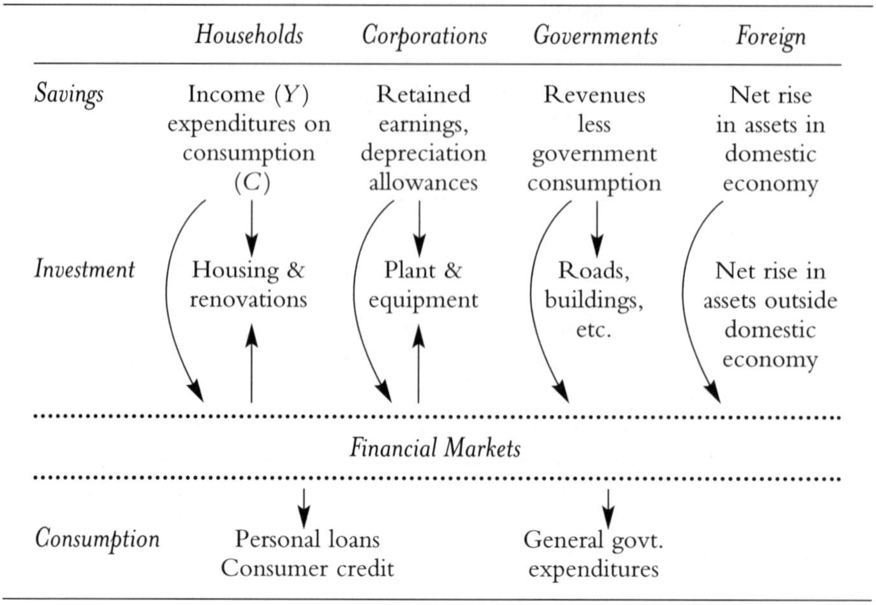

	Households	*Corporations*	*Governments*	*Foreign*
Savings	Income (*Y*) expenditures on consumption (*C*)	Retained earnings, depreciation allowances	Revenues less government consumption	Net rise in assets in domestic economy
Investment	Housing & renovations	Plant & equipment	Roads, buildings, etc.	Net rise in assets outside domestic economy

Financial Markets

Consumption	Personal loans Consumer credit		General govt. expenditures

Things are slightly more complex than suggested because a great deal of saving and investment never touches financial markets. Households use a considerable amount of their savings to build up the value of their residences. A family earning $70,000 a year that spends $20,000 of that income on adding a room to their house is investing in physical assets, counted in the national accounts as investment, but the household neither borrowed nor lent any funds in financial markets. Similarly, much corporate investment takes place outside of financial markets, as shareholders allow (or technically, direct) their corporations to reinvest revenues to replace depreciated capital and to expand plant and equipment. Moreover, governments often build up physical capital, such as roads, buildings, and sewage facilities, out of current revenues, not necessarily by borrowing from the markets. So a considerable proportion of investment never touches the market. What funds reach the market come from what is left over from income after each household, each firm, and each government has finished spending on consumption and investment. In other words, income minus absorption is what is placed on financial markets. Figure 10.6 helps to visualize what happens.

Funds come into financial markets from four sources: households, firms, governments, and the foreign sector. Household saving is the difference between income and consumption, some of which goes directly into

466

residential investment, the bulk of it, however, goes into the financial markets. Households also borrow back some money for consumption and investment purposes. What households put into the market, net of what they borrow back, is basically their income minus their absorption. The same reasoning fits firms (which, of course, do not consume) and the government.

An equation can show this in two ways:

(Eq. 10.10) $\qquad Y_L - A_L = F_L$

(Eq. 10.11) $\qquad S_L - I_L = F_L$

The subscript L refers to all the households, firms, and governments that are net lenders, Y is income, A is absorption, S is saving, and I is physical investment. F is the funds provided, F_L being the funds provided by lenders. That is, the income of lending units minus their absorption equals the funds lent on the market, and the savings of the lending units (income minus consumption or $Y_L - C_L$) minus the physical investments made by those units equals the amount they have left to put on financial markets.

Obviously, not all households, firms, and governments are net lenders. Many of them have absorption levels exceeding their incomes, and these borrow from the market. Whether they borrow for consumption (as for a large wedding) or investment (as for a new house), and whether they are households, firms, or governments, their absorption exceeds their income and their investments exceed their saving. So:

(Eq. 10.12) $\qquad Y_B - A_B = F_B$

(Eq. 10.13) $\qquad S_B - I_B = F_B$

where the subscript B refers to the households, firms, and governments that are net borrowers. Combined, the two absorption equations produce:

(Eq. 10.14) $\qquad Y_L + Y_B - (A_L + A_B) = F_L - F_B$

That is the income of the country is the total income of borrowers and lenders and the absorption the total absorption of the two. If funds lent exceed funds borrowed, then total absorption must be lower than income, and vice versa.

The two savings formulas produce:

(Eq. 10.15) $\quad S_L + S_B - (I_L + I_B) = F_L - F_B$

That is, all of the saving less all of the investment yields the net amount of funds on the market. If the country's saving is less than its investment, funds lent will exceed funds borrowed, and vice versa. In sum, the difference between income and absorption equals both the differences between saving and investment and the funds lent and borrowed on the financial markets.

How Financial Markets Influence Absorption and Income

Previous discussion has dealt with how the left sides of the formulas could drive the right. A decline in saving, an increase in investment, or a decrease in income could all cause funds borrowed to rise and funds lent to fall. But can the right side of the formula drive the left? For sure.

No matter how desperate a country's financial difficulties, it cannot spend (absorb) more than its income unless people in other countries are willing to give it credit. Oddly enough, the reverse is also common: no matter how sensibly a country runs its economy, it cannot help but absorb more than its income if other people in other countries are insistent on lending it money. Consider the United States in two periods: the 1980s and the late 1990s.

As described earlier in the chapter, in the 1980s American trade deficits sometimes exceeded $100 billion, the federal government deficit was high, private savings were mediocre, and even modest levels of investment kept absorption well above income. Yet, the country had little trouble in borrowing the additional funds. Even if Uncle Sam seemed a bit wasteful with his accumulated wealth, he certainly had the means—even if he didn't have the will—to pay off his debts. In the late 1990s, in contrast, the federal budget was in balance—indeed, in surplus—inflation was low and employment high. Particularly after the Asian crisis of 1997, funds poured into U.S. markets, and the effects of that shift were to produce a trade deficit as high as it had been in the 1980s. Uncle Sam didn't need to borrow, but an awful lot of people were lending him money because he took good care of it.

Even more dramatic was the effect of shifting patterns of lending to several of the Asian tigers—Korea, Thailand, Indonesia, and Malaysia. A great willingness to lend to the countries enabled the very high rates of investment similar to those shown in Figure 10.4c. Yet, a change in assessment (or sentiment) caused a sudden outflow of funds, with a consequent decline in investment (and income and consumption).

Later chapters explore the way these mechanisms work, but for the moment consider that, at root, they all trace how the availability of foreign capital affects the availability of funds for investment and consumption (partially through the interest rate mechanisms) and how those changes in turn affect income. As a case in point: the inflows of capital experienced by the Asian tigers led to high levels of investment, employment, and income, while the outflows had the opposite effect.

TRADE IMBALANCES AS PROBLEMS AND SYMPTOMS

Is a Trade Deficit a Bad Thing?

A trade deficit is not in itself good or bad. A country may be borrowing abroad to invest at home in capital improvements that have much higher benefits. After all, firms don't borrow funds if they think that they will not earn more on them than they pay in interest. Households and governments, of course, may not always be so calculating and borrow for personal consumption or for investments that are politically rewarding, even if economically dismal. This suggests two questions, neither easy to answer:

1. Is the trade deficit so costly that the service (interest and principal repayments) on the borrowings might be unsustainable? The benefits, for instance, might not be high enough to cover the costs of borrowing. Or, the benefits may be great, but they do not generate sufficient foreign exchange to keep up the payments on the debt.

2. Is the benefit, even where payments can be sustained, worth the cost?

With just a few twists, the same question can be raised of a trade surplus.

3. Are the investments made abroad as a consequence of the trade surplus as beneficial as expenditures that would be made domestically? Consider the case of Japan, which has had large trade surpluses. Would not the economy have done better if many of those funds were used to improve the economy at home—or simply to allow the Japanese to have more enjoyment in life?

Trade Imbalances, Capital Accumulation, and Growth

Long-term growth stems from several sources: increased physical capital, a more highly educated population, improved technology, and more efficient organization of firms and markets. Capital has received the most attention partly because it is easily measured and partly because it has, at least in the past, been highly correlated with economic growth. Capital accumulation is essential for economic growth over the long term. In the short term, a nation with substantial unemployment and underutilized physical facilities can grow simply by using its existing facilities more—that is, by getting close to full employment. At full employment, a nation can grow through better use of the existing capital—a better use deriving from greater education levels, technological change, wider markets, and/or greater specialization of production, to mention a few key elements. Still, the capital base has an important role, and a changing (and increasing) capital base has normally been associated with changing technology and higher educational levels. Without the accumulation of physical capital to produce more goods and services— more transportation facilities, more machinery, more buildings, more communications facilities, many of them embodying the new technology— the other sources of economic growth would have far less effect.

Growth in this sense derives from the *domestic* capital base. But what about the savings a country has lent abroad? Of what use is this to the country? Certainly it is part of a nation's capital base. Unlike the domestic base, however, which is held in physical form, the foreign base is held in financial form, a topic soon to be explored.

DOMESTIC BASE

The domestic base of a nation's capital is the total accumulation of everything that has been made, saved, and not used up. Statistically, it is the accumulated gross fixed capital formation plus changes in inventories, minus depreciation. Many economists argue for a broader interpretation of capital that would include (1) consumer durables such as cars, furniture, and appliances (now counted as consumption, even though they do not disappear during the year); (2) educational expenses; (3) expenditure on research and development; (4) computer software. The grounds for arguing a broader definition is that all of these things last from year to year, even though, as in the case of education and research and development, they are not physically present. Students struggling with a burden of student loans and heavy course loads may be surprised to learn that they are consuming and putting nothing aside for the future. Corporations spending millions on developing new products or processes surely regard what they are doing as a kind of investment, even though it is not resulting in plant and equipment. Certainly, not all educational expenses or R&D contributes, but neither does all capital. A factory at half capacity, a resort with few patrons, and a highway to nowhere are no more useless than the most obscure doctoral dissertation a congressman can dig up or the most hare-brained product development managers come up with. Inclusion of the items listed above roughly doubles the amount of "investment" the United States and many other developed countries make. A warning therefore is in order: investment, as defined by national income figures, is just one part of a broader group of investments, rather more difficult to trace, so all conclusions based just on the growth of physical capital should be taken with a grain of salt.

470

A "good" trade deficit in this context would be one in which the increase in absorption allowed higher spending on the items noted above (whether the broad or narrow idea of investment) such that the economic growth produced would enable the economy to service the debts incurred. A "bad" trade deficit is one in which either there is insufficient investment, or investment is so poorly targeted (factories that produce things people do not want, empty hotels, overly specialized educational training) that the economy can not sustain payments.

FOREIGN CAPITAL BASE

An accumulation of foreign assets is also an important part of a nation's capital base. The investments made abroad produce interest and profit, which are part of the income stream. As the discussion of multinational firms in Chapter 19 explains, foreign investments are also closely connected to the full exploitation of the value of innovations, inventions, and other forms of *proprietary* knowledge, serving therefore to increase employment in various knowledge-producing or processing jobs. If a particular firm or bank sees an opportunity to invest abroad at a higher interest rate (and same risk) than it does domestically, that income will yield a larger income stream than it will if invested in domestic capital. A nation whose foreign investments decline sees a drop in its income and jobs just as much as does a nation whose own physical capital decreases.

Note that foreign investment can be in financial form and need not be in physical form like domestic investment. Introductory textbooks explain that investment must be in physical form (or perhaps in human capital) to be counted as investment, not in financial form, which is just an income transfer. Yet, in this circumstance, strictly financial investments are to the nation true investments.

For the nation, an accumulation of foreign assets fulfills the criteria needed to be an investment—goods set aside in one period that can be used in a subsequent period without having to devote new resources to their creation. A Canadian purchasing a bond in the United States does not increase North American investment one iota, but does increase Canadian investment; in any future year, Canada can claim goods and services from the United States equal to that investment—and that is, from a national viewpoint, just as much an investment as is an increase in inventory or the purchase of machinery. The sale of the bond by the American has decreased U.S. claims on the rest of the world and is a form of international borrowing or disinvestment; in the future, Americans will have to provide the goods and services represented by that bond sale whenever the Canadian desires to cash in the bond. Since the United States has not physically set anything aside on selling the bond, no North American investment has occurred: U.S. disinvestment matches

Canadian investment, so the *net* effect on *world* investment is zero. The sum of all the nations' investments and disinvestments together should equal zero. No double counting should occur.

The Interplay of Domestic and Foreign Capital Stocks

The only way a country can have a trade deficit is to go into debt or sell off existing foreign assets. Castorians went into debt when they agreed to deliver more pelts the next year; they could also have borrowed money from some other source in Fabrica to pay the traders. If, in previous years, they had accumulated credits or bought assets in Fabrica, they could turn them in. A country with a surplus has to place the surplus in some financial form. The Fabricans left their surplus as pictures of beavers—an extension of *commercial credit*, to be technical. In a more modern economy, they could have received money and invested that in bonds or physical assets in Castoria.[*]

To the extent that a nation draws down its stock of foreign assets or incurs additional foreign debt, its domestic investment is not net investment. A firm that reduces a sinking fund[†] to build up its plant and equipment does not count the increased value of its plant as net new investment. In the same way, a country cannot count the increase in its domestic capital as net of whatever it has sold off or borrowed abroad to make those investments.

To see this better, consider the formula for net national product.

(Eq. 10.16) $GNP - Dp = NNP$

Enlarging this to show the components of GNP, *C, I, G,* and *X − M,*

(Eq. 10.17) $C + I + G - D + (X - M) = NNP$

If imports exceed exports $(M > X)$, then the stock of foreign investment is lowered. To pay for the deficit, the country must sell off foreign assets or borrow by selling their own assets to foreigners. The foreign investment of the country accordingly falls. In this sense, a trade deficit is much the same as depreciation and has to be subtracted from the country's net investment. We can show this by stating the trade deficit as $M - X$, which produces a positive figure if imports exceed exports. Restating Equation 10.12:

---

[*] Students sometimes ask, "Can't they buy goods with it?" Of course, but if they buy goods they no longer have a surplus. Chapter 11 handles the more special problem of gifts. Fabrica could *give* away its surplus and be left with no investment.

[†] A sinking fund is an accumulation of assets, usually in bank accounts and short-term bonds, that a firm puts aside in order to avoid borrowing to finance a future project.

Figure 10.7

U.S. DOMESTIC INVESTMENTS,
TOTAL INVESTMENTS, AND NET FACTOR RECEIPTS

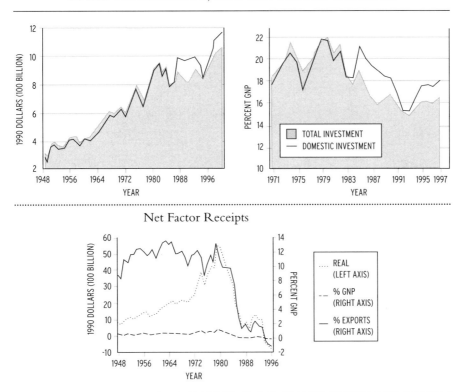

Net Factor Receipts

$$(Eq.\ 10.18) \qquad C\ +\ I\ +\ G - Dp - (M - X) = NNP$$

Unless *I* exceeds both *Dp* and *(M − X)*, the nation's capital base will shrink and its potential productivity in subsequent years is lowered.

THE COST

Nations whose net foreign investment position is negative—that is, who owe more than they have invested abroad—usually have more interest and profits payments flowing out of the country than coming in. Expenditures that otherwise could have been made on domestic consumption, investment, or government are instead spent on the profits and interest payments required to pay for another year's use of other nations' savings. These count as imports of

473

Figure 10.8
IRELAND: DOMESTIC INVESTMENTS, TOTAL
INVESTMENTS, AND NET FACTOR RECEIPTS

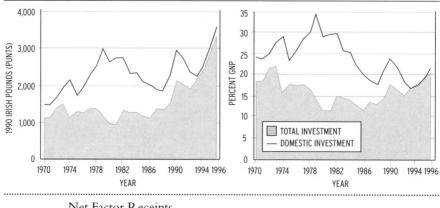

Net Factor Receipts

Note: Ireland borrowed very heavily to finance its capital expansion in the 1970s and 1980s. In some years more than half of all its investment was covered by borrowings from abroad, although in recent years Ireland itself has been able to provide nearly all its new capital itself.

services, but certainly do not give as much satisfaction as imported capital goods or consumption goods. Economically, it may be quite reasonable to borrow considerable amounts from abroad if the investments those borrowings allow are sound and help build capacity in the domestic economy; in such cases the payments abroad are only a small portion of the net economic benefits. When, however, the borrowing from abroad is used largely for consumption purposes and investment does not rise, future payments for those borrowings must come from the same economic base as before. Some examples can illustrate these points.

THE UNITED STATES

The United States entered the period after World War II with large trade surpluses and a considerable amount of foreign investments, and so long as it

474

continued to have trade surpluses its net foreign investment position improved. Its total investment—the increase in physical capital domestically and its financial stake abroad (*Id* + *If*)—continued to rise, and with that rise its net receipts from investment income also rose, such that from 1955 to 1981 total return on foreign investments was at least $50 billion in 1990 dollars in all but a few years. When the United States began to run trade deficits and borrow from abroad, however, its payments abroad rose sharply and net receipts from investment tumbled. The three panels of Figure 10.7 show what happened, using an item, net factor receipts, as a proxy for investment income. This figure, whose principal components are interest income and payments and profits of foreign-owned firms, is explained in more detail in the next chapter. When it is positive, the country is receiving more investment payments from abroad than it is sending.

Total American investment was higher than domestic investment from the beginning of the statistical series (1948) until 1983, with the exception of the years right around the two oil price crises of 1972 and 1978. After 1984, total investment was consistently lower than domestic investment. Until 1993, the United States received more from its foreign investments than it paid foreigners for their investments in the States, but the heavy borrowings from abroad (and to a lesser extent the selling off of foreign assets) changed net earnings from over $50 billion in 1979 to net payments of around $10 billion in 1996. These figures are tiny in comparison to American GNP, but significant as a portion of exports, where the shift amounts to about 13% of all exports. To put it another way, had the United States not borrowed in the 1980s, its balance of trade (on goods, services, and income) would be better by about 60 billion 1990 dollars, equivalent to about 12% of American exports of goods, services, and income.

THE CASE OF IRELAND

Ireland presents a different scenario marked by greater extremes. Ireland borrowed heavily from abroad and used a great deal of that to build up its physical capital. (It already had a solid educational base.) The result was far lower total investment than domestic investment and an increasing amount of payments for the borrowed money. Ireland has paid heavily for the extensive borrowing. At one point, it was paying nearly 15% of its GNP and 20% of its export receipts just to pay for what it borrowed. Nonetheless, it has been able to sustain payments because its GNP and exports have both grown vigorously (exports far more than GNP) and it has stopped the heavy borrowing from abroad.

Figure 10.9

BRAZIL: DOMESTIC INVESTMENTS, TOTAL
INVESTMENTS, AND NET FACTOR RECEIPTS

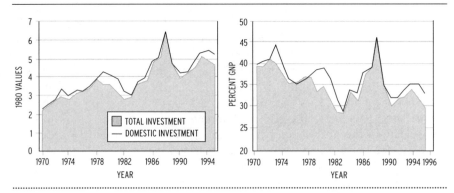

Net Factor Receipts

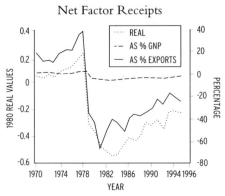

THE CASE OF BRAZIL

Brazil showed yet another pattern. Because it is a large country, Brazil's exports and imports tend to be a small proportion of GNP. Moreover, years of protectionist policies have reduced the percentage of trade in Brazil's economy even further, such that a relatively small boost to domestic resources provided by a series of trade deficits produced serious payments problems. As a percentage of GNP, the figures do not look bad, but the problem was that Brazilian investments were not producing the foreign exchange necessary to service the debt. As Chapter 1 indicated, Brazil's exports are a very small fraction of national income so a small percentage of GNP is a large percentage of exports. Factor payments grew to be more than half of all Brazil's exports, leading to a major debt crisis for the country. In real terms, too, the debts grew to be enormous.

COMPARING THE COUNTRIES

Ireland used the very extensive borrowing to build up its physical capital, although the cost has certainly been high. It has, nonetheless, been sustainable, and the decline in factor payments as a percentage both of GNP and of exports improves its sustainability. Brazilian borrowing was not nearly so high as a percentage of GNP, but it did not seem to help produce the foreign exchange needed to service the debt. While Ireland saw a sharp rise in exports and in exports as a percentage of GNP, Brazil did not and ended up in crisis. The American case is rather more difficult. Clearly, physical capital was not built up during the 1980s, yet the 1990s saw an expansion of the economy unmatched in the developed world. The probable answer is that the national income definitions of capital simply are not appropriate, or at least are insufficient, to account for growth. Higher spending on education, on research and development, and on computerization and telecommunication were only weakly reflected in physical capital. (Glass-fiber communication systems, for instance, are cheaper to install and build than the old copper wire systems and can carry vastly more information.) Moreover, the American trade deficit was to some degree an intergenerational transfer of saving, as younger Americans chose to consume (including building up durable goods and furthering their educations, as well as more frivolous activities) rather than save, while older Europeans and Japanese sought places to put their savings.

The rosy tint of the previous paragraph needs some darkening. Both Irish and American economic policy contributed to unnecessarily high trade deficits. The Irish let inflation get out of control, which, as Chapter 5 explained, leads to trade deficits. Brazilian economic policy suffered from hyperinflation and a related absence of effective fiscal and monetary controls. The Reagan tax cuts led to enormous fiscal deficits, yet private saving did not rise to cover the shortfall in saving. To counter the fiscal stimulus, the Federal Reserve used a high interest rate policy, which attracted the foreign funds that allowed the large trade deficits, but that very policy depressed investment in physical capital. Expenditures on further education and research in the United States were probably as much in spite of the economic policies of the 1980s as because of them.

Is a Trade Surplus a Good Thing?

Borrowers always seem to have the worst problems. What about the lenders? Whether the placing of additional saving abroad is a good or bad thing depends on the objectives of the country and its neighbors. With a given level of saving, the choice between domestic and foreign investment is, in a sense, a *portfolio* choice, with the nation deciding how many of its assets or debts it wishes to place at home or abroad. Too much foreign investment can lead to a weak domestic economy, as has been argued for Britain in the last decades of the previous century when half of all British saving (!) was going abroad. The same argument has been made for the Netherlands, as the expansive seventeenth-century economy led into a rentier eighteenth-century "Periwig" economy with vast sums invested in British bonds.[5] Too little foreign investment, on the other hand, means the forsaking of excellent foreign investment opportunities, the income from which will provide foreign goods and services for years to come. And as Japan enters the twenty-first century with sluggish demand at home and slowly growing markets, it, too, may begin to question how much of its wealth it wants to place abroad.

JAPAN: A LENDER'S PROBLEMS

As noted in Chapter 8, Americans have complained vigorously against Japan's seeming protectionism and often cite the large trade deficit the U.S. has with Japan as demonstrable proof. The main piece of evidence is the large and long-standing trade surplus with the United States, which runs back to the 1970s, although it only achieved a large size of $40 billion to $50 billion (as much as two-thirds of the entire American deficit) in the mid-1980s. The American public tends to equate trade surpluses with trade protectionism. Obviously, so runs the story, if a country exports a lot but holds down imports, then it will have a trade surplus. This argument, however, doesn't fit the income–absorption model at all. What is wrong?

For one thing, bilateral trade is not a meaningful figure. Sure, the U.S. imports a great deal more from Japan than it exports to Japan. But trade is multilateral, not bilateral. For example, the United States exports a considerable amount to oil producers in the Middle East that have earned large sums from exporting to Japan. While some 30% of Japan's exports go to the United States and only about 23% of its imports come from there, consider that only about 2.5% of Japan's exports go to the Middle East while about 10% of its imports come from there.[6]

More importantly, saving and investment determine trade imbalances. Japan's trade balance, including services and net income from abroad, was a little over $100 billion in 1997. So the savings-investment gap is also $100 billion. If the relation of saving to investment does not change, the trade balance cannot change. Importing more will just lead to an expansion of exports as resources freed from making import substitutes are used to produce exports. Unless something happens to increase Japanese investment or decrease Japanese saving, its trade surplus will persist. Chapters 12–15 examine in more detail the mechanisms at work. Both general equilibrium and absorption models, however, come to the same conclusion: protectionism reduces the amount of trade, not the trade imbalance.

The continued protection of Japanese agriculture and the structural problems the economy has in accepting imports, noted in Chapter 8, have undoubtedly depressed trade as a portion of the Japanese economy, as the figures from Chapter 1 showed. It would be good for Japan to trade more, but more trade in itself will not change the trade balance.

Last is the question of whether Japan is wise in investing so much abroad. From a practical point of view, the answer is positive. Japan's domestic economy has faltered throughout the 1990s: the stock market has fallen, interest rates are barely above zero, and firms are making scant if any profits. With such low returns on investment and much higher returns abroad, it is quite reasonable for individual investors, as well as the country as a whole, to invest its surplus abroad.

TOTAL INVESTMENT EQUALS TOTAL SAVING

A trade deficit measures the gap between domestic saving and domestic investment. When the United States has a $50 billion trade deficit, it means that foreign countries have saved $50 billion of income from goods they sold to the United States but did not collect on (much as the Fabricans did with the Castorians). Total domestic investment thus equals domestic saving plus foreign saving. To put it algebraically:

$$\textit{(Eq. 10.19)} \qquad Sp + Sg + (X - M) = Id$$

and $\quad$ *(Eq. 10.20)* $\qquad X - M = Sf$, where Sf = foreigners' saving

Thus: $\quad$ *(Eq. 10.21)* $\qquad Sp + Sg + Sf = Id$

Looking at the same issue from another angle, we could also say that total American investment was Id less $(X - M)$. In this case, $X - M$ is foreigners' investment and must be subtracted, as in the examples above, from total American investment. We do not violate the basic equality of investment to saving.

THE INTERNATIONAL CAPITAL MARKET AND NATIONAL SAVING

It is surprising, given the differences in saving rates among countries, how small net transfers are—that is, how little trade imbalances count as a portion of income or saving. High-saving countries tend to invest heavily in their

Figure 10.10
JAPAN-U.S. LENDING

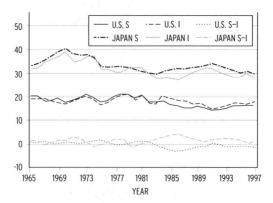

Note: The United States and Japan, like most other OECD countries, saw saving and investment rise and fall closely together, with high-saving Japan also a high-investing country. Gaps opened up a bit in the 1980s, but tended to close again in the 1990s.

home markets, such that *Id* and *Sd* are closely correlated.[7] In the late 1980s
there was some shifting away from that pattern, typified perhaps by the lending between Japan and the United States.[8]

Another way to look at the question is to examine the size of current
account deficits as a percentage of national incomes. Most studies have been
on a country-by-country basis, but recently Alan Taylor of Northwestern
University has been calculating a capital mobility index, which brings together
data from many countries. His index uses the current account imbalance as
a percentage of GNP, algebraically identical to the net capital movement.
Before World War I, trade imbalances ran between 3 and 6 % of the GNPs of
countries. In the 1920s they fell to less than 2% of GNP, rose in World War
II to about 3%, but then fell again in the 1950s to between 1.5 and 2.5% of
GNP[9]. For all our talk about globalization, capital flows, relative to national
output, were higher a century ago.

GOVERNMENT SAVING AND TRADE DEFICITS:
THE TWIN DEFICIT QUESTION

Government saving may play a vital role in national saving. Exactly what role
it plays is in dispute, so we begin there.

The Decline of Public Saving: Budgetary Deficits and the Trade Balance

A common argument about public debt is that "We owe it to ourselves," and it is therefore less serious a problem than if we owed it to outsiders. Most U.S. Treasury bills are indeed held by Americans. Most Canadian federal government debt is held by Canadians. But who holds a bond is no more important than who pays a tax; taxes can be passed on and so can debt. If the government sells all its debt to its nationals, its households and corporations may need to raise funds abroad. We cannot get around the relationship that $X - M = S - I$. For illustration, suppose private saving equals domestic investment and the government has a deficit, then:

$$(Eq.\ 10.22) \qquad Id\ +\ X - M = Sp\ +\ T - G$$

$$\text{if} \qquad Id = Sp$$

$$\text{then} \qquad (X - M) = (T - G)$$

Thus, *the budget deficit equals the trade deficit!*

While such a conjunction of having $Sp = I$ would be unusual, figures approximating it are not, and the lesson, in any case, need not be lost. Any change in $T - G$, given no change in Sp and I, will equal the change in $X - M$. Many critics of the Reagan administration argued that, in essence, the government deficits of those years *caused* the trade deficits, that the government borrowed private savings and spent it on government consumption. C. Fred Bergsten of the Institute of International Economics called the budget and trade deficits *the twin deficits* and argued that the elimination of the government deficit will make a major contribution toward eliminating the trade deficit.[10] Figure 10.1 showed that the deficit appeared as the United States entered the 1980s. The increase in the federal government deficit after 1982 was closely linked to the increase in the trade deficit, particularly in the early years of the decade. The reduction of the deficit (combined federal, state, and local) in 1987 may have contributed to the small improvement in the trade balance.

If the budget deficit decreases domestic saving, then it helps to create a trade deficit by widening the gap between Id and S. Should this occur it negates one of the standard defenses of an unbalanced budget—we owe all the debt to ourselves. The advantage of "owing money to others in the same nation" is that repayments are just transfers from one subset of people in the nation to another subset. Instead of taxpayers (Set 1) getting the goods produced in the nation, bondholders (Set 2) get the goods. The extent of the income redistribution is uncertain, because some individuals are in both sets, but the important factor is that the nation does still enjoy all the goods it produces. With foreign debt, however, the nation must produce a trade surplus, saving more than it invests. There are real costs involved, regardless of the income distribution effects.

Offsetting Effects

A decline in government saving does not automatically lead to an increase in the trade deficit. Much depends on what impact the decline in government saving has on private saving or investment. To take the U.S. case, it appears that the decline in government saving was the major contributor to the rise in the trade deficit in the 1980s, but the increase in government saving in the late 1990s has been in considerable part offset by a decline in private saving. For government saving to affect fully the trade balance, Y, Sp (private saving), and Id must be constant. If, however, a cut in taxes increased private saving, possibly as much as the amount of the tax cut itself, then domestic saving would be unchanged.[*] Why might offsetting effects arise?

1. People may react to a tax increase (particularly one not expected to last) by maintaining their consumption level through cutting savings, and vice versa with a tax cut. This follows from the idea of permanent income that Milton Friedman suggested as a description of household behavior. People, argued Friedman, tend to adjust their consumption to their idea of how much they will earn over their lifetimes. Changes in their income that they see as temporary cause them to adjust savings rather than expenditure. If they get a single bonus (winning a lottery, for example), they will only increase their consumption a bit, as if they bought an annuity with the winnings. (An annuity pays a predetermined sum every year, based on its earnings and a gradual run-down of its capital.) If their income rises and falls, they will tend to keep the same level of expenditure, saving more when it rises and less when it dips.

2. If the government withdraws services, people will have to pay for them themselves. So if nursing home support is cut, the families will put in more; if it increases, they will put in less.

3. Harvard's Robert Barro, among others,[11] harks back to David Ricardo as he argues that private and government savings tend to offset each other. His reasoning is that when governments run deficits, taxpayers recognize that future taxes will be higher and increase their rate of saving to compensate. If,

---

[*] The *permanent income hypothesis* arguments, as well as life-cycle hypotheses, suggest that changes in government taxes or expenditures are offset by the private-sector reactions. Those students familiar with those arguments might wish to pursue the question with some made-up examples.

for instance, you planned on supplementing your social security with $20,000 a year income, you might wish to set aside $400,000 (to yield 5% and leave your estate intact). If, however, you expected higher tax rates or that inflation would require $30,000 instead of $20,000 beyond social security, you would save more as the government deficit rose (and less as it fell). While logical, the model will only work if citizens are both rational and well informed, and while as economists we may assume the first, we cannot assume the second.

Arguments of this kind are not so much theory as observations of behavior. Yes, rational, fully informed households will increase their saving to offset government dissaving, resulting in little or no change in total domestic saving, but households are not always well informed and generally do not, or at least in some countries do not, so react. This may explain why the evidence for offsetting effects so far is mixed. U.S. figures do not show strong support for any counterbalancing in the mid-1980s,[12] although the late 1980s provide some support as the declining government deficits were offset by declining personal saving.[13]

In contrast to the American experience, Canadian figures seem to substantiate Barro's thesis, with private saving rising as government saving falls, falling as government saving rises. Canadian government deficits were larger on a percentage or per capita basis than American deficits, yet because private saving was high, Canada was able to run a number of trade surpluses in the 1980s. Figure 10.11 shows this pattern.

Figure 10.11 tracks government saving on the left-hand axis, private saving on the right. The very good mirror images of the two pairs of lines show that movements of government and private saving tended to offset each other throughout the two decades shown. The correlations do not tell us whether the offsets occurred because people anticipated future expenditure, or whether some other factor affects government saving one way and private saving the opposite way.

Figure 10.11

CANADA: A BARRO EFFECT?

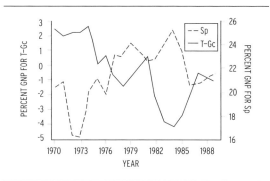

Theory, policy, and statistics come together on this question. If private-sector saving behavior is sufficiently isolated (by lack of information, appreciation of the information, or ability to act) from public-sector deficits, then fiscal policy can cause or eliminate trade deficits. At first blush, the U.S. figures seem to confirm that assessment, while the Canadian ones do not. Yet, if the information and its assessment are key, why should the Americans differ so much in their response from the Canadians? With all due respect to the True North Strong and Free, there is little to suggest to us that Canadians are more sophisticated about economic matters than Americans.[*]

More important, perhaps, than trying to demonstrate if Barro is right or not is to keep in mind that private and government saving may not be independent. Barro is certainly right some of the time, and almost always to some degree. Most economists in policy positions would probably reject the more extreme position that private and government savings always (or in the long run) offset each other and would opt for some middle ground.[14] The government deficits, at least in some situations, are the probable cause of trade deficits, but, since it is uncertain in what situations that is true, the simple prescription merely to cut the deficit is in fact simplistic. It may work and it may be, as Fred Bergsten argued for the Americans, "the only game in town," but its success is not assured.

PRIVATE SAVING

Private saving throughout most of the industrial countries has fallen as a percentage of GNP.[15] The American figures, for instance, show total saving falling below 15%, which would hardly cover depreciation of plant and equipment. Yet the American economy followed this period of low saving and investment with a decade-long economic expansion, while Japan, with savings often at twice the percentage of American investment, languished. Clearly, the correlation between gross fixed capital formation, as it is measured presently, and economic growth is not at all clear. Two things are possible: (1) saving is being underestimated or (2) the sources of growth are not strongly related to capital spending. The broader definitions of investment, including education, consumer durables, military spending (not in American capital formation figures), and computer software (just put in the American figures) typically raise expenditure in the industrial countries to around 30% of GNP. Since there are no direct measures of saving, an increase in investment automatically increases saving. That is, $I = (X - M) = S$, and $S - Sg = Sp$. If I rises, S rises. It still doesn't change the fact that a trade

---

[*] Clearly, other factors may also affect the statistical correlations. Our purpose here is not to apply exhaustive analysis, but to indicate general relationships. The IMF's Tamim Bayoumi figured that Barro effects might account for about 25% of an offset: that is, a $1 million increase in government deficit in many OECD countries was partially offset by a $250,000 rise in saving. See his "Saving-Investment Correlation," *IMF Staff Papers* (June 1990): 360-87. More recently the Bank of Canada has begun to calculate the offset at 50%.

deficit indicates that $I > S$, but it does raise the question of whether citizens of industrial countries are wildly profligate.

Demographic Change and the Saving Life-Cycle Hypothesis

Putting on rose-colored glasses for a moment, contemplate a plausible hypothesis: international trade imbalances may be nothing more (or less) than large intergenerational transfers, smoothing the consumption pattern of individuals and also of nations. Let us see why.

People tend to save most money in the years before retirement, when earnings are high but expected to fall. They save the least in retirement, in the years before they work, and in their early working years. That, in essence, is the *life-cycle hypothesis* of saving which is useful in domestic macroeconomics. Its international implications are of great importance because it suggests that a country's saving (as a percentage of GNP) can be predicted by observing its demographic profile. Moreover, the same intergenerational patterns of the working-age people lending to the young and the old using up (or not increasing) their saving extends into the international sphere.

The 1980s trade deficits of the United States and Canada, for instance, were the result of the large number of baby boomers (children born between 1946 and 1964) in the late school and early working years. As they move into their high-earning and -saving periods, North American saving is expected to rise. Western Europe and Japan, on the other hand, have relatively older populations, many of whom will be moving into retirement, and their saving is expected to fall. Given no sharp change in investment patterns, North America would then move into a trade surplus position. Table 10.1 illustrates the changes in *dependency ratio*—the number of those under 15 and over 64 years old as a percentage of the 15-64 age group, historically and as projected.

If saving is highest in nations with lower dependency ratios, as most studies suggest it indeed is, then the trade deficits of the United States should have turned into surpluses sometime in the 1990s, which they did not. Canada's is supposed to turn, but a bit later. Japan and Western Europe should develop deficits. This clearly depends on domestic investment not rising sufficiently in North America (or falling in Europe and Japan) to overcome the rise in saving.[16]

The life-cycle saving hypothesis suggests, then, that high-saving middle-aged people in Europe are lending resources to younger, lower-saving North Americans. When the Europeans and Japanese turn older, however, they will save less while North Americans save more. North Americans will repay their debt and in the process all groups will enjoy a smoother pattern of consumption over their lives. What appears to be a spendthrift period in North America evens out with a thrifty one in the longer run.

Table 10.1

SELECTED DEMOGRAPHIC VARIABLES, 1965—2025 (%)

Country	1965	1975	1985	Projections			
				1995	2005	2015	2025
Population under 15 / population 15-64							
United States	51	39	33	34	29	29	30
Japan	38	36	32	25	28	28	27
Germany, Fed. Rep. of	35	34	22	23	22	19	23
France	41	38	32	31	28	26	28
Italy	—	—	—	25	25	22	24
United Kingdom	36	37	29	31	31	31	31
Canada	57	41	32	30	27	25	28
Population 65 and over / population 15-64							
United States	16	16	18	19	18	21	29
Japan	9	12	15	19	26	33	32
Germany, Fed. Rep. of	18	23	21	24	29	31	37
France	19	22	20	22	24	27	33
Italy	—	—	—	22	25	28	32
United Kingdom	19	22	23	23	22	24	28
Canada	13	13	15	18	19	25	34
Overall dependency ratio							
United States	67	55	51	52	47	50	59
Japan	48	48	47	44	54	61	59
Germany, Fed. Rep. of	54	56	43	47	51	51	60
France	61	60	52	53	52	53	61
Italy	52	54	45	47	50	50	55
United Kingdom	55	59	52	54	53	55	59
Canada	70	54	48	48	46	50	61

Source: Paul R. Masson and Ralph Tryon, "Macroeconomic effects of projected population aging in industrial countries," *IMF Staff Papers* (September 1990): 457.

CONCLUSION

A principal thrust of this chapter has been to show the relationship of the saving-investment gap and the related absorption gap to trade imbalances—the trade gap, to give it a name. Patterns of causality are complex, but ample evidence suggests that shocks to the domestic gaps frequently give rise to the trade imbalances. If, indeed, trade imbalances emerge from deeply rooted patterns of saving and investment, then macroeconomic policy may be singularly ineffective in correcting them. Changes in tax structures, in controls over government expenditure, in incentives for private saving, or in encouragement of the proper long-run level of investment may be required to eliminate trade deficits or surpluses.

A second thrust of this chapter has been to indicate what the costs of trade imbalances are, both to the trade-deficit country and to the trade-surplus country. Is their control in fact the *central question* or is their size *incidental* to other, basically more important, economic goals, such as high levels of employment, efficient allocation of resources, and economic growth? We trust it becomes clear that the pursuit of balanced trade for its own sake is neither fruitful nor wise. Countries can live for generations with deficits or surpluses; the ultimate question is whether in so doing they are in fact reaching some optimal level of growth and employment.

A backward look is also instructive. Trade deficits do not arise because of other countries' trade policies. Protectionism reduces the total amount of trade and economic efficiency. Artificial boosting may increase trade, but it reduces efficiency. Neither affects fundamentally the balance of trade. If a country absorbs more than it produces, it will have a deficit; if it produces more than it absorbs, it will have a surplus.

The following chapter takes up several of the questions we have raised in this one. In particular, it examines how a trade deficit is financed to get at the problem of the cost not in terms of investment forgone (which we have covered here), but in terms of the interest costs of carrying a large load of debt. Moreover, it shows how one can use the balance-of-payments statement to develop far more precision and far greater insights into the international economic situation of any country.

APPENDIX: WHERE TO FIND THE NUMBERS

National account information for any member of the International Monetary Fund is available in *International Financial Statistics*. If you wish to do anything extensive with the figures, try to obtain the *IFS* CD-ROM, which has the figures as far back as the country was a member of the IMF, which in many cases is 1948.

To construct diagrams like those in the text, make the following adjustments. (1) Domestic investment is gross fixed capital formation plus increase in stocks. (2) National accounts give only a net figure for factor payments. We have handled it by adding the number to exports (in countries where the figure is normally positive) or to imports (where it is normally negative). Be careful to subtract the figure from imports, which are stated as a positive figure. Alternatively and more accurately, check the *Balance of Payments Statistics Yearbook*, which does not net the figures. The sum of the income receipts and payments, however, may not match the national accounts figures, so you then have to use the proportions in the BPSY to establish the amounts. (3) Saving is domestic investment plus exports minus imports plus net factor payments. (4) A deflator may be figured from GDP in current values and from GDP in real values. Divide the current GDP by the real GDP. Divide all other current figures by the deflator so created. Government investment figures are available in the *National Accounts Statistics Yearbook*, a United Nations publication, but they are many years behind. You can get a good idea of their amount using the *Government Financial Statistics Yearbook* and summing the capital expenditures of central, state, and local governments. Similarly, government saving can be approximated by establishing the deficits at the three (or two) levels of government. The difference between revenue and expenditure is, at least in theory, the difference between T and G.

VOCABULARY AND CONCEPTS

		Symbols	
Absorption	GNP		
Balance of trade	Income-absorption gap	S	I
Barro thesis	Life-cycle hypothesis	Y	A
Capital accumulation	(and trade imbalances)	X	M
Demographic change	Output (income)	Sg	Sp
Domestic capital base	Ricardian equivalencies	Id	Gc
Foreign capital base	Savings-investment gap	T	Dp
Funds	Trade imbalance	NId	NNP
Funds market	Twin deficit question	Sf	Sg
GDP			

QUESTIONS

1. $X - M$ is:
   a. the difference between exports and imports.
   b. the difference between domestic savings and domestic investment.
   c. the difference between production and absorption.
   d. the foreign savings a nation uses or the savings it places abroad.
   e. the difference between the amount of funds domestic lenders place on the market and what domestic borrowers take from the market.
   f. all of the above.
   Why?
2. "If markets clear, then we can have no trade deficit." Explain.
3. Assume that the Castorians and Fabricans trade together as described in the text's example, and that the Castorians fail to bring the usual number of beaver pelts to the market. To get the same number of trade goods, the Castorians agree to deliver next year an extra 2,000 pelts and the Fabricans supply their usual number of trade goods.
   a. How is this a trade surplus or deficit?
   b. How does the market clear?
   c. Who can absorb more than they produce and who less?
   d. Who is using whose savings?
   e. Who has invested what in whom?
4. Why are imports subtracted from $C + I + G + X$? Why not just count the domestic C, G, and I?
5. First-year textbooks usually teach that $S = I$, yet we can see here that domestic saving need not equal domestic investment. Why?
6. Korea's trade deficit in the 1980s declined sharply as growth and saving rose. After 1997, however, it seemed less likely that Korea would try the same solution again. Why?

7. Contrast and compare the American trade deficit in the 1980s with the Korean trade deficit of the same period.
8. Contrast and compare the trade deficits of Ireland, the United States, and Brazil.
9. What is the "twin deficits" problem? What are the arguments for T − G causing the decline in savings? What arguments are there against this?
10. Explain why a difference between domestic saving and domestic investment is also the amount the country borrows from abroad in the market for funds.
11. No matter how desperate a country's financial difficulties, it cannot spend more than its income unless other countries give it credit. The reverse is also true. Explain, using Brazil and the United States as examples.
12. The foreign capital base is held in financial form. Is that consistent with other economic interpretations of investment?
13. "Despite vast improvements in international capital markets, countries that save a great deal also invest a lot domestically, with only a bit flowing outside." What is the evidence for such a statement? Why might this be happening? Is it a new thing or something old?
14. One interpretation of the U.S. trade deficit in the 1980s is that it resulted from the Reagan tax cuts of 1982, which, as one wag put it, "raised the disposable incomes of all those who had not read Robert Barro and David Ricardo." Explain, showing the role of the decline in government savings and what the Barro effect is.
15. Trade imbalances in themselves are neither good nor bad. What makes a trade deficit bad? What makes a trade surplus bad? What makes them good?
16. "Government deficits are no problem because we owe all the money to ourselves." Even supposing that the government sells all its T-bills and bonds to residents, does the country avoid foreign borrowing?
17. Countries with trade surpluses are investors abroad. Is that always a good thing?
18. A 1991 newsletter from the Federal Reserve Bank of San Francisco reviewed the improvement in the U.S. balance of trade and concluded:

> The continued existence of U.S. trade deficits reflects an imbalance of national saving above investment [that is, $I > S$], not any fundamental decline in competitiveness.... But thinking that the U.S. is uncompetitive and "over the hill" can create undue attention for inappropriate short-term economic solutions such as greater protectionism, managed trade policy, or industrial targeting, particularly during the current period of macroeconomic stress. [Reuven Glick, *FRBSF Weekly Letter*, Number 92013, March 27, 1992.]

At root, do the problems of trade imbalances have much to do with trade policy? Are they problems of fiscal policy?
19. What in the pattern of demographic change might give Canadians or Americans hope for turning around their balance-of-payments deficits?

NOTES

1. *International Financial Statistics*, CD-ROM, March 1999. These figures are slightly lower than those given in balance-of-payments data.

2. The concept of absorption goes back to Sidney S. Alexander, "Effects of a Devaluation on a Trade Balance," *IMF Staff Papers* 1952: 263-78. By giving primacy to the domestic saving and investment patterns, the absorption approach fits in well with much of the current policy literature, and to some considerable extent our saving and investment model fits better into that framework than it does the Keynesian, which we expound in Chapter 12. See Thomas F. Dernburg, *Global Macroeconomics*, (New York: Harper and Row, 1989), ch. 9.

3. See, as a well-articulated statement of the position, C. Fred Bergsten, *America in the World Economy: A Strategy for the 1990s* (Washington: Institute for International Economics, 1988), chs. 1-5.

4. The budgetary deficit includes government investment, *Gi*. We include only government expenditures on consumption goods and services to figure government saving. This figure is for all governments: federal, state, county, and municipal.

5. See C.R. Boxer, *The Dutch Seaborne Empire: 1600-1800* (New York: Alfred A. Knopf, 1965).

6. *International Economic Review*, November 1995.

7. The classic article is M. Feldstein and Charles Horioka, "Domestic Saving and International Capital Flows," *Economic Journal* (June 1980): 314-29. Their findings have been confirmed consistently.

8. See also Bijan Aghevli et al., *The Role of National Saving* 15. (Washington: *IMF*, March 1990).

9. "Capital goes global," *The Economist*, October 25, 1997.

10. Bergsten, *America in the World Economy*, ch. 5. An interesting set of essays on the issues, quite approachable for undergraduates, is James M. Rock, ed., *Debt and the Twin Deficits Debate*, (Mountain View, Calif.: Bristlecone Books, 1991).

11. See Tamim Bayoumi, "Saving-Investment Correlations," *IMF Staff Papers* (June 1990): 370-72, and bibliography.

12. See Lawrence Summers and Chris Carroll, "Why Is U.S. National Saving So Low?" *Brookings Papers on Economic Activity* 2 (1987): 607-35.

13. See A. Lans Bovenberg and Owen Evans, *IMF Staff Papers* (September 1990).

14. Bayoumi measured the "Ricardian equivalence" or Barro effect in 10 countries, finding some correlation in almost all the countries tested.

15. We rely on Aghevli et al., *The Role of National Saving*. See also Olli Pekka Lehmussaari, "Deregulation and Consumption: Saving Dynamics in the Nordic Countries, *IMF Staff Papers* (March 1990); Bovenberg and Evans, cited above. For general readers, a review of these and several other related articles is in the June 1990 issue of *Finance and Development*.

16. The table and some of the discussion derive from Paul R. Masson and Ralph W. Tryon, "Macroeconomic Effects of Projected Population Aging in Industrial Countries," *IMF Staff Papers* (September 1990): 453-90. The table is from p. 457. Masson and Tryon also demonstrate several other macroeconomic effects (on the investment side) of the demographic trends that will also contribute to a shift toward North American trade surpluses.

Chapter Eleven

The Balance of Payments

OBJECTIVES

OVERALL OBJECTIVE   To demonstrate how the figures on balance-of-payments accounts mesh with those for national income, giving a more precise account of the nature of current account surpluses or deficits and of how surpluses were invested or how deficits were financed.

MORE SPECIFICALLY
- To familiarize the reader with the situations of several key countries.
- To indicate how to read a balance-of-payments statement, identifying the key accounts.
- To identify the basic principles involved in constructing the accounts.
- To relate the figures on the balance-of-payments to national income accounts.

....

WHY STUDY THE BALANCE OF PAYMENTS?

An ability to understand a balance-of-payments statement (BPS) is as important to an international economist as reading a corporate account is to a financial analyst. It is key to being able to combine theoretical with statistical analyses and contributes toward the always difficult art of taking general models and fitting them to individual cases. This chapter reveals that no two countries are alike—even two countries of the same size with the same trade deficit may face very different kinds of problems with differing degrees of seriousness. It isn't surprising, after all, that of three students in debt, one owing money to her parents, one to his bank with collateral to back it, and one to the guy with dark glasses who hangs around the pool hall, the last has the most trouble. Nor would we be surprised to find that the person who borrowed money and invested wisely would be better off than the one who used the money for an expensive wedding. Similarly, the nature of the international debt—and to some extent the cause of the debt—can vary immensely depending on how it is borrowed and what it was used for.

For anyone with a bent for accounting, or at least its theoretical side, BPS has its own fascination, if only for the crudity of its figures and the difficulties of its classification system. For those who just want to have the ability to find some concrete numbers to go with theory, BPS is an essential tool.

WHAT A BALANCE-OF-PAYMENTS STATEMENT SHOWS

A BPS shows:

1. The extent of a country's trade imbalance and in what categories (such as physical goods, tourism, or interest on debt) it had deficits or surpluses.

2. The extent to which a country went into additional debt, drew down foreign assets, paid back debt, or built up foreign assets.

3. The nature of the borrowing or investment that occurred. This includes the specifics of private borrowing and lending.

4. The activities of monetary authorities—the central banks and, in the United States, the Federal Reserve.

In all, a careful examination of a BPS can give a good sense of where international debt or credits were incurred, how debt was financed or credits invested, and what kinds of risks or advantages result from the particular patterns.

BALANCE-OF-PAYMENTS ACCOUNTING

The Nature of the Balance of Payments

Probably not one in a hundred economists, even those specializing in international economics, could explain every item on a payments statement, so readers should not feel overwhelmed when they first view a real BPS, with its great list of items.[1] Moreover, the statements have changed over the years and will continue to do so. The object of this chapter is to show how the balance-of-payments statement fits in with the discussions of national income in the previous chapter and to provide an introduction to using payments statements. The full significance of some of the material, particularly that under the monetary account section, will not emerge until later in the text, but it is important to develop a basic understanding of it at this point.

Payments and Claims

An imbalance of trade ($X > M$ or $X < M$, including services and factor income) always generates a claim by residents of one nation on residents of another. As Fabrica found when it traded with Castoria, it had not only a trade surplus, but also a claim on Castoria at the end of trading. Because it did not use all it received from exports on imports, it holds the surplus as a claim on another nation's goods and services that it can exercise at a later date. It can do only three things with its surplus:

1. Invest it, in which case it keeps the claim.
2. Pay back debts accumulated abroad, thereby cancelling a claim some other nation had on the country's future production.
3. Relinquish its claim by giving it to the residents of another country or by having it taken away, as would occur if a company in another country defaulted on a loan.

A nation with a trade deficit (Castoria) has to explain how it managed to obtain the means to buy imports worth more than the goods and services it exported. It could have done so in only three ways:

1. It used previous savings it had abroad, selling off its holdings of foreign bonds, banking accounts, and the like, and reducing its stake in foreign companies.
2. It *borrowed* through selling bonds, bills, bank accounts, shares in corporations, or the corporations themselves to foreign residents.
3. It managed to persuade foreign residents (or their governments) to give it extra goods or services, as, for instance, a form of economic or military aid.

What Balances

The principle behind any accounting balance statement is simple enough—the account must add up every payment that the nation received from the rest of the world and show what it did with what it received. (An *accounting* is, at root, a *telling*, an explanation.) Payments from abroad are *receipts* or *credits* and arise from all the nation's income from exports of goods and services, all the money foreign residents invested in the country, and all the gifts from abroad it received. The *payments*, or *debits*, account traces how the nation disposed of those receipts. The nation would use its foreign exchange receipts to import, to invest abroad, to retire foreign debts, and to make gifts. The receipts always equal the payments because the account just describes what happened to the receipts—or how they were *disposed of.* An alternative explanation, taking it the other way around, takes the receipts (or credits) and shows how the nation got the foreign exchange to make the payments (debits).

An analogy to a household works well: if a household has spent on consumption expenses more than it earned (its own trade deficit), it will discover that the difference between what it earned and what it consumed has been provided by income transfers from others. It may appear as a scholarship or gift (analogous to a current transfer), a loan from a bank, or simply credit received on a credit card. If the household has consumed less than it has earned and seeks to account for the difference, it can check for increases in its savings accounts, repaid loans, accumulations of cash in drawers and piggy banks, or gifts of cash to others. Even if it fails to find what happened to all the money it earned, it still tries to *account* for it and would have to note that it had an unexplained amount, known as an *error* or a *discrepancy.* Anyone who has tried to tote up a year's household expenses knows that it is almost always easier to figure out what was spent on living expenses than to trace through the complexities of borrowings (including credit cards charges not yet on the statement), repayments, investments, drawing down of assets, and even somewhat fatter piggy banks. The family knows it is ahead if it did not consume or give away what it earned, but just where the money is may be difficult to discover.

Balance-of-payments accounting is similar to the household example. Indeed, it may be more similar to household accounting than corporate accounting because, like household accounting, the country does not have the accurate statistics a firm has. The nation adds up all it has taken in from exports of goods and services, subtracts what it has spent for imports of goods and services, and then tries to figure out what made up the difference. It looks first at gifts and similar transactions where goods are given away with no claim taken in return, and these are typically fairly small (at most a few percent of GNP). Then it looks at investments. If it had a trade surplus and did not give it all away, then it will have made investments abroad. (Even if it is simply a case where goods have been shipped in December and payment is received in January, the balance of payments would count the goods as exports and the money not received by the close of the year as short-term investments.) Nations with trade deficits and insufficient gifts to cover those find that they have borrowed and they show a net inflow of foreign investment.

In practice, the accounting is far more complicated, partly because investment flows are so much larger than trade flows. As with the Peorias and Brandons of Chapter 1, the same households and firms may be borrowing in one category and investing in another. The central bank may be accumulating foreign investments while the commercial banks are reducing theirs. When all capital movements are taken together, they equal the net difference in the current account, but it never looks as simple as that.

THE STRUCTURE OF THE BALANCE OF PAYMENTS

Balance-of-payments presentations differ between countries, reporting agencies, and over time. The latest changes to the IMF's accounting, which most countries use, came in the 1997 reports, and it is this improved scheme, differing somewhat from previous ones, that we describe. The layout of the BPS has three main divisions, sometimes complicated by a number of items that do not fit cleanly: (1) the *current account*, which is the trade balance plus or minus current transfers; (2) the *capital and financial account*, which is largely a record of all the nation's borrowing and investment, except that done by its central bank; (3) the *monetary account*, which records the lending or borrowing done through the monetary authorities—the central bank (the Federal Reserve for the United States) and the national treasuries.

The Current Account

The current account shows the *net* change in a nation's international investment position—that is, whether it has increased or decreased its *net* claims on foreign residents. The current account is further subdivided into *merchandise trade, service trade, income services*, and *current transfers* accounts.

The balance of trade in goods, services, and income shows the extent to which exports and imports differ, and an item called *current transfers* indicates how many claims were relinquished or accepted without any matching credit or debt. Typical current transfers are foreign aid, immigrant workers' remittances (money immigrants send back home to their families), and pension payments across borders, all cases where a claim is transferred without receiving anything in return. Together, the three trade accounts and the current transfer account make the current account. The *current account balance* must always equal the net change in the investment position.[*]

---

[*] Note that this modifies somewhat our description in Chapter 10 of the trade balance as equaling the amount of indebtedness. There we said that debt indebtedness was equal to $X - M$, and that is 95% correct in most cases. Current transfers, however, can make a difference of a few percentage points.

THE TRADE ACCOUNTS

The current account balance indicates the change in net credit or debit position of the nation—the extent to which it built up net foreign assets or increased its net foreign debt. The balance on goods, services, and income tells how much the country saved: it is the $X - M$ of the formula $X - M = S - I$ and thus reflects the difference between domestic saving and investment.

The *balance on goods and services* records the value of all imports and exports of goods and services. It, in turn, is usually divided into trade in goods, known as *visible* or *merchandise trade*, trade in services, or *invisible trade,* and trade in *factor services*. The phrase *trade balance* is a bit ambiguous. In many accounts, including those of the IMF, it is equivalent to trade in goods, not including services. The popular media often fail to distinguish the balance on *goods* (or *merchandise trade*) from that on *goods and services*. Canada, for instance, rarely has a deficit on the merchandise trade account and never has a surplus on the services account, yet many Canadians think that Canada's merchandise surplus means it is exporting more than it is importing. In fact, the Canadian merchandise trade surplus has to be substantial to overcome the deficit in services.

Economists sometimes use *trade balance* to mean the balance on goods, services, and income. That is the practice in this book, which reserves the phrase "merchandise trade" or "trade in goods" to refer to goods alone. By itself, the merchandise or visible trade balance has almost no economic significance and it is odd that it still commands such interest. Whether people earn income from goods or services, whether countries borrow to pay for goods or services, or whether it is the good or the service we enjoy in the act of consumption little affects theory.

The merchandise trade account is clear enough, as are non-factor services, such as royalties paid on films, consulting fees, insurance, sales commissions, transportation, and tourism. More difficult is the *income account*, which handles payments and receipts for the use of capital. National income accounting considers interest and profits as a reward for the lender, who is providing the "service." When Canadians buy Cheerios made in Canada, some small proportion of their money will go to General Mills in the United States in the form of profits from its fully owned Canadian subsidiary. This rewards General Mills for the capital (and managerial and marketing skills) it has invested in Canada for decades. Similarly, the interest an American receives on a Canadian bond is a reward for providing the capital, and it has to be counted—as surely as it would be had he performed a job for the Canadians.

A far less important part of factor payments is that made to labor. Any payments by companies or governments to non-residents for labor services also count as income. A Saudi Arabian firm paying a group of Thai

---

FACTOR PAYMENTS: AN EXAMPLE

Only a small proportion of payments to nationals who work abroad come under the factor income category. Consider the three hockey-playing Penalité brothers, Jean, Jacques, and Daniel from Baton Elevé, Quebec. Jean plays for the New York Rangers, Jacques for the Montreal Canadiens, and Daniel for the Colorado Avalanche, though he maintains his residence in Canada. Because Jean is an American resident, the U.S. does not record his salary as being international. When Jacques and the Canadiens come to the United States to play, the team gets a payment from the Rangers and it is just counted as a service. Only Daniel, as a Canadian drawing a salary from an American firm, is classified as receiving *factor income*.

The distinction stems from the way the expenses of the firm are calculated. In figuring GDP, the entire wages, salaries, interest, and profits of the firm are counted. After that, the factor payments are taken out. In the case of the Rangers paying the Canadiens, Jacques's pay would not turn up on American figures. And Jean's pay, although it turns up, belongs to an American resident. Only Daniel's pay, as part of the American firm's expenses, turns up as American wages. If the company had hired Daniel just as an independent professional, it would be a service.

Note that Daniel's salary would be in Canadian GNP and America GDP.

---

construction laborers for building it a factory in Saudi Arabia (an arrangement that has been common) makes payments to factors (labor), but, because they are non-residents, it is recorded as imported factor services.

For most countries, labor factor payments are a very small part of their total income payments. In 1996, the worldwide figure for investment income was around $1.2 trillion, compared to $33 billion (3%) in labor income. The United States had $206 billion in investment income and only $170 million (0.08%) in labor income.[2] Labor factor payments are only important in countries that import a lot of temporary foreign labor, such as the oil-rich countries of the Middle East, and those that export the labor, such as the Philippines and Thailand. In 1997, the Philippines received $5.7 billion from labor income, about 14% of its income from goods and services, so despite spending a net $2 billion on investment income, its income account was positive.

CURRENT TRANSFERS (FORMERLY UNREQUITED TRANSFERS)

The goods and services balance does not fully show the changes of a country's net investment (or borrowing) with the rest of the world. This is because it does not include *current transfers*.* A particularly dramatic case is the payments the United States received from its allies for American expenditures on expelling Iraq from Kuwait; these served to reduce the current account deficit to the lowest in years. Normally, American current transfers are well under 1% of GNP, but these can be much higher percentages of the trade imbalance. In 1996, net transfers were just over (minus) $40 billion compared with exports of goods and services of over $1 trillion. Because the trade deficit was small that year, the transfers cut the current account deficit by 30%. In countries that have been important recipients of military and economic aid, the transfer figures can be quite significant, however.

Because of the current transfers, a nation's foreign capital stock may not change by the same amount as implied by the formula $X - M = S - I$. One of the more dramatic examples is El Salvador, which receives a lot of foreign aid and migrants' remittances. In 1995, El Salvador's exports were $1.6 billion, its deficit on goods, services, and income just about the same, $1.6 billion, but it received transfers of $1.4 billion. In 1997, the country's exports had risen to $2.4 billion and its deficit in goods, services, and income had fallen to $1.3 billion, while transfers remained about the same at $1.4 billion, so despite a trade deficit of 52% of its exports, it had a current account surplus. Trade-surplus nations that give foreign aid and run negative current transfer accounts do not, of course, see their foreign investments rise by the full amount of their trade surpluses. The extreme case here is Saudi Arabia, whose transfers in recent years have often approached or even exceeded the balance on goods, services, and income. In 1997, for instance, the Saudis transferred $15.4 billion abroad, when their trade surplus was $15.6 billion—over 20% of their exports.† These, of course, are the extremes; most nations have relatively small amounts of transfer, the world average transfer being a little less than 5% of exports. $X - M$ still measures the transfer of saving, but one must figure in the current transfers to determine net foreign investment.

---

* Such transfers are no problem in our domestic models, which tend either to be of one country or for all the world, because we can cancel out all of them—if Peter gives Paul $10,000 and Paul invests it, then it is Paul's investment and Peter's income. The $10,000 goes down on the income side as Peter's and on the expenditure side as Paul's and the national accounts balance. But if Peter lives in the United States and Paul in Canada, Canada would show $10,000 more in total expenditures (the investment) than it shows in earnings because no one in Canada earned that amount. Canadian statisticians cannot show Peter's income because it was not earned in Canada. It isn't a wage, interest, profit, or rent. To account for such payments, they must keep an item called current transfers.

† The formula for figuring a nation's net investment position, then, must include current transfers

$$Id = Sp + (T - Gc) + (M - X) + U$$

where U = the current unrequited transfers from foreigners.

The Capital and Financial Account

The remaining accounts explain how the current account deficit was financed—what combination of borrowing and selling off of foreign assets allowed the nation to have a current account deficit. In the case of a surplus, the remaining accounts tell how the nation invested the surplus it received. A small part of that activity takes place through actions of the central bank, and that is under the *monetary account*, but the bulk of capital movement is carried on by private banks, firms, public corporations, or governmental units other than the central bank.[*] These non–central-bank transactions go under the capital and financial account.

THE CAPITAL ACCOUNT: A NEW TWIST

Recently, the IMF and most countries have introduced a new account called the *capital account*. It is a small account that might more accurately be named a capital transfers account. (Just to confuse things, the financial account used to be called the capital account, so any pre-1997 source that refers to the capital account means the present financial account.) The new capital account handles a number of cases where a creditor country makes an adjustment to its foreign debt, forgiving foreign debts, reducing part of foreign debts, or suffering default, and the debtor country does the opposite. Several years ago, for instance, Canada forgave the debts of many Central African countries that had no prospect of paying back various foreign aid loans given to it. Before 1997, that item would have come under current transfers in the current account and sharply worsened the look of the Canadian current account for that particular year. Now it comes under the capital account because it isn't really a *current* unrequited transfer, but a past unrequited transfer that is being acknowledged. Another item under the new capital account is "migrants' remittances." (The account draws a fine line between the money sent home by non-resident workers, which is in current transfers, and that sent by workers who have become resident.)

THE FINANCIAL ACCOUNT

The *financial account* tracks where residents of a country placed the funds they moved or left abroad and where they borrowed foreign funds. Normally, when a country has a trade surplus, most of that surplus turns up as an increase in foreign investments of various sorts. If a country has a trade deficit, that deficit turns up as foreign borrowings and reduction in some foreign assets.

---

[*] This last is often described as non-monetary, meaning it was an action by some part of the government not connected with the central bank.

The financial account has three parts: direct investment, portfolio investment, and other investment. Portfolio investments involve no attempt to control the corporation—a Canadian private individual's investments in the shares of an American corporation are portfolio investments. Direct investments, in contrast, involve an active participation in the management, where foreign owners appoint the management and control budgets and much of the activity of the firm. Most direct investments are 100% ownership of the domestic subsidiary, such as Ford Motor Company's ownership of Ford of Canada. When a single foreign company shares ownership with a domestic company, forming a joint venture, or when two foreign companies own a single domestic company, it is still considered direct investment. The actual ownership percentage required to be classified as direct investment is determined by the country itself, and in some cases can be as low as 1%, but normally it is 15% or higher.[3]

One important characteristic of the accounting for direct investment is that the figures count not only new capital flowing from the home firm to its subsidiary, but the reinvested earnings of that company. So, if Canada's Great West Life Company uses its American profits to expand its Denver offices, the money is treated *as if* Great West had sent all its profits back to Canada and then sent them back to Colorado for investment. A large part of increased foreign direct investment occurs without additional transfers from the home firm, so an important part of foreign direct investment does not actually pass through the foreign exchange markets. (Worldwide, in 1996 $105 billion of the $318 billion in foreign direct investment flows were reinvested earnings. Of American foreign direct investment of $88 billion, $58 billion (two-thirds) were reinvested earnings.

Portfolio investments consist of shares (called *equity securities*) and bonds and bills (*debt securities*). Until recent years, BPS figures listed which investments were short-term and which were long-term. The idea was that short-term investments were more volatile than long-term investments. Nervous investors could move short-term funds out of a country more quickly than long-term funds. In fact, the differences in the liquidity of a 30-year bond and a 180-day short-term security are not great. If investors are frightened, they will quickly dump the long-term bonds as well as short-term funds.

The *other investments* item includes trade credits, bank holdings of funds, foreign accounts of governments, and any changes in holdings of the domestic currency that foreign central banks made.

The Monetary Account

A country also holds foreign assets or incurs debts through its monetary authorities. The Federal Reserve and central banks in other contries hold foreign treasury bills and accounts in other central banks, and changes in their holdings are described under the official or monetary account (presently listed as the *official settlements balance*). In the older, simpler times, when gold was an international money, the monetary account was called the *gold account* and recorded how much gold had flowed into or out of the nation.

A central bank's sales of foreign exchange (or gold) are *receipts* on the balance of payments, even though they are *debits* on the nation's holdings of foreign assets. It is just like people who transfer money from a savings to a checking account; they debit the savings, but credit the checking account. The Bank of Canada in 1996, for instance, bought US$5.5 billion of foreign assets, almost entirely foreign treasury bills. (See the discussion of the Canadian BPS below.) That is just as much a minus sign on the BPS as if a Canadian resident had bought foreign treasury bills. It is, of course, a plus sign for the assets of the Bank of Canada, just as it would be a plus sign in the Canadian resident's foreign holdings, but we are looking at the BPS, not the accumulated assets.

For non-accountants, this can be disorienting: a plus on the balance-of-payments account occurs when the central bank's assets are falling, a minus when they are rising. (Just keep in mind the savings and checking account analogy; moving money from a checking to a savings account is a debit on the checking account.) Consider, too, that an inflow on the capital account occurs when foreign assets are depleted or borrowings made.*

Errors and Omissions or Discrepancies

Because of the difficult nature of collecting balance-of-payments figures, recorded outflows and inflows almost never match closely. An *error* or *discrepancy* figure is entered to make up the difference. The discrepancy item in balance-of-payments statements is often so large that it overwhelms the current account imbalance, such that it becomes impossible to decide if the country had a current account surplus or deficit. A more detailed look is in order.

Balance-of-payments accounting involves many estimates. It does not have the accuracy of a corporation account and is more akin to GNP estimation than financial accounting. Tourism expenditure is difficult to assess. Undeclared or undervalued imports are tricky. As Chapter 1 noted, the world seemingly imports more than it exports. Illegal or simply unrecorded movements of

---

* Another warning for those who use the IMF's BPS figures. The *International Financial Statistics* CD-ROM contains changes in countries' liabilities and assets, by category—e.g., portfolio equity investment. A positive sign in assets means an increase in assets, which has been achieved by a payment or debit on the BPS account. That is, the asset sign indicates the increase in the savings account. Similarly, an increase in liabilities is a positive sign on the BPS and a decrease a negative sign.

capital, including *flight capital*, are notoriously hard to figure. Trade in illegal substances, a major part of the earnings of some less-developed countries, is also hard to count, since the dealers do not report regularly to governmental statisticians. It should not surprise people that the total figures for the payments side differ from those on the receipts side.

Since one set of figures merely explains what was done with the other, in concept they have to equal. While corporate accountants might bury a few small discrepancies in miscellaneous *expenditures or receipts* to hide what they cannot find, national income accountants do not expect to find every expenditure or payment. They just declare that they have a discrepancy, leave the figure that seems the most solid, and adjust the other. Very often the discrepancies are large—over $40 billion for 1991, 1992, and 1996 on the U.S. account.

Some clue as to what is in the discrepancy comes from the sensitivity of that figure to interest rates. A country with high interest rates finds that its discrepancy is positive: that is, its receipts appear to exceed its payments. When the interest rate falls, the discrepancy falls also.* This suggests that an important part of the untraced transactions is short-term capital funds. The sharp swings in the discrepancy, too, do not accompany legal, political, or consumption changes that would encourage or discourage smuggling. This is not to say that underestimation of imports, undeclared expenditures, illegal trade, or poor estimates do not play a part, but that they are unlikely to cause sharp swings from year to year.

Payments accounts often differ by several percentage points from the same statistics in national income accounts, alas. It usually takes several years of reworking the numbers before statisticians are satisfied with the results. (If occasionally some of the figures in this book do not jibe with others, we trust they originate in accounts that are as yet unreconciled.) Typically, the figure first published for a discrepancy is revised as more information comes to light. Anyone keeping track of a country's balance of payments should not simply add the latest year to past information but should go back several years.

Payments accounts may also differ between the organizations that collect and publish data. The most standard form is that which the IMF uses, which is what this book explains. Payments figures present some very tricky problems and a number of estimates, so perhaps this should not be surprising.

---

* Some countries that normally have negative discrepancies—that is, outflows appear larger than inflows—find that the discrepancy shrinks when their interest rates are high and rises when they are low.

USING BALANCE-OF-PAYMENTS STATEMENTS AS ANALYTICAL TOOLS

The American Balance of Payments

As suggested earlier, the U.S. balance-of-trade deficit may reflect a rate of saving that is by most standards too low. A more detailed examination of the capital account, however, may give additional information as to the potential difficulty, if any, and the cost of maintaining the service on foreign debt incurred.

Initially, note the structure and balances, using 1997 as the example.

1. The Balance on Goods, Services, and Income, equivalent theoretically to $X - M$, is –\$127.93 billion. This should also be equivalent to the difference between domestic saving and investment in the United States. Major differences in the way the statistics are collected and presented, however, cause the two figures to diverge; in this case, $X - M$ figured from national income accounts is –\$116.4 billion, about \$11 billion less.*

2. The American increase in net indebtedness in 1996 was higher than the trade balance indicates because current transfers were –\$38.88 billion. The current account balance shows how much the U.S. needed to borrow or run down its foreign assets. How, then, did it get the \$166.8 billion dollars it needed to cover its current account deficit?

3. The capital accounts tell most of the story. (a) \$387.62 billion of foreign funds flowed into American securities, \$355.52 billion of that into bonds and bills. Countering that were increases in American holdings abroad of \$79 billion, leaving a net inflow of \$308 billion, the largest net inflow in American history, following on the heels of the second largest inflow in 1996. (b) The "Other Investment" account showed a small net outflow of \$32 billion. The sub-accounts show a great deal of bank activity, with very heavy inflows into the United States as American banks saw their foreign-held deposits rise greatly over 1996. American banks also increased their foreign deposits and loans considerably. Foreign central banks, particularly those in East Asia, drew down their holdings in the United States as they sought to defend their currencies. The large inflows the United States experienced in debt securities and bank holdings represented in part the outflow from private citizens in Asia, dwarfing the \$14.15 billion outflow the monetary authorities used to counter it. To look at it from the Asian side, see the discussion of Thailand

---

* The sources of figures, the handling of items in inventory and shipment, and the counting itself are often very different, and normally are done by different government departments. No attempt is made to reconcile national income figures with BPS figures. So while the balance on goods and services theoretically matches $X - M$, it sometimes is off by as much as 10%.

Table 11.1

U.S. BALANCE OF PAYMENTS, 1996 AND 1997 ($ BILLIONS U.S.)

Current Account	1996	1997
Goods exported	613.98	620.28
Goods imported	− 803.23	− 877.28
Services exported	234.69	251.13
Services imported	− 152.77	− 163.72
Income: Credit	206.57	236.20
Income Debit	− 207.47	− 254.53
Balance on Goods, Services, and Income	− 108.24	− 127.93
Current transfers	5.86	
Credits	− 46.35	6.13
Debits		− 45.01
Balance on Current Account	− 148.73	− 166.80

below. (c) The direct investment account shows a $11.5 billion outflow. The combination of capital and current accounts does not tell the whole story, however. The current and capital and financial accounts combined yield a net inflow of $98.12 billion. Two items remain.

4. The last account on the page, the Monetary Account, often called the Official Account and in newer publications simply "Reserves and Related Items," traces what happened to the central bank's holdings of (or debts in) foreign exchange. In this case, it is what happened to the Federal Reserve's holdings of foreign exchange in other central banks. The item entered there is a negative $1.01 billion, which means that the Federal Reserve increased its holdings of foreign assets. Note once again, that the sign on the account is negative, just as people's chequing accounts are debited when they move money to savings accounts.

5. When the accountants had calculated all that they knew, the accounts did not balance. The balance showed a net inflow on the current, capital, and financial accounts of $98.12 billion. Adding the monetary account to that figure gives $97.11 billion. But that is impossible. The BPS is supposed to show both (a) how a country generated all the foreign credits it used for imports, gifts, and investments abroad, and (b) how a country used the foreign credits it received. In this case, the United States received $97.11 billion

Table 11.1 *continued*
U.S. BALANCE OF PAYMENTS, 1996 AND 1997 ($ BILLIONS U.S.)

Capital and Financial Account	1996	1997
Capital Account		
Credits	.52	.35
Debits	0.0	0.0
Financial Accounts		
Direct investment abroad	− 87.81	− 119.44
Direct investment in U.S.	76.96	107.93
Portfolio Investment Assets		
Equity securities	− 58.79	− 37.98
Debt securities	− 49.4	− 41.30
Portfolio Investment Liabilities		
Equity securities	12.25	65.10
Debt securities	370.82	322.58
Other Investment Assets	− 163.11	− 227.20
General government	− 0.69	0.18
Banks	− 98.19	− 151.08
Other	− 64.23	− 76.30
Other Investment Liabilities	87.55	194.95
Monetary authorities	40.52	− 14.15
General government	0.72	0.54
Banks	14.51	163.82
Other	31.81	44.74
Balance on Capital and Financial Account	188.98	264.925
Balance on Current and Capital and Financial Accounts	40.26	98.12
Discrepancy	− 46.93	− 97.11
Balance on Current, Capital and Financial, and Discrepancy	− 6.67	1.01
Monetary Account	6.67	− 1.01
Total Balance	0	0

CENTRAL BANKS HOLDING OBLIGATIONS OF OTHER CENTRAL BANKS

Central banks of most countries hold their foreign assets as treasury bills in other countries and use these assets from time to time to help cover current and capital account deficits. Central bank activity turns up in two places in the balance of payments. One is in the monetary account, which shows how much the central bank has added to or taken from its reserves. But the assets of central banks are always the liabilities of another country. If Germany's Bundesbank increases its holdings of American treasury bills and deposits, the Americans must show the inflow. This item turns up in the *other investment liabilities* account as an investment liability. So if the Bundesbank buys U.S. dollar treasury bills, which it may very well do to build up foreign exchange reserves, it is also lending the U.S. that money. The more detailed America's balance-of-payments account shows that central banks outside the U.S. placed $40.52 billion in the U.S. in 1996 and withdrew a net of $14.15 billion in 1997.[*]

---

more than it disposed of; something must have happened to those billions. Did the United States use the money for imports or foreign investments or perhaps for undeclared imports? No one knows. It is as if a couple discovers that their expenditure during the year was $1,000 higher their income (including any additional borrowings they made). They go on a hunt about the house to see if anyone has forgotten some hidden present or purchased some financial asset they did not record, and then go over their expenditures and investment accounts again. Finally, they conclude it cannot be found and write in an item called "Discrepancy." So what the accountants did here was to write in a discrepancy of −$97.11 billion, quite a substantial sum. In future years, the reporting will show it as lower, as more information comes to light.

The Canadian Balance of Payments

The Canadian balance of payments for 1997 (Table 11.2) shows a current account deficit of $9.26 billion U.S. (The IMF publishes all BPS accounts in U.S. dollars. Individual countries publish their figures in their own currencies.) Typically, Canada's merchandise trade balance is in surplus, but both the services and income accounts are in deficit. Canada's receipts for services performed for foreigners were only 65-70% of its payments until recently, when the figure rose to around 80%. The big subcategories—transportation, travel, and other—always show deficits. Nonetheless, the balance on goods and

---

[*] This is a change instituted recently. Previously, the holdings of central banks in the U.S. were under the monetary account.

Figure 11.1

CANADIAN FOREIGN BORROWING AND PAYMENTS, 1980-1997

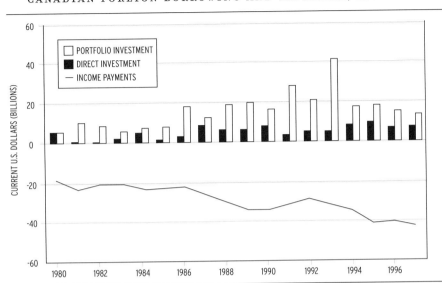

services alone was positive. Canada's current account deficits—and thus, too, its continually rising net foreign debt—stem from the very cost of that debt.

The US$42 billion outflow shown under income springs from the large amount of foreign investments, direct and portfolio, that have accumulated in Canada over many years. Canada has a considerable stock of its own foreign investments (indeed, per capita, Canadians' direct foreign investments are higher than those of Americans), but until 1997 it had only once earned over 50% of what it paid on foreign borrowings. A closer examination of payments figures shows what happened.

Canada borrowed abroad heavily in the period. Figure 11.1 shows the U.S. dollar amount of direct and portfolio investment placed in Canada and the amount of Canada's income payments abroad. On the current account, income payments abroad doubled from $20 billion to $40 billion over the period. The principal reason payments rose so sharply was the high amount of portfolio investment (the vast bulk in government bills and bonds) that came into Canada, particularly between 1987 and 1995). In the period 1980-97 as a whole, Canada borrowed US$87 billion in the form of direct investments and more than three times that much ($286 billion) in the form of portfolio investment, for a total of $384 billion. The extra $11 billion in investment income payments went to pay the interest and profits on the borrowings. (Repayments of the principal are in the financial account, turning up as a reduction in liabilities.)

Table 11.2

CANADA'S BALANCE OF PAYMENTS, 1996 AND 1997 ($ BILLIONS U.S.)

Current Account	1996	1997
Goods exported	205.16	217.42
Goods imported	− 174.45	− 199.86
Services exported	29.34	30.02
Services imported	− 36.14	− 36.36
Income: Credit	19.27	21.46
Income Debit	− 40.07	− 42.37
Balance of Goods, Services, and Income	3.13	− 9.7
Current transfers		
Credits	3.26	3.50
Debits	− 3.06	− 3.06
Balance on Current Account	3.23	− 9.26

These figures are not net of Canadian investment abroad. Indeed, Canadian direct investment abroad was heavier than the inflows—US$117 billion accumulated abroad against US$98 billion placed in Canada. And Canadians made some portfolio investment abroad—some US$87 billion. So the net change was that Canada's international asset position went another US$180 billion into deficit. While income payments from abroad rose by over US$8 billion, the net increase in income payments abroad was around US$12 billion.

Chapter 10 somewhat puckishly asked whether current account deficits were good things or bad things. The balance-of-payments can help assess that problem in a specific context. The income payments show the cost of the current account deficit—US$12 billion, which could otherwise be used for consumption or investment. This is not a huge sum in terms of GNP (2%) or exports (5%). Indirectly, however, it has contributed to the instability of the Canadian dollar because it turns a positive current account into a negative one and forces fresh borrowing. International investors look at current account balances as one of many elements influencing the exchange rate, and in this case it suggests that the Canadian dollar could go lower.

Moreover, the deficit was not used to build a domestic capital base. Investment fell as a percentage of GNP in the period. Some of the borrowed funds would have gone into other productive purposes, such as education or

Table 11.2 *continued*
CANADA'S BALANCE OF PAYMENTS, 1996 AND 1997 ($ BILLIONS U.S.)

Capital and Financial Account	1996	1997
Capital Account		
Credits	6.34	5.9
Debits	− .4147	− 0.4
Financial Accounts		
Direct investment abroad	6.83	− 14.04
Direct investment in Canada	− 11.63	7.13
Portfolio Investment Assets		
Equity securities	− 12.17	− 4.83
Debt securities	− 1.46	− 3.26
Portfolio Investment Liabilities		
Equity securities	6.08	5.46
Debt securities	8.78	8.12
Other Investment Assets	− 22.23	− 17.81
General government	− 0.12	− 0.53
Banks	− 15.17	− 5.20
Other		
Other Investment Liabilities	15.93	25.57
Monetary authorities	0	0
General government	− 0.16	− 0.51
Banks	12.71	24.63
Other	3.73	1.10
Balance on Capital and Financial Account	− 3.95	11.83
Balance on Current and Capital and Financial Accounts	− 0.72	2.59
Discrepancy	6.13	− 4.98
Balance on Current, Capital and Financial, and Discrepancy	5.50	− 2.39
Monetary Account	− 5.50	2.39
Total Balance	0	0

511

health care, but a great deal of it was just swallowed up in ordinary consumption expenses.

Borrowing through debt rather than equity also leads to potentially more volatile payments. Portfolio investors can sell all their holdings in a short period of time and flood the foreign exchange market with demands for other currencies. Direct investors have assets that are far less liquid. They do not sell off a factory or a mine on a computer terminal; indeed, they often continue to invest right through financial crises, as the discussion of Thailand below shows. Moreover, with their profits dependent on prosperity, they tend not to have dividends to remit when their host country is experiencing economic difficulties.

The BPS counts all profits earned by foreign firms, whether or not they are remitted abroad. If the company reinvests those earnings in Canada, BPS treats them under the financial account as if they are new investment flowing in under direct investment. In 1997, for instance, foreign corporations' profits in Canada were US$11.5 billion, but they only remitted US$6.2 billion, reinvesting US$5.3 billion in Canada.[8] The foreign exchange market saw only the US$6.2 billion. In some years, reinvested earnings make up over half of all new direct investment.

The current account deficit was covered by borrowing, largely in "other investment," and within that category further investigation reveals that heavy borrowing by Canadian banks made the inflow so high. Like the United States in 1996, in 1997 Canada found itself with its central bank reducing its reserves (by $2.39 billion) even though the combined current and capital and financial accounts were positive. Somehow, Canada had spent more than the accountants could trace, so they put in a "discrepancy" figure of $4.98 billion. In 1996, in contrast, the Bank of Canada increased its foreign holdings by $5.5 billion. The discrepancy item was positive, acknowledging $6.13 billion of unknown inflows from abroad.

Thailand's Balance of Payments

The Thai balance-of-payments statement shows dramatic changes between 1996 and 1997 and gives some insight into the currency crisis of the summer of 1997. In 1996 the current account deficit was very high, amounting to about 19% of all the current credits (exports of goods and services, income receipts, and transfers). This is high by international standards, but not unprecedented in Thailand's case. The trade deficit was not fed by high inflation or staggering government deficits, but by a very high level of domestic investment, fueled to a considerable degree by inflows of capital from abroad. In 1996, the other investment category indicates an $11.6 billion inflow of foreign capital, $2.9 billion of that from the banks and $9

Table 11.3

THAILAND'S BALANCE OF PAYMENTS, 1996 AND 1997 ($ MILLIONS U.S.)

Current Account	*1996*	*1997*
Goods exported	54,416	56,668
Goods imported	− 63,906	− 55,705
Services exported	17,070	16,006
Services imported	− 19,588	− 17,361
Income: Credit	3,969	3,733
Income Debit	− 7,355	− 7,309
Balance of Goods, *Services, and Income*	− 15,453	− 3,367
Current transfers		
Credits	1,651	1,359
Debits	− 891	− 909
Balance on Current Account	− 14,694	− 2,917

billion in the catch-all "other" category. Interestingly, the "other investment assets" category is positive; for Canada and the United States, it was a negative, indicating a building up of assets abroad. (Remember the chequing account analogy.) In this case, it indicates that Thais sold off or drew down their foreign assets and brought the money back home. Combining the drawdown of foreign assets and the new liabilities in the other account with the smaller net inflows in portfolio and direct investments reveals that the financial account surplus was well over $19 billion. Even though the discrepancy indicated untraced payments abroad, Thailand still had a comfortable overall balance of $2.167 billion, and its central bank purchased that much extra foreign exchange.

The crisis in the summer of 1997 shows a very different picture. Thailand had a much smaller trade deficit. The improvement in the current account, however, came when it became virtually impossible for Thais to borrow abroad. If you cannot borrow, you cannot go farther into debt.

The capital account is more striking. The increase in direct investment may reflect the continued confidence of firms working in Thailand, or simply the completion of existing projects. There was even a small net inflow of foreign money to buy securities. Thai outflows of money to buy securities were smaller than in the previous year. No big surprises there, but the "other

Table 11.3 continued
THAILAND'S BALANCE OF PAYMENTS, 1996 AND 1997 ($ MILLIONS U.S.)

Capital and Financial Account*	1996	1997
Direct investment abroad	− 931	− 532
Direct investment in Thailand	2,336	3,029
Portfolio Investment Assets		
Equity securities	1,164	3,441
Debt securities	2,421	861
Portfolio Investment Liabilities		
Equity securities	− 961	− 446
Debt securities	− 0	− 0
Other Investment Assets	2,662	− 1,588
General government	0	0
Banks	2,742	− 1,618
Other	− 80	30
Other Investment Liabilities	11,578	− 20,207
Monetary authorities	0	− 9,484
General government	− 58	524
Banks	2,909	− 3,286
Other	9,026	− 7,961
Balance on Capital and Financial Account	19,489	− 15,441
Balance on Current and Capital and Financial Accounts	4,795	− 18,658
Discrepancy	− 2,628	108
Balance on Current, Capital and Financial, and Discrepancy	2,167	− 18,257
Monetary Account	− 2,167	18,257
Reserve Assets	− 2,167	9,901
Borrowing from the IMF		2,437
Exceptional Financing	0	5,913
Total Balance	0	0

* Thailand does not calculate a capital account item.

investment" has some huge numbers in it. Thais were forced to pay back some $20.207 billion worth of foreign liabilities. Ignore for the moment the $9.484 billion that went to monetary authorities, and there is still around $10.7 billion. That makes a shift of $22.3 billion in that account between 1996 and 1997. In addition, the "other investment assets," which had been positive in 1996, turned to their more normal negative, adding another $4.2 billion, making the total about a $27 billion shift.

To counter this shift, the Thai central bank spent $9.901 billion of its assets, and borrowed and spent $2.437 billion from the IMF and another $5.913 billion from monetary authorities and private banks as exceptional financing.

The –$9.484 billion owed in the monetary authorities liability is the value of the Thai baht that Thailand's central bank deposited as collateral to secure the foreign exchange it needed when it borrowed from the IMF and through exceptional financing (see Chapter 18). To use the checkbook analogy, it is like giving a friend a postdated check to be cashed when his loan to you expires. You get the money now to spend, but there is still an outflow.

THE WORLD DEFICIT

Theoretically, one country's exports should be another country's imports and one country's transfers out should be another country's inward transfers. For years, the world has had a collective current account deficit, often over $100 billion a year. The IMF statisticians have been able to make a number of adjustments to the simple sum-totals of all the countries, but somehow, a world current account deficit remains. This occurs because of the difficulty of measuring, the tendency of government to be more careful about inflows than outflows of goods and services, hidden movements of capital to avoid taxation or detection, and the plain difficulty in making estimates.

For the record, the world collective balance-of-payments figures are shown in Figure 11.4.

Reading Payments Balances: Summary

The knowledgeable reading of a national balance-of-payments statement has its rewards and gives insight into a country's economy. Each nation, some-times each year, has its own characteristics that are impossible to summarize in a short space or by comparing some single balance within the accounts. The BPS does not reveal its secrets that easily. But it will reveal much and suggest many questions about an economy to the careful reader. If an examination of a BPS leaves more questions than answers, that—provided the questions are good ones—is a worthy result in itself.

Table 11.4

SUMMARY OF INTERNATIONAL TRANSACTIONS ($ BILLIONS U.S.)

	1990	*1991*	*1992*	*1993*	*1994*	*1995*	*1996*
Current Account (net)	−109.9	−113.4	−102.7	−63.7	−45.0	−41.9	−40.5
Goods	26.9	34.5	49.1	74.4	101.6	121.8	102.0
Credits	3445.3	3517.3	3736.1	3738.2	4222.7	5039.0	5291.0
Debits	3418.3	3482.8	3687.6	3663.7	4121.2	4917.2	5189.0
Services	−39.8	−42.3	−32.7	−21.4	−9.2	−16.7	2.7
Credits	866.0	898.4	989.0	1008.3	1103.5	1257.2	1330.7
Debits	905.9	940.7	1021.7	1029.7	1112.7	1273.9	1328.1
Income	−66.7	−71.3	−77.0	73.3	−85.9	−101.2	−98.9
Credits	846.5	876.6	899.6	904.3	966.3	1157.8	1214.9
Debits	913.1	947.8	976.6	977.7	1052.2	1259.0	1313.8
Current Transfers	−30.4	−34.3	−42.1	−43.4	−51.4	−45.8	−46.2
Credits	250.8	315.9	291.5	276.2	276.6	307.2	323.0
Debits	281.1	350.2	333.5	319.6	328.0	353.0	369.2
Capital Account (net)	14.8	12.7	17.6	17.5	19.8	17.5	19.6
Financial Account (net)	109.0	166.6	145.8	107.8	72.9	117.7	164.7
Direct investment	−37.5	−39.3	−22.5	−6.1	−15.4	11.0	12.6
Abroad	−238.3	−194.1	−191.7	−223.4	−252.4	−321.6	−318.1
In reporting economy	200.8	154.8	169.2	217.3	237.0	332.6	330.8
Portfolio investment	78.3	123.5	92.1	191.6	97.2	200.2	298.9
Assets	−183.8	−335.9	−357.4	−558.2	−328.7	−370.2	−582.7
Liabilities	262.1	459.4	449.4	749.8	425.9	570.4	881.6
Other investment	151.4	131.5	139.0	13.1	93.9	87.2	34.0
Assets	−498.2	20.2	−299.2	−427.3	−269.2	−676.5	−766.8
Liabilities	649.6	111.2	438.2	440.4	363.1	763.7	800.8
Reserves	−83.2	−49.1	−62.8	−90.9	−102.9	−180.7	−180.8
Net errors and omissions	−13.9	−65.9	−60.7	−61.5	−47.7	−93.3	−143.8

Source: Balance of Payments Statistics Yearbook, vol. 1, 1997, 9.

CONCLUSION

The balance-of-payments statement is an important source of statistics for international economists. The current account figures show how domestic imbalances of saving and investment have been reflected in the flows of goods and services, modified slightly by current transfers. The other parts of the payments statement show the results of myriad financial transactions that serve, net, to indicate the nature of a country's debt or foreign investments. Not only do we see that $I > S$, but just how the borrowing was done to allow those extra resources to enter the country. If $S > I$, then we can see how the country placed its savings abroad.

When facing the question of whether a given trade imbalance is "good" or "bad," consider not its size but the nature of the financial assets and liabilities it generated. The balance-of-payments statement shows not just the trade deficit but also the various categories of borrowings: short-term, long-term, private, government, and central bank. That information helps one to make a judgment on the *soundness* of the financing. Similarly, a country with a trade surplus will generate assets abroad, some of which may be quite vital and promising; others, like large amounts of low-yielding foreign treasury bills, look rather unpromising as long-run investments.

The analysis in Chapters 10 and 11, particularly the algebraic and statistical parts, has been static—that is, it has examined each year at year-end, much like a photograph. All the equations balance and all the accounts balance at that particular moment. But, like the economist who slipped on a banana and remained in equilibrium all the way down,[*] where an economy is at a given moment may be less important than where it ends up. Chapters 12-15 impart more of a dynamic to the situation, focusing on longer-run and more stable forms of equilibrium.

---

[*] "You just have to make the intervals short enough, and make your calculations quickly," he explained as he lay on the sidewalk, still maintaining that no good economist ever loses his equilibrium. "It is just that some equilibria last longer than others."

VOCABULARY AND CONCEPTS

Current account	Goods and services account
Current transfers	Goods or merchandise account
Debt and equity assets	Goods, services, and income account
Direct investment	Portfolio investment
Discrepancy	Reinvested earnings
Financial account	Visible trade

QUESTIONS

1. Choose a country of interest to you, find its balance of payments in *International Financial Statistics* or, if available, the *Balance of Payments Statistics Yearbook*, and, using the models in the text, set up its figures and make a short analysis.

    a. Make a short analysis of the relation of domestic savings to investment.

    b. Determine whether foreign borrowing (or investment) is greater than or less than the trade deficit.

    c. If the country has a current account deficit, how has it managed to import more than it exported? If it has a surplus, what did it do with its surplus funds?

    d. Come up with a quick "balance" showing the movements of capital— where the inflows were and where the outflows were.

    e. Identify the movement of funds into or out of reserves.

    f. If given multiple years, spot trends.

    g. If the country is a large debtor or creditor, identify, if possible, the item showing the debt service or at least composed mostly of debt service payments.

2. Explain the principal divisions of a balance-of-payments account. Why does the account always balance?

3. Why do some nations' payments balances have such a large "errors and omissions"? Can illegal shipments of drugs and arms account for such errors?

4. Suppose extraterrestrials are causing the world current account deficit. Is it legitimate to conclude that they will soon own the world?

5. Some countries make policy on the basis of their latest balance-of-payments statistics, particularly their trade deficits. People who have worked with such figures, however, are likely to furrow their brows and raise a very cautionary finger. Why?

6. A trade surplus is a claim on another country. What can the surplus country do with that claim?

7. Normally, there is not much difference between the current account and the balance on goods, services, and income. In what circumstances would the distinction between the two be important?

8. As an intern in an international bank, you are asked to give a quick assessment of a developing country's financial stability. What elements of the balance-of-payments statement would you look at? Why?

9. In what account would you expect to find the following (assume it is the American BPS):

   a. Profits of an American subsidiary in Canada that are reinvested in Canada.

   b. Profits of an American subsidiary in Canada that are returned to the United States.

   c. The money that Maria, the Peorias' maid, sends home to Guatemala.

   d. Royalties on this book. Brown's royalties? Hogendorn's royalties?

   e. The gift of a tractor to a farmers' group in Nicaragua.

   f. The Brandons' (Chapter 1) purchase of American assets.

   g. An increase in commercial credit offered by an American company to a foreign purchaser.

NOTES

A Note on Sources: The handiest source for balance-of-payments figures is *International Financial Statistics*, a monthly publication of the International Monetary Fund. Each country's balance of payments in moderate detail is listed along with a wealth of other financial information on the country. *IFS* also comes on CD-ROM, where the statistics are more extensive. Greater detail can be found in another IMF publication, *Balance of Payments Statistics Yearbook*; volume 1 gives much detail on a country basis, and volume 2 shows the material on a world basis. Both *IFS* and *BPSY* are available in most university libraries.

1. If you have a project that involves an intimate knowledge of many of the statement's items, you may want to use the latest edition of the *Balance of Payments Manual* (Washington: IMF).

2. *Balance of Payments Statistics Yearbook* (Washington: IMF, 1998).

3. See the *Balance of Payments Manual* (Washington, IMF, 1977), paragraphs 407-14.

4. *Balance of Payments Statistic Yearbook*, 44, 46, Tables B14, B15.

Chapter Twelve

Income and Price Effects

OBJECTIVES

OVERALL OBJECTIVE   To show that income and price level effects are mixed, often best approached through an aggregate demand and supply model, and to explore the interactions of price level, income, exports, and imports.

MORE SPECIFICALLY
- To explain and review the aggregate demand-and-supply model in its modern interpretations.
- To show how income effects impact on imports and trade balances
- To demonstrate how restricting imports, while appearing to give helpful economic stimuli, rarely does so in fact.
- To show the extra difficulties of adjustment when the terms of trade fall against a country.
- To assess, in a preliminary way, how the globalized economy affects domestic macroeconomic policy.
- To show how to use some of these ideas in studies of two events.

Chapter 10 demonstrated that the relationship between the investment-savings gap was the same as the balance on goods, services, and income, and noted that awkward current account imbalances sometimes emerge from too large a savings gap. Chapter 11 showed in more detail how to trace the complexities of a country's international payments. The next three chapters examine the principal mechanisms that connect the savings gap with the trade gap. The mechanisms are of two classes: income and price, with the price mechanisms divided further into effects on or of movements of the entire price level and effects from movement of the exchange rate.

521

To illustrate, suppose greater consumer optimism causes expenditure to rise. If the increase in expenditure causes *incomes* to rise, then imports, which are part of consumption, will also rise, but exports will be unaffected. If the increase in expenditure causes *prices* to rise, then exports will be less competitive and imports will be more competitive, causing $X - M$ to fall. Should the changes result in a balance of trade judged to be too negative, the government or central bank would then attempt to mitigate the problem through reversing the increase in expenditure or through allowing the currency to fall in value in foreign exchange markets. Both income and price effects are, however, rather mixed in practice, calling for a more detailed examination of the underlying macroeconomic mechanisms.

INCOME AND PRICE CHANGES

The Aggregate Demand-and-Supply Model

Long experience has taught three lessons about the relation of price levels to total demand. Lesson One is that increases in aggregate demand (AD), used sparingly and occasionally, can stimulate increases in output and accommodate increases in output that spring from higher productivity. Lesson Two, going a long way back to the Great Depression, is that sharp decreases in aggregate demand almost always create far more unemployment and less of a decline in the price level than a "rational" economy would have. People cease working even though reduced pay would still be adequate to keep them working. Lesson Three, as the 1970s brought home, is that repeated use of aggregate demand to stimulate an economy becomes addictive, stimulating only price rises, not output.

The AD/AS model (Figure 12.1) is a schematic way of representing both income and price effects. It is a deceptively simple diagram, almost a caricature of the way economies work; yet it helps visualize a number of rather subtle problems. Its virtue is that it is sufficiently close to an ordinary demand-and-supply diagram that it is easy to manipulate. Much of its similarity ends there: it is hardly a typical demand-and-supply model. True, the horizontal axis represents the total output of an economy, something like "quantity" in a demand-and-supply model. Since the model is extremely general, different writers label the axis "output," "income," or "GDP." The vertical axis, however, is not price, but the price *level*. As such, it does not measure opportunity cost (as do demand-and-supply diagrams) because when price levels change, opportunity costs do not.

Aggregate demand is the total demand for all goods and services. The AD curve shows that total demand for goods and services will be greater at lower price levels than at higher price levels. Since a lower price does not mean less of a sacrifice of other goods and services, but just a change in price level, why should AD be greater at lower price levels? The reasoning is that a given stock of money goes farther at lower price levels: if a family has $1,000 in a sugar bowl and another $9,000 in a bank account, and the price level falls to 80% of what it was before, they can buy $12,500 worth of goods. The family will feel wealthier and therefore spend more. The measure of the slope is unimportant for most economic arguments, so it is just shown as being a fairly steep negatively sloping line.

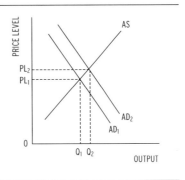

Figure 12.1

THE STANDARD
AGGREGATE DEMAND-
AND-SUPPLY DIAGRAM

The most common aggregate supply (AS) curve looks like a normal supply curve, and indicates that output increases as the price level rises.

Figure 12.1 shows that when aggregate demand rises from AD_1 to AD_2, both the price level and output rise, the price level rising from PL_1 to PL_2 and output rising from Q_1 to Q_2. The diagram therefore states, as it is presently drawn, that both income and price level effects will emerge from an increase in aggregate demand. The diagram, however, need not show that—this is a kind of "default" setting economists might draw when they have no particularly special argument to make. The shape and slope of the AS curve is in fact a central question.

Why should the total amount supplied increase when the price level rises and fall when the price level declines? It is not at all obvious. Consider it this way: output is the product of the number of hours worked times the output per hour worked, or the average productivity of labour. That is:

(Eq. 12.1) $\qquad H_L P_L = O$

where H is hours worked, and P is the average output per hour worked, and O is output.

The productivity of each hour worked derives from the amount of capital, the skills of the labor force, and the technology and organization present, most of which do not change rapidly. Over a period of a few years, the main element determining output is the number of people working and the hours they work. The price level should not affect the total hours worked and therefore it should not affect the total output of an economy. If José Papagrande is promised wages sufficient to purchase a sack of potatoes a week, it isn't important if the potatoes cost $10 or $100. He is working for the potatoes, not for the money.

Surely, a great part of the workforce has to work to provide the potatoes of life, and many would work—as their ancestors did and some of their cousins abroad still do—at near-starvation wages. But many are fortunate and have the food, shelter, and clothing sufficient to let them live comfortable and long lives. A great number of people in the workforce do not have to work and could trade their wages for a less costly style of life. At the margins of the workforce are many who have such a choice and therefore must balance paid work against unpaid work, improving their skills, or simply enjoying leisure. And, as first-year economics shows, it is the price on the margin that counts.

Those on the margin are young adults who can further their educations; older people who have sufficient funds to retire; and working couples with young children who could have one of them stay at home or work part-time while the other works full-time. People with elderly parents might wish to take the time to care for them. If the economy can reward these people with enough real goods and services, many of them will opt for employment; if it cannot do so, they will opt the other way. It is therefore the real goods and services offered that encourage people on the margins to enter the work-force—and that determine the level of wages. By this reasoning, a change in the price level should not change the balance between working and not working.

Sometimes the argument that fewer people work when rewards fall seems counter-intuitive. If the rewards for working go down, would it not be that people would want to work more to make ends meet? Most definitely in the short run, most certainly not in the long run. Try the following illustration.

Young Ashley Gray decided to postpone completing her university education to continue her work as a lab assistant. The pay was good and she purchased a new, rather sporty car; her parents, realizing that they would not have to help pay for her education for a few more years, remodeled their kitchen. Unfortunately, over the next several years, the price level rose considerably while Ashley's pay was unchanged, so she found it harder to get by. Often, she agreed to work overtime just to keep her apartment rent paid up. When she had to forgo her annual Caribbean trip, she deeply regretted her decision to continue working. Yet, she was in no position to quit because she had payments to make on the car and her family was unable to help with her education expenses. She resolved to disentangle herself, but two more years passed before she was finally able to leave the workforce to attend university.

About the same time, Ashley's twin brother, Asher, had finished his studies and found employment. He married, and he and his wife had a child on the way, so he was happy to have the job. True, the job was not as rewarding in real terms as it had been when he was hired, and the family had to economize

Figure 12.2

RELATIONSHIP OF HOURS WORKED TO AGGREGATE SUPPLY

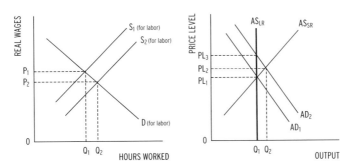

Note: Inflation causes real wages to decline, and companies hire more people, raising employment from Q_1 to Q_2. With higher employment, output rises from Q_1 to Q_2. If, however, people can untangle themselves from their obligations, both the supply of labor and the output level will return to their Q_1 positions.

more, but while he regretted the higher prices he did not regret having a job. Thus, while the marginal workers like Ashley continued working, new core workers like Asher were coming on the market with no reasonable possibility of exiting, so the hours worked rose, and with that output rose as well.

As the Ashleys of the world devise ways to leave the workforce, as parents with children decide that two jobs are not as rewarding as they used to be and adjust car ownership and mortgages so one of them can quit, and as people in their sixties decide that the rewards for working just aren't there any more, the workforce begins to shrink. Output falls back to its pre-inflation levels, except that the price level is higher. In the short run, then, lower real rewards do encourage people to work "to make ends meet." In the long run, however, the ends get adjusted and meet without the additional work.

The pair of diagrams in Figure 12.2 illustrates the idea. The panel on the left shows that inflation lowered real wages from P_2 to P_1. This in effect caused the supply of labor to shift to the right, meaning more people (Ashley *and* Asher) would work at any given wage. But when the Ashleys begin to realize that they are not getting the real goods and services they had expected, the supply of labor will shift back to S_1, with only Ashers left working.

The right panel shows how the aggregate supply curve represents this vignette. To begin, AD rises from AD_1 to AD_2. The diagram has two AS curves. The short-run AS (AS_{SR}) shows the situation as people like Ashley get caught and Asher joins them, as he must. The short-run effect of the inflation (the change from PL_1 to PL_2) is to create a larger labor force, allowing greater

525

Figure 12.3
AGGREGATE SUPPLY WITH RIGID WAGES

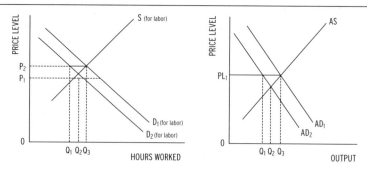

Note: A decline in aggregate demand causes the demand for labor to decline. If wages are rigid in a downward direction, hours worked fall to Q_1, as does output. If wages are not rigid, hours worked and output fall only to Q_2. As the economy adjusts to the lower employment levels, the AS curve may start to shift back toward its "normal" shape. Wages would then fall to P_1 and the price level would also fall to PL_1.

output, which rises from Q_1 to Q_2, while raising the price level to PL_2. The long-run AS (AS_{LR}) shows what output would be after the Ashleys of the world untangle their affairs and leave the workforce. It also shows what would happen if Ashley could have accurately anticipated the effect of inflation on real wages. If such accurate anticipation were the case, a change in the price level could deceive no one, output would be unchanged no matter what the price level, and there would be no short-run income effect. Ashley would never have gone to work if she had accurately anticipated what was going to happen. The long-run effect is simply that price levels rise to PL_3 and output is unchanged.

If AD shifts to the left, will output simply fall along the AS_{SR} curve? It may, but salaries and wages tend to be even less flexible downward than the first diagram suggests. In caricature, economists sometimes show them as being absolutely inflexible downward in nominal terms. If AD falls, labor unions do not rush to their employers with suggestions as to how far to cut wages; indeed, the very idea of management suggesting a wage cut is likely to provoke a strike. Non-unionized employees, of course, may not strike, but a lowering of their nominal wages can cause serious morale problems. In turn, the corporation faces increased monitoring costs and decreasing creativity. (Economists call this the *efficient wages* argument.) So, instead of the supply curve of labor continuing down in a straight line from the existing wage level, it makes a sharp left turn. The left panel in Figure 12.3 shows that at an existing price level P_2 and a demand for labor as in D_1, the hours worked would be Q_3. But, suppose the demand for labor were to fall to D_2. If, indeed, the supply of labor just extended out in a straight line, the hours worked would fall to Q_2, as a number of people would accept lower remuneration for doing the same work and the firm would just wait to see how many decided to leave. But if wages were extremely rigid in a downward direction, firms have no choice but to lay off people rather than cut wages. The supply curve turns horizontal and hours worked fall to P_1. An aggregate supply curve that incorporates this kind of rigidity has a flat portion, reflecting the sharp decline in output that occurs when wages are highly rigid downward.

In a long-run, well-informed, and quite rational world, of course, aggregate supply would be vertical at Q_3. So long as the lower nominal wages still buy a sack of potatoes, the José Papagrandes will accept lower pay. After a sharp decline in aggregate supply, as illustrated in Figure 12.3, it is quite likely that an increase in AD back to the original (from AD_2 to AD_1) can occur without any price increase. If people have just been laid off and are awaiting the phone call to go back to work, they are unlikely to demand higher wages.

Beyond just restoring output, however, a little more shifting of the AD curve might cause just a little inflation to help make essential adjustments in the labor force. Industries facing declining demand have a great difficulty in persuading their employees or unions to accept lower wages and salaries. However, with a wink and a nod, they may be able to persuade them to hold their nominal wages, while allowing real wages to fall. Union leaders do not want to go to the membership with the claim that they managed to keep management from cutting their wages by 10% and "gained" a cut of only 5%. But they could plausibly argue that they prevented any cuts, while knowing that a 5% inflation had in fact cut real wages. Psychologically, it is generally easier to accept a zero wage increase and a small inflation (which will not hit all members equally and is rather abstract) than it is to take the far more tangible pay cut immediately. Similarly, firms or industries with rigid prices that are suffering from declining demand may find it easier simply to leave their prices unchanged while inflation cuts away at their real value. Financial institutions, too, often back their loans with collateral in the form of real estate or buildings. If prices fall, the collateral may fall in value. Moreover, if the loans have been made at interest rates that anticipate no deflation, and there is a deflation, the banks will find that their borrowers have a more difficult time in repaying the debt. A little inflation finesses these problems and adds essential flexibility to the economy.

Continued use of a little bit of inflation, like continued use of many drugs, can create addiction. In countries with a history of inflation the entire institutional structure incorporates the anticipated inflation. Anyone thinking about taking a job has to calculate either a decline in real income or future raises, and thus demands more money to take a job. Contracts—labor and other—have COLA (cost-of-living adjustment) clauses. In Brazil, with a long history of inflation, even bonds, savings accounts, loans, and mortgages have COLA features to protect individuals and groups from the worst aspects of runaway inflation. Companies, knowing that they will have to adjust prices rapidly, set up means by which they can do so, sometimes to the point of not posting prices. Real wages and prices, in a sense, become rigid. Wages move up as fast as—and sometimes faster than—prices. The result is that the AS_{SR} keeps shifting upward. If the old levels of employment are to be regained, inflation must be even larger. (If everyone anticipates a 10% inflation, the AS will shift upward by 10%, so AD must rise by 20% if real wages are to be cut. But then people anticipated a 20% inflation, and so on.)

Figure 12.4 shows this pattern, named *stagflation* back in the 1970s. The country starts at AS_1 and AD_1 and an output of Q_1. The government would like AD to rise to AD_2 to stimulate an output of Q_2 but the country anticipates that move. Workers and employees demand higher wages, and employers, while unhappy, grant the higher wages because they, too, anticipate that they will be able to sell their goods at higher prices. As a result the price level rises from PL_1 to PL_2. Unless the government can manage to expand AD to AD_2, output will actually fall. If it wants to get out to Q_2, it will have to expand AD to AD_3. The result is an escalating inflation and no increase in output.

Figure 12.4

STAGFLATION

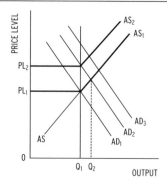

Note: When an economy becomes accustomed to inflation, people anticipate an increase in prices and bargain for wages with an inflation premium. Companies, also expecting inflation, grant those increases. As a result, the short-run AS shifts upward without any long-lasting increase in output.

Shifts in the Long-Run Aggregate Supply

Economic growth keeps the AS_{LR} shifting to the right as potential capacity rises with increases in the capital base, improvements in technology and organization, and improved workforce skills. Given no shift in AD, the price level would actually decline (as it did at the end of the nineteenth century and may, to some extent, have been doing at the end of the twentieth). After all, if everything gets cheaper to make or its (less measurable) quality improves, the price level will fall. Figure 12.5 shows this as AS_{LR} shifts to the right (from the AS_{LR1} to AS_{LR2}) and AD does not move and the price level falls to P_1. Because of the problems caused by deflation, governments normally make sure that aggregate demand rises enough to keep the same price level, shifting AD_1 to AD_2.

The AS curve can shift to the left, also. The obvious cases would be the effects of war or natural disaster. But a decline in the price of exports or a sharp rise in import prices also means that fewer goods are available. A shift from AS_1 to AS_3 represents such a case, with the price level rising from P_2 to P_3 as shown in Figure 12.5.

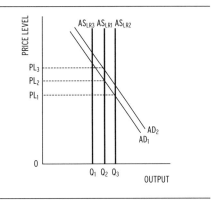

Figure 12.5

SHIFTS IN THE LONG-RUN AGGREGATE SUPPLY CURVE

Shocks to the Short-Run Aggregate Supply and Institutional Factors

A short-run AS curve carries certain institutional assumptions about the nature of wage settlement, of bargaining, or of price setting. If output falls when AD falls, it is not because of economic necessity, since the economy can produce just as much as it did before and apparently wants to produce it. Rather, no institutions exist to enable nominal wages and prices to fall quickly enough. Similarly, a movement upward in the AS curve comes about because of institutional factors. Wage increases in one sector may be immediately followed by "equity" raises in other sectors. Many contracts may have COLA clauses. In such situations, AS_{SR} would move upward whenever prices rose, whether that increase arose from wanton government spending or from a sudden rise in the prices of key imports.

INCOME EFFECTS

Almost always, imports rise when income rises. As Chapter 10 explained, imports are part of consumption, investment, and government expenditure, so as these rise imports also rise. The only possible exception to this pattern was the United States in the 1950s, when imports declined as a percentage of GNP despite rapid economic growth (although they did not decline in volume or value). This was due, perhaps, to the slow recovery of Europe and its inability to produce goods of interest to the American consumer. For the most part, however, imports are *income-elastic*, which is to say that any percentage change of income produces a larger percentage change in imports. One obvious result of that has been the way world trade has grown faster than world income.

An Injections and Leakages Approach

One way to understand income effects is to take the elements of national accounts used in Chapter 10 and postulate how they relate to changes in national income. To recall, some equations showed how expenditures equal income and the disposal of that income, in particular, $Id + X = S + M$, and $S - I = X - M$.

In the short run, all of the elements involved in the disposal of income (Sp, T, and M) are sensitive to income changes. All of the elements on the left side of the equation, however, are not particularly responsive to income changes. Government expenditures and most investment decisions are usually made on a yearly or multi-year basis. Exports are determined by demand in other countries or, sometimes, climatic conditions. Over the longer run, of course, investment increases—as do government expenditures—as income rises.

Figure 12.6, a variation on the standard Keynesian model of the income multiplier, helps illustrate and make more precise the way changes in income affect trade. The model uses the relationship $Id + X = Sd + M$, but connects the absolute amounts of each variable to income. The left side of the equation (Id and X) consists of two elements normally unrelated to the level of output; these are *injections*. The variables on the left are *leakages*—income not returned to the spending stream but saved or used on imports. Id and X, unchanging at any level of income, are horizontal. Domestic saving and imports, however, respond to changes in income, each rising in this diagram by 25% of any additional spending, together making an increase of 50%. So if spending rises by $1 million, saving and investment each will rise by $250,000.

The model shows three things: (1) the level of income at which the two sides of the equation will be equal, which is $1,000 million in the left panel; (2) the income multiplier, 2 in both panels, which is the amount by which income will rise after any new expenditure coming into the system has been respent; and (3) the amount of new imports generated from any change. The right panel shows the effect of an additional injection of $100 million. Since half of all new income is respent, income rises by $200 million before it generates the additional $200 million of savings and imports. The income multiplier in such diagrams is 1/CML—one over the combined marginal leakages of savings and imports. In this case, the slope of the S curve, or marginal propensity to save, is .25 and the slope of the M curve, or marginal propensity to import, is .25, and the combined slope is .5, so the income multiplier is 2.

Figure 12.6

INJECTIONS AND LEAKAGE DIAGRAM

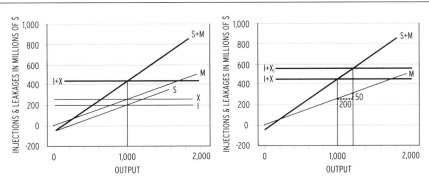

Note: In the left panel, the two horizontal schedules for injections, I at $200 million and X at $250 million, together form $I + X$ at $450 million. The two leakages, which at zero income are $50 million and 0, both rise at a slope of .25. The *combined leakage* schedule, $S + M$, rises at a slope of .5. Equilibrium occurs where $S + M = I + X$, which in this case is $1 billion. The right panel shows exogenous shifts of $I + X$ of $100 million with output rising by $200 million. Of the original injection, $50 million is drawn out for saving and $50 million for imports. Consumption (not seen on the diagram) rises by $50 million.

Many first-year textbooks use multipliers of three or four, probably reflecting the old days when the United States had relatively few imports and lower tax rates. A moment's reflection, however, suggests that multipliers cannot be that high today. A country like Canada, for instance, sees 40% of all its expenditures go to imports and over 30% go into taxes (exclusive of transfers). Rising income causes tax revenues to rise, while the government expenditures are largely planned in a previous period, so government saving increases. Add private savings of perhaps 10% and the saving rate would be around 40%. The combined leakage would therefore be .8. This is, admittedly, the average and not the marginal rate, but with imports income-elastic and tax rates progressive, the marginal rate must be even higher. The multiplier, even with the average rates suggested, would be 1/.8 or 1.25. The American rate would be closer to 2, but certainly not three or four.

The last thing the right panel shows is how much imports rise as a result of the changes. Suppose, for instance, that the reason $I + X$ increased was solely because exports rose. Would that mean that the trade surplus would rise by $100 million? No, because the additional injection of $100 million causes income to rise by $200 million, and with that rise in income of $200 million, imports will rise by a quarter of all new expenditure—$50 million. The panel also shows that an increase in income of $200 million increases imports by

Figure 12.7

SAVINGS-INVESTMENT GAP AND TRADE GAP

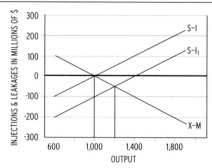

Note: This figure shows the same information as the previous figure, but the schedules are arranged differently. A decline in saving or a rise in investment leads $S - I$ to shift to the right. Output rises by 100, but a trade deficit of 50 opens up.

$50 million. Suppose, instead, the increase in injections was due solely to an increase in investment; however useful for the economy the $100 million in new investment, the trade deficit would worsen by $50 million and net new investment would only be $50 million.

$S - I = X - M$ and Income

One way to show clearly the relationship between a change in income and the trade deficit is to set up the model so that the savings-investment gap equals the trade gap, $S - I = X - M$. This produces a diagram as in Figure 12.7, where $S - I$ is a positively sloped line, a constant (I) being subtracted from a rising figure (S). $X - M$ is a negatively sloped line, the figure that rises with income (M) being subtracted from a constant (X). While the income multiplier is not particularly obvious here, the trade gap stands out. Figure 12.7 shows some of the same information as Figure 12.6. $S - I$ crosses $X - M$ at an income of $1,000 million just at zero, so trade is balanced. However, when investment rises by $100 million (or saving falls by $100 million), $S - I$ shifts to the right. Income rises, but with it a trade deficit of $50 million develops.

Figure 12.8

GNP AND IMPORTS IN CANADA AND THE UNITED STATES

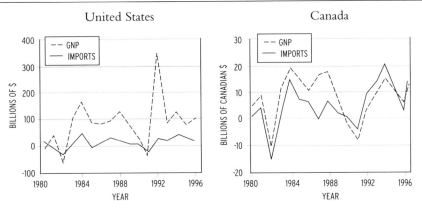

Source: IFS, 1999.

SOME INTERNATIONAL IMPLICATIONS

Trade Surpluses May Be Signs of Recession

A trade surplus, when it originates from declining imports, is a sign of an economy in trouble. As an example, American imports rose when GNP rose and fell when it fell, as Figure 12.8 shows. (In the entire 17-year period only 1997 has income and imports moving in opposite directions.) Canada shows not only the same direction of change for GNP and imports, but also a much closer relationship between the volume of the change in GNP and change in imports. (Canadian imports grew from 30% to 43% of GNP during the period, reflecting structural change as well as high income-elasticity of imports. Still, when GNP fell, so did imports.)

The relationship in the diagram does not isolate income effects from price or structural changes that might also be occurring and it does not always work so well for some countries, but the relationship between income and imports is quite obvious and, in countries with a great deal of trade, is virtually always very strong. When economies go into recession, income falls, and with it their imports. That is one reason why Japan's economic troubles have spilled over into the neighboring areas; with a sluggish economy, Japan is not drawing in the imports it had in the past.

JAPAN'S TRADE SURPLUS AS AN INCOME EFFECT

Japan has in fact been mired in a deep and long-lasting recession since the early 1990s. Real GDP growth was less than 1%, 1990-97, and was negative in some years, including 1998 and with an expectation that the country is on the verge of being the first industrialized nation to suffer a fall in GDP lasting three straight years.[1] Unemployment is very high by Japanese standards (though no higher than in the United States), and there has been a sharp downturn in property values. During most of the period, U.S. economic growth was strong, and growing income was sucking in imports.

The recession has led directly to lower Japanese imports, while the U.S. expansion has caused higher imports. Many Japanese imports from and exports to the United States are high-tech items, the income elasticity of which is above average, with sales especially subject to the business cycle. Econometrically, a fall of one percentage point in Japan's growth rate for a year causes a rise in Japan's trade surplus of about $5 billion.[2]

What Starts as an Income Effect May End Up as a Price Effect

The AD/AS model suggests that over time what begins as an income effect ends up as a price effect. An expansion stimulated by rising AD would therefore cause higher imports due to the income effect, leaving exports untouched. As people left the workforce and real incomes declined, however, price effects would replace the income effects, imports rising and exports falling.

Trade Deficits Help Control Domestic Inflation

Expenditures made abroad keep domestic AD down. For a dramatic example, consider Malaysia. The Malaysian economy looked much like the Thai economy in the mid-1990s, with very heavy portfolio capital inflows and a rapidly expanding money supply, but it had very little inflation. The reason is that imports are such a large part of total expenditure that most of the new expenditure created went outside Malaysia. Instead of inflation, it got a whopping trade deficit. To be more explicit: from 1990 to 1997, the narrowly defined money supply rose by 340% (and the broad money supply by 380%), the price level rose by only 34%, but the trade deficit rose from less than 2% of GDP to as much as 9% in some years, averaging 6% of GDP. So a great deal of what would otherwise have generated domestic expenditure went abroad.[3]

American inflation, similarly, would have been higher in the 1980s and again in the late 1990s—all other things being equal—had there not been trade deficits. Trade acts as a kind of a safety valve to let out excess demand pressures.

Figure 12.9
A DECLINE IN IMPORTS PRODUCES
PRICE AND INCOME EFFECTS

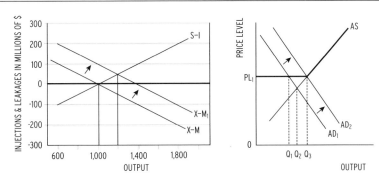

Note: The left-hand panel shows only income effects of a decline in imports. The right-hand panel shows the same situation on an AD/AS diagram, indicating both income and price effects. The right panel carries the assumption of price rigidity of the left panel such that there is a pure income effect.

Restricting Imports to Promote Short-Term Economic Growth

Theoretically, a nation could increase its income by reducing imports. The reduction in imports would cause total injections and AD to rise and thus stimulate domestic growth—in situations where there was already considerable unemployment. To wit, consider Figure 12.9.

Using the same figures as the previous income diagrams, suppose import restrictions shift the import schedule by $100 million. This shift causes $X - M$ to rise by $100 million in the left panel. As a result, income rises from $1,000 million to $1,200 million. The higher income, however, causes additional imports of $50 million, so although a trade surplus emerges, it is only $50 million, not $100 million. The right panel starts at a recession level of Q_1, but the import restrictions cause AD to rise from AD_1 to AD_2 and, with the AS flat at that point, income rises by what we know from the left panel is $200 million to Q_3.

Precious little evidence exists to show such situations. Almost always, declining imports are associated with declining income. Consider what some of the problems are:

1. AS would have to be horizontal upward as well as downward. If AD demand rises and AS has some upward slope, the price level will rise, making imports more attractive, dissipating the effect of the higher import restrictions.

The longer the time period and the greater the shift of AD, the less horizontal is an AS curve. Higher price levels also discourage exports, and AD would tend to fall back to the right. Such a situation suggests that the use of import protection to stimulate employment requires special and short-lived circumstances.

2. Other countries can retaliate, which would shift exports down.

3. As the economy struggled to manage without so many imports, its economic efficiency would fall, moving the long-run AS curve inward, forcing the price level further upward.

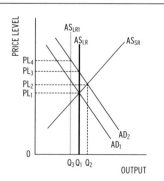

Figure 12.10

COMPLICATIONS FROM PROTECTIONISM CAN LEAD TO A LARGER INFLATION

The result of trying to restrict imports could be quite serious inflation. Figure 12.10 shows (1) the effect over the longer run as the short-run AS curve turns more vertical, and (2) the effect of the increasing inefficiencies, which moves the AS curve inward also. Starting at PL_1, AD_1 rises to AD_2, as in the right panel of Figure 12.9. This time, however, Figure 12.10 spans a longer period of time and the AS curve slopes upward, which would give a price increase to PL_2, and then to PL_3, as people with other opportunities leave the workforce. Then, with the added inefficiencies in the economy, the long-run AS curve shifts inward to AS_{LR1} and the price level rises to PL_4.

The Difficulty of Adjusting to Worsening Terms of Trade

A sharp worsening of a nation's terms of trade means that the same amount of exports purchases fewer imports. This decreases the aggregate supply because the same resources produce a lower output, just as surely as had a blight struck the major export crop. In terms of the formula for deriving AS from the hours worked, the productivity of labour declines. That is:

$$H_L(P_{L\downarrow}) \quad \rightarrow \quad AS\downarrow$$

Figure 12.11 shows AS_{LR} shifting from Q_1 to Q_2—the dark vertical line to the gray one. With AD unchanged but fewer goods available, prices will rise from PL_1 to PL_2. Many governments in this situation find themselves in deep trouble. Sometimes the government or central bank deliberately attempts to stimulate demand to raise the income back to Q_1 by raising AD to AD_2.

More often, situations like this lead to unintended increases in AD: the government's budget goes deeply into deficit because lower real incomes and an inability of taxes to keep up with inflation depress real revenue. In any case, the increased AD will only produce more inflation, as the price level rises to PL_3.

The panel on the right adds another complication: because of numerous COLA contracts, corporations with limited competition, and other institutional problems, the increased price of imports causes a sharp increase in the short-run AS curve, from AS_{SR} to AS_{SR1}. Now, output could still be Q_2 at price level PL_2, but any shifting of AD will result in an even higher price level—PL_4—than in the left panel.

Figure 12.11

REACTIONS TO WORSENING TERMS OF TRADE

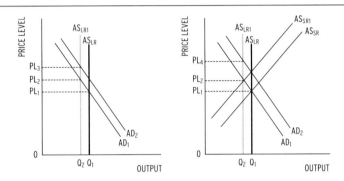

Note: As terms of trade worsen, AS_{LR} shifts to the left, but attempts to restimulate the economy cannot bring back the old employment levels. Worse, the increase in cost of living may kick in cost-of-living adjustments and shift AS_{SR} upward.

The price rise is in itself not good. Worse, it makes it very difficult to expand exports if the price level is rising. Exports begin to fall and budget and trade deficits worsen.

Income Effects Spill Beyond Borders: Foreign Repercussions

In a global economy, it may be misleading to think of expenditures on imports as leakages. American imports increase income in Canada and Canadian imports do the same in the United States. Just to use average figures: if the United States imports an extra $1 billion worth of goods from Canada, this might generate $1.2 billion in income (an income multiplier of 1.2), of which 40%, or $480 million, would be imports, typically about 80% of that—

$384 million—from the States. The United States, in turn, would see its income rise by $384 million times the multiplier, a small amount of which would go to Canada, and the process would continue.

Generally, the bilateral effects of the repercussion effects soon peter out, but in a global sense, American expenditure abroad produces income everywhere, and all of those imports produce income somewhere else. From a global point of view, the only "leakage" in the income system is that into private and government savings. Yet it is rarely in the interest of a single country to stimulate its economy in order to take advantage of the repercussions. The repercussion effect on any one country is too small to offer much reward, while the risks of running a larger trade or budget deficit may be far higher. As usual, domestic policy predominates over global policy.

In the late 1980s, when the United States had enormous trade deficits brought on by the drop in savings that occurred after the 1982 tax cuts, Treasury and State Department officials would argue that Japan and Germany needed to expand their economies and increase imports. They referred to these countries being "the locomotive economies" that would bring the rest of Europe and Asia to prosperity in their train. They used it so often, in fact, that the Germans grew quite testy at the phrase and the Americans had to ask their diplomats not to use it. Some back-of-the-envelope estimates illustrate why the idea was not popular.

Assume, cavalierly, that for either Japan or Germany any rise in income will increase imports by one-third of that amount (marginal propensity to import of .33), and of that increase in imports, .25 will be spent in the United States. (Both estimates are probably far too high, particularly the MPM of .33 for Japan.) This means a $12 billion rise in income would produce $4 billion worth of imports, only $1 billion of which would be spent in the United States. For each billion dollars' worth of reduction in the U.S. trade deficit, Germany, with a GNP of $883 billion in 1988, would have to increase its GNP by 1.36%. Japan, with a larger GNP, would have to expand it by 0.57%. The U.S. balance-of-trade deficit in 1988 was around $130 billion; even if Japan and Germany had expanded their incomes by 10% above their otherwise projected levels, the help for the United States would not have been great.

Using more sophisticated econometric modeling, Paul Krugman and Richard E. Baldwin calculated that if the whole rest of the world increased its income by 5%, the resulting increase in U.S. exports would not come close to eliminating the U.S. deficit problem.[4] It is no wonder the Germans grumbled that the Americans should put their house in order (that is, decrease the budget deficit) and were not about to risk their domestic price stability for some vaguer international good.

But take a situation that is potentially far more serious—a global recession or perhaps a depression as threatened in 1998 or occurred in 1931. Certainly in 1931 and possibly in 1998, increases in expenditure in several countries would have been good things. While the United States in 1998 wisely allowed a substantial current account deficit, it clearly could not revive the rest of the world on its own, hence its calls to Japan and Europe to increase their spending. While the Japanese, given that they were in recession, agreed it was a good idea, they had trouble putting policies in place. The Europeans, and particularly the Germans, nervous about the introduction of the new euro currency, were extremely reluctant to make any bold move.

The difficulty in cooperating is a systemic problem. Every country would like to be a free rider on another country's expansion. Yet, no mechanism exists to get the other country to expand, given that it, too, is a free rider: hence the need for international cooperation and institutions to help avoid this kind of problem. As Chapter 18 explains, the countries of the world were far better able to cooperate in 1998 than they were in 1931.

Globalization Blunts Domestic Policy Thrusts

A more integrated world poses challenges for domestic policy-makers. Consider just a few.

- It is harder for a single country to get out of a recession. With imports a much larger percentage of GNP, an expansion of AD will (a) be weaker because the income multiplier is lower, and (b) have immediate effects on the current account balance. A lower interest rate also is a helpful way to end a recession, but increasingly integrated capital markets mean that lower interest rates lead rapidly to capital account deficits. The combination of capital and current account deficits is likely to lead to a lower foreign exchange value for the currency. In itself that may not be bad, but, as Chapter 15 will indicate, it could trigger cost-push pressures by shifting the AS_{SR} upward.
- It is harder to avoid spillover effects from neighboring economies. With increasing percentages of GNP in exports, a recession in a trading partner will quickly spread domestically. An unexpected expansion next door may introduce higher exports piled onto an already climbing domestic AD, causing inflation.
- The domestic economies of countries differ in their response to changes in aggregate demand. In some an expansion of AD may cause a rise in output with little price effect. In others, the same rise in AD may produce mostly inflation. In some, a bit of inflation (with the wink and nod) may grease the wheels of change, allowing adjustments of real wages with little trouble. In yet others, the same increase in AD could cause serious inflation. The same prescription does not fit all, yet each may find that spillovers make it hard not to take the same medicine.

Figure 12.12

CAPITAL INFLOWS CAN BRING TROUBLE: THAILAND

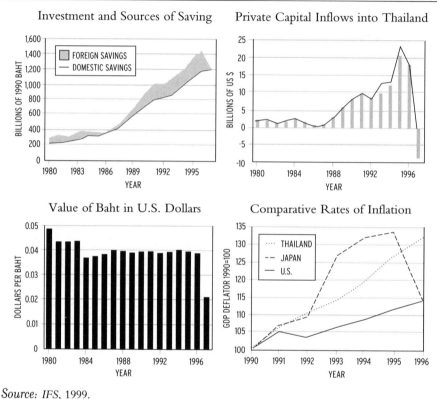

Investment and Sources of Saving

Private Capital Inflows into Thailand

Value of Baht in U.S. Dollars

Comparative Rates of Inflation

Source: IFS, 1999.

PRICE AND INCOME: TWO INTRIGUING CASES

External Shocks: Thailand in the 1990s

Thailand provides insight into the difficulties smaller countries face when private capital inflows are large, and provides an intriguing model for shocks from the outside. It also, along with the discussion in Chapters 11 and 14, provides insight into those "Asian tigers" that received heavy inflows of private capital in the 1990s.

In capsule form this is what happened. A large inflow of capital stimulated greater investment causing income to rise, which in turn brought in more imports without any immediate stimulus to exports. The price level also rose,

540

making it more difficult for exports to compete and imports became more competitive with domestic alternatives. Even with high rates of domestic saving, absorption came to exceed income as investment rose beyond the level the saving could finance, creating a large trade deficit (8% of GNP). Often when a country experiences inflation the foreign exchange value of its currency falls, but the capital inflow kept up the price of the Thai baht, granting exporters no relief from the rising price level. Now for the detail.

The upper left panel of Figure 12.12 shows domestic investment in Thailand. The bulk of it was financed through high domestic savings, but foreign capital provided substantial amounts (the shaded area). These levels of domestic investment were high—generally over 30% of GNP—so even though foreign saving provided only part of domestic investment, it was a substantial portion of GNP.

The upper right panel shows the amount of private portfolio capital inflows into Thailand. The bar is the total inflow from foreigners. The line shows the net inflow. In some years Thai investors were reducing their foreign assets, so net inflows exceeded the inflow from foreign investors. It was the sudden drop in this capital inflow—a turnaround of nearly $30 billion—that triggered the crisis in 1997.

The bottom left panel shows the value of the Thai baht in U.S. dollars. It remained quite stable, around four U.S. cents, from the mid-1980s to 1996. In the meantime, however, moderate inflation ate away at Thailand's competitive position. Thailand's chief trading partners, the United States and Japan, both had lower inflation. Japan's situation was critical because after having a large increase in price level in 1992-93, the increase slowed, turning into a drop—a sharp deflation—between 1995 and 1996. With its price level having risen farther than that of its trading partners, Thailand's exports were in trouble.

As Chapter 15 will show in more detail, price competitiveness involves both the level of the exchange rate and the relative rates of inflation of a country and its trading partners. Even without extensive detail, however, it is clear that Thailand would have been increasingly uncompetitive as its price level rose against a stable foreign exchange rate. It is impossible to separate out the income and price effects without extensive econometric work, but it is clear that exports rose less quickly than did imports and GNP during the 1990s, rather gradually opening up a trade gap. Imports rose as income rose, but exports, more dependent on foreign demand and price levels, could not keep up the pace. The gap was only closed after the crisis of 1997 when a combination of declining income and more costly exports lowered imports, and the lower baht encouraged more exports, as shown in Figure 12.13.

Figure 12.13

THAILAND: TRADE AND GNP

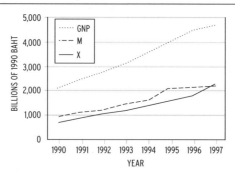

Source: *IFS*, 1999.

Internal Shocks: The United States in the 1980s

While Thailand shows a situation in which the principal factor of change was external, the United States in the 1980s showed the effects of internal stimuli: sharply falling savings coincident with a large tax cut caused consumption to rise as a portion of GNP. To control previous inflation and reduce the new inflationary pressures from the government deficit, the Federal Reserve ran a very tight money policy, raising real interest rates. The interest rates, higher than most other developed countries, caused an inflow of capital that increased the price of the dollar, leading to higher levels of imports and stagnant exports.

As was noted in Chapter 10, savings fell sharply in the United States after the tax cuts of 1982. Investment fell also, both in percentage and real terms, but not as far as savings because of foreign borrowings. Figure 12.14 shows how the country came to rely increasingly on foreign sources to finance its domestic capital investments.

The Federal Reserve was already taming the rapid inflation of the 1970s so had to intensify its very tight monetary policy, which raised interest rates in real terms and attracted funds from abroad. The left panel of Figure 12.15 shows how inflation declined (the solid line), but as it declined real interest rates rose sharply to historically high levels. (Real rates have tended to be around 3% over the past two centuries.) Foreign investors are more likely to respond to nominal rates, however, and the right panel compares American rates with those on similar assets of Japan and Germany.* American rates were four or five percentage points above comparable German and Japanese rates through 1985 and remained substantially above them until 1990. In addition,

---

* Comparing financial instruments between markets presents certain difficulties, so we have used a common instrument—the amount paid for three-month deposits in the three currencies in the London Eurocurrency markets. This is discussed at greater length in Chapter 16.

Figure 12.14

THE U.S. IN THE 1980S: DOMESTIC AND FOREIGN SAVINGS

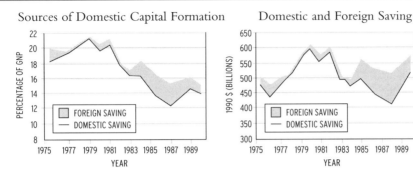

Source: IFS, 1999.

Figure 12.15

THE U.S. IN THE 1980S: INTEREST RATES

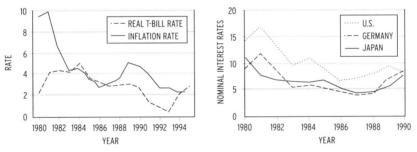

Source: IFS, 1999.

the high real rates put an enormous strain on many developing countries that had borrowed heavily, leading to a debt crisis. A great deal of flight capital then headed into the United States.

In Figure 12.16, the right-hand panel shows the increase in the value of the dollar. It takes the value of the dollar in two units of account—the SDR, which is a weighted average of key developed countries, including the U.S., and the ECU, a weighted average of European currencies. In addition, it uses one of several measures that attempt to figure in purchasing power, and that demonstrates that the dollar could buy considerably more abroad in 1984 and 1985 than it could before or after.

Should it be any surprise that exports had a major struggle, while imports zinged along? Figure 12.17 shows how exports and imports behaved in the period. Notice that exports—in real terms—actually fell from 1981 to 1986.

Figure 12.16

THE U.S. IN THE 1980S: AN INFLOW
OF FUNDS DRIVES UP THE DOLLAR

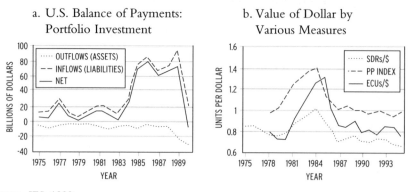

a. U.S. Balance of Payments:
Portfolio Investment

b. Value of Dollar by
Various Measures

Source: IFS, 1999.

Figure 12.17

U.S. TRADE IN THE 1980S

Exports and Imports in Real Terms

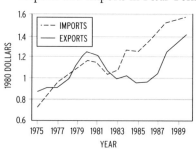

Source: IFS, 1999.

CONCLUSION

An understanding of income and price effects goes a long way toward under-standing many aspects of the international economy. The income and AD/AS models provide ways to understand how current account imbalances come about and how national economies interact through trade and capital flows. Still, the discussion has yet to touch on the big international financial markets that produce the capital flows, or on the role of money, two very big subjects to which the book now turns.

VOCABULARY AND CONCEPTS

Aggregate demand
Aggregate supply
Combined Marginal propensity
Cost-of-living adjustment
Foreign repercussions
Income effects

Injections
Leakages
Long-run aggregate supply
Price effects
Short-run aggregate supply
Wage rigidity

QUESTIONS

1. "Trade is affected by price and income effects. In the short run there are both price and income effects. In the long run, however, we have only price effects." Explain, using the AD/AS model to make your point.

2. Explain, using price and income mechanisms, how:
    a. a decrease in domestic saving as a proportion of income causes a trade deficit.
    b. an increase in investment does the same.
    c. an increase in government saving eliminates a trade deficit.
    d. a recession causes a strong trade surplus

3. Show each of the changes in question 2 with a diagram relating $S - I$ and $X - M$ to the level of national income.

4. Assume that 16% of the workforce is on the margin, like Ashley Gray, and that an unanticipated inflation raises the price level by 20%. Before the inflation, the country's output was $1 billion. A quarter of the marginal workers will leave the workforce after one year, another quarter after two years, and so on. Assuming no change to productivity and no further change in aggregate demand, what will happen to real output in each of the next four years? Assuming the two points you have are part of a line, draw the AS curves for each year. When does the short run become the long run?

5. Referring to the situation in number 4 above, what will happen to $X - M$, all other things being equal? Explain why imports at first are likely to show more change than exports.

6. In the 1950s and 1960s, economists often assumed that prices would be extremely rigid downward and that a country could get quite close to an inflationary point without having an inflation. Were they to have employed the AS model, it would have been a backwards L-shaped AS curve. This implies that countries needing to rid themselves of trade deficits will experience recession and those with trade surpluses will have inflation. Demonstrate.

7. Thailand has weak labor unions, many independent small businesses, a fiscally conservative government, and little experience with rapid inflation. Brazil has strong labor unions and strong labor legislation, a number of quite dominant firms, fiscally reckless governments, and a history of high inflation. Which country is likely to see AS_{SR} shift quickly and greatly?

8. Basically, the leakages and injections models are short-term and work best on the horizontal portion of the AS curve. Explain.

9. Draw an injections and leakages diagram using the following data. At an income of 200, $S = 20$, $M = 40$, $I = 30$, $X = 40$. I and X are exogenously determined. MPS $= .2$, and MPM 0.25. What is the equilibrium level of income? Assume exports were to rise by 20, what is the new income?

10. Use the same data as in the previous question with one exception. Assume that $X = 40$ only at an income of 200 and that it slopes downward at a slope of 0.1. What is your new conclusion? Why could X slope downward?

11. Explain why an increase in tariffs would have no success at reducing a trade deficit.

12. The foreign repercussion effect shows that leakage into imports is not as complete as leakage into savings. Explain.

13. The impact of expansion of European countries on the U.S. balance-of-trade deficit in the late 1980s would probably have been too small to change that deficit significantly. Explain, using the foreign repercussion effect and some rough-and-ready estimates.

14. Distinguish the kinds of shocks that affect the short-run AS from those affecting long-run AS?

15. Using a shift in the long-run AS curve, explain why it is difficult for countries to avoid inflation or restore employment.

16. Explain why globalization makes domestic policy more difficult.

17. The studies in the text of Thailand and the United States show two serious balance-of-payments problems. Contrast and compare them.

NOTES

1. Richard Katz, "Economic Anorexia: Japan's Real Demand Problem," *Challenge* (March–April 1999): 77-101.

2. See William R. Cline, *International Economic Policy in the 1990s* (Cambridge, Mass.: MIT Press, 1994), ch. 4.

3. *International Financial Statistics*, CD-ROM (Washington: IMF, March 1999).

4. Paul R. Krugman and Richard E. Baldwin, "The Persistence of the U.S. Trade Deficit," *Brookings Papers on Economic Activity* 1 (1987): 1-55.

Chapter Thirteen

Interest Rates, Prices, and Foreign Exchange

OBJECTIVES

OVERALL OBJECTIVE   To examine the interrelationships of interest rates, price levels, and capital market imperfections and exchange rates.

MORE SPECIFICALLY
- To present the basic institutional elements of foreign exchange markets and to place the astronomical amounts of foreign exchange traded in perspective.
- To develop a model that explores how interest rates influence the value of currencies, using the return-on-assets model.
- To develop a model based on price level differences, working out purchasing power parities.
- To explore the relation of the international financial markets to domestic financial markets, noting the importance of a continued separation of the two markets.

⋯⋯⋯⋯⋯⋯⋯⋯⋯⋯⋯⋯⋯⋯⋯⋯⋯⋯⋯⋯⋯⋯⋯⋯⋯⋯⋯⋯⋯⋯⋯⋯⋯

Exchange rates, capital flows, and interest rates have to this point remained in the background. This chapter brings them to the fore. The first topic it addresses is the nature of the foreign exchange markets themselves. Second, it examines how the value of a country's currency is determined. The two theories, not necessarily incompatible, are *interest rate parity* and *purchasing power parity*. The first holds that interest rates between countries tend toward the same value, given due considerations for risk, liquidity, and informational factors. The second holds that, at least in the longer run, what currencies actually buy—their real values—determine exchange rates. Finally, we consider the integration of the domestic and international financial markets and how interest rates abroad influence domestic rates.

THE FOREIGN EXCHANGE MARKET

> The Finance Minister looked grim as his currency was undergoing a series of attacks on the foreign exchange market. "I don't understand," he said to one of his advisers. "We have the budget deficit under control, our inflation is low, and the economy is doing well, yet our currency is under attack. What do I have to do?"
>
> "Look," replied his adviser. "There are 25-year-old kids in suspenders sitting in front of computer monitors playing games—and they're playing them with our money."

The anecdote has enough truth to be funny, but play and the type of play—like that of children or ropes—has clear limits. No bank lets its foreign exchange trader have a great deal of play. But a close look at the foreign exchange market is in order.

Like many commodities, national currencies are bought and sold in an international market. (To be more precise, banks buy and sell existing deposits of money in the banking system. If Barclays Bank in England sells £10 million to Citibank of New York, Citibank gets a deposit in an English bank and Barclays gets a deposit in an American bank.) Currencies make ideal commodities for big, efficient markets. Unlike many manufactured goods, they are homogeneous—one U.S. dollar is the same as another, one French franc is the same as another. Unlike agricultural commodities, they do not deteriorate (nothing like a late delivery of pig bellies). And the transportation cost is virtually nothing—just a notification via electronic media. Unlike goods, however, currencies are not traded for their own sake but for what they can buy. Ultimately, the value of a pork belly depends on what people will pay for the bacon; with currencies, there is still another step, as that currency is just a generalized claim on a nation's resources.

Few figures in economics are as astronomical as those for the foreign exchange markets. In the late 1990s estimates were that trading of currencies amounted to $1.2 trillion a day in the three major markets of New York, London, and Tokyo. With stupendous volume and such an ideal product, the markets are highly efficient. Whether they give a realistic value to a currency based on its long-run prospects is more debatable.

The Structure of the Market

The foreign exchange market has two levels. One is like a retail market, that between the banks and their customers, and the second is more of a wholesale market between major banks, a few other large financial institutions, and central banks. The press focuses on the wholesale market, but the retail market drives the wholesale market.

CUSTOMERS AND BANKS

Bank patrons have a variety of instruments available to engage in buying and selling foreign exchange. The vast majority of market participants buy and sell foreign exchange through their banks, a smaller number through securities dealers or brokerage houses. Consider a typical transaction.

The New York importer, Knight Stillman, orders Scotch whiskey from Olde Reekie Distilleries in Edinburgh, Scotland, at a cost of £10,000. The bill is *invoiced* in sterling (another word for British pounds)—Stillman's obligation is legally to deliver sterling. Any way that Stillman pays, it goes through a bank.

1. Stillman could just send a U.S. dollar check, having looked up the exchange rate in the newspaper. Reekie, however, would not be pleased if in the interim the exchange rate has fallen against the dollar (so they wouldn't get enough pounds) and would dun for the remainder. It may say nothing if the dollar has risen against the pound.

2. If Stillman does a lot of business with British suppliers, it may itself have an account in Britain. It would draw a check on that account and then replenish it from time to time by sending its British bank a U.S. dollar draft—if that draft were short of the amount paid out to Reekie, the British bank would not care so long as the account was not overdrawn. In many countries—but not the United States, where such practices are prohibited by law—a company can acquire a foreign currency account in its own country and simply draw on it. Canadian companies routinely establish U.S. dollar accounts at their Canadian banks. In such cases the Canadian bank holds a deposit in an American bank through which the checks clear. The Canadian bank then replenishes its deposits, should they fall.

3. If Stillman does not do regular business in Britain, it can request its bank to make out a check, like a cashier's check or certified bank draft, in the foreign currency. It costs more per transaction than having a foreign account, but the costs are a very small part of a large transaction like this.

4. If the two companies are unfamiliar with each other, they may choose one of a dozen or more *instruments of credit*—various letters of credit and commercial acceptances that come into play when the goods are delivered. In essence, Reekie could send Stillman a form that, when signed, acts as a draft on Stillman's account. Usually, these are guaranteed by one or both banks involved in the transaction. They are sometimes not for immediate payment, but for payment in 30, 60, or 90 days, and may be *negotiable*—that is, they can be sold at a discount to banks. (In such a case, they would be means of finance as well as means of exchange.) Throughout the nineteenth century and well into the twentieth, such guaranteed, future-payment letters, known as *bills of*

exchange, were the principal means of financing trade, and a vigorous market for their discount and sale grew up in London. Indeed, the London Royal Exchange traded such bills from the 1500s until its closing in 1920, when the growth of telex and telephone transfers eliminated the need for a large bourse.[1]

THE INTERBANK MARKET

Banks wish to avoid holding excessive amounts of any one currency. A British bank, having given Reekie a credit in *sterling* (British pounds), faces a risk that the U.S. dollars it holds might fall in value. Consider this more closely.

All of the possible means by which Stillman can pay Reekie involve a bank buying dollars and selling sterling. (A dollar check to Reekie would have to be cashed in a British bank; a sterling draft on Stillman's British bank would be replaced by a dollar check; an international bank draft in sterling causes the bank to buy Stillman's dollars; and any of the instruments of credit eventually end up with a bank buying dollars.) If the pound is worth us$1.50, then some bank ends up holding $15,000 and agreeing to pay out £10,000. In the course of a day—or, indeed, a few hours—a major bank will handle millions of dollars worth of transactions, most considerably larger than this one. Some of the transactions will have the bank—call it Lloyds, one of the large British banks—buying sterling, others selling sterling, but suppose that not very long into the day Lloyds notices that it is selling quite a bit more sterling than it is receiving, while it is also accumulating a great deal of U.S. dollars. Lloyds has already established some guidelines as to how much it wishes to have of various currencies. It knows that it could get into trouble if it holds too many dollars.

1. For one thing, Lloyds wants to keep its risks down. To do so, it wishes to match its assets and liabilities so that they are in the same currency. Even if the exchange rate is £1.00 = $1.50, the bank does not want to see 150 million *dollars* in assets backing 100 million *pounds* of liabilities. If the dollar should slip in value, the bank would face a severe loss. While it might gain if the dollar should rise, it is not primarily in the business of speculating and is not routinely going to "bet the bank" on the foreign exchange market.

2. In addition, U.S. dollars do not count as bank reserves in Britain. When Lloyds reports to the Bank of England how much it has held in reserve against its deposits, it cannot use foreign exchange as a primary reserve. If, for instance, Lloyds wants to hold 2% of its assets for settling accounts with the other British banks, it cannot use the U.S. dollars.[*]

---

[*] The numbers are for example only. Formal reserve requirements are declining in percentage worldwide, and some countries, such as Canada, have ended them entirely. Britain, in this

3. While not willing to bet the whole bank on speculation, Lloyds will have authorized its managers—who in turn control the kids in suspenders at the computer monitors—to do some limited speculation on the rise or fall of the dollar. If they are speculating against the dollar, they may, within their established *speculative limits*, reduce their dollar holdings.

4. In the very short run—a matter of hours, often—Lloyds may expect a change in its balances. Perhaps in the morning there is more demand for sterling, in the afternoon for dollars. The bank may not wish to face the transaction costs of selling in the morning and then rebuying in the afternoon, and may decide to let some imbalances ride.

In this particular case, suppose Lloyds decides that its need for reserves, its mismatched assets and liabilities, and its speculative feelings on the dollar suggest it should sell off $10 million—"small potatoes" in the huge international market. At this point, Lloyds would use the interbank (wholesale) market to sell.

The interbank market is almost a cybermarket—a computer-connected market, having no central bourse or city. The participants are principally the large banks and a few big brokerage houses. Regional banks in the United States buy and sell "retail" to the larger banks. Virtually all of the large sales are made through banks in London, New York, and Tokyo. In the late 1980s, London was doing about twice the volume of New York or Tokyo. Frankfurt, Hong Kong, Singapore, and numerous capital cities have smaller markets, usually for their own currencies against a few major ones. The Canadian foreign exchange market, for instance, has roughly two-thirds of its trades between the U.S. and Canadian dollar, around 30% between the U.S. dollar and other currencies, and only 3% between the Canadian dollar and other currencies.[2] The computer connections are open between all major banks during the business day, and if, say, a Canadian bank doesn't find the price it wants for its currency in Toronto, it knows what New York or, if early enough in the day, London has been offering. Later in the day, it might see what the currencies are going for in Tokyo. Because of the geographical spread of the three centers, the market never sleeps. When New York opens, London has already been open for five hours. When New York closes, Tokyo is just opening (and is open before the American west coast markets close). When Tokyo closes, London is already open.

The traders work with batteries of computers and a constant flow of data. They trade either directly with other banks or through foreign exchange brokers, dealing and confirming electronically. Most banks are constantly in the

---

sense, is a bad example because it, like Canada, has had no formal reserve requirements. Banks still keep deposits at their central banks for settling accounts with other banks and vault cash (an amount that is growing, due to the vast number of automatic teller machines), but their size is determined by the banks.

market, even if they have no need to change their portfolios, looking for an opportunity to make a little money by buying and selling currencies at slightly different rates. That way, when they do enter the market to balance their own portfolios, they are up-to-the-second on market information and the purpose of their own sale is disguised. (That is, no one will know whether Lloyds is just speculating a bit or balancing its portfolio.) Brokers try to make money on a spread between buying and selling rates, often very small—and they don't have to be very large when trading billions. The banks, of course, make money between the "retail" rates they charge their customers and the inter-bank rates they pay other banks. The business is highly competitive, and rates are often quoted to the ten-thousandth of a cent.

Big international investors—mutual funds, hedge funds, commodity brokers, insurance companies—all go through the banks. In situations when funds are moving out of a country in large amounts, the international investors have to ask their agents to sell their stocks, bonds, or various short-term assets and deposit them in their accounts in a local bank. Then they tell the bank to purchase another currency with that deposit. The banks find that their customers are asking for huge amounts of foreign currency and few foreign banks want to make new deposits. Their foreign exchange traders are busy selling and selling. Like a ship's anchor rope stretched taut in a storm, there is little play in a real rout.

Visualizing the Foreign Exchange Market

The foreign exchange market is in one sense a flow—millions of units of different currencies coming out of different pipes into a vast vat, some pipes pouring in, some only at a trickle. The resultant ratios of currencies in the vat determine the exchange rate. Throughout the first part of 1998, for instance, about US$71 entered the market for every $100 Canadian, resulting in a price of US$0.71 for the Canadian dollar. Then in the fall the flow of U.S. dollars slowed while that of Canadian dollars increased, leading to only US$65 for every $100 Canadian and a consequent fall of the Canadian dollar to 65 cents. Market participants try to guess the future prices, of course, and withhold currencies if they think the price is "too low," but they are constantly reassessing their position.

In another sense, the market has two stocks of currencies exchanging. All the currency offered in one hour, or one day, or one year, represents an exchange of a stock of each currency. This somewhat more abstract idea is useful because traders themselves must have a sense of the amounts of currency that will be traded in a given period of time so that they can judge if the price at any one instant is a reasonable one—whether they should turn down or accept with alacrity that price. It also allows the use of the familiar demand-and-supply diagrams to talk about currency values.

A century ago the great Cambridge University economist, Alfred Marshall, made some cautionary comments on using supply and demand:

> When demand and supply are in stable equilibrium, if any accident should move the scale of production from its equilibrium position, there will be instantly brought into play forces tending to bring it back to that position; just as, if a stone hanging by a string is displaced from its equilibrium position, the force of gravity will at once tend to bring it back to its equilibrium position....
>
> But in real life such oscillations are seldom as rhythmical as those of a stone hanging freely from a string; the comparison would be more exact if the string were supposed to hang in the troubled waters of a mill-race, whose stream was at one time allowed to flow freely, and at another partially cut off. The demand and supply schedules do not in practice remain unchanged for a long time together, but are constantly being changed; and every change in them alters the equilibrium amount and the equilibrium price, and thus gives new positions to the centers about which the amount and price tend to oscillate.[3]

Both the demand and supply of a currency derive from other demands and supplies—that is, people do not want the currencies for their own sake, but for the goods, services, or assets they buy. Over a short time the highly volatile demand for assets dominates the movements of exchange rates, like the millstream's troubled waters. Over the longer run the demand for goods and services dominates the demand for assets, like the end of the string to which the ball is tethered. Consider the difference between the sources of demand and supply over a year and over an hour.

The balance on the current account indicates the value of the funds that a country spends and receives on its imports of goods, services, income, and transfers. That is usually 80% or more of a country's expenditures and receipts. The rest is the net amount that is borrowed or lent. This is to say that the amount demanded and supplied of a currency over the period of a year arises principally from the goods and services, not from the demand and supply of financial assets. This is, so to speak, the location of the branch from which hangs the string that holds the stone. The bouncing around in small time periods, however, springs from the changes in interest rates of short-term assets and speculation on the value of the currency.

Picture a foreign exchange market with just two currencies, the American and Canadian dollars. Consider the trade in the market to represent all the trade in currencies done within a single month. The demand and supply will then show the average price, even if the hourly or daily price is dancing around like Marshall's stone in the millrace.*

Figure 13.1 shows a demand-and-supply diagram for U.S. dollars with their price in Canadian dollars (Cdn$). The horizontal axis is the number of dollars traded; the vertical axis is the price of the dollar as expressed in Canadian dollars per U.S. dollar.† The demand for dollars slopes downward because at a lower price, people will be able to get more American goods and to buy up American assets cheaply, and, as the price gets lower and farther away from its presumed long-run equilibrium, traders and speculators will want to purchase it. The supply of dollars slopes upward because any attempt to persuade the Americans to put more dollars on the market requires greater incentives—they will not buy unless foreign goods, services, and assets are cheaper or they expect the American dollar to be worth less.

At a price of the U.S. dollar at Cdn$1.30, well below where the diagram shows equilibrium, the Americans would not buy so many Canadian goods and assets because their prices would be high in U.S. dollar terms, while the Canadians would gladly purchase many dollars to buy American goods that appear so inexpensive. A shortage of U.S. dollars (*ac* on Figure 13.1) would result and the Cdn$1.30 price could not hold. Similarly, a very high price of Cdn$1.60 for the U.S. dollar would encourage Americans to purchase Canadian goods and assets, but fewer Canadians would want to buy American goods and assets, so a surplus of U.S. dollars *(ac* in Figure 13.1) would result. Only at the equilibrium price of Cdn$1.50 would the market clear and exactly as many dollars would be offered as would be demanded. Traders with a good sense of the patterns of demand and supply could presumably set the price quite close to a clearing equilibrium.

---

* In their pure form, demand-and-supply curves represent all potential offerings of goods and demands for goods at a large range of prices for a given period of time. It assumes, to be more precise, that all goods are sold at a single price for whatever time period is covered. That is a rather awkward assumption for a market where the price is changing every minute. As with many models, it is sometimes best not to look too closely, and just assume that the price is a kind of an average.

† A guaranteed error on the first hour test for somebody! Everybody, including the authors, has to check the axes very carefully; it is very easy to forget that dollars are on the horizontal axis and then to put the price as cents per mark on the vertical. That happens because we can speak of DM2.5 per $1.00 or US$0.40 per Deutschmark. If in doubt, substitute apples for Deutschmarks because we never speak of buying a dollar with three apples. Most currencies are quoted as units per U.S. dollar—e.g., 2.5 Deutschmarks, 8.0 francs, 180 yen *per dollar*. The exceptions are two: (1) the Canadian (and Australian) dollar, which might be quoted either way: Cdn$114 = US$1.00 or US$87.8 = Cdn$1.00. (2) The British pound sterling. Since the pound is one of the very few currencies with a larger unit value than the dollar, it is normally quoted as dollars per pound—e.g., $1.80 = $1.80/£1.00, not pounds per dollar, which is £0.56 = £1.00 / $1.80.

Figure 13.1

DEMAND AND SUPPLY FOR U.S. AND CANADIAN DOLLARS

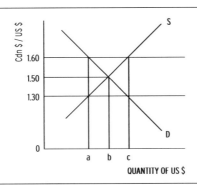

The Government's Role in Stabilizing the Value of a Currency

Most countries try to stabilize the value of their currencies, or at least keep them from swinging too widely. The wisdom of doing so is discussed in Chapter 15, but the fact of the matter is that countries are very active in manipulating their currency values, and an understanding of the mechanism is essential.

Countries and traders prefer reasonably stable exchange rates and governments can help or hinder that objective. Governments can operate either indirectly, by influencing the demand and supply of currencies, or directly, by entering the foreign exchange market. Indirectly, governments may try to alter the demand and supply of currencies through manipulating interest rates and the trade balance itself. Directly, the central banks enter the foreign exchange market to influence the price of currencies.

INTERVENTION IN THE FOREIGN EXCHANGE MARKET

This direct means is *intervention in the foreign exchange market*. Any government, through its central bank, can trade in its own currency, increasing the market's demand or supply. If the United States *monetary authorities* (the Treasury and the Federal Reserve Board) saw the dollar falling and did not want it to fall, they could try to stop that fall by purchasing U.S. dollars on the foreign exchange market. If the European Central Bank did not want the euro to rise, it could sell more euros.

Technically, the purchases and sales of foreign exchange go through the central banks, and, in the case of the United States, through its Federal Reserve System, specifically through the Federal Reserve Bank of New

York. Suppose, in a concerted action, the Federal Reserve Bank of New York (acting for the Federal Reserve System) and the new European Central Bank decided to halt the dollar's slide against the euro. Each bank would enter the foreign exchange market and purchase substantial amounts of dollars with euros. The Fed would use what euros it had already accumulated (its *foreign exchange reserves*) when the dollar was high, plus whatever it could borrow from other sources. The European Central Bank, of course, has an endless supply of euros that it can use, and it would put the dollars it bought into its foreign exchange reserves.

One of the more dramatic examples of intervention in the last 15 years came during the winter of 1987-88. The U.S. dollar came under much downward pressure in December 1987. The *Federal Reserve Bulletin* describes the events:

> The announcement on December 10 that the U.S. trade deficit had jumped to a record $17.6 billion in October underlined the difficulties in reducing the U.S. external imbalance and had a strong market impact. As traders rushed to liquidate their dollar positions, the dollar gapped downward 1 ½ to 2 percent within a few minutes of the announcement. The U.S. authorities entered the market in concert with several European central banks, to restrain the dollar's decline. The next day, when market conditions again deteriorated, the Desk reentered the market. Over the two-day period the U.S. authorities purchased $351 million against marks and yen.

And a few weeks later, after continued uncertainty in the market:

> Against this background, the dollar again came under strong downward pressure as the year drew to a close. U.S. corporations and Japanese banks sold dollars in thin holiday markets, at a time when most banks in Europe and the United States were unwilling to adjust their position ahead of the year-end. The U.S. monetary authorities intervened heavily in concerted intervention operations. During the period December 16 through December 31, the Desk purchased a total of $1,707 million, approximately half of which was against marks and half against yen. By early morning January 4, the dollar had declined to record lows.[4]

In December 1987 the Federal Reserve bought over $2 billion worth of U.S. currency (with marks and yen). The *Bulletin* does not indicate how much the Canadian, German, and other European and Japanese governments spent, but it was considerable. All in all, it is likely that in the last quarter of 1987, central banks spent somewhat over $30 billion to ease the dollar's fall,

Figure 13.2

INTERVENTION IN THE FOREIGN EXCHANGE MARKET

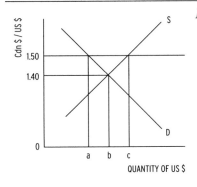

Note: How many dollars should be bought up from the market to bring the price up to Cdn$1.50? At a price of Cdn$1.50 the quantity supplied of dollars will be even greater than it is at Cdn$1.40—*0c*—while the demand for dollars will be less—*0a*. To cover this gap, the monetary authorities put *ac* on the market. The value of that in Canadian dollars is *ac* × 1.5, a rectangle formed by *ac* and reaching up to the Cdn$1.50 price. A similar exercise will show that a market equilibrium below the desired exchange rate will call forth a sale of dollars and purchase of Canadian dollars.*

led by Germany and Britain, each of which bought over $10 billion, and Japan, which bought over $8 billion.

Figure 13.2 visualizes what the monetary authorities do. Here the *D* and *S* represent the market forces independent of any *monetary intervention*. In contrast to Figure 13.1, the demand for dollars has fallen and the supply risen. These forces have pulled down the price of the dollar to Cdn$1.40, from the desired rate of Cdn$1.50. At Cdn$1.40 *0b* of dollars would be traded. The Bank of Canada and the Federal Reserve would like the price at Cdn$1.50. To do so, they have to buy up the U.S. dollars with Canadian dollars.

THE VAST SUMS TRADED

Pundits writing of the foreign exchange market like to impress their readers by citing the enormous amount of currency that is traded. Figures of $1.2 trillion a day dwarf the paltry billions of dollars central banks might spend on a market to support a currency. But the figures are not describing like phenomena. Because the extra cost of making another trade is so inexpensive, foreign exchange traders trade the same deposit many times a day. If the Bank of Canada adds $100 million of Canadian deposits to the market (to keep the price of the Canadian dollar down), that $100 million may be traded many, many times before it settles. It only takes a few seconds to make a trade, and a hundred banks may be interested in holding some of those Canadian dollar

---

* Some students show the monetary authorities' purchases and sales by shifting the demand-and-supply curves. There is a technical problem in handling the diagram that way, because a shift of, say, the supply curve for Cdn$ to the right in Figure 13.2 implies that the intervention would be the same at any price, and that is not what is meant at all. There is an intervention of different amounts, depending on the market's equilibrium price.

deposits as their own positions change and as they estimate which way the market is going. The same $100 million could easily generate a billion in trades even though at the end of the day the net amount moved is only $100 million.

INTEREST RATE PARITY

A serviceable model for handling the immediate pressures determining the value of a currency compares the interest rate within the country with the interest rates outside the country, adding elements of speculation. In this model, interest rates between countries determine the value of the exchange rates so it is usually called the *interest rate parity model*. It has a horizontal axis of the domestic expected rate of return and the vertical of the exchange rate. It has two schedules, one for the returns on domestic assets (RODA) and a second for the return on foreign assets (ROFA).

Consider a large American mutual fund with a lot of cash it is putting into the money market—that is, short-term assets, particularly Treasury bills, in both the American and Canadian markets. Suppose the American T-bill rate is 4.5% and the Canadian is the same. Market participants do not expect that the exchange rate between the Canadian dollar and the American dollar will change.

Figure 13.3 shows an initial situation in its left panel (bold lines) where the American dollar is worth $1.50 Canadian dollars (Cdn$1.00 = us$0.67). The interest rate in both countries is 4.5%, but then the Federal Reserve allows interest rates to fall, while the Bank of Canada holds them up. The change in domestic interest rates causes RODA—the return on domestic (U.S.) assets— to shift to the left to 4%. The return on Canadian assets is unchanged and, with the expectation of no change in the exchange rate, more funds shift to Canada. The Canadian dollar rises against the U.S. dollar, shown on this dia-gram as a decline in the price of the U.S. dollar to $1.40.

A key element in the diagram is the slope of the ROFA curve. If a given interest change causes a large change in the value of the currency, ROFA is steep; if it causes only a small change ROFA has a shallow slope. If investors viewed the Canadian and American dollars as perfect substitutes for each other, ROFA would be horizontal—all American short-term funds would shift to Canadian assets. (Just imagine what would happen if the Federal Reserve Bank of San Francisco tried to lower interest rates below what the Federal Reserve Bank of Chicago was trying to achieve; all funds would shift to Chicago.) But the two assets are not the same. The Canadian market for T-bills is not quite so liquid as the American, and sales or purchases of T-bills that would leave the American market virtually unaffected may be large

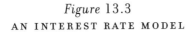

Figure 13.3

AN INTEREST RATE MODEL

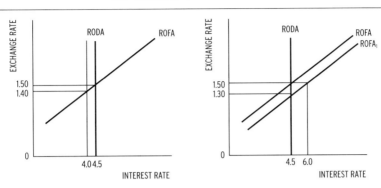

Note: The initial position in the left panel—the bold lines for ROFA and RODA—assumed that the market does not expect the change in the exchange rate. Interest rates in both Canada and the United States are 4.5%. The right panel shows what happens when the market anticipates a change.

enough to affect substantially the Canadian price of T-bills. Moreover, as the Canadian dollar rises in value, the chances that it might fall increase. Since assets in the two currencies are not perfect substitutes and the higher the Canadian dollar rises, the more the risk is that it will fall, RODA has an upward slope.

In this case, assume that a number of long-run indicators suggest that the Canadian dollar will rise in value. This means that the anticipated return on foreign assets (ROFA) is higher. Even if the interest rate in Canada is the same as the American—4.5%—the investor can expect an additional gain when the Canadian dollar rises. If, for instance, the Canadian dollar rose by a mere 1.5% over the year, it would increase the return, measured in U.S. dollars, to 6%— 4.5% in interest and 1.5% in exchange rate gains. In this case, the ROFA curve moves to the right as in the right panel. (At a price of $1.50, investment in Canadian assets would produce 6%.) This movement causes the Canadian dollar to rise in value and the U.S. dollar to fall in value. There is no precise way to indicate how much that rise or fall would be, so the figure of $1.30 is just to show the direction. (ROFA shifts because expectations have changed: at any interest rate the Canadian dollar is likely to rise against the U.S. dollar.)

Expected Values: Clarifications and Extensions

Financial analysts usually describe the expected change in an exchange rate as "an *expected* value." An expected value is a statistical concept, more readily applied to situations that repeat themselves often than to a single occurrence. If two people bet the coin on the flip of a quarter, the expected loss or gain is zero. That is, over numerous flips, neither bettor will lose or gain. The expectation on any individual flip, however, is either a 25-cent loss or a 25-cent gain. It usually takes a great number of flips to have the number come out close to 50% for each. If the expected value of the U.S. dollar in Canadian dollars is $1.50, unchanged from the present, it would mean that financial analysts have weighed the chances that the Canadian dollar will rise or fall and have come up with an *expected value* reflecting no change. But they may have evaluated the chances it would rise by 10% were the same as it would fall by 10%, and perhaps they only found a little chance it would actually stay the same. They do not literally expect the Canadian dollar will be unchanged, only that a bank or fund continually betting on the Canadian dollar will find that over time it rises as much as it falls. Since no one knows exactly what will happen in any one period, the expected value is the one they will use.

Table 13.1 shows a set of assumptions about a currency. Researchers have defined three separate *scenarios*, known in statistics as *states*. In the first scenario, several events come together, such as an improvement in export prices for the country's goods, that could raise the value of the currency by 20%. In the second scenario, events develop such that no change would occur, and in the third, the currency would fall by 20%. The researchers then ascribe probabilities that each scenario might occur, as in the third column. (The probabilities must add up to one.) The fourth column shows the product of the probability times the change. The sum of the three probabilities is the expected value of the change. In this case, researchers and pundits have decided that the currency is probably not going to change at all and that its chances of rising or falling are equal.

Table 13.1

ASSUMPTIONS ABOUT A CURRENCY

State/Scenario	Movement	Chances	Product
1	+ 20%	.2	4%
2	0	.6	0
3	− 20%	.2	− 4%
Expected value (change)			0

One curious implication of using expected values is that institutions may begin to shift their portfolios, even if they do not expect the value of the currency to change. If the chances of a negative movement increase, the expected value will fall, even though the chances that no change will occur may still be above 50%. Table 13.2 illustrates how a change would occur:

Table 13.2
NEGATIVE MOVEMENT

State/Scenario	Movement	Chances	Product
1	+ 20%	.1	2%
2	0	.6	0
3	− 20%	.3	− 6%
Expected value (change)			− 4%

Even though institutions still hold the probability of no change to be the most likely outcome, the chances of a rise in the currency have declined and the chances of a fall have increased, so the expected value of the change is now − 4%. To cover the increased possibility of loss, institutions would begin to sell the currency. (And the ROFA curve would shift to the right.)

THE LONGER RUN:
PRICE LEVELS AND PURCHASING POWER PARITY

Like the stone in the millrace that hangs from a string tethered to a tree limb, a currency will tend to center around a value that reflects more long-run factors. On what basis does the market develop an *expectation* that a certain exchange rate will come about? The principal base is the relation of purchasing powers between countries. If Canadian prices are lower than those in the United States, Canadian exports will be inexpensive and imports expensive, leading to a Canadian current account surplus. The current account surplus means that more U.S. dollars are being offered to buy Canadian dollars. The exchange rate can only remain unchanged if the Canadians are willing to build up foreign investments and the U.S. will tolerate large debts. But capital imbalances have their limit, and governments and markets become jittery as they grow to be more than a few percent of GNP. And, as Chapter 15 demonstrates, the economic pressures of trade surpluses usually increase the price level, while deficits cause it to stagnate and in some cases actually decline. So either the increased demand drives up Canadian prices or it drives up the value of the Canadian dollar. (Or, the decreased demand could drive down prices in the U.S.) Thus, relative prices are a key element in any long-term assessment.

Absolute Purchasing Power Parity

In the latter part of 1998, the Canadian dollar was worth around us$0.65 on the currency markets. If, however, a Canadian family had spent a thousand Canadian dollars on a typical market basket of goods, it would have had a basket worth us$850. A Canadian family earning $50,000 in Canadian funds would, on average, be able to purchase as many goods and services in Canada as would an American family earning $42,500 in the United States. This implies an exchange rate of us$0.85 = Cdn$1.00. If the Canadians were "snowbirds" spending much of the winter in the American South, their money could only purchase goods and services worth us$32,500. The comparison of what can be purchased suggests that the exchange rate should have been us$0.85 = Cdn$1.00. If such *absolute purchasing power parity* determined the Canadian dollar, economists would have expected it would soon rise, because it was severely *undervalued* on the foreign exchange market. This is a striking difference, unusual for countries with similar living standards. How could it occur?

The Canadians cannot carry their basket of goods and services with them when they travel, which is to say that many things they consume cannot be traded. The basket includes a pile of services like haircuts, home and office rent, medical services, and video rental fees, most of which are cheaper in Canada than the United States. But it is *tradable* goods that directly influence exchange rates. Moreover, retailers may adjust to the lower purchasing power in Canada such that even many tradable goods are cheaper in Canada. In one case, noted in October 1998, an inkjet printer was priced at $300 in the U.S. and the identical item at $400 in Canada; at the exchange rate, it should have been $450 in Canada.

Economists have known for years that absolute purchasing power doesn't work. The first statistical studies were carried out in the aftermath of World War II, when the United States was trying to figure out how to compare incomes between European countries in order to parcel out Marshall Plan aid. Simple exchange rate translations did not work, so economists took the typical market basket from each country and priced it in the others. One thing they found, and that has consistently turned up since then, is that per capita income figured at exchange rates is always quite different from that figured at purchasing power rates; moreover, the poorer the country, the greater the difference between the exchange rate translation and the actual purchasing power. Thus Italy, one of the poorest countries, showed a much greater difference than did Great Britain between income figured at purchasing power and income figured at exchange rates. (This makes the discrepancy between the Canadian and American figures all the more remarkable, since per capita income is only somewhat lower in Canada than the United States.)

Relative Purchasing Power Parity

Absolute PPP is best for comparing actual standards of living, but it never works well to predict exchange rates. More useful, though trickier, is to compare *changes* in purchasing power within two countries—in the short run tradable goods change more slowly than do price levels, so a percentage change in the price level might be a good indicator. To be more specific, the percentage change in the price level of one nation compared with the percentage change in the price level of another determines the alteration in the relative values of their currencies. As an example, suppose France had an inflation that doubled its wholesale price index and the United States had no inflation. Then if the French franc was initially at US$0.20, we would expect that it would now fall to US$0.10.

Usually, however, both nations are inflating at the same time, though some at more rapid rates than others. That is harder to do in the head and a formula is in order.

$$(Eq.\ 13.1)\ \frac{PPPa}{PPPb} \times \frac{Ca_0}{Cb_0} = \frac{Ca_1}{Cb_1}$$

where $PPPa$ = index of the purchasing power of currency *a* in the current period, with the base year set at 100.

$PPPb$ = index of purchasing power of currency *b* in the current period, with the base year set at 100.

Ca_o and Cb_o = value of currencies *a* and *b* in terms of each other (Ca/Cb) in the base period.

Ca_1 and Cb_1 = value of currencies *a* and *b* in current period.

As an example, suppose the United States had an inflation of 100% over a given period and France had one of only 50%. In the initial period the exchange rate was Fr5 = US$1.00. To handle this example, make both countries' price indices 100 in the base year and determine the new price index: the new French price index is 100 + 50 = 150, and the American is 100 + 100 = 200. (Be careful to express the figures on a base of 100, otherwise the formula would predict that a country with a 2% inflation would see its currency halve in value against a country with a 1% inflation!)

Then: $\quad \dfrac{150}{200} \times \dfrac{5}{1} = \dfrac{3.75}{1}$

The French franc would tend toward a value of 3.75 to the dollar.

Figure 13.4
PPP ESTIMATE AND REAL VALUE OF THE
CANADIAN DOLLAR IN U.S. DOLLARS

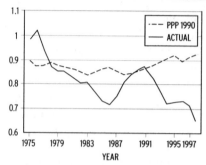

Note: The result of the exercise shows that the predicted values of the Canadian dollar are often far from the actual value. The PPP schedule takes the 1990 value of the Canadian dollar and figures inflation, using the GDP deflator, from that point. Where the broken line goes down, Canadian inflation exceeded American inflation, and where it goes up the reverse is true. The actual value of the Canadian dollar, however, was for the most part well under that predicted value, indicating a persistent undervaluation in terms of purchasing power.

Source: IFS, 1999, national accounts tables.

Gustav Cassel first put forth the theory of relative purchasing power parity in a series of articles published during World War I. The war had unleashed inflation, but this varied from nation to nation. Cassel figured that simple adjustment of exchange rates would restore the pre-war trading relations. The nations, however, attempted to restore pre-war gold parities and pre-war price levels and only adjusted exchange rates when they were forced to. Indeed, the creation of many new states in Central Europe and the destruction of older industries and establishment of newer ones may have fundamentally altered the relationship of domestic to international purchasing power, making purchasing power theory useless.

Cassel's ideas, whether followed or not, made good sense and the theory of purchasing power parity is in common use among bankers as an important indicator of foreign exchange movements. No modern bank report on foreign exchange is complete without some purchasing power observations, and they have a remarkably good track record in predicting the extent of exchange rate movements. The statistics can be frustrating and debatable at points, but the method has been remarkably durable. It must, of course, be used with considerable caution because, as the previous chapter explained, interest rates are also important determinants of exchange rates.

Figure 13.5

UNITED STATES AND CANADIAN REER AND NEER

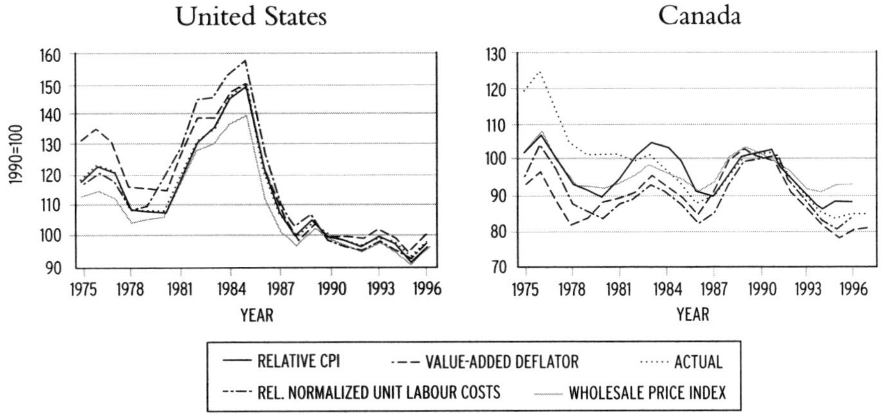

Source: *International Financial Statistics Yearbook*, real effective exchange rate indices.

Figure 13.4 shows purchasing power parity used to explain the difference in the values of the U.S. and Canadian dollars, and demonstrates both the strength and weakness of the PPP approach.* In this case, which students can easily reproduce, the figure uses the GDP deflators in the United States and Canada to compare purchasing power and runs the formula (Eq. 13.1) for every year.

The IMF provides a more complete and statistically sophisticated set of figures for the major industrial countries. The IMF figures take into account all the major trading partners of each country, weighted by the amount of trade with that country. British trade, for instance, is heavily with European countries, but also with the United States and Japan, so the calculation is somewhat more complicated. Moreover, the IMF uses several bases to compare price levels. Figure 13.4 used the GDP deflator, but the GDP deflator and also the consumer price index take into account many things that are not tradable. It does not make a great deal of difference to exports and imports if haircuts, hotel rooms, and restaurant meals are expensive or inexpensive because they do not enter trade. Some economists argue for the use of the wholesale price index, or its equivalent, because it measures mostly goods and contains more tradable items. Others argue that labor costs—expressed as the "normalized unit labor costs"—are the most important. (Unit labor costs are

---

* More complex modeling uses five or six trading partners, with different weights for each. The benefit of using U.S.-Canadian trade is that 75% of Canada's trade is with the U.S., and the other countries do not greatly affect the purchasing power parity.

the cost of labor per unit of output.) Not only is the string tied to a branch, but no one is certain which branch it is tied to!

Figure 13.5 shows the "real" values (known as the REER, or real effective exchange rate) of both the Canadian and American dollars, as figured by various indices. Rather than using a price in one currency, the "actual" value of the currency derives from another index, weighted again by the amount of trade with each country; the IMF calls this the nominal effective exchange rate, or NEER. Unlike PPP, which uses a base-year exchange rate, the real value calculation uses the current year's exchange rate.

The heavy black line is the NEER or actual exchange rate, weighted by the trading partners' rates. The index is set to 1990, so all lines converge there. In the American case, note how the actual rate and the various predictors move together. In no year was the NEER lower than all of the real indices and for the most part it was between the various measures of the real rate. We may not know to which branch the string that holds the stone is attached, but the branches all appear close.

The diagram based on the IMF data for the Canadian dollar looks more plausible than Figure 13.4, but it still shows a far greater difference than the American dollar between the actual rate and the various real rate measures. Should the Canadian dollar be 80% of or 100% of its 1990 value? The heavy black line indicating the NEER value only joins the pack of other figures in the early 1980s, indicating overvaluation before that period. The REER measures are also more dispersed than the American measures. This suggests that by 1996 the Canadian dollar was overvalued in relation to the consumer price index (CPI) and labor costs, but undervalued in relation to the value-added deflator and the wholesale price index. The branches on this particular tree appear to be far apart and it is no wonder, perhaps, that the Canadian dollar has always bounced around in the foreign exchange markets.

INTERNATIONAL AND DOMESTIC FINANCIAL MARKETS

One of the more important and in a sense more problematic issues is the degree of integration of the world financial markets. The press often gives the impression that global markets are highly integrated with vast sums sweeping over the world like tidal waves, while individual countries struggle helplessly to control their own financial markets, drowned one moment in capital inflows, left high and dry the next. However dramatic the picture, it has a considerable degree of hyperbole. Two key points in the argument have already been made in Chapter 10:

1. Net capital flows, as measured by current account imbalances and compared to GNP, are much lower today than a century ago.

2. Countries in which saving is high also have high levels of investment, and countries with low savings have low levels of investment. In other words, high savers are not transferring their savings to low-saving countries where, presumably, scarce capital would earn more.

To these two points, this chapter adds a third, entirely consistent with those two observations:

3. Interest rates are not the same between countries by any of numerous attempted measures. Differences in information, risk, scale, and scope of national markets mean that assets are not identical, so that partial and significant market segmentation remains.

Interest Rates Remain Different

While economists sometimes speak of *the* interest rate as if there were one such rate, they recognize it is a fiction and that they are speaking of a basic short-term rate, above which rises a structure of different rates. As in any capital market, particular interest rates accrue to particular assets because the assets differ in liquidity, term, risk of default, and availability of information. Is it reasonable to expect that a similar asset in several different countries will carry the same nominal interest rate? A glance at any summary of international financial conditions will show this to be false.

Why don't investors put all their money where nominal rates are the highest? The problem is that the currency might change in value. As Chapter 16 will show, it is quite possible to invest in another country without any foreign exchange risk, but the cost of covering the risk that the exchange rate will change is equal to the difference in the interest rates between the two countries. Only if international investors bear foreign exchange risk (or there is no risk) will nominal rates be the same. It follows that the difference in interest rates might be ascribed to foreign exchange risk.

The risk of exchange rate change, therefore, should be connected with purchasing power. This raises the possibility that real interest rates, which already incorporate price level changes, would tend to be the same. If interest rates in the United States were 7% and the inflation 3%, while in Canada interest rates were 7% and the inflation 1%, the real rates would be 4% and 6% respectively. Since the Canadian dollar would be expected to rise about 2% with a 2% lower inflation, the expected return on the Canadian dollar should be 9%. Funds would accordingly flow into Canada until the real interest rates between Canada and the United States were the same.

Figure 13.6
COMPARATIVE REAL BOND YIELDS

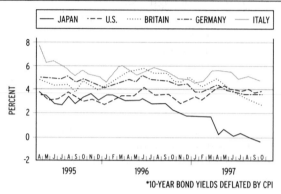

Source: The Economist, October 25, 1997.

The RODA/ROFA diagram explicitly recognizes that the returns are *expected* and carry in them an anticipation about potential exchange rate changes. Over the longer run, the relative purchasing power parity model implies that differences in changes in real purchasing power determine where the nominal rates settle. Another way to put this is that real exchange rates (the nominal rate minus the rate of inflation) should tend to be equal. Hence, ROFA should shift according to the percentage change in the price levels of the two countries, and real interest rates should be the same. Do real interest rates behave this way? No. Real interest rates, if anything, are more different than nominal rates, as Figure 13.6 shows.

The argument on real interest rates assumes that changes in purchasing power are the principal or only determinants of exchange risk and that the concern is long run. Several other factors are important, however, as was earlier demonstrated. The ability to service foreign debt, changes in productivity, or continued large savings-investment gaps could all change exchange rates without a direct relation to price level comparisons. Perhaps more important is that it is the *cost of the risk, not the risk itself,* that determines the premium. If the willingness to bear financial risks changes, riskier currencies will lose value whether or not their fundamentals have changed. A little more modeling can help illustrate these points.

A Model of the Funds Market

Chapter 10 discussed how the funds that reached the financial markets were the difference between income and absorption of particular households, firms,

Figure 13.7
LOANABLE FUNDS

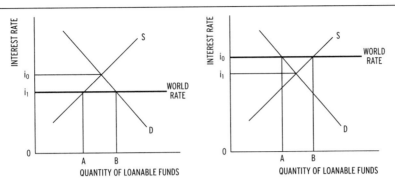

Note: Both panels in Figure 13.7 show that the demand and supply of loanable funds are sensitive to interest rate changes. As described above, if this were the entire market, the country would have an interest rate of i_o. When the country is open to the rest of the world, however, the story is different. For convenience, suppose this country is small enough that its borrowing or lending does not change the predominant world interest rates. The diagram can thus show the (hypothetical) world interest rate as a horizontal line. If the economy of the small country were entirely integrated financially with the world economy, the world interest rate would determine domestic interest rates. In the left panel, borrowers will not pay i_o if they can borrow at the world rate of i_1. At the lower world rate, they will borrow $0B$ of funds. Lenders, unable to get i_o, will not put as much on the market, limiting the supply of funds to $0A$. The result is that AB of funds comes from outside the country. In the right panel, the world interest rate is above the point where the domestic equilibrium would be. Since lenders can get a higher rate abroad, they lend $0B$. Borrowers, however, are constrained by the higher interest rate and borrow only $0A$. AB is the amount the country lends abroad.

and governments, and the demand for those funds arose from households, firms, and governments whose absorption exceeded their income. The decision to put funds on the market or to borrow funds is partially related to interest rates such that the loanable funds market can be expressed in a diagram. The higher the interest rate, the more people will be willing to place on the market. They will save more from their incomes and also may forgo some investment in their own homes in order to lend funds to others. Firms may find that projects they wished to undertake with retained earnings seem less advisable in light of higher returns on the capital markets. At the same time, of course, borrowing will fall as it becomes more expensive. These elements produce a characteristic loanable funds diagram like Figure 13.7. The supply and demand of loanable funds, in the absence of any international market, would produce an interest rate of i_o.

Recall also from Chapter 10 that the difference between funds lent and funds borrowed is also the difference between saving and investment and is the trade imbalance (the balance of goods, services, and income). Thus, trade deficits are always associated with inflows of capital and lower interest rates than there would otherwise be, and trade surpluses with the opposite conditions.

Figure 13.7 suggests intriguing implications for national income and policy. Given the locations (intercepts) and slopes of the supply and demand for funds, world interest rates determine the levels of domestic savings and investment (with implications for long-run economic growth), the investment-savings gap, and the trade imbalance. Given, further, that the country has significant respending effects and some unemployment, it also helps determine national income. In addition, it suggests that the principal effect of a shift in the supply or demand for funds is a change in the trade balance. If investors feel more positive and increase the amount they are willing to invest at any given interest rate, and domestic lenders are not willing to lend any more at the given interest rate, the demand for funds shifts and the supply does not. Instead of dampening the demand for new investment and stimulating some additional saving, the additional funds come from abroad and the country gets a larger trade deficit. A similar shift would happen if the government's deficit increased and its demand for funds rose. Figure 13.8 shows this effect.

For convenience, the country has no trade imbalance to start. An improved investment climate encourages firms to invest more at given interest rates and the demand for funds shifts from D to D_1. Without the international market available, interest rates would rise to $i_{(d)}$, the parentheses just to indicate it is not an allowed outcome in this diagram. Investment would therefore not rise to $0C$, but only to $0B$, and domestic saving would rise to $0B$. With the international market available, however, investors can borrow freely abroad and have no need to pay domestic savers any more. As a result, there is no more saving, but more investment, as imported funds rise to AC, an amount equal to the trade deficit. Other variations on the diagram are possible. Tax measures to increase saving, for instance, would shift the supply curve to the right.

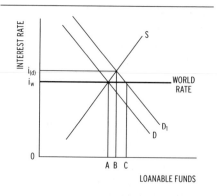

Figure 13.8

LOANABLE FUNDS, WITH INCREASED GOVERNMENT DEFICIT

Figure 13.9

LOANABLE FUNDS, WITH CURRENCY RISK PREMIUM

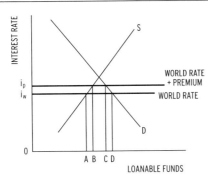

Note: Figure 13.9 shows a second line, world rate + premium (risk). This establishes an interest rate of i_p and, compared to Figure 13.7 in the left-hand panel, reduces the foreign borrowing from *AD* to *BC*. Even with a stable world interest rate, a country could find that changes in the risk premium altered its domestic interest rate, and with that the train of other changes enumerated above.

Figure 13.10

CHANGE IN RISK TOLERANCE

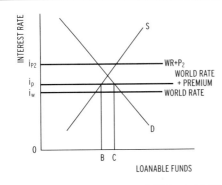

Note: The sudden change in tolerance for risk causes the world rate + premium $(WR + P)$ to rise to $WR + P_2$, and interest rates to rise to i_2. At these interest rates, demand for funds falls back to $0B$ and the supply of funds increases to $0C$, with a trade surplus instead of a trade deficit.

The problem with the models in Figures 13.9 and 13.10 is that they have interest rates that are the same between the country and the rest of the world, ignoring currency risk. To incorporate foreign exchange risk, Figure 13.9 adds a currency risk premium.

The model gives possible insight into what occurred in 1997-98 when an economic collapse in Thailand somehow led to collapses in several other Asian tigers and then to serious problems in virtually all world markets. Thailand's difficulties led investors worldwide to reassess their situations and caused the tolerance for risk to fall. As a result, all risky assets fell in value as a general *flight to quality*, as finance people call it, occurred. Not only currencies, but all less risky assets fell in value—stocks, particularly technology stocks, below-investment-grade bonds (junk bonds), and even higher-grade bonds in countries whose currencies became suspect. Figure 13.10 shows the change in the risk tolerance as a large increase in the risk premium. As a result, the country changes from having a trade deficit to having a surplus, but also experiences a decline in investment.

The American investment bank, J.P. Morgan, calculates an index of risk tolerance, working off the idea that the "appetite for risk" changes in more or less predictable patterns. While the prediction is still difficult, the work does suggest that when the stock and bond markets show less risk-taking activity, it also is reflected in movements away from the riskier currencies.[5]

Preferred Habitats and Segmented Markets

Not only do assets differ by risk, liquidity, and information; the market to which they sell differs as well. Buyers of securities differ in their abilities to evaluate particular sets of information, their need for liquidity, and their tolerance of risk. These differences serve to segment markets, turning what in the abstract is a single market into a series of partially overlapping markets. An asset might sell well to a well-defined group of buyers, for which the liquidity, risk, and informational challenges pose no particular problem, but when it moves out of the particular segment, it must offer higher rates to attract people for whom it poses ever-greater difficulties. To use another financial term, it has to lure buyers out of their *preferred habitats* into ones in which they are less comfortable.

The nature of the investment, hence its underlying risk, may be difficult for potential lenders to evaluate. Perhaps a core group really understands, say, the complexities of a new software company and the risks inherent in the business, and they might be willing to lend money at quite reasonable rates. As the company seeks to borrow beyond the core, however, costs rise because lenders have more trouble in evaluating the prospects of the company. If the underlying investment does not require specialized knowledge, then the instrument itself could. A complex derivative might seem forbidding, even though its actual risk could be quite low. It is far easier to understand a savings deposit or the purchase of a bond.

Buyers differ in the risk and kinds of risk they wish to tolerate. Some buyers are very nervous about how the values of some assets bounce around (assets with high volatility); others do not worry about that so long as they have a guaranteed return throughout the period. Buyers have different liquidity requirements, too. A retail store, setting aside its Christmas earnings in January, knows that it will need the money soon again. In contrast, a pension fund may not need the money for 30 years. Higher rates may entice nervous buyers to take greater risk or those in need of liquidity to become a little less liquid, but it is costly to the buyer and seller.

One way the market divides into segments is between one group of buyers that are sensitive to international interest rates and another group that are not. Call the first the *globalized segment* and the second the *insulated segment*. The globalized segment looks like the model shown in the figures above. The insulated segment, however, cannot take advantage of international interest rates in the same way. Consider why a great deal of the financial market may be insulated.

- Borrowers lack information on potential lenders in other countries, and the potential lenders have little information on the borrowers. If Trudy Truenorth drives across the Bluewater Bridge that links Sarnia, Ontario, with Port Huron, Michigan, and presents her plan for expanding her business to a bank or group of investors there, she will have far more difficulty in securing funds than if she talked to Ontario bankers. The banks and investors in Port Huron cannot easily—which is to say, cheaply—handle the evaluation of the project. It isn't that funds don't flow across borders, or that Trudy's bank might not borrow in New York and use some of the funds to lend to her, but that Trudy herself cannot borrow. Borrowing isn't as easy as picking up an electric toaster and taking it back. (Trudy would have no trouble depositing a check, however, although she might be surprised at the charges if it is a Canadian dollar check.)
- It is not only small investors that have difficulty; even large financial institutions specialize in their own country and are far more familiar with their own country's markets, securities, companies, and buyers than they are with other major markets. Such familiarity gives them a competitive advantage against foreign firms but limits their knowledge of other countries' markets.
- Instruments are not the same between countries, nor are markets. The principal short-term instrument in Canada, for instance, is a bankers' acceptance (in essence, a postdated check certified by the bank), not a T-bill. The market for bankers' acceptances is somewhat more liquid and active than that for Canadian T-bills. Indeed, probably the United States, Japan, and Great Britain are the only countries with T-bill markets large and vigorous enough to be the main short-term financial market in the country. This means that managers interested in foreign investment have to know the local markets and instruments as well as the companies. Otherwise, they may have difficulties with liquidity.

A segmented market model cuts the two markets apart and controls the amount of flow between them. Figure 13.11 shows a domestic market split into two segments, the globalized and the insulated. The globalized segment is very sensitive to international interest rates and behaves much as the open

Figure 13.11
INSULATED AND GLOBALIZED DOMESTIC MARKET SEGMENTS

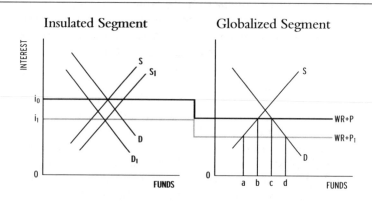

economy model shown above. When world interest rates fall, it imports more capital. Firms having access to the international market borrow from there and those financial investors that normally operate in the international market continue to do so, even though the returns are lower. So the import of capital and the trade deficit open up in the usual way.

The insulated market in the left panel is only insulated, not isolated. As the larger firms with access to international markets borrow there, some of their borrowing is shifted away from the insulated market. As lenders who formerly lent to the world market turn to higher domestic returns, more funds come on to the insulated segment. As a result, both the demand-and-supply curves shift and the interest rate in the insulated segment also falls. (The curves shift because the prices of competitive funds have shifted.). Figure 13.11 shows such a situation.

World price (plus any risk premium) is originally the black line at $WR + P$. The globalized segment of the market is importing bc of capital. The insulated segment has a higher interest rate at i_0. The black line shows that the two rates are different, which comes from the partial separation of the two markets. When world interest rates plus the premium fall to $WR + P_1$, capital imported rises to ad. Because some money that would otherwise have been borrowed in the insulated segment is now borrowed internationally, the demand for funds falls there from D to D_1. Because some funds that would normally have been placed in the international market are diverted to the insulated segment, the supply of funds rises to S_1 and the interest rate falls in the insulated segment. The diagram assumes that the extent of separation between the two markets continues to be the same, such that the difference between the interest rates in the two markets is the same. The gray line shows the two interest rates and the difference between them.

CONCLUSION

The enormous flows of funds through foreign exchange markets may mask the fact that the underlying net movement of funds from country to country is comparatively modest. Exchange rates, key in such transfers, retain elements of risk that are difficult to model or quantify. Both the interest parity and purchasing power parity models give insight into their movements, but neither alone or in combination appears to be a complete explanation of where short-run or long-run equilibria should lie. While the world financial markets are integrated, the degree of integration is not so great as to make interest rates the same between countries or to transfer savings from country to country on the scale (compared to GNPs) that it occurred a century ago. National financial markets still have substantial segments whose interest rates are separate from rates on world markets, and only respond partially to movements in international rates.

All this sets the stage for the introduction of monetary policy, the topic of the next chapter.

VOCABULARY AND CONCEPTS

Expected value
Foreign exchange reserves
Funds market
Interest rate parity
Intervention (in foreign
  exchange market)
Preferred habitat

Purchasing power parity
  Absolute
  Relative
RODA
ROFA
Segmented markets

QUESTIONS

1. Indicate what options a non-financial company has to make a payment in a foreign currency?
2. How do banks pay one another?
3. Try using a supply-and-demand foreign exchange diagram for the Mexican peso, worth about US$0.10. Since it is pesos that are being purchased, they go on the X-axis. Be careful about the Y-axis (pesos/$ or $/peso?). Show what would happen if interest rates rose in Mexico. Show what would happen if people feared the peso would fall in value? If the price of oil, a big Mexican export, rose?
4. The money traded on the foreign exchange market is hugely in excess of the amount of underlying payments that are made. Why is this so?
5. What was the authors' point in quoting Marshall?
6. Experiment with the interest rate parity model (RODA/ROFA). Use Figure 13.3 to find the following: (a) a rise in American interest rates; (b) a fall in Canadian rates; (c) indications of a bad wheat harvest in Canada; (d) an LDC crisis that will create a lot of "flight capital" looking for safe places to invest.
7. In May of 1999, the Canadian dollar rose to US$0.69 after being as low as 65 cents. The Bank of Canada then cut interest rates. Using the interest rate parity model, but with the Canadian dollar on the X-axis, show these changes.
8. Using expected value, explain how the expected value of a currency could fall, even though no one expects it to fall. Will it then fall?
9. Figure the following purchasing power parities, all based on the Mexican peso equaling 10 U.S. cents in 2000.
   a. By 2002 the U.S. has had 8% inflation and Mexico 16%.
   b. Now suppose the U.S. had 10% and Mexico 5%.
   c. With 1995 = 100, the price index in 2000 in the U.S. is 150 and the Mexican is 200. By 2000, the U.S. price index is 160 and the Mexican is 220.
10. Purchasing power parity is broadly true, but its measurement raises many problems. What are they?

11. A funds market diagram suggests that trade imbalances are, in a sense, the product of an imbalance between domestic saving and investment. The idea reinforces what Chapter 10 explained, but it adds an interesting dynamic. Explain how the supply of and demand for funds, combined with the funds available in the international market, determine the current account imbalance.

12. Simple observation shows that interest rates are not the same between countries. Explain how differences in risk can make markets different. Show what the effect of greater risk for a country's currency is on its borrowing and trade imbalance.

13. Use the theory of segmented markets to explain why interest rates differ between countries or among different markets within the same country.

NOTES

1. *The ABC of the Foreign Exchanges* is a marvelous book about how exchanges worked. George Clare published the first edition in 1892, and as of the mid-1960s George Crump was handling the 13th edition. A great number of libraries have older copies; they are fascinating reading for the economic antiquarian.

2. Against third currencies, the Canadian dollar, like virtually every other currency, is converted first into U.S. dollars and then into the third currency. For example, the Canadian buying yen purchases U.S. dollars and then buys yen with the U.S. dollars. See Rob Ogrodnick and Judy DiMillo, "Survey of the the Canadian foreign exchange and derivatives markets," *Bank of Canada Review* (Winter 1998-99): 3-28.

3. Alfred Marshall, *Principles of Economics* (1910), 425-26.

4. From "Treasury and Federal Reserve Foreign Exchange Operations," *Federal Reserve Bulletin* (April 1988): 210-11.

5. See "Time to whet investor's appetites," *The Economist,* February 24, 1996.

Chapter Fourteen

Money in the Global Economy

OBJECTIVES

OVERALL OBJECTIVE   To relate money and monetary policy to interest rates and economic activity and to examine the interplay between domestic and international monetary factors.

MORE SPECIFICALLY
- To frame the discussion by examining monetary theory, (1) showing the demand for liquidity, velocity approaches, and portfolio approaches and (2) connecting these models with previously developed models of the demand for funds and the AS/AD model.
- To show how flows of funds between countries can have a monetary effect if the central bank purchases and sells foreign exchange.
- To demonstrate how central banks that purchase and sell foreign exchange generally counterbalance the effects of their purchases with other monetary tools.
- To examine the role of money in correcting serious balance-of-payments difficulties.
- To illustrate the monetary problems created by large capital flows, and to further develop the monetary transmission mechanism, using Thailand as an example.
- To explore a model of external balance involving both fiscal and monetary policy.

....

To this point, money has stood in the shadows as the text has tried to look, in Leland Yeager's evocative phrase, "beyond the veil of money and prices."[1] But money, as does any veil, partially conceals, and thus has some very real

579

effects. To explore these effects in their global setting, this chapter first looks at money in national economies and then introduces the elements to make it an international analysis.

THREE WAYS OF LOOKING AT MONEY'S RELATION TO REAL OUTPUT

Money and Velocity

The most basic approach is that of money and the speed with which it is spent, or velocity. The model works best under the assumption that a predictable and reasonably constant relationship exists between an economy's stock of money and its total economic output. People spend money at a more or less given speed and the combination of the two produce the nominal GDP. So $MV = GDPn$—money times velocity equals nominal GDP. More fully, nominal GDP is the real GDP in a base year times the price level, here called P, so the formula is:

$MV = PY$

where M is the money stock, V is velocity,
P is the price level, and Y is the nominal GDP.

The sticking points with the velocity approach have been the constancy of velocity and the difficulty of defining the money stock. Perhaps 30 years ago it was an easier proposition. Funds that were ready to be spent had to be in the form of currency or checking accounts, and people had to go to their bank, broker, or life insurance agent to convert less liquid accounts into usable cash. When held as currency or checking account, the funds were ready to be spent, so the money supply (cash and checking accounts) was a reliable predictor of the amount of expenditure. Today, savings and money market accounts allow checks and often other forms of debit, and, even where they do not, a visit to an automatic teller machine or a home PC transfer can move the funds quickly. It is no longer obvious what can be counted as the ready pool of money that is to be spent. As a result, the different measures of money supply—M_1, M_2—have proliferated, and it is very difficult to establish a regular base or velocity. While it is quite obvious that a sharp increase in the money supply on almost any level of measurement is inflationary and a decrease usually deflationary, it appears more difficult to manage an economy's activity through the money supply alone.

In the 1970s and 1980s, some central banks tried to control their economies through setting a money supply as a target, but velocities proved to be quite unstable—that is, the relation of the money supply (however defined) with GDP was not as regular as the bankers expected or as it had been in the past. The benefit of such *monetarism*, as it was called, may have been as much political as economic in that it gave further reason for reducing what had been exceedingly high growth rates of money in the 1970s.

Money as Part of a Portfolio

A second way to look at money is to look at it as part of a portfolio. Instead of looking at three alternatives for holding assets—money, time deposits, and securities—think of a continuum ranging from money and highly liquid assets through longer-term bonds, stocks, and finally goods themselves. When the money supply rises, people find that their portfolio holds too much cash, so they shift into T-bills and bonds (depressing interest rates) and goods to build up the value of their physical assets. The lower interest rates stimulate investment and the greater purchases of durable goods raise consumption. The result is that AD shifts to the right. In some situations, too, the increase in money causes people to shift into foreign assets.

The Demand for Liquidity

A third way of understanding the connection of money with the real economy is the liquidity approach. Interest rates are the price of funds available for borrowing, but they are also the price of money. Money, in its function as a means of storing value in a liquid form, has a value somewhat different from and beyond what it actually buys. To build up a stock of money, households not only have to save beyond their own absorption, but they cannot lend to others all that they have accumulated. Consider two famous literary skinflints: Dickens's Ebenezer Scrooge and George Eliot's Silas Marner. Both lived penuriously despite their substantial incomes. But Scrooge transferred his claim on resources to others—for a price, of course. Marner, in contrast, liked to see his money pile up as coin that he would count up frequently, so neither he nor anyone else could exercise his claim on goods and services. Marner's *liquidity preference* was much higher than Scrooge's, indeed, considerably higher than normal.

The desire to hold money for itself poses problems for the economy because changes in that desire affect total spending. If people act like Marner, spending less than their income but not lending their claims on resources so that others may exercise them, aggregate demand falls. Scrooge, while unlikely to have caused a stampede in consumer spending, provided others

Figure 14.1
A DEMAND AND SUPPLY OF MONEY DIAGRAM

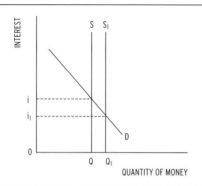

Note: The X-axis shows the amount of money and the Y-axis the real interest rate. The supply of money is vertical because the assumption here is that the monetary authorities can control it and that it is not sensitive to interest rates. The demand for money, sometimes called the demand for liquidity or D_L, is a downward sloping curve. An increase in the money supply from Q to Q_1 will lower interest rates from i to i_1.

with the means to absorb more than their incomes. Marner, however, let no one else use his claims. Too many Marners can lead to a decline in aggregate demand, and in turn, as Chapter 12 demonstrated, a decline in output, prices, or some combination of the two.

Liquidity is the speed with which an asset can be turned into cash. Whenever a household or firm lends money to someone else, it loses its ability to exercise its claim on the economy for the period of the loan. The time can range anywhere from a few days to many years. The interest on the loan pays for the lenders' loss of liquidity as well as for their saving—that is, their generation of an unused claim on resources. In the absence of interest, there would still be saving because people have to set something aside for emergencies and old age. In the absence of interest payments, however, a great deal of that saving would not be lent. Economics has therefore built up a series of models to deal with the demand for money.

To begin with, people hold money for its potential use, whether it is for emergencies, for the ordinary purchases of the week, as yet unexecuted, and sometimes just in anticipation that prices will fall. In more formal phrasing, the first use of money—emergencies—refers to the *precautionary motive* for holding money, the second the *transactions motive*, and the third the *speculative motive* for holding money. Typically, as an economy's wealth rises, people carry higher money balances. Without anyone being a miser, there is a kind of Marner effect as more funds are held in idle balances.

The motives for holding money are ways of explaining what lies behind velocity. If the demand for money itself rises, velocity will fall. Everyone becomes a bit of a Marner so the same amount of money will not sustain the same output as before.

Figure 14.2
EFFECTS OF AN INCREASED MONEY SUPPLY

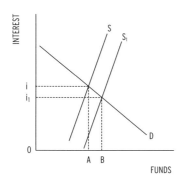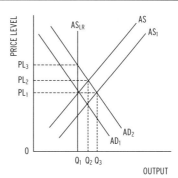

MODELING THE EFFECTS OF THE MONEY SUPPLY

The most standard diagram that illustrates the relation of the money supply to interest rates shows the supply of and demand for money, or in some models, the supply and demand for liquidity. Figure 14.1 shows it in its simplest form.

The idea behind Figure 14.1 is that when interest rates are low, firms and households are not particular about the size of their money balances because they are not forgoing much income. When interest rates are high, however, they will watch their money balances more closely and not let them get so high. Even old Silas Marner might have been tempted to lend some of the money from his chest if interest rates were high enough.

Figure 14.2 shows the connection between increases in money and aggregate demand. The left panel shows an increase in the supply of loanable funds that was stimulated by the increase in reserves and money. As new money comes into the system, loanable funds rise and nominal interest rates fall. Whether *real* interest rates fall or not depends on what happens to output and the price level, as will be discussed below. In turn, aggregate demand shifts outward. Figure 14.2 shows this in diagrammatic form.

The shift in AD has three possible outcomes. (1) It produces a mixture of price and income effects and the new equilibrium is where AD_2 crosses the AS curve, such that prices rise to PL_2 and output rises to Q_2. (2) It fails to stimulate income at all, running into a vertical long-run AS curve, the AS_{LR}; in this case prices rise to PL_3 but output remains at Q_1. (3) The economy is expanding already and a shift in AD merely accommodates that expansion. The expanded economy means that output is greater at any price level, so the diagram has an AS_1 to show that expansion. The long-run AS curve, not shown, would be at Q_3. If the AS curves have shifted, the price level would not rise.

583

MARKETS FOR FUNDS AND MARKETS FOR LIQUIDITY

As noted at the outset of this chapter, the two interest rates—that in the market for liquidity and that in the funds market—have to be the same. That equalization comes about through the income and price level mechanisms just described. If the central bank adds just enough money to replace what Silas Marner has set aside, other people will use Silas's claims on resources. If it adds more than what Silas took out and the increase produces an income effect, income rises and, with a rise in income, savings rise, as shown in Figure 12.6. In that sense, the new money produces new loanable funds, which create their own savings. Silas does not get any return, but whoever creates the new money gets it.

If, on the other hand, the extra money increases prices rather than real savings, the *real* money supply does not rise. The real money supply is the nominal money supply deflated by the price index, so if the money supply is $100 billion and it rises to $110 billion in nominal terms, but the inflation is 10%, the real money supply is unchanged. While initially borrowers may have had an advantage in that nominal interest rates fell before lenders realized an inflation was in progress, once lenders came to anticipate the inflation they demanded an *inflation premium* to cover the increase in the price level. In this example, it would be 10% plus whatever they were getting on the loan. Borrowers are willing to pay the extra premium because they realize that the goods they produce will sell for 10% more. But, other than a short burst of activity while the economy adjusts, nothing real changes.

Additional money, then, can serve to replace money that is hoarded, allowing the claims of the hoarder to be exercised by another party. In some situations, new money may stimulate income and output, producing new claims on resources that can be exercised without raising the price level. To the extent that prices rise, the nominal interest rate will rise with the price level change. The interest rate in the funds market through these three mechanisms comes to be the same as that in the liquidity market.

Another element in the picture is the velocity of money. The demand for money can alter velocity, but *monetarists* have held that velocity is fairly stable and are interested in more long-run effects. For expositional clarity, the examples given with Marner and Scrooge carry the presumption that velocity does not change. If increases in velocity and/or a falling price level came as Marner stashed his hoard, total *real* spending need not fall and no money need be added. Suppose the Marners of the economy stashed 10% of the money supply, but everyone just cut down the amount of money they held as cash and checking accounts, yet spent the same amount; velocity—GDP/MS— would rise by 10%. If velocity did not rise, a lower price level would also neutralize the effect of hoarding. It is unlikely, however, that either velocity or price level changes would fully compensate for the increased hoarding of money.

MONETARY POLICY

Central banks can exercise some control over interest rates and the money supply, attempting to keep an economy growing without significant inflation. After the severe inflations of the 1970s, monetary authorities, acting on the advice of monetarists, began to emphasize control over the money supply itself as their principal target. The idea was to keep a money supply growing at about the rate of the economy. If demand for investments rose, they would let the interest rates rise, and if the demand fell, let the interest rates fall. As in the Silas Marner analogy, they would replace just as much money as he put in his trunk, and perhaps a little more to enable the economy to purchase the larger potential output that occurred as AS shifted outward.

One of the principal problems that arose was what to count as the money supply. The narrow definition is always currency plus checking deposits, but in recent years even checking deposits have become blurred with the introduction of checkable savings accounts and checkable money market funds. Moreover, in practice the banks had to be concerned with changes in the demands for liquidity. If they cannot predict what Silas is putting in his chest—or how long he intends to keep the new coins there—they cannot accurately predict how much money is the right amount.

In recent years many central banks have turned to targeting inflation. New Zealand, Canada, and Britain have specifically noted inflation targets, while Germany and several other continental countries have implicitly done so. Rather than being concerned about the money supply, the banks try to control interest rates such that prices are stable. If they can keep the economy with low inflation, they know that, whatever Silas puts in his trunk and however rapidly potential GDP is growing, they are allowing the right amount of money. In a sense, inflation targeting finesses—gets around—the question of what money supply to choose and what velocity to count on.

NATIONAL MONEY SUPPLIES AND GLOBAL FLOWS

The critical link between national money supplies and international money flows is the extent to which the monetary authorities purchase or sell foreign exchange themselves. As Chapter 13 illustrated, monetary authorities frequently do so, mostly to influence the value of their currencies in the foreign exchange markets. While they may not be attempting to hold their currency to a particular value, they still do not want to see it soar or plummet.

How International Money Flows Affect Countries' Money Supplies

A closer look at the underlying banking process helps to show the connection between the international flows and the domestic money supplies.

TRANSACTIONS WITH NO INTERVENTION

Consider for a moment how a check in dollars sent to a British bank clears. The mechanism is not the same as a normal domestic check sent on to the central bank. Suppose, as in the example in Chapter 13, that the American firm Knight Stillman imports a considerable amount of whiskey from Olde Reekie Distilleries of Edinburgh and sends Reekie a check for $1.5 million. Reekie deposits that check in its British bank, Lloyds, receiving credits for £1 million at the exchange rate of US$1.50 = £1.00. What does Lloyds do with the check? If Lloyds had received sterling, it would be no problem, for it would just send the sterling check on to the Bank of England, where it would receive credit, and the Bank of England would debit the bank on which it was drawn. Lloyds cannot send its dollar checks to the Bank of England, however. The Bank of England holds no account for the American bank on which the check was drawn and will not credit a British bank for foreign currency it holds.

Unable to use the Bank of England for clearing the check, Lloyds will deposit the check in an American bank. The American bank has a regular checking account for Lloyds and credits the check to that account in the same way it would any other depositor. In some cases that American bank may be a Lloyds subsidiary, for most of the major foreign banks have operating subsidiaries in the United States—and most major American banks have subsidiaries in London and other financial centers. When a subsidiary is not available, or not convenient, foreign banks have working relationships with numerous American banks, called *correspondent* banks, which establish ordinary deposit accounts for them. Once the check enters the banking system it was issued in, it clears normally.

The T-account for the commercial banks shows the British end of this set of transactions. Lloyds credits Reekie with £1 million (B1) and uses the dollars as backing, increasing its foreign exchange assets by £1 million (A1). But the T-account also shows a decline of £1 million in Other Depositors' accounts (B2). Why does that come about? It occurs because at this point the banking system is fully loaned out—that is, the commercial bank reserves can support no more deposits. If, for instance, the British reserve requirement were 10%, then 10% of all deposits must be in the form of reserves. If the deposits rise but reserves do not, the banking system must build up its reserves by reducing its lending. The T-account shows that process, with loans down

586

Table 14.1

BRITISH COMMERCIAL BANKS' T-ACCOUNT

Assets			Liabilities		
A1	FX	+ £1 mn	B1	Olde Reekie	+ £1 mn
A2	Loans (Net	− £1 mn ± 0)	B2	Other Depositors (Net	− £1 mn ± 0)
C1	Reserves	+ £1 mn	D1	Other Depositors	+ £1 mn
C2	Loans	+ £1 mn			
C3	[Loans	+ £9 mn]	D2	[Other Depositors	+ £9 mn]
E1	Reserves	− £1 mn	F1	Other Depositors	− £1 mn
E2	[Loans	− £9 mn]	F2	[Other Depositors	− £9 mn]

by £1 million (A2), as are deposits (B2). The net result is that total deposits in sterling (British pounds) neither rise nor fall.*

The T-account for the Bank of England shows no activity because it is not involved. Even if Lloyds sold its £1 million deposit to another British bank, such as Barclays, all the Bank of England would do would be to credit Barclays and debit Lloyds, still making no net change in liabilities or assets, as G and H show.

The Bank of England Intervenes

Now suppose that the Bank of England finds that the pound is rising on the foreign exchange market and it does not want it to do so. It therefore *intervenes in the foreign exchange market*, entering the market and buying the $1.5 million from Lloyds. When it gets the dollars, it credits Lloyds with the £1 million and uses the foreign exchange it gained to back that credit. The Bank of England's T-account shows its liabilities to the commercial banks rising by £1 million (J), and the Bank's assets (held as foreign exchange, normally as T-bills in other countries) rising also by £1 million (i).

---

* Where banks have low or no reserve requirements like British banks or Canadian banks, they keep far less than 10% as reserves. The money multiplier is constrained more by the size of currency and withdrawals than by reserve requirements. Nonetheless, the general point is still valid. Every additional deposit created will create additional currency withdrawals, forcing the banks to use their own reserves to buy currency from the central bank. To maintain their essential reserves, they still have to sell off foreign assets.

Table 14.2

THE BANK OF ENGLAND'S T-ACCOUNT

Assets			Liabilities		
G		$\pm$ o	H		$\pm$ o
I	FX	$+ £1$ mn	J	Commercial Banks	$+ £1$ mn
K	T-bills	$- £1$ mn	L	Commercial Banks	$- £1$ mn

The Bank of England's purchase of foreign exchange has the same effect on the money supply as its purchase of Treasury bills or bonds from the banks. Every time it buys a pound's worth of foreign exchange, it credits the bank with *new* reserves of a pound. The middle section—I—of the commercial banks' T-account shows the reserves of the commercial bank up (C1). Initially, this allows Lloyds to make new loans of £1 million (C2). The higher loans create new deposits, shown as *other deposits* in D1. The new reserves, however, are *high-powered money* (part of the monetary base) and will sustain deposits worth a multiple of their amount. If we again assume the British banks want to keep 10% of their deposits as reserves, the £1 million in new reserves would support £10 million in new deposits, which shows as an additional £9 million to the £1 million on the first round (D2). To create these deposits, the banking system issued £9 million in new loans (C3). Both figures showing the potential expansion (C3 and D2) are in brackets.

Counterbalancing Monetary Policy: Foreign Exchange Sterilization

When central banks expand the money supply through foreign exchange purchases, they often offset that monetary impact by selling T-bills. Were they not to do so, they fear the unwanted expansion of the domestic monetary base would create too much money. Continue following the T-account above by supposing that the Bank of England, although it wanted to keep the pound from rising, did not want the money supply to rise. The Bank could then *sell* T-bills to its commercial banks, removing the new reserves at the same time it is creating them. The T-account shows the Bank of England's assets falling by £1 million as it sells off T-bills (K). (Its total portfolio of assets has now changed, since it now holds more foreign exchange and fewer T-bills, but the portfolio's value is the same as it was before the Bank intervened to purchase the foreign exchange.) As the British commercial banks purchase the T-bills, the Bank of England debits their accounts (L).

Figure 14.3

CHANGES IN CANADIAN MONETARY AUTHORITIES' HOLDINGS OF
FOREIGN EXCHANGE ASSETS AND CLAIMS ON THE GOVERNMENT*

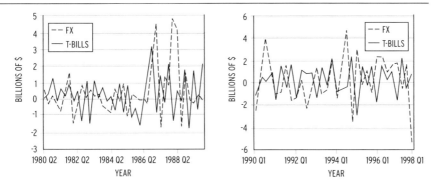

Note: The accordion pattern, the solid line moving opposite to the broken line, shows that sales of foreign exchange were generally partially matched by purchases of T-bills, and vice versa.

On the commercial banks' T-accounts, the effect of the Bank of England's activity is to reduce reserves at E1, reduce deposits by £1 million at F1 (assuming the Bank of England purchased from a depositor), and reduce any actual or potential expansion of money, shown at E2 and F2. The central bank thereby reverses the expansionary round activity and the potential monetary expansion shown under C and D. The act of removing the new reserves created by purchasing foreign exchange carries the antiseptic name of *sterilization.*

To examine what would happen if Lloyds had issued a check so that Olde Reekie could buy something from the United States and the Bank of England had intervened to keep the price of sterling from falling, just reverse all the signs. The result should show a monetary contraction. If the Bank of England purchased T-bills, the contraction would be reversed.

---

* The phrase "monetary authorities" here refers to both the Bank of Canada and the Canadian Treasury Department. The Bank of Canada sends its foreign exchange holdings (normally in the form of foreign treasury bills) to the Treasury, which in turn gives the Bank of Canada Canadian T-bills. A person looking at the regular reports from the Bank of Canada cannot perceive how much of its "claims on the government" came from purchases of T-bills or other Canadian government assets and how much from purchase of foreign assets. *International Financial Statistics*, however, distinguishes the holdings by referring to "monetary authorities" and not double-counting. The same is true in the United States, if the Federal Reserve turns over foreign exchange to the Treasury. Some of the "claims on government" in the tables are bonds, not bills, but the vast bulk are T-bills.

Figure 14.4
CHANGES IN FOREIGN EXCHANGE HOLDINGS OF BANK
OF CANADA AND COMMERCIAL BANK RESERVES

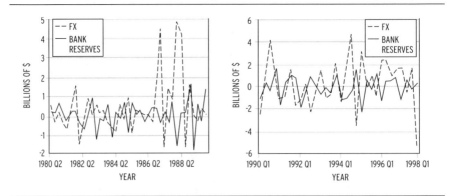

PREVALENCE OF MONETARY COUNTERBALANCING

Monetary counterbalancing is a very common—indeed, routine—practice. The quarterly Canadian figures on foreign exchange accumulation and monetary reserves through the 1980s and 1990s, a period when the Bank of Canada sometimes bought and sometimes sold foreign exchange, show an accordion-like pattern. Figure 14.3 shows the pattern on a quarterly basis, between 1980 and 1997. While every quarter does not have a counterbalancing pattern, the great majority of them do. The Bank of Canada's assets were, of course, growing over this period so the counterbalancing was not always complete.

The size of the foreign exchange that the Bank of Canada accumulates or depletes over a year is very large in comparison to the Canadian monetary base. In the U.S. dollar crisis of 1987 and 1988, the Bank of Canada built up its holdings of foreign exchange by $11 billion; Canadian commercial bank reserves were about $6 billion and reserve requirements were about 5%. Had Canada failed to counterbalance the effect of all these purchases, reserves would have tripled and the money supply could have risen 20 times that amount—$440 billion. Of course, the Bank of Canada allowed no such thing. As Canada's reserve requirements fell to zero in the 1990s, bank reserves fell and the potential impact of small changes in them increased. Often the swings in foreign exchange holdings on a quarterly basis exceeded the amount of Canadian bank reserves. The Bank of Canada was not about to let bank reserves swing so wildly as its holdings of foreign assets. As Figure 14.4 shows, bank reserves moved in a very different pattern—neither the same nor opposite. As a consequence of the counterbalancing activities, bank reserves are far less volatile than the Bank of Canada's holdings of foreign exchange.

Table 14.3

CONTROLLING AN OUTFLOW OF FOREIGN EXCHANGE (BILLIONS)

European Central Bank			European Commercial Banks		
	Assets	Liabilities		Assets	Liabilities
FX	− 2	− 2 CBD*	Reserves	− 2	− 2 Reserves
Advances	+ 1	+ 1 CBD	Reserves	+1	+1 Advances
Securities	+ 1	+ 1 CBD	Securities	− 1	
(Repos)			Reserves	+1	

*   commercial bank deposits

COUNTERBALANCING IN COUNTRIES WITHOUT BIG T-BILL MARKETS

North American students are familiar with monetary policy that works through the T–bill markets, but most countries in the world do not have T–bill markets that are large and liquid enough for a central bank to execute monetary policy. Indeed, the United States, Britain, Canada, and to a lesser extent New Zealand and Australia are probably the only countries that use T–bills as their principal tools. Most other countries use advances to their commercial banks or *repossession agreements*, called *repos*, where the central bank purchases for a short period of time a commercial bank's liquid assets (T–bills, other short-term assets) and then sells them back to the commercial bank.

Suppose, for instance, the new European Central Bank (ECB) experienced an outflow of foreign exchange and wished to reduce its impact on European commercial banks. Table 14.3 demonstrates how this would be done.

In the first line, the outflow of foreign exchange is reflected in the ECB's decline in foreign exchange assets and in the commercial banks' loss of 2 billion in reserves. This could cause the money supply to fall precipitously, so the ECB provides advances of 1 billion. Since it is the creditor and lending the money, the advances are its asset and the liability of the commercial banks. But the advances allow the commercial banks to increase their reserves by 1 billion. To further supplement its action, the ECB makes a repossession agreement with various commercial banks, taking their securities as assets, and crediting them with 1 billion additional reserves. The result is that the banking system now has as many reserves as before the foreign exchange outflow. The central bank's use of advances and repos has allowed the same kind of counterbalancing effect as does the purchase of T–bills.

Table 14.4

EASING AND TIGHTENING MONEY (MILLIONS)

	Bank of Canada		Canadian Commercial Banks	
	Assets	*Liabilities*	*Assets*	*Liabilities*
FX	− 100	− 100 CBD*	Reserves − 100	− 100 Deposits
	+ 1	− 100 Gov. dep.	Reserves + 100	+ 100 Gov. dep.
		+ 100 CBD		

* commercial bank deposits

Some countries manipulate where they place the government accounts or accounts of government-owned financial institutions such as agriculture banks or savings banks. Canada, for instance, can hold government balances either at the Bank of Canada or in the commercial banks. When the Bank of Canada wants to ease money, it shifts funds into the commercial banks' accounts and when it wants to tighten money it shifts the government accounts back to itself.

The Bank of Canada experiences a loss of \$100 million in foreign exchange. The banks experience a drop in their reserves and deposits of \$100 million. To remedy this situation quickly, the Bank of Canada moves \$100 million of government deposits from its accounts into the commercial banks' accounts. This restores the banks' reserves.

THE ROLE OF MONEY IN CORRECTING SERIOUS BALANCE-OF-PAYMENTS DIFFICULTIES

The monetary account of the balance of payments shows how much foreign exchange the monetary authorities of the country purchased or sold. Since every purchase the central bank makes of foreign currency generates additional reserves, the monetary account is also a measure of the amount of bank reserves generated in the period covered. When private capital inflows do not cover the entire current deficit, the monetary account shows the country sold foreign exchange. (Recall that it is a positive sign on the balance of payments.) When private capital outflows do not reach the level of the current account surplus, the country accumulates foreign exchange. Consider the monetary implications of this relationship.

FOREIGN EXCHANGE AND BANK RESERVES: A CLARIFICATION

The meaning of *foreign exchange reserves* and *domestic banking reserves* sometimes can be a bit confusing. Foreign exchange reserves are the assets a country's monetary authorities hold, enabling them to buy up their own currency, if needed, when its value slumps on the foreign exchange market. These assets, as we saw in the chapter on the balance of payments, are largely Treasury bills and other short-term assets of other major countries, but also include various deposits with the International Monetary Fund, and, as a secondary reserve, gold. Such reserves, along with T-bills and other claims on the domestic government, are part of the assets of the monetary authorities.

Banking reserves are reserves of the commercial banks; they are part of their assets and defined as vault cash—the currency in the banks and their automatic teller machines, and deposits with the central bank (or Fed). As such, they are liabilities of the monetary authorities. They do not include foreign exchange.

- A current account deficit not fully financed from funds coming into the financial account leads to a decline in both foreign exchange and monetary reserves. When it is not fully counterbalanced, this leads to a contraction of the money supply.
- A current account surplus not fully used in private placement of funds abroad leads to an increase in both foreign exchange and monetary reserves. Not fully counterbalanced, this leads to an expansion of the money supply.

Now consider the consequences. In the first case, the money supply falls, which would trigger higher interest rates, lower aggregate demand, and a decline in income, the price level, or some of both. If the price level falls, that will make imports more expensive and export cheaper, which will tend to improve the trade balance. That is:

$$C\&F{\downarrow} \rightarrow R_{FX}{\downarrow} \rightarrow R_M{\downarrow} \rightarrow MS{\downarrow} \rightarrow i{\uparrow} \rightarrow AD{\downarrow} \rightarrow PL{\downarrow} \rightarrow M{\downarrow}, X{\uparrow} \rightarrow C{\uparrow}\&F$$

This is to say that the current and financial accounts (*C&F*) fell, leading to a decline in the monetary authorities' reserves of foreign exchange (R_{FX}), leading to a decline in monetary reserves (R_M), which caused interest rates (*i*) to rise. With higher interest rates, aggregate demand (*AD*) fell. Being on a vertical AS curve, the price level (*PL*) declined, making imports (*M*) more expensive, which caused them to fall, and exports (*X*) become cheaper, causing them to rise. In turn, the current account improves. (The velocity of money approach moves directly from the decline in the money supply to the price level change.)

The mechanism just described has been known for over two centuries. Called the *price-specie mechanism*, it acted to describe the way economies responded to flows of gold and silver (known as *specie*). In the days of the gold standard (see Chapter 17), a country's foreign exchange reserves were gold reserves. Economists perceived that when gold reserves rose, the price level rose, and when they fell, the price level fell.

But the price-specie mechanism had a hitch. Gold outflows were usually accompanied not by immediate changes in the price level but by financial panics and recessions—that is, the outflow caused income rather than prices to fall. Since imports decline when income declines, a decline in aggregate demand causes imports to decline, so the flow would appear:

$$C\&F\downarrow \ \to \ R_{FX}\downarrow \ \to \ R_M\downarrow \ \to \ MS\downarrow \ \to \ i\uparrow \ \to \ AD\downarrow \ \to \ Y\downarrow \ \to \ M\downarrow \ \to \ C\uparrow\&F$$

Another consequence of the outflow of capital was that an increase in interest rates would cause an inflow or slow the outflow of capital. Hence, a great deal of the adjustment would come through the capital account. To wit:

$$C\&F\downarrow \ \to \ R_{FX}\downarrow \ \to \ R_M\downarrow \ \to \ MS\downarrow \ \to \ i\uparrow \ \to \ C\uparrow\&F$$

Long before World War I, European central banks had practiced some degree of counterbalancing activity, increasing their lending to commercial banks when gold flowed out of their countries and decreasing the lending when gold flowed back in. Such activities were not usually enough to completely offset the capital flows but were sufficient to moderate their impact and to avoid sharp financial panics. One of the principal ideas behind the creation of the Federal Reserve System in the United States in 1913 was to have an institution that could moderate the effects of the capital flows and the sharp financial panics that followed the outflows. Indeed, with the single, enormous exception of the 1930-33 crisis, the United States has not since experienced any devastating credit crunches or unwarranted monetary expansions attributable to foreign capital flows. (Some economic historians have argued that if President Andrew Jackson had not closed the Second Bank of the United States—to some extent a central bank—the United States would not have experienced the sharp financial panic of 1837.) The use of the central bank to moderate the effect of international currency flows is clear in the preamble to the Bank of Canada Act of 1935, which states that the Bank's purpose is:

> to control and protect the external value of the national monetary
> unit and to mitigate by its influence fluctuations in the general level of

production, trade, prices and employment, so far as may be possible within the scope of monetary action....

The choice of the word "mitigate" is significant. It was not supposed to counteract the effect of capital flows but to make them milder.

How Monetary Policy Affects Trade and Capital Movements

When a country has an inflation larger than those of its trading partners, it has more difficulty exporting and finds imports look cheaper, so tends to develop a trade deficit, as Chapter 13 discussed. The usual cause of large inflation is an overexpansion of money so it is not hard to connect monetary policy with trade deficits. Similarly, very tight monetary policy that keeps inflation rates down usually improves a country's trade balance against its partners, whose inflations are larger.

The portfolio view of money adds another element: as the money supply rises, households and firms find their money balances are too large. They try to shift their portfolios into less liquid or more secure assets. Not only does the demand for goods rise, increasing aggregate demand, but the demand for foreign assets rises. The expected return on foreign investment rises, as in Figure 13.4. Capital starts to flow out of the country. Suppose monetary authorities (1) do not let the currency fall in value but keep buying it up on the foreign exchange market and (2) keep counteracting the contractionary effect of their actions. Unless good fortune strikes, the country is going to be in for a rough time.

To illustrate these ideas, suppose that Brazil's currency, the real, is worth US$1.00, but that monetary expansion, while modest for Brazil, is still larger than that in Brazil's major trading partners. Brazilians with extra cash will try to move it to safer assets because the *expected return* has risen due to the increased probability that foreign currency will appreciate against the real. Figure 14.5 shows the situation with an interest-rate parity model. As the probability that the real will fall in value rises, the return on foreign investment rises. With speculation against the real rising, the central bank can

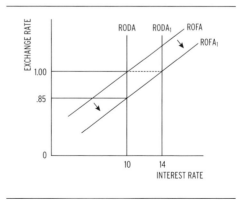

Figure 14.5

VALUE OF A CURRENCY FALLS WITH EXCESS MONEY

only maintain the real at $1.00 if it raises interest rates to 14%. Otherwise, the real will fall to 85 cents.

Prime interest rates in Brazil begin at around 10%. They do not change much as the money supply expands because people demand an inflation premium. $ROFA_1$ represents the changed expectations about the return on foreign as compared to domestic assets. This will push the exchange rate down to US$0.85. If the Brazilian central bank intervenes in the foreign exchange market to keep it up, it must also be sure that domestic interest rates rise to 14% (at $RODA_1$) or else the outflow will continue until it pushes the real down to 85 cents.

Money and Floating Exchange Rates

When central banks allow their countries' exchange rates to float, they neither buy nor sell foreign exchange. This leaves their money supplies unaffected. Instead, if the value of their currency changes, the capital and current account balances have to offset each other exactly since the monetary account will necessarily be zero under such circumstances. Suppose that a rise in several commodity prices increased Canada's exports by 20%. If all the exporters bring back their foreign exchange and buy Canadian dollars, they must buy the dollar deposit from an existing holder, since the central bank will not create any more deposits. The Canadian dollar will rise in value. The higher value of the dollar will make exporting less profitable and encourage more imports. The mechanism is thus:

$$\$\uparrow \; (X\downarrow - M\uparrow) \; \downarrow$$

The flow diagram shows that the currency ($) rises in value and discourages exports, causing them to fall, and stimulates imports, causing them to rise, and thereby reduces the trade surplus. Unless some exporters decide to leave some of their currency abroad in the form of short-term investments, the process will end up offsetting any existing imbalance in the financial accounts. A trade deficit, unaccompanied by a matching inflow of capital on the financial account, would produce the opposite.

$$\$\downarrow \; (X\uparrow - M\downarrow) \; \uparrow$$

As means of correcting payments imbalances, depreciation and appreciation of a currency are much more direct than price-level or income changes. The monetary effects, if any, come from how the changing trade balance alters economic activity and in turn the demand for money, as Chapter 15 explains.

THE PROBLEM OF LARGE CAPITAL FLOWS

What should countries do when they receive very large capital inflows such that the inflow of foreign exchange rising from their capital account overwhelms a modest current account deficit or adds to a current account surplus? Many of the East Asian countries (and some Latin American ones) had only modest trade deficits but huge capital inflows. The United States in the 1920s had trade surpluses and huge capital inflows—partly private and partly from foreign governments as repayments on money lent them during World War I.

The conundrum is this: the foreign exchange coming in is a claim on the resources of foreign countries and the only way to exercise that claim is to spend the foreign exchange. If the central bank buys it all up and then just holds it as foreign exchange reserves in the form of foreign T-bills, then the bank earns a minimal interest rate while the foreign investors reap a substantial reward. It was even more dramatic in the old days when the reserves would be held as gold, which paid no interest. If the foreign capital inflow does not stimulate a larger trade deficit, it does not alter the investment-savings gap. Economists sometimes say that this means that no *real transfer* has taken place, in the sense that there is no net borrowing of goods and services. The country does not invest a larger portion of GNP than it had previously. All that has happened is that the central bank has picked up foreign assets in exchange for allowing foreign investors to increase their ownership of domestic assets.

When central banks counterbalance their purchase of foreign exchange with the sale of Treasury bills or reduction in bank advances, they create a fiscal effect. As the central bank's portfolio changes from holding high-yielding domestic assets to low-yielding foreign assets, the central bank makes less money. Since the surpluses of central banks go into government coffers, the governments lose what is often an important source of revenue.[*]

The IMF estimates that, in the 1990s, $575 billion worth of capital inflow into developing countries—just about half of the total inflow—ended up as foreign exchange reserves. The owners of the funds received high returns, while the governments received only the T-bill rates of the developed countries. The cost of the difference between the returns foreigners received on these assets and the interest the monetary authorities received amounted to around $10 billion.[2]

---

[*] In some countries the central banks themselves sell securities to their own banks. This is a liability on the central bank, balanced by a reduction in its holdings of commercial bank reserves. The central banks, of course, must pay a much higher interest rate than they are receiving from the foreign deposits.

Figure 14.6
THAI FOREIGN EXCHANGE RESERVES

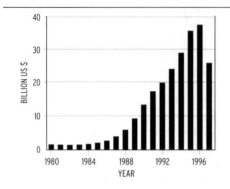

Note: The scale on Figure 14.6 is in dollars and the others in baht, which is why holdings of foreign exchange fall in 1997 in 14.6 and not in 14.7. *IFS* accounts are not complete, so the assets do not normally quite match the liabilities.

Figure 14.7
KEY CENTRAL BANK ASSETS

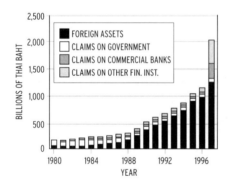

Figure 14.8
KEY CENTRAL BANK LIABILITIES

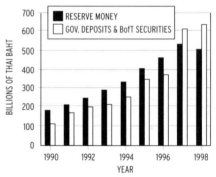

Source: All data for Figures 14.6-14.9 from *IFS*, 1999. Foreign exchange reserves and central bank assets and liabilities are found in "monetary authorities"; commercial bank data are under "deposit money banks"; more money supply information is in "monetary survey."

Thailand in the 1990s

Thailand's experience in the 1990s serves to illustrate many of the points raised above—how the monetary systems respond to a heavy increase in private investment, how real transfers take place, and how, ultimately, the economy can get into deep trouble. Chapter 12 introduced some of the problems that faced the Thai economy in the 1990s, noting that the baht was held to a value of about four U.S. cents until a crisis in 1997, and that private capital inflows were heavy. The inflow of capital allowed Thailand to augment its otherwise considerable domestic savings. The question here is how the monetary authorities reacted. Thailand had a trade deficit throughout most of this period but, year in and year out, the capital inflows were larger than the trade deficits, the difference being made up by the Bank of Thailand's purchases of foreign exchange, which Figure 14.6 shows.

Figure 14.7 shows that the purchases of foreign exchange led to a considerable expansion of the assets of the Bank of Thailand. The white parts of the bars are the foreign exchange, while the other assets—government securities and advances to the banks and other financial institutions—were small until the 1997 crisis. Since the Bank held only a few government securities (claims on government) and had few advances to banks (claims on commercial banks and on other financial institutions), it could not use the counterbalancing tools that North American and European banks use. It was, however, partially successful.

Figure 14.8 shows how the Bank tried to control the monetary expansion. Reserve money includes currency and commercial bank reserves, the latter the base for the expansion of loans. While reserve money did double, the Bank kept it from expanding even more by keeping all new government deposits at the central bank and by selling its own securities to the banks and public. Whenever such securities are purchased, bank reserves fall. Essentially, the black bars show the expansion, and the white bars show how the Bank mopped up a good proportion of the bank reserves created by the purchases of foreign exchange. Had the Bank not sold the securities and accumulated the government deposits, the values in the gray bars would be much greater than those of the black bars, almost doubling the amount of reserves created.

Figure 14.9 takes the *transmission mechanism* another step to the commercial banks. The upper left-hand panel shows the two most important elements in the commercial banks' assets column—the amount of reserves and the amount of loans. Because reserves are so much smaller than loans, the diagram uses two scales, with reserves measured on the right and loans on the left. (The proportion of loans to reserves is about 1:25 in most years.) In the seven years from 1990 to 1996 reserves tripled (from 51.5 to 167 billion baht, or 3.2 times) and loans also tripled (from 1,408 billion baht to 4,687 billion baht, or

Figure 14.9
THAI COMMERCIAL BANKS: KEY FIGURES

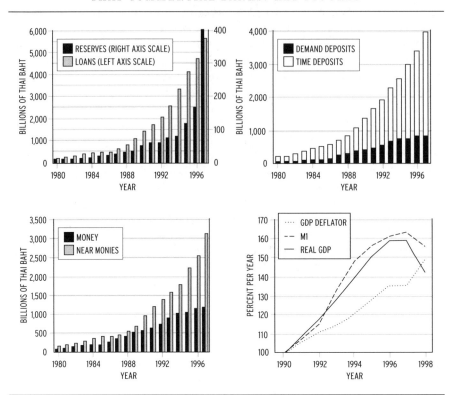

3.3 times). The right panel shows the growth in the banks' demand and time deposits. The demand deposits are the largest item in the narrowly defined money supply and the time deposits are the biggest item in the broadly defined money supply. The remarkable growth was largely in the time deposits.

The lower left panel shows the expansion of money and the near-monies—principally savings and other deposits that have to be converted to checking accounts to be spent. Together, the money and near-monies make up a broad definition of the money supply usually associated with the designation M_2.

Finally, the lower right panel shows the growth of the narrow money supply (M_1) compared with the price level and the change in real GDP. Thailand was fortunate in that its economy was expanding rapidly such that M_1 did not much outpace the 50% rise in real output. At the same time, there was a small decline in velocity of M_1 (and M_2), so inflationary pressures were much mitigated. Despite a 60% rise in the money supply, prices until 1998 had risen only about 35%. That is not in itself good and certainly contributed to the trade deficit, but by developing world standards it isn't bad, and it is similar to that many industrial countries experienced in the 1970s.

Such a situation is not necessarily disastrous. Thailand faced a number of additional problems. (1) The banking system itself, awash in funds, lost its ability to distinguish potentially successful projects from likely losers and engaged in what, in retrospect, was reckless and indiscriminate lending. Loans rose 350%, many going for projects with little chance of succeeding. (2) Perhaps more fundamentally, Thailand may have been approaching the limits of the growth it could achieve without major increases in the education of its labor force, which has lagged well behind the other Asian tigers. (3) Thailand's trading partners had much lower inflations, and Japan, in particular, was in a recession. Topping that off, the yen fell in value against the dollar—to which the baht was pegged—making Thai exports even less competitive in Japan. The first two items are largely outside the scope of the present chapter, although necessary for background, and Chapter 12 has looked at the price competitiveness question. Suffice it to say that rising labor productivity would have relieved some of the inflationary pressures and allowed Thailand to compete better at the existing exchange rate.* As it was, Thailand's inflation was increasing the costs of its exports much faster than prices were rising in its markets. At the same time, imports to Thailand were falling in price relative to their domestic substitutes.

DR. HINDSIGHT MAKES A DIAGNOSIS

Thailand's macroeconomic policy was by no means a mistaken one. The bulk of the new capital that flowed in was indeed used for the import of goods and services, and investment rose to high levels. Given the decision to peg the baht at four cents and the difficulty of quickly increasing productivity, a modicum of inflation was appropriate for widening the trade gap, allowing a larger transfer of real goods and services to Thailand. The $38 billion that the Bank of Thailand accumulated and held in low-yielding T-bills may not have been the best form of investment, but the total private capital inflow was over $110 billion during the period, so the bulk of the inflow was indeed turned into a real transfer.

What could Thailand have done? Dr. Hindsight would have recommended a policy to let the value of the baht rise with the inflow of capital.

---

* Productivity in itself, as Chapter 2 showed, does not change the balance of trade, but if the exchange rate is fixed, the adjustment to changing productivity must be through the price levels of the country and its trading partners.

This would, of course, have produced a trade deficit, perhaps somewhat larger than the one Thailand had. Indeed, one could argue that Thailand should have had a larger trade deficit. After all, the central bank is just sitting there with $25 billion earning less than 5% return. Thai exporters and firms competing with imports were going to get squeezed, whether it was because domestic costs were rising, due to the inflation, or because the baht was rising. A more expensive baht would also have slowed the inflow of capital. Not only would it make domestic assets more expensive to outsiders, it would increase the chance that the baht would fall in value, making investments in Thailand somewhat riskier. It is now obvious that the financial system was not equal to the task of using the flood of domestic and foreign savings wisely, so it might have been the better part of wisdom to introduce more uncertainty into the value of the baht. As it was, Thai investors were overly confident that the exchange rate would be unchanged, encouraging them to borrow heavily from abroad. Chapter 16 explores the exchange rate factors further.

MONETARY AND FISCAL POLICY TOGETHER

The constraints on monetary policy posed by highly liquid capital markets have led to the development of a model associated with Professors Trevor Swan, Robert Mundell, and the IMF's Marcus Fleming. For convenience and to describe the model this book adapts, call it the external-internal balances or EXIN model. The model works off the idea that the *external balance*—essentially the balance of the trade and capital accounts—responds more readily to changes in monetary policy than it does to fiscal policy. The principal reason for the ready response is the ability of interest rates to attract or repel short-term capital. *Internal balance*—the satisfactory resolution of inflation and employment—responds to both fiscal and monetary policy. The effect of fiscal contraction or expansion, however, is much greater on the internal balance than on the external.

The EXIN model broadens the vertical axis to include more than fiscal policy, incorporating the overall economic situation exclusive of monetary factors. This would include the level of expectations of profit and the expectations of consumers as well as the government's fiscal policy, so the vertical axis is *the non-financial stance*. Anything that affects the level of aggregate demand *except* monetary policy goes on it. (Be careful here: the vertical axis is not the actual movement of AD, only what it would be if money did not matter.)

Figure 14.10

INTERNAL AND EXTERNAL BALANCES

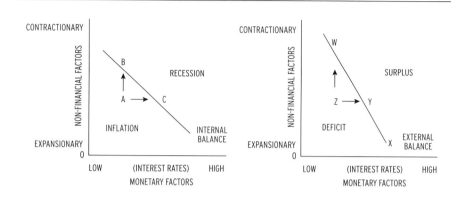

Internal Balance

The left panel in Figure 14.10 shows the differing patterns of internal response on the EXIN diagram. Take first the structure of the diagram. The vertical axis represents the non-financial balance, with a tendency to produce high aggregate demand at the bottom, and to have low aggregate demand at the top. The horizontal axis shows monetary policy, with the highest (most contractionary) interest rates on the right and the low (expansionary) interest rates on the left. A point in the lower left-hand corner, accordingly, would represent a combination of expansionary real factors and expansionary monetary ones; a point in the upper right would represent a contractionary combination. A point on the upper left corner represents an economy where, in the absence of expansionary monetary policy, a low aggregate demand would tend to create recession, but low interest rates stimulate investment and consumption to offset the otherwise sluggish economy. (Aggregate demand would be low because people might be saving larger percentages of their income and expectations of profitable investments were poor.) A point in the lower left corner represents a situation in which the real factors (again, perhaps a highly positive outlook for investment) are restrained with high interest rates.

The line labeled internal balance shows the border between recession and inflation—presumably some ideal of low unemployment and little inflation. Any point in any of the territory to the northeast is a recessionary point, and any point in any of the territory to the southwest is inflationary. For whatever reason, interest rates may not be sufficiently counterbalancing the real pressures for expansion or contraction and a nation can be at a position not on the border. Certainly, higher interest rates discourage investment and stimulate saving, but so do changes in expectations, in demographics, and in the microeconomic effects of taxes on saving and investment. As a result, the internal balance responds reasonably well to both fiscal and monetary policies.

The distance from point A of the left panel, where the economy is in inflation, is about the same to point B as to point C. Point B has the non-financial factors somewhat contractionary (perhaps due to a contractionary fiscal policy or pessimism among investors), counterbalanced by an expansionary monetary policy. Point C is at a point where investment would exceed saving were it not balanced out by a contractionary monetary policy. Any point below the internal balance line would be an expansionary one, presumably continuing with inflation, and any point above that line would be creating too much unemployment.

External Balance

The right panel in Figure 14.10 shows the external balance, which is a balance on the *combined current and financial accounts.*[*] A combination of capital inflows and reduced trade deficits can keep a country's exchange rate stable without need for monetary intervention. Anywhere along the external balance line the value of the currency is stable and monetary intervention does not occur. The territory to the northeast of the line is a surplus on the financial and current accounts; everything to its southwest is a deficit. The external border is steeper than the internal balance curve because the financial account balance is highly sensitive to interest rate changes. The current account balance is probably insensitive to interest rates. But the addition of the financial accounts causes the greater sensitivity to interest rates.

The border between an external deficit (a deficit on combined current and financial accounts) is quite vertical. Its vertical nature means that horizontal movements toward or away from the curve are less than vertical ones—for example, if a country is in deficit, with a policy mix at Z, then it needs to move from Z to Y if it uses monetary policy. Policy affecting non-financial factors, however, would have to be stronger to move from Z to W. While changes in the balance of trade would take some time, interest rates need not change enormously to cause an inflow or outflow of capital. As interest rates rise, income and/or prices will fall with some effect on correcting the trade imbalance, but the principal effect will be an inflow of short-term capital. As they fall, the opposite will occur.

---

[*] In the IMF presentation of payments balances, as shown in Chapter 11, the combined current and financial accounts would include the current account and the capital and financial account. For convenience here we call the financial and capital account simply the financial account. (Many sources still refer to it as the capital account.)

Point W in the right panel of Figure 14.10 shows an external balance achieved with non-financial factors such that saving would greatly exceed investment (perhaps because of a very conservative fiscal policy), which holds down aggregate demand, partially counterbalanced by relatively low interest rates—similar to the situation of Germany at several points in the last decades. The conservative fiscal policy causes a trade surplus by reducing income and holding down prices, while the low interest rates encourage the capital outflow to accompany the trade deficit. (Remember that the external balance is the *combined* financial and current accounts, so that a point on the balance line can have a current account surplus matched by a financial account deficit, or vice versa.) Point X looks more like the American pattern in the 1980s, with strong budget deficits causing pressures for aggregate demand to rise while high interest rates, and the accompanying high capital inflows, contribute to trade deficits. The country still can stay close to external balance if the capital inflows overcome the current account deficits. Nothing in the EXIN model deals with solving a trade deficit; it just shows whether the financial and current accounts are in balance.

Note that a country can only move off the external balance line if its monetary authorities are intervening in the market. So long as the monetary account is at zero, the other two accounts have to balance out. A country can only have a deficit on the combined financial and current accounts if the monetary account is positive—that is, the central bankers are selling foreign exchange.

Put the two curves together and difficulties stand out. Figure 14.11 has four zones. In Zone 2, outside both the external and internal balance lines, there is both a recession and a payments surplus. The solution to both problems is a set of policies that encourage greater investment and/or consumption for the non-financial axis and lower interest rates for the monetary axis. Zone 4 shows both inflation and a payments deficit; contraction through encouraging more saving and discouraging investment, accompanied by higher interest rates (which also encourage saving and discourage investment), is surely the way to right both the internal and external balances.

So far no problem. Suppose, however, that a nation is in Zone 4 at point A; unable to control the budget or other non-financial factors raising aggregate demand, it opts for a very tight monetary policy, trying to move to point C. If it gets anywhere outside the external balance line, however, it enters Zone 3, generating a surplus on the combined current and financial accounts, partly as a result of the decreased economic activity and partly as a result of the short-term capital inflow. Point C lies where there is internal balance but surpluses on the combined current and financial accounts. If, instead, the country uses fiscal policy, successfully decreasing aggregate demand, it moves toward point B on the internal balance; this places it at the edge of Zone 1, with an internal balance but still a payments deficit. If it persists in using contractionary fiscal policy, it is going to have to move all the way to D to reach external balance, and at that point it will be in a major recession. The reason is that the low interest rates are failing to attract capital (or repelling too much domestic capital). Zones 1 and 3, accordingly, are very troublesome because the solutions to the internal problem and the external problem call for opposite policies. When both boundaries between internal and external balances appear on the same diagram, two anomalous zones appear (1 and 3), where policies that improve one balance make the other worse. An increase in interest rates moving the country from C to D, for instance, improves the internal balance but produces a high capital inflow.

In some senses, all nations should aim for point E, where the external and internal balances cross; that is not an easy matter. The monetary policy must keep interest rates where they help create just the right economic incentive to invest, while yet moving short-term capital in a way to keep the balance on the current and financial accounts neutral. If monetary policy alone cannot bring about a balance, it is up to other policies affecting non-financial elements to do so. There is no way, for instance, to move from point C in the preceding example (Figure 14.11) to point E (equilibrium) without using policies affecting *both* axes. Yet fiscal policy is very hard to use strictly to regulate GNP—government taxes and expenditures have multiple purposes and, possibly regrettably, macroeconomic management is

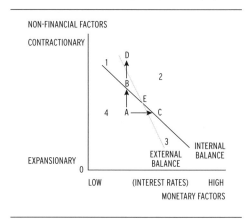

Figure 14.11
EXIN MODEL:
BOTH BALANCES TOGETHER

not normally a high priority. Moreover, even effective fiscal policy may not work, requiring the institution of other, rather slower-acting policies such as tax reform. It is highly unlikely the government could work directly and quickly to change any of the other factors affecting the non-financial axis.

The EXIN model is an interesting tool, one that policy-makers often use. American economists have often suggested that Germany through the 1980s had a positive balance of payments only because it constrained its economy too much. This would be a point between E and G in Figure 14.11. U.S. policy in the 1980s had reasonably good internal balance, but poor external balance, placing it between points E and F on Figure 14.11. Canada in the late 1980s had high interest rates, greater inflation than the United States, large fiscal deficits, and trade deficits, placing it in Zone 4, about the height of point C, but well to its right. The policy prescription would therefore be to decrease the fiscal deficit and lower interest rates. Canada did indeed do that in the mid–1990s, moving toward E.

CONCLUSION

Global capital flows normally affect national money supplies because central banks try to give some stability to their currencies' exchange rates, purchasing or selling foreign exchange. Domestic monetary policy affects a country's balance of payments through its effects on output and price levels. Often, central banks try to counterbalance the monetary effects of their foreign exchange operations, but with mixed success and sometimes at a considerable cost. Generally speaking, monetary policy affects exchange rates more quickly than does fiscal policy. But it is impossible to complete the picture without looking at exchange rate policy far more closely, which is where the book now turns.

VOCABULARY AND CONCEPTS

Counterbalancing monetary policy
EXIN diagram
External balance
Inflation premium
Inflation targeting
Internal balance
Intervention in the
  foreign exchange market

Liquidity preference
Monetary authorities
Monetarism
Portfolio interpretation of effect of
  changing money supplies
Sterilization
Velocity of money

FINDING THE NUMBERS

Choose a country that you know has had large capital inflows or outflows. Then examine the changes in the assets of "monetary authorities" (*International Financial Statistics*, CD-ROM) to see if it sold off or accumulated large amounts of foreign assets. Check the assets also to see if it counterbalanced the sale or purchase of foreign exchange through sales of government securities (liabilities to the central government) or bank advances (liabilities to deposit money banks, known as DMBs). Check the liabilities side to see if the liabilities to DMBs changed substantially and to see if other kinds of liabilities have grown, for instance, government deposits or central bank bonds. This would be a sign that the central bank is trying to mitigate the effect of purchasing or selling foreign exchange.

If it does not appear that complete counterbalancing took place, examine further the expansion of commercial bank assets and deposits, using the *IFS* table called "deposit money banks." Then check the change in money supply under "monetary survey." Money is normally checking accounts plus currency. Quasi-money includes various time deposits, and the broad money supply is money plus quasi-money.

QUESTIONS

1. Why was Marner's behavior more likely to cause a recession than Scrooge's?

2. What has been the concern in recent years over the velocity approach to money? Include in your answer both the velocity and the definition of money.

3. How can additional money lead to more loanable funds? Under what conditions could it do so in real terms?

4. Demonstrate, using a T-account, why an inflow of foreign exchange—that is, purchases of domestic currency with foreign currency—does not affect the money supply if the central bank does not intervene.

5. Demonstrate on a T-account what happens when a central bank intervenes. Suppose, for instance, that the Federal Reserve buys $1 billion worth of foreign exchange.

6. Show on a T-account how the Federal Reserve could counterbalance those purchases with open market operations (purchases or sales of T-bills).

7. "The goal of a stable exchange rate may in fact cause a very unstable money supply." Explain.

8. How do central banks that do not have big T-bill markets counterbalance the effects of foreign exchange intervention?

9. Explain how a trade surplus could lead to a monetary expansion. Explain how that monetary expansion could then end the trade surplus. Do the same for a trade deficit. Include in your answer the expected reaction of the price level and employment level to changes in aggregate demand.

10. Many central banks were founded or developed with the idea of mitigating the effects of sudden changes in capital flows. Were they trying to insulate the domestic economy from global effects?

11. Why does a rapid expansion of the money supply often lead to a sharp deterioration of the foreign exchange rate?

12. How does a trade imbalance tend to be self-correcting when a country allows a floating exchange rate?

13. Sometimes developing countries get large capital inflows. Their central banks try to keep the currency from rising and buy up a great deal of foreign exchange. Is there a cost in this?

14. Explain the Thai experience, using the charts shown. For a project, bring them up to date. Another project could take Korea, Malaysia, Indonesia, or the Philippines, which had somewhat similar patterns.

15. Why did Dr. Hindsight want the Thai government to have floated the baht?

16. Using the EXIN model, suggest where Thailand was in 1996? In 1997? Consider your own country in the present year and debate where you think you should place it.

17. Why is the external balance more sensitive to monetary policy?

NOTES

1. Leland Yeager, *International Monetary Relations* (New York: Harper & Row, 1966).

2. David Folkerts-Landau et al., *International Capital Markets: Developments, Prospects, and Key Policy Issues, 1997* (Washington: IMF, 1997), 28-29, 64-66.

Chapter Fifteen

Exchange Rate Adjustment

OBJECTIVES

OVERALL OBJECTIVE   To show the different exchange rate regimens—the policies countries have toward fixing or floating their exchange rates.

MORE SPECIFICALLY
- To frame the discussion by examining monetary theory, (1) showing the demand for liquidity, velocity approaches, and portfolio approaches and (2) connecting these models with previously developed models of the demand for funds and the AS/AD model.
- To see how and when foreign exchange rate changes correct payments imbalances.
- To explore how exchange rate changes affect aggregate demand.
- To look closely at how exchange rate changes affect aggregate supply, noting particularly the domestic setting, the extent to which all prices are set against the exchange rate, and the willingness of the government to accommodate price increases.
- To show how foreign exchange control has worked and note its limitations.
- To look at devaluation and upward revaluation as explicit policies.
- To examine more closely the problem of slow adjustment to exchange rate changes, particularly the J-curve and Marshall-Lerner conditions.
- To show how to handle exchange rate changes with the EXIN model.

....

Chapter 15 focuses on exchange rates and their relation to macroeconomic policy. Previous chapters have already explored parts of the question. Remaining, however, are numerous questions about government policy and habits in dealing with their exchange rates, and the effects of exchange rate changes on underlying economic processes and on trade and investment.

WHAT COUNTRIES REALLY DO

In the abstract, countries can follow several regimens:

- A fixed exchange rate, where the national currency is tied to another currency or a basket of currencies weighted by the importance of trade with each partner. Typically, the central bank sets a high and a low point, at which it will intervene to stabilize the currency. Such *bands* may be narrow (for instance, 2.5%) or broad (5-10%).
- A floating rate, where the central bank never intervenes.
- A floating rate where the central bank intervenes to take out peaks and valleys when the market itself seems to be failing.
- A more-or-less fixed rate that is known only to the central bank and exchange traders who can surmise what is going on, but that can be floated at any time. (The Canadian dollar has often had this pattern.)
- One of the arrangements above combined with *exchange control*, in which anyone moving currency must have that transaction approved by the government.

A number of countries practice fixed exchange rates. Argentina has pegged its peso to the U.S. dollar as part of an anti-inflationary policy. From January 1991 through the time of writing this text (1999), the Argentine peso remained between US$1.00 and US$1.01. Most Western European currencies have been pegged to a weighted average of their currencies, which, in effect, pegged them to the German mark. In preparation for the advent of the euro, a single currency for all of Europe, the countries kept their exchange rates in very narrow bands. Thailand, as the previous chapter explained, pegged its currency to the U.S. dollar, although at some points it had tried pegging it to a basket of currencies.

In practice, no countries allow completely floating rates; every country's balance of payments shows often considerable changes in foreign exchange reserves. Even Canada and Peru, the only countries with declared floating exchange rates in the 1950s and 1960s, have shown a great deal of evidence of central bank intervention in the foreign exchange market. Indeed, about the only time that governments do not intervene is when their currencies are in free fall and it would do no good. In 1997, for instance, Thailand gave up on pegging the baht after it had spent only about a third of its considerable foreign exchange reserves.

The IMF summarizes currency arrangements in the following table.

Table 15.1

INTERNATIONAL CURRENCY ARRANGEMENTS

	Number of Currencies	Examples
Currency pegged to		
U.S. dollar	21	Argentina; some oil producers
French franc	15	Former French colonies
Other currency	11	Nepal to the Indian rupee
SDR	2	Libya; Myanmar
Other currency composite	17	Iceland; Jordan
Flexibility limited *vis-à-vis* a single currency	4	Saudi Arabia (U.S. dollar)
Cooperative arrangements	12	Members of European Monetary Union
Managed floating	48	Brazil; Korea; Thailand
Independently floating	51	Canada; Peru; Philippines; Mexico

Sixty-six countries fix their currencies against another currency. Most of these peg against the U.S. dollar, but some former French colonies have pegged to the French franc and continue against the euro. Several other small countries peg against larger neighbors. The price of petroleum is fixed in U.S. dollars, hence the number of oil producers pegging to the dollar. The SDR, explained in Chapter 17, is, among other things, a weighted basket of the world's major currencies. What the IMF calls "limited flexibility" is a wide-band arrangement. The cooperative arrangement is that of the Western European countries, explained later. Most countries, however, have one or another degree of floating currency. Thailand's unofficial pegging of the baht at four U.S. cents was a *managed float*. Canada's dollar is *independently floating*, although, as noted above, this has not meant that the Bank of Canada abstains from intervention, as other chapters have shown.

The variety of systems—and the absence of any countries that never intervene—suggests foreign exchange policy itself has a very important function. The ability to influence the value of a currency on the foreign exchange market is simply too valuable a tool for countries to abstain from its use.

While, clearly, the advantage of some degree of exchange rate stability helps traders and investors, this is probably not the primary reason for countries to choose their policies. The reasons are more macroeconomic, principally in the way exchange rates help the countries adjust to payments difficulties.

THE ROLE OF THE EXCHANGE RATE IN ADJUSTING TO PAYMENTS DIFFICULTIES

As the last chapter pointed out, changing the exchange rate is normally an efficient way to adjust to a trade imbalance or abnormal capital flow. If it is necessary to increase exports and decrease imports, why go through the trauma of pushing down the domestic price level to do so? And why suffer an inflation to rid the country of a trade surplus or to turn a capital inflow into a trade deficit? The case for letting exchange rates float is strong, but, as with so many other things in economics, it has its limitations. What may work in one situation may not work in another, and what may work for one country may not for another. A closer look is in order.

First, some basic vocabulary. A currency that is floating and decreases value is said to *depreciate*, and the government is said simply *to allow depreciation*. If the currency is fixed, or has been unofficially fixed and the government removes support, people say the country *devalued* its currency. The opposite phrases are *appreciation* and *upward revaluation*. Since systems themselves are mixed, the proper choice of words is not always clear. If Argentina has to let the peso fall, it will definitely *devalue* the peso. But consider Thailand. It had not declared an official exchange rate of four U.S. cents but had maintained the baht at that price for half a decade. So did it *devalue* the baht or allow the baht to *depreciate*?

Exchange Rate Shocks: Correcting Payments Imbalances

The object of letting a currency change values is to shift resources between the *trade-sensitive sector* consisting of imports, import substitutes, and exports and the *non-tradable sector* (or *trade-insensitive sector*) consisting of goods and services that are not easily or normally traded. If a country allows its currency to depreciate, prices will rise for goods in the trade-sensitive sector such that more exports and more import substitutes are made. If there is to be no inflation, prices in the *non-tradable* sector must go down. The opposite is true when a currency appreciates. Chapter 12 showed that income models indicate that devaluation—insofar as it is successful—increases aggregate demand. Unless the country is in the very special circumstance of facing a horizontal AS curve, devaluation is going to cause some degree of inflation. Price–level

Figure 15.1

A DEVALUATION CAN PRODUCE AN INCOME EFFECT

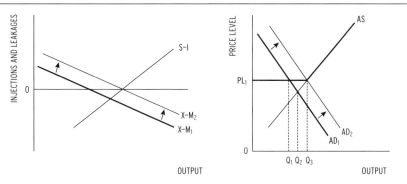

Note: A devaluation stimulates exports and discourages imports causing $X - M$ to shift to the right. Because substantial employment existed at the time of the devaluation, the increased aggregate demand increases employment, not prices. In turn, saving rises. The $X - M$ curve shifts along the $S - I$ curve. As a result $S - I = 0$ at the same point as $X - M$ does. The right panel shows the effect of a rise in AD on prices and income, assuming a flat short-run aggregate supply curve.

models also suggest that lowering domestic prices is difficult; thus, prices in the non-tradable sector are unlikely to fall. What happens is that the devaluation allows the trade-sensitive sector to outbid the non-tradable sector for resources, and this is done at the cost of some inflation. Policy-makers just hope that a shift of resources can be made with relatively little inflation. The following section explores these questions.

AGGREGATE DEMAND AND INCOME EFFECTS

As Chapter 14 suggested, a change in the exchange rate could be an effective move. But price effects, whether through devaluation or a lowering of the price level, cannot end a trade imbalance unless they also change $S - I$ and $Y - A$. So the question is how a *price effect* that changes the relation of exports and import substitutes to the prices of other goods can also change saving or investment.

A stimulus to the trade-sensitive sector could cause an income effect, which would in turn raise saving and reduce the savings-investment gap. If the economy has many unemployed resources, the stimulus increased exports and decreased imports give to the economy will generate more income, part of which will be saved. This process is easy to see as an injections and leakage diagram. Figure 15.1 shows a situation in which a devaluation raises exports and lowers imports, thereby shifting $X - M$ to the right. As it does so it increases real income, and as real income increases so does saving.

Figure 15.2

DEVALUATION PRODUCING INCOME AND PRICE-LEVEL EFFECTS

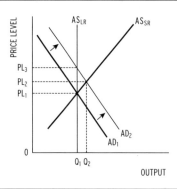

Note: An increase in aggregate demand stimulated by a depreciation of the exchange rate may produce a mix of income and price effects if the aggregate supply is not vertical. In this case, the shift produces an increase in output of Q_1Q_2 and an increase in the price level from PL_1 to PL_2. If the AS were vertical, the effect would be simply an increase in the price level to PL_3. The higher level of prices would squeeze exporters once again, and AD would tend to fall back (not shown), but at a higher price level.

To complete the scenario and make some of its underlying assumptions specific, The right panel shows a situation in which the increase in aggregate demand did not cause prices to rise. The reason prices did not rise is that the AS curve is horizontal. Since horizontal AS curves are probably not that common, situations in which a devaluation could cause *only* an improvement in the trade balance and not some inflation are also likely to be uncommon. As noted in Chapter 10, many payments deficits come about when an economy is expanding rapidly or suffering from inflation, with aggregate demand very high. Only in cases such as Canada's in 1998, where commodity prices fell sharply and the economy was experiencing low inflation, might depreciation have some useful income effects.

The more likely scenario is that the devaluation will lead to some income-induced price increases and partially undo the price effect of the devaluation. The devaluation will therefore have to be larger than initially anticipated to take effect. If, however, the AS were vertical such that there is no income effect, the price effect of the devaluation would be completely undone. Prices would keep rising until the trade deficit rose again to siphon off the excess domestic demand, as Figure 15.2 illustrates.

MONETARY MODIFICATIONS

When devaluation stimulates the economy—nominal or real—the demand for money rises. The rise in the demand for money causes a decrease in the amount of funds offered in the funds market, raising the interest rate, and in response savings rise and investment falls. $S - I$ therefore shifts to the left.

More elaborate models—variations on the ISLM model—can show just what level of income will produce a payments situation under fixed rates

Figure 15.3
INTEREST RATE EFFECTS OF DEVALUATION

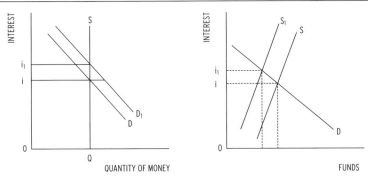

Note: The left panel of Figure 15.3 shows how interest rates shift from *i* to *i₁*, as a result of the demand for money shifting from *D* to *D₁*, which was itself a result of the higher AD. The right panel shows how the increased *demand* for money results in a decreased *supply* of funds being supplied to the funds market.

where no monetary intervention is necessary. Suffice it here to note that income or price levels must rise and that, given an unchanged money supply, interest rates will rise, choking off some investment and consumption and closing the savings-investment gap, which, of course, also closes the trade gap. If devaluation causes a real income effect, savings will also rise as a response to the higher income.

Aggregate Supply Effects

LIMITING PRICE EFFECTS OF DEVALUATION

Devaluations often also shift the short-run aggregate supply. The initial effect of a devaluation is to increase prices in the trade-sensitive sector, but the non-tradable sector may not have a simultaneous decline in prices. The effect will be to shift short run AS to the left, as Figure 15.4 shows. The diagram also includes the shift in AD incorporated in Figure 15.2. Even though the price level rises, it should not rise as much as the prices of traded goods. If the only thing feeding the increase in AD is $X - M$, $X - M$ will shrink as prices rise. Any inflation that would completely undo the effects of the devaluation would remove the stimulus for the price increases. Therefore, domestic inflation dampens—but does not eliminate—the price effect of devaluation, weakening its effectiveness.

To illustrate the shift of both curves, consider a scenario that might have developed in the United States during the Reagan years. Suppose the dollar had fallen earlier and further than it did and that, as a consequence, the trade balance moved to a surplus. This would have meant that over $100 billion of goods and services from abroad would not be available. The fall in the dollar would have put pressure on the AS curve to shift leftward, and the disappearing trade deficit would have increased AD well beyond what it actually was. Unless absorption fell, inflation would have risen sharply. That inflation would partially undo the effect of the devaluation, perhaps requiring another devaluation.

The AS_{SR} curve probably would not have moved far. The U.S. imports about 10% of its goods and services. A fall in the value of the dollar by 20% could increase the price of imports by that amount, but that would be only a 2% increase in all costs. Even that is unlikely because oil prices are stated in dollar terms and many other exporters to the United States would hold their prices down. In an economy such as Canada's, which imports far more and would likely pay the full amount of the price change,[*] the change is not enormous. A 20% rise in the 40% of GDP that Canada imports would cause the price level to rise by 8% at the most, assuming that all the price increase can be passed on. Even if that 8% did cause some further rounds, it is unlikely it would reach 20%. In such a case, although the decline in the dollar would cause some changes in the price level, they would be insufficient to counter the exchange rate effect. What happens to AS depends very much on the structure of the domestic economy.

Figure 15.4

EFFECTS ON AGGREGATE SUPPLY

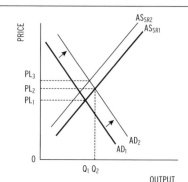

Note: Devaluation can cause a leftward shift in *ASsr* as well as a shift in AD. Increased prices would limit the movement of AD to the right, but not cancel it completely.

THE STRUCTURE OF THE DOMESTIC ECONOMY

The extent to which prices increase after devaluation depends very much on the situation in the underlying economy. Brazil has experienced large price effects almost instantaneously. Sweden and Ireland saw a slower creep of inflation, but had enough to eventually undo the price effects of their devaluations. Canada experienced very little effect at all, even less than the increase

---

[*] Because it would not have a beneficial terms of trade effect, Canada being too small to affect world prices very much.

in the price of imports themselves. What characteristics of the economies, then, cause the differences in reaction?

As explained, devaluation, to be successful, has to shift resources into exports and import substitutes. It has to increase saving or decrease investment. The political economic factors may, however, prevent both these things from occurring. Inflation and devaluation are one way of working out deep political problems. Typical *political* problems they can solve include the following:

- Governments often use inflation as a means of funding projects, maintaining high payrolls, paying for extensive social services, and keeping up pensions without collecting the taxes necessary to do so. Brazilian state and federal parties use their payrolls to reward supporters, much as American cities have done for over a century. The difference is that Chicago can't print money, but Brazil can.

- Protectionist trade policies also support the protected groups (unions in protected industries and the owners of protected firms) and have limited the power of international competition. They shift resources away from potential exporters. Years of such policies have often left countries with export sectors dominated by commodities, which are rather price-insensitive, with few exports in manufacturing or agricultural products such as fruits and wines, which are more price-sensitive. In Latin America, Africa, and some other areas where incomes are low, protectionism has tended to discriminate against the agricultural sectors. Conversely, in highly developed countries, the agricultural sectors are protected and other sectors suffer. This means that exports cannot quickly expand and the adjustment occurs through declining imports.

- To protect themselves against inflation, numerous interest groups press the government or employers for various forms of indexing. COLA clauses for wages, pensions, and social security are common. Some countries, such as Brazil, have indexed savings accounts and, of course, indexed bonds. The indexing creates numerous problems.

- Indexing protects only those powerful or persuasive enough to gain protection. Often, too, the cost of living overstates the amount of inflation because of built-in indexing errors (as with American social security), so those whose income is indexed tend to get larger proportions of output.

- Indexing causes prices to rise very rapidly. The economy does not have a period of grace between the increase in AD and the realization that prices have risen. Those people, like Ashley Gray, who are on the margins of the workforce, anticipate that they will not earn what they expect at current wages and will not accept a job that does not have a wage high enough to withstand the expected inflation or a COLA clause. As a result, wages rise immediately when prices rise.

• Governments and central banks have very little ability or willingness to tolerate the amount of unemployment that occurs when the AS shifts up sharply. As a consequence, they increase AD, accommodating to the higher prices and undoing the effect of the devaluation. Many economists see this not as simply accommodation, but *validation*, indicating to those who pushed for the higher prices that their moves were correct.

Stopping inflation and the accompanying currency depreciation hurts the very groups that support the government. Governments that manage to balance their budgets have to reduce whatever discretionary expenditure they have, cut payrolls massively, and reduce pensions. Members of powerful labor unions (if such exist) no longer enjoy the jump they had on less-organized workers when they got their COLA and the others did not. Firms that routinely gave in to labor's demands, knowing they would soon be bailed out by inflation, have to bargain hard, increasing tensions. If protectionism is also reduced—as is usual—the sectors that had been unable to win political favor benefit and those that had gained favor lose it. Political leaders get caught in what is both a political and moral dilemma. Not only are they cutting their political base, but they have imposed substantial adjustment costs on economies that may not yet have the means to adjust rapidly. New export industries may not be on the point of emerging; old industries may not know how to cut costs quickly; and unemployed workers may be unwilling or unable to gain new skills or move across regions.

A MICROECONOMIC LOOK

How many goods have their price changed by devaluation? The usual base is to take imports as a percentage of GNP and work from there. But the effect could certainly be much wider than that because the opportunity cost for any exportable good or any potential import substitute rises. Figure 15.5 shows that not just the exports and imports will change in price, but the prices of potential exports and import substitutes in domestic markets.

Before devaluation, the price of imported widgets in Figure 15.5 is World Price 1. After devaluation it is World Price 2. It is not just imported widgets Q_1Q_4 that will rise in price, but all the imported widgets and

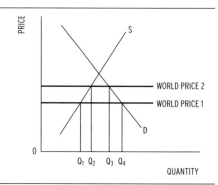

Figure 15.5

THE LIMIT PRICE ARGUMENT

620

Figure 15.6

PRICE LEVEL EFFECTS OF DEVALUATION

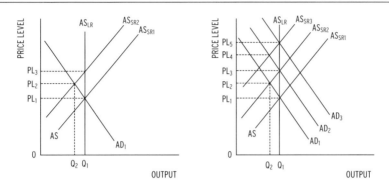

domestic widgets as well: $0Q_3$. Devaluation, accordingly, increases prices across large sectors of the economy. The effect is similar for exports. As exports rise in value, the exported widgets, as well as all the widgets sold domestically, rise in price.

Note that these are *partial equilibrium* arguments, assuming that the only product whose price moves is the widget. Could a 20% devaluation cause *all* prices to rise by 20%? That is unlikely. If the money supply is unchanged, it is even more unlikely. Certainly, the velocity of money could rise, but it cannot do so without limits. If incomes do not rise, or do not rise sharply, people will have less money left over for other goods, after purchasing their widgets, and the prices in the non-tradable sector should fall. The left panel in Figure 15.6 shows what would happen.

In protecting themselves against price increases, firms and workers cause AS_{SR} to shift sharply to the left. In the left panel, the government does not accommodate them by shifting AD, and a recession takes hold, causing income to fall from Q_1 to Q_2. In the right panel, the government expands AD, but it generates a further round of AS moving leftward and further accommodation. The left panel of Figure 15.6 assumes that firms and workers attempt to pass on virtually the entirety of the price increase of the devaluation, such that AS shifts to AS_{SR2}. The magnitude of that shift shows up on the vertical AS curve as the distance between PL_1 and PL_2. But the actual increase in prices is only to PL_2 because AD has not shifted. This might be because the central bank kept the money supply very tight, causing investment to fall. What this means is that output has fallen from Q_1 to $Q_2.$ The decline in employment is in the non-tradable sector, which, given no increase in AD, will eventually have to cut its prices if the country is to return to Q_1.

The problem is that in the short run the producers of exports and import substitutes are having to bid resources away from their existing uses by offering higher prices. They can do so, given the devaluation. But price rigidity slows the transfer of those resources as prices do not fall elsewhere in the economy. Unemployment is thus much more severe in the short run than in the long run and the government will be sorely tempted to increase aggregate demand to alleviate it. The right panel in Figure 15.6 shows this process. After the initial shift of AS_{SR1} to AS_{SR2}, pressures build on the government and central bank to increase aggregate demand to rid the country of the unemployment. They do so, and AD shifts to AD_2 while prices rise to PL_3. People are back working, but the trade deficit, of course, reappears.

Add now another element: *expectations*. Suppose that devaluation has been frequent. Labor unions and managers know to expect a certain degree of inflation, and set their bargain and their prices (to the extent they can) with a degree of inflation built in. People who might only demand a real 2% increase in wages will find themselves demanding 10% if they expect an 8% inflation. Exporters and producers of import substitutes know that they will come in for a period of low margins with perhaps some unemployment as inflation increases costs and the exchange rate does not change. But periodic devaluations reduce that constraint. That is, indeed, what devaluations are supposed to do in order to keep the economy operating efficiently. The problem is that it removes any constraints on the next round of wage and price increases. To illustrate this, the right panel of Figure 15.6 shows yet another round of price increases, beginning with a shift of AS_2 to AS_3 and a rise in the price level to PL_4; after a short time, the economy experiences another decline in employment, so the government allows AD to rise to AD_3, which kicks up prices to PL_4. Successive rounds can follow, and each may have larger shifts in AS as people try to get ahead of the inflation.

Now, *if* workers could not expect a devaluation and *if* firms could not count on raising prices, they would order their affairs differently. Moreover, *if* governments could not count on devaluation to end payments problems, they, too, would try to keep inflation down. So, goes the argument, a fixed exchange rate, tied to a currency of a low inflation country, will feed back into more moderate wage demands. While there may be some temporary unemployment and bankruptcies as those firms who doubt the government's will are shown to be wrong, eventually the cost-push elements will be controlled.

The argument above has more theoretical vestments. It has a following among both European central bankers and international organizations. Most of the models, usually mathematical, show that it is important for the government to have a *credible commitment*, or to achieve *credibility*, and for the anticipations to be consistent with what the government will do. Credible policies show two important effects: a moderation of the inflation and a reduction in dislocation.

If wages and prices are set too high, expecting an increase in aggregate demand that does not occur, unemployment will be considerable, lasting a long period of time, and capacity utilization will fall, reducing profits. If wages and prices are set too high for exports in anticipation of a devaluation that does not occur, then, too, those industries will experience unemployment, poor capacity utilization, and perhaps bankruptcy. If people respond fairly quickly to the unemployment by lowering wages and to the undercapacity by lowering prices and bargaining harder on wage deals, realizing that their expectations were proving wrong, then the dip in employment and profits may be short. Economists call this *adaptive expectation*. If, however, everyone believes the government and immediately jumps to the solution, rather than pushing to see if the government will really keep its word, there will be very little displacement. Wages and prices will not rise much and the government will not be tempted to expand aggregate demand to catch up with the rising costs. This is forward-looking rational expectation with credible commitment. Devaluation will be unnecessary. As a consequence, the economy fares better.

While this may seem a very rosy prediction, it is a key factor in the reasoning that many countries have for joining the European Monetary System (described in the next chapter), which ties their currencies to the German mark. It clearly lay behind the strategies of John Major in the United Kingdom, and of Ireland, where it is cited as being a major factor in the decline of inflation and control of the trade deficit. In 1991 Sweden joined the European Monetary System to try to end its successive rounds of devaluation and inflation.

The Irish case is of particular interest. When its very large current account deficits occurred in the 1970s and early 1980s (discussed in Chapter 10), it was pegged to the British pound, which had experienced frequent depreciations. Then it began to peg its exchange rate against an average of European rates, which, in essence, fixed it to the German mark. It was then able to cut its rate of inflation (to less than 3% in 1990) and achieve current account surpluses from 1987 onward. Growth rose to 5% a year. Unfortunately, unemployment, which was running around 15%, continued at those high rates for some years. Note, however, that unemployment did not worsen, nor is there any evidence that it had been responsive to macroeconomic measures. Certainly, the use of high aggregate demand in the 1970s and early 1980s had little or no effect on its level.[1]

THE ARGENTINE CASE

Argentina had been plagued by rampant inflation for decades. The left panel of Figure 15.7 shows the consumer price index and the right indicates the

Figure 15.7
ARGENTINE CONSUMER PRICES

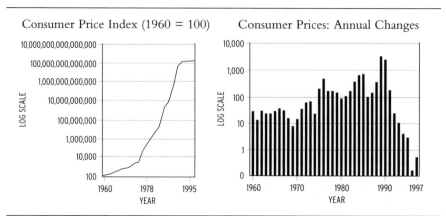

percentage change of prices for each year. So great was the inflation that the diagrams use log scales to show their size. An Argentine who lost a peso in a desk drawer in 1960 and found it again in 1991 could use it to purchase one-*trillionth* of what it could have bought when he lost it! When the peso got to be 1,000 to the dollar, the government declared a new peso, worth a thousand old pesos. When the zeros on the new pesos began to get too long, it declared a new currency, the *austral*, worth a thousand of the new pesos. When the *austral* got to be 1,000 to the dollar, the government introduced a peso once again ($1,000^4 = 1$ trillion). This peso, however, was tied to the U.S. dollar at 1 peso = 1 U.S. dollar in January of 1991 and has stayed there for 8 years. The year 1989 saw prices rise 3,080%; in 1996 there was no inflation.

Many countries have tied their currencies to the dollar, swearing they will never abandon the connection. As Mark Twain said of quitting smoking: it isn't hard at all, he'd done it many times. It is not intention; it is execution. Argentina's last fixed exchange rate plan was an integral part of a very deep economic reform; indeed, the fixed exchange rate was not an end in itself, merely a means to build the credibility needed to end the inflation.[*]

Argentina had developed an economy very sensitive to price increases. COLA clauses were in all major labor contracts, in pension arrangements, and in any ordinary contracts. A manufacturing firm could not agree to deliver items at the current price of 1,000 pesos in six months if those pesos might

---

[*] Professor George Halm of the Fletcher School, who taught in Germany until the Nazis drove him out, recalled an incident in the 1920s when the Nazis were just a fringe group. He met a small group of them during the devastating German inflation of 1923 and asked them how they would handle the inflation. "We would make it illegal to raise price," he said, "and shoot those who violated the law." This is not the type of execution the Argentines had in mind, being under a democratically elected government at the time.

be worth only 10% of what they were at contract signing. And a retailer wouldn't agree to deliver 10,000 pesos in six months if the peso fell only by half. Taxes incurred in January and paid months later would be worth a fraction of what they were at the point they were incurred, so government revenues fell to a fraction of the government's expenditures. As elsewhere in Latin America, Argentines kept large amounts of U.S. dollars as precautionary and speculative balances, and kept accounts in U.S. dollars simply because the Argentine currency was so unstable.

The package to end the inflation consisted of several important items.

• The Bank of Argentina was prohibited from buying government debt, except under extreme conditions. If the government was to have a deficit, it had to borrow the money from private sources. Nor was it to undertake active monetary policy, using bank advances or repos. It took a few years to unwind, but by 1997 the Bank's principal assets were over 70% foreign exchange, 26% government debt, and 4% bank advances.

• The Bank of Argentina could issue currency *only if* the currency were *fully* backed by U.S. dollars (or other equally high-quality foreign assets). This rather draconian measure works through a *currency board*. The currency board intervenes in the foreign exchange market, always purchasing dollars when the supply of dollars rises and selling them when it falls. This means that the money supply within Argentina is tied strictly to the flow of foreign exchange, much as it was in countries in the days of the gold standard. When the currency board sells dollars, it must reduce currency in circulation and bank reserves have to fall. This is a very powerful check on inflation from within the country.

• It allowed free convertibility of the peso into dollars, allowed domestic accounts in U.S. dollars, and even allowed domestic contracts to be written in dollars. Many Argentines already had substantial holdings of U.S. currency, as protection against inflation, and had become accustomed to doing their accounts and calculations in U.S. dollars, so the step legalized what had been going on anyway. All it did was to tie the peso to the U.S. dollar so that dollars did not need to be in circulation. (They are not, for the most part, but it is no problem to pay or get paid in U.S. dollars.)

A look at the T-accounts of the central and commercial banks in Argentina (Table 15.2) shows how restrictive the rules can be. Suppose that there is a $10 million outflow of deposits from Argentina such that the currency board sells $10 million more than it buys. Line 1 of the table indicates that monetary authorities' assets fall by $10 million, as do commercial bank deposits at the Bank of Argentina, Argentine commercial bank reserves, and deposits in the

EXCHANGING PESOS AND DOLLARS IN ARGENTINA

One Argentine who had just returned from finishing an agricultural degree in the United States commented on the difference between Argentina when he left and when he returned. When he left in 1993, he had to seek special permission to purchase dollars, demonstrating his acceptance at the American university, and was allowed only a limited number of dollars. He was granted a license to get the dollars and took it to a bank. The process took days. When he returned to Argentina in 1996, he had carefully put some dollars aside. He asked a friend where he could turn them in to get pesos. "Anywhere," said his friend, pointing out kiosks, and all the banks on the street, "and all at one peso equals one dollar." He was amazed. Argentines have come to view the free convertibility of the peso into the dollar as part of their political, as well as economic, freedom.

commercial banks.* The central bank, however, cannot counterbalance this movement by purchasing T-bills. Could it use advances to banks or repos? It might, but it has another problem—it has lost its backing for 10 million pesos worth of currency, which it would repurchase from the commercial banks. The banks would scramble to get the currency. They can only do this by allowing their loans to fall; as the loans and deposits they create fall, the demand for currency declines and the public turns some currency into the banks (lines 2 and 3). The Bank of Argentina buys back the currency, granting the banks credit for the currency they turn in. It all balances, but the result is a decline in deposits by $10 million.

Since bank reserves are now restored, can loans be expanded back to where they started? No. If the banks lend more money, the public will demand more currency, and the banks have no way of getting that currency. In Argentina, currency forms over 60% of the money, a sharp contrast to figures for developed countries like Canada, where it is only 18%. This means that many of the new loans, rather than being redeposited into other banks, are taken out as currency. This reduces the deposit and money multipliers.

Argentina's fixed exchange rate is part of a strong anti-inflationary program designed to give credibility to the government's intentions to maintain low inflation. It is only one part of major reforms intended to "tie the government's hands," so that it cannot repeat the monetary abuses of recent decades. Unable to use the central bank to create additional money, the government has been forced into major fiscal reforms, both increasing revenues and decreasing expenditures. To cut expenditures and raise money, it engaged in major privatizations—even road maintenance is partially privatized and

---

* The $ sign also stands for pesos; indeed, it is originally a Spanish symbol, basically the *8* referring to the "piece of eight," a Spanish coin worth about one dollar.

Table 15.2
ARGENTINE T-ACCOUNTS (MILLIONS)

	Bank of Argentina			Argentine Commercial Banks	
	Assets	Liabilities		Assets	Liabilities
1. FX	− 10	− 10 CBD	Reserves − 10		− 10 Deposits
2.		− 10 currency	Loans − 10		− 10 Deposits
3.		+ 10 CBD	Reserves + 10		+ 10 Deposits
Net FX	− 10	− 10 currency	Currency − 10		− 10 Deposits

drivers find themselves paying a peso every few miles in exchange for a decently maintained road. To promote competition, it lowered trade barriers. It has, moreover, stuck with its policy of a fixed exchange rate, even though it has faced several periods of currency outflow and absolute declines in the money supply as a result. While output and employment have suffered, most Argentines feel the avoidance of inflation has been worth the price. Principally on the basis of his economic policy, President Carlos Menem was elected to a second term, and a constitutional amendment was required to allow him to seek office again. Neither of the two leading political coalitions advocates an abandonment of the tie to the dollar.

For most countries, the Argentine solution would be too severe. The restrictions on monetary policy are unnecessary for many countries, whose governments have been more responsible. Most of the East Asian countries, for instance, lacked a history of rapid inflation. Countries with strong anti-inflationary monetary policy, as shown below in the discussion of Canada, can face depreciation without consequent inflation. Besides, in East Asia, the problem until 1997 was the inflow of foreign currency. If the Argentines experience a major inflow of dollars, they would find themselves creating a great deal of money, and the same laws that tie the hands of the government to create money prevent it from the moderate creation of money under a strong dollar inflow. (Further discussion is in Chapter 18.)

THE CANADIAN SITUATION

In contrast to many of the countries in Latin America, Canada has held its price level remarkably stable, notwithstanding two major depreciations of its currency. In the 1990s, despite the large amount of trade as a percentage of GDP (close to 80%) and a 30% increase in the cost of the U.S. dollar, consumer prices rose less than 15%, less than 2% a year. The Canadian dollar fell

Figure 15.8

CANADIAN DOLLAR AND INFLATION, 1990—1998

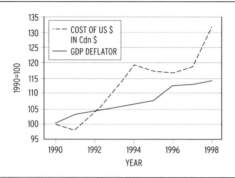

17.5%, from 87 cents to 72 cents, from 1991 to 1994 and 11%, from 73 cents to 65 cents, in 1996-98 (Figure 15.8). How could this happen with so little impact on the price level?

The answers are several. (1) The 1991-93 period was accompanied by lower tariffs, with both the Canada-U.S. Free Trade Agreement and the Uruguay round cuts coming in, and invigorated competition on the retail level, including the entry of Walmart and numerous "big box" retailers. Fighting hard for market share, firms were reluctant to raise prices, particularly since they expected little inflation. Of the major industries, only the automobile industry actually passed on all of the price increases to the market. Reading materials, furniture, household appliances, clothing, and audiovisual equipment all kept their price increases far under the decreased value of the dollar, but most even under the price increases in the American market. Audiovisual equipment actually saw price decreases.[2] What this means is that AS did not shift upward as the devaluation occurred, allowing the tight money policy to continue without inducing more extensive unemployment. (2) It is possible that Canada was just fortunate in that the increased competition and lower tariffs coincided with the decline in the value of the Canadian dollar. But the decline in the dollar in 1996-98 also appears to have stimulated very little inflation. Partly, this reflects the continued intensity of retail competition, partly the decline in prices of a number of imports from countries whose currencies have fallen much farther than the Canadian dollar. It may also reflect a decline in the prices of the non-tradable sector, although that is as yet unclear. (3) The Bank of Canada came increasingly to target the inflation rate and let the exchange rate move. If, as in the 1990s, the lower Canadian dollar did not interfere with inflation control, the Bank did not attempt to control its value.

EXCHANGE CONTROL

Any law that interferes with the free exchange of one currency for another is a form of exchange control. Exchange controls range from very mild measures, such as that requiring that all purchasers of foreign exchange have a license, the vast majority of which are automatically granted, to the draconian, where every exporter must turn over its foreign earnings to the government, every importer must have a license to purchase foreign exchange, every party that wants to move money abroad for travel, investment, or education must have a license, and every party that wants to bring in capital also must explain why and be given permission.

Although later used by some of the most democratic countries, exchange control had its origins with Stalin and Hitler.[3] Both attempted to preserve their countries' gold stocks by controlling the purchase of foreign exchange using the more severe measures described above. By the end of World War II every European country and many Latin American countries had their own forms of exchange control, turning trade, travel, and repatriation of foreign earnings into a complex bureaucratic process with extensive intergovernmental negotiation. As many new countries were formed in subsequent decades, they tended to follow the practices of their former colonial masters. The International Monetary Fund (see Chapter 17), founded in 1947, was given the task of gradually persuading countries to reduce their exchange controls. Most of the Western European countries eliminated the last vestiges of exchange control in the 1970s, but until the Thatcher government Britain still retained restrictions on how much of their private savings its residents could spend abroad. Many Latin American, Asian, and African countries maintained their exchange controls into the 1990s and, indeed, a number of countries still persist. Nigeria and Brazil, the largest countries on their continents, still have them.

Consider the experience of Peru after World War II. The Peruvian currency was the sol and in 1945 it was worth about 15.5 U.S. cents, or 6.5 soles to the dollar. Under pressure from powerful urban interest groups, the government tried to keep the price of imported food and other essentials down by fixing the exchange rate at the 1945 level, even though inflation was moving along at 30% or so a year. As Peruvian prices rose, imports appeared cheaper and many people wanted to import. Lacking sufficient foreign exchange the government established an exchange control system, rationing foreign exchange, and issuing permits to purchase it only to those it favored. Exporters suffered because the government insisted they turn over all their foreign exchange earnings and receive only 6.5 soles per dollar. Exports of mining products and cotton fell considerably. Figure 15.9 demonstrates what happened.

The Peruvian government rationed its expected foreign exchange receipts (represented as dollars) at the line marked Quota. At a price of 6.5 soles to the dollar, exporters were forced to limit their exports and they brought in only the Quota amount of dollars. Demand, however, was great at 6.5, amounting to Q^*. Since that amount could not be supplied, all those between the Quota and Q^* could not buy dollars. Measured by the scarcity, the sol was actually worth no more than about 5 cents, or 21 to the dollar. (This would be a guess for the actual situation, but the black market price was even higher.)

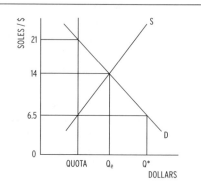

Figure 15. 9

FOREIGN EXCHANGE
CONTROL IN PERU

Foreign exchange restrictions transfer an enormous amount of power to whoever decides who gets the license. Figure 15.9 shows that a dollar could be purchased for soles and sold for 21 soles (or, the goods imported with the dollars could be sold for the equivalent price). The license, in essence, was worth about 15 soles per dollar. The temptation to bribe and be bribed was enormous, as was the invention of absolutely convincing reasons why someone just had to have that foreign exchange so even an honest and conscientious official would be persuaded to grant the request. In Peru's case, the exchange control did not last long enough for the kind of systematic bribery that has emerged in many countries. At one point, however, the government had granted import licenses to goods and not granted the licenses to buy the foreign exchange. Ships that came to port with goods that had been ordered with import licenses were forbidden to unload and the port became so clogged that the government did away with the exchange controls and ordered the army to help unload the ships.

In 1948 the government decided previous policies were a mistake and reduced most of the exchange control. The sol went to about 14 per dollar, or 7 cents. Was that a decline in value from 15 cents (6.5/$) or a rise from 5 cents (21/$)? As many Peruvians had argued, the exchange control was in fact a "hidden devaluation," and the actual devaluation that followed only reflected what had already occurred. Exports did recover and the economy had reasonable growth well into the late 1960s, when a left-wing military group took control and reintroduced exchange control. Subsequent military and civilian governments failed to re-establish the prosperity that had seemed plausible in the 1960s.

JOIN THE ARMY, MAKE A KILLING

Since the army has ruled Nigeria for all but ten of its 39 years as an independent country, many Nigerians have joined up with the dream of getting rich. Pay and conditions are tough but for any soldier lucky enough to make it to brigadier or general, the possibilities have been wondrous: a state governorship or the directorship of a state company, bringing millions of dollars within reach.

One of the easiest ways corrupt officials have got at this money is by exploiting the dual exchange rate. The official rate nowadays is 22 naira to the dollar, the market rate about 89 naira. The official rate is reserved for government contracts—and Sani Abacha, the soldier-president who died in June, was generous in giving import contracts to his cronies, many of them generals.

The system works like this. The lucky recipient borrows money from the bank (generals figure prominently on bank boards) and buys many more dollars at the official rate than are needed to buy the imported goods. The goods are then bought (unless the importer forgets this stage) and the rest of the dollars sold on the street at the market rate.

General Abdulsalam Abubakar has said that he will abolish the dual exchange-rate system, but not until the end of the year. Will this allow a last quick slurp at the trough? Some of the lucky ones are feeling the pinch. They have, after all, spent lavishly on such necessities as mansions, cars, extra wives, trips to Europe, and school fees. Many lost money they put into shady banks which collapsed or were shut down by the government. It is not safe to assume that Nigeria's top military officials feel rich enough to retire forever to their villages.[*]

Devaluation, in this sense, worked because prices already had risen, reflecting the scarcity of foreign exchange. There was, in a sense, no shift upward in AS because that had already occurred. Consequently, the devaluation—if that is what it was—did not cause any change in the rate of inflation.

THE ONCE-AND-FOR-ALL
DEVALUATION AFTER GREAT INFLATION

A situation somewhat analogous to devaluation after exchange control is devaluation after great inflation. Devaluation is an important means to re-establish a country's trade competitiveness after it has suffered a severe inflation. Cassell's original ideas to use purchasing power as a guide to re-establishing exchange rates after general severe inflation was sound, and

---

[*] *The Economist* (October 17, 1998): 52. (Note that the new civilian government made important moves in 1999 to correct this problem.)

post-World War I Europe was almost an ideal place to use such a policy. Different rates of inflation in each of the countries, different borders, and vastly changed economic conditions had thrown the pre-war exchange rates vastly out of alignment, and the simplest approach might have been a once-and-for-all resetting of exchange rates, with the high-inflation countries devaluing. Instead, some of the countries undertook the monumental task of trying to force their price levels lower, a task they failed to accomplish.

One of the more dramatic examples of the economic consequences of avoiding devaluation after inflation was that of Britain in 1925—a failure so great as to cause Winston Churchill, then the Chancellor of the Exchequer, to lose his place in the Tory leadership until the outbreak of World War II. As Chapter 17 explains, Britain had not pegged the pound against other currencies since World War I. Churchill thought it was time to do so, but did not seem to recognize that pegging the pound at the pre-war rate (US$4.80 = £1.00) would leave it greatly overvalued. John Maynard Keynes, recognizing what was about to happen, penned a pamphlet, *The Economic Consequences of Mr. Churchill* (following his *Economic Consequences of the Peace*), in which he predicted that pegging the pound at that high rate would lead to a trade deficit, a capital outflow, and a recession. Keynes turned out to be right. It is one thing to be like Argentina or Ireland and use a fixed exchange rate to hold an existing exchange rate; it is quite another to try to force prices down.[4]

Devaluation to Stimulate a Lagging Economy

For a nation with substantial unemployment far to the left of where AS_{SR} and AS_{LR} meet, devaluation looks like an attractive way to increase national income. Some nations have used devaluation for just that purpose. France in the late 1920s under the pretext of "going on the gold standard" purchased gold extensively, thereby increasing the supply of francs and holding down the value of the French franc.[5]

The difficulty with using devaluation to stimulate income comes in the hidden assumption of the income diagram—the horizontality of the aggregate supply curve. The devaluation will increase real income only insofar as there is a pool of unemployed labor (and other idle factors) that, because prices are rigid in a downward direction, cannot be employed at current prices and wages. Besides, the income that a trade surplus produces, while it does cut foreign debt, does not by definition contribute to absorption. So it is only the added consumption from the multiplier effect that is a net contribution to absorption. That is, you cannot eat (or absorb) your exports.

Perhaps it is best that devaluations are not often successful in stimulating large increases in income because such policies are successful only insofar as they "make beggars of their neighbors." France's trade surplus in the late

Figure 15.10

SELECTED ASSETS AND LIABILITIES OF GERMAN CENTRAL
BANK AND MONEY SUPPLY, QUARTERLY DATA, 1970‑1973

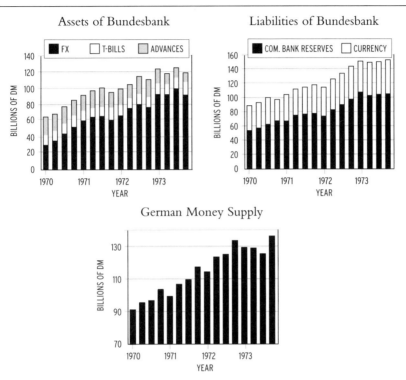

Source: IFS, 1999.

1920s was England's deficit and whatever additional AD was created in France came at the expense of lower AD in the United Kingdom. If the policy-makers are going to be Keynesian, there are surely better ways to expand aggregate demand than beggaring one's neighbor.

REVALUATION (UPWARD VALUATION)

To this point the discussion has centered on devaluation. Partly, this derives from the ease of explaining models in just one context. But countries adjust their exchange rates upward as well as downward, and not all of the models can be reversed.

In the great exchange rate crisis of 1971-72, it was not the United States that devalued but Germany, Japan, and Switzerland that revalued. Why should it be the countries with heavy current and capital account inflows that make the change? After all, while a heavy capital inflow is not "a good thing" to an economist, it is not as bad as having a heavy outflow. Often, the onus is on the troubled debtor, not the grumbling creditor.

The answer lies in what Chapter 13 showed: it is impossible for most countries to *sterilize* a heavy inflow on the balance of payments. The central bank counterbalances through selling T-bills or reducing advances to commercial banks. It may not have enough of either to counteract the inflow. Consider the case of Germany's Bundesbank from 1970 to 1973, as shown in Figure 15.10. An inflow of short-term capital caused the Bundesbank to purchase large amounts of foreign assets. Difficult to counterbalance, these expanded bank reserves and the money supply.

Worries about the size of the American current account and budget deficits drove international investors to pull money out of U.S. dollars and into Germany, Switzerland and Japan. The figures for the Bundesbank show that holdings of foreign assets rose DM51 billion from the first quarter of 1970 to the third quarter of 1972. The holdings of T-bills and advances to banks in the first quarter of 1970 were only DM34 billion. The bank had no way of sterilizing or even moderately counteracting the monetary effect of the inflow, even were it to cut all its holdings of T-bills and bank advances to zero. This led to a large expansion of the money supply from DM90.6 billion to DM133 billion in the fourth quarter of 1972, as shown in the bottom panel of Figure 15.10. To prevent further expansion of the money supply and consequent inflation, the Bundesbank allowed the DM to float and cut down its intervention.

Germany and Switzerland did not want their money supplies to rise and create an inflation. That might have corrected the payments problems, but they viewed the cost of inflation as too great. They therefore opted for revaluation to make their exports less competitive and increase their imports.

PRICE SENSITIVITY: WHAT HAPPENS WHEN PRICE EFFECTS WORK SLOWLY

To this point, the short-run problem of most significance has been that of the unemployment that might be generated if the short-run AS curve rises after devaluation. There is another quite serious effect, also short run and also dangerous. An exchange rate change may have a short-run price effect opposite to that expected and the trade balance will worsen. At the very least the response to the change in prices will be weak, although in the right direction.

The Necessary Demand Conditions

The worst-case scenario requires some special conditions. The Marshall-Lerner theory (after Abba Lerner, who took one of Alfred Marshall's models to illustrate these points) conjures up a specter to haunt policy-makers who try devaluations. What the M-L theory says, in essence, is that a devaluation will work only if the demand for a nation's exports and that nation's demand for imports are sufficiently elastic; to be more precise, the two elasticities, added together, have to exceed 1, or the devaluation will make the trade balance worse.

Take a simple example. Suppose the U.S. dollar and the Canadian dollar are, as they were for a number of years, at par—a U.S. dollar equals a Canadian dollar. Suppose further that the Canadians spend about $100 million a month on imports from the U.S. and the Americans spend $100 million on imports from Canada. Now suppose Canada devalues its dollar by 20%. Will the devaluation increase exports and decrease imports?

Suppose the Canadian demand for imports is highly inelastic—indeed, it has an elasticity of zero. It certainly would be low in the very short run because almost all the imports have already been ordered and virtually all are invoiced in U.S. dollars. The Canadians would therefore import the same quantity of U.S. goods and would have to pay 20% more for them. The result: $120 million Canadian on the market where there had been only $100 million before.

And, to make things more difficult, suppose the Americans had a demand for Canadian exports of zero elasticity.* Since the Americans do not need any more imports from Canada, they will pay only 80 cents for the Canadian dollar—and only $80 million U.S. are put on the market. Those dollars equal $100 million Canadian at the new exchange rate of US$0.80 = Cdn$1.00. The result: a trade deficit of $20 million Canadian. Summarized on Table 15.3, it is Set 1, the first pair of comparisons.

Now suppose, as in Set 2, the demand elasticity of Canada's imports is still zero, but that its exports had an elasticity of 1—that is, a 20% decrease in price triggers a 20% increase in volume, which means total revenue is unchanged (Set 2 in Table 15.3). In such a situation, Canada's importers would respond by placing Cdn$120 million on the market, but the American importers would offer the same US$100 million. The value in Canadian dollars of those $100 million is Cdn$120. The balance of trade is unchanged.

Or suppose, as in Set 3, that the elasticity of Canada's imports was 1, and that of the U.S. for Canadian exports was zero. In that case $100 million Canadian trades for $80 million U.S. The US$80 million is worth Cdn$100 million, which again gives us no change in the trade balance.

---

* This is actually unlikely even in the very short run because most of the invoices are also in U.S. dollars.

Table 15.3

EFFECT OF 20% DEVALUATION OF CANADIAN DOLLAR
UNDER DIFFERENT ELASTICITY ASSUMPTIONS

Set	Importer	Elasticity	US$		Cdn$	Balance of Trade
1	Canadian	0			120	− 20
	U.S.	0	80	=	100	
2	Canadian	0			120	0
	U.S.	1	100	=	100	
3	Canadian	1			100	0
	U.S.	0	80	=	100	
4	Canadian	.75	85	=	102	+ 13
	U.S.	.75	92	=	115	

The two extreme examples with an elasticity of zero and the other of 1 just meet the Marshall-Lerner condition that *the sum of the two elasticities must equal at least 1 for the balance of trade to improve.* The same would be true of any other combination of elasticities—e.g., 0.5 for each of the demands. Anything that adds up to more than 1 will improve the balance of trade. Set 4 shows a situation in which both the demand for imports and the demand for Canada's exports are inelastic (0.75), but the effect is quite positive. Canadian importers reduce their consumption of American goods to US$85 million, worth Cdn$102 million.[6] The U.S. importers from Canada will spend 15% more Canadian dollars, but need only purchase them at 80 cents so will offer US$92 million. The trade balance improves by Cdn$13 million.

Elasticities in Practice: An Assessment

Most economists agree that nearly always there exist the minimum elasticities required to avoid the Marshall-Lerner bind. A.C. Harberger's studies have shown that the short-run elasticities of demand for imports into a typical country are at least as high as 0.5 or 1, while the elasticity of demand for the same typical country's exports is at least 2 and usually higher. The result is that the Marshall-Lerner minimum conditions (that the sum of the elasticities of the demands for a nation's imports and exports exceed 1) are almost always satisfied.

Theoretically, a number of factors contribute to the adequacy of the elasticities. The first is the question of time. The longer the time period, the higher the elasticities. In the very short run (usually a few months) elasticities are probably very low. As noted in the discussion of Canada, above, the currency of invoice is important. Most trade is invoiced in U.S. dollars and therefore a country devaluing against the United States dollar will find that its imports, already ordered or on the way, do not fall and its importers simply have to fork up the extra money to pay for these imports. The saving grace here, however, is that exports are also invoiced in U.S. dollars, so the U.S. importers cannot reduce the amount of U.S. dollars they have agreed to pay. Accordingly, the situation will tend toward the very minimum Marshall-Lerner condition with the sum of the elasticities close to 1.

The opposite occurs if the nation devaluing is also the nation of the currency of invoice—the United States would find that import prices would not rise immediately, but export prices would not fall either. Again, the Marshall-Lerner condition would be just barely met. The examples can also be worked for nations who tie their currencies to the dollar—e.g., Thailand, more or less tied to the U.S. dollar, trading with Japan, not tied to U.S. dollar. If the dollar falls against the yen and the currency of invoice is the dollar, Thai imports would not fall, but neither would its receipts from exports.

The demand for imports is usually far more elastic than that for the goods themselves. The reason is that, as imports fall in price, they not only increase the total sales of the good, but also displace domestic supplies. Elasticities of imports are also fairly high because of the increasing amount of substitutability. A great deal of trade, as Chapter 3 showed, is *intraindustrial*—that is, trade within the same industry as automobiles for automobiles, appliances for appliances, or airplanes for airplanes. Because such goods are close substitutes, elasticities are high.[*]

Many years ago, an economic journalist questioned the effect the devaluation of the U.S. dollar would have on this "wheat- and jumbo-jet-exporting nation." The phrase nicely summarizes the problem of the rapid response of exports. Cutting the price of wheat is probably not going to bring in more foreign exchange since demand elasticities for foods are highly inelastic. Similarly, many capital goods are not strikingly price-sensitive. If an airline needs jumbo jets, it orders them. If it doesn't need them, it doesn't order them simply because they are 10% off. Demand, of course, can shift between Boeing and Airbus, but demand as a whole for many large-ticket capital goods may not be highly elastic. (The saving grace here is that the export market for many capital goods is highly imperfect. If Boeing does not think that lower prices will sell more aircraft, it won't cut the price; and no other

---

[*] In the short run, intra-firm trade may be less elastic. A firm that builds a plant in one country to supply a plant in another cannot quickly switch when the exchange rate changes. Such a situation is particularly important in the trade of intermediate goods. See, for instance, Jane Sneddon Little, "Intra-firm Trade: An Update," *New England Economic Review*, Federal Reserve Bank, Boston (May/June, 1987): 46–51.

Figure 15.11

J-CURVE EFFECT

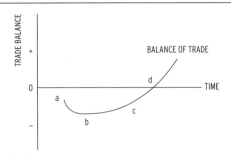

Note: The country devalues at point *a*. The ensuing months see the balance of trade worsen to point *b*, whereupon it improves. At point *c* it is the same as it was when devaluation occurred. At point *d*, the trade deficit ceases. The critical period is *a-c*, the width of the J.

American firm makes jumbo jets. Given the larger profit margin, however, Boeing may add features to the airplane or give more favorable service arrangements, using non-price competition to further its sales.)

J-Curves

Typically, a country that devalues its currency sees a fall or no improvement in its trade balance for several months or longer, and then an improvement. The trade balance, plotted over a time period, looks like a J (Figure 15.11). Since Marshall-Lerner type effects are most likely in the very short run, it is quite possible that a country's trade deficit will worsen immediately after a devaluation or depreciation of its currency, as the full effects of the price change will take some time to work their way through the economic system. Some of the non-price changes noted above may take even more time to be effective.* As the months move on, the trade balance ceases to worsen, then, as the elasticities rise, it begins to improve, often quite rapidly. In such cases, the devaluing country must have the foreign exchange funds to prevent further declines in its currency over the initial few months after devaluation.

If the bottom of the J is deep or wide so that recovery does not appear to be taking place, the country may be tempted to devalue again. Or, under floating rates, the market itself may perceive that no improvement is forthcoming and thus may force a further depreciation. J-curve becomes added onto J-curve in such a situation, which can worsen rapidly, as Figure 15.12 shows.

If a country faces a J-curve effect, it must have the foreign exchange funds to prevent further declines in its currency over the initial few months after

---

* If a company decides that foreign profits will be gained more effectively by selling an improved and more costly to make product than by lowering its price, it may take several years to develop the product.

Figure 15.12
REPEATED DEVALUATIONS AND SUCCESSIVE J-CURVES

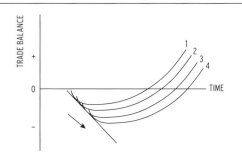

Note: A series of repeated devaluations or declines in the value of a currency causes a series of J-curves to form. Because the market (or central bank) does not wait until the curve begins to turn upward, it keeps introducing new price declines. As a result, the balance of trade appears to worsen, following the line more or less tangent with the edges of the J-curves.

devaluation. Otherwise, it might face new pressures for devaluation and put itself once again in the downward sloping part of the J. One of the problems suggested for floating rates has been that, without monetary intervention, the exchange rate will keep declining, putting the country into situations where the demand and supply of imports are highly inelastic. Such a pattern has been suggested for the United States in the 1980s, although a recent article argues strongly against that interpretation.[7]

Three Last Bracing Thoughts on Marshall-Lerner

1. *If devaluations won't work, lowering the price level will not work either.* Almost all the discussion of Marshall-Lerner is in the context of devaluation, yet the alternative of deflation (price effects only) depends equally on the two elasticities of demand for imports being high enough. The world is in a fine state if neither deflation nor depreciation works, because all that leaves for policy is the reduction of national incomes.

2. *If income effects eventually become price effects, recession won't work either, because the price system will ultimately adjust.* As prices of exports fall because of highly inelastic demand, foreign exchange receipts will fall, and as import prices rise, import demand will not be choked off enough. The only reason why lowering the price level might *look* as if it would work is that it is a more gradual process than devaluation and might avoid the downward section on the J-curve.

3. *If devaluation doesn't work, an increase in the value of a nation's currency will work.* That suggestion takes the breath away. Logically, this is true, yet no nation has ever proceeded to carry this out, which rather suggests that few people believe that Marshall-Lerner conditions prevail.

NEW ZEALAND'S J-CURVES

New Zealand provides some evidence of both kinds of J-curves. In the early 1980s New Zealand let its dollar fall and saw some response in improved trade. Like Sweden, however, New Zealand was unable to control its inflation. In the later 1980s it let the dollar tumble. We can see some lagged effects of this strategy, but, again, the underlying problems were not solved (although successive governments have been working on it).

Figure 15.13

NEW ZEALAND: J-CURVE, 1979-1985

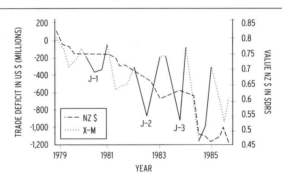

The New Zealand dollar depreciated in value considerably during the 1979-85 period, as indicated on the right-hand axis. The trade balance is measured along the left-hand axis. There appear to be three J-curves in this period, one following the depreciation of the N.Z. dollar during 1979, a second following the slide of the dollar in 1981, and a third following its continued slide in 1982. The 1984 devaluation showed only a small J effect.

This is not to dismiss the problem of high inelasticity. Rather, it is to suggest that some countries will respond more quickly to devaluation than others, and to counsel patience.

EXCHANGE RATE CHANGES AND THE EXIN MODEL

The EXIN model suggests some interesting interpretations of what happens when the exchange rate changes. A currency that falls in value stimulates exports and discourages imports, making it possible to have a better trade balance (and general improvement in the payments balance) at any given

Figure 15.14
EXCHANGE RATE CHANGES

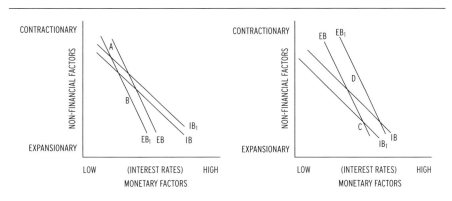

combination of fiscal and monetary policy position—that is, the external balance shifts to the left. The effects of the depreciation of the currency, however, change the internal balance as well. With the trade deficit smaller or with a trade surplus, aggregate demand is higher for any given combination of fiscal and monetary policy and the internal balance shifts to the right.

The left panel of Figure 15.14 shows the shifts in the curves, using *IB* to mean internal balance and *EB* to mean external balance. A falling currency might help a country in the area marked out by box *A*—suffering a payments deficit but also an economy that is underperforming. Many of the Western European countries in the Great Depression had this situation and devalued their currencies to try to get an economic boost as well as to improve their payments situations. (The policies did not work because other countries retaliated by doing the same thing.) If successful, the devaluation would shift both the external and internal balance borders onto *A*.

Brazil in 1998-99 exemplifies box *B*. It has had both a serious trade deficit and is experiencing inflation. The removal of central bank support for the Brazilian real may help alleviate the trade deficit, but it makes domestic balance harder to achieve. The shift in the internal and external balances brings Brazil closer to external balance, but much further away from internal balance. It will have to raise interest rates and follow tight fiscal policies if it is to get an internal balance. If it does not do so, eventually the inflation will drive the real lower again.

The right panel shows a situation in which a currency rises in value. The external balance shifts to the right and the internal balance shifts to the left. That is, at any level of interest rate and an unchanged fiscal policy, *X* − *M* will be a lower figure, but aggregate demand will be less. Point *C* could represent the United States either in the mid-1980s or late 1990s. With a low dollar, the country would have had inflation but a reasonable external balance. The rise in the dollar, however, took pressure off the internal balance, allowing low inflation, but worsened the trade deficit. IB_1 passes through point C, but EB_1 has moved far to the right. Point D could represent Japan in the late 1990s. Suffering from a recession and having a trade surplus, a rise in the yen would help reduce an embarrassing trade surplus, but it would almost undoubtedly worsen the recession.

CONCLUSION

Changes in exchange rates can trigger a large number of further changes: aggregate demand, aggregate supply, and price levels normally are all affected. This means that any change in the exchange rate must necessarily involve adjustments to monetary and fiscal policy. Indeed, in some cases it may also involve social and political changes. Sometimes, too, the beneficial effects of exchange rate changes are delayed or mitigated by the slowness of the economy to adjust and of exporters to respond to the change in incentives. Exchange rate adjustment is accordingly neither cure-all nor poison; rather it is part and parcel of a more general pattern of health or disease.

VOCABULARY AND CONCEPTS

Appreciation

COLA clauses

Credibility (of monetary authorities)

Depreciation

Devaluation

Exchange control

Fixed rate

Floating rate

Indexing (of prices)

J-curve

Limit price argument

Managed float

Marshall-Lerner condition

Non-tradable sector

Pegging

Trade-sensitive sector

Upward revaluation

PROJECTS

1. Check the latest data to see if the Argentines are still holding down inflation and keeping the peso equal to a dollar.
2. Find a country that has had frequent devaluations (you might try Sweden or Ireland in the 1970s or 1980s) and see if they show any signs of J-curves.
3. Examine the foreign exchange holdings of countries that allow their exchange rates to float. Do they show substantial sales or purchases of foreign exchange?

QUESTIONS

1. "The ability to influence the value of a currency on the foreign exchange market is simply too valuable a tool for countries to abstain from its use." What is monetary intervention used for?
2. Explain, using both an $S - I = X - M$ diagram and an AD/AS diagram, how devaluation can stimulate income and/or price-level effects. What happens if the money supply is not changed after a devaluation?
3. How can protectionism limit the effectiveness of devaluation?
4. If inflation is built into the political system, can devaluation ever be truly effective?
5. Explain why some countries see their price level rise rapidly after a devaluation, while others find it only rises modestly.
6. Why might an end to inflation and successive devaluations also mean an end to the government in power?
7. Given that many goods in the economy could be traded, why doesn't the domestic price level rise immediately after a devaluation?
8. What is the importance of credibility in fixing an exchange rate?
9. Explain why Argentina was able to end its inflation and peg its peso to the dollar, while Brazil was not.
10. How could Canada sustain a substantial decline in the value of its currency without generating significant inflation?
11. Explain why exchange control opens up opportunities for bribery or extortion. Use a demand-and-supply diagram.
12. "It is one thing to be like Argentina or Ireland and use a fixed exchange to hold an existing exchange rate; it is quite another to try to force prices down." Why is it difficult to try to force a deflation through adopting an overvalued currency?
13. What are the advantages and disadvantages of using devaluation to stimulate a weak economy?
14. A fixed exchange rate is a double-edged sword. It holds down inflation if the currency is weak. But it causes inflation if the currency is strong. Explain.

15. Explain the Marshall-Lerner condition and why it is only likely to happen in the short run.
16. Explain what a J-curve is and why it is important to recognize that they occur.
17. Try to place several countries of your choice on the EXIN framework and see what happens when you adjust the exchange rate.

NOTES

1. See Jereon J.M. Kremers, "Gaining policy credibility for a disinflation," *IMF Staff Papers* (March 1990): 116-35. See also *The Economist*, May 25, 1991, 111.

2. See Therese LaFleche, "The impact of exchange rate movements on consumer prices, *Bank of Canada Review* (Winter 1996-97): 21-32.

3. See "The cash don't work," *The Economist*, December 19, 1998, 98-100; Leland Yeager, *International Monetary Relations* (New York: Harper & Row, 1966): 322-24.

4. See Yeager, *International Monetary Relations*, 277-80.

5. Ibid., 285-86.

6. The figures: .75 = %dQ/dP; .75 = %dQ/.2; %dQ = .2*; .75 = .15. Fifteen percent of 100 is 15, so Canadian imports fall to US$85.

7. The Federal Reserve Board's Ellen E. Meade concluded that the J part was relatively shallow (for the U.S.) and that we cannot explain the U.S. balance-of-payments problem as a series of continuing J-curve effects. The article has some general discussion of interest also. Meade, "Exchange Rates, Adjustment and the J-curve," *Federal Reserve Bulletin* (October 1988): 633-44.

Chapter Sixteen

International
Financial Markets

OBJECTIVES

OVERALL OBJECTIVE   To provide an overview of international financial markets, showing the extent to which they fulfill the functions of financial markets, and then to analyze the economic implications of key changes in the markets.

MORE SPECIFICALLY
- To show how financial markets provide liquidity, information, and means for sharing risk and to examine these in an international context.
- To indicate the size of domestic and international capital markets, with explicit attention to the Eurodollar market.
- To demonstrate the functions of derivative and swap markets, illustrating in particular the characteristics of forward markets for currencies and their implications for covered interest rate arbitrage.
- To discuss the ongoing changes in international capital markets, including disintermediation, securitization, and risk unbundling.
- To introduce some of the problems that have emerged from large international flows of capital, including a discussion of a flight to quality and the role of hedging and speculation.

···

THE FUNCTIONS OF FINANCIAL MARKETS

Financial markets move funds—which represent the claims lenders have on resources but choose not to exercise—to borrowers who wish to use those resources. Such funds may move either through intermediaries such as banks, insurance companies, or mutual funds or directly through the purchase and sale of financial assets such as bonds, commercial paper, or corporate shares. Financial markets have three key functions: (1) to provide liquidity; (2) to allocate risk among the parties, frequently pooling risks so that they are shared; and (3) to provide information to allow participants to better assess and price their risk and loss of liquidity. Large financial markets almost always perform all these functions better than small ones, providing economies of scale (number of total transactions) and scope (the number of different kinds of financial instruments they have).

Liquidity

Liquidity is the ease with which an asset can be turned into cash. It can emerge from short maturity assets, as, for instance, a savings account, or a deposit "on call" (that is, a deposit that the borrower can retrieve on very short notification), or from having a good secondary (resale) market for long-term assets. The holder of a 90-day U.S. treasury bill, for instance, cannot receive payment from the government until the bill matures, but would have no problem selling the bill to someone else who would be willing to wait. Similarly, a company depositing money in a bank may receive a negotiable certificate of deposit, which allows it to sell the rights to the deposit and interest to any other company.

For an asset as secure as an American T-bill, the main risk in purchasing the bill is that the interest rate will rise before the bill matures, lowering its resale value. Typically, then, a T-bill presents very little *credit risk* (the borrower will pay for sure), but has *interest rate risk*. For less secure assets, buyers take the credit risk that the market's assessment of the likelihood of repayment will change (as in a Brazilian bond), and so they may have to sell at a discount to what they expected.

Liquidity is less in smaller markets. A person holding a five-year corporate note from an obscure Finnish corporation he knows personally to be reliable has no credit risk. But if he is suddenly faced with the need for some cash and wants to sell the note, he will find very few potential buyers who also know the reliability of the firm. He must wait, holding his price, until a knowledgeable buyer with a desire to invest comes along; alternatively, he can sell at a considerable discount to people who, lacking knowledge of Finnish companies, consider the investment risky or who do not feel that this type of investment, however secure, fits their investment portfolios at this time. Such secondary markets are described as "thin."

Liquidity is higher in larger markets because the secondary markets are much more active. The volume of sales in stock and bond markets is very much greater. The more unusual assets (e.g., Finnish *markkaa*-denominated bonds) have very small secondary markets and so are less liquid. The larger the market, however, the more likely it is that even the more unusual assets will have decent secondary markets. Borrowers will have lower costs in good secondary markets because they may issue a longer-term security, yet the lender may treat it as only a somewhat riskier short-term commitment.

Risk-Sharing and Allocation

Markets allow the sharing of risk in many marvelous ways. Depositors in banks know that some of the banks' borrowers will default, but recognize that the bank normally prices its loans to cover a typical amount of non-payments so that all depositors share the risk. Far better for 10,000 people to lend to a bank and have it lend to 1,000 people than to have those thousand go personally to wealthier friends and relatives to borrow, as was the pattern into the early part of the twentieth century. Individuals lending directly to firms can build a portfolio to protect themselves from a large loss from any one company in difficulty. These reflect a pooling of risk and portfolio benefits.

Markets can also match up opposite risks. Firms that will be hurt if the Canadian dollar falls can trade off that risk to firms who fear it will rise. Firms fearful of increases in interest rates can find trade-offs with those who fear a decrease in interest rates. In such situations the total amount of risk in a market declines. Most of these arrangements work through derivative and swap markets, discussed later in the chapter.

Information

Lastly, markets provide information that allows the pricing of risk and liquidity. Banks do vast amounts of research. Brokers and mutual funds have extensive research operations, and independent companies assess bond and country risks. It is not that they eliminate risk, but they can allow risk to be priced appropriately: if the risk of default is higher, lenders must make sure that they have priced their loans such that they can take some losses and still make money.

THE ADVANTAGES OF LARGE MARKETS

Larger markets provide more liquidity for more kinds of assets. Because of the size of the American economy, most secondary American financial markets are larger and therefore more liquid than other markets in the world. The markets for U.S. treasury bills and bonds allow a company to buy or sell quickly, and they are so large that an individual company's purchases and sales

Figure 16.1
CAPITAL MARKETS, 1995

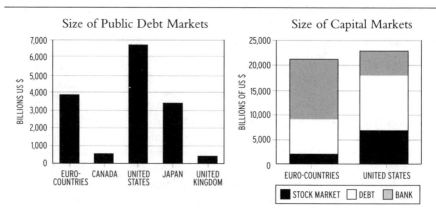

Source: IMF, *International Capital Markets*, November 1997, 23.

do not normally significantly affect the price. That simply is not true of the market for Canadian, Australian, or New Zealand T-bills. Nor has it been true in Europe, where T-bill markets are rather small. Even with the introduction of the euro, where all financial instruments are denominated in the same currency, important differences in risk exist between Italian, Portuguese, and German euro-denominated T-bills, just as there is a difference between Canadian bonds denominated in U.S. dollars and American bonds. (The *sovereign spread* is the difference between two bonds of different countries in the same currency.) The left panel Figure 16.1 shows some comparative figures on the size of the government bond markets.

The United States has by far the largest market in public debt, which includes short-term assets such as T-bills as well as medium- and long-term assets like bonds. The countries presently using the new euro have a market about 60% the size of the American market. Japan has a large government debt market, as do Canada and the U.K.

The right panel shows indicators of the larger capital markets, including the stock market, debt securities (bills and bonds), and bank assets. Here the American market is still dominant by size, but the emerging European market, to the extent that it becomes highly integrated, is close in size, and large enough to have virtually all of the advantages of scale and scope of the American market. At present, however, it still lacks the integration needed.

Larger markets also provide for more kinds of assets and for the secondary markets to support them. Financial wizards have a way of coming up with new kinds of instruments all the time. Each of the new innovations needs primary markets and good secondary markets. Otherwise, the cost of borrowing becomes too high as lenders demand high interest rates for loss of liquidity. Only really large markets can manage good secondary markets in a large variety of instruments—that is, to have the scale and scope to keep costs down.

AN OVERVIEW OF THE INTERNATIONAL MARKETS

International capital markets have all the complexities of national markets compounded by international elements. There are two classes of international activity. (1) *Cross-border* or *traditional markets* are those in which investors place their money in foreign banks or buy securities in another country, using the currency of the other country. A Canadian buying American stocks is engaging in a cross-border purchase, and a Canadian borrowing in the U.S. is taking a cross-border loan. Activity in such markets has grown considerably. (2) *Eurocurrency markets* are international markets where the accounts are kept and securities issued not in the currency of the country but in some other currency. An American company can deposit or borrow U.S. dollars in London or issue securities denominated in German marks in London as well.

The Eurocurrency Market

The Eurocurrency market consists of issues of loans, deposits, and securities denominated in currencies *other than* the currency of the nation in which the deposit is made or the securities are issued. Like any national market, the Eurocurrency market has bank loans, securities for short, medium, and long term, and a great variety of instruments among these. Unlike national markets, however, the debt is not denominated in the home currency.

When a security is issued or a loan made in a currency other than that of the nation in which it is issued, it is called a *Eurocurrency* debt. A British bank taking deposits in U.S. dollars and lending in U.S. dollars is making *Eurodollar* transactions. An American investment house syndicating securities denominated in Japanese yen (but not issued in Japan) is selling *Euroyen* securities. A European company borrowing long term and issuing bonds denominated in SDRs is also in the Eurocurrency market.

No logical reason exists why debt should have to be denominated in the currency of the debtor or that of the creditor. Indeed, it need not be denominated in any specific currency at all. Companies issue bonds in both SDRs and ECUs.* The practice is hardly new. Medieval European merchants often stated debt in terms of coins of known quality but no longer minted, or minted with

---

* An SDR is a unit of account the IMF uses. It consists of 35.19% euros, 27.2% yen, 10.5% British pounds, and 58.821% U.S. dollars. An ECU is a European currency unit, made up of a weighted basket of European currencies. See *IMF Survey*, January 11, 1999, 5.

Figure 16.2

INTERNATIONAL CAPITAL MARKET COMPARED WITH
DOMESTIC MARKETS IN SELECTED MAJOR COUNTRIES

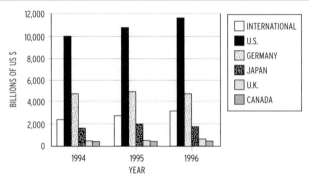

Source: IMF, *International Capital Markets*, November 1997, 23; also Annex 4, 184-99.

less gold content than earlier coins; bills drawn at fairs might be stated in Venetian gold ducats of 1480, meaning the gold content of those earlier ducats.[1]

Virtually every major industrial country has a *Euro-* version of its domestic currency.* Bank deposits and loans, particularly of shorter duration, are predominantly in U.S. dollars, hence the phrase "Eurodollar market", which often applies somewhat loosely to all the Eurocurrency markets. Because the longer-run value of the U.S. dollar is uncertain, many longer-term securities are issued in currencies other than the U.S. dollar.[2] A borrower wishing to pay a low interest rate may choose to issue its debt in a currency expected to be stable or to rise in value. Manitoba Hydroelectric, the provincially owned electric utility, for instance, borrowed in Japanese yen. The corporation thereby traded off a lower interest rate against the risk that the currency will not rise in value. Manitoba Hydroelectric gets its revenue in Canadian and American dollars, which have fallen in value against the yen, so has found its debt burden rising as it has had to pay more to buy the yen to service its debt.

The international capital market—including both traditional and Eurocurrency markets—is much smaller than total domestic markets. Total domestic markets are about US$26 trillion, compared to a "mere" $3.2 trillion for the international market. Still, that $3.2 trillion makes the international market larger than the domestic capital markets in all countries but those of the United States and Japan, as Figure 16.2 shows.

---

* *The Economist*'s weekly tables list Australian dollars, Austrian schillings (bonds only), Belgian francs, British pounds, Canadian dollars, Danish and Swedish crowns, French francs, German marks, Dutch guilders, Italian lira, Japanese yen, Spanish pesetas, Swiss francs, and U.S. dollars. One supposes that London will soon have its own version of the new euro, the Euroeuro.

ORIGINS OF THE EURODOLLAR MARKET

Before World War I, London was the chief financial market for the world. In the interwar decades, New York gradually came to overshadow London as the most important financial market. The dollar remained strong while the sterling faltered, and all of London's financial acumen could not attract a large amount of foreign deposits denominated in sterling. British exchange control during World War II and into the postwar period made the position of the London banks even worse. While London withered as a market, New York waxed stronger. Was London to disappear as a major international financial center? No, thanks to the invention of a new class of financial instruments—Eurodollars.

In the 1950s a momentum began to build in Europe for a new kind of capital market, one free of the limitations of using only domestic currencies to denominate debt. The impetus came from a number of governmental decisions that, by hindsight, seem unwise in their impact on the New York and London capital markets. Basically, both the British and American governments were concerned about the amount of short-term lending their banks were making abroad and restricted them, through controls and taxes, from lending more. The British restrictions came in 1957 and the American in 1963, with the effect of sharply reducing the loans the two biggest capital markets in the world could make. The American market remained open for Canada and many Third World countries, but the Japanese and the Europeans lost their source of short-term dollar financing. Where could they turn to borrow and lend in the world's major currency?

For years, London banks had checking accounts in foreign currencies, principally dollars. Any individual or business could open a dollar account with a London bank, depositing dollars and writing checks in dollars. In the 1950s many Communist bloc countries had begun to make dollar deposits in London to have the security and liquidity associated with dollars, yet to avoid the scrutiny and possible freezing of their funds that would occur were they to hold dollars in an American bank.* London banks realized that they could use such accounts to provide the basis for lending dollars rather than sterling. They could thereby avoid the restrictions on the foreign lending of sterling and at the same time take advantage of the world's demand for dollar-denominated loans and deposits. They began to promote the idea of making dollar deposits with them and in turn they would make dollar loans. Soon the name "Eurodollars" came to apply to such transactions.

---

* The term "Eurodollar" appears to have derived from a Soviet-owned bank in France, the Banque Commerciale pour l'Europe du Nord, whose cable address was EUROBANK. Because the Russians were among the first extensive users of such accounts, they were called Eurodollars.

Most investors were not interested in putting dollars into London simply for current account use. Rather, they wished to make short-term deposits for periods of a few weeks to a few months. While the British did pay some interest on the regular *external* checking accounts, investors sought higher returns and London was ready with a variety of means for providing what was sought. It soon developed deposits for money *on call* (whenever the depositor requested), 30, 60, and 90 days, and followed the American lead immediately when in 1961 American banks developed the certificate of deposit.*

The popularity of Eurodollars grew rapidly. They were convenient—that is, the *transaction costs* of borrowing or lending were lower. European borrowers of dollars did not need to develop contacts with American banks and could instead deal with their own banks. American banks and corporations with dollars to lend found it much easier to lend these dollars to European banks than to try to place the dollars themselves in Europe. They thus avoided the problems of credit risk and lack of knowledge concerning local markets and conditions. The aggravating difference in business hours between Europe and America could be avoided by Europeans who dealt in dollars with European banks. Finally, there was also a crucial competitive factor. British banks found that dollar-denominated deposits were an excellent way to attract additional deposits and, by running leaner operations, they could reduce the *spread* between what they paid for deposits and what they charged for loans below what New York could.

Again, U.S. regulations were partially to blame for the early boost to the Eurodollar market. (They certainly were not the entire cause of the market's growth because it remains vigorous today after all the regulations that contributed to its rapid growth have been relaxed.) The Federal Reserve regulated the interest rates, time periods, and reserve requirements on time deposits. American banks had to hold 5% of all time deposits as reserves, while European banks could use their discretion, which frequently meant they carried no reserves specifically for the Eurodollar deposits. This meant that an American bank with a $100,000 savings deposit could lend only $95,000 of it, while the European bank with the same deposit could lend it all. At 10% interest, the European bank would earn $500 more a year and could therefore undercut the American rate.[3] American banks also could not pay interest on the shorter-term deposits (e.g., CD deposits of less than 90 days). Moreover, when interest rates rose sharply in the 1970s as a response to worldwide inflation, American banks found themselves up against a regulatory ceiling on interest rates they could pay to secure funds. Many of their big depositors therefore just moved their money to the Eurodollar market, which was not so constrained.

---

* A certificate of deposit or CD is a negotiable interest-bearing certificate indicating a fixed sum has been deposited and will be paid back on a given date.

American banks did not want to miss out on the Eurodollar action, and large numbers of them moved to London to accept Eurodollar deposits and issue loans. All the major banks and many smaller ones (forming joint banks to operate abroad) opened London banks.[4]

The Eurodollar Bank Loan Market Today

Some banks, particularly the London banks, have been successful at collecting Eurodollar deposits, but frequently do not have ready places to lend the money. A vigorous market developed in which banks with surplus Eurodollars could sell them to other banks with ready borrowers. The market is much like the foreign exchange market, with large amounts of Eurodollars traded in blocks and frequently going through several banks on their way to the final borrower.

Longer-Term Securities

While Eurodollar deposits and loans were the principal short-term instruments in the Eurocurrency market, the securities market developed somewhat differently. It began with the issue of bonds—long-term securities—denominated, at first, predominantly in dollars, but soon in a variety of other currencies as well. The advantages of issuing a Eurocurrency bond lay in the ability to tap an international capital market with one bond issue rather than having to employ the more complex and considerably more expensive method of issuing *parallel bonds* in several national markets. Eurocurrency bonds also had more freedom from national rules, which lay most heavily on the issue of bonds to nationals in the country of issue; a Dutch firm issuing Eurodollar bonds and selling them in France was far less constrained than if it offered guilder bonds in the Netherlands and incidentally sold some in France as well.

The medium-term markets developed more slowly than either the short- or long-term markets. Secondary markets were thin, forcing many buyers to hold securities until their expiration. It has only been since the 1980s that the medium-term markets for securities have grown vigorously and come to fill out the market.[5] Nonetheless, the medium-term markets are still considered illiquid. The British and European banks have been particularly innovative in their approach to the medium-term market. One invention was the *floating rate note* or FRN, where the borrower is guaranteed receipt of a certain amount of capital, but the interest rate paid goes up or down depending on market conditions. Normally such rates are expressed as percentages above a base rate, which in the case of the Eurodollar markets is the *London Interbank Offer*

Table 16.1
T-ACCOUNT FOR EURODOLLAR BORROWING

American Banks		London Bank		Banque de Paris	
Assets	Liabilities	Assets	Liabilities	Assets	Liabilities
± 0	Deposits GM − 1m Lloyds + 1m	U.S. deposit + 1m	GM + 1m		
± 0	Lloyds − 1m BdeP + 1m	Loan to BdeP + 1m U.S. deposit − 1m	GM + 1m	U.S. deposit + 1m	Loan from Lloyds + 1m
± 0	BdeP − 1m Pechiney + 1m			U.S. deposit Loan to Pechiney + 1m	− 1m
± 0	Pechiney − 1m Various payees of Pechiney +1m				

Rate (LIBOR).[*] LIBOR is the interest rate banks pay each other to borrow short-term funds in the Eurodollar market.[6]

EURODOLLARS, T-ACCOUNTS, AND MONETARY EXPANSION

In the years when the Eurodollar market was growing rapidly, some observers began to question whether Eurodollars could have a multiple expansion like domestic currency. Closer examination indicated that it was unlikely. What banks are trading in the Eurodollar market are deposits in American banks. If General Motors deposits $1 million in Lloyds Bank in London, Lloyds gains a deposit in an American bank. Lloyds may lend it to another bank, but what it is lending is still the $1 million in an American bank. When a bank lends the $1 million to a commercial borrower, the borrower will spend the money

---

[*] A floating rate note in the U.S. would normally be expressed as a percentage over the Treasury-bill rate.

for whatever project it has on hand. Some of the money may go back to the United States, and some will be converted by the users to the currency of the country they live in. The T-account in Table 16.1 illustrates the process.

In the first set, General Motors deposits $1 million in Lloyds in London. Lloyds notifies its correspondent American bank, and the bank credits Lloyds with the deposit and the bank from which it is drawn debits GM. Lloyds now has a Eurodollar deposit, which is its liability, and an asset, its account in the American bank. In the second set, Lloyds lends the $1 million to the Banque de Paris. Once again, the dollar deposit changes ownership in the U.S., American banks crediting the Banque while debiting Lloyds. Lloyds now holds a deposit from GM and a promise to pay from the Banque de Paris, which in turn holds as a liability a debt to Lloyds and keeps the deposit as an asset.

Obviously, the Banque de Paris did not borrow the money to admire it but to lend it, which it does to the aluminum producer, Pechiney. The third set shows this with the American deposit moving again from one party to another. The Banque de Paris substitutes the Pechiney loan for its U.S. deposit. Finally, Pechiney spends the money it has borrowed and the various payees get checks drawn on American banks. If Pechiney's payees want another currency, they will have to sell their dollar deposits to their own bank for domestic currency. That would just shift the ownership of the American deposit to their bank.

To have some kind of monetary expansion from this activity, deposits somewhere would have to expand. In none of the movements on the T-accounts did American deposits or reserves expand, so nothing happened to the American monetary system. Nothing would happen in France, either. As Pechiney or its payees turned dollars into francs, their banks would get the dollars. If their banks wished to sell the dollars, they would end up selling them to some company that wanted dollars. The ownership of the American deposit would go from the French bank to whoever sold the francs to the French bank. Lastly, the Eurodollar market itself will not have a multiple expansion because none of the money that has been lent to Pechiney has been redeposited in the Eurodollar market. Thus, withdrawals from the Eurodollar market are 100%.

DERIVATIVE AND SWAP MARKETS

The Concept

One of the principal ways financial markets work to reduce risk is through derivative and swap markets. A derivative market sells instruments or arranges agreements in which two parties establish claims contingent upon the future price of an asset. Abstractly, the claim would be:

If on a future date agreed upon, the price of Asset X differs from a price both parties set today, then one party will pay the other an amount based on the difference, the seller paying the buyer if the price is lower and the buyer paying the seller if the price is higher.

As an example, Canada's Big Moose Exporters has shipped goods worth 100,000 Canadian dollars and is expecting to receive a payment in 90 days. The Canadian importer, Canadian Citrus Importers, has to pay 65,000 American dollars (100,000 Canadian dollars at the current exchange rate) in 90 days. Big Moose fears that by the time it receives payment, the Canadian dollar will be more expensive. Canadian Citrus fears the Canadian dollar will be worth less, making it more expensive to settle its debt. Table 16.2 illustrates the gains and losses to each party.

Table 16.2

DERIVATIVE AGREEMENT

	Will receive	Must Pay	US$0.67 = Cdn$1.00	US$0.63 = Cdn$1.00
Big Moose	us$65,000	Cdn$100,000	us$67,000 = Cdn$100,000	us$63,000 = Cdn$100,000
Canadian Citrus	Cdn$100,000	us$65,000	Cdn$100,000 = us$67,000	Cdn$100,000 = us$63,000

Big Moose and Canadian Citrus figure their profit margins on a basis of Cdn$1.00 = us$0.65. As the exporter, Big Moose will receive U.S. dollars; as the importer, Canadian Citrus will receive Canadian dollars. But their debts are in the opposite currencies. If the Canadian dollar rises to us$0.67, Big Moose will have been short by us$2,000 (about Cdn$3,000) as it converts its payment to Canadian dollars, but Canadian Citrus will be able to purchase us$67,000, $2,000 more than it needs. If the Canadian dollar fell to us$0.63, Big Moose would gain an extra amount of Canadian dollars, but Canadian Citrus would be short.

Managers of the two companies just happen to discover each other's needs in a casual meeting in a coffee shop. Realizing that they can help each other out, the two companies consider alternatives. They could just swap receipts, Canadian Citrus turning over its Canadian dollars to Big Moose in exchange for Big Moose's U.S. dollars. They would therefore make a primitive version of what is called in the market a swap.

Alternatively, they could make an agreement on the value of the exchange rate they will use in 90 days, using the current rate, for instance of us$0.65 =

Cdn$1.00, and if the exchange rate changes the winner on the exchange rate change will compensate the loser. (Such a price need not be and is not normally at the current exchange rate, as explained below.) If the price of the Canadian dollar is US$0.67 on that date, Canadian Citrus (the importer) will compensate Big Moose by 2 U.S. cents on the dollar or US$2,000. If the price is US$0.63, Big Moose will pay Canadian Citrus. The instrument or arrangement is therefore contingent upon—or *derived from*—the future price of Asset X, hence the term "derivative." The most common arrangements deal with exchange and interest rates: if interest rates rise, A pays B so much; if interest rates fall, B pays A so much.

The arrangement reduces risk. Big Moose has to calculate its profit margins on the goods it is exporting. It has no problem for domestic sales in figuring what it must get in revenues, but internationally, it stands a chance of losing on an unexpected change in the value of the Canadian dollar. Even the 2-cent change in the example above is about 3% of the 65 cents; this might be a substantial cut in the firm's margins. Big Moose is quite happy to forgo the opportunity to make more money if the Canadian dollar is lower than anticipated for the certainty of receiving one Canadian dollar for every 65 American cents. Canadian Citrus is in the opposite position. It has to make calculations on what prices to set on the imported goods, and it does not want the goods suddenly to rise in price by 3%. By making an agreement with each other, the two firms eliminate the foreign exchange risk. Since the companies no longer face the possibility that they will suffer from an adverse turn in the exchange rates, they can make their prices lower, passing to the buyers some of the savings from the reduction of the risk.

Note that the party that pays does not lose and the party that collects does not win; both parties break even. If the Canadian dollar ends up at 67 cents, Canadian Citrus finds that its costs of buying U.S. dollars are lower by 2 cents on the Canadian dollar, which is exactly what it needs to pay Big Moose. If the Canadian dollar ends up at 63 cents, Big Moose is able to purchase all the Canadian dollars it counted on for 63 cents and use the two cents left over to pay Canadian Citrus. Since both parties were avoiding speculation, they are happy to complete their agreements. (In essence, they traded the chance to win on the change of the Canadian dollar in order to have the certainty of not losing.)

The example above depended on having Big Moose and Canadian Citrus knowing about each other and having a coincidence of wants—one wanted to sell and one wanted to buy just the right amount on the right date. Derivative financial markets serve to make this process a great deal smoother, matching parties and needs. The markets can be either through an intermediary or *brokered*. The vast majority of currency derivative activity uses the banks as intermediaries, but a great deal of other forms of coverage—against changes in interest rates, for instance—use organized futures exchanges or more specialized *over-the-counter* (OTC) arrangements set up by a bank or financial house. OTC arrangements are *brokered*, meaning that the financial institution that helps match the parties and oversees the conduct of the arrangement does not in itself take any ownership of the assets involved.

Forward Exchange

The oldest and still most-used way to cover foreign exchange risk is a forward contract, which uses banks as intermediaries. Using the example above, Big Moose Exporters makes a contract with the Royal Bank of Canada, promising to deliver to the bank US$65,000 at a specified future date in exchange for Cdn$100,000 on that date. The bank enters the interbank forward market. The market for forward currencies runs off the same network as does the spot market. Banks trade currencies for future delivery (for 30, 60, 90, 180, 360 days, etc.) with each other. Rather than Big Moose finding an importer itself, which would involve finding another party with the same amount and dates required, the banks themselves act as intermediaries and the market they create serves to match the different banks. The banks also serve to guarantee payment. The banks assess the ability of the firm signing a contract with them to deliver the currency when required, and the banks trust one another to fulfill their contracts.

A bank's inability to fulfill a contract is known as *Herstatt Risk*, after an Austrian bank that went bankrupt while still a party to many forward contracts. Fortunately, the risk of non-fulfillment is very low.

ARBITRAGE BETWEEN FORWARD AND T-BILL MARKETS

What if there are more buyers than sellers at any given price? Clearly, the price will rise, but the degree to which it normally moves is sharply constrained. If the bank does not like the price the market offers, it can cover on its own. The Royal Bank, acting on a vastly larger scale than Big Moose, has signed contracts agreeing to deliver Cdn$10,000,000 for US$6,500,000. Table 16.3 shows the bank's situation as Contract 1. Royal has two ways of covering: it can find matching forward contracts to receive $10 million Canadian and pay out US$6.5 million (row 2), or it can move money into Canadian T-bills that will mature with the requisite Cdn$10 million, as shown in the bottom rows. Suppose again the forward rate—the price of the Canadian dollar due in 90 days is 65 American cents. Today's price—the spot rate—is, however, 64.5 cents. Instead of using the futures market, at the existing price of 65 cents, Royal Bank purchases the Canadian dollars right away on the spot market for US$6,450,000, reducing its holdings of American T-bills and putting its new Canadian dollars into Canadian T-bills.

Table 16.3
ROYAL BANK'S ALTERNATIVES TO COVER
ITSELF AFTER MAKING CONTRACT 1

	To receive	*To deliver*	*Cdn T-bills*	*US T-bills*
Contract 1	US$6.5m	Cdn$10m		
Contract 2	Cdn$10m	US$6.5m		
T-bill moves			+ Cdn$10m	– US$6.5m

Note: Having made Contract 1, Royal Bank will be assured that it will have the Cdn$10 million either by finding a matching contract (Contract 2 on the bottom left) or by moving its T-bill holdings (top right two boxes).

Which method Royal chooses depends on the difference between interest rates in the two countries. Suppose, as often was the case in the late 1990s, the discount on T-bills (their interest rate) was the same in both countries. Royal Bank therefore loses no interest in changing assets, and when the contract is due, it gets 65 cents for what cost it 64.5 cents. Since a half a cent on 65 cents is 0.77% for 90 days, over 3% annually, at no risk, many banks would do the same. This would raise the spot rate and depress the forward rate until they were the same.

Royal Bank is not speculating here at all. It does not make any difference what happens to the value of the Canadian dollar—it will gain half a cent. If it were *speculating*, it would not move the T-bills but would wait until the contract was due and purchase the Canadian dollars when the price went down, hoping it could get them for less than 65 cents. In the situation described, however, Royal Bank is performing *arbitrage*—the near simultaneous buying and selling of an asset in two markets. It *arbitrages* between the forward market and the T-bill market by simultaneously making a forward contract and moving T-bills.

An individual firm could also avoid the forward market if the price seemed too steep, using much the same method. Big Moose could borrow American dollars, using its expected receipts as collateral, then take the money back to Canada and either invest it or use it to pay down existing debt. A large firm with high liquidity could sell some American short-term assets and buy Canadian short-term assets to cover a similar exposure. The difficulty with the small firm doing this, however, is that it would have to pay considerably more than T-bill rates to borrow and the arrangements would be time-consuming. A forward contract with a bank is much simpler and inexpensive.

COVERAGE AND FOREIGN BORROWING AND LENDING

The discussion in Chapter 13 on interest rate parity noted that investors who desire to have their investments fully covered against exchange rate fluctuation cannot gain from differences in T-bill rates between countries. At this point, the reason for that becomes clearer. Unless speculation is high, *the difference in interest rates between countries determines the forward rate, hence the cost of coverage.* A closer look is in order.

The example above of Royal Bank using the T-bill market to arbitrage had the interest rate being the same between the United States and Canada. Suppose, instead, the interest rate had been much higher in Canada, as it was back in 1993. Investors were discounting Canadian debt far more than American debt, the difference being about 3% per annum. (This meant that the value of Canadian dollars to be delivered in one year was 3% p.a. less than American dollars delivered after the same period.) Banks would gladly hold Canadian assets, paying 3% more than American assets, if they were guaranteed American dollars in payment. In essence, this is what a forward contract does—it promises the bank American dollars for Canadian dollars, allowing the bank to put its assets into Canadian T-bills. On the other hand, if banks had to deliver American dollars, they would have to sell a Canadian T-bill and buy an American T-bill, losing 3% p.a. on the deal. The result of this is that firms selling U.S. dollars get a 3% p.a. premium and those that buy U.S. dollars with Canadian dollars pay a 3% p.a. penalty (or discount). Hence the rule: the forward currency of the high interest rate currency sells at a discount to its spot.

At first exposure, some people find the idea mind-bending, but consider it in terms of present value. The present value of Canadian dollars received in the future was lower than the present value of American dollars received at the same time. The forward contract is for the future exchange and reflects the difference. An asset for future receipt of the currency with the lower present value sells for less than the one for the currency with the higher present value. To check how this works consider the actual rates in February 1993, shown in Table 16.4, when Canadian interest rates were much different from American rates.

FORWARD RATES AND COVERED INVESTMENTS

Because forward cover costs the same as the interest rate differential, it is not sensible to invest in another country to get higher interest rates and then to cover, because covering will cost the same amount as the extra interest earned. The same is true for saving money on borrowing, but covering to cut the risk.

Table 16.4

FORWARD RATE ON CANADIAN DOLLAR
AND SHORT-TERM INTEREST RATES

	1-month	3-month	6-month
Exchange Rates			
Spot rate US$.7931=Cdn$1.00			
Forward Rates	0.7911	0.787	0.789
difference	0.002	0.0061	0.0122
discount (per annum)	0.030	0.0308	0.0308
Interest rates %			
US T-bill	2.75	2.88	3.04
Cdn T-bill	5.87	6.18	6.31
difference	3.12	3.3	3.27
US commercial paper	3.08	3.1	3.2
Cdn Bankers' Acceptances	6.06	6.24	6.46
difference	2.98	3.14	3.26
Eurodollars			
Cdn$	6.06		
US$	3.18		
difference	2.88		

Note: Table 16.4 does a broader comparison than just the T-bill rates, since there are many short-term interest rates. Bankers' acceptances (debts guaranteed by commercial banks) are much more common in Canada than the United States, for instance. What the table shows is that the difference between spot and forward, expressed as a yearly interest rate, is about 3%, as are the differences between all the principal short-term interest rates.

The situation in 1993 when American interest rates were 3% below Canadian rates serves to illustrate the problems of covered investments. Why didn't Jean Jacques Canadien, facing an interest rate of 10% in Montreal, drive down to Plattsburgh, New York, and borrow there at 7%? J.J. could certainly have done so, but if he wanted to *cover* his risk, he would not save anything. If the Canadian dollar fell in the interim, Jean could have lost far more than the 3% he saved annually by borrowing in the United States. Certainly bank officers would not leave much of their bank's portfolio in such an uncovered position. Once the cost of cover is added, however, virtually any savings from lower interest rates disappear. When J.J. went to buy forward cover, he found that the forward Canadian dollar was selling at a premium of 3% to the spot. And that is because the cost of selling the Canadian dollar forward very closely matches the discount on the interest rate differential.

FORWARD RATES IN THE FINANCIAL PAGES

When Canadian short-term interest rates actually dipped below American rates in 1996 and 1997, the forward Canadian dollar sold at a slight premium to the spot, but the differences in short-term rates throughout the late 1990s were very small. The following is from January 22, 1999. The Canadian forward is at a slight premium to the spot. The American T-bill rate was about a tenth of a percent above the Canadian T-bill rate. Following the rules strictly, the Canadian dollar therefore should have been at a slight discount. The problem when interest rates are so close, however, is that the assets are not strictly comparable. Eurodollar rates, for instance, were above the Canadian short-term rates.

Table 16.5

FORWARD RATES

	$1 US in Cdn$ =	$1 Cdn in US$ =
U.S./Canada spot	1.5178	0.6588
1 month forward	1.5179	0.6588
2 months forward	1.5179	0.6588
3 months forward	1.5179	0.6588
6 months forward	1.5174	0.6590
12 months forward	1.5163	0.6595
3 years forward	1.5148	0.6602
5 years forward	1.5141	0.6605
7 years forward	1.5038	0.6650
10 years forward	1.4928	0.6699
Canadian dollar in 1999: High	1.5020	0.6658
Low	1.5475	0.6462
Average	1.5197	0.6580

Source: *Globe and Mail*, January 23, 1999, B23.

The figures indicate, too, that the forward market functions to cover foreign exchange risk up to 10 years. Back in the 1960s, it was rare to find any contracts longer than 12 months forward. The longer contracts show how much the financial markets have developed.

Speculation can make forward rates differ markedly from where the forward interest rate arbitrage would place them. The existence of gaps that could be easily arbitraged is a sign that financial institutions are passing up a sure thing for the chance of gaining more from a change in the exchange rate. A currency whose forward rate is below the value determined by interest rate arbitrage is in trouble because the market is so sure it is going to fall that banks are turning down sure arbitrage profits in order to speculate.

The same reasoning works in the other direction: high interest rates may attract foreign short-term investments—but only if they are *uncovered*. If Polly Platt in Plattsburgh, New York, had purchased Canadian securities, she could have received 10% compared to perhaps 7% at home. However, if she had wanted the security of knowing the Canadian dollars would buy the same amount of American dollars they did when she made the investment, she would have to sell the proceeds of her investment in the forward market for their various due dates. Indeed, had Polly not covered, she would have taken a sharp loss because the Canadian dollar fell from 78.6 American cents in May of 1993 to 72.2 American cents in May of the next year, a nice little 8% fall that would have wiped out all her gains. J.J. would be telling people what a good speculator he was.

Futures Markets

Participants in forward markets know one another and trust one another to fulfill their contracts—the bank knows its customer and the banks know one another. The bank takes the risk the customer will not be able to deliver on the promise, and it takes only a tiny risk that its counterparty banks will not pay. Participants in futures markets, however, deal with counterparties unknown to them. Big Moose knew Royal Bank would pay, but it could not be sure that Canadian Citrus would pay. Thus futures markets need mechanisms to maintain confidence in the market.

Futures markets exist for foreign exchange, although the forward markets are very much larger. Futures are much more important in interest rates and in stock market indexes, as well as in commodities. There are also forward markets for interest rates, but the futures markets for them are much larger.

Big Moose and Canadian Citrus serve well to show the mechanics of futures markets. Suppose Big Moose decides to use the futures market instead of the forward market. It buys Cdn$100,000 on the futures market in Chicago. Canadian Citrus Importers also sells Cdn$100,000, and through the market the two become party and counterparty to a deal. Forces of demand and supply in the futures market would have established a *strike price*—the exchange rate at which they will deliver the currency on a given day. For convenience, suppose that American and Canadian interest rates are just about the same, so the strike price they choose is exactly the same as the spot price—65 American cents for a Canadian dollar.

If at any time before the contract matures, the Canadian dollar rises above the strike price, Canadian Citrus, the seller of Canadian dollars, must provide the market with enough money to cover the difference for the buyer. If, for instance, the Canadian dollar rose to 66 cents, Big Moose would need another cent to buy a Canadian dollar at the agreed upon price. Therefore, a Cdn$100,000 contract would require Big Moose to provide the futures exchange with US$1,000 (Cdn$100,000 x .01). This is called *marking to market*. If the Canadian dollar rose another cent, Canadian Citrus would have to provide another $1,000. If the Canadian dollar fell a cent below the strike price, it would be Big Moose that would provide the exchange with the $1,000. When the due date comes, the futures exchange will pay what it has in escrow to the other party. (The actual delivery of the currency is not required.) If the Canadian dollar had risen to 67 cents, the buyer would take the $2,000, which, combined with the buyer's $65,000 receipts from its exports, would provide the $67,000 the buyer needed to buy Cdn$100,000 on the spot market. If for some reason the seller had defaulted by failing to mark to market, the buyer would be given the money on deposit right away.

Marking to market enables futures exchanges to avoid losses and the participants to deal with parties unknown to them. The very spectacular losses in the futures markets of Barings Bank and of Orange County, California, caused no harm to the counterparties and trading continued without a ripple. Barings Bank, through an improperly supervised trader in Singapore, was speculating on the Nikkei stock market index, betting that it would rise while it was falling. As the Nikkei index fell, Barings had to put up larger and larger amounts to mark to market. When it could no longer do so, it lost all that it had put up to the counterparties, throwing the firm into bankruptcy. A similar thing happened to Orange County, although the derivatives were a bit more complicated. Nonetheless, the county's default in the market did not hurt the counterparties or the market itself.

OPTIONS

Closely related to futures are *options*. Options come in two kinds—*puts* and *calls*. A put gives one party the right to force the counterparty to provide the good at the strike price. But the first party need not exercise the option. In the example above, for instance, Big Moose might be willing to take a small loss but would be nervous about losing more than 5 cents on the dollar. So Big Moose would purchase an option to *call* Canadian dollars at 70 cents. The counterparty, however, has no right to ask the owner of the option to guarantee against a decrease in the price of the dollar. Since this is a "heads I win, tails you lose" situation for Big Moose, the counterparty would insist on a flat payment for its exposing itself to the risks. Canadian Citrus Importers would want a *put* option, guaranteeing that the counterparty would buy Canadian dollars at, say, 60 cents, should the importer exercise the option.

INTEREST RATE FUTURES AND OPTIONS

The futures markets in interest rate futures and options have played an important role in international financial markets and anyone trying to understand

Figure 16. 3

SIZE AND COMPOSITION OF
EXCHANGE-TRADED DERIVATIVE MARKETS

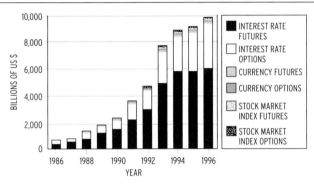

Source: IMF, *International Capital Markets*, 1997, 17

the markets should have at least a nodding acquaintance with them. What is actually bought and sold are not assets called "interest rate futures," but rather future T-bills or treasury bonds, and the parties settle on the price they will pay for the T-bill or bond at a specified future date. The discount on the bond, of course, is the interest rate.

As in the foreign exchange markets, some parties can suffer considerably if interest rates fall unexpectedly and others if they rise unexpectedly. For an illustration, consider the situation of an American bank, which has assets largely in loans and mortgages at fixed interest rates with terms extending from a several months to many years. Its liabilities, however, are heavily in deposits, which are very short term. Should interest rates rise unexpectedly, the bank will see its deposit flee or else have to increase interest rates paid on them. (If it expected interest rates to rise, it would have raised the cost of loans.) Consumer Credit, Incorporated, however, has the opposite situation. This company specializes in holding the consumer loans that retailers make. It buys these loans from many retail companies and knows that these assets are highly interest-rate sensitive. Its liabilities, however, are mostly bonds and forms of commercial paper it has issued. Thus, if interest rates fall, it has difficulties because it earns less, yet is still committed to the interest rates stated in its bonds and commercial paper. The function of the futures market is to bring together companies with such opposite risks.

Figure 16.3 shows that the value of derivatives traded in the organized derivative markets rose sharply between 1986 and 1996, from US$618 billion to nearly US$10 trillion. The bulk of these have been in interest rate futures and options, with currency and stock market derivatives much smaller.

665

Swaps

A *swap* is an arrangement in which one firm trades a stream of income with another firm. Big Moose and Canadian Citrus could have arranged their affairs that way. Big Moose would swap, suppose, a million dollars of its annual revenue in U.S. dollars for an equivalent amount of Canadian dollars from Canadian Citrus. The price of doing so, of course, might include some speculation of where the Canadian dollar was going to go, but a secure contract could be signed. Such a deal would normally be brokered by a bank, which would oversee the contract and handle the payments. Both firms would end up with the currency they wanted without any foreign exchange risk.

Firms use swaps for both foreign exchange and interest payments. One of the more common arrangements is a swap of a stream of fixed interest rate payments for one that is variable. A bank, for instance, may prefer a stream of income closely connected with current interest rates so that its loans could increase their yield when it had to raise its payments to depositors. In such cases, the bank may agree to swap the fixed payment proceeds from its loans for a variable stream of income, the variable rate based on the American T-bill rate or LIBOR plus a percentage. In that way, the bank can continue to specialize in making loans at fixed rates, knowing it could trade them off (perhaps for a price) for variable rates. Table 16.6 exemplifies such a swap.

Table 16.6

AN INTEREST RATE SWAP

Chase Manhattan	Bank of Nova Scotia
Loan in Cdn$, fixed interest to Company 1	Loan in US$, variable interest to Company 2
Loan to Company 1 variable interest, US$ from Company 2	Loan to Company 2 Fixed interest, Cdn$ from Company 1

Chase Manhattan lends money to Company 1, a Canadian company wishing to pay fixed interest in Canadian dollars. The loan does not fit Chase's portfolio wishes precisely, so it seeks a swap. Chase finds the Bank of Nova Scotia, which has lent U.S. dollars at a variable rate to one of its American borrowers, a loan, too, that does not fit the Bank of Nova Scotia's portfolio. In Table 16.6 the loan above the dotted line represents the situation of both banks before the swap. The two banks agree to swap the payments, while

Figure 16.4
VALUE OF SWAPS, 1987–1995

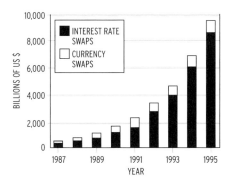

each keeps the credit risk (and the customer). The resultant situation is shown below the dotted line. If need be, either bank could find another bank with which to swap only the currency or fixed vs. variable interest, separating the risk even further.

As with derivatives, the value of the assets covered by swap agreements has risen very sharply since 1987, as Figure 16.4 shows.

Over-the-Counter Markets

There are futures and sometimes options for stock exchange indexes, for the credit risk on groups of bonds (e.g., bonds from a single country), and for the more popular individual stocks. The phrase "over-the-counter" (OTC) refers to arrangements brokered by financial institutions that have no large, highly organized markets. The needs may be too highly specialized for there to be thousands of buyers, but not so obscure that a bank could not find a few hundred buyers interested in becoming counterparties to the agreements. Moreover, an OTC agreement can be tailored carefully to fit the needs of party and counterparty, while the exchange-traded derivatives are highly standardized—e.g., lots of 100,000 Canadian dollars over the next three months. If a company wants to trade an odd amount for the longer period of one year, it cannot use the organized market, but a bank would be able to arrange a proper OTC agreement for it.

The IMF estimates that OTC markets (including swaps) are at least twice as large as the more organized derivative markets and have been growing faster. This trading is becoming consolidated among the largest banks. In the United States, for instance, the top eight banks have over 90% of the OTC business, reflecting the importance of scale and scope in this kind of trading.[7]

CONTINUING CHANGES IN THE INTERNATIONAL CAPITAL MARKET

All capital markets, national and international, are experiencing four major changes: (1) increased *liquidity*; (2) greater *disintermediation,* which is a move away from using banking intermediaries; (3) more *risk unbundling;* and, possibly, (4) a *decrease in transparency*. At the same time the markets are undergoing these changes, the organization of the market itself is changing as the lines between banks and other financial institutions are blurring.[8]

1. *Liquidity.* Changes in communication, computerization, and the increasing sophistication of modern finance allow large amounts of capital to be mobilized very rapidly. The ease with which financiers have been able to raise the capital to take over large corporations is just one of many illustrations of the ability of modern markets to generate capital funds.

2. *Disintermediation.* As noted earlier in the chapter, lenders can place their money with banks and let the banks do the lending for them, or they can lend directly to the borrower through purchasing securities. In recent decades, intermediated lending has lost market share to direct lending. Where corporations in past decades relied on banks for much short-term and medium-term financing, they now issue more bonds, medium-term securities, and short-term securities known as *commercial paper*. A company with a good reputation, working with an investment banker or brokerage house, can arrange an issue of securities and pay smaller fees than it would if it borrowed from a bank. The banks can only try to help the corporations place (sell) their securities, competing with investment bankers and brokerage houses. In Canada, for instance, corporate loans have steadily declined as a proportion of bank's assets, replaced by consumer loans, where the banks are still strong.

Such *securitization*, as it is sometimes called, substitutes a security for funds that have been traditionally drawn from retained earnings or bank loans. Rather than build apartments, developers build condominiums with the buyers providing the capital up front. Mall developers sell shares in long-term leases. Banks, rather than using deposits to support housing loans, often sell off securities to finance the mortgages. Roughly one-third of all U.S. mortgages are financed through issues of securities rather than through bank deposits. Corporations with heavy capital costs have cut their dependence on banks by selling part of the organization to a leasing company (financed by a new issue of stock) and using the proceeds of the sale to expand in another area.[*]

---

[*] As an example, Union Carbide sold one of its plants to a new company it created, then leased back the plant. The new company raised money through stockbrokers and paid its shareholders with the rents from Union Carbide. Union Carbide took the money from the sale of the plant and used it to invest elsewhere. Look, Ma, no banks.

Table 16.7

DISINTERMEDIATION IN SELECTED INDUSTRIAL COUNTRIES

	Assets of Institutional Investors		Institutionalization of Household Savings	
	1985	1995	1985	1995
Canada	26.4	35.9	24.5	31.4
France	11.4	23.4	15.7	27.3
Germany	12.8	19.0	19.6	28.9
Japan	10.2	22.6	32.2	34.8
Norway	13.0	21.9	25.1	37.5
Spain	3.2	15.0	2.9	24.4
United Kingdom	26.7	31.6	...	52.0
United States	43.8	54.6	33.4	45.3

Note: The IMF defines institutional investors as insurance companies, pension funds, and investment companies (largely mutual funds). The table shows such intermediaries' increased share of domestic financial assets. Canadian institutional investors in 1985, for instance, had 26.4% of all domestic financial assets and 24.5% of household savings; by 1995, they held 35.9% of domestic financial assets, including the 31.4% of household savings.

Source: IMF, *International Capital Markets*, 1997, 135.

The development of high-yielding, somewhat less secure bonds, known as *junk bonds*, has been a key element in the takeover battles of recent years.* In addition, many industries that suffered greatly during credit crunches in the past have reduced their dependence on bank credit through leasing and other securitized programs.

The words to describe the processes are not yet settled in meaning. Most writers describe the increase in direct lending as "securitization." Others call it "disintermediation"—ceasing to use intermediaries and define "securitization" in a narrower way, meaning the repackaging of loans, where a bank takes a group of loans, such as mortgages, puts them into a separate company, and issues securities backed by those loans. "Disintermediation," however, also has two uses: the banking community refers to it as the movement away from using banks as intermediaries. Because the investors are simply changing intermediaries, this might more properly be called *re-intermediation*. Table 16.7 shows the extent of this re-intermediation, here called *disintermediation*.

3. *Unbundling of risk.* Risk unbundling is the ability of the financial market to take what used to be a package of risks all bundled together and separate

---

* The bonds do not receive a high rating from bond-rating companies and thus are ineligible to be purchased by many trust and pension funds. They are somewhat riskier, but they pay well enough to keep buyers coming.

the risks, selling them to the parties who can handle them best.[9] Consider the following situation.

Injuries forced Denny Downhill to give up his Olympic skiing hopes, but the expertise he gathered in his years as ski bum—and an MBA—provided him with great insight into what makes a successful ski resort. Denny has identified a promising project in Chile and is gathering a group of investors to finance it. The problem Denny faces is this: his knowledge is about what makes a resort successful and he has made a good study of the Chilean company and concluded the project is excellent, the New Zealand and Chilean partners experienced, and the chances of success great. But Denny has no special expertise about two other risks investors will face: (1) the foreign exchange risk involved in building a resort with Chilean pesos, with income expressed largely in pesos yet payment in U.S. dollars, and (2) the risk that interest rates will be higher at the time Denny refinances the project. The Chilean company would prefer to pay in pesos with interest rates fixed for the next four years. Denny doubts he could place such a package at any reasonable interest rate because investors would charge a considerable amount to shoulder all those risks.

"There must be a way to break up this risk," Denny muses, "so that my investors group can take the risks of the operation's success, while we can pass on the foreign exchange risk and the interest rate risk. Other people fear the peso will rise and interest rates will fall; if I could only find them I could lay off some of my risk." Denny, in other words, is looking for ways to *unbundle* the risk. That way, he can maximize the value of his expertise and lower the costs of investing to all the parties concerned. Can he do it? Probably.

   a. There is no forward exchange trading for the Chilean peso, but Denny can find an OTC market for it. Or, his bank may be able to arrange an OTC swap.
   b. Once he has the dollars from the swap, Denny's bank can arrange an interest rate swap, trading his regular payments, vital to his planning, with someone who would arrange variable payments, key to his being able to place his securities. (Or, his bank may be able to arrange an interest rate derivative.)

Denny would be left largely with the kinds of risk he knows how to manage—the credit risk of the skiing operation, which is based on its success. Other parties have the risks they know how to manage and Denny does not have to be a specialist in international finance as well as in resort construction and management. The modern financial market has allowed him to unbundle the risks of the project.

4. *Reduced transparency*. A number of the changes occurring in financial markets today have the effect of making it harder to assess underlying risk. Financial institutions are probably carrying more "contingent liabilities," agreeing, for instance, to buy up unsold securities, to support a secondary market, or to guarantee securitized transactions. The health of the intermediary is much harder to judge when liabilities are only contingent upon a failure somewhere else. The practice of syndicated loans virtually stopped after LDC debt defaults, but these began again, and various risk-pooling and other innovative financial devices often make it quite difficult to perceive the underlying risk. Moreover, a number of economists fear that in the process of short-circuiting the banks, the information-gathering and risk assessment in the market have declined. The riposte to that suggestion is that the separation of credit, interest, and exchange rate risk places risk with specialized holders, each better able to assess the risk than a more generalized institution.

5. *Changing roles of intermediaries*. As the markets have changed, so have the institutions in the market. There has been a blurring of the traditional lines between a commercial bank—which accepts deposits, holds reserves, and makes loans—and an investment house or merchant bank—which underwrites and places securities issues. In the U.S., where the 1933 Glass-Steagall Act (recently expired) sought to separate the deposit-taking banks from merchant banks, banks have used holding companies to buy investment houses and investment houses have set up banks. Abroad, where the lines were less clear but still visible, the process has also occurred. It is a necessary adjustment to the changes in market liquidity.

IMPLICATIONS OF THE CHANGES

Monetary Policy

The availability of outside sources to finance corporate capital expenditures reduces the effectiveness of monetary policy. Canada's 1987-89 attempt to keep its interest rates 3-4% higher than U.S. rates, much higher than their historic spread, attracted a great deal of short-term capital and may not have had a significant effect on choking off domestic investment, much of which is financed from abroad. The argument, seemingly simple, is actually more subtle.

Much economic theory assumes that raising the interest rate affects the economy evenly, cutting off only the lower-yielding investments, but that may not have been what was occurring. The argument has two strands. *Capital availability* or liquidity theory argues that banks do not rely exclusively on interest rates, but *ration* the quantities of loans they make. In a period of economic expansion, banks do not immediately raise interest rates to serve only those who can pay high rates; instead, they ask their customers to delay receiving loans until the money is available. A queue thus forms, and bankers lend the money as available. (Rationing and queuing is quite common in many industries during boom periods, as the firms have to consider not just the short-run advantage but their long-term relation to their customers.) *Market segmentation theory* argues that the household and small business sectors are more dependent on bank finance than is the large corporate sector. Larger corporations can use retained earnings, issue commercial paper (short-term debt), or borrow from foreign markets or foreign affiliates.

Investment borrowing may be highly *price inelastic*, since it is a derived demand from increased consumer spending or foreign spending. (Ask an executive from almost any firm if a 1% rise in the interest rate is going to change the firm's plans. Few will admit their decision is so finely tuned.) Instead, lower money supplies rationed credit and tended to target those industries most dependent on bank credit—e.g., construction and some forms of new capital investments. While quite willing to invest, builders or potential housing buyers were met with requirements such as banks refusing to lend more than 50% of the value of a house, which essentially cut many of them out of the market. As such industries have come to use securitization to sidestep extensive use of bank credit, they have become less sensitive to changes in the money supply. Since reducing the money supply no longer has the same rationing effect, interest rates must be raised much higher to induce firms to postpone investment plans.[10]

Many borrowers, unhappy with domestic interest rates, can borrow abroad at lower rates. So long as they are willing to shoulder the foreign exchange risk, they can have their funds to invest. The funds they borrow give them command over resources domestically and, given relatively full employment (or a vertical AS), will squeeze some other group out. As the borrowing abroad increases, the value of the currency rises (under floating rate systems), as the Canadian dollar did in the late 1980s. This hits exports and import-competing goods. Under fixed rates, the capital inflow causes inflation while the exchange rate remains unchanged, squeezing the same groups. Restrictive monetary policy, while it reduces household and small business investment, falls heavily on exports and import-competitive goods—the *exchange-rate-sensitive* sector. Aggregate demand falls not because, as traditionally expected, investment falls, but because exports fall and imports rise.

Supervision and Monitoring

Authorities find it far harder to monitor and regulate the financial markets than before. Certainly one problem is the number of different countries and conflicting jurisdictions. Perhaps more important has been the increase in securities, by nature harder to monitor than bank loans, the rise in contingent liabilities, and the newer and more complex financial instruments that have been developed. Declining transparency and increasing liquidity are like a flood of dark water to those charged with monitoring financial markets.

CONCLUSION

Chapter 18 carries the discussion further, showing the darker side of the changes in the international financial markets. For the present, consider the importance of the good side of international finance—its abilities to move capital inexpensively, to reduce international interest rate disparities, to match borrowers with unusual requirements to those lenders who understand them. However fashionable it has become to decry the international market for its failings or to search for a quick fix, the question is how to fix what does go wrong without preventing it from achieving what goes right.

VOCABULARY AND CONCEPTS

Covered investments
Cross-border capital markets
Derivative
Disintermediation
Eurocurrency markets
Eurodollar market
Forward exchange
Forward markets
Forward-spot arbitrage
Futures markets
Information (in capital markets)
Interest rate futures and options

Liquidity
London interbank market
Marking to market
Options
Over-the-counter markets
Risk unbundling
Risk-sharing
Securitization
Sovereign spread
Swaps
Transparency

QUESTIONS

1. Explain the functions of financial markets and the advantages of large markets in fulfilling those functions.
2. Compare the European and American financial markets for size and integration.
3. Explain what a Eurocurrency asset is and why it exists.
4. Follow a typical Eurodollar transaction through the banking system. Explain why there is little or no multiple expansion of Eurodollars.
5. What is a derivative? From what is it derived?
6. Explain how Big Moose and Canadian Citrus can reduce their risk through making a swap or derivative arrangement.
7. Explain the difference between forward and futures markets.
8. Suppose T-bill rates in the United States are 5% and in Canada they are 4%. Would the Canadian forward dollar be at a premium or a discount to the U.S. forward dollar? How much of a discount or premium would that be on a 90-day contract with an exchange rate of us$0.75 = Cdn$1.00?
9. If you invest abroad to take advantage of higher interest rates on safe assets like T-bills, can you cover your foreign exchange risk and still make more money than at home?
10. Explain the importance of marking to market as it affects (a) the functioning of the futures market and (b) the need for liquidity of a firm that holds a futures contract.
11. Virtually all non-financial companies state in their annual reports that they use derivatives, but they are never leveraged—that is, they do not speculate. Explain what they mean and why this is so.
12. Explain what a swap is.
13. Explain what securitization is.
14. What is meant by the unbundling of risk?
15. What major changes have affected international capital markets and how have they changed monetary policy?

NOTES

1. "It was mainly in order to escape the effects of incessant changes in the value of coins on bill rates that [medieval] merchants adopted the device of issuing bills in terms of some fictitious unit of stable value. As a result, bills drawn in actual currencies were usually quoted at a discount against fictitious units, and they fluctuated more widely. The relative stability of exchange rates in terms of fictitious units was in sharp contrast with the instability of such units in terms of the actual currencies of the countries concerned." Paul Einzig, *The History of Foreign Exchange* (London, 1964), 83.

2. *The Economist* has no bond listing for Belgian francs, Italian lira, Spanish pesetas, or Swedish crowns. It does not list, although they exist, rates for SDR and ECU bonds.

3. Some writers confused the reserve requirement on checking accounts (at that time around 18%) with those on savings (then 5%). Eurodollars were a near money, competitive with CDs and short-term savings deposits, whose reserve requirements were 5%.

4. The history of the market has been covered in a number of places. An early analysis is Paul Einzig, *The Eurodollar System* (London, 1965). See also R.B.R. Johnson, *The Economics of the Eurodollar Market* (London: Macmillan, 1983), ch. 2; Gunter Dufey and Ian Giddy, *The International Money Market* (Englewood Cliffs, N.J.: Prentice-Hall, 1978), ch. 1; Jan S. Hogendorn and Wilson Brown, *The New International Economics* (Reading, Mass.: Addison-Wesley, 1979), ch. 5.

5. Maxwell Watson et al., *International Capital Markets: Developments and Prospects* (Washington: IMF, 1988), 36.

6. See Adrian Hamilton, *The Financial Revolution* (New York: Free Press, 1986), 57. Hamilton also mentions numerous other floating rate instruments.

7. IMF, *International Capital Markets*, 1997, 17-18.

8. International capital markets change rapidly. Those interested in recent developments may wish to check one of two regular reviews of the market. (1) The IMF publishes an annual survey in January of each year, *International Capital Markets*. It contains a general discussion, often some background study, and a number of important tables and statistics. (2) Every year in the last week in March *The Economist* publishes a survey of world banking.

9. Christopher James, "Off-Balance Sheet Banking", *Economic Review*, Federal Reserve System of San Francisco (Fall 1997): 21-36; Thomas Simpson, "Developments in the U.S. Financial System since the Mid-1970s," *Federal Reserve Bulletin* (January 1988): 1-13.

10. The credit-rationing argument and the argument that higher interest rates now squeeze exports and import-substitutes is from Watson et al., *International Capital Markets*, ch. 3. In brief and more explicit form it is in Russell Kincaid, "Policy Implications of Structural Changes in Financial Markets," *Finance and Development* (March 1988): 2-6.

Chapter Seventeen

International Monetary Institutions (I)

OBJECTIVES

OVERALL OBJECTIVE   To discuss in a historical context the development of the institutions of the international financial system, exploring their strengths and limitations.

MORE SPECIFICALLY
- To explore the way in which the gold standard worked, the conditions that allowed it to work, and its strengths and weaknesses.
- To examine the troubles of the 1920s and 1930s, with particular focus on the development and collapse of the international financial system.
- To look at the issue of the real transfer in the context of World War I debts.
- To see how the Bretton Woods system was designed to remedy flaws in the earlier system, looking closely at the adjustable peg system and the International Monetary Fund.
- To examine the conditions under which the Bretton Woods system flourished and the conditions that led to the elimination of some of its key elements.

....

Chapters 17-19 look at the international system as a whole rather than, as did Chapters 10-15, the situation of the individual nation in a global economy. As a *system*, the international economy is a group of parts that work together. The parts are best described as *institutions*. An institution can be an organization like the International Monetary Fund, but it can also be a pattern or routine—a way of reacting to events that is consistent and accepted as the usual way of doing things. Most of the institutions of the international system are of the latter kind, although they may have become more formalized in recent decades. No international organization enforced the gold standard, established the American dollar as the currency that central banks would hold to back their own currencies, or told countries to raise interest rates when capital was fleeing those countries. Indeed, economic organizations that were both international and intergovernmental were absent before World War I and scarce before World War II. The International Monetary Fund, the World Bank, GATT, and dozens of other international organizations did not emerge until after World War II. Their emergence was not accidental; rather, they were designed to remedy problems that had earlier emerged in a world without them; they were established to mitigate some of the instabilities of earlier systems. It is toward these issues that this chapter 17 turns.

Key to understanding any international financial system are three elements: (1) *exchange rate regimens*: the extent to which exchange rates are fixed or floating, the ways of controlling the exchange rates, and the kind of backing countries keep for their currencies; (2) *adjustment*: the ways in which countries and their banking systems adjust to international disturbances; (3) *international cooperation*: the extent to which several governments work together internationally and the nature of that cooperation, which can range from an occasional meeting to the creation of a supranational organization. The way in which these elements of the system have evolved over the last century shows how the system as a whole worked and failed, and provides essential background for thinking of the future. This chapter covers the world system until 1973 and the collapse of the Bretton Woods arrangements. Chapter 18 takes up the story from there.

THE INTERNATIONAL SYSTEM
UNDER THE GOLD STANDARD

The classic gold standard, in use from roughly 1870 to 1914, had permanently fixed exchange rates, a few well-understood rules of how to handle payments troubles, and virtually no intergovernmental cooperation. It coincided with, and perhaps fostered, a great increase in capital and trade flows, and supported quite high levels of international trade imbalances. Prices during the period were stable or even falling. The gold standard was also associated with stable or falling prices, and some financial panics and recessions, which may have unnecessarily reduced economic growth and employment.

The gold standard as a generally accepted system did not exist "from time immemorial." It flourished only during the 35 years of European peace between the Franco-Prussian War and World War I, a period characterized by rapid technological change that begat a vast increase in commerce and international investment. The growth of commerce happened to coincide with the discovery of large amounts of gold and silver, and improved means to extract them, such that both commerce and specie (gold and silver coinage) grew together.

In the eighteenth century governments minted coins in both gold and silver. Both governments and the commercial banks also issued notes (currency) equivalent in face value to the coins, but whether or not the notes could be converted to gold or silver—that is, whether the notes were *convertible*—depended very much on the time and place. During the wars with Napoleon, the British pound was not convertible, and convertibility to gold was not restored until the early 1820s. In its early days, the United States was officially *bimetallic* —it redeemed currency in gold and silver, but in practical terms it was on a silver standard until the Civil War (1861-65), when the currency became non-convertible. It was 1879 before the United States government made its currency convertible only to gold and ceased to purchase silver. France also based its notes on either gold or silver.

Bimetallism had curious aspects, partly because the supplies of gold and silver both expanded rapidly in the nineteenth century. In the early days of the Republic, the United States Treasury, for instance, stood ready to buy 15 ounces of silver and pay in notes that it would redeem for 1 gold ounce—that is, a 15:1 ratio. As the price of silver fell against gold to 15.5:1, silver holders would buy an ounce of gold from the American government for 15 silver ounces, then sell the gold for 15.5 ounces of silver. The U.S. Treasury accumulated a great deal of silver until the ratio was changed in the 1830s. But the problem reappeared in the 1870s as silver production rose faster than gold production. So bimetal countries were on a standard of whichever metal was increasing production the fastest.

As silver production outstripped gold production in the last three decades of the nineteenth century, silver-based currency was potentially inflationary. Gold production, while occasionally causing deflation, was still expanding at a rapid enough rate to allow the considerable growth that the world underwent in that period. More practically, governments could not afford to keep buying and coining silver while giving up their gold, nor could they keep changing the ratio between silver and gold and claim they had a standard. In a sense, then, the gold standard was kind of an accident.[1] Silver production was expanding too quickly, but gold production was rising at a pace that, given the growth of output, was just right to allow modest increases in money.

Bimetallism became a huge controversy in the United States in the 1890s (some years after the U.S. had in fact moved to the gold standard). A large and populist element of the Democratic Party considered the gold standard an evil. The Democratic contender for the 1896 presidential election, William Jennings Bryan, thundered, "You shall not crucify mankind upon a cross of gold." In a much gentler way, L. Frank Baum took Dorothy down the Yellow Brick Road, where she discovered that the Emerald City (the prosperity at the end of the road) was all an illusion.

The Gold Standard in its Prime

Before the advent of paper currency and central banks, coinage was in gold or silver and a nation's monetary base was directly dependent on the availability of the circulating gold and silver. A deficit on the capital and current accounts would lead to an outflow of specie and a shortage of currency.

As banknotes (currency issued by private banks and the government) came into use in the nineteenth century, banks and governments found they could keep as reserve gold worth only a fraction of the notes they issued, establishing, in essence, the kind of fractional reserve system we have today that derives from checking accounts.* Those people transferring funds abroad exchange their notes for gold, which they could in turn convert to a foreign currency. If there were a deficit on current and financial accounts in such a situation, the outflow of gold would cause multiple contractions, as the banknotes issued would have less backing and prudent banks would cease to issue new notes as existing notes were retired. Or, as happened from time to time, customers would demand gold from their banks all at once, causing a run on the banks and financial panic.

The late nineteenth and early twentieth centuries brought the growth of central banking, the appearance of banknotes issued by the government and central banks, the growth of checking accounts, and a decline in privately issued banknotes, establishing the domestic monetary system more or less as described in introductory texts. Banknotes were redeemable in gold. Central banks, where they existed, held gold to back the banknotes they issued and the deposits of commercial banks they held—that is, they backed the monetary base with gold. Many countries, including the United States, Canada, China, and most of Latin America had no central banks.† There, commercial banks held gold (silver in China) to back their currencies, but, typically, only a small fraction of their notes would be backed by gold.

Whenever the nation had a deficit on the current and financial accounts, customers would be seeking gold for their notes. In countries without central banks, commercial bank gold reserves would fall sharply, forcing the banks to contract credit. Currencies issued by the national treasuries would also be

---

* Before checking accounts were common, banks issued their own notes. A borrower would receive banknotes, fractionally backed by gold, and these notes circulated as currency. It is only in the twentieth century that banknotes have become monopolies of the central bank and government.

† The Fed dates from 1913. The other nations established their central banks in the 1930s.

redeemed for gold and the gold sent abroad (to London, normally). The result would be a sharp drop in the money supply. Where there were central banks, the commercial banks would ask the central banks for gold, which would be granted, but the decline in commercial bank deposits and gold caused a decline in the money supply.

The essence of the gold standard was the legal obligation of countries to buy and sell gold to all comers at some fixed price. Around 1900, the United States was doing this at approximately the same price that had been in use since long before the Civil War—$20.67 per ounce.* Anyone visiting an office of the U.S. Treasury was able to sell gold to the Treasury in the form of coins, bars, or gold dust, collecting the fixed price of $20.67 an ounce minus only a service charge of a quarter of a percent. Anyone with dollars in hand could visit that same office and buy gold at the identical price, but with the 0.25% charge added on. A little thought will show that the mutual agreements to buy and sell gold at fixed rates meant that the exchange rate of one currency in terms of another was also fixed.

Consider what ensued if the American dollar started to fall in value against the pound sterling in the foreign exchange market in London, then the largest in the world. Holders of dollars never needed to accept a highly unfavorable rate. Instead, they could take the dollars to a bank or office of the Treasury, redeem them in gold, then ship the gold to Britain, selling it for pounds sterling. Say that in 1900 the amount of a debt to be paid in London was £1,000. Americans would find that a gold bar weighing 235.414 ounces would be worth exactly £1,000 if sold in London. By American law they could buy this bar for exactly $4,866, including service charges. The *mint parity* of the pound to the dollar was thus $4.866 to £1.00. If they were to purchase one such bar and ship it by sea to London, the additional cost of shipping and insuring might amount to $26, making the total cost $4,892. As long as the price of pounds on the London foreign exchange market remained above £1.00 = $4.892, traders would benefit by shipping gold instead of using the foreign exchange market.

Conversely, British buyers of dollars would ship gold to the United States any time their £1,000 sterling were to buy them less than $4,840 on the foreign exchange market. There was thus a floor for the price of a pound at $4.840 and a ceiling of $4.892, with 5.2 cents (about 1%) spread between the two prices known as *gold points*. Since spread was determined by shipping costs, which fell throughout the period, the spread gradually diminished to around ½ of 1% (0.5%) at the outbreak of World War I.

---

* This was not the usual avoirdupois weight, but a slightly heavier troy ounce—12 of which make up a troy pound, which is lighter than the 16 ounce avoirdupois pound. Yes, trivia fans, an ounce of gold is heavier than an ounce of lead, but a pound of gold is lighter than a pound of lead!

Figure 17.1

CURRENCY STABILITY AND THE GOLD STANDARD

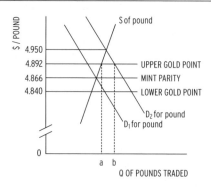

By the last quarter of the nineteenth century, it was seldom necessary for the typical trader or even bank actually to ship any gold. Instead, specialized *bullion dealers* acting as arbitrageurs would ship gold whenever the spread opened too widely.

Figure 17.1 illustrates how the gold standard worked. Suppose mint parity is $4.866 and transportation charges were about one-half of one percent. With the demand for pounds at D_1 there is insufficient incentive either to ship gold to Britain or to export it from Britain. If, however, the demand for pounds increased to D_2, it would be cheaper for those buying pounds to eschew the foreign exchange market and buy gold and ship it to Britain instead. Once the pound reached $4.892 in the foreign exchange markets in New York or London, dealers would begin to purchase gold in the United States and ship it to England. How much would they ship? Enough to fill the gap between demand and supply at the upper gold point—*ab*. Conversely, if the pound fell in value below $4.84, dealers would ship gold from Britain at the lower gold point. Sales of gold thus served to fix the price of the dollar and pound to a narrow range.

The true golden age of the world's money markets made trade and international investment easy. Private citizens of all occupations and nationalities could exchange major currencies without fear of a change in value—and, in fact, no major currency *did* change in value throughout the period. It was a time of almost unbelievable convenience for foreign trade and investment, with currencies exchanged against one another at fixed rates that were not expected to and did not change from year to year and decade to decade. What is more, the rates were in part selected for ease of calculation. Consider these typical gold standard rates from 1913:

German mark = 1 British shilling
U.S. dollar = 50 British pence, thus 2 U.S. cents = one British penny
Italian lira = 10 British pence = US$0.20 = 1 Austro-Hungarian crown
Russian rouble = US$0.50
Swedish crown = Norwegian crown = Danish crown = US$0.25

Another remarkable thing about the gold standard period was the degree of trade imbalances it allowed. So long as people believed that the system would work, they were willing to tolerate trade imbalances much larger than they have in recent decades, as Table 17.1 shows.

Table 17.1
TRADE IMBALANCES AS PERCENTAGES OF GNP UNDER
GOLD STANDARD AND IN THE POSTWAR PERIOD

	Average Current Account Balance		*Average Current Account Balance*
Gold Standard		*Postwar*	
United Kingdom	4.5	United States	0.0
Germany	1.8	Japan	0.7
Italy	0.6	Germany	0.9
Sweden	− 2.7	France	0.2
Norway	− 2.5	United Kingdom	0.0
Denmark	− 2.6	Canada	− 1.5
Australia	− 3.7	Belgium	0.0
Canada	− 7.7	Norway	− 2.1
		Finland	− 1.6
		Greece	− 3.1

Source: Tamim Bayoumi, "Saving-Investment Correlation," *IMF Staff Papers* (June 1990): 360-87.

Adjustment Under the Gold Standard

Under the gold standard, adjustments to international imbalances happened quickly. Unfortunately, many times it was income, not price levels, that adjusted. The nineteenth-century financial histories of both Canada and the United States are filled with panics that came about when British banks called in North American loans and credit dried up precipitously.

By the early years of this century, however, central banks were acting to mitigate (not counter) the contractionary effects of outflows or the expansionary effects of inflows. In those days, the principal monetary tool was the discount rate offered by the central bank for loans to other banks. If central banks wanted to cushion the fall in the money supply, they would lower the discount rate, encouraging the commercial banks to take advances from them and hold the advances as reserves. Substantial evidence dating from as early as 1890 shows that commercial bank reserves remained much steadier than the strict gold standard rules would have allowed them, showing that partially counterbalancing monetary policy is over a century old.[2] Indeed, one of the principal reasons for forming the Federal Reserve System was to partially insulate the U.S. from the bank panics and ensuing recessions that had occurred whenever gold flowed out of the U.S. In a sense, bankers came to value predictability in the domestic credit markets over predictability of international reactions.

A trade-off involving some sacrifice of the automatic nature of the gold system for stability in domestic currency markets was not a bad one so long as the central bankers paid attention to the medium and longer term, raising interest rates when needed to conserve the gold stock. They could, in essence, take the sharp edge off a panic, allowing the market more time to adjust, if necessary, to higher interest rates. Indeed, so long as gold served as a base both for the monetary system and for international transactions, the bankers had little choice but to allow the longer-term adjustments.

Dampening the effects of gold outflows and inflows required some form of monetary reserves that was not immediately monetized. As yet the distinction between domestic banking reserves and international or foreign exchange reserves had not yet emerged. Gold served to back both, but the link was not as direct as in earlier times because central banks could regulate how much gold was required to back a given money supply.

End of the Gold Standard

During World War I, it became increasingly difficult to buy and sell gold. At first it was merely unpatriotic to put a strain on one's country's finances by buying gold. Britain used many means to pretend that it would still redeem currencies in gold, yet making sure it did not have too many takers. What is clear is that by the end of the war the old standard was dead.[3]

The Gold Standard as a System

The gold standard had credible fixed exchange rates, backed by the widespread assumption that, while central banks might occasionally have followed counterbalancing policies, a gold outflow would cause a domestic contraction that would end any threat to the currency's viability. Domestic economies did indeed adjust, and there is ample evidence of stable or falling price levels from 1870 through World War I. (Part of this came from the dramatic decline in costs of production and transportation—often called *technological deflation*—and part through recessions that forced all prices down.) The private capital market flourished and was able to support trade imbalances that were very large by modern standards.

THE 1920S: PEGGED EXCHANGE RATES

The Way the System Worked

World War I and its associated inflations and economic dislocations brought about the demise of the gold standard. Many of the European countries substituted paper money and cheap coinage for gold and denied what was then called *convertibility*—the right to turn currency into a gold equivalent.* (The U.S. allowed this right until 1933.) No longer could a Frenchman go to his bank and get gold for francs; he would have to have his bank buy whatever currency he wanted on the foreign exchange market. The United States remained fully convertible, but few other countries would allow their notes to be turned into gold in order to purchase U.S. dollars.

Without gold transfers to hold their currencies steady, central banks began to buy and sell foreign exchange much as they have done ever since. They still held gold, but rather than selling the gold to the public they would trade gold with other central banks in order to buy or sell that country's currency. If Britain, for instance, found the pound falling in value, it could transfer gold to the Federal Reserve and receive dollar deposits in return. The Bank of England could then use those dollars to buy up excess sterling. If Britain found the pound rising in value, it might buy some gold back from the Federal Reserve. At the same time, many countries began to keep their reserves not as gold reserves but as foreign exchange reserves, again, much as they have done since. (In the 1920s, only about 25% of all reserves were in foreign exchange.) Because of the way countries used both gold and foreign exchange as backing, the system is sometimes called the *gold-exchange system*.

While the Americans enjoyed the roaring twenties, Europe was not nearly so prosperous. Germany experienced a hyperinflation and the international system was under constant strain from high French and British war debts owed to the U.S. and reparations payments the Germans owed to the French and British. Without gold convertibility, the values of currencies in foreign exchange markets could fluctuate and central bank intervention was neither

---

* Convertibility today means the ability to change a currency into foreign currency without having an exchange license—the absence of exchange control.

always consistent nor regular. Chapter 15 noted Britain's aborted return to gold under Churchill. The French franc was very unstable during most of the period, with some pegging, but with much heavy speculation against it. The German mark, suffering from the hyperinflation of 1922-23, fell to about four trillion to the dollar.

In short, the gold standard in the 1920s was what one specialist called a "façade."[4] In fact, it was a mixture of floating exchange rates with frequent and extensive intervention to peg the exchange rate, with many of the pegs (or par values) set at inappropriate levels.[5]

War Debts, Reparations, Tariffs

During World War I, Britain and France and their allies had borrowed large sums of money (about $10 billion) from the United States, principally from the government. When the war was over, they demanded enormous reparations from Germany to cover the cost of the war. (Germany had demanded reparation payments from France after the Franco-Prussian War of 1871.) Eventually, they scaled down their demands to just what they would have to pay the United States for war debts. For this to work, the Germans had to develop a trade surplus with the United States and use the dollars so gained to pay Britain and France, who would then repay the U.S., with whom they needed balanced trade. The United States could be paid back for the goods and services it had transferred to France and England during the war by goods and services from Germany. Because the money to pay back the debts at some point had to emerge from something real moving—a net surplus of goods and services for those paying—the issue is known as *the real transfer problem*.

Table 17.2 shows what would have been necessary. In the first line Germany has a trade surplus of US$1 billion. The German trade surplus means that German income exceeds German absorption (and savings exceed investment) by $1 billion. But Germany has agreed to pay Britain a vast amount of money as reparations—a transfer that, under the present form of balance-of-payments presentation, is under the *capital account*. So the German savings are transferred to Britain in the second line. Germany's current account shows a trade surplus and an outflow under unrequited transfers of $1 billion, giving it a balance of zero.

Britain has unchanged trade balance. The $1 billion in payments from Germany comes in as a capital transfer and goes out under the same category. Britain thereby reduces its indebtedness abroad. Britain's current absorption is unchanged, but it is able to use the transfer from Germany to reduce its net indebtedness.

The United States, in order to use the German savings, runs a trade deficit of $1 billion, which it pays for with the $1 billion in loan repayments from

Table 17.2

MAKING WAR DEBT REPAYMENTS WORK

	Germany	Britain	U.S.
Trade	+ $1 billion	no change	− $1 billion
Capital	− $1 billion	+ $1 billion − $1 billion	+ $1 billion

Great Britain, which is under the capital account. The U.S. has $1 billion more worth of goods and services to use, but sees its foreign assets fall by $1 billion—which is what it wants if it is to get paid back.

The only way this could have worked is if the United States ran a trade deficit and Germany a surplus. U.S. domestic investment had to exceed U.S. domestic saving ($Id > Sd$) for imports to exceed exports ($M > X$). The world did not work that way, unfortunately. The U.S. raised tariffs considerably in 1922, making it harder for Europe to export and reducing the volume of trade. As Chapter 2 noted, tariffs reduce the volume of trade but do not in themselves alter trade balances. The smaller volume of trade, however, made the interest and repayment of capital much larger as a percentage of all exports. Sterling was probably overvalued in 1925, making exports difficult, the German economy was in chaos, and only the franc, some of the time, was undervalued. Domestic price levels showed little sign of decline, and neither massive devaluation nor deflation was practical.

Instead, what interest and reparations payments there were (about $5 billion) came from private lending ($8-$9 billion). Europe had higher interest rates than the U.S. and European national and municipal governments frequently sold bonds on the New York markets. When the dollars so gained were converted to domestic currencies, the governments bought them and used them to repay the U.S. government. Thus a private capital flow helped pay the public debts, as illustrated in Table 17.3. It was, in a sense, a house of cards, and it collapsed after the October 1929 stock market crash on Wall Street. That particular financial panic might have been just a historical curiosity instead of a world trauma had it not removed a key card from the pile. The private loans to Europe stopped, and with their cessation, gold began to flow out of Europe—first from Austria, then from Germany, then from France.

Looming over it all was the Smoot-Hawley Tariff. President Hoover had originally intended lower tariffs, but the momentum in Congress produced sharply higher tariffs. In itself, however unwise, the tariff would merely have made the world less efficient and lowered trade, not worsened trade balances.

Table 17.3

WAR DEBT "REPAYMENT" WITHOUT A REAL TRANSFER

	Germany	*Britain*	*U.S.*
Trade	no change	no change	no change
Financial	+ $1 billion		+ $1 billion
Capital	− $1 billion	+ $1 billion − $1 billion	+ $1 billion

Coming as it did, when it did, it decreased the chances of any country developing a trade surplus with the U.S. and spread despair in Europe.

Tentative Steps in International Financial Cooperation

In seeking to get its debt repayments, the United States sponsored two international meetings to deal with the problem, the first, following the German hyperinflation, led to the Dawes Plan, and the second, in 1929, led to the Young Plan, both named after Americans. In retrospect, these were the first intergovernmental meetings ever to address any financial or economic problem. The Young Plan led to the establishment of the first intergovernmental and international institution, the Bank of International Settlements (BIS), which was to handle the international war debt and reparation payments. It also pioneered a system of repackaging debt and selling it in the form of new securities—an early form of securitization. Some of the German reparation debt was securitized and the resultant securities sold to investors; 1929, however, was not a good year for floating new issues. The BIS is still in existence, playing a key role these days in coordination of banking regulations, as in the Basel Accord. It still holds bonds issued under the Young Plan on its books. Practically, however, the efforts of the two plans and the BIS had no effect on repayment of debts. The American government recovered only about $2.7 billion of its claims of just over $10 billion, and that was from its own private lending.

The Financial Collapse

The collapse of the international monetary system did not follow immediately after the October Wall Street crash, nor after enactment of the Smoot-Hawley Tariff of 1930. It fell more like a pile of cans than a house of cards: a period of uneasiness (1930) followed by one can, then two, then the whole

688

pile coming down over the summer of 1931. Like so many macroeconomic phenomena, it was real and monetary at the same time. As loans from New York dried up and no signs of new ones were forthcoming, the inflow of dollars to Europe ceased. As their currencies began to fall in value, European central banks tried to intervene, but they lacked the gold or foreign exchange to do so successfully. Nor could they isolate their own money supplies from the outflow of gold and their monetary base; instead, they let interest rates rise with the hope that it would keep funds from exiting. Banks failed and people panicked (rightly so), withdrawing their money from the banks.

The problems were especially great for Britain because many foreign banks (including central banks) held sterling as reserves. When the foreign central banks came to intervene in the foreign exchange market, they sold the sterling for gold and used the gold to buy dollars to intervene. Every time the Austrian bank spent a million pounds of its sterling reserves, it used up not only a million pounds of its foreign exchange reserves but a million pounds of Britain's gold reserves as well. So the roughly 20-25% of reserves that were in foreign exchange disappeared, causing international reserves to fall sharply. As the process continued, Britain's ability to redeem currencies in gold came under doubt.[*] Several central banks cleared out their holdings of sterling bonds, including the Bank of France. Despite a considerable number of loans, arranged hurriedly with the U.S. Treasury, the pressure against the pound proved too great and Britain announced on September 15, 1931, that it would no longer redeem currencies in gold. The declining monetary bases in Europe and the attempts to keep capital from fleeing by raising interest rates caused investment to fall sharply, just at a time when it needed to be encouraged. The result was a recession that turned into a full-scale depression.

Pressure then came on the American Treasury. The United States had no problem with trade deficits, but it still was redeeming currency in gold for all comers, and many investors preferred gold to dollars.[†] As a result, banks and the U.S. Treasury lost gold. Rather than replace the lost reserves, the Fed decided that the decline in gold reserves mandated a decline in the money supply so that the smaller gold holdings would be close to the currency in

---

[*] Gone was the old assurance that, if Britain just raised interest rates, it could attract money from anywhere. Because New York was such a good alternative capital market, raising British interest rates no longer worked effectively.

[†] Ironically, when the U.S. went off the gold standard in 1933, it prohibited its citizens (not just residents) from holding gold and was one of the last major countries to restore that right. Samuel Insull, the utility magnate, commented that if two men went down the street in 1929, one with his pockets full of gold, the other with them full of whiskey bottles, the latter was the criminal and the former the good citizen. By 1934, the former would be the criminal and the latter the good citizen.

circulation.* As a consequence, interest rates rose in the U.S. throughout 1931 and 1932, turning the recession into a depression. Finally, in 1933, the U.S., too, ceased to redeem currency in gold, severing the link. Gold became exclusively an intergovernmental medium, but even in that case few governments stood ready to sell gold at the simple request of another.[6]

Assessment of the 1920s "Gold-Exchange Arrangements" as a System

The international system of the 1920s was an unstable system during an unstable period. Temporarily pegging exchange rates left considerable uncertainty about where the price would be in the future. The severance of the domestic monetary base from inflows and outflows of capital meant that governments were under less pressure to expand or contract as the balance of payments dictated. The good side of this was that certain unnecessary recessions could be avoided, but the downside was that governments, businesses, and labor were under no great pressure to keep the price level down. Also on the good side, the U.S. was able to sterilize all gold inflows and so avoid inflation. On the downside, the European countries trying to develop a trade surplus with the U.S. were forced into deflationary policies or into frequent devaluations. Economies, in a sense, became less flexible, although whether the inflexibility caused the frequent devaluations or the reverse is unclear.

International cooperation began in a series of attempts to solve the war debts issue. Relations between the Bank of England and the Federal Reserve Bank of New York were strong and consultation regular. There was, however, no international institution to provide any additional reserves or any formal procedures for central banks to borrow from one another.

Key to the difficulties of the 1920s system was the unsatisfactory reserve base and, ultimately, the unwillingness of central banks to lend when private capital could not or would no longer do so. Some might argue, in a "what it could have been" way, that had the Federal Reserve stood ready to help Britain out in the early 1930s, private capital would not have panicked. There never would have been a run on the sterling or the ensuing collapse of world reserves.†

---

* The Federal Reserve claimed, perhaps rightly, that it needed to keep the gold to back its issue of currency notes and that it could not hold more Treasury bills. That constraint was removed shortly, but the Fed still did not reflate the economy.

† The Federal Reserve considered the request for a loan, but took longer than the market was willing to wait. We could perhaps add that, had sterling not collapsed, Europe's economy would have recovered, Hitler would not have risen to power, and World War II would not have occurred. You never know.

THE GREAT DEPRESSION

Released from the need to redeem currencies in gold, governments were free to reflate and increase demand. But the prevailing wisdom was not Keynesian; it would be nearly a decade before Keynes's ideas were well understood. The freedom was, therefore, not well used. The currency experience of the 1930s was a mixture of floating rates, pegged rates, and experiments in exchange control, the last in Nazi Germany. Few observers at the time, or indeed since, considered the 1930s experiments with floating rates successful, since they appeared to disrupt trade and foreign investment.

The outbreak of World War II brought exchange control in virtually every country except the United States. As Chapter 15 explained, the value of a currency is maintained by rationing foreign currencies through a system of licenses, and exporters are required to turn in any foreign exchange and accept the government's official value for it, despite much higher black market rates. Such a system has affects similar to quotas on imports, but it also includes any other use of foreign exchange—for travel, repayment of loans, or remittance of profits. It seriously distorts the price system and may, perhaps, have been justified during the war, but its use in peacetime made little sense. The system in the 1930s lacked international cooperation, a generally agreed upon set of rules, stable exchange rates, and any reserves but gold. Domestic problems were so serious that they always took precedence over international cooperation or coordination.

THE BRETTON WOODS SYSTEM: 1947–1973

The Bretton Woods Conference of 1944 introduced major changes to the international monetary system, changes that were to endure for 25 years. As World War II finally turned in favor of the Allies, the governments of Britain and the United States turned some of their thoughts to the postwar economic and political order. Many of our current international institutions were designed to prevent a rerun of the 1930s. The United Nations, particularly its Security Council, was intended to keep any new Hitler from power. The International Monetary Fund and the associated understandings, known as the Bretton Woods system, were intended to control or eliminate the currency speculation, frequent changes in currency values, and lack of means to make economic adjustments characteristic of the previous three decades. The British, French, and Americans had begun discussions on the postwar economic order as the war progressed, but in 1944 a final conference was held at the orange-roofed Mount Washington Hotel in the New Hampshire mountain resort of Bretton Woods. Representatives of some 44 nations attended,

Figure 17.2
CENTRAL BANK INTERVENTION

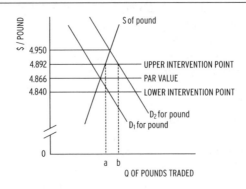

but the principal action was between the British delegation, headed by none other than John Maynard Keynes, and the American delegation, headed by a Treasury official, Harry Dexter White.

The conference hammered out two important features of the postwar world, the International Monetary Fund and a set of rules for an exchange rate system, known as the *adjustable peg*.

Exchange Rates under the Bretton Woods System

Under the Bretton Woods adjustable peg, governments fixed their currencies in terms of gold and used their foreign exchange reserves (and borrowings from the newly created IMF) to keep their exchange rates from falling below their target. While technically the currencies were fixed to gold, in practical terms they were fixed to the U.S. dollar, which served far more than gold did as reserves and as a means for intervening in the foreign exchange market. When the value of their currencies rose toward the target ceiling, the governments would buy back the foreign exchange (largely U.S. dollars), replenishing their reserves and repaying their loans. In the 1950s Britain, for instance, defined the pound in terms of gold so that £1.00 = $2.80. It would allow fluctuation around that par value of about 3 cents either way, giving a floor price at $2.772 and a ceiling at $2.828. If the pound fell toward the floor or hit the ceiling, the Bank of England would intervene in the market, *pegging* the rate.

The diagram for showing intervention (Figure 17.2) looks very much like the gold standard diagram. The difference is that, instead of private dealers moving gold when a gold point was reached, the Bank of England itself intervened to purchase or sell sterling in the way it still does today.

Figure 17.3

ADJUSTING THE PEG: BRITAIN DEVALUES THE POUND

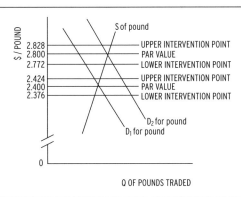

When the fixed rate became untenable, however, the country would change the rate, this being the *adjustable* element. Thus in 1967, after several years of attempting to maintain the old rate, Britain devalued the pound from $2.80 to $2.40. It removed the peg, so to speak, and repegged the rate at a point it thought it could defend. Figure 17.3 shows the situation in which Britain found itself in 1967. After a number of years in which the demand and supply of the pound had kept the price at around $2.80, demand for the pound fell sharply, from D_1 to D_2.* The amount of intervention the Bank of England would have to undertake to peg the pound at $2.772 or above would be enormous. So, instead, Britain announced that, henceforth, it would peg the exchange rate to within 1% of $2.40 rather than $2.80. That is a devaluation and downward adjustment of the peg.

Nations announced their par values and only changed them if they had a *fundamental disequilibrium*—and then this would be done in consultation with the IMF. One reason for the consultation was to prevent the kind of competitive devaluations that had occurred in the 1920s, when nations sought to stimulate their economies by devaluing. Another reason was to have international advice in seeking alternatives to revaluing the currency.

Nations were also to strive to remove the exchange controls they had placed on their currencies during the Great Depression and World War II. The agreement set no specific dates, but by the mid-1950s most industrial countries had removed all significant controls. (Britain freed almost all transactions, but until the 1970s still clung to a restriction on how much British residents could take abroad.) Third World countries persisted in using exchange control.

---

* Historically, the supply of pounds also rose, but that makes the diagram unnecessarily crowded, so we just move one curve.

Figure 17.4

U.S. WHOLESALE PRICE (FINISHED GOODS) INDEX, 1951-1980

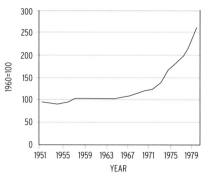

Source: IMF, *International Financial Statistics Yearbook*, 1981.

The whole thrust of the adjustable peg system was toward pegging, not adjustment. Governments were to try to use domestic monetary and fiscal policies to correct payments difficulties, and repegging was to be used only as a last resort. Keynes himself helped design the International Monetary Fund system and supported the thrust toward exchange rate stability. Keynes put considerable value on stable expectations for government policy as means for keeping capital costs down and investment up; support of stable exchange rates was consistent with that goal.[7]

The system worked well until the late 1960s. A strong U.S. dollar, produced by consistent American trade surpluses, high U.S. gold reserves, and a low rate of U.S. inflation, anchored the system. Countries, in fact, were pegging their currencies to the U.S. dollar and holding dollars rather than gold as reserves. While the high rate of U.S. private investment abroad caused deficits on the combined capital and current accounts throughout the period, other countries welcomed the increase in foreign exchange reserves (at least through the 1950s). The rise in dollar holdings abroad, moreover, was not so rapid as to cause undue expansion of the money supply in other countries. Figure 17.4 shows the wholesale price index for finished goods in the U.S. during that period, indicating the low rates of inflation before 1965.

Between 1951 (the slowing down of the Korean War) and 1967 the wholesale price level for finished goods rose about 10.5%. That is an average rate of less than 0.75% a year. Given the upward bias of a price index, deriving from its failure to reflect quality changes, there was probably no inflation at all. The dollar provided an excellent anchor for the whole system. But the upward turn afterward set the whole system adrift.

SPECULATION AND THE ONE-WAY OPTION

Difficulties with the Bretton Woods system arose when the U.S. price level increased sharply in the late 1960s. Its balance of trade worsened, and it had become obvious that the U.S. gold supply was not going to be used to back the currency. As the inflation and trade balance problems continued, they put serious strains on the system, which were aggravated by great currency speculation that was endemic in the system.

To see why speculation was high, consider the case of Great Britain in 1967 when it devalued the pound. Up to the very day on which the pound was devalued (a Sunday, of course, when markets are closed), the Bank of England was buying enormous quantities of pounds in a last-ditch attempt to maintain the rate at the level of £1.00 = $2.772. By doing so, the Bank of England (and other monetary authorities who pitched in to help) set up a situation whereby speculators might win but could not lose.

An example will show this *one-way option*. Imagine yourself the treasurer of Transatlantic Enterprises, a London-based subsidiary of an American company that in 1967 had £50,000 in cash assets. You suspect the pound will be devalued on the weekend because it has been battered heavily for several weeks. So you convert all £50,000 into dollars at the rate of £1.00 = $2.772, receiving $138,600. If the devaluation does not occur, you can buy back whatever sterling you need on Monday at a rate very close to what you sold them for, less rather minor bank charges. After all that pressure, the pound is not going to rise to its ceiling and certainly it is not going to be revalued upward, so the risk of loss from an upward movement of the pound is minuscule. But if the pound is devalued, then you stand to gain. Had it been the weekend of October 27, 1969, you would have awakened Monday morning to find the pound down to £1.00 = $2.40, and you could then have repurchased your £50,000 for $120,000, a neat $18,600 profit; that is better than 13% for one weekend. The one-way option was that you can't lose but can win, and it encouraged enormous speculative currency movements.

The one-way option forced governments to be dishonest about their exchange rates. To avoid massive speculations, finance ministers and undersecretaries never spoke of devaluations except in the most condemning of terms. If on Monday the ministers met to decide whether to devalue on the Friday, no minister emerged from the meeting to give an inkling of what had transpired. No comment would be made beyond the firm assurance that "the government is prepared to defend the existing parity at all costs." For this reason, a government defending a fixed rate continues to issue reassuring statements, often wholly untrue, right up to the very hour of the devaluation. As long ago as 1551, the Duke of Northumberland, in charge of English finances, denied firmly that the pound would be devalued at the very time he was arranging its devaluation.

Under a floating rate system, the one-way option disappears. Since the central bank does not regularly intervene, the exchange can move up or down, much as do shares on the stock market. If the pound had been floating in 1967, it would already have been in the $2.40 neighborhood and nobody could have made 13% on a weekend. Speculation, of course, continues, as it does in the stock and commodities markets, but the "heads I win, tails I don't lose" aspect of adjustable parities disappears.

While speculation was a problem, particularly near the end of the adjustable peg system, governments acted together to provide other central banks with considerable financing to peg their exchange rates. The system was designed so that scrambling to find additional finance to fight speculation (as Britain had to do in 1931) would not be necessary. There would be a ready, reasonable, and sufficient source of additional reserves. That source would be the International Monetary Fund.

The International Monetary Fund

THE DESIGN OF THE SYSTEM

At Bretton Woods, the British, led by Lord Keynes, advocated a powerful institution that could create new international reserves in the same way as a central bank can expand the domestic money supply of a country. Countries wishing to settle debts could make a limited amount of overdrafts (borrow) from a so-called clearing union. When they borrowed, the clearing union would credit the countries' accounts with *bancor*, which the nations could then turn over to surplus countries in exchange for their currencies. In essence, each nation would agree to receive the bancor much as it took gold. The bancor could also be used to back domestic currency issues and be held as reserves of the central bank. On a T-account, the clearing union could expand world reserves as needed by the stroke of a pen.

Table 17.4
CLEARING UNION

	Assets	Liabilities
	Loan to Debtor Nation +100	*Bancor* +100

The United States pushed through a much more conservative proposal. Each member nation of a new organization, the International Monetary Fund, received a quota that bore some general relation to the value of its wealth and trade.* The country would pay a quarter of its quota in gold and the remainder in its own currency. The Fund could in turn lend these monies to countries having difficulty defending their exchange rates. Not only would this increase the stability of exchange markets, but it would give the Fund some degree of control over its members. If the 1931 crisis had reappeared in 1951, Britain would not have had to try to make on-the-spot arrangements with other powerful central banks like the Federal Reserve but could go to the IMF

Table 17.5

FUND QUOTAS AND VOTES

Country	% Votes
United States	18.2
Germany	5.9
Japan	5.7
France	5.1
United Kingdom	5.1
Saudi Arabia	3.2
Italy	3.2
Canada	2.9

directly, following an established procedure. If members violated a rule of the Fund—one, for example, was not to devalue by more than 10% without prior consultation—then the Fund could deny loans to that country. The IMF soon organized a secretariat and technical staff to help make studies and offer advice. The power to send or withdraw a technical mission gave additional control over member nations. Finally, the IMF was given a very special weapon (never actually used) called the *scarce currency clause*. This allowed the Fund to declare scarce the currency of a country with a large trade surplus. It might do this if the surplus country were accumulating large amounts of reserves and showing no sign of trying to reduce that surplus. If the currency was declared scarce, all other countries could apply discriminatory exchange controls against the offender.

Such power, although certainly not enabling the IMF to dictate policy, was considerable, and the Fund's designers were not careless about its control. They were not about to adopt a one-country, one-vote rule, such as employed in the United Nations General Assembly. Nor did the idea of key members with veto power (as in the UN Security Council) appeal to them. Instead, voting in the IMF was apportioned according to the quotas, the vote being directly proportional to the quota size. Early in the Fund's existence, this meant that the United States, with 24.3% of the votes, and Great Britain, with 11.5%, could control the Fund. Quotas have been altered considerably since. Table 17.5 indicates the percentages for the most dominant countries as of 1996.

---

* The actual figure was based on payments to the International Postal Union, a handy proxy because payments to it had evolved to reflect income and population.

Figure 17.5
LENDING BY THE IMF

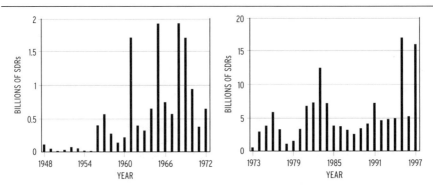

Note: The right and left panels are to different scales. The measurement is in the IMF's unit of account, the SDR (more below), which in 1997 was worth about US$1.37.

LENDING OPERATIONS OF THE IMF

One of the main functions of the IMF is to lend money to nations having difficulty keeping their exchange rates from falling. Such loans have served to stave off many a devaluation, giving time for the nation to make adjustments and convincing speculators that the nation had enough backing to keep its currency from falling. By the end of 1997, the Fund had lent around US$240 billion, the vast bulk of it after 1981. Figure 17.5 shows the total yearly lending over the history of the fund.

HOW THE FUND WORKS: THE BASIC STRUCTURE

The Fund is, as noted above, a pool of currencies. As the Fund's needs rose, national quotas for IMF members were raised several times, each requiring the one-quarter gold and three-quarters currency contribution. Recent increases in the quota have used foreign exchange in place of the gold (e.g., Germany could give three-quarters in marks and one-quarter in francs).* The Fund encouraged central banks to include the gold and foreign exchange deposited with the Fund as part of their official reserves. Each nation could borrow from the Fund an amount equal to 125% of its quota. That borrowing was divided into five *tranches* ("tranche" is French for slice, but usage rhymes "tranche" with "ranch"). A borrowing country could get the first tranche

---

* That foreign exchange may be in any hard currency normally used as a reserve—dollars, yen, and German marks are fine, but no Haitian gourdes or Peruvian soles.

(the *reserve tranche*, called in the old days the *gold tranche*) simply by asking for it; after all, it was the country's gold to begin with. When the country desired to borrow more than the gold tranche, however, it had to ask the Fund. The IMF's permission to borrow became more and more difficult to obtain as the nation borrowed each successive tranche up to the *supertranche,* the last 25%. That basic system continues today.

Technically, the IMF describes a nation's borrowing as a *purchase,* because the borrowing nation pays for the foreign currency it buys by depositing its own currency with the Fund. When Argentina borrowed SDR 292.5 million (about US$400 million) worth of foreign currency in 1991, for instance, it paid for it with 417.69 million Argentine pesos. When it paid back the foreign exchange, it *repurchased,* to use the Fund's word, its own pesos.[8]

MODIFICATIONS TO THE ORIGINAL SCHEME

The Fund has come under considerable pressure to expand its lending operations and at the same time has sought sources of funding beyond quota increases to help meet this pressure. As a result, the basic structure of IMF finances has changed considerably, although the bulk of these changes occurred after 1973. Early ones include borrowing by the Fund and stand-by arrangements.[9]

Borrowing by the Fund. The Fund in 1962 made an agreement, continued to this day, with 10 industrial nations (the Group of Ten) called the General Arrangements to Borrow (GAB), a credit line that presently can amount to SDR 18.5 billion. (Again, if a major currency is under attack, it cannot be used. If the U.S. dollar should need aid, the $4.25 billion of the U.S. line of credit would be useless.) Originally, the GAB could only be used to finance loans to the Group of Ten, but since 1983 some of the money can be used for weaker countries. None of the money borrowed is part of a country's quota. Additional sources of funding, developed later, are discussed in the following chapter.

Stand-by Arrangements. From its very early days the Fund has frequently negotiated *stand-by arrangements* with countries, where it agrees that, if needed, it will lend to a nation out of its various facilities. It established such arrangements, originally in 1952, because the use of the tranches beyond the reserve tranche is not automatic and requires time to negotiate. A stand-by arrangement is evidence that a country has immediate access to foreign exchange, which may well calm the markets for its currency, even if this exchange is never used.

The founders of the IMF could hardly have envisaged an organization with 167 members,* nor could they have foreseen the needs and difficulties of new nations. The IMF soon learned, however, that it could not play the role of a private banker with a spendthrift customer and simply deny loans when the nation asked for more help. The *conditionality* of the upper credit tranches gave the IMF an opportunity—or perhaps forced upon it a duty—to do more than just deny loans; it had to give counsel and advice and monitor that the advice was taken. The IMF would send advisers, who would suggest certain programs—following them would secure new loans, while ignoring them would lead to the denial of new loans.

RESERVE CURRENCIES

When many central banks hold their foreign assets in securities of another country, that currency is known as a *reserve currency*. The principal reserve currency in the 1920s was sterling. In the 1930s and for a period after World War II, those countries continuing to use sterling as a reserve were part of what was called the *sterling area*. Sterling's weakness (constantly under pressure to fall in value) made it less attractive than the dollar and, as noted above, the dollar became the principal reserve currency after the war. In more recent years, central banks have kept wider portfolios of foreign currencies, particularly the stronger German mark, Japanese yen, and Swiss franc.

The difficulty with using currencies like the Deutschmark or Swiss franc as reserve currencies is that their domestic financial markets are small and, compared to the dollar and sterling markets, rather illiquid. A nation seeking to buy a considerable amount of German marks (in the form of German government bonds) could drive up bond prices, and drive them down when it sold off the marks. Moreover, if the German government tried to keep the DM stable by intervening in the foreign exchange market, German reserves would undergo a number of shocks that would make it difficult for the Bundesbank to keep the DM stable. In the larger, more liquid U.S. (and Eurodollar) markets, such changes would be a ripple, not a wave.

A curious property of those nations whose currencies are used as reserves is that their trade deficits are, in effect, covered by the central banks that pick up the excess foreign exchange reserves. Whenever other countries buy up dollars to keep their own currencies from rising (i.e., the dollar from falling),

---

* In 1944 there were only three independent countries in Africa (Ethiopia, Liberia, and South Africa), three in the Caribbean (Cuba, Haiti, and the Dominican Republic), and three in the Far East (Japan, China, and Thailand). The Communist countries did not join.

their reserves, and hence world reserves, rise automatically. So whenever the U.S. ran a deficit on the capital and currency accounts, world reserves tended to rise, leading to rather special problems.

The U.S. trade deficit of the mid-1980s provides an illustration. From 1984 through mid-1987 that deficit was covered by large private capital inflows from abroad, but in the latter part of 1987 foreign central banks began to pick up billions of dollars, accounting for a great deal of the SDR 84 billion rise in world reserves discussed in the following chapter. The dollar, however, was not an ideal reserve because it was tending to fall in value, so the central banks were buying up an asset declining in value. The U.S. trade deficit, in essence, was paid for by central banks investing in U.S. Treasury bills. The Americans gave hope from time to time that they would end the deficit, but the Europeans and Japanese complained that the additional reserves so created were preventing adjustment and letting the American deficit plunge on.

In the 1960s, the U.S. had a trade surplus, but also a heavier capital out-flow, much of it in the form of foreign direct investment. European central banks, to keep their currencies from rising against the dollar, bought large amounts of U.S. dollars, which they held in the form of U.S. T-bills. The Europeans complained the Americans were "buying them out with their own money," because European holdings of T-bills were poor investments compared to the direct investments of the U.S. in Europe. Americans, in turn, claimed that the Europeans should either let the *real transfer* take place (by running trade deficits, particularly by letting in more American agricultural goods) or stop complaining.

SPECIAL DRAWING RIGHTS

Worries about whether the U.S. dollar could continue to be a strong reserve base caused economists to try to think of some means to replace the dollars as reserves. The reliance on the dollar as a reserve currency was much in discussion in the 1960s. As foreign holdings of dollars swelled and the U.S. gold base shrank, some bankers feared a repeat of the 1931 British scenario. Others were just annoyed that the U.S. was in a position to run deficits indefinitely. This was before the period when the U.S. had a trade deficit, but the combined current and capital accounts had been in deficit for many years. Indeed, the U.S. had to run a deficit on the combined current and capital accounts if world reserves were to expand. If the U.S. sensibly stopped doing so, then world reserves might shrink. What could the world possibly use if the dollar ceased to be appropriate? In an attempt to replace U.S. dollars as foreign exchange reserves and avert a possible crisis similar to that of 1931, central bankers agreed to create a Special Drawing Right. The SDR is a unit whose value is determined by a basket of key currencies. But it is also a right to draw foreign exchange from another central bank, acting almost like gold. Despite initial enthusiasm, the SDR has never become a very important reserve.

At a meeting of the IMF Board of Governors in 1967, a new plan was presented, the result of four years of study by the technical staffs of the Group of Ten. Over the next six months, accompanied by an enormous amount of discussion, the details of the reform were hammered out as an amendment to the articles of the IMF. The details were as follows:

1. A new category of reserves called *special drawing rights* (SDRs) was established separate from the general accounts of the IMF but still part of the Fund's operations.

2. Any IMF member was eligible to participate and any member could opt out. (The two great opponents of the SDR, France and South Africa, finally decided to participate in the scheme.)

3. The initial allocation of SDRs, made on January 1, 1970, was SDR 9.4 billion. Of this, SDR 3.4 billion was made available at once, SDR 3 billion in 1971, and the last SDR 3 billion installment in 1972. (An SDR was worth $1.00 at the time.) Subsequent allocations occurred in 1979, 1980, and 1981. The IMF expected that it would create additional new SDRs every five years. However, 85% approval of the IMF is required for new issues, meaning that token opposition suffices to stop any new issue. The formula used to allocate the new reserves was based on voting strength in the Fund; hence, rich countries benefited far more than poor.

4. Holders of SDRs (which must be central banks) can exchange them for foreign currency directly with another country. As this resembles the way gold used to be employed as a reserve, the SDRs, not surprisingly were nicknamed "paper gold." Initially, the SDRs were even defined in terms of gold, with the dollar designation being understood to mean the dollar at $35 per ounce of gold. However, in 1974 after the dollar had begun to slide and the gold price rose, the IMF began to express the value of the SDR as a moving average of major currencies. (The weights at present are U.S. dollar 40%, German mark 21%, Japanese yen 17%, French franc 11%, and British pound 11%.) SDRs are little affected by currency devaluations (other than that of the dollar, which is 40% of the basket). They hold a substantial advantage over gold in that interest rates (60% of the weighted average of short-term interest rates in America, Japan, Germany, and Britain) are paid to any country that holds SDRs in excess of its initial allocation, that interest rate in effect being paid by the countries using the SDRs and thus holding less than their quota. This seems to make a great deal more sense than the use of gold, which not only bears no interest, but takes up storage space, must be guarded, and has many industrial uses.

The transfer of SDRs occurs on the accounts of the IMF. The paying country is debited and the recipient country is credited. Thus there are no pieces of paper called SDRs, just numbers in books and on computers. There is no requirement for corrective action or IMF supervision, as with the Fund's credit tranches. However, even though the IMF need not approve a transaction involving SDRs, the recipient country must agree, and does have the right to refuse acceptance.*

Perhaps the most hotly debated of all the topics concerning the SDR was *reconstitution*. After using SDRs, must a country eventually return to its original position by buying them back? If so, how soon? Some countries advocated repayment as if an SDR were a temporary loan. Others wanted no reconstitution at all, as if the SDR were just like gold or foreign exchange. The result of the debate was a compromise. All SDRs may be used, but the average daily holdings by a country over a five-year period must be no less than 30% of its average daily allocation of SDRs. The result is that a country using no more than 70% of its allocation has no problems and the SDR is "good as gold." If it uses 80% for six months, it must *reconstitute* (buy back) enough SDRs to reach 40% of its allocation in some subsequent six-month period. It would do so by exchanging holdings of foreign currency for the SDRs of some other country.

SDRs as reserves have never become as important as economists expected; indeed, no new ones were issued between 1981 and 1997, although in 1997 the IMF Board of Governors voted to allow a modest one-time issue of additional SDRs.[10] (None, as of 1999, had been issued, however.) The reasons for not issuing more SDRs are several.

1. Central banks are doing quite well relying almost exclusively on foreign exchange for reserves. As gold has become a secondary reserve asset, nations have come to rely almost exclusively on foreign exchange reserves, despite the higher risks of holding a fluctuating currency. Virtually all nations have sundered the tie between gold or foreign exchange reserves and their domestic currency and money issues.

2. As the U.S. ran enormous trade deficits in the mid-1980s and persuaded other nations' central banks to buy up many of the surplus dollars, world reserves grew very large. Not counting gold, they jumped by 20% in 1987.

---

* There is one exception: when a country is "designated" by the IMF—ordinarily this would be a country with a very large and growing stock of reserves—then it *must* accept SDRs in exchange for its own or some other convertible currency. The obligation ends when the designated country has acquired SDRs up to three times its own allocation. For example, a country allocated $100 in SDRs after designation would be obligated to accept $200 worth of additional SDRs from other countries. After the required maximum figure is reached, the designated country can continue to accept the SDRs of others if it wishes, but it does not have to. This clause has never been used.

Because the tie with gold no longer exists, foreign central banks that buy U.S. dollars can only turn them in for more U.S. dollars, so they are left with the choice of letting their own currencies rise in value or increasing their holdings of dollars. In some senses, the U.S. has not needed reserves because it has been able to persuade, cajole, or force other nations to accumulate dollars.

3. Most of the problems faced by the international monetary system are problems of *adjustment*, not problems of inadequate reserves. Additional reserves *per se* would not end the U.S. deficit or solve the problems of indebtedness in less-developed countries.[*]

4. More reserves could be inflationary. By postponing adjustment, deficit countries would continue in deficit, and the surplus countries would be forced to maintain high trade surpluses and/or to let their price levels rise, as argued in the previous chapter. Even the non-oil-producing LDCs, many of whom were heavily indebted, did not use their SDRs to the fullest possible extent, retaining 40-60% of their allocations. Actual patterns of retention appeared to be determined by portfolio considerations of the balance between foreign exchange and SDR holdings and the risk and interest on each. An increase in SDRs would not, and did not, automatically lead to their being spent to perpetuate a deficit.[11]

BORROWING: SWAP LINES

By the mid-1960s, the resources of the IMF looked small compared to the speculative movements of currencies that countries were experiencing. The IMF worked well enough for small, Third World countries at that time, but it would not have the resources to fight a run on a major currency. As a response to this problem, most of the industrialized countries developed short-term arrangements for lines of credit with each other called swap lines. Most of these are bilateral agreements to lend each other up to several billion dollars if called upon. Many of these arrangements have been in place since the early 1960s, although they have to be renewed as frequently as four times a year.

THE END OF THE BRETTON WOODS SYSTEM

The end of the Bretton Woods system came in 1973. Continued American inflation, triggered by the large budget deficit emerging from the costs of the

---

[*] This is not to say that they might not be part of the solution. If new SDRs were issued to heavily indebted nations, for instance, they (or 70% of them) could be used to pay off the debt. Such a simple solution, however, carries with it a large number of problems. Most economists would like some mixture of increased adjustment ability along with some debt relief.

war in Vietnam and increased social programs, was pushing the purchasing power parity value estimates of the U.S. dollar far out of line from the German mark, Swiss franc, and currencies closely tied with them. The OPEC oil crisis was driving up the cost of U.S. imports. U.S. gold reserves, still important in that period, were falling and doubt was considerable that they would ever be used anyway. The rising tide of inflation was lifting the system's anchor off the floor, and with the chain at its bitter end, a round of speculation against the dollar ensued. The governments called a hurried conference in Washington in December 1971. Meeting in a room at the centrally located Smithsonian Institution, the central bankers and treasury and finance officials realigned currencies, noting, as usual, that the arrangement was "for eternity." This Smithsonian Agreement was shaky at the start, failing to engender confidence or change governments' policies.

In January of 1973, speculation on the Swiss franc rising caused a large movement of funds into Switzerland, which the Swiss could not sterilize. Rather than face an inflation, the Swiss allowed the franc to float upwards. While such a move is reasonable from the experience over the last decade and a half, it exposed the weakness of the Smithsonian Agreement. Within a few weeks there surged a veritable tidal wave of speculation out of weak currencies and into German marks, Swiss francs, and Japanese yen. The Bundesbank alone was rumored to have purchased $6 billion to $7 billion worth of currency in a week. As Chapter 16 showed, central banks rarely have enough other assets to sell to counterbalance inflows of this magnitude. Germany could have reduced all its bank advances to zero and sold what few government securities it had, and it still could not have checked the expansion of reserves. Currencies were once again realigned, but the capital flows did not cease. Finally, on March 11, 1973, governments announced that they would no longer peg their currencies. Eternity had lasted little more than a year. The Bretton Woods period, begun with a bang, closed with a whimper.

THE BRETTON WOODS SYSTEM: AN ASSESSMENT

Under Bretton Woods, at least in its heyday, exchange rates were fixed but could be adjusted. Domestic flexibility had declined considerably, as few countries saw prices falling and high levels of unemployment were not tolerated. As a consequence, there was far more pressure for international cooperation and building up of reserves. The cooperation, through the IMF, helped in adjustment (through its approval of exchange rate changes and its advisory capacity) and in the ability to maintain trade imbalances. The sharp increase in the holdings of U.S. dollars allowed a large expansion of international reserves, and while this increase was perhaps excessive at times, it was important in keeping reserves at high levels. Indeed, when the U.S. no longer would redeem dollars in gold, it was gold, not dollars, that ceased to be the international reserve!

The Bretton Woods System was a good one for its time. It worked in a period when international capital flows were modest, compared to the present markets, when a single financial market and a single currency dominated, and where that currency's purchasing power was quite stable. It worked in a period when full employment levels could be achieved with only modest inflation and when a slowing of growth could bring income adjustments without large-scale unemployment. Times changed, however, and the Bretton Woods system could not survive the changes. What would replace it in the decades to follow? And what kind of system can we now build? These questions are the focus of the following chapter.

VOCABULARY AND CONCEPTS

Adjustable peg
Bimetallism
Bretton Woods system
Convertibility
Fundamental disequilibrium
GAB
Gold points
Gold standard
Gold-exchange system
International Monetary Fund
Mint parity
One-way option

Par value
Pegged exchange rates
Quotas
Reparations
Reserve currency
SDR
Specie
Stand-by arrangements
Swap lines
Tranche—reserve, regular, super
War debts

QUESTIONS

1. Compare the gold standard, the 1920s gold-exchange system, and the Bretton Woods system, indicating what each was and how much each depended on exchange rate flexibility, flexibility of the domestic economies, and explicit international cooperation.

2. "Although some people speak of the gold standard as some kind of golden age, the fact is that it lasted only about 35 years and was enabled almost accidentally by the moderate expansion of gold production." Explain.

3. Explain how the gold standard worked, indicating what gold points were.

4. One sign of the strength of the gold standard in its prime was the large size of trade imbalances. Explain why they are considered large and why they are signs of strength.

5. Why were the war debts owed to the United States not repaid? Explain, using the concept of the *real transfer*.

6. What was the role of the Smoot-Hawley Tariff in bringing on the Great Depression?

7. Explain the Bretton Woods exchange rate system and show the adjustable peg. Under what circumstances could a country change its peg? How was this an improvement over what had occurred in the 1920s?

8. Why did the inflation in the United States contribute to the end of the Bretton Woods system?

9. Why can speculation actually be worse under a fixed rate than a floating rate system?

10. Explain how the IMF works. Where does it get its funds? How can countries get funds from it? What are the restrictions on borrowing?

11. Even when the IMF asks a country to do something that is utterly reasonable by economic standards, it sometimes faces heavy criticism. Why?

12. What is an SDR? Why were they created? Explain how they work.

13. What led to the end of the Bretton Woods exchange rate system?

NOTES

1. The historical discussion comes from Leland Yeager, *International Monetary Relations* (New York: Harper and Row, 1966), 251-53. For extensive discussion and analysis of the various issues and events covered in this chapter, see Mark Brawley, *Turning Points: Decisions Shaping the Evolution of the International Political Economy* (Peterborough, Ont.: Broadview Press, 1998).

2. Arthur I. Bloomfield traces the relationship of the discount rate to the reserve ratio in 11 European nations. "The fact that, for five of the eleven [central] banks examined, discount rates and reserve ratios did *not* characteristically move in opposite directions— even on an annual average basis—indicates that the link between discount rate changes and movements of gold was not so close or general under the pre-1914 gold standard as is supposed." Bloomfield, *Monetary Policy under the International Gold Standard, 1880-1914* (New York: Federal Reserve Bank of New York, 1959).

3. "The date when England 'returned to gold' after the war is a landmark in world history, but it is very difficult to determine the date when England left the gold standard to which she returned in 1925." W.A. Brown, Jr., in Ragnar Nurkse, *International Currency Experience*, vol. 2 (Geneva: League of Nations, 1944), 28; quoted in Yeager, *International Monetary Relations*, ch. 15.

4. W.A. Brown, Jr., ibid.

5. For a good summary of the whole period, see Yeager, *International Monetary Relations*. For more depth, see Nurkse, *International Currency Experience*, 2 vols.

6. See Yeager, *International Monetary Relations*; Nurkse, *International Currency Experience*, 2 vols. volumes.

7. Allan Meltzer, *Keynes's Monetary Theory: A Different Interpretation* (Cambridge, 1989).

8. Borrowings and repayments, described as purchases and repurchases, are in the beginning pages of the IMF's *International Financial Statistics*, a monthly publication available in almost any university library. They are not in the annual yearbook.

9. The basic arrangements are described in the Introduction to each month's *International Financial Statistics*.

10. *IMF Survey*, August 3, 1998, 246.

11. Robert G. Murphy and George M. Von Furstenberg, "An Analysis of Factors Influencing the Level of SDR Holdings in Non-Oil Developing Countries," *IMF Staff Papers* 18 (June 1981): 310-37.

Chapter Eighteen

International Monetary Institutions (II)

OBJECTIVES

OVERALL OBJECTIVE   To explore the institutional reaction to the three great shocks after 1972—the oil crisis, the Third World debt crisis, and the financial panic in East Asia—and to evaluate the increasing pressures toward fewer currencies.

MORE SPECIFICALLY
- To examine the impact of the oil crisis of the 1970s and the subsequent inflation.
- To assess the floating exchange rate system that emerged as a result of the rapid and varying rates of inflation.
- To contrast and compare the two debt crises of the period—the Third World debt crisis of the 1970s and the Asian tiger crisis of 1997-99.
- To study the institutional reaction to the debt crises, with particular emphasis on the IMF.
- To examine the discussions about reducing the number of currencies in the world in light of optimum currency area ideas.

....

An international financial crisis reveals problems previously hidden and hastens the calls for reform. When institutions fail, people start thinking about ways to improve or replace them. The gold standard did not survive World War I. The makeshift arrangements of the 1920s could not survive the financial crises that preceded the Great Depression. The Bretton Woods system could not survive the oil shocks and inflations of the early 1970s. The last three decades of the century were to see a new series of crises and further institutional change. These troubling events—accompanied by some degree of financial panic—

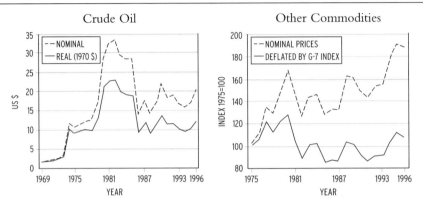

Figure 18.1

THE PRICE OF A BARREL OF OIL
(ARABIAN CRUDE) AND OTHER COMMODITIES

Source: IMF, *International Financial Statistics Yearbook*, commodities prices tables, various years.

were the oil price shocks of 1972 and 1978, the Third World Debt crisis beginning in 1982, and the panic that spread from East Asia in 1997.

THE OIL CRISES

The petroleum industry has had a history of shortage and glut, each shortage accompanied by dire warnings that the world was about to run out of oil. In the 1930s and 1940s more of the control of oil had fallen into the hands of the large integrated major companies. These companies maintained a standard price for oil, no matter where it was pumped from, based on a base price set for the Persian Gulf plus any transport costs from that region—the "gulf-plus" system. By the late 1960s, this price was $1.80 a barrel, reflecting the inexpensive oil flowing from the Arabian Peninsula. Many oil-producing countries felt that they could get more than this and that they could wrest power from the large oil companies. The growth of independent producers, refiners, and distributors meant that they could act effectively on such an evaluation. Moves by Libya and OPEC—the Organization of Petroleum Exporting Countries—changed power relationships and led to the producing countries maintaining output restrictions. By 1973 OPEC had seized the price-setting ability and raised the price of a barrel of oil. The left panel of Figure 18.1 shows how the price of oil changed after 1969.

The diagram shows four periods: (1) the first oil shock, 1972-77, which drove prices from $1.80 to $10 to $12 a barrel; (2) the second oil shock,

Figure 18.2
ANNUAL CHANGE IN THE CONSUMER PRICE INDEX
OF G-7 COUNTRIES (WEIGHTED BY 1975 GDPS)

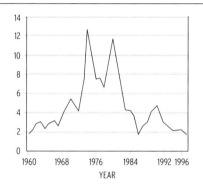

Note: The weighting is based on 1975 GDPs, converted to SDR values. The G-7 countries are: United States, Japan, Germany, United Kingdom, France, Italy, Canada.

Source: IMF, *International Financial Statistics Yearbook*, various years.

beginning in 1978-81, which pushed prices over $30 a barrel; (3) the collapse in oil prices (1981-85); (4) a period in which oil prices ranged between $15 and $21 a barrel (1985-96). (A period of oil prices below $15 began in 1997.) Each of the first three periods triggered financial crises. In contrast to the price of oil, other commodities' prices rose only for a short period of time. (The IMF began its price index of non-oil commodities only in 1975. Prices of most commodities were rising in the early 1970s, however.) After 1982, the index, in real terms, was below 100 from 1981 through 1994.[1]

Inflation and Retrenchment

When the price of oil first started to rise, many economists in developed countries worried that the high prices of oil would cause imports to rise and severely depress aggregate demand. To counter this supposed deflationary effect, monetary policy was eased, leading to inflation. The price hikes of 1978, however, were met with much tougher monetary policy, causing a sharp rise in real interest rates.

In the 1970s, virtually all countries experienced large and unanticipated increases in their price levels, followed by very pronounced decreases in inflation. The consumer price index in the United States, for instance, rose only by about one-third from 1960 to 1970 but doubled between 1970 and 1980. In the next decade it rose about 50%, and in the 1990s it rose by only about one-third, back to 1960s rates of increase. The other industrial countries followed roughly the same pattern, although in some countries inflation was more severe and in some less so. Figure 18.2 shows the annual weighted average inflations of the seven most important industrial countries (the G-7). Figure 18.3 shows the pattern from 1965 through 1985 in six of the countries.

Figure 18.3
INFLATION, 1965-1985, SELECTED COUNTRIES

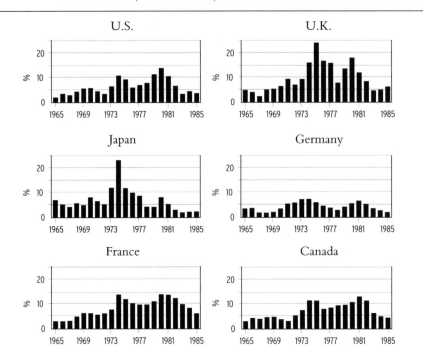

Inflation, as measured by consumer price indexes, rose sharply after the two major increases in oil prices of 1972-73 and 1978. Inflation declined swiftly in the 1980s and by the 1990s it was down to about 2% a year. Given the typical errors in the CPI that overstate inflation, a 1-2% inflation is not really an inflation in the sense that a person on a fixed income will not lose real income.

As Figure 18.3 indicates, while some countries had lower inflations than others and Japan brought its inflation under control quite quickly, the overall pattern is much the same in each of the countries—low inflation in the 1960s, followed by a peaking in the 1970s and then a decline in inflation in the 1980s. American inflation, interestingly, was the second lowest over the period, bettered only by Germany's.

When most net oil-importing countries eased credit to avoid deflation in the early 1970s, real national income did not respond to the expansion of demand. The result was higher prices, but little increase in output—*stagflation*—inflation with high unemployment. The oil producers could not immediately use their increased funds and dumped them into financial markets, and the banks scrambled to find useful places to put them. As the stagflation continued, economists and central bankers began to reflect on the more conservative monetary theories, which argued that the expansion of money in itself did nothing in the long run (in this case, even the apparent short run) but push up prices. At the same time, the financial markets adjusted to the unexpected inflation as savers demanded and borrowers conceded high inflation premiums, which tended to shift AS to the left in the AD/AS diagram. The reaction to the 1978 crisis was therefore opposite to that of 1972—a tightening that produced a sharp drop in the rate of inflation.

Figure 18.4

GOVERNMENT BOND
YIELDS OF G-7 COUNTRIES

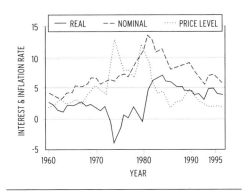

The unanticipated changes in the rate of inflation caused the real rates of return to be quite erratic in the period. A real rate of return is the interest rate minus the inflation rate ($i - \Pi = r$, where i is the nominal interest rate, Π is the rate of inflation, and r is the real interest rate). Theoretically, real rates are easy to define, but practically, it is difficult to choose an inflation indicator and comparable investment assets to use. Figure 18.4 uses the government bond yield (short-term, if available) and the consumer price index, again weighted by the countries' GDPs, to produce a quickly understood diagram.

Nominal interest rates lagged behind inflation until the late 1970s, allowing real rates to fall into the negative numbers. In 1978, however, the sharp increase in the cost of living was matched—or overmatched—by a sharper increase in nominal rates, causing real rates to rise. As inflation fell, however, nominal rates once again lagged behind the change in inflation, and real interest rates continued to rise until 1984.

FLOATING EXCHANGE RATES

One of the first institutional reactions to the rapid inflation was the adoption of floating exchange rates. The underlying conditions made it extremely difficult to have a fixed exchange rate system. To return to Marshall's "stone on a string in the millrace" analogy, no one knew where the string was tied (i.e., purchasing powers were moving erratically) or how much water would be surging through the millrace (i.e., nominal interest rate differentials were moving unpredictably). It is not surprising that most countries had to establish floating exchange rate systems.

Economists did not greet floating rates with the dread that had accompanied the floating rates of the 1930s. Germany and Switzerland, after all, had allowed their currencies to float to keep inflation *down* and many people thought that the U.S. dollar should have been lower in value. Canada had floated its currency in 1949, never again declared a par value, and had a relatively good experience. Peru's floating currency was part and parcel of a more open economy and the IMF had never seen much need for complaint. Given the size of speculative funds and the increased liquidity of capital markets, pegging rates seemed impossible. Moreover, many economists were convinced that market-determined exchange rates would be more stable, lacking the one-way option, and more reflective of underlying costs than government-determined rates. To be sure, experience with floating rates revealed a number of problems, but none of them were insuperable. Every criticism of the floating rate seemed to have a decent riposte.

Cost of Trade

International trade and investment are more costly and complicated when currencies change frequently in value. As Chapter 16 showed, the financial markets responded with a great array of risk-reducing devices, such as long-term forward instruments, futures, swaps, and various over-the-counter arrangements. World trade and investment continued to increase without any sharp break. But forward coverage is not free, and, for the smaller firm, it is complicated. Travelers, who sometimes could use such coverage, cannot be bothered (in the sense that the bother is a cost) and sometimes get stung, holding a declining currency. Moreover, truly long-run investments cannot be covered.

Given the fact that nations have different rates of inflation, investors would probably prefer floating rates, which would distort costs less than would fixed rates. If British Industries builds a plant in Canada to serve the North American market and the Canadian inflation is more than the American, British Industries is certainly better off if the Canadian dollar can fall in value than if it stays the same while costs rise. Nor is it really true that fixed rates eliminate the costs of coverage. Central banks have to hold much larger amounts of low-yielding foreign exchange assets in their reserves; the cost is to a large extent shifted from the private to the public sector.

Financial Problems

Financial, tax, and cost accounting problems are considerable under floating rates and the solutions to the problems are often rather awkward. A money-losing (in euros) German subsidiary of an American company, for instance, could turn up on the American accounts as improving the company's profits because the accounts require the value of the whole German plant to be stated in dollars. If the euro rose in value, the increase in the value of the plant could easily be more than the operating loss. In a sense, the German subsidiary has helped the parent, but only if the parent is about to or can sell it, which may not be an option. While management might understand the ambiguity, recognizing that in one sense the plant has contributed to profits and in another it has not, tax collectors cannot be equally philosophical, assessing a profits tax that is both paid and not paid.

Again, a floating rate may be preferable to fixed rates, given disparate rates of inflation, which have their own accounting problems. The better solution is little or no inflation in all major countries and consequently fewer changes in exchange rates.

Irrational Currency Movements

Currency movements under floating rates have not proved as sensible as anticipated. Despite the fact that the free market is at work, some currencies appear overvalued and some undervalued—in the judgment of most economists. Whether this is the fault of speculators or of countries' increasing reliance on interest rate policy is unclear, but very large current account imbalances are offset by large short-term capital inflows. Either the market has been often in error or the economists and central bankers are wide of the mark.

Several economists have argued convincingly that rational economic decision-makers can cause exchange rates to *overshoot*. The arguments center on the timing of the response of spot and forward exchange rates, interest rates, and prices, the details of which need not concern us here.[2] Stock markets, commodity markets, and, to a lesser extent, bond markets all show patterns of overshooting, and, however inconvenient, it seems to be true also of foreign exchange markets. Suffice it to note that information in markets is asymmetrically distributed and much key information is unknowable, meaning that expectations are important in short-term movements.

Again, it is unlikely that the Bretton Woods system as it stood could have produced better exchange rates. As two IMF economists commented, "The hybrid system that has been in place since 1973 has proved resilient to large shocks to the international monetary system; it is doubtful whether the Bretton Woods system would have withstood the two major oil price increases."[3]

Inflation

A floating rate may give a country the ability to keep on inflating without suffering any more severe consequence than the continued fall in the foreign

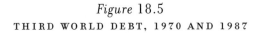

Figure 18.5

THIRD WORLD DEBT, 1970 AND 1987

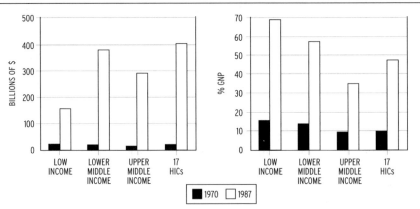

Note: The World Bank divided the Third World countries into three main groups based on their income per capita and created a fourth group, drawn from the others, of the 17 countries with the highest total debt: Argentina, Bolivia, Brazil, Chile, Colombia, Costa Rica, Côte d'Ivoire, Ecuador, Jamaica, Mexico, Morocco, Nigeria, Peru, the Philippines, Uruguay, Venezuela, and Yugoslavia. All of these countries are from the middle-income groups.

exchange value of its currency. Any pressure for price stability exerted by the outflow of reserves under a fixed exchange rate system is thereby ended. The argument cuts both ways. By cutting loose from fixed values, Germany and Switzerland avoided severe inflations in the early 1970s. By staying with fixed exchange rates, many Asian tigers created inflations. Fixed rates restrain inflation only when the low-inflation country can anchor the system and when the country fixing the exchange rate is in danger of having capital outflows. Otherwise, it can spread inflation.

As Figure 18.2 showed, the world has had both high and low inflations with floating exchange rates. Inflation rates in the late 1990s have been the lowest in decades—so low that even a sober-sided magazine like *The Economist* argued that the world was in danger of a deflation, and a grim reaper with a scythe labeled "Deflation" stalked its cover.[4]

Fixed rates are also incompatible with inflation targeting, one of the most interesting monetary policy developments of the 1990s. As of 1999, New Zealand, Canada, Australia, Britain, and Sweden were all using the inflation rate as the sole target for monetary policy. To this point, the targeting has been successful in holding down inflation, while its effect on employment is still under question, although unemployment rates, while initially high, have tended to move closer toward those of other countries. It seems likely that

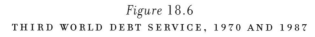

Figure 18.6

THIRD WORLD DEBT SERVICE, 1970 AND 1987

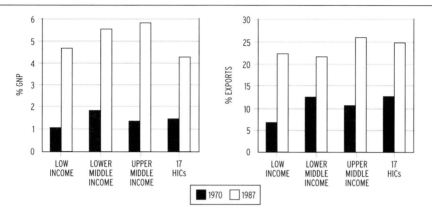

other central banks will adopt inflation targeting. A central bank cannot target *both* inflation and the exchange rate. The interest rate, which keeps up the value of a nation's currency in the foreign exchange market, may be the one that keeps inflation below the target range. The interest rate that keeps down the value of a nation's currency may be the one that is inflationary.[5]

THE DEBT CRISES

Fifteen years separated the first debt crisis from the second. The first crisis was triggered when Mexico could not meet payments on its debt in 1982. Within months, it appeared that every Third World country was in trouble and few could get any credit in international financial markets. The second came when Thailand allowed its currency to fall in 1997—again, within months credit was exceedingly difficult to obtain.[6] The crises shared a number of common features and differed sharply on others.

Elements in Both Crises

1. In the years before the crisis, foreign borrowing rose sharply and then declined precipitously, leaving countries with debts that were difficult to service and causing sharp declines in living standards.

Figures 18.5 and 18.6 contrast countries' public debt positions between 1970, just before the oil price rise, and 1987, five years after the crisis triggered by Mexico's default. They do so in four different ways: (1) by total debt; (2) by debt as a percentage of GNP; (3) by interest payments (debt service) as a percentage of GNP; and (4) by interest as a percentage of exports.

Even given that these growing debts are in nominal rather than real terms, the increase in indebtedness is astounding, from $39 billion to $826 billion, from small fractions of their national incomes to large portions of it. The interest charges on the debt alone rose from 1-2% of GNP to

Figure 18.7

MEXICO: CHANGES IN
FINANCIAL LIABILITIES

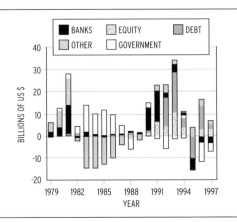

4-6%, and 20-25% of all export receipts were going just to pay the interest on the debt. In some senses, the countries owing the most were not in the most trouble. Brazil had (and still has) the highest international public debt, but it was paying only about 2.4% of its GNP for interest payments. (Jamaica had to pay 17.3% of its GNP.) The low-income countries owed a great deal, but they had been unable to tap the international financial markets, and their debt was largely to other governments, which gave them better terms. It was the upper middle-income countries that borrowed the most and, in a sense, got in the most trouble.

Mexico's capital flows do not look that different from those of Thailand, shown in Chapter 14. Like the Asian tigers in the 1990s, Mexico borrowed capital from abroad, resulting in higher levels of capital formation. And, like those Asian countries after 1997, the inflow of capital reversed very suddenly for Mexico, as Figure 18.7 shows.

Mexican liabilities to foreign residents rose sharply in the 1970s. Figure 18.7, relying on published IMF data that begin with 1979, shows the crisis years, with a very sharp increase in foreign borrowing in 1981, most of it by Mexican banks or by "Other," which would include the government-owned corporations. (To see the private flows, just ignore the white sections of the bars.) In 1982, the private borrowing ceased, with government borrowing replacing private borrowings. Much of that was emergency funds lent to the government or liabilities of government-owned corporations the government had to take over. Borrowing from abroad did not resume until 1990. Note, too, the very different character in the 1990s, with much more private debt and equity.

Figure 18.8

MEXICAN DOMESTIC INVESTMENT AND SOURCES OF SAVING

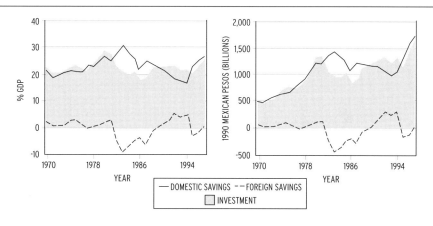

As Mexican income swelled in the 1970s, investment rates rose to nearly 30% of GDP, high by Latin American standards, but the decline in oil prices produced a sharp drop in investment, as Figure 18.8 shows.

The change in capital flow had an impact on total investment. In both panels, the gray area is the total domestic capital formation, the black line is the domestic savings, and the broken line the foreign savings as measured by the current account balance. In the early 1970s, the vast bulk of capital formation came from domestic savings, with only a small percentage provided from abroad. When Mexico defaulted, its ability to borrow abroad stopped abruptly and it struggled to pay back debts, already hampered by the decline in oil prices. In 1983, Mexico had a trade surplus of 10% of GDP and a reduced national income, bringing severe hardship. Not only was per capita income down, but 10% of that was going to creditors. All the white space between the upper black line and the shaded area represents an excess of saving over investment produced at a very considerable hardship. The low level of investment, too, made it much more difficult for Mexico to generate additional income to generate new savings or foreign exchange.

The effect on production and incomes was very severe. Growth rates that had been substantial and well ahead of population growth slowed such that per capita income began to fall. The left panel of Figure 18.9 shows the trend for all Third World countries, while the right panel shows it for Mexico.

All groups of countries had plausible rates of economic growth preceding 1980, although more detailed analysis would show that the increase in oil prices in 1972 had hurt a number of countries severely. At the same time, the oil producers are included in the statistics, and their income obviously

719

Figure 18.9

EFFECT OF DEBT CRISIS ON ECONOMIC GROWTH

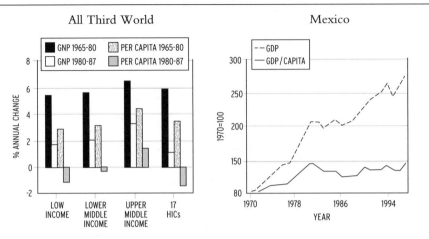

increased until 1981. Mexico, an oil producer, shows a typical oil-producer situation.

It is too close to the 1997 crisis to have a complete set of figures, but the economies of the Asian tigers have all been in serious trouble, with sharp declines in output. In addition, several other countries, particularly Brazil, Argentina, and Mexico, have been forced into sharp slowdowns.

2. Preceding the crisis, much of the new capital was placed in investments whose return was low and not oriented toward generating the foreign exchange required to service the foreign debt. Before the first crisis, some of it just went into increased government consumption.

Many of the Latin American and African countries damaged by the first debt crisis had not used the funds borrowed in such a way as to increase the potential output of the economy, and, in particular, to increase the exports needed to service the foreign exchange debt. Most of the South American countries were at the time strongly protectionist, with overvalued exchange rates that created economic incentives to push capital into inefficient protected industries and not into exports. The number of government-owned corporations, often with reputations for inefficiency already, used any extra funding to continue in the same vein. The countries that were to become the Asian tigers, in contrast, had far more open economies and fewer government corporations. Their record of investment returns was better and, after a few years of trouble, they were able to resume the high rates of growth they had experienced before the debt crisis.

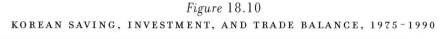

Figure 18.10

KOREAN SAVING, INVESTMENT, AND TRADE BALANCE, 1975-1990

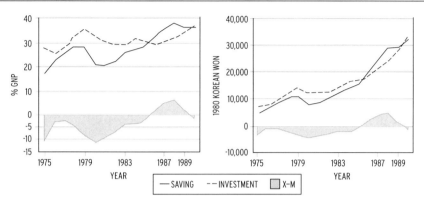

The contrast in the way the economies reacted to the first debt crisis is quite striking. Once foreign funds were unavailable and some of the debt had to be paid back, countries had to generate a trade surplus, which is to say the savings-investment gap had to become positive. The Latin American countries achieved this by constricting their economies and depressing output, such that *I* fell below *S*. The future Asian tigers, after a brief period of trouble, raised domestic savings rates and expanded exports, with the result that the debt fell very sharply as a portion of both GDP and exports. Korea provides an example of the kinds of changes that occurred.

Korea's borrowing had peaked in 1980, and by the time of the 1982 crisis the country had already started on a path of increasing saving as a percentage of GDP, due in part to banking reforms that raised returns on saving. Real investment hardly changed at all in 1982, while savings increased steadily. The result was a surplus on the current account by 1986 and continued rapid growth. The pattern is much the same for Thailand, Malaysia, and Taiwan.

Moreover, exports were driving growth, expanding faster than GDP such that debt fell sharply as a percentage of exports.

Figure 18.11

KOREA'S NET FACTOR PAYMENTS AS PERCENTAGE OF GNP AND EXPORTS

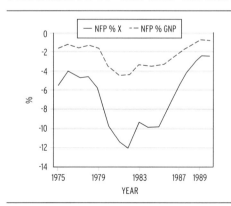

721

The other Asian tigers, similarly, saw such an expansion of exports that their debt payments declined sharply as a percentage of GDP. Korea, as shown in Figure 18.11, was able to reduce its debt service from 12% of export receipts to just over 2% and to reduce the export receipts from 4% to about 1% of GDP.

The Asian tigers' success was in a way their undoing in the 1990s. High rates of saving caused funds to pour into domestic financial institutions, large companies generated huge retained earnings, and the addition of foreign funds to the heap strained the ability of the business community to find high-yielding investments. The evidence, on a micro level, is the great number of companies that defaulted on their loans, unable to earn a return that exceeded their interest payments. Broader evidence is more scattered but consistent with the idea that capital productivity fell, and fell sharply. One sign, for instance, is a decline in the ratio of new investment to increases in output, the *incremental capital-output ratio* in much of East Asia. While this decline could represent a shift in investment into more capital-intensive projects such as housing, mining, or chemical refining, that is probably not the case. Rather, the countries are running out of high-yielding investment opportunities.[7] Regrettably, countries that were rather poor squeezed a great deal of savings out of the population and squandered too much of it on low-yielding projects like office buildings, hotels, and factories that made products with limited markets. The errors they made were not on the scale of those in Latin America in the 1970s, but the consequences are similar.

3. The lack of orderly exit procedures delayed the settlement of the situation, pro-longing the unsettled period following the collapse.

An *exit procedure* resolves the disputes over who will get paid and how much the parties will get and pay. An ordinary domestic bankruptcy is a formalized exit procedure. At least in Europe and North America, the rules are straightforward. The law sets out who gets paid first, who gets paid after that, and so on. The owners of a corporation and many of their creditors lose some or all of their investments, but if the company is economically viable once it has no debt payments, some other firm will buy it at a fraction of what was spent to build it and then will operate it. Moreover, once the original creditors have lost their claim, the new company can borrow money without exposing its new creditors to the errors of the past owners. The new owners may have to pay a premium because previous experience was not good, but the firm's debt-to-equity ratio will be vastly improved, and if it posts good earnings it may have little trouble in establishing credit again. When bankruptcy is drawn out, however, the physical equipment and workers stand idle, even though they could be employed profitably by another company.

The nature of the debt differed greatly between the two crises. In the first, the debt was overwhelmingly public debt—i.e., government debt. Even when the debt started out as being separate from the government itself (as in the heavy borrowings of the government-owned corporation), the government had guaranteed the debt and ended up owing it. The problem with government debt is that it is *sovereign debt* (debt of sovereign countries), and it is not subject to any bankruptcy law. Without a bankruptcy law establishing a priority among creditors, *every* creditor has an equal say on any settlement at less than the full value owed. A typical loan to a government has what is called a "negative pledge"—a clause worded in such a way that each of the lenders can veto any settlement reached between the other creditors and the defaulting government. Small creditors, in the hope that the large creditors will buy them off with better terms, often hold up the procedure. Negotiations therefore drag on, and the parties are unable to come to any settlement. Despite numerous urgings to eliminate the negative pledge, it is still in place on almost all syndicated loans.[8]

In the 1997 crisis, the debt was private, as was a great deal of the lending. But the problem has been that the countries themselves have weak and unclear bankruptcy laws. Moreover, the political pressures of well-connected banks and other lenders have slowed attempts by the governments to get better laws. In essence, large banks and wealthy lenders stand to lose a great deal of their money and want to keep down their losses as much as possible by making other groups pay. The losses are there, but with the laws rather vague, it is unclear what proportion is to be taken by banks, bondholders, noteholders, those who extended credit, and so forth. Any settlement is going to hurt someone, and the government doesn't want to hurt anyone that is powerful. As a result, reform of the law and settlement of many bankruptcies remains hung up.

4. The events in one country spread rapidly to other countries and threatened the stability of the international financial system.

In the early 1980s crisis, the banking system itself was threatened. If several major banks had failed, the entire financial system may have collapsed. Banks have so many reciprocal obligations in their forward market and swap activities that the failure of just a few would leave others holding unfulfilled obligations. It would be like a shotgun blast at a switchboard—some connections would still work, but a great number would not and the system might not survive the damage. In 1997, it was not the banks themselves so much as the broader financial markets that were endangered. Consequently, capital was suddenly unavailable for many firms and governments that were not otherwise in serious difficulty. The financial aspects deserve closer scrutiny.

Table 18.1

EMPIRE BANK, 1980

Assets	($ millions)	Liabilities and Net Worth ($ millions)	
Loans	700	Deposits	750
T-bills	85		
Reserves	22.5		
Buildings, etc.	17.5	Equity	75
	825		825

Financial Instability as Cause and Consequence

CONTAGION

Why should a large group of countries suddenly and simultaneously get in trouble? Why should a crisis, for instance, spread so quickly from Mexico to Argentina or from Thailand to Korea? There is not now, nor was there in 1982, enough trade between the countries for changes in trade or income of one country to affect the other. Economists have suggested some possible connections.[9] (1) All the countries are responding to the same external change. In 1982, for instance, the combination of the collapse in oil prices and the increase in real interest rates would have been the same on any oil-producing country. (2) Lenders are forced to rid themselves quickly of any questionable assets. This could be either because of a "herd mentality," where each investor is safest moving within the herd, or because a particular crisis served as a wake-up call, alerting investors to dangers they had not previously recognized were there.

The 1997 crisis lacks an obvious outside trigger. The only serious candidate is the depreciation of the yen against the dollar and therefore against the Asian currencies pegged to the dollar. But only the Thai baht appears to have been seriously overvalued and the collapse occurred rather a long time after the yen fell in value.

Evidence that foreign investors reacted in the same way to all countries comes from the Eurobond markets. The difference between dollar-denominated government debt of sovereign countries—known as *sovereign spread*—shows interesting changes. Previous to the crisis of 1997, the sovereign spread moved independently for each country, but after the crisis, all the countries' sovereign spreads not only rose, but rose or fell together.

Table 18.2

EMPIRE BANK AFTER LOAN DEFAULTS

Assets	($ millions)	Liabilities	($ millions)
~~Loans~~	~~700~~	Deposits	750
Loans	630		
T–bills	100		
Reserves	7.5	~~Equity~~	~~75~~
Buildings, etc.	17.5	Equity	5
	755		755

THE ENDANGERED BANKING SYSTEM IN 1982

Consider the problem in 1982 through the examination of a fictional bank, "Empire Bank," an aggressive lender to Third World countries. In 1980, Empire's balance sheet looked like Table 18.1.

Empire is in reasonable shape. It has 3% of deposits in reserve. Its equity—what it owes its shareholders—is the difference between what it has in assets and what it owes creditors, in this case $825 - 750 = 75$. What happens, however, if a number of its loans go sour? If it suddenly finds itself with loan defaults of $70 million, its loan portfolio will fall to $630 million and the bank will lose most of its equity (Table 18.2). (With only $630 million in its loan portfolio and deposits unchanged, it will have only $5 million in equity left.) If it loses another $10 million, it will be bankrupt, having fewer assets than liabilities.

Empire Bank, as shown, had far more equity in relation to its loans than most banks in 1982. Most banks were highly leveraged—that is, they had relatively little equity and much debt. Many had less than 3% equity. When defaults began, the banks found themselves with insufficient capital. Had they honestly recorded what their loans were worth, their books would have shown them bankrupt. These were major banks and their failure would have devastated the banking system, so the banks pretended the loans were merely non-performing and continued to pretend to charge interest, adding it to the unpaid loans. The banks' reluctance to officially declare losses was another reason it was so hard to settle the debt issue.

Figure 18.12

PRIVATE CAPITAL FLOWS INTO AND OUT OF THAILAND

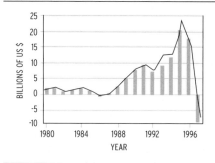

Note: The line shows the total private capital flow, exclusive of direct investment, into or out of Thailand, and the bar shows the figure net of capital outflows. In some years capital outflows were negative—investors bringing back funds from abroad—so the net can be higher than the gross.

THE ENDANGERED FINANCIAL MARKET IN 1997

The picture presented in Chapter 16 of a highly liquid, risk-reducing, and efficient international capital market, creating some tricky but not impossible problems, contrasts with the darker image of vast flows of short-term capital pouring in and out of country after country, panicking financial managers, and sudden and highly destructive changes in liquidity. Is liquidity too great?

Chapter 14 examined how the large capital inflows into Thailand expanded the money supply. The country was hardly ready for the sharp turnaround that occurred in 1997. Figure 18.12 shows the sudden change in the flow of private capital.

Between 1996 and 1997, private capital changed from an inflow of $15.5 billion to an outflow of $7 billion—a $22.5 billion change. Thailand was not alone in facing this problem, as its problems soon spread to Korea, Malaysia, and Indonesia.

But why should the difficulties of one country whose trade is only about 1% of all the world's trade have such far-reaching effects? Within months of the collapse of the Thai baht, its scenario was repeated in Korea (about 2% of world trade), Malaysia, Indonesia, the Philippines, and there were serious threats to Hong Kong, Taiwan, and even Brazil. Moreover, borrowers in financially sound countries began to experience trouble reissuing securities or renewing bank loans.

Finance people describe what happened as *a flight to quality*. As the likelihood of default on securities and loans increases, financial institutions compensate by shifting their portfolios to the most secure and high-grade securities they can find. International figures show some sign of this shift in 1996. Private capital flows for debt securities headed for the United States and, to a lesser extent, to Germany, Japan (despite Japan's very low interest

726

Figure 18.13
FLOWS OF PRIVATE DEBT CAPITAL TO THE U.S., GERMANY, JAPAN, AND CANADA

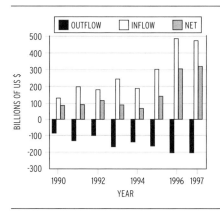

Note: The figure shows private debt securities—bonds, medium term assets, notes, and T-bills. The net inflow, which had not been above $100 billion before 1995, jumped sharply to over $300 billion in both 1996 and 1997. The United States was by far the biggest recipient of this inflow—some $281 billion in 1997, compared with $20 billion for Germany, $15 billion for Japan, and $3 billion for Canada.

rates), and Canada. Even the Netherlands and Switzerland and the somewhat less secure members of the G-7 industrial countries (the United Kingdom, France, and Italy) had net outflows of short-term capital. Figure 18.13 shows the net inflows of debt capital of the four principal recipients.

THE CONSEQUENCES OF FLIGHT TO QUALITY

To represent all financial players, imagine a financial organization holding a portfolio of treasury bills and short-term commercial notes. This particular imaginary organization is an offshore, lightly regulated fund on the island of Guernsey called Hedgehog Fund. It owns assets whose face value is $400 million, so that if no defaults occur Hedgehog will have $400 million in one year. Barb Espinoso, the chief financial officer, likes to keep the fund very simple such that her wealthy, but not financially sophisticated, clients can understand what Hedgehog is doing.

Since some borrowers will fail to pay in full, Hedgehog establishes four categories or ratings for its holdings, going from A, where payment is certain, to D, where there is the greatest chance of non-payment. To start, Barb proposes the Fund buy $100 million in each of the four categories. The $100 million in Group A assets would have a future value of $100 million. No defaults are remotely possible, so the expected value of those future payments is also $100 million. Securities in this group are selling at 95.238, which works out to be a 5% interest.

Table 18.3
HEDGEHOG'S PORTFOLIO

Rating Group	Future Value	Percentage Paying	Expected Future Value	Present Value of Expected Future Value	Yield Required
A	100	1.00	100	95.238	.0500
B	100	.975	97.5	92.857	.0769
C	100	.95	95	90.477	.1052
D	100	.90	90	85.714	.1667

For those rusty about interest rate figuring, the interest on a non–interest bearing security is its future payment minus its cost today, divided by its cost today. That is

$$(FV - PV) / PV = i,$$ where FV is future value, PV is present value, and i is the interest rate. Thus $(100\text{-}95.2381) / 95.2381 = .05$.

Hedgehog's experts work hard on figuring the probabilities of default within each group and conclude that 97.5% of the securities they have in Group B will pay in full, but 2.5% will default, 95% of Group C will pay, and 90% of Group D will pay. This gives Hedgehog an idea of how much it will get from each group when the securities mature, what can be called the *expected future value* (fourth column). Hedgehog then figures the present value of all those expected future values, using the 5% it can get on the most secure bonds as the rate for discounting.

The formula for present value is: $PV = FV/(1 + i)$. (To get the present value of the expected future value, Hedgehog discounts the expected future value—such that the $PV = EFV/(1 + r)$.) For Group B that is $97/1.05 = 92.857$. This means that any security in Group B with a face value of $100,000 would have to sell for $92,875 or less for Hedgehog to be interested in buying. Were Hedgehog to buy any single bond in Group B with a face value of $100,000, it would have a yield of 7.69%. The purchase price of $92,875 divided into the gain (on those bonds that do not default) of $7,143 gives 7.69%. If Hedgehog had many such bonds, each of which it bought for $92,857, it would receive an average of $100,000 at the end of the period ($92,857 × 1.0769), the same amount it would get if it bought Group A bonds at a 5% discount. To put it another way, the extra discount of $2,381 on each of 97.5% of the bonds that did not default can earn—at the discount of 1.0769—just enough to cover the defaults. (If Hedgehog had $10 million in assets, the defaults would be $250,000 and the present value of those defaults is $238,100.)

Table 18.4

HEDGEHOG'S PORTFOLIO WITH MARKET STRESS

Rating Group	Future Value	Percentage Paying	Expected Future Value	Present Value of Expected Future Value	Yield Required
A	100	1.00	100	95.238	.0500
B	100	.975	97	92.857	.0769
C	100	.90	90	85.714	.1667
D	100	.85	85	80.952	.2353

Hedgehog prefers, of course, to pay less than the amounts it sets as its maximums. Often it can do so because the market as a whole tends to overdiscount securities of lower ratings—that is, the market does not pay as high as 84.76 and 79.5 for securities in the C and D groups, even though the best estimates of Hedgehog's blue-ribbon team of finance experts have proven correct in the past. Hedgehog's experts have also noted that the B group of higher-grade securities is generally insufficiently discounted. Hedgehog takes advantage of this difference by selling its A and B securities in order to purchase additional lower-grade securities.

When firms or countries that issued bonds in one of the lower groups show distress, so that the chances of default rise, the value of all the bonds in that group fall. Table 18.4 shows the situation that would confront Hedgehog. The items that have changed in value are Groups C and D. As the probability of default of some of the assets has risen, their expected present values have fallen.

Another thing that is likely to happen is that the movement into the securities in Group A will raise their prices, lowering yields in that group. Table 18.5 shows the securities in Group A rising in price to $97 per $100 face

Table 18.5

RISING PRICE OF BETTER SECURITIES

Rating Group	Future Value	Percentage Paying	Expected Future Value	Present Value of Expected Future Value	Yield Required
A	100	1.00	100	97.000	.0309
B	100	.975	97	94.575	.0574
C	100	.95	90	87.300	.1455
D	100	.90	85	82.450	.2129

value. This reduces the interest rate to .0309, which means that assets in the other groups have less of a discount. The expected present values of the securities in Groups A and B rise. Because of the increased chances of default, however, the securities in Groups C and D are still considerably below their values as shown in Table 18.3.

Consequences of this are:

1. All bonds in the same group become riskier, even though any single bond may be just as safe as before. Even though financial institutions use far more sophisticated models and classifications than the one shown here, they still have limits in assessing any single security. It is, in fact, a variation of the *lemons* problem. Buyers in the market are unable to distinguish the really poor performers—the lemons—from the other members of the group; all members of the group have to suffer. Even if some of the buyers can indeed distinguish the good from the bad, they cannot keep the price from falling if most buyers cannot make that distinction.

2. Many financial institutions take a heavy hit on their equity—the shareholders' stake.

3. A great many financial firms suffer serious liquidity problems as the present value of their portfolios falls and the market "excessively" discounts bonds that are probably quite safe.

4. Most firms compensate for these problems by fleeing toward bonds that are highly liquid and very safe. This serves to assure the firm's owners and reduces the cost of any borrowing the firm might have to try to do.

The first question is to assess its equity. If Hedgehog had held $100 million in each category, the present value of its assets would be $364 million in Table 18.3, $355 million in Table 18.4, and $361 million in Table 18.5, involving losses of $3 million to $11 million. It is far more likely that Hedgehog's assets would be much more heavily weighted toward Groups C and D and its losses would be much higher. If it held $25 million each in Groups A and B and $175 million each in Groups C and D, its loss would be $16.7 million. If Hedgehog had a lot of derivative contracts based on the same estimates, its losses could even be greater (see box).

The key question is whether shareholders still have anything left after losing millions of dollars? The larger loss above is about 4% of their original assets; some funds have less leverage—the relation of their ownership base to their debts—than that. Today, due to the Basel Accord, banks are supposed to have about 8% in equity, so they could sustain a blow of this size. Hedgehog could be technically bankrupt. It could, of course, wait the crisis out, reasoning that—even with the increase in defaults, the market is still

HEDGE FUNDS AND DERIVATIVES

To further increase its profits, Hedgehog uses the derivative markets. Believing that the market as a whole undervalues (overdiscounts) Groups C and D, it agrees to buy a number of them in the future. By the time the securities are closer to maturation, the market will have recognized that the chances of default are lower than it earlier anticipated and heavy discount will disappear. The actual value of the securities on the market will be higher than Hedgehog agreed to pay for them, and it will get payments from its counterparties in the derivative agreements.

Hedgehog may also believe the market is underdiscounting the B-level securities, thus the chances of a default or delay in payments are actually a bit higher than the market seems to assess. As a result, Hedgehog sells futures on these securities, expecting that when the contract expires the securities will be slightly cheaper than the market anticipated. Hedgehog will get money from its counterparties. Hedgehog managers say their fund is *arbitraging* between the two markets, reducing the difference in the discounts, but, because estimates of future returns are part of the picture, it is also speculating.

If a scenario develops as in Table 18.5, however, Hedgehog loses on both deals. Moreover, it will have to *mark to market*, making daily deposits with its bank or exchange, so that it gets into a serious liquidity problem

The year 1998 saw additional complication for many of the hedgers (both banks and funds). As prices fell on lower-quality securities, the market became quite illiquid. Holders were reluctant to sell in the hope of a higher price and buyers were unwilling to buy for fear of lower prices. As a result, almost all lower-grade debt worldwide fell in value, and many borrowers (not in themselves lemons) found themselves unable to refinance. It was at this point that the Federal Reserve eased monetary policy after earlier, less effective easings. The expectation was that as more reserves came into the market, banks would feel freer to buy or buy as repos poorer-grade securities, and that they would feel freer to make loans.

overly discounting the C and D shares. But what if Hedgehog also faces a liquidity problem? Suppose it had a lot of derivative contracts and had to keep placing money in the market as its positions worsened. It may be unable to meet its commitments and may be forced into bankruptcy.

Given that it believes its investments are basically sound—that there really are not as many lemons in the group as the market thinks—could Hedgehog borrow new funds or, more soundly, raise additional equity? The problem is that this is just the situation when equity would be very expensive, as investors would fear they would just be putting money into a large sinkhole.

Institutional Reaction to the Debt Crises

Both borrowers and lenders made errors that were very costly, not only for those who made the errors but for the people of the deeply indebted countries, and very nearly for the people of creditor countries, who narrowly missed systemic financial collapse. The questions policy-makers faced were both short-term—how to get the borrowers and lenders out of the mess—and long-term—how to prevent the scenario from recurring.

THE 1982 CRISIS

Relieving and restructuring debt. Negotiations for handling the debt problem were similar to those in the 1920s aimed at the war debts problem. The negotiations began by trying to restructure debts so that the countries could meet the payments and ended with substantial debt relief, yet the debts continue to hang on for decades.

Like the 1924 Dawes Plan negotiations, the first efforts to relieve debt burden were essentially restructuring agreements where the interest payments were reduced by increasing the maturity of the loans. These were, however, little more than stopgap measures because the debts were larger than many countries could expect to pay. The next step, similar to the 1929 Young Plan, was to securitize the debt and sell it off to the private markets as *exit bonds*. A debtor country could agree, for instance, to pay half of what it owed a syndicate of banks. The banks would forgive half the debt and then issue bonds for the other half, guaranteed by the governments. Since it was more likely that the debtor countries could service the debt at a lower value, there proved to be a market—albeit heavily discounted—for these bonds.

Debtor countries also experimented with debt-for-equity swaps. Such arrangements allowed foreign direct investors to pay off some of a country's debt and, in turn, receive local assets. To make this attractive, the investors would get quite a bit more domestic currency than they could just by purchasing it on the foreign exchange market. In a few cases, environmental groups used this arrangement to set aside land in developing countries as reserves. Nonetheless, the initial arrangements did not prove adequate to handle much of the debt.

It was 1990 before a more comprehensive plan was put in place. Nicholas Brady, Secretary of the Treasury under President Bush, proposed the plan, which bears his name. Exit bonds, now known as Brady bonds, would have collateral as backing, with the collateral being supplied by the World Bank and the IMF. Moreover, the IMF would have more supervisory powers over the countries that took advantage of the program, and the loans it made for such purposes would be *conditional* on the performance of the country.

Basically, the countries would be offered far more generous credit terms in exchange for agreeing to being closely supervised by the IMF. To achieve this, the assets of both the IMF and World Bank were increased.

Controlling banks' exposure to risk. To avoid another threat to the banking system, the central bankers of the key G-7 countries worked with bankers at the Bank for International Settlements (noted in Chapter 17) to devise a framework for bank regulation and supervision. This document, revised regularly, the *Core Principles for Effective Banking Supervision*, usually called the Basel Accord, provides guidelines for national monetary authorities. The key provision, adopted by all industrial countries, is that each commercial bank should hold enough equity to take a loss of 8% of its loans and other claims on all but the safest creditors (the G-7 countries themselves). Empire Bank, with its loans of $700 million, would have to have $56 million in equity. The actual agreement is rather more complicated and is revised continually.* While it took banks some years to build up their equity to the amount required, most today have the 8%. This means that their shareholders are far more concerned that the banks not overextend themselves, and, perhaps more important, the shareholders, not the economies of the countries, will take the blow if defaults again become widespread.

Increasing information in the market. If good risks are being lumped in with bad risks because it is impossible to sort them out, increased and more up-to-date information should distinguish the lemons from the rest. If a major failure is needed to provide a wake-up call, then perhaps more information will warn both lenders and borrowers before the alarm goes off so that they can head off the crisis. The IMF has developed a Code of Good Practices on Fiscal Transparency to try to get member countries to be more open on their budgetary practices, and it is developing a similar code on monetary and financial policies. It also has encouraged countries to allow more information about their economies to be distributed, and, indeed, a vast amount of information is now available at the IMF Web site (www.imf.org). Countries to which the IMF has lent money are subject to IMF surveillance, part of which consists of a private report to the government. A summary of the discussion is usually published and also made available on the Web.[10]

---

* Initially, the banks were asked to have at least 4% in equity and the rest could be in *subordinated debt*, the last debt to be paid off in case of bankruptcy. Regulations over the risk exposure of derivatives and swaps and the appropriate amount of equity to hold against them have been contentious, but they are also included.

The Response of the IMF

The crises caused several changes in the IMF.

1. In its Bretton Woods conception, the IMF was to provide funds for short periods (three years) at no more than 125% of the country's quota. The increase in oil prices followed by the debt crisis of 1982 gave rise to requests for larger and longer-term funds, and the IMF's rules were changed to accommodate.

2. The increased need for funds caused the IMF to increase the quotas of its members and to seek supplementary financing.

3. The advisory or supervisory role of the IMF increased as private banks, bondholders, and government lenders all sought more than just a promise that an indebted country would repay.

4. As the IMF's advisory and supervisory roles grew, it came under increasing criticism for what it advised, not just from the countries it was advising but from outside as well.

INCREASED PROVISION OF FUNDS

Beginning in the 1970s as a reaction to the oil price increases, the IMF began to provide a group of supplementary ways to borrow. Countries would no longer be limited to their five tranches but could tap other *facilities* created for restricted purposes or countries with certain types of difficulties.* Many of these facilities were in existence for only short periods of time, although there are still outstanding loans under some. Still extant are:[11]

• The Extended Fund Facility (EFF), established in 1974 for countries that were hurt by the sharp rise in oil prices, allows countries to borrow more for longer periods of time. Presently, qualifying countries can borrow up to 300% of their quota, although no more than 100% in one year. Virtually all the Fund's lending to the Asian countries affected by the 1997 crisis has been through the EFF.

• The Compensatory and Contingency Financing Facility (CCFF), established in 1988 to supplement a similar facility going back to 1963, allows countries that face a sudden and severe external shock to borrow extra amounts of funds. A country could find, for instance, that the price of its main export had

---

* Technically, countries do not borrow and repay from the Fund's General Resources Account. Instead, they "purchase" other currencies with their own and "repurchase their own currencies." In some of the newer facilities, however, the countries technically take loans and repay them. While for the most part it is possible to avoid the awkwardness of describing a very-loan-like transaction as a purchase of currency, anyone reading the IMF accounts or discussing them closely needs to know their terminology.

Table 18.6

DRAWINGS AND BORROWING FROM THE IMF, 1996-1998 (SDRS)

	1996	1997	1998
General Resources Account	5,271	16,113	20,586
Stand-By Arrangements (not lent out)	2,471	13,255	12,098
Supplemental Reserve Facility		4,100	8,726
Extended Fund Facility	2,625	2,750	6,331
Supplemental Reserve Facility			675
CCFF (Buffer stock)	174	107	2,157
Structural Adjustment and Enhanced Adjustment Facilities	709	731	896
Total	5,980	16,843	21,482

Source: IMF Survey, March 8, 1999, 77.

fallen, that import prices of some essential goods had shot up, or that tourism had dropped off severely due to unrest, and any such reason might qualify it for additional borrowing. In 1998, Russia used this facility, on the grounds that earnings from its oil exports had fallen sharply when the price of oil fell.

• The Supplemental Reserve Facility (SRF) was especially designed for the 1997 crisis and began in December 1997. The IMF notes that "it is for member countries experiencing exceptional balance of payments problems owing to a large short-term financing need resulting from a sudden and disruptive loss of market confidence reflected in pressure on the capital account and the members' reserves." Moreover, it is to be used when the danger of contagion is great. Any borrowings under these facilities are normally to be repaid within a year and a half but they may be extended by a year. The Fund has lent to Korea and Russia under this category.

• Structural Adjustment and Enhanced Structural Adjustment Facilities, established in 1986 and 1987, go far beyond the Fund's historical provision of funds for balance-of-payments purposes. The Fund lends them to countries that have long-term balance-of-payments difficulties *and* are making serious efforts to address their serious structural problems. While the other facilities allow "drawings" on the fund, secured by the borrower's own currency deposits, the SAF and ESAF are straight loans, the money being raised by the Fund from wealthier members for this purpose. SAF funds are limited to 70% of the nation's quota, but ESAF funds can be 250% of the quota.

As an example of the use of these facilities, by 1996 Argentina had borrowed about 375% of its quota of SDR 1,537 million. The normal (GRA) would allow it only SDR 1,844 million, but Argentina has just over SDR 4 billion from the extended fund facilities.[12] Pakistan, while not so much in excess of its quota, had tapped more facilities getting SDR 15.3 million from the buffer stock facility and SDR 123 million from the Extended Fund Facility. It had another SDR 278 million from the SAF and SDR 202 from the ESAF. In addition, the IMF was holding SDR 394 million in stand-by agreements.

The 1997 financial crises, combined with extensive troubles in Russia, led to the largest amount of credit the fund had ever issued. Table 18.6 shows the size of debts to the IMF (including stand-by facilities that had not yet been lent) at the end of 1998.

EXPANDED RESOURCES

The IMF has expanded its resources in two ways: by raising the quotas and by borrowing directly from governments. In addition, it has authorization to borrow from private sources, but it has never done so. The IMF has reviewed its quotas 11 times, increasing them after seven of those reviews. The last quota increase was for January 1998. In addition to the General Arrangements to Borrow discussed in Chapter 17, the Fund in 1997 completed a New Arrangement to Borrow (NAB) with 25 countries participating, allowing the Fund to borrow up to SDR 34 billion (US$45 billion) if needed. Resources are nonetheless limited. The total assets of the Fund in 1999 were around SDR 1 billion, which seems an impressive sum. However, much of that was not truly usable.

1. Many currencies it holds are *soft*, so hedged about by exchange restrictions that they are of little or no use in making international payments. Others are *hard* enough, but so unimportant no one wants them anyway— e.g., the Guatemalan quetzal. In the early years of the Fund, loans were almost exclusively in U.S. dollars. However, in the 1970s the Fund began to lend many other currencies (including the quetzals and Malaysian ringgit, but only in very small quantities); most of the lending is in the currencies of the developed nations, and still heavily in U.S. dollars.

2. Roughly one-quarter of the Fund's assets are likely to be already lent out at any given time. As repayment is scheduled over three to five years, this portion of the IMF's assets is effectively immobilized. The IMF does earn some small interest on its loans, but it is unimportant.

3. Finally, much of the Fund's holdings are unusable because these are the currencies under attack. If the Argentine peso is facing difficulties and the Fund's holdings of pesos are high, it makes no sense to lend out the pesos just used by Argentina to purchase foreign currency. When the U.S. dollar fell in value in the late 1980s, the Fund had to reduce its lending of U.S. dollars for fear of driving it down farther. Even the NAB includes the Thai baht and Malaysian ringgit, neither of which could be lent at present.

INCREASING SUPERVISORY OR SURVEILLANCE DUTIES

As the length and amount of IMF lending rose, the Fund's role began to switch from advisory to supervisory, or as the IMF puts it, "surveillance." As Chapter 17 noted, the Fund could never act like a commercial bank, just giving and denying loans, but had to have some means of assuring that they would be repaid. Under the Brady Plan, the IMF became key to the "exit strategy" for the Third World debt crisis. When the commercial banks agreed to the Brady bonds, they needed assurance that the countries would maintain payment on the bonds; otherwise they would have to sell them for very low prices. The IMF was the logical institution to oversee the countries' macroeconomic policies and cajole them into sound policies that would allow continued servicing of the debt. The demands for more information and transparency that followed the 1997 crisis persuaded the IMF to release much more information than it had previously, letting the world know more of the kinds of advice it was giving governments.

The breadth of policies that the IMF discusses, advises upon, and considers in granting and continuing its financial support of debtor countries is considerable. As the IMF itself has put it:

> Structural policies are also examined since they are germane to macroeconomic developments and policies. In recent years, surveillance has taken more account of regional, social, industrial, labor market, income distribution, governance, and environmental issues, where these have important implications for macroeconomic policies and performance.[13]

THE IMF AND ARGENTINA

The policy memorandum of Argentina to the IMF gives an idea of the things the IMF presses governments to do. The report began with a review of the economy, indicating that Argentina had 4.5% growth in 1998, less (but still substantial) unemployment, a worsening terms of trade, and a somewhat larger current account deficit, amply covered by capital inflows. It then continued to note the following areas.

Macroeconomic policies. The budget deficit, which was supposed to be no more than 1.1% of GDP, was a tenth of a percentage point higher due to increased costs associated with flooding, greater arrears in tax payments, and lower payments in government pension plans, as individuals shifted to private plans. The provincial debt was within the target of 0.2% of GDP. The target ceilings on growth of public debt, however, were met with some margin, as was the ceiling on the expansion of the net domestic assets held by the central bank.

Fiscal reform revenues. The government broadened the base of the value-added tax, introduced a minimum corporate income tax based on assets, and made a number of other smaller changes. At the same time the government made improvements to the coordination of state and federal tax collection, tax auditing, and administration of court cases involving tax payments.

Expenditures. The government increased its attempts to promote cost-effective public expenditures and to monitor waste and unethical conduct. The World Bank and the International Development Bank agreed to help the country adopt measures to improve the efficiency, targeting, monitoring, and control of social programs. It also leased to private companies its national airports and began preparations to privatize its mortgage bank and to sell off its remaining interest in YPF, formerly the national oil company.

Other. The government also improved the bank surveillance system, passed a law reducing the cost of dismissing workers, and tried to improve education and judicial systems.

The memorandum then indicates that the government intends to reduce its deficit further, improve tax administration, continue budgetary reform, increase education expenditure, improve the effectiveness of its food welfare program and reform social security. It is also intending to pass a Fiscal Responsibility Law to set limits on the indebtedness of the government, constrain growth of current public expenditure to the growth of the GDP, and establish a fiscal stabilization fund to smooth out the cyclical changes. It also will continue its already substantial privatization program. It will work on continued labor market reform and improve its economic regulatory regime.[14]

Criticisms of the IMF Policies

DEBTOR COUNTRY COMPLAINTS

The IMF faces frequent criticism from the countries it is advising. Often the advice it gives is sound enough, but it is politically unpopular. Suppose the Fund must advise a country suffering from high inflation, sagging exports, and a growing debt problem. It might call for the reduction of a government deficit, devaluation and elimination of exchange control, and the elimination of subsidies on fuels and food. Such a program would tend to shift income *toward* the rural areas, *toward* people who had not been able to secure import licenses, *toward* exporters and producers of import substitutes (but not to those who depended on imported materials), and *toward* those on more fixed incomes.

Consider the domestic political situation, represented in many Latin American, African, and some Asian countries. For years, they have had policies that protected industry, kept the exchange rate overvalued, and built large bureaucracies with extensive economic regulations. Industrialists and unions enjoying protection from imports and fairly generous import licenses are going to be hurt, while those that might have become exporters did not come into existence or power, at least. Small agriculturists who would enjoy export markets and higher food prices typically lack power. (Indeed, one of the reasons the Asian tigers did so well was that their small farmers were strong and their industrialists were not highly dependent on protection.)* The regulations, particularly the import controls, created extensive opportunities for bribery and extortion. The inflations forced labor unions, pensioners, and investors to seek inflation indexing and those that had enough power secured it. Politicians in some countries, like the old city political machines in the United States, keep themselves in power by providing jobs directly to their supporters. As an instance, 78% of the expenditure of the Brazilian state of Minas Gerais goes to its employees.

The IMF's advice, however productive for a healthy economy, hurts the strong and helps the weak (not necessarily the rich and the poor, just the well organized and the unorganized). If the weak were strong, they would have had these advantages already. The advice is sure to bring howls of rage from the labor unions and industrialists dependent on import licenses or from oft-suborned officials who grant licenses. Even if the IMF orders just what the finance minister wants to do, he must pretend that he is doing it only with extreme reluctance. Obviously, in many situations, the IMF may not be able to have many of its policy recommendations accepted at all.

Equally interesting, however, is that many finance ministers and presidents may prefer to have the IMF "tie their hands behind their backs." In no other way can they override the powerful interests that wish to preserve their privileges and in so doing create new interests to back superior economic policies. The minister must fold his hands, weep a few crocodile tears, and tell his constituents that what the government used to do is impossible while under such terrible pressure from the IMF. The minister may even rail against the IMF in public, while in private he may support or even suggest the policy. Politicians and business people are inventive. Surely they can come up with new ways of maintaining their political bases and new ways to invest that are more productive.

---

* Korea, Japan, and Taiwan all had extensive land reforms, designed to weaken the power of the rural landlords. (Credit the first two to General Douglas MacArthur and the third to Chiang Kai-shek, seeking to consolidate his power.) Both Thailand and Malaysia have had governments reluctant to support the ethnic Chinese business community and partial to the more rural Malay and Thai farmers. The motives were profoundly political, but the effects were to create more open and successful economies.

ENDING BRAZIL'S INFLATION REDUCED INEQUALITY

A combination of foresighted Brazilian leaders and IMF pressure led to an ending of Brazil's decades-old inflation, beginning in 1993. The end of inflation shifted income. Politically powerful groups had protected themselves with inflation-adjustment clauses to the detriment of others. Under inflation, the government by law indexed wages, pensions, and financial assets to the rate of inflation. When inflation was especially rapid, the values of financial assets were often adjusted on a daily basis to the inflation. Wages and pensions were adjusted, but so quickly that the large number of workers outside the formal economic sector had no protection whatsoever.

The low inflation of the late 1990s maintained the real value of wage increases granted in 1994 and 1995. At the same time, imports became cheaper and prices of many manufactured goods actually fell. In particular, the prices of manufactured goods fell relative to those for services, which employ poorer people. As a result inequality declined, as did levels of absolute poverty. The unorganized poor, therefore, benefited from IMF advice.[15]

CREDITOR COUNTRY COMPLAINTS

Criticism of the specific policies. Most economists accept the importance and basic duties of the IMF, but many object to specific policies. Just as many economists criticize the Federal Reserve's economic policies but do not question the need for the institution, so many critics come down hard on IMF policies. The IMF response to the Asian tiger crisis of 1997 led to a particularly spirited debate between the IMF's economists and a group of economists centered at Harvard University. It has been in some ways the classic dispute between those who think that the monetary and fiscal policy advocated and implemented is too restrictive and deflationary and those who feel it is essential. Some of the debate even reached the popular press when *Business Week* had a lead article in which it claimed that the reason the countries in Asia were finally doing better is that they were rejecting the IMF's advice, a claim that proved surprising to the IMF and anyone following the situation closely.[16]

Moral hazard. This occurs when protection against harm causes riskier behavior. As an example, some financial economists claim that deposit insurance contributed to the savings and loan crisis in the United States because it eliminated the incentive for depositors to pay attention to the financial security of the institution where they placed their money. So the question is whether the IMF, by "bailing out" countries that have deep troubles, creates sufficient moral hazard as to encourage more troubles. Given the depth of the troubles that countries have when they apply for IMF help, the moral hazard argument seems far-fetched. It is hard to imagine that the Korean government was careless enough to let the country sink into years of recession because they thought the IMF might bail them out. It is a bit like arguing that the fire department is a bad idea because it creates a moral hazard that people will be more careless, knowing that the fireman will put out their fire—the magnitude of the hazard is vastly larger than that of the compensation.

More realistic than the moral hazard argument is the point that in some cases the IMF seems to send millions of dollars to countries with seemingly little effect. Like foreign aid, it becomes a burden on the taxpayer with rather uncertain gains. That, of course, is why the IMF has been given such extensive supervisory powers.

The IMF has relied on an overly simplistic free-enterprise approach. The essence of this complaint is that the promotion of open economies in both trade and finance has been too *laissez-faire.* There has been an overreaction to the extensive misuse of state institutions, so that many countries, including the Asian tigers, were ill-prepared to handle the financial and social consequences of a rapid opening of their economies, particularly in the financial sphere. An underdeveloped financial sector and inexperienced and weak regulators contributed to the poor investments that brought about the East Asian crisis. Moreover, the low level of education in some countries (such as Thailand) placed sharp constraints on the kind of growth the country could have. Yet, if the IMF were to become more proactive, rather than being essentially reactive, then it would find itself even deeper into national government policies, being perhaps even more prescriptive than it has been.

CURRENCIES AND GOVERNMENTS: HOW MANY CURRENCIES?

What difference does it make when countries have different currencies? Does every one of the 181 IMF members need to have its own currency?[*] (Eleven of them in Europe have decided that they do not.) Even when central banks are well-behaved, separate currencies introduce foreign exchange risk, raising the cost of capital; they divide capital markets, making small markets where a larger one would be cheaper; they raise the cost of foreign transactions; and they make cross-border price comparisons difficult. When central banks are ill-behaved or simply unskilled, they can introduce monetary chaos. Indeed, given the scarcity of good policy economists, small countries often have difficulty in getting or keeping top people for their central banks, and when

---

[*] In one case, a country has three currencies. China has its own yuan and Hong Kong has its dollar. Taiwan, although governed separately, is a province of China, and it, too, has its own currency.

they do, they have to take them out of some other activity nearly as important. The loss of the head of the Bank of Thailand to the private sector, for instance, took a steady hand away from the central bank just before the crisis of 1997.

Still, central banks were established (or grew) with the idea that national monetary policy has an important role to play. A key motivation for forming the American Federal Reserve System was that it could reduce the monetary impact of the inflows and outflows of gold, which had been the cause of many of the financial panics in the previous century. The Bank of Canada, founded in 1935, was "to regulate credit and currency in the best interest of the economic life of the nation ... and generally to promote the economic and financial welfare of Canada."

The question is partly one of where monetary policy works, particularly the size of the area that should be included. Eleven European nations have decided to go with a single currency, the euro for the whole area, and there is talk of several countries just adopting the U.S. dollar, including Canada, Mexico, and Argentina. What are the considerations in such arguments? The problem goes by the name of the *optimum currency area* question.[17]

A Case in Point: Canada and the 1997 Asian Crisis

The Canadian dollar fell from US$0.74 in January 1997 to US$0.645 in July 1998. Its fall did not reflect higher domestic inflation (indeed, it was lower than Canada's main trading partners) or unusually low interest rates; rather, it was a result of the decline in commodity prices caused by the Asian crisis. How that crisis affected Canadians depended very much on the size of the currency area and whether the currency had a fixed or floating exchange rate.

Start with what happened: the Canadian dollar fell 13% in value from early 1997 to mid-1998. The lower dollar stimulated exports, principally of manufactured goods (which were already growing), and dampened imports. Both owners and workers in manufacturing, located principally in Ontario and Quebec, benefited from the troubles of those in commodities, most of whom were outside those provinces. Consumers and retailers (who absorbed a great part of the price increases of imports) suffered, as did the "snowbirds"— retired Canadians living part of the year in the southern U.S. Commodity producers would have benefited to a small degree because the Canadian dollar price of their goods would be 13% higher than its already depressed price. Should the depressed commodity prices have persisted, the capital and labor involved in commodity production would eventually have shifted to the areas where the economy was expanding.

The Bank of Canada reacted to the difficulty by maintaining its focus on holding the rate of inflation between 1% and 3%. With inflation already near the low part of that band, the federal government in surplus, and the economy still showing a lot of slack, the Bank continued to let the money supply rise and maintained interest rates very close to American rates, despite the declining dollar. While this did not do much for the producers of the affected commodities other than to keep their debt service down, it did help the manufacturing and service sectors to expand.

Had the Bank of Canada been using a fixed exchange rate system, it would have been forced to raise interest rates, probably rather steeply, to hold the Canadian dollar up. With the rate of inflation already low and a modest degree of wage inflexibility (particularly in the highly unionized mining and forestry sectors), such a policy would have been disastrous, leading to widespread unemployment and outright deflation. Just look to what happened in the same period to New Zealand. It and Australia were faced with similar dilemmas. Australia followed Canada's policies. New Zealand, fearful of the inflationary consequences of a lowered N.Z. dollar (AS shifting to the left and AD to the right), raised interest rates sharply, plunging the country into a severe recession. Australia's real GDP grew by 4% and New Zealand's fell by nearly 2%.[18]

Now, in a kind of caricature, suppose that the commodity problems were all in the western provinces of Canada, which had become a separate country, Canada West. The "western dollar" would fall in value much farther than did the Canadian dollar. Without a large manufacturing and service base, it would take far longer for different exports to become established or expand. The commodities might become more competitive, but, as is often the case, their prices tend to be set by world markets in which western Canada is only a small player. Since the countries are separate, the Westerners could not easily migrate to the east, and would have to stay in Canada West to tough it out. In the meantime, Ontario and Quebec would not get any benefit from the lower commodity prices through a lower dollar. Snowbirds from Canada West would have a hard time while those from old Canada would see no change.

The Bank of Canada West would undoubtedly try to mitigate the decline in income, but it would be facing a much tougher problem than did Canada as a whole because the productive base has shrunk. As explained in Chapter 12, a sharp drop in the value of exports is akin to a natural disaster, shifting the long-run AS curve to the left. This limits the scope of monetary policy.

Under somewhat different circumstances, the scope for monetary policy in Canada West might have been broader. If Canada West had a large manufacturing base that could expand to take up the slack left when commodity prices fell, mildly expansionary monetary policy might also have replicated what the Canada-wide policy did. Or, the problem may have been principally monetary to begin with. Suppose, for instance, the problem was one of an incipient financial panic caused by the bankruptcy of a few large firms and the instability of a key commercial bank. In this case, the quick provision of additional liquidity would be effective.

Now suppose Canada had decided to use the American dollar. The result would start out roughly the same as it was with Canada West as a separate country. If the Asian crisis caused the American dollar to fall, it would not be by much, and the effect of this decline would be spread over both countries. Canadian manufacturers would get no particular boost, nor would its service sector. Canada West, meanwhile, would remain a pocket of severe unemployment.

In the longer run, both capital and labor would leave Canada West. Labor, lacking easy immigration to the United States, can only go "back east." Some capital would leave Canada, but, given continued separation of markets, some would move east. The resulting downward pressure on wages and interest rates might eventually make Ontario and Quebec more competitive and stimulate the economy there, but the process would be much slower than it would be with the exchange rate change and an independent monetary policy. We remain skeptical about the benefits of Canada adopting the American dollar.

What Makes a Currency Area Optimum?

Single currencies seem to work best when the area they cover (1) has high labor mobility, (2) has moderate price and wage flexibility, (3) experiences the same economic shocks, and (4) has a system of interregional governmental transfers. Consider the case of Canada above. The shock of lower commodity prices was not uniform over the country and had the unusual effect of promoting growth in a region far from the ones most affected by the initial shock. The effect was moderated to some extent, however, by the higher governmental revenues produced as the economy nonetheless expanded, some of which were transferred to negatively affected areas. Labor mobility and price flexibility also may serve to ease the problems, should they persist.

The problem with having a separate currency for Canada West is that only the third condition—the economic shock—is fulfilled. The entire West suffers from the low commodity prices, but the labor cannot move to the other area, prices in the West are not particularly flexible, and there would be no system of intergovernmental transfers. The problem with having Canada use the American dollar is that only the moderate wage flexibility condition is fulfilled, and Canada is probably less flexible than the United States. The other three conditions are not fulfilled. Canada is suffering far more than the United States is suffering from the same economic shock; labor cannot easily emigrate; and greater revenues to the American Treasury are not going to be redistributed to Canadian provinces.

The Euro

Over a period between January 1, 1999, and July 2002, when all national currency notes are withdrawn, 11 European nations will convert all their currencies into a single currency, the euro.* While no actual euro bills or coins will circulate until January 2002, all the member exchange rates are fixed against the euro, the financial markets are converting to using the euro, and the central banking institutions are in place. The move is bold with large risks. The policy-makers see it, however, as the essential last step in creating a single market in Europe, bringing with it large gains in efficiency and further tightening the many bonds that hold Europe together in a peaceful, democratic, and productive society. It has been driven more by the political vision that rose from the rubble of World War II than it has by economics. What perils the euro faces are therefore of critical concern.

CAPSULE VIEW OF THE MONETARY ARRANGEMENTS

As of the summer of 2002, the 11 European countries will be using the same currency, not just in accounting, but in their pockets and vending machines. Somewhat like the American Federal Reserve System, the national central banks remain, but policy is set and directed from a single European Central Bank. It decides whether credit is to be extended to commercial banks, whether T-bills are bought and sold (and which ones), and how much intervention takes place on the foreign exchange market.

PROBLEMS AS AN OPTIMUM CURRENCY AREA

Most observers are concerned about how the various national and regional economies are going to respond to a single currency. Consider the four main issues of any currency area: labor mobility, price and wage flexibility, response to the same economic shocks, and intergovernmental transfers. The last is the only one where Europe has a mechanism in place. The other three all appear to have problems:

1. Europe has less labor mobility than the United States and Canada. Certainly there are large numbers of Italian families in Germany and the Volvo factory at Gothenburg has signs in Swedish, Finnish, and Serbo-Croatian, but mobility is not what it is in North America.

---

* The countries are Austria, Belgium, Finland, France, Germany, Ireland, Italy, Luxembourg, the Netherlands, Portugal, and Spain. Greece would like to join. Other European Union countries—Britain, Denmark, and Sweden—have opted out for the present.

2. Price and wage flexibility is less than in North America. Most labor unions have historically been more closely linked with governments and have chosen solutions that are national in scope, rather than on a company-by-company basis. Bargaining is generally with an employer's group and the wage of, say, a welder with 10 years' experience would be the same in all companies, and border-to-border. Union membership and support are much greater. It is not that unions cannot accept lower wages and work something out with the employer when things are tight, but they normally have not done so.

3. The continent is large and varied and unlikely to be suffering from the same shock at the same time. There may be depressed areas and booming areas without any obvious means of spreading the prosperity.

Econometric models have added to the skepticism, suggesting again that Europe is hardly an optimum currency area because of the way shocks affect it differently and the lack of labor mobility.[19]

CAUSE AND EFFECT

While skepticism seems in order, it is well to consider that lack of mobility, price rigidity, and differential reaction to economic shocks may be results of separate monetary systems. Without the need to migrate, people have not migrated or created the institutional structure to do so (for instance, even something so simple as international real estate companies). Without the need to bargain in such a way as occasionally to take a cut in wages, neither union nor company knows how to go about it. And with separate monetary systems, monetary shocks may be more national than international. Those in favor of the single currency recognize potential problems but believe the polity is strong enough to solve them.[20]

Dollarization

Throughout Latin America and some other parts of the world, such as Russia, the American dollar is, to one degree or another, a parallel currency. Like the tourist and the clerk, people think in terms of dollars, seeing through the local currencies, much as a hiker might see through the rushing waters of a stream to the stepping stones below the surface. Thin lines of that recognizable green of American money (a $50 or $100 bill) rest along the backs of many a wallet with all the multicolored stuff in front. Safety deposit boxes and safes contain stacks of American dollars. No one knows for sure how much American currency is outside the U.S., but consider this: American monetary authorities have issued over $1,600 dollars worth of currency *per American resident*. It is unlikely that American residents themselves hold that much cash. The

---

DEALING IN DOLLARS

"How much is that carving?" the tourist asked the Brazilian clerk. She paused a moment, checked her list of the dollar prices of the items, and then converted them to cruzeiros on her calculator. "Two million five hundred thousand cruzeiros." The tourist put the 2,500,000 into his calculator, dividing by the exchange rate to arrive at the dollar price, about $45. "Fair enough," he commented as he handed over his credit card. Who knows, by the time the charge goes in, the cruzeiro might fall another 50%, and the gift shop owner probably anticipated that in the initial dollar pricing.

---

comparable Canadian figure is 40% of that—$995 Canadian dollars, or about $660 American dollars.[*] Some of the currency is used for illegal activities, but a great deal of it is simply held by nervous savers around the world who prefer a cache of non-interest-bearing greenbacks to any asset denominated in local currency.

Not only have saving and transactions become dollarized. In many cases, contracts themselves are in dollars. The process is most advanced in Argentina, where dollar contracts (including wage contracts), dollar bank deposits, and other dollar assets are perfectly legal alongside peso contracts. U.S. dollar accounts and other short-term assets, sometimes called Argendollars, are an important part of the money supply. Indeed, Argentina counts both peso and dollar accounts in both its narrow money supply and broader definitions.

As Argentina has become more dollarized, the effectiveness of any devaluation of the peso is reduced. A devaluation would penalize only those whose wages and salaries were in pesos, while rewarding those who had chosen dollar values. It may not give exports much of an advantage if many of the exporters' costs were already in dollar terms. Moreover, it would have truly weird monetary effects as dollar holdings would rise in value (as measured in pesos), and peso values would fall (as measured in dollars).

When the Brazilian real fell in value in 1998, pressures rose against the Argentine peso. To allay fears, Argentina suggested it was considering moving entirely to the dollar. Would such a move be sensible? After all, Argentina and the U.S. are not an optimum currency area, labor is not mobile between them, they do not have the same economic shocks, and neither government is likely to aid a stricken region in the other. Why, then, move to the dollar?

---

[*] Canadians are less wealthy than Americans, meaning the demand for currency is lower. Moreover, Canadians have begun substituting debit cards for cash in transactions between $20 and $100 and currency per capita has fallen. Still, that does not explain why Americans hold 2.4 times the currency Canadians do.

First, take the macroeconomic aspects. (1) It may further increase credibility. Argentina has stripped its own central bank of virtually all of its power to create money by moving to a currency board. The next step—to give away total power—may not be so great. (2) The dollar is so much a part of the economy now that any outflow of dollars would in itself be sharply recessionary, and there is little the government can do about it, given the reduction of central bank powers. Indeed, any reflation in pesos would not give companies the dollars they need to fulfill domestic contracts signed in dollars. (3) The economy and polity have begun to shape themselves around a low-inflation, non-accommodative monetary policy and dollar prices. Prices and wages are probably far more flexible (nominally) than they were in the recent past, as indeed they must be.

Using the dollar might also protect Argentina from financial panics. Just as a few bankruptcies and difficult times in Michigan do not cause a panic to sell all Michigan-based assets and just as financiers are not staring at the relation of Michigan's foreign debt to its gross state product, people should not worry if the same things happen in an Argentina entirely on the American dollar. The analogy is not perfect because Argentina would still be tracking its income, trade, and GDP and a negative economic performance may depress the whole country, but it has merit. If there is no peso to fall, there is no risk of it falling.

Lastly, the numerous microeconomic advantages of having a single currency would persist—foreign exchange risk would disappear, prices could be compared more easily, and transactions would be that much cheaper.

DÉJÀ VU ALL OVER AGAIN

The economic questions the world faces as it enters the twenty-first century are much the same as they were a century before. We have seen them before. (1) To what extent can price level movements and adjustments occur without causing excessive unemployment and hardships? (2) To what extent can or should governments and their monetary authorities attempt to ease the burden of adjustment? (3) To what extent does or should adherence to an international system reduce the freedom of governments to use seigniorage as a major way of gaining resources? (4) What kinds of international institutions should there be to ease adjustments or correct errors of the market?

Unemployment and Monetary Ease

Even as the world moved to general acceptance of the gold standard in the 1870s, central banks had begun to experiment with ways of reducing the full impact on the banking and price level. Churchill's failed attempt to return to the gold standard indicated just how difficult it was to push price levels down.

The Fed's insistence on sterilizing the inflow of gold (and the high tariffs) showed how difficult it was to persuade a creditor country to accommodate debtor countries.

The Bretton Woods system still was oriented toward price stability and flexibility. But it bought more time for the changes to occur. Countries were encouraged not to change their exchange rates, and few did in its first 20 years of existence. At the same time, however, policy economists were increasingly convinced that attempts to reduce the price level were doomed to failure and that attempts to adjust price levels would be very costly. Such an understanding, coupled with fixed exchange rates, is inherently inflationary. Since the debtor countries cannot deflate and cannot change their exchange rate, the creditor country must inflate (or, as the U.S. did, just keep lending more money).

The inflation of the 1970s, however, gave economists pause. Price-level flexibility is not necessarily a "given" around which everything else fits, but it may in itself be endogenous. The extent to which alterations in the money supply or rate of inflation can be deliberately used effectively—that is, without creating the seeds of its own destruction—became a topic that is still critical. The fuzzy line between policy that *accommodates* and policy that *validates* is critical in every policy decision. As countries begin to contemplate giving up their own currencies, it seems the world is back to the questions of the acceptance of the gold standard in the 1870s.

Seigniorage

Another lesson, going back well into the nineteenth century, is that in critical situations, nations rarely give up seigniorage, which is a kind of taxation. For the American government fighting the Civil War, the European governments in World War I, and the many countries simply short on revenue-generation but long on the ability to spend, the benefits of inflation exceeded the principal of keeping the currency stable. The gold standard did not collapse because of some commodity crisis or a worldwide depression, but because governments spent more than they had and were able to sever the fixed bond of their currencies to other ones. Again, the moves in the last decade or so for giving up national currencies are partly based in the desires of a polity to constrain how their government can raise funds.

The International Institutions

The creation of international institutions has carried with it the same problems of accommodation and validation. As the chapter has argued, most of the moves of the IMF are not validative—that is, they have little moral hazard, given the seriousness of the problem. But to avoid validation, the institutions themselves have taken increasingly greater powers so that what help they give is accompanied by the proper subsequent behavior. To make an analogy, it is like any small community or a family. When bad behavior has occurred, it is not necessary to punish it but to make sure it doesn't happen again. The decision between punishment and additional control is never easy.

VOCABULARY AND CONCEPTS

Basel Accord	The euro	IMF facilities
Brady bonds	Exit bonds	Moral hazard argument
Contagion	Exit procedures	Optimum currency area
Debt service	First debt crisis	Overshooting
Dollarization	Flight to quality	

QUESTIONS

1. How did the policy reactions of monetary authorities in developed countries differ between the 1972-73 increases in the price of petroleum and the 1978 rise?
2. Real interest rates changed dramatically between 1973 and 1983. What was the probable cause of those changes? What was the consequence for Third World borrowers?
3. Evaluate floating exchange rates, indicating their costs and benefits.
4. Contrast and compare the 1972 and 1997 debt crises. Examine and explain each of the major points of comparison.
5. Show how in each crisis foreign borrowing rose, then fell precipitously, and show the consequences of such changes.
6. It appears that much of the resources borrowed from abroad failed to generate sufficient income or foreign exchange. What is the evidence for saying that?
7. Explain the problem countries have because of the lack of an orderly way to default.
8. Did the financial crises spread from one country to another because they had extensive trade links, because they reacted to the same external shock, and/or because they created the same external shock?
9. Explain how a large number of defaulted loans could have endangered the entire banking system of the world?
10. What are the evidences of a flight to quality in 1997? What were the consequences?
11. Using the portfolio matrices (as in Table 18.3), illustrate why a fund or bank would flee risky assets for safe ones. Why does the situation get worse when the bank or fund holds derivatives?

12. Why is sovereign debt more difficult to default on than private debt?

13. Explain the role of exit bonds and the need for increased IMF surveillance.

14. How has the Basel Accord served to strengthen banks against the possibility of extensive losses?

15. What changes have been made in the IMF as a response to the crises?

16. What kind of things does the IMF oversee in its surveillance role?

17. Debtor countries often complain about the policies their governments take when pressured by the IMF. Sometimes, indeed, the policies may be mistaken, but often the complaints come for other reasons. What are they?

18. What is the moral hazard problem with the IMF's lending? Does it seem to you to be an important one? Explain.

19. The Canadian reaction to the decline of its export sales in 1997 and 1998 was to allow the Canadian dollar to fall. In what way would the economic reaction have been different if Canada had been using the American dollar? Does this mean that Canada is an optimum currency area?

20. Examine the four elements that make for an optimum currency area. Then explain why Canada and the United States or the 11 European countries that use the euro are *not* optimal. (Just because it isn't optimal, does not mean that ways might not emerge to make it work.)

21. One of the principal worries about the euro is that there will be larger pockets of unemployment, which will in turn destabilize the political arrangements. Why might this be so?

22. What would be the advantages and disadvantages of Argentina using the American dollar? Of Brazil doing the same?

NOTES

1. The G-7 deflator is derived from the consumer price indices in the seven leading industrial countries, weighted by their 1975 GDPs. See Figure 18.2.

2. The standard article is Rudiger Dornbusch, "Expectations and Exchange Rate Dynamics," *Journal of Political Economy* (December 1976). See also Robert A. Driskill, "Exchange Rate Dynamics," *Journal of Political Economy* (April 1981).

3. Joyce Horne and Paul Masson, "International Economic Cooperation and Policy Coordination," *Finance and Development* (June 1987): 28-31.

4. *The Economist* of Feb. 20, 1999, has both a lead article, "The New Danger," and "Could it happen again?" *The Economist*, February 20, 1999, 15-16, 19-21.

5. On inflation targeting, see Guy Debelle, Paul Masson, Miguel Savastano, and Sunil Sharma, *Inflation Targeting as a Framework for Monetary Policy* (New York: IMF, 1998). On Canada's experience, see Gordon G. Thiessen, "The Canadian experience with targets for inflation control," *Bank of Canada Review* (Winter 1998-99): 89-107. On Australia and New Zealand, see "On Target," *The Economist*, September 6, 1997, 81.

6. We omit the Mexican "Tequila crisis" of 1994, partly because its effects were more limited and partly because of space considerations.

7. See *World Economic Outlook* (New York: IMF, October 1998), 83-87.

8. Nicholas Brady, the American Secretary of the Treasury under Presidents Reagan and Bush, called for such a change in 1989 (*IMF Survey*, March 20, 1989, 90-92), and 10 years later Alassane Ouatarra, Deputy Managing Director of the IMF, made the same call (address to Midwinter Conference of the Bankers' Association for Foreign Trade, February 3, 1999, available at the IMF Website: www.imf.org).

9. The following material has been used: Taimur Baig and Ilan Goldfajn, *Financial Market Contagion in the Asian Crisis, Working Paper of the International Monetary Fund* (Washington: IMF, 1998); Guillermo Calvo, "Capital Inflows and Macroeconomic Management: Tequila Lessons," *International Journal of Finance and Economics* 1 (July 1996); Chinn and Menzie, *Before the Fall: Were East Asian Currencies Overvalued?*, NBER Working Paper 6491 (Cambridge, Mass.: MIT Press, 1997); C. Fred Bergsten, "The Asian Monetary Crisis: Proposed Remedies," Statement to the Committee on Banking and Financial Services, U.S. House of Representatives, November 13, 1997; Joseph Whitt, "The Role of External Shocks in the Asian Financial Crisis," *Economic Review*, Federal Reserve Bank of Atlanta, Second Quarter (1999), 18-31.

10. An increasing amount of information is available. Check the IMF Web site at www.imf.org. Look for the area labeled SDDS (Special Data Dissemination Standard). For a general discussion, see Alassane D. Ouattara, "The International Financial Institutions: A View from the IMF," address to the Midwinter Conference of the Bankers' Association for Foreign Trade, February 3, 1999. Available at IMF Web site.

11. The details in the following discussion are from the "Introduction" to *International Financial Statistics,* section 2, and from "IMF Financing Helps Members Pursue Sound Policies," *IMF Survey Supplement,* September 1998, 16-20.

12. The figures are available in the beginning pages of *International Financial Statistics*.

13. "Scope of Surveillance Expands to Include Broader Range of Institutional Measures," *IMF Survey*, Supplement, September 1998, 11-14, quotation at 11.

14. *Argentina Policy Memorandum*, January 11, 1999. IMF Web site: www.imf.org

15. "The rise and retreat of the consumer," *The Economist*, March 27, 1999, 4.

16. *Business Week,* February 8, 1999. The IMF's reply was made the next week, February 15. It is also on the IMF Web site.

17. The founding article on this issue is Robert Mundell, "A Theory of Optimum Currency Areas," *American Economic Review* 51 (1965): 657-65.

18. "G'day, Goldilocks," *The Economist*, March 6, 1999, 66.

19. See Barry Eichengreen, *European Monetary Unification: Theory, Practice and Analysis* (Cambridge, Mass.: MIT Press, 1997); James Forder, ed., *The European Union and National Macroeconomic Policy* (London: Routledge, 1998); Francesco Giordano, *The Political Economy of Monetary Union: Towards the Euro* (London: Routledge, 1998); C. Randall Henning, *Cooperating with Europe's Monetary Union* (Washington: Institute for International Economics, 1997); Paul Welfens, ed., *European Monetary Union: Transition, International Impact and Policy Options* (Berlin: Springer-Verlag, 1997).

20. Tamim Bayoumi and Barry Eichengreen, "Shocking Aspects of European Monetary Integration," in F. Giavazzi and F. Torres, eds., *Adjustment and Growth in the European Monetary Union* (New York: Cambridge University Press, 1993), 193-229. See also various studies of the Bank of Canada cited in Chantal Dupasquier and Jocelyn Jacob, "European economic and monetary union: Background and implications," *Bank of Canada Review* (Autumn 1997): 3-28.

Chapter Nineteen

Multinational Firms, Foreign Direct Investment, and Globalization

OBJECTIVES

OVERALL OBJECTIVE   To examine how foreign direct investment and multinational firms fit into the global economy, with particular interest in the extent to which multinational firms can operate without close reference to the market.

MORE SPECIFICALLY
- To examine foreign direct investment, gauging its size and importance.
- To show that FDI has been around for over a century.
- To build a model that shows why FDI exists.
- To demonstrate why the firm coordinates some activities and the market others.
- To define the space in which the firm can operate without direct reference to the market.
- To look at several specific issues involving multinational firms.

....

Chapter 1 began with a discussion of the way globalization restricted the use of many accepted means of achieving social and political ends. Put more broadly, globalization weakens the nation-state, at least as its powers are presently employed. But to whom, if anyone, does that power pass? Is it to a higher level of international authority, such as the WTO or IMF or the European Union government? Is it the unconscious market? Or might it be the very conscious activities of a group of executives of some multinational corporation? People frustrated by ineffective national policies may rail against an odd mixture of them all: currency speculators, multinational firms, the IMF, the WTO, and the market.

However conscious their decision-making, IMF and WTO officials will undoubtedly point out that what they are doing is trying to get the market to work, to have firms and households respond to real costs and benefits, not political rents. The multinational corporate official will respond that the firm is just responding to or anticipating market changes. Such a statement is true, but can in some senses be disingenuous or at least simplistic. Analytically, we can get closer. This chapter looks specifically at the relation of the multinational firm and the market, trying to define more precisely what power a firm might have and what powers it does have, however much people may wish to think it is some unconstrained force.

The scope of the chapter does not go so far as to examine the large firm's political activities—how the firm itself shapes the laws under which it operates. As other chapters have pointed out, the influence of producers tends to overwhelm the interests of consumers in trade law, and an international firm is little different from domestic firms in that regard. (It may have less political clout or legitimacy, but it may have more money.) Rather, the chapter assumes the legal and political framework is independent of the firm. Readers may take that as a simplifying, but highly useful, assumption.

FOREIGN DIRECT INVESTMENT AND THE MULTINATIONAL FIRM

Foreign direct investment (FDI) is investment outside the investor's country in which the investor exerts a degree of control over the company. Normally the investor in such case is not an individual but a foreign corporation (whose ownership in turn may be widespread). The management in the home (or investor) country has considerable direct control over their subsidiary, including the right to determine the board of directors and management, and normally controls the choice of upper management and large capital expenditures. In most cases, the foreign subsidiary is registered as a separate company for legal and tax reasons, and the parent company owns 100% of its shares. In a significant minority of cases, the foreign investment is a *joint venture* paired with a domestic company,[1] is made up of two or more foreign companies,[2] or is just the foreign company with domestic investors holding portfolio interests.[3] Portfolio investments, in contrast, are those in which the investor has no hands-on control—bonds, preferred shares, or small amounts of common shares.

FDI sometimes forms a large part of a country's foreign assets—both the United States and Canada, for instance, have around 35% of all their foreign assets in the form of direct investments, as Figure 19.1 shows. The income produced from FDI can also form a substantial portion of domestic profits.

After-tax profits of American foreign subsidiaries have been above 15% of American profits in recent years, and in the late 1990s foreign subsidiaries of American corporations invested sums that were around 8% of all new American investment.[4]

Multinational firms (MNFs) are large firms with substantial operating units in several countries. They include many large manufacturing firms, such as General Motors, Exxon, and Nestlé, as well as a number of service firms in retailing (Woolworths, active for decades), food service (McDonald's and Mr. Donut), financial services (Sun Life

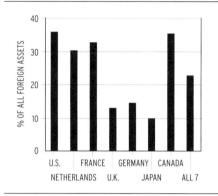

Figure 19.1

FDI AS A PERCENTAGE OF FOREIGN ASSETS IN SEVEN KEY COUNTRIES

and KPMG, the auditing firm), and increasingly transportation (Air Iberia and American Airlines in South America) and communications (AT&T). FDI counts all the foreign investments of MNFs, but also catches smaller firms with investments in only one foreign country, which some writers do not consider multinationals. Figures for FDI are more readily available than they are for one group or one writer's definition of MNF.

Even foreign direct investment, nevertheless, is difficult to measure. Statisticians can easily measure *flows* during a year because new capital transferred and retained earnings of subsidiaries are reported on the balance of payments. The *stock* of foreign direct investment, however, is not the sum of the flows since some investments are marvelously successful and others are duds. It is not difficult to get stock values of a country's holdings of foreign bonds or shares traded on a stock market. But a subsidiary with no traded shares is much more difficult to value. This explains why only 18 countries, fortunately including all major industrial countries, keep regular figures on the stocks of their foreign investments, but with the exception of Canada none of these series go back before 1980. In the absence of estimates of stock values, researchers have often used *book values*, what the parent company reports as the value of the subsidiary on its balance sheet, but these tend to be rather lower than the imputed value of companies' shares. Using what figures are available, nonetheless, FDI appears to have developed over the last 150 years in four periods.

1. The initial thrust, 1865-1914, found national firms extending themselves across borders. Estimates of the size of foreign direct investment in the

THE MEAT PACKERS: A HISTORICAL EXAMPLE

Before the railways, the age-old pattern was for a surrounding countryside to supply food to the nearby city. With the opening of the rail lines to the American West, western cattlemen could drive their herds to the nearest rail terminal and sell them there. The cattle were then sent live to the cities, where they were auctioned, slaughtered, and butchered. A number of entrepreneurs realized that sending live cattle east was wasteful, as many of the cattle died and all lost weight. A carcass, shipped in refrigerated railcars, could age on the route, increasing in value as it rolled toward its markets.

They began to put the plans in effect in the 1870s. The plans required considerable coordination as well as investment in specialized boxcars, which the railways (with heavy investments in feeding yards along their tracks) were reluctant to do. So the packers purchased their own cars, established cold storage on the eastern end and slaughterhouses in the West, and allowed the carcasses to age properly while in transit. Instead of an auction of live cattle on two ends of the track, there was one auction, at which the packers bought the meat; after that, the packers owned it all the way until it got into the butchers' shops. Moreover only a few companies—e.g., Swift, Cudahy, Armour, Canada Packers—had the capital and talents to put together such national networks.

Going international was a small step for the packers. Once they figured out how to control and monitor their managers, supervise procedures to maintain standards, and keep generating capital, the international network was just another step. For Canada Packers, it was just a railway that crossed the border, though much was transshipped to lake freighters. For the American companies, it meant moving the carcasses from a boxcar to a ship, and then, on the other end, into a boxcar again. The distance was longer, the timing more critical to avoid overripe meat, but it was still feasible. By the 1890s the British were eating meat raised in Nebraska and slaughtered in Chicago.

The process went one step further when British companies began to source beef from Argentina to compete with the Americans, and in 1907 the Americans opened up operations in Argentina, also to supply the British market. By World War I, both British and American firms were also operating in southern Brazil.[5] The pattern ended when Britain established "Imperial Preference" tariffs for members of the British Empire in the 1930s and successive Argentine governments discriminated against exports. Perhaps it is as well they did not re-establish the British market because the Common Agricultural Policy would have destroyed it again.

early period are tricky. The principal guideline to get an impression of the size of FDI in the early period is to compare their book value with estimates of GNP.* (This compares a capital stock with an output of another capital stock, but no figures are available about the output of foreign subsidiaries or the capital stock of countries.) The book value of American corporations' foreign subsidiaries was 7% of estimated GNP in 1914.

2. Retrenchment and defensive operations occurred from 1919 to 1945, when a great deal of investment was defensive and total investment fell sharply as a percentage of economic activity. High tariffs forced a number of companies that had previously exported to establish foreign plants, a process particularly marked in Canada. In 1929, just before the onset of the Depression, the book value of American-owned subsidiaries was still 7% of GNP, but this had fallen to around 3% just after World War II.

3. The postwar decades (1948-80) at first were dominated by American firms, but firms from many other countries later became involved in FDI. American foreign investment climbed once more to the 7% figure. In the 1960s, the issue of foreign direct investment became a topic of concern in many countries, the phrase "multinational firm" was coined, and a large number of studies began.

4. During the period at the end of the century, (1980-present), public concern about multinational firms seemed to ebb while FDI rose very sharply, far outpacing the growth of output. The pattern of investment, like that of trade, was increasingly an interpenetration as FDI levels, both inward and outward, rose in all major industrial countries.

FDI IN RECENT YEARS

World Figures

The United Nations placed the book value of foreign direct investment in 1971 at a figure that works out to US$512 billion in 1990 dollars.[6] The estimated market values the IMF uses in its series are somewhat higher.[7] By

---

* Historically, the common measurement has been "book value"—the value of the foreign subsidiary as kept in the books of the parent, which was usually the sum of all investments made in the subsidiary minus depreciation. Book value, however, is something created out of tax and accounting rules, and is not an assessment of what the company feels its subsidiary is worth. In knowledge-based companies, book value has very little to do with how the market values the firms, nor should it: Microsoft has had about the same market value as General Motors, but only a tiny fraction of GM's book value. For successful companies in any business book value is far too low, so statisticians must come up with an estimate of the value of the subsidiary. Given these caveats, the numbers are nonetheless interesting and, insofar as they indicate trends, of considerable validity.

Figure 19.2

INDICATORS OF DIRECT INVESTMENT

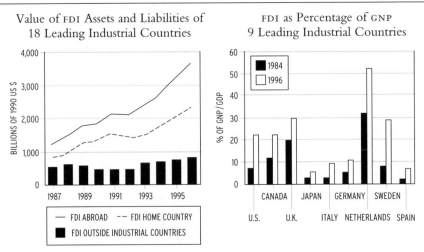

Value of FDI Assets and Liabilities of
18 Leading Industrial Countries

FDI as Percentage of GNP
9 Leading Industrial Countries

Note: The countries included are U.S., U.K., Japan, France, Germany, Netherlands, Canada, Australia, New Zealand, Austria, Switzerland, Italy, Spain, Ireland, Sweden, Norway, Finland, Denmark. No figures are available for Belgium and Portugal. The amounts of FDI not included in this set are small compared to the total. This is not to say that Chilean investment in Argentina is unimportant, but it won't affect the total in a way that would be seen on the diagram.

Source: Calculated and summed from *IFS*, 1999, and deflated by the U.S. deflator.

1980, not yet including figures from France, Sweden, and Switzerland, the figure was $675 billion. Figure 19.2 shows the more recent figures.

The estimated stock of FDI held by the 18 largest industrial countries, which is the vast bulk of FDI,[8] rose from US$1.4 trillion (1990 dollars) to $3.1 trillion in 1996. Growth of FDI rose fairly steeply from 1987 to 1991, flattened, and then took off at an even greater pace in 1993. The dotted line shows FDI in the 18 countries, the vast bulk of which, of course, is provided by others of the same 18 countries. The difference, shown with the columns in the left panel, is investment the 18 countries made outside one another, principally in Asia and Latin America.

The right panel uses a somewhat narrower base to get a longer span. (In 1984 six of the countries in the left panel had not begun reporting.) Note how much FDI grew as a portion of GNP (GDP for some countries where GNP was not available). Not on the diagram because it would ruin the scale is Switzerland, whose FDI stood at 66% of GNP in 1984 and 263% in 1996.

The Leading Investors

American FDI has been dominant since World War II. In 1975, over half the book value of FDI was American.[9] In 1996, however, American FDI was 42%, by estimated value of FDI of the 18 largest countries, as Figure 19.3 shows.

Figure 19.3

SHARES OF FDI BY INVESTING COUNTRIES, 1986 AND 1996

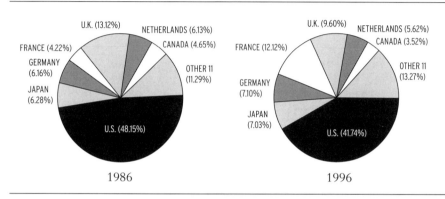

The American share of FDI fell somewhat between 1986 and 1996, mainly because of increases in the shares of France, Germany, and Japan. The story is not the changes in percentage share, however, but the sheer growth in FDI, which far outpaced the growth of GNP. Consider American investment shown in Figure 19.4.

Figure 19.4

AMERICAN FDI

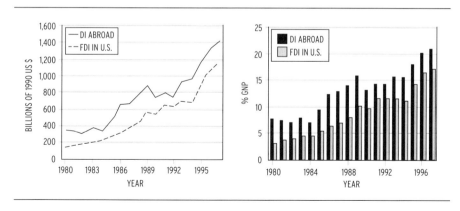

Figure 19.5

FDI IN CANADA AND CANADIAN FDI, 1948-1997

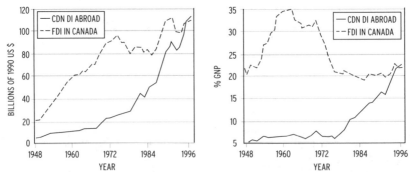

Note: Because the amount of FDI has long been a concern in Canada, the figures run back to 1948. Numbers in *IFS* balance-of-payments statistics are always in U.S. dollars, hence the right-hand panel is deflated by the U.S. GDP deflator. The right-hand panel used GNP figures from the *IFS* national accounts tables and the average Canadian dollar price in U.S. dollars to convert to U.S. dollars in order to figure the percentage.

Source: IFS, 1999.

The left panel shows American FDI in real terms. The black line shows American investment abroad and the broken line investment of other countries in the United States, both of which have risen sharply. The right panel shows American FDI as a percentage of GNP. The numbers are market value estimates, not book values, and so are somewhat higher as portions of GNP than the historical figures cited. That said, since 1985 FDI has grown strikingly as a percentage of GNP, from the earlier pattern of around 7% to over 20%. Foreign direct investment in the U.S. has also risen, from 3% to 17%.

The Canadian Situation

The Canadian experience is particularly interesting because of the intense concern Canadians had about the dangers of foreign direct investment, epitomized in Kari Levitt's *Silent Surrender* (1970) and in the founding in 1973 of the Foreign Investment Review Agency, which during the decade of its existence demanded that all fresh foreign ownership over a certain value follow certain guidelines and have its approval. (It was accompanied by a marked decline in FDI in Canada.) Canada had the heaviest foreign direct investment (mostly American, but substantial British also) of any of the major industrial countries and a weak manufacturing sector. The fear was that most of the critical decisions would be taken in headquarters outside of Canada and it would be left a "branch-plant economy." As Figure 19.5 shows, FDI, while growing and strong in Canada, was overtaken by Canadian direct investments abroad, a trend so new and startling that most Canadians have yet to realize it.[10]

FDI in Canada was very high as a proportion of the economy, peaking at 35% of GNP in 1962 and hitting US$96 billion (1990 dollars) in 1974 and not hitting that figure again until 1988, when the Canadian economy was considerably larger. Canadian direct investment abroad remained very modest until the late 1970s, when it began to accelerate, and it accelerated even more in the mid–1990s.

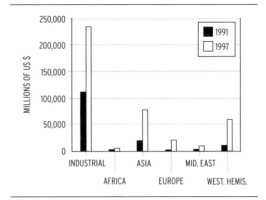

Figure 19.6

FDI FLOWS BY HOST AREAS (NEW INVESTMENT)

HOST COUNTRIES

As Figure 19.2 showed most FDI, like most trade, is between developed countries. What may not be clear from that diagram is that FDI in non-industrial nations has fallen from around 40% to between 25% and 30% of all FDI. Figure 19.6 shows that the flows of FDI remain heavily oriented toward developed countries and appear to be increasingly so. Balance-of-payments data on flows of new FDI (including reinvestment of retained earnings) indicate a trend toward increasing investments in developed countries. Only some Asian countries and some Latin American countries received important increases in investment.

FDI and Trade

Because most national firms are also multinational firms, and because historically many began as exporters or importers, they are heavily involved in world trade. Around 99% of American trade, for instance, involves a multinational as one of its parties—for example, multinational Walmart purchasing from a Taiwan clothing producer, or Walmart purchases from multinational SONY. Confining this definition strictly to American firms, 80% of U.S. exports and nearly 50% of U.S. imports involve American multinationals. Trade within the same firm—e.g., Ford Canada to American Ford—amounts to a bit over one-third of American trade.[11] What light can economic theory throw on these developments?

761

THE THEORY OF FOREIGN DIRECT INVESTMENT

The Problem of Direct Investment

Despite their early origins, it was the 1960s before multinational firms received either a name or widespread attention. Business writers praised the efficiency-producing, capital-moving, and technological-transferring form of organization. Some political scientists sounded notes of caution; others sounded alarms. What manner of beast was this *multinational firm*? How did it differ from a domestic firm? Could the economist help? Perhaps, but when economists went to their tool-boxes to try to address some of the issues raised, they found their tools were at best awkward and their arguments unconvincing. International trade theory was firmly based on highly competitive markets, and *independent* exporters and importers, yet it was clear a great deal of trade occurred between affiliates of the same firm. Classical economics postulated single-product, single-location entities and, in truth, explained the existence of *any* firm awkwardly. The profession, it appeared, would have to go back to the drawing boards.

Early interpretations of foreign direct investment saw it as a capital movement—with those areas having a surplus of capital exporting it in various forms to capital-scarce regions. It was an alternative to portfolio investment but responded to the same forces. If so, then much of the current interpenetration of investments is hard to explain. Why would a single nation be both the host to FDI and an investor abroad itself? Why has the bulk of FDI gone to countries with adequate capital? Viewing FDI simply as a form of capital flow, responsive to interest rates and risk premiums, has not been particularly helpful.[12] Instead, economists have increasingly viewed the MNF as an organizational response to certain kinds of market imperfections and to view a it in the same way as they would a national firm.[13]

Why Any Firm Exists

Readers who have seen the American public TV program, *This Old House,* might think about the business relationships involved in the house renovation projects. The owners of the house have an architect and at least a general contractor, who may do some work with his own crew but subcontracts most work to others. The owner may bring in other specialist firms also. The renovations use perhaps a dozen small companies, all bringing their own equipment and many their own materials. A very complex network of bids, cost estimates, contracts, personal relationships, and financing underlies the projects. Moreover, a few people, principally the general contractor, have to coordinate the whole project. All the firms involved are very small, in some cases just a single person, contacted through the trade union, agreeing to come in on a daily basis. The whole operation is primarily coordinated through the market.

Contrast the house construction business with a large automotive company. Its line workers don't come in with their own tools, nor do they make individual bids on what they are going to do that week. People in management do a wide variety of tasks, none of which have they bid on, and only occasionally are consultants brought in for particular tasks. The designers and engineers work on developing a new model, marketing studies what to make and how to sell it, and the bulk of the process of moving the new model from idea to the garages of the world is closely coordinated *within* the company, not, as in construction, between independent people and businesses. While today automotive firms do much more contracting than they did in the past, it is still an industry largely of *administrative* coordination rather than of *market coordination*.

All allocational decisions are at some level administrative, involving managerial judgment. The farmer, although he may be in an industry that approaches perfect competition, decides what to plant, when to plant, when to harvest, and what equipment to use. A vertically integrated banana company has to decide several years ahead how many banana plants to put in, and how the bananas are to be shipped and ultimately retailed. If the farmer or managers err and find they have grown too much or too little, they lose money. It is unlikely that either will go out of business right away as the perfect competition models would have it, but continued bad judgment will lead even quasi-monopolists to perform badly, losing market share or the confidence of their shareholders and setting themselves up for a takeover bid. The market, accordingly, provides a check on management's judgment, but it does not supplant the need for managerial judgment.

A firm may have to make a large number of judgments before the market can check on it. Think of what goes into a new automobile model or new airplane before it makes even its first sale, or, more mundanely, what Gillette puts into a new razor model. The market comes in only very late in the process to give its judgment. The firm supplants or *internalizes* the market to a greater or lesser degree before submitting its decision to the market. The key question, then, is why firms in some industries internalize so much activity, while in other industries relatively little is internalized.

The reason is that using the market has costs, known as *transaction costs*.[14] A contract has costs associated with it, particularly the difficulties of specifying the thousands of "what-ifs" to cover the actions to take when meeting anticipated or unanticipated problems. These are *contingencies*—contingent upon event X occurring, the contract specifies Y action is taken. If costs run more than estimated because material costs are higher, then party A pays, or party

A and B pay half each, etc. When the future is quite uncertain or the time period is long, it becomes very hard to specify all the contingencies, hence the contract is *incomplete*, raising risks for both contracting parties. If the firm does the activity itself, hiring people on salary or wages and building its own equipment, it does not have to worry about how another party will react to a specific problem that might emerge. The firm itself will take all the loss or gain for any judgments it has made.

Another type of transaction cost arises from the difficulty the firm has in transferring its information, knowledge, and skills to another party. It faces two problems. (1) What it has to transfer is what some call a set of *routines*, a culture involving how the firm goes about solving problems, identifying opportunities, maintaining and improving production efficiency, and dealing with suppliers and customers. This kind of knowledge is not easy to transfer, takes time to develop, and is most easily accomplished within an organization rather than through some separate training program.[15] (2) The outside party has no way of assessing the value of something so imprecise as learning another company's culture and hence cannot pay its full value.

A different way to look at transaction costs is to see the difficulty a firm has as it tries to extract from the market the value of its knowledge or culture. This is the question of *appropriability*. A company that comes up with a series of new products, technical innovations, or new market opportunities or one that has established itself as making reliable products and being a good credit risk needs at least to get back the cost of what it has done, and preferably get back something beyond that. Economics handles this, somewhat awkwardly, as a form of *rent*. The special capabilities of a firm are usually unique, meaning a completely inelastic supply; they thus command a *rent*. Because eventually the firm's skills can be replicated or superseded, these rents are limited in time; technically they should be called not *rents*, but *quasi-rents,* but economists usually don't bother with the distinction. The problem is that the market cannot pay anything like the full rent these skills could command were it not for various market imperfections.

Consider a licensing arrangement, where the licensor confers rights to a product or process and teaches the licensee how to use it. The licensee has no sure idea it can gain as much from the license as the licensor has or thinks it must of necessity discount any return it figures. The licensor has no idea just what the buyer is going to use them for. It may find the transfer far too costly either in terms of manpower or, more importantly, in the threat to its markets as it creates a competitor. (It makes no difference if it has been able to charge enough, but if it guesses wrong, it will lose.) So the licensor must discount its returns from the licensee. The uncertainty of the situation causes the licensee to bid too low and the licensor to demand too high a price. The alternative would be a very complex, extremely costly contract. As a result, the firm chooses not to license but to exploit the product itself.

Figure 19.7
TRANSACTION AND ADMINISTRATIVE
COSTS RELATED TO COMPLEXITY

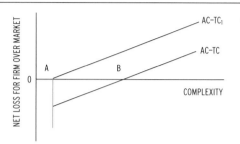

Source: Adapted from Richard Langlois and Paul L. Robertson, *Firms, Markets, and Economic Change* (New York: Routledge, 1995), 32, who adapted their model from Morris Silver, *Enterprise and the Scope of the Firm* (London: Martin Robertson, 1984).

As a firm becomes more complex, adding product lines and integrating vertically, it becomes increasingly difficult to manage, incurring *administrative costs.* A more complex administrative structure slows decision-making and distorts information. The increasing range of products proves an ever-greater challenge to top management to understand what is happening in diverse product and geographical markets. In particular, the diverse firm has considerable difficulty in allocating capital between competing internal projects.[16]

As a result administrative costs rise with complexity. Figure 19.7 shows the relationship of the balance between *AC* and *TC* and increasing corporate complexity. The short vertical line indicates the absolute minimum size of the firm, below which it would be very difficult to use a market—such as the small contracting firms. The range of things a firm does would stop growing where *AC − TC* crosses the zero line.

Over time, the *AC − TC* line can shift. General competitive pressures tend to push it to the left as markets develop new instruments and understandings and as uncertainty declines in maturing markets. But idiosyncratic factors, such as technological change causing different scale operations, changing market conditions, or new corporate developments, could cause the line to move either rightward or leftward.

The range of a firm's activity is determined by a balance between the costs of using the market to purchase or sell materials, technology, and other services from independent contractors and the costs of doing the same within a firm. The vertical line in Figure 19.7 shows the theoretical minimum firm size, and *AC − TC* the pattern of *AC* rising with complexity while *TC*s are unchanged. The firm's size would therefore be at point *B*. Over time, transaction costs usually fall, so the firm would tend to become less complex and *AC − TC* would drift to the left, as shown by *AC − TC₁*, and the firm would have the complexity shown at point *A*.

Benefits of Coordination and the Benefit of Firms

The question of why multinational firms exist is simply a variant of the question of why firms exist, just as the question of what benefit MNFs might create is the same as what benefit any firm might create. Take the cases in which the benefit firms create derives from their coordination efforts.

The coordination of research and design, production, and distribution of goods and services is essential for economic efficiency and progress. Both firms and markets coordinate activities, and the balance between transaction and administrative costs determines which of them coordinates and the cost of doing so. The benefits of good coordination are considerable. Coordination of production and sales avoids costly inventories or equally costly shortages. Coordination of innovative products or services and their manufacture and delivery (including the information the ultimate consumers need) allows rapid innovation and technological progress without an excessive number of unnecessary failures. The costs of achieving that coordination may also be considerable.

To model this, take a situation in which companies can achieve considerable economies of scale by increasing production and distribution, but they must do this in one jump such that the market cannot feel its way toward a new equilibrium. The example is the production and distribution of bananas. Independent sailing ships that picked up bananas along with other cargo in the Caribbean were first introduced to the seaports of the United States in the mid-nineteenth century. When they got to port, assuming the bananas had not ripened too soon, the captains then found buyers, but in the beginning the arrangements were not well organized. Growers, local buyers, ship captain, and distributors in east coast cities were all separate. The more visionary captains, planters, and distributors could see the possibilities of a very large market for this tasty and exotic fruit, although it is doubtful they would have imagined that it would eventually be second only to the apple in popularity. To do this properly, they would need large plantations dedicated to banana production, steamships with ice or refrigeration, and a distribution network that could take the bananas rapidly from the ships to their retail markets, one that, like the meat packers, soon came to use refrigerated railcars. The question was how to coordinate the expansion, particularly since it could not be done gradually, but had to be done in a number of carefully planned leaps.

Consider the problem in a simple game matrix (Table 19.1). The possible actions of distributors are to set up to handle 1 million or 2 million bananas, and the shippers are set up to ship either amount. The numbers refer to the profits that would be made, the left number the distributors' profit, the right one the shippers'. The upper left quadrant shows that if both choose the conservative course, thereby avoiding risk, both will earn 5. If, as in the upper

Table 19.1

COORDINATION MATRIX FOR BANANAS

	Shippers	
Distributors	*Ship 1 million*	*Ship 2 million*
Handle 1 million	5, 5	5, − 5
Handle 2 million	− 5, 5	10, 10

right, the shipper sends 2 million and the distributor cannot handle them, the distributor earns 5 but the shipper loses 5. If the distributor gears up to handle 2 million with extra warehouse space, more retail stores lined up to take the bananas, and more wagons to deliver the bananas and then the shipper fails to come through, the distributor loses 5 and the shipper still gets 5 (lower left). Only if both cooperate at the 2 million level will the high profits be realized, but that exposes both parties to a risk of non-fulfillment.

The usual solution for such a game is the upper left because there both parties minimize their risks. Neither party on its own will move to the 2 million position for fear the other party will not. In game theory parlance, the upper left solution is called a *Nash equilibrium*. The lower right is also an equilibrium, but the risks are too high for it to be reached without special arrangements.

The gain from coordination in the matrix is 10 (the upper-left Nash solution compared with the optimal solution of the lower right). Through contracts and other devices firms may solve the problem or a single, unified firm might plan the coordination. Suppose, for instance, that transaction costs were 5 and administrative costs 2; both market and firm could create the benefit of 10, but the market's way would be more expensive by 3. It could be the other way around, with the market being more efficient. In some cases the AC or TC might exceed the benefit of 10, so that only the firm or the market would achieve the coordination. And some coordination may simply yield too little to be worth the cost. Schematically, with B = benefit of coordination, and TC and AC equaling transaction costs and administrative costs respectively, we get the schema presented in Table 19.2.[17]

Either the market, through contracts, or the firm, through administrative actions, can solve the problem to get to the 10,10 solution. Contractual parties, for instance, might agree to compensate the other if they fail to meet the target. But if transaction costs are high, it might be expensive, time-consuming, and risky to come to any contractual solution, and, as occurred with bananas, the firm replaces the market. Alternatively, the firm might prove to be an expensive way of organizing coordination and the normal processes go on through the market.

Table 19.2
COORDINATION AND BENEFITS

	Situation	Result
1.	$B > AC > TC$	Benefit created through market
2.	$B > TC > AC$	Benefit created by a firm
3.	$TC > B > AC$	Benefit created by a firm
4.	$AC > B > TC$	Benefit created through market
5.	$B < TC$ or AC	No benefit created

The net gain from having a firm do the coordination cannot exceed B. In situation 2, the tendency would be for a firm to form, but if legislation or other political factors blocked its formation the benefit would still occur. The cost of coordination would be higher by $TC - AC$, but the benefit would still occur. In situation 1, a legal monopoly might prevent the market from coordinating and the net benefit would be reduced by $AC - TC$. In situations 3 and 4, no benefit would occur if the cheaper route were blocked.

Factors Determining Whether Firms May Operate Abroad

Not every firm, not even every large firm, has extensive operations outside its home country. This is because the benefit and the balance between transaction and administrative costs differ within a country from what they are between countries. Consider some of the key elements.

1. *Locational factors.* There may be no benefit at all in coordinating operations across borders and there may be no benefit to appropriate from bringing in innovative products or methods. A firm would have to have some locational advantage to producing in more than one place. Many software producers have only one principal location where the vast bulk of the development occurs. This may be because they can take advantage of the external economies that reside in cluster development. But it is also because the product they make is light, faces low or zero tariffs, and, beyond translation into major languages, does not need modification for different markets. The same is also true of almost all computer components; their production is knowledge- and capital-intensive, with manufacturing labor a very small part of total costs, while they are so light that air transportation is sensible. Interestingly, the weight of American exports has been declining steadily—a real dollar's worth of exports today weighs only 30% of what it did in 1969.[18]

In other cases, foreign production is the only way to go. A restaurant chain, an airline, or a bank has to perform its services in multiple locations.

The trend in manufacturing for flexible factories with just-in-time delivery has also shifted some production to locations closer to their markets. Automobile firms, for example, encourage their suppliers to locate close to them, whether it is next to a new plant in their home country or abroad, so that all the firms in the chain of suppliers (the *value chain*, in managerial phraseology) can keep their inventories down.

2. *The nature of the firm's special abilities.* Some firms' skills may fit only their own country. Legal firms and tax specialists (and software producers of tax-related materials) get their edge because they are intimately familiar with one country's laws. This gives them no competitive edge in another country. Others may benefit because of their political connections—road or defense contractors, for instance. Retailers sometimes find that their particular abilities fit just one country, an example being Marks and Spencer, a British retailer for years dominant in the British market yet never able to operate successfully abroad. A number of quite successful Canadian firms have taken a financial bath in the American market, too. Canadian mall developers, in contrast, have been very successful in the American market, perhaps because they have developed the political skills to mesh the interests of many layers of government and the private sector.

3. *Nationalist legislation.* The firm may be unable to operate in the other countries because of laws favoring national firms. Financial services (particularly banking and insurance), communications, and often transportation have, at least until recently, been reserved for nationals in many countries. Before 1929, many multinationals were in communications (AT&T, which later sold to ITT), insurance (Equitable Life, New York Life, Sun Life of Canada), railroads, and even city streetcar systems. (Brazilian Traction, a Canadian company that is now a financial conglomerate called Brascan, started life building and running the street railways in Brazil, and expanded to providing electricity and gas.)* As it became fashionable for countries to own their own utilities and control more of their own financial systems, many of these companies reduced their holdings or were bought out entirely.[19]

In some cases, local manufacturers have the market tied up with the aid of various laws. Canadian beer companies, for instance, like the environmental advantages of bottles because their weight keeps foreign companies from shipping in beer. Beer in Ontario is sold through Brewers' Retail Outlets—cooperatively administered retail stores owned by Canadian beer companies.

---

* Brazilian Traction, Light and Power Company, now Brascan, began converting the mule-driven street railways of Rio de Janeiro and Sao Paulo to electricity, much as its founder had done in Toronto and Winnipeg. Because the company needed electricity, it soon expanded to become the main electricity and gas supplier for Brazil's southeast. As the operations were made national or municipal, Brascan used its compensation money to make investments in Canada, where it now controls several large corporations. *The Canadian Encyclopedia Plus* (1996).

LICENSING ACROSS BORDERS

Very often firms will license across national borders where they would not license within the same country. If they can restrict the licensee from selling back into the home market, then they do not risk losing sales to their own licensee. Even then, licensing problems are considerable.

A 1983 study of the market for licensing technology showed just how many difficulties there are.[20] Potential buyers are uncertain about the value of new information. In addition, they are concerned that technology may change, leaving them at a disadvantage to their competitors, and so they may wish to purchase a license not only for current technology but for future improvements, a greater uncertainty. The licensor is reluctant to make a license for "current and future technology" because it will have to share the fruits of any technological breakthrough with a licensee without being able to renegotiate the contract. The licensor, accordingly, has less incentive to improve its licensed product or technology. The licensor is also anxious to get in on any improvements the licensee might make to the licensed product or technology and tries to write a contract whereby any such improvements come back to it automatically—without any payment. The licensee does not like this type of contract because if it makes any key improvements, it will not be rewarded for them. It therefore has less incentive to make improvements.

In England, the pubs are generally owned by the brewers. It is hard to break into markets like that.

4. *Transaction costs.* Licensing is less risky across national borders, which means transaction costs are lower. Why would Coors license a Canadian company to brew its beer, but not an American company? Part of the answer is that it would be expensive to break into the Canadian market, as indicated above. The other part is that Coors can make a licensing agreement that prevents the Canadian seller from exporting Coors beer. If Coors undercharges the Canadian company, it need not fear the Canadian firm will use the savings so gained to export into the American market. If it had licensed an American brewer on the east coast, it would have been unable to prevent the brewer (or distributors) from selling anywhere in the country. Interstate commerce cannot be blocked; international commerce certainly can.

5. *Higher costs of being international.* Costs of being in more than one country may be higher. This is certainly true for small and medium-sized companies, which have to set up special offices, have added tax and legal complications, and in some cases have to change their managerial structures. For companies already established the addition of another country to the market is probably not much more expensive. Because of the higher costs,

many writers have suggested that the firm's unique capabilities must be greater than those of competitive domestic firms—that is, it must have a larger rent or else it will not be profitable to operate in the other country.

In sum, the points above suggest that the total benefit and the balance between administrative and transaction costs are somewhat different internationally than domestically. The $AC - TC$ line in Figure 19.7 would lie to the left of the one shown both because the complexity is greater (raising AC) and because some of the risks of licensing are less (lowering TC).

POSSIBLE REASONS FOR THE RECENT INCREASE IN FDI

Why might FDI have increased so sharply over the last decade? One reason is that opportunities to invest in services have increased greatly. The privatization, denationalization, and partial deregulation of utilities and financial services have opened up opportunities for firms to operate in other countries and intensified competition. Air Iberia, the Spanish airline, owns several airlines in South America, including the old state-run Argentine airline. CN, one of the two Canadian railroad companies, owns Illinois Central and a large chunk of the Upper Midwest railroad system. Telecommunications companies, responding to liberalization of domestic markets and riding the technological waves, have expanded into one another's turf, forming a number of mergers and joint ventures in an almost dizzying set of mergers and buy-outs. Finally, with financial services also undergoing liberalization, companies are expanding abroad there also. An interesting case, for instance, is the merger of ING and the Bank of Boston, principally a defensive reaction to try to gain scale economies.

In other cases, new skills developed in large domestic markets have proven to work well in foreign markets. Wal-Mart, which entered Canada in 1994, was by 1998 Canada's largest retailer. The big-box stores like Staples, Office Depot, and Home Depot are in all the major Canadian cities and in several other countries. Most of the big restaurant franchisers are abroad, McDonald's being the most famous, but you can Dunk your Donuts in Tokyo and go to a Pizza Hut in Bangkok, should you get a hankering for that sort of thing.

Lastly, the move to flexible factories has encouraged more production closer to the market served. Like shopping malls, which tend to have the same stores in them from city to city, manufacturing centers have many of the same groups of firms—sometimes including those that audit them, do their market research, or handle their advertising. The supply pipelines would be too long to service the new manufacturing from far away, but the need to have the same standards and groups of companies is still there.

CANADIAN NATIONAL RAILWAYS BUYS ILLINOIS CENTRAL

The purchase of Illinois Central by a Canadian rail company demonstrates how privatization and increasing trade also increase international investment and the opportunities for in-firm coordination.

The Canadian National Railway Company (CN), one of two Canadian railway companies, was formed as a government-owned corporation in 1919 when a number of smaller railways were beginning to fail. The government privatized it in 1995 by offering shares to the public. It is national, with over 15,000 miles of track in Canada, and stretches from coast to coast and down into Chicago and Detroit. To extend its reach, it purchased Illinois Central for just under US$2.4 billion (about 20% of CN size). Illinois Central owns the Illinois Central and Chicago Central railroads. This gave CN a corridor to New Orleans. It also made an alliance with Kansas City and Southern Railroad allowing it to use KCSR's track, which brings it farther across the prairies and makes a connection in Laredo with the Mexican railway. CN management expects to gain savings from more efficient use of engines, cars, and track and plans to build business as the materials and industrial goods trade rises between the three countries. The new arrangement allows CN and Illinois Central to avoid changes of cars in the overcrowded stock railyards and opens quicker service for shippers sending goods between Canada and the Gulf Coast or other parts of the American Midwest.[21]

EXTENT OF THE FIRM'S FREEDOM FROM MARKET CONSTRAINTS

No matter how much internal coordination, a firm is constrained at some point by the market. Even in the old days when oil companies controlled oil from exploration stages until the gasoline reached cars' gas tanks, they were still subject to market forces emanating from new supplies and the price people were willing to pay. The vertical integration meant that the market did not direct each stage—expected new supplies did not send a price signal to explorers to reduce their searches, for refiners to increase their capacity, or for distributors to build new gas stations. The company simply looked at the expectations and commanded all those things. Nor were the cooperative arrangements between the major oil firms—although often remarkable—ever sufficient to insulate the firms from new suppliers.

Still, market allocation can be different from administrative allocation. Suppose, for instance, new banana planters decided they wanted to find independent markets, but transaction costs were higher than administrative costs. Even though the new suppliers might have cheaper bananas, they may not be able to deliver them more cheaply. Suppose the big banana multinational, Pulpo (Octopus), has a benefit from coordination of $100, with the (administrative) cost of coordination being $25, leaving it with a net benefit of $75. The independant cooperative El Calamar (Squid), which deals with independant distributors, gets the same benefit from coordination of $100, but the cost of coordinating a group of independants is $50. Calamar is no threat to Pulpo unless it can produce bananas for $25 less than Pulpo does. Algebraicly, the *entry condition* for Calamar is that the difference between its production costs and Pulpo's production costs must be at least equal to the difference between the administrative and transactions costs, $(TC - CA) = (PC_P - PC_C)$, where PC is production costs and the subscripts refer to Pulpo and Calamar.

Over time, transaction costs tend to fall. The unique abilities of a firm become less special and the rate of technological change slows down, making the technological and competitive environment more predictable. The reduced uncertainty allows the development of contracts, understandings between parties, and modes of behavior that become routine. While still huge, automobile companies are far less vertically integrated than they have been in a century[22] and huge independent suppliers like the Canadian-based Magna have grown, even designing the interiors of some cars.* Changes in the oil business have led to the first open market (including futures and options) in oil in nearly a century. There are independent explorers, producers, refiners, and distributors. Even the large integrated oil producers do not necessarily sell their oil to themselves or buy it from themselves, and even when they do, they have a market reference point at each stage. Interestingly, bananas still tend to be vertically integrated, although the companies no longer own the shipping lines and various antitrust settlements have turned what was once a monopoly into a reasonably competitive oligopoly. (Whether bananas, which compete with many different fruits, ever comprised a real monopoly is another question.)[23]

When industries are changing rapidly, as they are today with computers, software, communications, and the Internet, it is difficult to speak of a market price or indeed of a cost. Firms are forward-looking and look toward future costs and future prices, which are by nature imprecise. Production experience curves (Chapter 3) lower prices over time, bringing opportunities for uses as yet unknown. As the price of computers and peripheral equipment fell, whole sets of new uses developed—personal communications and information-gathering on the Internet, digital photography and development, and awesome computer games, to name a few. To speak of an equilibrium price when equilibrium is changing rapidly may not be meaningful, as Alfred

---

* General Motors, which had lagged behind Chrysler and Ford in using outside suppliers, managed to spin off (create a separate company by giving shares in the new unit to the stockholders of the former parent) Delphi, its parts division, in 1999.

Figure 19.8

ALLOCATIONAL DECISIONS BY FIRM OR MARKET

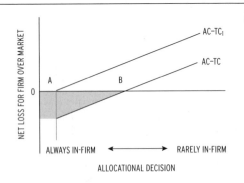

Note: With allocational decisions arranged from the kind always in the firm and those rarely done in the firm, the *AC* − *TC* line sketches out the area in which a firm is free from ready market constraints—essentially, the shaded area.

Marshall himself argued a century ago.[*] It is difficult in an industry that is changing rapidly—whether it has large firms or small firms, national or multi-national—to see how the market can be much of a check on the firms in anything but a long run.

A variant on Figure 19.7 helps illustrate the points above. While Figure 19.7 took the increasing complexity as a problem affecting the firm's total costs, Figure 19.8 looks at each decision as having a cost of its own, arranging all decisions a firm takes with the ones farthest from any market checks on the left and those closest to the market on the right. A decision on whether to promote one of two people would be on the left side, a decision on whether to make a part or buy it from an outsider would be in the middle, and a decision about which contract to sign would be on the right. *AC* − *TC* is still the same.

ISSUES MNFS RAISE

Many issues that arise in the context of MNFs arise only because the MNF is doing what the market would do anyway and it happens to be the agent that people focus on. Any decision that lies to the right of point *B* on Figure 19.8

---

[*] "That is the real drift of that much-quoted and much-misunderstood doctrine of Adam Smith and other economists that the normal or "natural" value of a commodity is that which economic forces tend to bring about in the long run. It is the average value which economic forces would bring about if the general conditions of life were stationary for a run of time long enough to enable them all to work out the full effect. The fact that the general conditions of life are not stationary is the source of many of the difficulties that are met with in applying economic doctrines to practical problems." Alfred Marshall, *Principles of Economics*, 1910, 427.

would not differ between firm and market. With the general tendency for $AC - TC$ to drift to the left, it is probably also true of decisions in the proximity of point B. That still leaves an area worthy of discussion.

The Branch-Plant Economy

If all the corporate headquarters are located outside a country, what opportunities do the people of that country have for high level work, participation in major decisions, and the high living standards that top management brings? Does the country end up a body with no head, its citizens only getting chances to advance to high ranks by moving to the headquarters' country? Thoughtful Canadians brought up these questions in their debates about FDI in the 1970s. When free trade in automobiles began, for instance, the design of the slightly different Canadian versions of the parent company's cars and a number of other important and creative tasks were no longer needed. Virtually all manufacturing seemed to be the same. Canadians could be creative in only a very circumscribed area of activity. While this was largely an effect of the Canadian tariffs that had attracted so many plants in the first place and driven manufacturing costs up too high to be competitive, the solution to the problem was unclear. Declining tariffs meant that even the limited scope available to local decision-makers would disappear, as it had in the automobile industry. As the statistics on FDI show, once tariffs fell, Canadian FDI rose sharply. As the automobile industry reduced its vertical integration and began buying from more and more independents, Canadian parts producers expanded in size and themselves became multinational.

In a sense, upper management skills are a factor of production—one of the sort that is created through experience. As companies build up their particular abilities, they become the low-cost producers of those abilities and, given typical market imperfections, they often become multinational in the process of appropriating the value of what they know best how to do. Countries trade goods and services; they also trade managerial skills in packages known as firms. The way to provide the high-level jobs with great decision-making powers is to have some multinationals of one's own, not to pressure firms to delegate decisions that they ordinarily would make centrally.

TRANSFER PRICING

A transfer price is the price of a product or service moving within a corporation. Within a country a firm may have no particular reason to give a part a price. If an automobile firm makes a muffler and installs it in a vehicle, it need not have a price for the muffler. It may have one, if the one division makes the muffler and the other does the assembly, but such internal prices frequently do not closely mirror any market price.[24] When parts cross national borders, however, they must have prices. In the old days, the tariff was a major factor, but now transfer prices have a major impact on the corporation's profit and therefore on the profit that can be taxed by government. If a shipment of mufflers is valued at $1 million and tax authorities insist it should be $800,000, that lowers the domestic subsidiary's costs by $200,000, hence raising its profits by the same amount. At a 30% corporate tax rate, that is $60,000 for the government.

Tax authorities would like corporations to use "arm's-length" prices—equivalent market prices. But the problem is that much of what a corporation transfers has no market price. It is in the gray area of Figure 19.8 and possibly in accounting's gray area as well. "There is," said an accountant explaining dealings with Canadian Customs, "a price below which it cannot be and a price above which it cannot be, but the range is sometimes quite large and we just compromise in the plausible area." A muffler would be easy to value, but licenses, managerial advice, technical help and designs, and all the really useful help transferred between parent and subsidiary defy easy valuation. After all, if they had a price, they could be traded in the market and the firm would not be necessary.

Gray areas can be exploited (by both firm and tax authorities). Will the firm exploit them? That depends on the possible gain. There is first a cost: any departure a company makes from its normal accounting procedures involves a cost because figures have to be adjusted or because division managers will use the prices as real costs or benefits and adjust their behavior. If the imported product is priced artificially high to avoid high taxes, subsidiary managers will price their product higher and sell less, which is not the object. Instead of transferring profit to the exporting unit, it reduces sales. The subsidiary manager would have to be given specific instructions or another set of costs to use. The more complex the company, the less likely it is to play with its transfer pricing for tax purposes. With costs of changing the transfer-pricing scheme substantial, firms need a good tax incentive to go ahead with any scheme. Because taxes on profits are very similar between industrial countries, the gains to be made in tax savings rarely exceed the losses that would occur from fouling up the accounting system.

Oil companies in the old days used to keep their profits "at the wellhead" by pricing oil much higher than its cost of extraction. Where their oil was in Third World countries, they did indeed save on taxes. Note, however, that the oil industry had a simple product—crude oil—not a thousand different products, and they were anxious to use that price to keep out independent competition at the refining level, which the high import price also accomplished. Since the 1970s, independent markets and a market price for oil have emerged, so the companies can no longer play that particular game.

MNC or Globalization?

Does it ever work to put pressure on a multinational to accomplish something that the market is not doing on its own or something that many people believe the market should not be doing on its own? Whether the aim is the reduction of global warming, better treatment of employees, preservation of the environment, or improvement in human rights, must the pressures always be on governments singly and in combination to change the market incentives or institute a system of penalties? If the particular decision is in the gray area (literally of Figure 19.8, but figuratively rather broader), it can work. If a firm is deciding whether to develop product A or product B in Australia, and Australians have a preference for A because of the technological direction it might go, the firm could probably comply easily. If the firm has a choice between manufacturing in a police state or a democracy and the costs are not so different as to allow producers in the police state to compete with it, it will likely choose (or can be persuaded to choose) the democracy. The sacrifice for cooperating is not such that it much weakens the firm, at least in the short run. Indeed, in cases where specialization in one of several centers or in one of several directions will be, so far as mortals can see, successful, the decision may be costless. The closer to the edge of the gray area one gets, however, the more the firm has to lose. And, since the market is liable to be able to do the same thing within a short period of time, the less the firm will be able to change things.

It is generally newer industries that have $AC - TC$ placed far to the right and large gray areas, so it follows that countries or pressure groups will have greater success in dealing with new and innovating firms than they will in older areas, such as textiles or appliance manufacturing, where the $AC - TC$ has moved to the left.

CONCLUSION

As we have argued throughout the text, the passing of some power from national governments to more abstract market forces is often quite beneficial, particularly given the tendency for national governments to become the agents of domestic producers rather than of domestic consumers. As Chapter 1 indicated, we see very many useful things for governments to do and are not discomforted by moderately activist governments. But globalization is not some evil: on balance it carries more benefits than difficulties. If on occasion we need to rethink our aims and methods so that they might be made compatible with the rising tide of globalization, that is no bad thing.

VOCABULARY AND CONCEPTS

Administrative coordination	Market coordination
Administrative costs	Multinational firm
Allocational decision	Nash equilibrium
Appropriability	Quasi-rent
Book value	Rent
Branch-plant economy	Stock of direct investment
Flow of direct investment	Transaction costs
Foreign direct investment	Transfer pricing
Internalize	

PROJECT

Bring up to date any of the statistical diagrams in the chapter. Figures on FDI stocks are in the *Balance of Payments Statistics Yearbook* (*BOPSY*) at the end of each country's figures. As of this writing, only 18 countries had this information. The same figures are also available on the *IFS* CD-ROM. End-of-period stock figures for other foreign assets and liabilities are in the same listings. GNP (gross national income) and GDP are available in *International Financial Statistics* and the *IFS* CD-ROM. The financial flow figures come from the *BOPSY* in the capital and financial accounts.

QUESTIONS

1. Back in the 1960s there was a joke: "The Swedes stay home and mind their own business, the Americans go abroad and mind everybody else's business, and the Swiss stay home and mind everybody else's business." It may have been true then, but it certainly is not true today. Demonstrate.
2. What is the difference between an MNF and FDI? Between direct investment and portfolio investment?
3. Why did the meat packers establish themselves as companies in Europe? That is, why did they just not sell their beef to other companies once it got to the American port?
4. What is the evidence that FDI has risen sharply in the last decade?
5. Since FDI is rising faster than GNP and exports, is there any evidence it is displacing exports? How does the Canadian situation throw light on the question? (Hint: look at the expansion of exports and intraindustrial trade noted in Chapter 3.)
6. Since capital is scarce in less-developed countries, one would expect that FDI, to the extent it is a capital movement, would be flowing heavily toward capital-scarce regions. Is it? By Chapter 19 are you surprised it isn't?

7. "All allocational decisions are at some level administrative, involving managerial judgment." Comment, explaining the difference between the allocational decisions and the closeness to the market of a farmer and those of a computer software company.

8. Explain what transaction costs are and in what circumstances they could be high.

9. Use figure 19.7 to explain why firms' growth is constrained. What would cause $AC - TC$ to shift to the left? To the right?

10. How can coordination bring benefits? Use the game matrix to demonstrate the benefits of coordination.

11. Sometimes markets do just fine in making coordinative operations. Indeed, they probably do well most of the time. But what might make coordination difficult—that is, make transaction costs high?

12. Why are some firms national but not multinational?

13. What may be the cause of the sharp increase in FDI?

14. The difference between the cost of coordination within a firm and between firms partially insulates a firm's decisions from the market. Explain, using Figure 19.8.

15. What are the problems of living in a branch-plant economy? How has the problem developed, or perhaps even been resolved, in Canada?

16. Why have firms resisted using their prices between national subsidiaries to make tax savings?

17. Take a situation in which you know of a group that wants to put pressure on large firms. How might you evaluate whether such pressure could be effective, given the structure of the arguments in this chapter?

NOTES

1. For example, Anaconda-Erichson, a Swedish-American joint venture in the U.S. in wire manufacture.

2. Caltex, a joint venture of California Standard Oil (Chevron) and Texaco, has served Far East markets for many years.

3. Imperial Oil, Exxon's Canadian subsidiary, has such an arrangement, with the majority of the shares in Exxon's hands and the minority widely spread.

4. The figures for total foreign assets and liabilities, available only for 18 major industrial countries, are in two places: (1) at the end of the balance-of-payments statements figures on the *IFS* CD-ROM, and (2) the *Balance of Payments Statistics Yearbook* (*BOPSY*). Portfolio and bank holdings are listed as "EPS" for end-of-period stock, while FDI holdings are described as "Direct Investment Abroad" and "Foreign Direct Investment in Rep.[represented] Economy." Total profits figures come from the *Federal Reserve Bulletin*'s presentation of the American income accounts.

5. The description of the domestic development is drawn from Thomas Horst, *At Home Abroad*. The Latin American material is from Mira Wilkins, *The Emergence of Multinational Enterprise* (Cambridge, Mass.: Harvard University Press, 1970), 189-90.

6. United Nations, Department of Economic and Social Affairs, *Multinational Corporations in World Development*, 1975, 139.

779

7. To judge by some overlapping years. The U.S. still keeps book and "market" values, with the latter about 20% higher than the former.

8. By book value, the countries accounted for all but 2% of FDI in 1985. United Nations Centre on Transnational Corporations, *Transnational Corporations in World Development*, 1980.

9. Ibid.

10. Extensive analyses of the increase in Canadian FDI, as it was developing in the early 1990s, is in Stephen Globerman, ed., *Canadian-Based Multinationals* (Calgary: University of Calgary Press, 1994).

11. John Cantwell, "The Relationship Between International Trade and International Production," in David Greenaway and L. Alan Winters, *Surveys in International Trade* (Oxford: Oxford University Press, 1994), 309-20.

12. A good review of earlier theory is in John H. Dunning, *Explaining International Production* (London: Unwin Hyman, 1988), 120-39.

13. The theory jelled in the 1970s. See John McManus, "The Theory of the International Firm," in Gilles Paquet, ed., *The Multinational Firm and the Nation State* (Toronto: Collier-Macmillan, 1972), 66-93; Wilson B. Brown, "Islands of Conscious Power," *MSU Business Topics* (Summer 1976): 37-45; J.H. Dunning, "Trade, Location of Economic Activity and the Multinational Enterprise: A Search for an Eclectic Approach," in B. Ohlin et al., eds., *The International Allocation of Economic Activity* (London: Macmillan, 1977).

14. The basic framework of transaction cost analysis goes back to Ronald Coase, "The Nature of the Firm," *Economica* 4, New Series (1937): 386-405.

15. Richard Langlois and Paul L. Robertson, *Firms, Markets, and Economic Change* (London: Routledge, 1995), 15-17.

16. *Journal of Finance*, 52, 1 (March 1997) had a group of related articles on this topic. See David J. Denis, Diane K. Denis, and Atulya Sarin, "Agency Problems, Equity Ownership, and Corporate Diversification"; Owen Lamont, "Cash Flow and Investment: Evidence from Internal Capital Markets"; Jeremy C. Stein, "Internal Capital Markets and the Competition for Corporate Resources."

17. See Wilson Brown, *Markets, Organizations, and Information* (Toronto: Wiley, 1992), 54-58.

18. David Wessel, "Alan Greenspan has a truly weighty idea," reprinted from *Wall Street Journal* by *Globe and Mail*, May 20, 1999, B15.

19. See Wilkins, *The Emergence of Multinational Enterprise*; Mira Wilkins, *The Maturing of Multinational Enterprise* (Cambridge, Mass.: Harvard University Press, 1974).

20. See Richard Caves, Harold Crookell, and J.P. Killing, "The Imperfect Market for Technology Licenses," *Oxford Bulletin of Economics and Statistics* (August 1983): 249-67.

21. Information from Canadian National Railways Web site: www.cn.ca

22. Langlois and Robertson, *Firms, Markets, and Economic Change*, 46-67.

23. See Brown, *Markets*, 193-201; Robert Read, "The Banana Industry," in Mark Casson et al., *Multinationals and World Trade* (London: Allen & Unwin, 1986); Read, "The Growth and Structures of Multinationals in the Banana Export Trade," in Read, *The Growth of International Business* (London: Allen & Unwin, 1983).

24. See H. Thomas Johnson and Robert S. Kaplan, *Relevance Lost: The Rise and Fall of Managerial Accounting* (Boston: Harvard Business School Press, 1987). See also Brown, *Markets*.

Index